Fodor's 90 France

Fodor's Travel Publications, Inc.
New York and London

ISBN 0-679-01768-2

Fodor's France

Editor: Lisa Cussans
Area Editor: Simon Hewitt
Coordinating Editor: Gillian O'Meara
Editorial Contributors: Judy Allen, Donna Dailey, James Etheridge, John P. Harris, Andrew Heritage, Ann O'Connor, Carla Power, Caroline B.D. Smith, Anne Willan
Art Director: Fabrizio La Rocca
Cartographer: David Lindroth
Illustrator: Karl Tanner
Cover Photograph: Jean–Paul Naciret/Leo De Wys

Design: Vignelli Associates

Special Sales

Fodor's Travel Publications are available at special discounts for bulk purchases (100 copies or more) for sales promotions or premiums. Special editions, including personalized covers, excerpts of existing guides, and corporate imprints, can be created in large quantities for special needs. For more information write to Special Marketing, Fodor's Travel Publications, 201 East 50th Street, New York, NY 10022. Enquiries from the United Kingdom should be sent to Fodor's Travel Publications, 30–32 Bedford Square, London WC1B 3SG.

Manufactured in the United States of America
10 9 8 7 6 5 4 3 2 1

Contents

Menu Guide *493*

Index *499*

Maps and Plans

Foreword

This is an exciting time for Fodor's, as we continue our ambitious program to rewrite, reformat, and redesign all 140 of our guides. Here are just a few of the new features:

★ Brand-new computer-generated maps locating all the top attractions, hotels, restaurants, and shops

★ A unique system of numbers and legends to help readers move effortlessly between text and maps

★ A new star rating system for hotels and restaurants

★ Restaurant reviews by major food critics around the world

★ Stamped, self-addressed postcards, bound into every guide, give readers a chance to help evaluate hotels and restaurants

★ Complete page redesign for instant retrieval of information

★ ITINERARIES—The experts help you decide where to go

★ FODOR'S CHOICE—Our favorite museums, beaches, cafes, romantic hideaways, festivals, and more

★ HIGHLIGHTS—an insider's look at the most important developments in tourism during the past year

★ TIME OUT—The best and most convenient lunch stops along exploring routes

★ A Traveler's Menu and Phrase Guide in all major foreign guides

★ Exclusive background essays create a powerful portrait of each destination

★ A mini-journal for travelers to keep track of their own itineraries and addresses

We'd like to express our gratitude to Simon Hewitt, our Area Editor, and to Gillian O'Meara, our Coordinating Editor, for their help in preparing this new edition.

Special thanks also to Colette Martin of Paris's Tourist Board; Jean-Pierre Martinetti, head of A.R.T.L., Corsica's regional tourist agency; Alexandre Lévy of the Toulouse-Midi-Pyrénées regional tourist board; and also to Brigitte Doignon and Florence Danjean.

While every care has been taken to ensure the accuracy of the information in this guide, the passage of time will always bring change, and consequently, the publisher cannot accept responsibility for errors that may occur.

All prices and opening times quoted here are based on information available to us at press time. Hours and admission fees may change, however, and the prudent traveler will avoid inconvenience by calling ahead.

Fodor's wants to hear about your travel experiences, both pleasant and unpleasant. When a hotel or restaurant fails to live up to its billing, let us know and we will investigate the complaint and revise our entries where the facts warrant it.

Send your letters to the editors of Fodor's Travel Publications, 201 East 50th Street, New York, NY 10022.

Highlights '90 and Fodor's Choice

Highlights '90

Culture in Paris, fun in the provinces—that seems to be the legacy of the Revolution Bicentennial celebrations in France in 1989.

After a decade of frantic change, Paris is finally shedding its scaffolding. 1989 saw the **Louvre**—recently pushed into the back seat by the success of the Musée d'Orsay, the science museum of La Villette, and the glistening Institute of the Arab World—finally move back into the limelight upon the completion of its famous **glass pyramid.**

The controversial pyramid, set to become as familiar a landmark as the Eiffel Tower, crowns a vast new entrance hall that includes shops, café, restaurant, and ticket counters (whose automatic ticket machines help avoid long lines). The once-cramped Louvre has emerged better organized and more spacious, though remains stiflingly hot in July and August. There is also, now, the chance to examine the rediscovered towers and walls of the medieval Louvre.

Away to the west of Paris, as a counterpoint to the Louvre, the giant glass and concrete arch of **La Tête Défense** is now the linchpin of the aggressively cityscaped suburb of La Défense. The world's most spectacular vista extends between this arch and the Louvre—via Napoleon's **Arc de Triomphe,** resplendent after cleaning and restoration, and **place de la Concorde,** whose grimy, flaking monumental statues of enthroned matriarchs (representing French cities) have reemerged in golden grandeur.

One way of keeping track of new developments in Paris is to pay a visit to the **Pavillon de l'Arsenal,** a handsomely restored glass-roofed building on the edge of the Marais, opened in 1989. Drawings, maps, photos, and scale models chart the changing urban scene, complemented by temporary exhibitions with architectural themes. Entrance is free.

The **Bastille Opera,** nearby, which was aimed to bring a traditionally élitist pastime to a mass audience, underwent a stormy baptism in 1989 as Musical Director Daniel Barenboim quit after a pay dispute. The public opening of the new opera house was consequently delayed until early 1990.

The word "stormy" does less than justice to the weather in **Nîmes** (Provence) one day in the fall of 1988, when an unprecedented **flash-flood** left thousands homeless and swamped the town's famous Roman remains. Things are pretty much back to normal, with the magnificently preserved amphitheater again the stage for bullfights rather than water polo. Modern architecture enthusiasts should note that Nîmes has underlined its "renaissance" by constructing the new **Costieres sports stadium,** widely acclaimed for its architecture and unique crowd-fencing system: Whole sections of fencing can swivel around at the press of a button, thereby avoiding the risk of overcrowding.

Also in southern France, a new **perfume museum** opened in Grasse—fragrance capital to the world—and two stylish **hotels** opened in Nice. The self-styled "Queen of the Riviera" has long struggled to match its tourist appeal with good hotel accommodation—so the arrival of the **Elysée Palace** near the seafront, and the more intimate **Beau Rivage** downtown, is more than welcome.

For travelers on a tight budget, a new chain of hotels known as **Formule 1** has sprung up nationwide. Rooms are unpretentious but cost only 110 francs per night for one, two, or three persons.

1989 was a boom year for the French leisure industry. Several amusement parks opened their doors, stealing a march on the European Disneyland east of Paris, plans for which are now well under way.

Chief of the new parks is the **Parc Astérix** at Plailly, just off the A1 expressway 32 kilometers (20 miles) north of Paris. The park is inspired by the popular French cartoon here Asterix and his fellow Gauls, whose adventures take place during the Roman invasion of France 2,000 years ago. An eastern France counterpart, the **Nouveau Monde des Schtroumpfs,** opened at Hagondange, just off the A31 expressway between Metz and Luxembourg. Some $100 million has been plowed into the 100-acre site, yielding such goodies as a Time Tunnel, City of Water, Metal Planet, and three-dimensional movie-cinema, not forgetting the Village of the Schtroumpfs (the cute blue dwarves known as Smurfs in English).

A vacation center combining sporting activity and health treatment has opened at Anglet on the Atlantic coast between Bayonne and Biarritz. The $10 million **Atlanthal** complex comprises hotel and thalassotherapy (or seawater therapy) center with heated pool, mudbaths, gym, weight-training, saunas and Turkish bath, as well as golf and tennis facilities.

For a slightly different type of vacation, **Center Parcs,** a leisure idea that has proved a success in Holland and Germany, has established a new "vacation village" at Verneuil-sur-Avre, 110 kilometers (70 miles) west of Paris. The village, made up of shops, restaurants and 650 cottages, is centered around a luxurious swimming pool equipped with wave machines and water slides. Peace and quiet is guaranteed: The village is set in a forest and cars are banned.

The **French rail system** continues to consolidate its reputation as the best in the world. A new branch of the TGV (High Speed Train) was opened in 1989 between Paris and Nantes on the Atlantic coast, slashing travel time from 3½ to two hours. Of even greater tourist interest will be the new run between Paris and the southwest, scheduled to begin operation in 1990. This will put Bordeaux at three hours from the capital instead of 4½, with stops at the historic towns of Poitiers and Angoulême. Tours and the Loire Valley—one hour instead of two—will become within day-trip range of Paris, while the delightful old town of Vendôme, formerly a rickety two hours away, will take just 40 minutes to reach.

The new TGV trains, to have distinctive blue and white livery, have been timed at 255 mph during practice runs, though for safety reasons they will content themselves with a mere 190 mph for passenger journeys. The new trains can hold 485 passengers and will be sound-proofed, air-conditioned, and equipped with telephones and even "boardroom" type cars. All TGV trains serving the Atlantic coast will leave from Gare Montparnasse (Bordeaux trains used to leave from Gare d'Austerlitz). It is no surprise that the Spanish government has placed a giant order for TGV rolling stock with the aim of cutting train travel time between Paris and Madrid from 20 hours to eight hours by the year 2000.

In Paris, a new branch of the super-fast suburban train system (RER-C) has been opened linking the Invalides/Eiffel Tower to the northern suburbs, interconnecting with the Métro network at La Muette and Porte Maillot. The new line rockets over the Seine (along a long-disused bridge) near the Eiffel Tower.

A new way of traveling down the Seine was launched in 1989, called **Bat-O-Bus.** Unlike the existing Bateaux Mouches, this is a passenger boat service with six stops between the Eiffel Tower and the Hôtel de Ville. Ticket prices —30 francs—are no giveaway, but this is a fine way to enjoy some leisurely sightseeing while avoiding the Métro.

Chief development on the **French road network** in 1989 was the opening of the Laon–Reims section of the A26 expressway. There is now an uninterrupted expressway run from Calais to Strasbourg (640 kilometers/400 miles).

On the **political front:** Barring accidents, 1990 should see President François Mitterrand enter his tenth year in office, with his popularity, and that of the center-left government led by Michel Rocard, riding high. The French economy has enjoyed a mini-boom in the late eighties, with inflation restricted to a modest 3% per year and the lingering after-effects of Black Monday finally forgotten.

1989 saw elections for town and city mayors, with traditional left–right voting patterns halted by personalized,

American-style campaigns that saw a new generation of charismatic politicians elected: Michel Noir in Lyon, for instance, and Robert Vigouroux in Marseille. Paris mayor (and hapless presidential challenger) Jacques Chirac received across-the-board approval of the dynamic way he runs the capital.

Hostility to a planned subway system led to the downfall of Marcel Rudloff, veteran mayor of Strasbourg, and reflected a nationwide surge in support for the Green (Ecologist) Party. This suggests that the French have at last awoken to environmental problems; lead-free gas is making a tentative appearance at the pumps. The price of gas in France—unleaded or not—remains, however, among the highest in Europe.

1989 also witnessed European Parliament elections and provoked much talk of the European Ideal, in which France is a firm believer. Symptoms included a government decree for children to study foreign languages at grade school. After the French Revolution Bicentennial of 1989, the "Greater Europe" of 1992 (when customs formalities within the European Community will be abolished) is the next major event on everyone's lips.

Fodor's Choice

No two people will agree on what makes a perfect vacation, but it's fun—and can be helpful—to know what others think. We hope you'll have a chance to experience some of Fodor's Choices yourself while you're visiting France. For detailed information about each entry, refer to the appropriate chapters within this guidebook.

Hotels

La Cour des Loges, Lyon (*Very Expensive*)
Crillon, Paris (*Very Expensive*)
Le Palais, Biarritz (*Very Expensive*)
Westminster, Le Touquet (*Very Expensive*)
Angleterre, Paris (*Expensive*)
Grand Hôtel de Cala Rossa, Porto-Vecchio (*Expensive*)
Mas du Langoustier, Ile de Porquerolles (*Expensive*)
Château de Bellecroix, Chagny (*Moderate*)
L'Hostellerie du Vieux Cordes, Cordes (*Moderate*)
Louvre, Nîmes (*Moderate*)

Restaurants

Boyer–Les Crayères, Reims (*Very Expensive*)
L'Espérance, St-Père-sous-Vézelay (*Very Expensive*)
Le Grand Véfour, Paris (*Very Expensive*)
Georges Blanc, Vonnas (*Very Expensive*)
Joël Robuchon, Paris (*Very Expensive*)
Château d'Esclimont, near Maintenon (*Expensive*)
Le Centenaire, Les Eyzies de Tarsac (*Expensive*)
Hiély-Lucullus, Avignon (*Moderate*)
Mas de la Chapelle, Arles (*Moderate*)
Au Gourmet sans Chiqué, Strasbourg (*Inexpensive–Moderate*)

Historic Towns and Villages

Les Baux de Provence
Beaune
Cluny
Cordes
Laon
Rocamadour
St-Emilion
Troyes
Vendôme

Drives

The Seine Valley from Mantes-la-Jolie to Rouen
The Voie Express Georges Pompidou (Paris) along the north bank of the Seine
Through the Beauce from Chartres to Vendôme
Along the Route du Vin (wine road) in Alsace
Along the banks of the Loire between Blois and Saumur
Across the Marais Poitevin from Niort to La Rochelle
The Gorges du Verdon in the Alpes de Haute-Provence

Across the Camargue from Aigues-Mortes to Saintes-Maries-de-la-Mer

Along the Scali di Santa Regina (D84) from inland Corsica to the coast at Piana

Museums

Musée des Beaux-Arts, Dijon
Musée Condé, Chantilly
Musée Ingres, Montauban
Musée Matisse, Le Cateau-Cambrésis
Musée National de l'Automobile and Musée Français du Chemin de Fer (National Car and Train Museums), Mulhouse
Musée de l'Oeuvre Notre-Dame, Strasbourg
Musée d'Orsay, Paris
Musée Unterlinden, Colmar

Works of Art

Apocalypse Tapestry, Angers (castle museum)
Bayeux Tapestry, Bayeux (Musée de la Tapisserie)
Gericault's *Raft of the Medusa*, Paris (Louvre)
Grünewald's *Issenheim Altarpiece*, Colmar (Musée Unterlinden)
Janmot's *Poem of the Soul* painting cycle, Lyon (Musée des Beaux-Arts)
Rodin's sculpture *The Burghers of Calais*, Calais
Sculpted tombs, Dreux (Chapelle Royale)
Stained glass, Chartres (cathedral)

Churches and Abbeys

Abbey of St-Savin, St-Savin
Basilica of Ste-Madeleine, Vézelay
Cathedral, Amiens
Cathedral, Bourges
Mont-St-Michel
Notre-Dame, Guebwiller
Notre-Dame-la-Grande, Poitiers
Ste-Foy, Conques
St-Urbain, Troyes

Gardens

Château of Vaux le Vicomte
Château of Versailles
Château of Villandry
Jardin du Thabor, Rennes
Jardin des Tuileries, Paris
Musée Rodin, Paris
Orangerie, Strasbourg

Streets and Squares

Cours Mirabeau, Aix-en-Provence
La Croisette, Cannes
Main street, Riquewihr
Place de la Bourse, Bordeaux
Place du Capitole, Toulouse
Place Stanislas, Nancy

Place Vendôme, Paris
Place des Vosges, Paris

Châteaus and Castles

Chambord, Loire Valley
Chenonceau, Loire Valley
Fontainebleau, Ile de France
Hautefort, Périgord
Josselin, Brittany
Pierrefonds, Oise
Vitré, Brittany

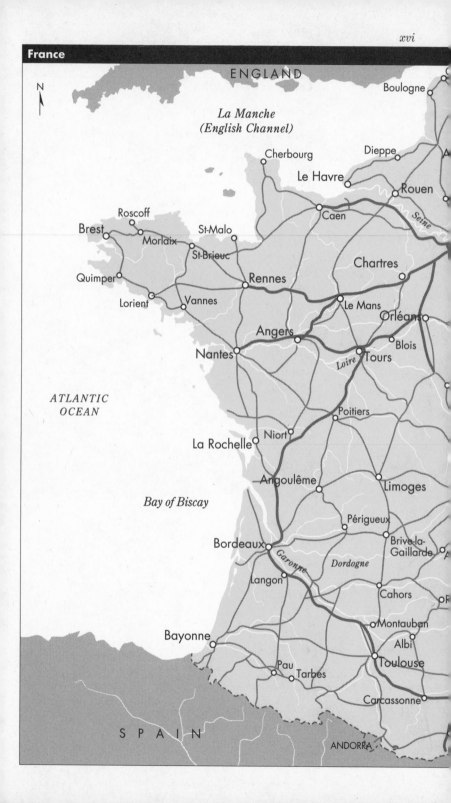

Calais
BELGIUM
Lille
Arras
Amiens
Cambrai
St. Quentin
LUXEMBOURG
Beauvais
Reims
Metz
Paris
Châlons-sur-Marne
Nancy
Strasbourg
Rhine
WEST
GERMANY
Troyes
Auxerre
Mulhouse
Belfort
Bourges
Beaune
Dijon
Besançon
Nevers
SWITZERLAND
Montluçon
Macon
Bourg-en-Bresse
Saône
Clermont-Ferrand
Lyon
Rhône
ITALY
Chambéry
Aurillac
Le Puy
Grenoble
Rhône
Rodez
Montélimar
Millau
Avignon
Nîmes
Monte Carlo
Montpellier
Aix-en-Provence
Nice
Cannes
Narbonne
Marseille
Toulon
Perpignan
0   50 mi
0   75 km
Mediterranean Sea
Corsica

Corsica
Bastia
Calvi
Corte
Ajaccio

World Time Zones

Numbers below vertical bands relate each zone to Greenwich Mean Time (0 hrs.).
Local times may differ, as indicated by lightface numbers on the map.

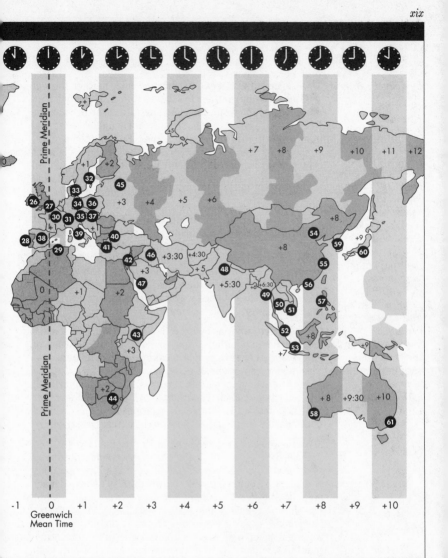

Mecca, **47**
Mexico City, **12**
Miami, **18**
Montreal, **15**
Moscow, **45**
Nairobi, **43**
New Orleans, **11**
New York City, **16**

Ottawa, **14**
Paris, **30**
Perth, **58**
Reykjavík, **25**
Rio de Janeiro, **23**
Rome, **39**
Saigon, **51**

San Francisco, **5**
Santiago, **21**
Seoul, **59**
Shanghai, **55**
Singapore, **52**
Stockholm, **32**
Sydney, **61**
Tokyo, **60**

Toronto, **13**
Vancouver, **4**
Vienna, **35**
Warsaw, **36**
Washington, DC, **17**
Yangon, **49**
Zürich, **31**

Introduction

by John P. Harris

Born in England, John P. Harris has lived in a small village in the south of France since 1975. He has written numerous articles for both French and British newspapers and magazines, including the London Times, *and is the author of* France—a Guide for the Independent Traveler *(Macmillan, London 1987).*

France is neither too hot nor too cold, neither too wet nor too dry, neither too flat nor too crammed with inconvenient mountains. At any rate, that is what the French say. They think that countries should be hexagonal in shape and about 600 miles across. Spain is too square, Norway is frayed at the edges, l'Angleterre (which is what they usually call Great Britain) is awkwardly surrounded by cold water, Switzerland landlocked and too small, and the United States too large (you cross three time zones and then get the same depressing dinner). After God created France, He belatedly realized that He had gone too far: It was too near perfection. "How can I restore the balance?" He asked Himself. Then He saw what to do—He created the French. That is a French story. The French enjoy grumbling about themselves or, rather, about other French people, but in the same breath they admit that there is only one civilized way for people to live, and that is the French way, *la civilisation française.*

On the other hand, a chorus tells us that the French are a nation of individualists, and, indeed, at each corner of *l'hexagone,* there are people speaking strange languages— Basque, Breton, Flemish, Alsatian, Provençal and Catalan —many of whom (especially Bretons) get rather prickly if you call them French. And yet almost all of them feel that nonhexagonal ways of life are deviations from the civilized norm: barbarous, if not verging on the extraterrestrial.

My wife and I have been living in France for 15 years, and we have come to the conclusion that there is something to be said for this view. Our fellow-villagers are kind, patient, and friendly, behaving with natural dignity and good manners, like most of the other French people we meet (except Parisians in the rush hour). If we were to try to live in outlandish ways, doing the wrong things at the wrong times, we might meet with greater tolerance than in some other countries, but our life would be less easy and pleasant. Visitors to France, whether they stay a week or a year, will have a better time if they "go native" as far as they find it practicable—and when and where they don't, they should be philosophically aware of the drawbacks of trying to behave as in dear old Birmingham (AL or U.K.). This essay is about the French way of life as it impinges on the visitor, particularly the Anglo-Saxon visitor. (I am using the word "Anglo-Saxon" as the French use it. To them, Louis Armstrong, Robert Burns, James Joyce, and Frank Sinatra are representative Anglo-Saxons; Beowulf and King Alfred have nothing to do with it.)

Let's look at the French timetable. Most of them are up early, gulping a *café au lait* and getting to work by 8. By 10, Parisian executives are fuming because their London contacts haven't yet answered the phone (it's only 9 in England). There is no coffee break.

At noon, they are hungry. Work stops for two hours or longer. Museums and small shops close. *Le déjeuner* (called *le dîner* in the country) is a sacred rite. Fast-food outlets have multiplied, but the norm is a proper meal, taking an hour and a half; a surprising number, even of those who work in central Paris, manage to get home for it. However, the increasing number of women at work means that six lunches out of ten are eaten at restaurants or canteens; substantial freshly cooked affairs, eaten with serious critical attention. The French grew rich in the '60s: Back in 1920, they each ate nearly three pounds of bread a day—now it is just under a pound, with a corresponding increase in the consumption of meat, fish, and cheese. Less wine is drunk, but more of it is of higher quality. Quality is important. Bread, butter (margarine is for Americans and such), eggs, chickens, and cheese—basic things like these—can be had in perfection in France if you take time and trouble and pay the price. Rich and poor alike pay as much attention to bread and butter and eggs and the contents of the water jug as rich Anglo-Saxons might pay to the choice of steak and claret.

There is a typical restaurant in our nearest market town (pop. 6,000). It has only one menu: copious hors d'oeuvre, a fish dish or a light meat dish, a more serious meat dish, vegetables in season, a good cheese board, fruit or ice cream. It's always full by 12:30. A couple from San Francisco who stayed in a rented cottage in our village were hardly ever able to use it. They used to get up at 9 and have an Anglo-Saxon sort of breakfast, and so they were hopelessly out of phase with the commercial travelers (up at 6) who form the restaurant's main clientele. You can't start your lunch there at 1:30 or 2, and there are no doggy bags in France. We are in the Midi, where an early start and a siesta are convenient (many of the shops don't reopen until 3:30). However, the couple happily developed the picnic habit: France is God's own country for picnicking, if only you get to the *charcuterie* and the *boulangerie* and the *pâtisserie* well before they close at noon.

Back to work for another four-hour stretch. No tea or coffee break. Are the French mighty toilers? Yes and no. I have conducted oral language examinations in France and in England. The French expect me to keep on examining nonstop from 8 to 12:30 and again from 2 to 6:30. The merciful (lazy?) English think six hours of attentive interviewing per day, with breaks mid-morning and mid-afternoon, are all the human mind can stand. French schoolchildren have a much longer day than do Anglo-Saxon ones and have more to learn (enormously more than American children, who seem to the French to leave serious learning until university, if then; though U.S. postgraduate degrees are respected).

On the other hand, wage earners and schoolchildren have many leisure days. In the '80s, the average industrial worker put in 1,872 hours of work in the United States, 1,750 in Great Britain, but only 1,650 in France. Five weeks' paid vacation is the official minimum, and there are many public holidays. The children have Europe's longest school day, but they also have the longest vacations. The French have become addicts of leisure in the past two decades. They are the world's champions in ownership of *résidences secondaires:* One family in ten has a second house in the country, where they go on weekends and vacations, causing astounding traffic jams as they flee the cities.

But many French people want to be their own bosses. The price of independence is hard work. A motorized grocer comes to our village on Tuesday and Saturday. He and his wife seem happy working a 70-hour week. He takes one week's vacation a year. To him, company men seem featherbedded: 50% of all who work have secure tenure in their jobs, 27% buy their enterprise's products at reduced rates (electricity workers are given current almost free, for example), 24% get automatic promotion by seniority, 24% get six weeks' paid vacation or more; and there are all kinds of fringe benefits. But our grocer clings to independence. So do small family enterprises: the modest hotels, restaurants, little shops and garages that give such good service on a personal basis.

If he finishes his day's work at 6 or 6:30, will our average Frenchman call in at his favorite café for a chat and an aperitif on his way home? Probably not, nowadays. In the past, the café was used as a sort of extra living room for meeting friends or professional contacts, or even for writing novels if you were Jean-Paul Sartre or Simone de Beauvoir. But today, an average of two hours and 50 minutes is spent watching television at home, which reduces the time available for social life.

This is sad. The number of cafés has diminished. Fortunately, there are still a lot left, and how convenient they are for the visitor! Anglo-Saxon bars and pubs may be seen by the French as somber haunts where customers take refuge from the wife and children while getting soused as rapidly as possible. On the terrace of a French café, you can bask in the sun or enjoy the shade of a multicolored parasol, sipping a cool beer and keeping an eye on life's passing show, while your near and dear toy with popsicles or write letters. A small black coffee entitles you to spend an hour or two—no hurry. But in our market town, the cafés do good business only in the summer, when the tables are set out under the plane trees in the avenue, and then half the customers are "foreigners"—Parisians, Britons, the Dutch. . . .

While we are on the subject: It seems odd to the Anglo-Saxon that in France beer is generally considered a non-alcoholic drink. When you tell the French that some people at home succeed in getting nastily drunk on it, they say "But they must drink several glasses!" Indeed. A Frenchman will spend half an hour sipping a quarter of a liter. One sees few drunks in France, except in the north.

Nonetheless, alcoholism exists. The cause, usually, is excessive regular consumption of wine. The average is 73 liters a year, but it is those who drink substantially more than a liter a day who pay the price; they don't get rowdy, they succumb at last to cirrhosis of the liver. Let's not be gloomy. The French live fractionally longer than do Americans or Britons, and a moderate amount of daily wine is thought to be good for the health.

I mentioned the aperitif hour to talk not only about cafés but about friendliness. Some people—notably Americans—complain that the French are inhospitable and standoffish. The fact is that they are great respecters of privacy. If the Englishman's home is his castle, the Frenchman's apartment or house is his lair. People simply do not pop into one another's lairs, drinking casual cups of coffee and borrowing half a pound of sugar. They need a neutral place in which to socialize. Britons (more or less, depending on whether they live in the north or the south) come somewhere between typical French people and the American middle class. According to Paul Fussell (*Caste Marks*, 1983): "Among the [American] middles there's a convention that erecting a fence or even a tall hedge is an affront." And he quotes William H. Whyte, Jr., who was told: "The street behind us is nowhere near as friendly. They knock on doors over there."

It's different in France. People in the Midi, where we live, just love to talk, and even to listen. But our village neighbors are timid about entering our house. If they want to ask us something they will wait until we meet, or stay on the doorstep, or phone (from 50 yards away). They penetrate our house, and we penetrate theirs, when specifically invited—for aperitifs or dinner—and the occasion is rather formal. No potluck meals on the spur of the moment. That is how they behave among themselves, too. It's not because we are foreigners.

So when do we talk? If there was a café in our village, that would be the place, but the village is too small. Fortunately, there are only a few days in the year when open-air life is impossible, and there are benches everywhere, in the sun and in the shade. The villagers—and we—sit there for hours, chatting. Are you staying in a small country hotel or renting a vacation place? The locals really are interested in you, your habits and tastes, the number and ages of your children, your work, where you come from, and so forth, and are longing to impart a discreet selection of their own personal details. Of course you *may* be invited home. There are no rules about this sort of thing. And if there were, the French would take pleasure in breaking them.

When talking with the French, there are conventions that should be observed if you don't want to be thought a barbarian by people who are unaware of Anglo-Saxon attitudes. You must say *Bonjour,* followed by *Monsieur, Madame, Mademoiselle, Messieurs, Mesdames,* or *Messieurs-dames* much more often than you would think necessary (on entering a small shop, for instance) and *Au revoir Monsieur* (etc.). Hands are shaken frequently (by colleagues at work, morning and evening, and by the most casual acquaintances). *Bon appétit* can replace *Au revoir* shortly before mealtimes. On going through a door, a certain amount of *après-vous*-ing is normal, with *Pardon* if you go through first, turning your back. Getting on first-name terms is a sign of much greater intimacy than in England or the United States. Rush-hour Parisian life is more brutal, of course, and, as elsewhere in the world, the driving seat of a car exerts a malign influence. In England, a headlight flash sometimes means "After you"; in France, it means either "After me" or "I am a criminal and I expect you are, too, so watch it, chum, the cops are round the corner."

Back home from the café, there is, of course, television, about which the French have mixed feelings. At one and the same time, they envy the number of channels available to American viewers and feel superior about the low intellectual quality of American television, as reported by French sources. Old movies are the favorites. Lengthy and serious discussion programs have a wide audience, and so does *Apostrophes,* a literary program devoted to new middlebrow and highbrow books.

Le dîner (called *le souper* in the country) is at around 8, for rich and poor. It's a lighter meal than at midday, with soup replacing hors d'oeuvre. The schoolchildren will have finished their homework by then. Bed follows not long after. But the movies, after a sharp fall as television established itself in every home, have resisted well. Except in Paris, films are dubbed into French, a practice deplored by intellectuals. (Visitors to Paris who want to see a movie in the language it was made in should look for the abbreviation *v.o.*, meaning *version originale;* otherwise, they'll experience such shocks as seeing the space traveler in *"2001, A Space Odyssey"* pressing the button marked "English" at the satellite debriefing computer, only to receive the question *"Quelle est votre nationalité?"* to which the able astronaut replies, without blinking an eyelid, *"Américaine.")*

Almost all employed people now have a two-day weekend, usually Saturday and Sunday, but Sunday and Monday for many shop workers. Schoolchildren have Wednesday free. In recent years, the French have revolutionized their leisure habits: Jogging, swimming, soccer, gymnastics, tennis, and vigorous bicycling (for fun, not transport) are practiced, mainly on weekends, by large numbers of all social classes.

Sunday is a day for enjoying oneself. Though 85% of the population declare themselves Catholics, only 15% of those go to church every week. There is a fairly strong anti-Church sentiment among many, even among those who say they are Catholics (but the traditional warfare between priest and primary-school teacher, the one reactionary and the other attached to Republican ideals, is a thing of the past). Divorce, the pill, and safe legal abortion are widely accepted, even by practicing Catholics, who politely conceal their smiles when celibate ecclesiastics denounce such facilities.

The great Sunday ritual takes place at noon or soon after. Four out of ten will visit friends or relations. 60% of families do more cooking on Sundays than on other days. This is also a big day for restaurants who feature a special menu with somewhat higher prices. Half the French end their Sunday lunch with a fresh fruit tart or some sort of *gâteau*, which is why the pastry shops are open in the morning and why you see Frenchmen carefully carrying flat cardboard boxes. Then a quarter of the population takes a little siesta.

An essay such as this has to contain rash generalizations, unless it is to be five times the length, hedging every statement with ifs, buts, and exceptions. Is there an average French person? Obviously not. There are the rich and the poor, for example. But in the Anglo-Saxon world, there seem to be more class differences, apart from money, than in France. The Anglo-Saxon blue-collar worker—to speak only of food, an important enough subject—chooses different meals from the élite and eats them at different times. Not so in France where, however, income differences can be greater. The poor, in France, like champagne, oysters, and foie gras, but they get them less often than do the rich. The same is true of other aspects of life. The gulf between one class and another is not one of tastes and aspirations; rich and poor are in broad agreement on what constitutes a pleasant life. The poor are simply further away from it than are the rich.

Many of the unskilled sector and of the unemployed are North African immigrants, a reminder of France's colonial past. Frictions develop in rundown areas that have turned into ghettos. Extreme right-wing groups, notably the *Front National* under Le Pen, have picked up racist votes, capitalizing on the fear of insecurity. Theft and violent robbery have increased, but not as much as awareness of them. French enthusiasts for bringing back the death penalty are incredulous when told that the number of murders in France today is no greater than in 1825, when the population was half its present size. You are in no more danger of being murdered in France than in Britain, and in nine times less danger than in the United States.

Changing France. . . . I was there in 1947, and I said to myself: "How wonderful! But it can't last." On the whole it has. The surge of prosperity in the '60s brought improvements to French life, with some drawbacks (traffic in Paris, for example), but basic traditions die hard. The young ape foreign fashions, with a fast-food/motorcycle/mid-Atlantic pop noise/comic-strip culture, but they grow out of it. Official morality has changed. Contraception used to be forbidden; Paris was famed for its elegant brothels, but women had to go to London for diaphragms and to Switzerland for abortions. All that has gone. In 1988, the rise of AIDS caused a quickly smothered quarrel among bishops about the sinfulness of condoms, which are readily available. *Le topless* is seen on most beaches, and total nakedness on some. But the family remains a powerful cohesive unit, *jeunes filles* are very often *sérieuses* (an important word: "responsible" rather than "gloomy"), and foreign tourists looking for an easy lay can do better elsewhere.

What do they think of us? Corresponding to the Anglo-Saxon stereotype that depicts all Frenchmen wearing berets and pointed beards, waving their arms wildly and being saucy with the girls, the French picture Americans as rich, generous, overweight, and likely in world politics or personal relationships to behave like well-meaning bulls in china shops and the English as either tall, silent, inhibited, masochistic, and scrupulously honest or as drunken, sadistic, soccer-watching vandals. Of course nobody really believes any of this, but if you are going to attach a national label to yourself, you might as well be aware of the cliché lurking at the back of the mind.

"Happy as God in France" say the Germans, exaggerating a bit. Anglo-Saxons come in two sorts: those who love France and those who don't. It's a matter of taste and character. The former find it easy to slip into the French way of life for a week or a month or permanently. The latter are better off in Paris or on the Riviera. There, at a price, arrangements can be made to suit inflexible millionaires from Texas or the Middle East; you might even be able to get a classic dish served with milky breakfast coffee at three in the afternoon, shielded from the shudders of the natives. But really, the French are canny operators when it comes to enjoying *le douceur de vivre*, the sweetness of life. If you follow their example while in France, you can't go far wrong. (One way of going wrong might be to quote almost any paragraph from this essay to them; at any rate, it will start a vigorously French argument.)

1 Essential Information

Before You Go

Government Tourist Offices

Contact the French Government Tourist Offices for information on all aspects of travel to and in France.

In the U.S. 610 5th Ave., New York, NY 10020 (tel. 212/315–0888); 645 N. Michigan Ave., Chicago, IL 60611 (tel. 312/337–6301); 2305 Cedar Springs Rd., Dallas, TX 75201 (tel. 214/720–4010); 9401 Wilshire Blvd., Beverly Hills, CA 90212 (tel. 213/271–6665); 1 Hallidie Plaza, Suite 250, San Francisco, CA 94102 (tel. 415/986 –4174).

In Canada 1981 McGill College, Suite 490, Montreal, Quebec H3A 2W9 (tel. 514/288–4264); 1 Dundas St. W., Suite 2405, Box 8, Toronto, Ontario M5G 1Z3 (tel. 416/593–4723).

In the U.K. 178 Piccadilly, London W1V OAL England (tel. 01/491–7622).

Tour Groups

Care to balloon over the Loire Valley, sip wine with a countess in Burgundy, or just hop aboard a whistle-stop tour of the country's most famous highlights? Then you may want to consider a package tour. Creative itineraries abound, offering access to places you may not be able to get to on your own as well as the more traditional spots. They also tend to save you some money on air fare and hotels. If group outings are not your style, check into independent packages; somewhat more expensive than package tours, they are also more flexible.

When considering a tour, be sure to find out exactly what expenses are included (particularly tips, taxes, side trips, additional meals, and entertainment); governmental ratings of all hotels on the itinerary and the facilities they offer; cancellation policies for both you and the tour operator; and, if you are traveling alone, what the single supplement is. Most tour operators request that bookings be made through a travel agent— there is no additional charge for doing so. Below is a sampling of the many tour options available. Contact your travel agent or the French Government Tourist Office for additional resources.

General-Interest Tours **American Express Vacations** (Box 5014, Atlanta, GA 30302, tel. 800/241–1700 or, in Georgia, 800/637–6200) is a veritable supermarket of tours; you name it—they've either got it packaged or will customize a package for you. **Globus Gateway** (150 S. Los Robles Ave., Suite 860, Pasadena, CA 91101, tel. 818/449–0919 or 800/556–5454) offers the hectic but comprehensive 15-day "La France." **Jet Vacations** (888 7th Ave., New York, NY 10106, tel. 212/247–0999 or 800/JET–0999) features "Paris & Châteaux Country" and "Paris, Burgundy, Provence & the Riviera." **Trafalgar Tours** (21 E. 26th St., New York, NY 10010, tel. 212/689–8977 or 800/854–0103) offers a moderately priced, two-week "Best of France" program. The 17-day "Best of France" package from **Hemphill/Harris** (16000 Ventura Blvd., Suite 200, Encino, CA 90024, tel. 818/906–8086 or 800/ 421–0454) is distinctly top of the line (and priced accordingly).

Special-Interest Tours Wine/Cuisine	**Travel Concepts** (373 Commonwealth Ave., Suite 601, Boston, MA 02115-1815, tel. 617/266–8450) serves up such specialties as "Champagne and Cuisine with Mrs. Charles Heidsieck" (of Heidsieck Champagne fame), "Burgundy: History, Wine & Cuisine with Countess De Loisy," and, for the serious wine-lover, a week-long seminar at the University of Wine in the Rhône Valley.
Art/Architecture	**Past Times Arts and Archaeological Tours** (800 Larch Lane, Sacramento, CA 95864-5042, tel. 916/485–8140) escorts the curious through the strange world of prehistoric cave art in southern France. Its "Paris Art Museums and Historic Neighborhoods" is a tour that tells as well as shows.
Cycling	**Sobek Expeditions** (Box 1089, Angels Camp, CA 95222, tel. 209/736–4524) gets the blood flowing with its "Tour de France" ride through the French countryside from Burgundy to the Bay of Biscay.
Ballooning	**Buddy Bombard Balloon Adventures** (6727 Curran St., McLean, VA 22101-3804, tel. 703/448–9407 or 800/862–8537) takes groups of a dozen or fewer into the gentle breezes above Burgundy and the Loire Valley during its three-night to six-night tours. Fine dining back on the ground is an added touch.
Barge Cruising	Drift in leisure and luxury through Burgundy, Champagne country, and other scenic areas on any of four tours with **Floating Through Europe** (271 Madison Ave., New York, NY 10016, tel. 212/685–5600).
Singles and Young Couples	**Trafalgar Tours** (*see* General-Interest Tours) offers "Club 21–35," faster paced tours for travelers who are not afraid of a little physical activity—whether it's bike riding or discoing the night away.
Music	**Dailey-Thorp Travel** (315 W. 57th St., New York, NY 10019, tel. 212/307–1555) offers deluxe opera and music tours, including "French Festivals." Itineraries vary according to available performances.

Package Deals for Independent Travelers

Self-drive tours are popular in France, and **The French Experience** (171 Madison Ave., New York, NY 10016, tel. 212/683–2445) has put together nine different routes, including "The Châteaux Experience" with stays at private châteaus and manor houses. **Abercrombie & Kent International** (1420 Kensington Road, Oak Brook, IL 60521, tel. 312/954–2944) adds the option of a chauffeur to its somewhat pricier deluxe driving tours. **Air France** (666 5th Ave., New York, NY 10103, tel. 212/247–0100) offers week-long air/hotel packages to Paris and the Riviera. **Pan Am Holidays** (800/THE–TOUR) and **TWA Vacations** (800/GETAWAY) have similar flexible packages. "France à la Carte" is a menu of hotel packages available in Paris and Nice from **The French Experience** (see above).

When to Go

On the whole, June and September are the best months to be in France, since both are free of the mid-summer crowds. June offers the advantage of long daylight hours, while slightly cheaper prices and frequent Indian summers (often lasting well into October) make September an attractive proposition.

Try to avoid the second half of July and all August, or be prepared for inflated prices and huge crowds on the roads and beaches. Don't travel on or around July 14 and August 1, 14, and 31. July and August can be stifling in southern France. Paris can be stuffy in August, too, but it is pleasantly deserted (although many restaurants, theaters, and small shops are closed).

The skiing season in the Alps and Pyrenees lasts from Christmas to Easter; do not go in February if you can avoid it (vacation time for schoolchildren). Anytime between March and November will offer you a good chance to soak up the sun on the Riviera, though, of course, you'll tan quicker between June and September. If Paris and the Loire are among your priorities, remember that the weather is unappealing before Easter. If you're dreaming of Paris in the springtime, May (not April) is your best bet.

Climate The following are average daily maximum and minimum temperatures for Paris and Nice.

Paris								
Jan.	43F	6C	**May**	68F	20C	**Sept.**	70F	21C
	34	1		49	10		53	12
Feb.	45F	7C	**June**	73F	23C	**Oct.**	60F	16C
	34	1		55	13		46	8
Mar.	54F	12C	**July**	76F	25C	**Nov.**	50F	10C
	39	4		58	15		40	5
Apr.	60F	16C	**Aug.**	75F	24C	**Dec.**	44F	7C
	43	6		58	15		36	2

Nice								
Jan.	55F	13C	**May**	68F	20C	**Sept.**	77F	25C
	39	4		55	13		61	16
Feb.	55F	13C	**June**	75F	24C	**Oct.**	70F	21C
	41	5		61	16		54	12
Mar.	59F	15C	**July**	81F	27C	**Nov.**	63F	17C
	45	7		64	18		46	8
Apr.	64F	18C	**Aug.**	81F	27C	**Dec.**	55F	13C
	46	8		64	18		41	5

Updated hourly weather information in 235 cities around the world—180 of them in the United States—is only a phone call away. Telephone numbers for **WeatherTrak** in the 12 cities where the service is available may be obtained by calling 800/247–3282. A taped message will tell you to dial the three-digit access code to any of the 235 destinations. The code is either the area code (in the United States) or the first three letters of the foreign city. For a list of all access codes, send a stamped, self-addressed envelope to Cities, Box 7000, Dallas, TX 75209. For further information, phone 214/869–3035 or 800/247–3282.

Public Holidays January 1, Easter Monday, May 1 (Labor Day), May 8 (VE Day—a new holiday and not observed as extensively as the others), Ascension Day (five weeks after Easter), Monday after Pentecost, July 14 (Bastille Day), August 15 (Assumption), November 1 (All Saints), November 11 (Armistice), and Christmas Day. If a public holiday falls on a Tuesday or a Thursday, many businesses and shops and some restaurants close on the Monday or Friday, too.

Festivals and Seasonal Events

Top seasonal events in France include the Monte Carlo Motor Rally in January, February's Carnival in Nice, the Cannes Film Festival in May, Paris's French Open Tennis Championships in May, the Festival du Marais in Paris in July, July's Bastille Day, and the September Autumn Festival in Paris. Contact the French Government Tourist Office for exact dates and further information.

Jan. International Circus Festival, featuring top acts from around the world, is held in Monaco.

Mid- to late Jan. Monte Carlo Motor Rally, one of the motoring world's most venerable races, has its finish line in the streets of Monaco.

Mid- to late Feb. Carnival of Nice provides an exotic blend of parades and revelry during the weeks leading up to Lent.

Late Mar. to early Apr. Prix du President de la République takes place at Auteuil Racecourse in Paris.

Mid- to late Apr. Monte Carlo Open Tennis Championships get under way at the ultraswanky Monte Carlo Country Club.

Apr. to Sept. Sound and Light Shows (son-et-lumière), historical pageants featuring special lighting effects, are held at many châteaus in the Loire Valley.

Mid- to late May. Cannes Film Festival sees two weeks of star-studded events.

Mid-May. International Marathon of Paris leaves from the place de la Concorde and ends at the Château de Vincennes, in Paris's eastern suburb. **Monaco Grand Prix** races through the streets of Monaco.

Late May to mid-June. Lyon International Festival spells three weeks of artistic celebrations, held at various locations in Lyon.

Late May to mid-June. French Open Tennis Championships get under way at Roland Garros Stadium in Paris.

Mid-June to mid-July. Festival du Marais, including everything from music to dance to theater, is held in Paris. (Tickets: 68 rue François-Miron, 75004 Paris, tel. 48–87–74–31.)

Mid-June. Strasbourg International Music Festival features concerts in various city cathedrals and halls. (Tickets: 24 rue de la Mésange, 67081 Strasbourg, tel. 88–56–04–77.) **Grand Steeplechase de Paris** is a popular horse race at Auteuil Racecourse, Paris.

Late June. Grand Prix de Paris, a major test for equine three-year-olds, gets under way at Longchamp Racecourse.

Early July to early Aug. Festival of Avignon affords almost an entire month of top-notch theater throughout Avignon. (Tickets: Bureau de Festival, 8-bis rue de Mons, 84000 Avignon, tel. 90–82–67–08.)

Mid-July. Grand Parade of Jazz provides nearly two weeks of musical entertainment in Nice.

July 14. Bastille Day, a national holiday commemorated throughout the country, celebrates the Storming of the Bastille in 1789—the start of the French Revolution.

Mid- to late July. Festival of Lyric Art and Music brings nearly three weeks of musical entertainment to Aix-en-Provence. (Tickets: Palais de l'Ancien Archevêché, 13100 Aix-en-Provence, tel. 42–23–34–82.)

Mid-July to late Sept. Festival Estival of Paris hosts classical concerts in churches, museums, and concert halls throughout the city. (Tickets: 5 pl. des Ternes, 75017 Paris, tel. 42–27–12–68.)

Mid-July to early Aug. International Fireworks Festival features spectacular displays of pyrotechnics in Monaco.

Late July. Tour de France, the world's most famous bicycle race, has its finish line on the Champs-Elysées on the penultimate Sunday in July; all Paris turns out to cheer.

Sept. Music Festival of Besançon and Franche-Comté hosts a series of chamber music concerts in and around Besançon. (Tickets: 2d rue Isenbart, 25000 Besançon, tel. 81–80–73–26.)

Mid-Sept. to Dec. Festival of Autumn is a major arts festival held throughout Paris. (Tickets: 156 rue de Rivoli, 75001 Paris, tel. 42–96–12–27.)

Early Oct. Prix de l'Arc de Triomphe, a venerable annual horse race, is held at Longchamp Racecourse in Paris.

Oct. *Vendages* (grape harvest) **festivals** are held in the country's wine regions.

Late Nov. Les Trois Glorieuses is Burgundy's biggest wine festival, featuring the year's most important wine auction and related merriment in several Burgundy locations.

Dec. 24 Shepherd's Festival, a Christmas celebration, featuring midnight mass and picturesque "living cribs," is held in Les Baux, Provence.

Late Dec. to early Jan. Christmas in Paris spells celebrations, especially for children, during the school holiday.

What to Pack

Pack light: Baggage carts are scarce in airports and railroad stations, and luggage restrictions on international flights are tight. Airlines allow two pieces of check-in luggage and one carry-on piece, per passenger. Each piece of check-in luggage cannot exceed 62 inches (length plus width plus height) or weigh more than 70 pounds. The carry-on luggage cannot exceed 45 inches (length plus width plus height) and must fit under the seat or in the overhead luggage compartment.

Clothing   What you pack depends more on the time of year than on any particular dress code. Northeastern France is hot in the summer and cold in the winter. You'll need a raincoat or an umbrella for Paris any time of the year and a sweater or warm jacket for the Mediterranean areas during the winter.

For the cities, pack as you would for an American city: cocktail outfits for formal restaurants and nightclubs, casual clothes for sightseeing. Jeans, as popular in France as anywhere else, are acceptable for sightseeing and informal dining. However, a jeans-and-sneakers outfit will cause raised eyebrows at theaters or expensive restaurants or when visiting French families. The rule here is to dress up rather than down. The exception is in young or bohemian circles where casual dress is always the rule.

Men and women who wear shorts will probably be denied admission to churches and cathedrals, although there is no longer any need for women to cover their heads and arms. For the beach resorts, pack something to wear over your bathing suit when you leave the beach. Wearing bathing suits on the street is frowned upon.

Most casinos and nightclubs along the Riviera require jackets and ties. They are the place for chic cocktail dresses and tuxedos, if you like to dress formally. Casual dresses and slacks outfits are also appropriate.

Miscellaneous You'll need an adapter for hair dryers and other small appliances. The electrical current in France is 220 volts and 50 cycles. If you are staying in budget hotels, take along small bars of soap; many do not provide soap or limit guests to one tiny bar per room.

Carry-on Luggage New rules have been in effect since January 1, 1988, on U.S. airlines regarding carry-on luggage. The model for these new rules was agreed to by the airlines in December 1987 and then circulated by the Air Transport Association with the understanding that each airline would present its own version.

According to the model, passengers are limited to two carry-on bags. For a bag you wish to store under the seat, the maximum dimensions are 9 inches × 14 inches × 22 inches, a total of 45 inches. For bags that can be hung in a closet or on a luggage rack, the maximum dimensions are 4 inches × 23 inches × 45 inches, a total of 72 inches. For bags you wish to store in an overhead bin, the maximum dimensions are 10 inches × 14 inches × 36 inches, a total of 60 inches. Your two carry-ons must each fit one of these sets of dimensions, and any item that exceeds the specified dimensions will generally be rejected as a carry-on and handled as checked baggage. Keep in mind that an airline can adapt these rules to circumstances, so on an especially crowded flight, don't be surprised if you are only allowed one carry-on bag.

In addition to the two carry-ons, the rules list eight items that may also be brought aboard: a handbag (pocketbook or purse); an overcoat or wrap; an umbrella; a camera; a reasonable amount of reading material; an infant bag; crutches, a cane, braces, or other prosthetic devices on which the passenger is dependent; and an infant/child safety seat.

Note that these regulations are for U.S. airlines only. Foreign airlines generally allow one piece of carry-on luggage in tourist class in addition to handbags and bags filled with duty-free goods. Passengers in first and business class are also allowed to carry on one garment bag. It is best to check with your airline ahead of time to find out what their exact rules are regarding carry-on luggage.

Checked Luggage U.S. airlines allow passengers to check in two suitcases whose total dimensions (length plus width plus height) do not exceed 60 inches. There are no weight restrictions on these bags.

Rules governing foreign airlines vary from airline to airline, so check with your travel agent or the airline before you go. All the airlines allow passengers to check in two bags. In general, expect the weight restriction on the two bags to be no more than 70 pounds each and the total dimensions on the first bag to be 62 inches and on the second bag, 55 inches.

Taking Money Abroad

Traveler's checks and major U.S. credit cards—particularly Visa, often going under the name of France's domestic equivalent, Carte Bleue—are accepted in the larger cities and tourist areas. In small towns and rural areas, you'll need cash. Even in the larger cities, many small restaurants and shops operate on a cash basis. You won't get as good an exchange rate at home as abroad, but it's wise to exchange a small amount of money into French francs before you go to avoid long lines at airport currency-exchange booths. Most U.S. banks will change your money into francs. If your local bank can't provide this service, you can exchange money through **Deak International.** To find the office nearest you, contact the headquarters (630 5th Ave., New York, NY 10111, tel. 212/635–0515).

For safety and convenience, it's always best to take traveler's checks. The most recognized traveler's checks are **American Express, Barclays, Thomas Cook,** and those issued through major commercial banks such as **Citibank** and **Bank of America.** Some banks will issue the checks free to established customers, but most charge a 1% commission fee. Buy part of the traveler's checks in small denominations to cash toward the end of your trip. It will save you having to cash a large check and ending up with more francs than you need. You can also buy traveler's checks in francs, a good idea if the dollar is falling and you want to lock in the current rate. Don't forget to take the addresses of offices where you can get refunds for lost or stolen traveler's checks.

Getting Money from Home

There are at least three ways to get money from home: (1) Have it sent through a large commercial bank with a branch in the town where you're staying. The only drawback is that you must have an account with the bank; if you don't, you'll have to go through your bank, and the process will be slower and more expensive. (2) Have it sent through American Express. If you are a cardholder, you can cash a personal check or a counter check at an American Express office for up to $1,000; $200 will be in cash and $800 in traveler's checks. There is a 1% commission on the traveler's checks. American Express has a new service available in France and most major cities worldwide, called **American Express MoneyGram.** Through this service, even non-cardholders can receive up to $5,000 cash. It works this way: you call home and ask someone to go to an American Express office or an American Express MoneyGram agent located in a retail outlet and fill out an American Express MoneyGram (it can be paid for with cash or any major credit card). The person making the payment is given a reference number and telephones you with that number. The American Express MoneyGram agent calls an 800 number and authorizes the transfer of funds to an American Express office or participating agency in the town where you're staying. In most cases, the money is available immediately on a 24-hour basis. You pick it up by showing identification and giving the reference number that was phoned to you by the person who purchased the American Express MoneyGram. Fees vary according to the amount of money sent. For sending $300, the fee is $22; for $5,000, $150. (For the American Express MoneyGram location nearest your home and for locations overseas, call 800/543–4080.) You do not have to be a cardholder to use this service. (3) Have it sent through **Western Union.** (The U.S. number: 800/325–6000.) If you have a MasterCard or Visa, you can have money sent for any amount up to your credit limit. If not, have someone take cash or a certified cashier's check to a Western Union office. The money will be delivered within two business days to a bank in the city where you're staying. Fees vary with the amount of money sent. For sending $1,000, the fee is $69; for $500, $59.

French Currency

The units of currency in France are the franc (fr.) and the centime. The bills are 500, 200, 100, 50, and 20 francs. Coins are 10, 5, 2, and 1 francs, and 50, 20, 10, and 5 centimes. At press time (May '89), the exchange rate was about 6.29 francs to the U.S. dollar, 4.5 to the Canadian dollar, and 10.6 to the pound sterling.

What It Will Cost

Inflation in France has been low in the late '80s, around 2%–3% annually. Air and car travel in France can be expensive (gas prices are above average and tolls are payable on most highways). Train travel, though, is a good value.

Hotel and restaurant prices compensate for the expense of travel. Prices are above average in Paris, on the Riviera, and in the Alps during the skiing season (worst here in February). But even in these areas, you can find pleasant accommodations and excellent food at moderate prices. In rural areas and throughout northern France, it is difficult to spend much even if you want to! Hotels in the Loire Valley are not high priced, but try to book well ahead in summer.

Taxes All taxes must be included in affixed prices in France. The initials TTC (toutes taxes comprises—taxes included) sometimes appear on price lists but, strictly speaking, are superfluous. By law, restaurant and hotel prices must include 18.6% taxes and a service charge. If you discover these have rematerialized as additional items on your bill, kick up a fuss.

Sample Prices The following prices are for Paris; other cities/areas are often cheaper.

Coffee in a bar: 3.80 francs (standing), 6 francs (seated); beer in a bar: 6 francs (standing), 8.50 francs (seated); Coca Cola: 6–10 francs a can; ham sandwich: 12–15 francs; one-mile taxi ride: 20–25 francs; movie-theater seat: 30–35 francs (30% cheaper on Monday); foreign newspaper: 8 francs.

Passports and Visas

Americans All U.S. citizens require a passport for entry into France. Applications for a new passport must be made in person; renewals can be obtained in person or by mail (see below). First-time applicants should apply well in advance of their departure date to one of the 13 U.S. Passport Agency offices. In addition, local county courthouses, many state and probate courts, and some post offices accept passport applications. Necessary documents include (1) a completed passport application (Form DSP-11), (2) proof of citizenship (birth certificate with a raised seal or naturalization papers), (3) proof of identity (driver's license, employee identification card, or any other document with your photograph and signature), (4) two recent, identical, two-inch-square photographs (black and white or color), (5) $42 application fee for a 10-year passport (those under 18 pay $27 for a five-year passport). Passports are mailed to you in about 10 working days.

To renew your passport by mail, you'll need completed Form DSP-82, two recent, identical passport photographs, and a check or money order for $35.

At press time, U.S. citizens needed a visa to enter France, but this may be discontinued soon; check with the French Consulate or the nearest French National Tourist Office.

Canadians All Canadians require a passport for entry into France. Send a completed application (available at any post office or passport office) to the Bureau of Passports, External Affairs (Ottawa, Ont. K1A 0G3). Include $25, two photographs, a guarantor, and proof of Canadian citizenship. Applications can be made in person at the regional passport offices in Edmonton, Halifax, Montreal, Toronto, Vancouver, or Winnipeg. Passports are valid for five years and are nonrenewable.

Visas are required by Canadian citizens to enter France. Obtain details from the French Consulate or the French National Tourist Office.

Britons All British citizens need passports, applications for which are available from travel agencies or a main post office. Send the completed form to a regional Passport Office or apply in person at a main post office. You'll need two photographs and will be charged a £15 fee. The occasional tourist might opt for a British Visitors Passport. It is valid for one year, costs £7.50, and is nonrenewable. You'll need two passport photographs and identification. Apply at your local post office.

Visas are not required for British citizens entering France.

Customs and Duties

On Arrival There are two levels of duty-free allowance for travelers entering France: one for those coming from an EEC country and the other for those coming from anywhere else.

In the first category, you may import duty-free: 300 cigarettes or 150 cigarillos or 75 cigars or 400 grams of tobacco; five liters of table wine and (1) 1½ liters of alcohol over 22% volume (most spirits), (2) two liters of alcohol under 22% by volume (fortified or sparkling wine), or (3) three more liters of table wine; 75 grams of perfume; 375ml of toilet water; and other goods to the value of 2,400 francs (620 francs for those under 15).

In the second category, you may import duty-free: 200 cigarettes or 100 cigarillos or 50 cigars or 250 grams tobacco (these allowances are doubled if you live outside Europe); two liters of wine and (1) one liter of alcohol over 22% volume (most spirits), (2) two liters of alcohol under 22% volume (fortified or sparkling wine), or (3) two more liters of table wine; 50 grams of perfume; ¼ liter of toilet water; and other goods to the value of 300 francs (150 francs for those under 15).

Any amount of French or foreign currency may be brought into France, but foreign currencies converted into francs may be reconverted into a foreign currency only up to the equivalent of 5,000 francs. Similarly, no more than 5,000 francs may be exported and no more than the equivalent of 2,000 francs in foreign currency may be exported.

On Departure
U.S. Customs

U.S. residents who are bringing any foreign-made equipment from home, such as cameras, would be wise to carry the original receipt with them or to register it with U.S. Customs before leaving home (Form 4457). Otherwise, you may end up paying duty on your return. You may bring home duty-free up to $400 worth of foreign goods, as long as you have been out of the country for at least 48 hours. Each member of the family is entitled to the same exemption, regardless of age, and exemptions can be pooled. For the next $1,000 worth of goods, a flat 10% rate is assessed; above $1,400, duties vary with the merchandise. Included for travelers 21 or older are one liter of alcohol, 100 cigars (non-Cuban), and 200 cigarettes. Only one bottle of perfume trademarked in the United States may be brought in. However, there is no duty on antiques or art over 100 years old. Anything exceeding these limits will be taxed at the port of entry and may be taxed again in the traveler's home state. Gifts valued at under $50 may be mailed to friends or relatives at home duty-free, but no more than one package per day can be sent to any one addressee and no perfumes costing more than $5, tobacco, or liquor can be mailed.

Canadian Customs

Canadian residents have a $300 exemption and may also bring in duty free up to 50 cigars, 200 cigarettes, two pounds of tobacco, and 40 ounces of liquor, provided these are declared in writing to customs on arrival and accompany the traveler in hand or in checked-through baggage. Personal gifts should be mailed as "Unsolicited Gift—Value under $40." Request the Canadian Customs brochure *I Declare* for further details.

U.K. Customs

British residents have two different allowances: one for goods bought in a duty-free shop in France and the other for goods bought anywhere else in France.

In the first category, you may import duty-free: 200 cigarettes or 100 cigarillos or 50 cigars or 250 grams of tobacco (these allowances are doubled if you live outside Europe); two liters of table wine and (1) one liter of alcohol over 22% by volume (most spirits), (2) two liters of alcohol under 22% by volume (fortified or sparkling wine), or (3) two more liters of table wine; 50 grams of perfume; ¼ liter of toilet water; and other goods up to a value of £32.

In the second category, you may import duty-free: 300 cigarettes or 150 cigarillos or 75 cigars or 400 grams of tobacco; five liters of table wine and (1) 1½ liters of alcohol over 22% volume (most spirits), (2) three liters of alcohol under 22% by volume (fortified or sparkling wine), or (3) three more liters of table wine; 75 grams of perfume; 375ml of toilet water; and other goods to the value of £250.

No animals or pets of any kind can be brought into the U.K. without a lengthy quarantine. *The penalties are severe and strictly enforced.*

Traveling with Film

If your camera is new, shoot and develop a few rolls of film before leaving home. Pack some lens tissue and an extra battery for your built-in light meter. Invest about $10 in a skylight filter and screw it on the front of your lens. It will protect the lens and reduce haze.

Film doesn't like hot weather. If you're driving in summer, don't store film in the glove compartment or on the shelf under the rear window. Put it behind the front seat on the floor, on the side opposite the exhaust pipe.

On a plane trip, never pack unprocessed film in check-in luggage; if your bags get X-rayed, your pictures will be ruined. Always carry undeveloped film with you through security and ask to have it inspected by hand. (It helps to isolate your film in a plastic bag, ready for quick inspection.) Inspectors at American airports are required by law to honor requests for hand inspection; abroad, you'll have to depend on the kindness of strangers.

The old airport scanning machines—still in use in some Third World countries—use heavy doses of radiation that can turn a family portrait into an early morning fog. The newer models—used in all U.S. airports—are safe for anything from five to 500 scans, depending on the speed of your film. The effects are cumulative; you can put the same roll of film through several scans without worry. After five scans, though, you're asking for trouble.

If your film gets fogged and you want an explanation, send it to the National Association of Photographic Manufacturers (600 Mamaroneck Ave., Harrison, NY 10528). The association will try to determine what went wrong. The service is free.

Language

The French study English for a minimum of four years at school (often longer) but to little general effect. English is widely understood in major tourist areas, however, and, no matter what the area, there should be at least one person in most hotels who can explain things to you, if necessary. Be courteous and patient and speak slowly: The French, after all, have plenty of other tourists and are not massively dependent for income on English-speaking visitors. And while it may sound cynical, remember the French respond quicker to charm than to anything else.

Even if your own French is terrible, try to master a few words: The French are more cooperative when they think you're making at least an effort to speak their language. Basic vocabulary: *s'il vous plaît* (please), *merci* (thanks), *bonjour* (hello—until 6 **PM**), *bonsoir* (good evening), *au revoir* (goodbye), *comment ça va* (how do you do), *oui* (yes), *non* (no), *peut-être* (maybe), *les toilettes* (toilets), *l'addition* (bill/check), *où* (where), *anglais* (English), *je ne comprends pas* (I don't understand).

Refer to the Traveler's Vocabulary and Menu.

Staying Healthy

There are no serious health risks associated with travel in France. However, the Centers for Disease Control (CDC) in Atlanta cautions that most of southern Europe is in the "intermediate" range for risk of contacting traveler's diarrhea. Part of this risk may be attributed to an increased consumption of olive oil and wine, which can have a laxative effect on stomachs used to a different diet. The CDC also advises all international travelers to swim only in chlorinated swimming pools, unless they are certain the local beaches and fresh-water lakes are not contaminated.

If you have a health problem that might require purchasing prescription drugs while in France, have your doctor write a prescription using the drug's generic name. Brand names vary widely from country to country.

The **International Association for Medical Assistance to Travelers (IAMAT)** is a worldwide association that publishes a list of approved English-speaking doctors whose training meets British and American standards. For a list of French physicians and clinics that are part of this network, contact IAMAT (417 Center St., Lewiston, NY 14092, tel: 716/754–4883. **In Canada:** 188 Nicklin Rd., Guelph, Ontario N1H 7L5). **In Europe:** Gotthardstrasse 17, 6300 Zug, Switzerland. Membership is free.

Shots and Medications Inoculations are not needed to enter France. The American Medical Association recommends Pepto Bismol for minor cases of traveler's diarrhea.

Insurance

Travelers may seek insurance coverage in three areas: health and accident, loss of luggage, and trip cancellation. Your first step is to review your existing health and home-owner policies: Some health insurance plans cover health expenses incurred while traveling, some major medical plans cover emergency transportation, and some home-owner policies cover the theft of luggage.

Health and Accident Several companies offer coverage designed to supplement existing health insurance for travelers:

Carefree Travel Insurance (Box 310, 120 Mineola Blvd., Mineola, NY 11501, tel. 516/294–0220 or 800/645–2424) provides coverage for medical evacuation. It also offers 24-hour medical phone advice.

Health Care Abroad, International Underwriters Group (243 Church St. W., Suite 100D, Vienna, VA 22180, tel. 703/281–9500 or 800/237–6615), offers comprehensive medical coverage, including emergency evacuation, for trips of 10–90 days.

International SOS Insurance (Box 11568, Philadelphia, PA 19126, tel. 215/244–1500 or 800/523–8930) does not offer medical insurance but provides medical evacuation services to its clients, who are often international corporations.

Travel Guard International, underwritten by Cygna (1100 Centerpoint Dr., Stevens Point, WI 54481, tel. 715/345–0505 or 800/782–5151) offers medical insurance, with coverage for emergency evacuation when Travel Guard's representatives in the USA say it is necessary.

Lost Luggage The loss of luggage is usually covered as part of a comprehensive travel insurance package that includes personal accident, trip-cancellation, and sometimes default and bankruptcy insurance. Several companies offer comprehensive policies:

Access America Inc., a subsidiary of Blue Cross–Blue Shield (600 Third Ave., Box 807, New York, NY 10163, tel. 800/851–2800).
Near, Inc. (1900 North MacArthur Blvd., Suite 210, Oklahoma City, OK 73127, tel. 800/654–6700).
Travel Guard International (*see* Health and Accident Insurance above).

Trip Cancellation Flight insurance is often included in the price of a ticket when paid for with American Express, Visa, and other major credit and charge cards. It is usually included in combination travel insurance packages that are available from most tour operators, travel agents, and insurance agents.

Renting or Leasing Cars

Renting If you're flying into Paris or some other city in France and are planning to spend time there, save money by arranging to pick up your car in the city the day you depart; otherwise, arrange to pick up and return your car at the airport. You'll have to weigh the added expense of renting a car from a major company with an airport office against the savings on a car from a budget company with offices in town. You could waste precious hours trying to locate the budget company in return for only a small financial savings. If you're arriving and departing from different airports, look for a one-way car rental with no return fees. If you're traveling to more than one country, make sure your rental contract permits you to take the car across borders and that the insurance policy covers you in every country you visit. Be prepared to pay more for cars with automatic transmissions. Since they are not as readily available as those with manual transmissions, reserve them well in advance.

Rental rates vary widely, depending on the size and model, the number of days you use the car, insurance coverage, and whether special drop-off fees are imposed. In most cases, rates quoted include unlimited free mileage and standard liability protection. Not included are Collision Damage Waiver (CDW), which eliminates your deductible payment if you have an accident, personal accident insurance, gasoline, and European Value-Added Taxes (VAT). The VAT on car rentals in France is a whopping 33.3%, the highest in Europe.

Driver's licenses issued in the United States and Canada are valid in France. You may also take out an International Driving Permit before you leave, to smooth out difficulties if you have an accident or as an additional piece of identification. Permits are available for a small fee through local offices of the **American Automobile Association** (AAA) and the **Canadian Automobile Association** (CAA), or from their main offices (AAA, 1000 AAA Dr., Heathrow, FL 32746-0001, tel. 800/336–4357; CAA, 2 Carlton St., Toronto, Ontario M5B 1K4, tel. 416/964–3170).

It's best to arrange a car rental before you leave. You won't save money by waiting until you arrive in France, and you may find the type of car you want is not available at the last minute. Rental companies usually charge according to the exchange rate of the dollar at the time the car is returned or when the credit card payment is processed. Three companies with special programs to help you hedge against the falling dollar, by guaranteeing advertised rates if you pay in advance, are **Budget Rent-a-Car** (3350 Boyington St., Carrollton, TX 75006, tel. 800/527–0700), **Connex Travel International** (983 Main St. Peekskill, NY 10566, tel. 800/333–3949), and **Cortell International,** 17310 Red Hill Ave., Suite 360, Irvine, CA 92714, tel. 800/228–2535). Other budget rental companies serving Europe include **Europe by Car** (1 Rockefeller Plaza, New York, NY 10020, tel. 212/245–1713, 800/223–1516, in California 800/252–9401), **Auto Europe** (Box 1097 Sharps Wharf, Camden, ME 04843, tel. 800/223–5555, in Maine 800/342–5202, in Canada 800/237–2465), **Foremost Euro-Car** (5430 Van Nuys Blvd., Van Nuys, CA 91404, tel. 800/423–3111), and **Kemwel** (106 Calvert St. Harrison, NY 10528, tel. 800/678–0678). Others with European rentals include **Avis** (tel. 800/331–1212), **Hertz** (tel. 800/223–6472, in New York 800/654–3001), and **National** or **Europcar** (tel. 800/CAR–RENT).

Leasing   For trips of 21 days or more, you may save money by leasing a car. With the leasing arrangement, you are technically buying a car and then selling it back to the manufacturer after you've used it. You receive a factory-new car, tax free, with international registration and extensive insurance coverage. Rates vary with the make and model of the car and the length of time it is used. Car-leasing programs in France are offered by Renault, Citroën, and Peugeot. Delivery is free to downtown Paris and to the airports in Paris. There is a small fee for deliveries to other parts of France. Before you go, compare long-term rental rates with leasing rates. Remember to add taxes and insurance costs to the car rentals, something you don't have to worry about with leasing. Companies that offer leasing arrangements include **Kemwel, Europe by Car,** and **Auto Europe,** all listed above.

Rail Passes

The **French Rail Pass** (formerly the **France-Vacances Rail Pass**) is a good value for those who plan to do a lot of their traveling by train. Unlike other passes, the French Rail Pass allows you to stagger your train travel time instead of having to use it all at once. For example, the four-day pass ($134 in first class, $99 in second), may be used on any four days within a 15-day period. Similarly, the nine-day pass ($224 in first class, $160 in second) may be used on any nine days within one month.

You must buy the French Rail Pass before you leave for France. It is obtainable through travel agents or through **French National Railroads** (610 5th Ave., New York, NY 10020, tel. 212/582–2110).

The **EurailPass,** valid for unlimited first-class train travel through 16 countries, including France, is an excellent value if you plan to travel around the Continent.

The ticket is available for periods of 15 days ($320), 21 days ($398), one month ($498), two months ($698), and three months ($860). For those 26 and under, there is the **Eurail Youthpass,** for one or two months' unlimited second-class train travel, at

$360 and $470. For travelers who like to spread out their train journeys, there is the new **Eurail Flexipass.** With this pass, travelers get nine days of unlimited first-class train travel, but they do not have to ride for nine consecutive days, since they can use the pass on any nine days in a 21-day period. The Flexipass costs $340.

The EurailPass is available only if you live outside Europe or North Africa. The pass must be bought from an authorized agent in the Western Hemisphere or Japan before you leave for Europe. Apply through your travel agent or **French National Railroads** (address above).

Student and Youth Travel

The **International Student Identity Card** entitles students to youth rail passes, special fares on local transportation, Intra-European Student Charter flights, and discounts at museums, theaters, sports events, and many other attractions. If purchased in the **United States,** the $10 cost of the ISIC also includes $2,000 in emergency medical insurance, plus $100 a day for up to 60 days of hospital coverage. Apply to the Council on International Educational Exchange (CIEE) (205 E. 42nd St., 16th floor, New York, NY 10017, tel. 212/661–1414). **In Canada,** the ISIC is available for CN $10 from the Association of Student Councils (187 College St., Toronto, Ontario M5T 1P7).

The **Youth International Educational Exchange Card** (YIEE), issued by the Federation of International Youth Travel Organizations (FIYTO, 81 Islands Brugge, DK-2300 Copenhagen S, Denmark), provides similar services to nonstudents under age 26. **In the United States,** the card costs $10 and is available from CIEE (address above) or from ISE (Europa House, 802 W. Oregon St., Urbana, IL 61801, tel. 217/344–5863). **In Canada,** the YIEE is available from the Canadian Hostelling Association (CHA) (333 River Rd., Vanier, Ottawa, Ontario K1L 8H9, tel. 613/476–3844).

An **International Youth Hostel Federation** (IYHF) membership card is the key to inexpensive dormitory-style accommodations at thousands of youth hostels around the world. Hostels provide separate sleeping quarters for men and women at rates ranging from $7 to $15 a night per person, and are situated in a variety of facilities, including converted farmhouses, villas, and restored castles, as well as specially constructed modern buildings. IYHF membership costs $20 a year ($10 a year for people under age 18) and is available in the United States through **American Youth Hostels** (Box 37613, Washington, DC 20013, tel. 202/783–6161). AYH also publishes an extensive directory of youth hostels around the world.

Economical **bicycle tours** for small groups of adventurous, energetic students are another popular AYH student travel service. The AYH 16-day tour of England for $1,500 (from New York) is a typical offering. For information on these and other AYH services and publications, contact AYH at the address listed above.

Council Travel, a CIEE subsidiary, is the foremost U.S. student travel agency, specializing in low-cost charters and serving as the exclusive U.S. agent for many student airfare bargains and student tours. CIEE's 80-page *Student Travel Catalog* and *Council Charter* brochure are available free from any Council Travel office in the United States (enclose $1 for postage if ordering by mail). In addition to CIEE headquarters (205 E. 42nd St., New York, NY 10017) and a branch office (35 W. 8th St. in New York, NY 10009), there are Council Travel offices in Berkeley, La Jolla, Long Beach, Los Angeles, San Diego, and San Francisco, CA; Chicago, IL; Amherst, Boston, and Cambridge, MA; Portland, OR; Providence, RI; Austin and Dallas, TX; and Seattle, WA.

The **Educational Travel Center,** another student travel specialist worth contacting for information on student tours, bargain fares, and bookings, may be reached at 438 N. Frances St., Madison, WI 53703, tel. 608/256–5551.

Students who would like to work abroad should contact **CIEE's Work Abroad Department** (205 E. 42nd St., New York, NY 10017). The council arranges various types of paid and voluntary work experiences overseas for up to six months. CIEE also sponsors study programs in Europe, Latin America, and Asia and publishes many books of interest to the student traveler. These books include *Work, Study, Travel Abroad: The whole world handbook* ($8.95 plus $1 postage); *The Teenager's Guide to Study, Travel, and Adventure Abroad* ($9.95 plus $1 postage); and *Volunteer! The Comprehensive Guide to Voluntary Service in the U.S. and Abroad* ($4.95 plus $1 postage).

The Information Center at the **Institute of International Education** (IEE) has reference books, foreign university catalogues, study-abroad brochures, and other materials that may be consulted by students and nonstudents alike, free of charge. The Information Center (809 UN Plaza, New York, NY 10017, tel. 212/883–8200) is open from 10 AM to 4 PM , Mon.–Fri. and weekdays, until 7 PM Wednesday evenings. It is not open on weekends or holidays.

IIE administers a variety of grant and study programs offered by U.S. and foreign organizations, and publishes a well-known annual series of study-abroad guides, including *Academic Year Abroad, Vacation Study Abroad,* and *Study in the United Kingdom and Ireland.* The institute also publishes *Teaching Abroad,* a book of employment and study opportunities overseas for U.S. teachers. For a current list of IIE publications with prices and ordering information, write to Publications Service, Institute of International Education (809 UN Plaza, New York, NY 10017). Books must be purchased by mail or in person; telephone orders are not accepted.

General information on IIE's programs and services is available from its regional offices in Atlanta, Chicago, Denver, Houston, San Francisco, and Washington, DC.

For information on the **Eurail Youthpass,** *see* Rail Passes, above.

Traveling with Children

Publications   *Family Travel Times* is an 8–12-page newsletter published 10 times a year by **TWYCH** (Travel with Your Children, 80 8th

Ave., New York, NY 10011, tel. 212/206–0688). Subscription includes access to back issues and twice-weekly opportunities to call in for specific advice.

Family Travel Organizations **American Institute for Foreign Study** (AIFS, 102 Greenwich Ave., Greenwich, CT 06830, tel. 203/869–9090) offers a family vacation program in France specifically designed for parents and children.

Families Welcome! (1416 2nd Ave., New York, NY 10021, tel. 212/861–2500 or 800/472–8999) is a travel agency that arranges French tours brimming with family-sensitive choices and activities. Two other travel arrangers that understand families' needs (and can even set up short-term rentals) are **Paris Accueil** (231 Spruce St., New Windsor, NY 12550, tel. 914/565–6951) and **The French Experience** (171 Madison Ave., New York, NY 10016, tel. 212/683–2445).

Hotels The **Novotel** hotel chain allows up to two children to stay free in their parents' room, and offers a free breakfast as well. Many Novotel properties have playgrounds. (For international reservations call 800/221–4542.) **Sofitel** hotels offer a free second room for children during July and August, and over the Christmas holidays. (For international reservations call 800/221–4542.) **Club Med** (40 W. 57th St., New York, NY 10019, tel. 800/CLUB–MED) has a "Baby Club" (from age four months) at its resort in Chamonix; "Mini Clubs" (for ages four to six or eight, depending on the resort), and "Kids Clubs" (for ages eight and up during school holidays) at all its resort villages in France except in Val d'Isere. In general, supervised activities are scheduled all day long.

Villa Rentals **At Home Abroad, Inc.,** 405 E. 56th St., Suite 6H, New York, NY 10022, tel. 212/421–9165. **Villas International,** 71 W. 23rd St., New York, NY 10010, tel. 212/929–7585 or 800/221–2260. **Hideaways, Int'l.,** Box 1270, Littleton, MA 01460, tel. 508/486–8955. **B. & D. de Vogue,** 1830 S. Mooney Blvd. 113, Visalia, CA 93277, tel. 209/733–7119 or 800/727–4748. **Meeting Points,** 5515 S.E. Milwaukee Ave., Portland, OR 97202, tel. 503/233–1224. **Vacances en Campagne,** Box 297, Falls Village, CT 06031, tel. 203/824–5155 or 800/553–5405.

Home Exchange See *Home Exchanging: A Complete Sourcebook for Travelers at Home or Abroad* by James Dearing (Globe Pequot Press, Box Q, Chester, CT 06412, tel. 800/243–0495; in CT 800/962–0973).

Getting There On international flights, children under two not occupying a seat pay 10% of the adult fare. Various discounts apply to children aged two to 12. Reserve a seat behind the bulkhead of the plane, which offers more leg room and can usually fit a bassinet (supplied by the airline). At the same time, inquire about special children's meals or snacks, offered by most airlines. Ask in advance if you can bring aboard your child's car seat. (For the booklet *Child/Infant Safety Seats Acceptable for Use in Aircraft,* write Community and Consumer Liaison Division, APA-400 Federal Aviation Administration, Washington, DC 20591, tel. 202/267–3479.)

Getting Around The **French National Railways** (SNFC) accommodates family travel by allowing children under four to travel free (provided they don't occupy a seat); by allowing children four to 11 to travel at half fare; and by putting "family trains" on many lines, equipped with nurseries, play areas, and even activity organizers.

Baby-sitting Services First check with the hotel concierge for recommended child care arrangements. Paris agencies: **American College in Paris** (31 av. Bosquet, 75007 Paris, tel. 45-55-91-73); **Baby Sitting** (18 rue Tronchet, 75008 Paris, tel. 46-37-51-24); **Kid Service** (17 rue Molière, 75001 Paris, tel. 42-96-04-16); **Medical Students Association** (105 blvd. de l'Hôpital, 75013 Paris, tel. 45-86-19-44); **Grethe's Babysitters and Au Pairs** (57 rue des Moines, Paris 75017, tel. 47-00-53-39).

Pen Pals For names of children in France to whom your children can write before your trip, send a self-addressed, stamped envelope to **International Friendship League** (55 Mt. Vernon St., Boston, MA 02108).

Miscellaneous Contact the **CIDJ** (Centre d'Information et de Documentation pour la Jeunesse, 101 quai Branly, 75015 Paris, tel. 45-67-35-85) for information about activities and events for youngsters in France.

Hints for Disabled Travelers

In France Facilities for the handicapped in France are better than average. The French government is doing much to ensure that public facilities provide for disabled visitors and has produced an excellent booklet—*Tourists Quand Même*—with an English glossary and easily understood symbols, detailing facilities available to the disabled in transportation systems and museums and monuments, region by region. The booklet is available from French national tourist offices and the main Paris Tourist Office, or from the **Comité National Français de Liaison pour la Réadaptation des Handicapés** (38 blvd. Raspail, 75007 Paris, tel. 45-48-90-13).

A number of monuments, hotels, and museums—especially those constructed within the past decade—are equipped with ramps, elevators, or special toilet facilities. Lists of regional hotels include a symbol to indicate which hotels have rooms accessible to the disabled. Similarly, the SNCF has special cars on some trains reserved exclusively for the handicapped and can arrange for wheelchair-bound passengers to be escorted on and off trains and helped to catch connecting trains (the latter service must be requested in advance).

A helpful organization in Paris is the **Association des Paralysés de France** (17 blvd. Auguste-Blanqui, 75013 Paris, tel. 45-80-82-40), which publishes a useful hotel list.

Free baby-sitting for physically and mentally handicapped children is provided by the **Foundation Claude Pompidou** (42 rue du Louvre, 75001 Paris, tel. 45-08-45-15; phone between 2 and 6). Services are available at all times.

In the U.S. Tours that are especially designed for handicapped travelers generally parallel those for nonhandicapped travelers, albeit at a more leisurely pace. For a complete list of tour operators who arrange such travel, write to the **Society for the Advancement of Travel for the Handicapped** (26 Court St., Brooklyn, NY 11242, tel. 718/858-5483). Annual membership costs $40, or $25 for senior citizens and students. Send a stamped, self-addressed envelope.

Moss Rehabilitation Hospital (12th St. and Tabor Rd., Philadelphia, PA 19141, tel. 215/329-5715) answers inquiries regarding specific cities and countries and provides toll-free telephone numbers for airlines with special lines for the hard of hearing and, again, listings of selected tour operators.

The **Information Center for Individuals with Disabilities** (2743 Wormwood St., Boston, MA 02210, tel. 617/727-5540) offers useful problem-solving assistance, including lists of travel agents that specialize in tours for the disabled.

Mobility International (Box 3551, Eugene, OR 97403, tel. 503/343-1284) has information on accommodations, organized study, and so forth around the world.

The Itinerary (Box 1084, Bayonne, NJ 07002, tel. 201/858-3400) is a bimonthly travel magazine for the disabled. *Access to the World: A Travel Guide for the Handicapped* by Louise Weiss is useful but out of date. Available from **Facts on File** (460 Park Ave., New York, NY 10016, tel. 212/683-2244). *Frommer's Guide for Disabled Travelers* is also useful but dated.

Hints for Older Travelers

The **American Association of Retired Persons** (AARP, 1909 K St. NW, Washington, DC 20049, tel. 202/662-4850) has two programs for independent travelers: (1) *The Purchase Privilege Program*, which offers discounts on hotels, airfare, car rentals, and sightseeing, and (2) the *AARP Motoring Plan*, which offers emergency aid and trip-routing information for an annual fee of $33.95 per couple. The AARP also arranges group tours, including apartment living in Europe, through two companies: **Olson-Travelworld** (5855 Green Valley Circle, Culver City, CA 90230, tel. 800/227-7737) and **RFD, Inc.** (4401 W. 110th St., Overland Park, KS 66211, tel. 800/448-7010). AARP members must be 50 or older. Annual dues are $5 per person or per couple.

When using an AARP or other identification card, ask for a reduced hotel rate at the time you make your reservation, not when you check out. At restaurants, show your card to the maitre d' before you're seated, since discounts may be limited to certain set menus, days, or hours. When renting a car, remember that economy cars, priced at promotional rates, may cost less than cars that are available with your identification card.

Elderhostel (80 Boylston St., Suite 400, Boston, MA 02116, tel. 617/426-7788) is an innovative 14-year-old program for people 60 and older. Participants live in dorms on some 1,200 campuses around the world. Mornings are devoted to lectures and seminars; afternoons, to sightseeing and field trips. The all-inclusive fee for two- to three-week trips, including room, board, tuition, and round-trip transportation, is $1,700-$3,200.

Travel Industry and Disabled Exchange (TIDE, 5435 Donna Ave., Tarzana, CA 91356, tel. 818/343-6339) is an industry-based organization with a $15 per person annual membership fee. Members receive a quarterly newsletter and information on travel agencies and tours.

National Council of Senior Citizens (925 15th St. NW, Washington, DC 20005, tel. 202/347-8800) is a nonprofit advocacy group with some 4,000 local clubs across the country. Annual membership is $10 per person or $14 per couple. Members receive a monthly newspaper with travel information and an identification card for reduced-rate hotels and car rentals.

Mature Outlook (6001 N. Clark St., Chicago, IL 60660, tel. 800/336–6330), a subsidiary of Sears Roebuck & Co., is a travel club for people over 50, offering hotel and motel discounts and a bi-monthly newsletter. Annual membership is $9.95 per couple. Instant membership is available at participating Holiday Inns. *Travel Tips for Senior Citizens* (U.S. Department of State Publication 8970, revised September 1987) is available for $1 from the Superintendent of Documents, U.S. Government Printing Office, Washington, DC 20402.

In France   Senior citizens (men over 62 and women over 60) enjoy reduced museum admission (usually 50%) and cheap train tickets (the **Carte Vermeil**, available at stations throughout France; the Carte Vermeil costs about 80 francs a year and entitles the holder to discounts of up to 50%, depending on when you travel). Senior citizens should keep their passports or identification card with them at all times.

Further Reading

An erudite, perceptive, and witty survey of France and its people is Theodore Zeldin's *The French* (Pantheon); Joseph T. Carroll's *The French—How They Live and Work* (David & Charles) is in a similar vein. A summary of recent social, political, and economic developments is provided by John Ardagh's *France in the 1980s* (Penguin).

Nancy Mitford's *The Sun King* (Crown) is a readable approach to the regal grandeur of the 17th century, while Alfred Cobban's *History of Modern France* (Pelican) provides workmanlike coverage of trends and events from the death of Louis XIV up to 1962. If you prefer your history in a fictional setting, pick up Victoria Holt's fictional memoir of Marie Antoinette, *The Queen's Confession* (Doubleday).

Books about French wine are frequent, but Steven Spurrier's pocket-sized *French Country Wines* (Putnam) is unusual in its thorough treatment of lesser-known (and often good-value) wines. Architecture buffs should read Henri Focillon's *The Art of the West* (Cornell U. Press) for a thoughtfully illustrated, scholarly exposé of Romanesque and Gothic architecture.

Charles Dickens, in a *Tale of Two Cities* (Bantam), and Ernest Hemingway, notably in *A Moveable Feast* (Scribner), are just two authors who have written about Paris in English. One author whose descriptive powers and latterday relevance seldom disappoint is Emile Zola. His novels are situated mostly in Provence or in Paris—by and large the Paris we know today, emerging from mid-19th-century reconstruction amid back-street squalor and brash glamour, all tellingly depicted in such works as *La Curée, L'Assommoir*, and *Nana* (Penguin).

Historian and archaeologist Dorothy Carrington has written the well-documented *Granite Island: A Portrait of Corsica*, which gives a thoughtful insight into the islanders' archaic beliefs, infamous vendettas, and complicated internal politics.

Several good thrillers set in France include the following: *Assignment in Brittany* (Fawcett), by Helen MacInnes; Pierre Salinger's *The Dossier* (Doubleday); Philip Loraine's *Death*

Wishes (St. Martin); and *Most Secret* (Amereon) by Nevil Shute.

Arriving and Departing

Since the air routes between North America and France are among the world's most heavily traveled, the passenger has many airlines and fares to choose from. But fares change with stunning rapidity, so consult your travel agent on which bargains are currently available.

From the U.S. by Plane

Be certain to distinguish among (1) nonstop flights—no changes, no stops; (2) direct flights—no changes but one or more stops; and (3) connecting flights—two or more planes, two or more stops.

Airports and Airlines The U.S. airlines that serve France are **TWA** (tel. 800/892–4141), **American Airlines** (tel. 800/433–7300), **Delta** (tel. 800/241–4141), and **Pan Am** (tel. 800/221–1111). All fly to Paris's Charles de Gaulle (Roissy) Airport (tel. 48–62–22–80) and Orly (tel. 48–84–32–10). Pan Am also flies to Nice.

Flying Time to Paris From New York: 7½ hours. From Chicago: nine hours. From Los Angeles: 11 hours.

Discount Flights The major airlines offer a range of tickets that can increase the price of any given seat by more than 300%, depending on the day of purchase. As a rule, the further in advance you buy the ticket, the less expensive it is and the greater the penalty (up to 100%) for canceling. Check with the airlines for details.

The best buy is not necessarily an APEX (advance-purchase) ticket on one of the major airlines. APEX tickets carry certain restrictions: they must be bought in advance (usually 21 days); they restrict your travel, usually with a minimum stay of seven days and a maximum of 90; and they penalize you for changes—voluntary or not—in your travel plans. But if you can work around these drawbacks (and most can), they are among the best-value fares available.

Charter flights offer the lowest fares but often depart only on certain days, and seldom on time. Though you may be able to arrive at one city and return from another, you may lose all or most of your money if you cancel your ticket. Travel agents can make bookings, though they won't encourage you, since commissions are lower than on scheduled flights. Checks should, as a rule, be made out to the bank and specific escrow account for your flight. To make sure your payment stays in this account until your departure, don't use credit cards as a method of payment. Also, don't sign up for a charter flight unless you've checked with a travel agent about the reputation of the packager. It's particularly important to know the packager's policy concerning refunds if a flight is canceled. One of the most popular charter operators is **Council Charter** (tel. 800/223–7402), a division of **CIEE** (Council on International Educational Exchange). Other companies advertise in Sunday travel sections of newspapers.

Somewhat more expensive—but up to 50% below the cost of APEX fares—are tickets purchased through companies, known as consolidators, that buy blocks of tickets on scheduled airlines and sell them at wholesale prices. Here again, you may lose all or most of your money if you change your plans, but at least you will be on a regularly scheduled flight with less risk of cancellation than a charter. Once you've made your reservation, call the airline to make sure you're confirmed. Among the best-known consolidators are **UniTravel** (tel. 800/325–2222) and **Access International** (250 W. 57th St., Suite 511, New York, NY 10107, tel. 212/333–7280). Others advertise in the Sunday travel sections of newspapers as well.

Yet another option is to join a travel club that offers special discounts to its members. Three such organizations are **Moments Notice** (40 E. 49th St., New York, NY 10017, tel. 212/486–0503); **Discount Travel International** (Suite 205, 114 Forest Ave., Narberth, PA 19072, tel. 215/668–2182); and **Worldwide Discount Travel Club** (1674 Meridian Ave., Miami Beach, FL 33139, tel. 305/534–2082). These cut-rate tickets should be compared with APEX tickets on the major airlines.

Enjoying the Flight If you're lucky enough to be able to sleep on a plane, it makes sense to fly at night. Many experienced travelers, however, prefer to take a morning flight to Europe and arrive in the evening, just in time for a good night's sleep. Since the air on a plane is dry, it helps, while flying, to drink a lot of nonalcoholic liquids; drinking alcohol contributes to jet lag. Feet swell at high altitudes, so it's a good idea to remove your shoes while in flight. Sleepers usually prefer window seats to curl up against; those who like to move about the cabin should ask for aisle seats. Bulkhead seats (adjacent to the Exit signs) have more leg room, but seat trays are attached to the arms of your seat rather than to the back of the seat in front.

Smoking If smoking bothers you, ask for a seat far away from the smoking section. If the airline tells you there are no nonsmoking seats, insist on one: FCC regulations require airlines to find seats for all nonsmokers.

From the U.S. by Ship

The *Queen Elizabeth 2 (QE2)* is the only ocean liner that makes regular transatlantic crossings. However, the *Vistafjord* of the Cunard Line sails to and from Fort Lauderdale, Florida, to Marseille, France, in repositioning crossings. These crossings occur when cruise ships are taken to or from North America and Europe as one season ends and another begins. Some sail straight across, often at reduced rates to passengers. Others stop at several ports of call before heading to open sea. Arrangements can be made to cruise one way and fly one way. Since itineraries can change at the last minute, check with the cruise lines for the latest information.

Cunard Line (555 5th Ave., New York, NY 10017, tel. 800/221–4770, in New York 212/880–7545) operates four ships, including the *QE2* and *Vistafjord*. The *QE2* makes regular crossings April through December, between Baltimore, Boston, and New York City and Southampton, England. Arrangements for the *QE2* can include one-way airfare. The *Sea Goddess I* and *Sea Goddess II* sail to and from Madeira, Portugal, and St. Thomas, the U.S. Virgin Islands, for their repositioning crossings. Cunard Line offers fly/cruise packages and pre- and postland packages. For the European cruise season, ports of call include Southhampton; Madeira; Marseille; Hamburg, Germany; Genoa, Rome, Venice, and Naples, Italy, Monte Carlo, Monaco; Malaga, Spain; Piraeus (Athens), Greece; Copenhagen, Denmark; and Stockholm, Sweden. Ports of call vary with the ship.

Royal Viking Line (750 Battery St., San Francisco, CA 94111, tel. 800/634–8000) has three ships that cruise out of European ports. Two of the ships make repositioning crossings to and from Fort Lauderdale, Florida, and Lisbon, Portugal. Fly/cruise packages are available. Major ports of call, depending on the ship, are Copenhagen, Denmark; Stockholm, Sweden; Bergen, Norway; Hamburg, Germany; Leningrad, USSR; Barcelona, Spain; Venice, Italy; Dubrovnik, Yugoslavia; Villefranche, France; Corfu, Greece; and Lisbon.

American Star Lines (660 Madison Ave., New York, NY 10021, tel. 800/356–7677, in New York 212/644–7900) makes transatlantic crossings in spring and fall to and from Greece and Barbados, British West Indies. The crossings are regular cruises, with ports of call in Portugal, Italy, Turkey, and the Greek Islands. Summer cruises are from Piraeus (Athens), Greece, to the Greek Islands and Turkey. Fly/cruise packages are available.

Check the travel pages of your Sunday newspaper for other cruise ships that sail to Europe.

From the U.K. by Plane, Car, Train, and Bus

By Plane The major airlines operating between the United Kingdom and France are **Air France** (tel. 01/759–3211), **British Airways** (tel. 01/897–4000), and **British Caledonian** (tel. 01/668–4222).

The route from London to Paris (journey time: one hour) is the busiest in Europe, with up to 17 flights daily from Heathrow (Air France/British Airways) and four or five from Gatwick (British Caledonian), all to Charles de Gaulle (also known as Roissy). There are also regular flights—geared mainly to businesspeople—from the new London City Airport in the Docklands; direct flights to Paris from several regional U.K. airports, including Manchester, Birmingham, Glasgow, and Southampton; and flights from London to Nice, Lyon, Bordeaux, Marseille, Clermont-Ferrand, Caen, Quimper, Nantes, Montpellier, and Toulouse, as well as from Manchester to Nice. Remember, though, flying to France is often absurdly expensive. Charter flights (contact **Nouvelles Frontières**, 1–2 Hanover St., London W1R 9WB, tel. 01/629–7772) or the thrice-weekly British Caledonian service between Gatwick and Beauvais, north of Paris, offer the best value.

By Car There is no shortage of Channel crossings from England to France; all boats (and Hovercraft) welcome motor vehicles. The quickest and most frequent routes are between Dover/Folkestone and Calais/Boulogne: Sealink and P & O run 16 daily services in summer and at least 10 in winter. The Dover–Calais journey time is 75 minutes.

Each of the other routes has geographic advantages to offset its comparative slowness. Ramsgate–Dunkirk (Sally Line: 2½ hours) offers excellent restaurant and duty-free facilities, plus minimum fuss at port terminals; Newhaven–Dieppe (Sealink: 4½ hours) lands you in pretty Normandy; Portsmouth–Caen/

St-Malo (Brittany Ferries: six hours) can take you either to Brittany (St-Malo) or within striking distance of Paris (Caen); while Portsmouth–Le Havre/Cherbourg (P & O: six hours), Plymouth–Roscoff (Brittany Ferries: eight hours), and Poole/Weymouth–Cherbourg (Brittany Ferries: eight hours) all cater to drivers from Wales and southwestern England.

The Ramsgate–Dunkirk service operates several times daily, the rest at least once a day (Weymouth–Cherbourg summer only). The Hoverspeed crossings between Dover and Boulogne/Calais take just over half an hour but are suspended during heavy winds and, therefore, unreliable in winter. Whichever route you choose, it is advisable to book ahead. Prices and time-tables vary according to season, time of day, and length of stay, so contact the relevant ferry operator for details: **Sealink** (tel. 01/834–2345), **Sally Line** (tel. 0843/595566), **Brittany Ferries** (tel. 0705/827701), **P & O** (tel. 01/734–4431), and **Hoverspeed** (tel. 0304/216205).

By Train Traveling by train from London to Paris and other French cities can mean a lot of hassle—in the form of purposeless waiting, lengthy lines, and a pervading air of either dilapidation (British Rail) or indifference (French officialdom). If there are no unforeseen delays, the journeys from London to Paris via Dover or Folkestone take around seven hours. The trip via Newhaven–Dieppe—offering the cheapest prices to those aged under 26—takes nine hours. Check train/ferry prices with Sealink/British Rail, since there are numerous variations, depending on the time, season, crossing, and length of travel. The faster and more convenient Hovercraft service via Dover–Boulogne takes under six hours, but remember that Hovercraft are more affected by high winds and are relatively expensive (around £40 each way, although five-day mini-vacations are good value at just over £50). There are also good-value five-day trips to such destinations as Lyon, Avignon, and Cannes. For addresses, see above.

Paris is the hub of the French train system and a change, both of train and station, is often necessary if your destination lies farther afield. There are, however, direct trains from London to Strasbourg, Lyon, the Alps, the Riviera, and the Pyrenees.

By Bus For those who prefer bus to train travel, a London-to-Paris bus journey can be a rewarding experience (and costs only a little over £40 round trip). **International Express** (tel. 01/439–9368) runs four daily *Citysprint* buses in summer from Victoria Coach Station to the rue Lafayette in Paris near the Gare du Nord; these buses use the Hovercraft crossing, and the journey time is around 7½ hours. Three daily buses from Victoria to the Porte de la Villette on the outskirts of Paris use traditional ferries for the Channel crossing and take a bit longer (nine to 10 hours).

A number of U.K. companies operate under the International Express banner to 40 destinations throughout France. The *Riviera Express*—run in conjunction with French Leave vacations—leaves Victoria two mornings a week for such resorts as Nice, St-Maxime, and Cannes, with a relaxing overnight stop in Auxerre (fare is around £150 round trip). The Atlantic coast is also served by International Express, with at least one bus a day to Bordeaux and Biarritz in mid-summer (journey time 24 hours; price approximately £100 round trip);

twice a week, the Bordeaux service is extended to Lourdes via Tarbes. There is also regular service from London to Chamonix and the Alps (21 hours; around £85 round trip).

Eurolines (tel. 01/730–3433) operates an express service that runs overnight to Grenoble, from where there are connecting services to Nice and Marseille (return trip to Nice costs around £130). Eurolines also runs a fast bus service to Lyon four days a week in summer, leaving London mid-evening and reaching Lyon the following afternoon (around £75 round trip).

Staying in France

Getting Around France

By Plane Air France operates France's domestic airline service, called **Air Inter,** with flights from Paris to all major cities and many interregional flights. For long journeys—from Paris to the Riviera, for instance—air travel is a time saver, though train travel is always much cheaper. Most domestic flights from Paris leave from **Orly Airport** (tel. 48–84–52–52). For details, check with the local airport or call Air Inter (tel. 45–39–25–25).

By Train The SNCF is generally recognized as Europe's best national train service: It's fast, punctual, comfortable, and comprehensive. The high speed TGVs, or *Train à Grande Vitesse* (average 255 kph/160 mph), are the best domestic trains, operating between Paris and Lyon/Switzerland/the Riviera (and, at press time, were scheduled to link Paris with Nantes and Bordeaux by 1990). As with other mainline trains, you may need to pay a small supplement when taking a TGV at peak hours. Unlike other trains, you *always* need a seat reservation—easily obtained at the ticket window or from an automatic machine. Seat reservations are reassuring but seldom necessary on other mainline French trains, except at certain busy holiday times.

If you are traveling from Paris (or any other station terminus), get to the station half an hour before departure to ensure yourself a good seat. The majority of intercity trains in France consist of open-plan cars and are known as *Corail* trains. They are clean and extremely comfortable, even in second class. Trains on regional branch lines are currently being spruced up but lag behind in style and quality. Food in French trains can be good, but is poor value for the money.

It is possible to get from one end of France to the other without resorting to overnight train travel. Otherwise you have the choice between high-priced *wagons-lits* (sleeping cars) and affordable (around 75 francs) *couchettes* (bunks), six to a compartment (sheet and pillow provided). Special summer night trains from Paris to Spain and the Riviera, geared to younger people, are equipped with disco and bar to enable you to dance and drink the night away.

Fares Various reduced fares are available. Senior citizens (over 60) and young people (under 26) are eligible for the **Carte Vermeil** (85 francs) and **Carré/Carte Jeune** (150 francs) respectively, with proof of identity and two passport photos. The SNCF offers 50% reductions during "blue" periods (most of the time) and 20% the rest of the time ("white" periods: noon Friday through noon Saturday; 3 PM Sunday through noon Monday). On major holidays ("red" periods), there are no reductions. A calendar of red/white/blue periods is available at any station, and you can buy tickets at any station, too. Note that there is no reduction for buying a round-trip *(aller-retour)* ticket rather than a one-way *(aller simple)* ticket.

By Bus France's excellent train service means that long-distance buses are rare; regional buses, too, are found mainly where the train service is skimpy. Excursions and bus holidays are organized by the SNCF and other tourist organizations, such as **Horizons Européens.** Ask for the brochure at any major travel agent, or contact **France-Tourisme** (214 rue de Rivoli, 75001 Paris, tel. 42–60–30–01).

By Car
Road Conditions
Roads marked A *(Autoroutes)* are expressways. There are excellent links between Paris and most French cities, but poor ones between the provinces (principal exceptions: the A62 between Bordeaux and Toulouse; and the A9/A8 that runs the length of the Mediterranean). It is often difficult to avoid Paris when crossing France; this need not cause too many problems if you steer clear of the rush hours (7–9:30 AM and 4:30–7:30 PM). Most expressways require you to pay a toll *(péage);* the rates vary and can be steep. The N *(Route Nationale)* roads and D *(Route Départementale)* roads are usually wide, unencumbered, and fast (you can average 80 kph/50 mph with luck). The cheap, informative, and well-presented regional yellow Michelin maps are an invaluable navigational aid.

Rules of the Road You may use your home driver's license in France, but must be able to prove you have third-party insurance. Drive on the right. Be aware of the erratically followed French tradition of giving way to drivers coming from the right, unless there is an international stop sign. Seat belts are obligatory, and children under 12 may not travel in the front seat. Speed limits: 130 kph (81 mph) on expressways; 110 kph (68 mph) on major highways; 90 kph (56 mph) on minor rural roads; 60 kph (37 mph) in towns. French drivers break these limits and police dish out hefty on-the-spot fines with equal abandon.

Parking Parking is a nightmare in Paris and often difficult in large towns. Meters and ticket-machines (pay and display) are commonplace (be sure to have a supply of 1-franc coins). In smaller towns, parking may be permitted on one side of the street only, alternating every two weeks: Pay attention to signs. The French park as anarchically as they drive, but don't follow their example: If you're caught out of bounds, you could be due for a hefty fine and your vehicle may be unceremoniously towed away to the dreaded compound (500 francs to retrieve it).

Gas Gas is more expensive on expressways and in rural areas. Don't let your tank get too low (if you're unlucky, you can go for many miles in the country without hitting a gas station) and keep an eye on pump prices as you go. These vary enormously: anything from 4.50 to 5.30 francs/liter. At the pumps, opt for "super" (high-grade/4-star) rather than "essence" (low-grade/2-star).

Breakdowns If you break down on an expressway, go to the nearest roadside emergency telephone and telephone the breakdown service. If you break down anywhere else, find the nearest garage or, failing all else, contact the police.

By Boat France has Europe's densest inland waterway system, and canal and river vacation trips are popular. You can take an all-inclusive organized cruise or simply rent a boat and plan your own leisurely route. Contact a travel agent for details or ask for a *Tourisme Fluvial* brochure in any French tourist office. Some of the most picturesque stretches are found in Brittany, Burgundy, and the Midi. The Canal du Midi between Toulouse and Sète, constructed in the 17th century, is a historic marvel. Request further information from French national tourist offices, or try **France-Anjou Navigation** (Quai National, 72300 Sablésur-Sarthe) or **Bourgogne Voies Navigables** (Maison du Tourisme, 89000 Auxerre).

By Bicycle There is no shortage of wide, empty roads and flat or rolling countryside in France suitable for biking. The French, themselves, are great bicycling enthusiasts. Bikes can be hired from many train stations (ask for a list at any station) for around 30 francs a day; you need to show your passport and leave a deposit of around 200 francs (unless you have Visa or Mastercard). You must usually return the bike to a station within the same *département* (county or region). Bikes may be sent as accompanied luggage from any station in France; some trains in rural areas transport them without any extra charge.

Telephones

Local Calls The French telephone system is modern and efficient. Telephone booths are plentiful; you will nearly always find them at post offices and often in cafés. A local call costs 12 centimes per minute (minimum tariff 73 centimes); half-price rates apply weekdays between 9:30 PM and 8 AM, from 1:30 PM Saturday, and all-day Sunday.

Pay phones work principally with 1- and 5-franc coins (1 franc minimum). Lift the receiver, place the coin or coins in the appropriate slots, and dial. Unused coins are returned when you hang up. A vast number of French pay phones are now operated by cards *(télécartes)*, which you can buy from post offices and some tobacco shops, or *tabacs* (cost: 40 francs for 50 units; 96 francs for 120).

All French phone numbers have eight digits; a code is only required when calling the Paris region from the provinces (add 16–1 for Paris) and for calling the provinces from Paris (16 then the number). The number system was changed only in 1985; therefore, you may still come across some seven-digit numbers (in Paris) and some six-digit ones (elsewhere). Add 4 to the start of such Paris numbers, and the former two-figure area code to provincial ones.

International Calls Dial 19 and wait for the tone, then dial the country code (1 for the United States and Canada; 44 for the United Kingdom), area code (minus any initial 0) and number.

Approximate daytime rate, per minute: 9.50 francs for the United States and Canada; 4.50 francs for the United Kingdom. Reduced rates, per minute: United States and Canada, 5.75 francs (2–10 AM) or 7.25 francs (8 PM–2 AM/10 AM–2 AM Sunday and holidays); U.K., 3 francs (9:30 PM–8 AM/2 AM–8 PM Saturday/all-day Sunday and holidays).

Operators and Information To find a number in France or to request other information, dial 12. For international enquiries, dial 19–33 plus the country code.

Mail

Postal Rates Airmail letters to the United States cost 4.20 francs for five grams; to Canada, 2.80 francs for 5 grams; these prices increase by 60 centimes per 5 grams up to 20 grams total. Letters to the United Kingdom cost 2.20 francs for up to 20 grams. Letters cost 2.20 francs within France; postcards cost 2 francs within France and if sent to Canada, the United Kingdom, and Common Market countries; 2.80 francs to the United States and elsewhere. Stamps can be bought in post offices and cafés sporting a red TABAC sign outside.

Receiving Mail If you're uncertain where you'll be staying, have mail sent to **American Express** (tel. 800/543–4080 for a list of foreign offices), **Thomas Cook,** or to the local post office, addressed as **Poste Restante.** American Express and Thomas Cook have a $2 service charge per letter.

Tipping

The French have a clear idea of when they should be tipped. Bills in bars and restaurants include service, but it is customary to leave some small change unless you're dissatisfied. The amount of this varies: 30 centimes if you've merely bought a beer or a few francs after a meal. Tip taxi drivers and hairdressers about 10%. Give ushers in theaters and movie theaters 1 or 2 francs. In some theaters and hotels, coat check attendants may expect nothing (if there is a sign saying *Pourboire Interdit*— Tips Forbidden); otherwise give them 5 francs. Washroom attendants usually get 5 francs, though the sum is often posted.

If you stay more than two or three days in a hotel, it is customary to leave something for the chambermaid—about 10 francs per day. In expensive hotels, you may well call on the services of a baggage porter (bell boy) and hotel porter and possibly the telephone receptionist. All expect a tip: Reckon on about 10 francs per item for the baggage boy, but the other tips will depend on how much you've used their services—common sense must guide you here. In hotels that provide room service, give 5 francs to the waiter (this does not apply to breakfast served in your room). If the chambermaid does some pressing or laundering for you, give her 5 francs on top of the charge made.

Gas station attendants get nothing for gas or oil, and 5 or 10 francs for checking tires. Train and airport porters get a fixed sum (6–10 francs) per bag, but you're better off getting your own baggage cart if you can (a 10-franc coin—refundable—is sometimes necessary). Museum guides should get 5–10 francs after a guided tour, and it is standard practice to tip tour guides (and bus drivers) after an excursion.

Opening and Closing Times

Banks Banks are open weekdays, but have no strict pattern regarding times. In general, though, hours are from 9:30 to 4:30. Most banks, but not all, take a one-hour, or even a 90-minute, lunch break.

Museums Most museums are closed one day a week (usually Tuesday) and on national holidays. Usual opening times are from 9:30 to 5 or

6. Many museums close for lunch (noon–2); many are open afternoons only on Sunday.

Shops Large shops in big towns are open from 9 or 9:30 until 6 or 7 (without a lunch break). Smaller shops often open earlier (8 AM) and close later (8 PM) but take a lengthy lunch break (1–4). This siesta-type schedule is systematic in the south of France. Corner groceries, often run by immigrants *("l'Arabe du coin")*, frequently stay open until around 10 PM.

Shopping

If you ask any Frenchman to identify a region by product, he'd probably think first in alcoholic terms—of such local wines and brandies as cognac, Armagnac, Calvados, and marc. Food would be next on the list: foie gras in the southwest, mussels and oysters on the Channel and Atlantic coasts, olives and herbs in Provence, sausages and sauerkraut in Alsace, and nougat in Montelimar. Most regions have their own cheeses.

As for clothes, Paris is the firm fashion capital. Traditional regional strongholds (Lille for textiles, Calais for lace) have little clout these days, though good clothes can be bought everywhere and are invariably cheaper outside Paris (*see* Shopping sections in individual chapters for details).

VAT Refunds A number of shops, particularly large stores and shops in holiday resorts, offer VAT refunds to foreign shoppers. You are entitled to an Export Discount of 20–30%, depending on the item purchased, often only applicable if your purchases in the same store reach a minimum 2,400 francs (for U.K. and Common Market residents) or 1,200 francs (other residents, including American and Canadian).

Bargaining Shop prices are clearly marked and bargaining isn't a way of life. Still, at outdoor markets and flea markets and in antique stores, you can try your luck. If you're thinking of buying several items, you've nothing to lose by cheerfully suggesting to the storeholder, *"Vous me faites un prix?"* ("How about a discount?").

Sports and Fitness

France has no shortage of sports facilities. Many seaside resorts are well equipped for **watersports,** such as windsurfing and waterskiing, and there are swimming pools in every French town. In winter, the Alps and (somewhat cheaper) the Pyrenees and Vosges boast excellent **skiing** facilities—both for downhill *(ski alpin)* and cross-country *(ski de fond)*.

Biking (*see* Getting Around by Bicycle) is a popular pastime and, like horseback riding *(equitation)*, possible in many rural areas. The many rivers of France offer excellent **fishing** (check locally for authorization rights), and **canoeing** is popular in many areas. **Tennis** is phenomenally popular in France, and courts are everywhere: Try for a typical *terre battue* (clay) court if you can. **Golf** and **squash** have caught on recently; you may be able to find a course or a court not too far away. The French are not so keen on **jogging,** but you'll have no difficulty locating a suitable local park or avenue.

The sport that is closest to French hearts is *boules* or *pétanque* —an easy-to-grasp version of bowling, traditionally played beneath plane trees with a glass of *pastis* (similar to anisette) at hand. The local *boulodrome* is a social focal point in southern France.

Beaches

It is ironic that France's most famous coastline should possess the country's worst beaches. But there it is: Sand is in shorter supply along the Riviera than pebbles. There are sandy beaches, of course, but they are seldom large or particularly clean, since the Mediterranean behaves like a large lake, with minimal tide to wash away the litter.

By far the best French beaches are those facing north (toward the Channel) and west (toward the Atlantic). Many are so vast that you can spread out even at the most popular resorts (like Biarritz, Royan, Dinard, or Le Touquet). The most picturesque beaches are those of Brittany; the Brétons, the most seafaring of French people, will provide a hearty and well-equipped welcome to sailing enthusiasts.

Best bets for family vacations include the coast west of Bordeaux around Arcachon (good choice of accommodations and amusements), and the northern coast between Calais and Le Touquet (for a more invigorating climate and tranquil beachcombing). Larger resorts are invariably equipped with landlubbing sports facilities like golf, tennis, and horseback riding; Le Touquet is unbeatable for this.

Dining

Eating in France is serious business. This is two-big-meals-a-day country, with good restaurants around every corner. If you prefer to eat lighter, you can try a *brasserie* for rapid, straightforward fare (steak and french fries remains the classic), a picnic (a *baguette* loaf with ham, cheese, or pâté makes a perfect combination), or one of the fastfood joints that have mushroomed in towns and cities over recent years. Snack possibilities—from bakeries *(patisseries)* to pancake/roast chestnut streetsellers—are legion.

French breakfasts are relatively skimpy: good coffee, fruit juice if you insist, and croissants. You can "breakfast" in cafés as well as hotels. If you're in the mood for bacon and eggs, however, you're in trouble.

Mealtimes Dinner is the main meal and usually begins at 8 PM. Lunch—starting at 12:30 or 1—can be as copious as you care to make it.

Precautions Tap water is safe, though not always appetizing (least of all in Paris). Mineral water—there is a vast choice of both still *(eau plate)* and fizzy *(eau gazeuse)*—is a palatable alternative. Perhaps the biggest eating problem in France is saying no: If you're invited to a French family's home, you will be encouraged, if not expected, to take two or three servings of everything offered.

Ratings Highly recommended restaurants are indicated by a star ★.

Category	Cost*: Major City	Cost*: Other Areas
Very Expensive	over 450 francs	over 350 francs

Expensive	250–450 francs	200–350 francs
Moderate	150–250 francs	100–200 francs
Inexpensive	under 150 francs	under 100 francs

per person for a three-course meal, including tax (18.6%) and tip but not wine

---

Lodging

France has a wide range of accommodations, ranging from rambling old village inns that cost next to nothing to stylish converted châteaus that cost the earth. Prices must, by law, be posted at the hotel entrance and should include taxes and service. Prices are always by room, not per person (ask for a *grand lit* if you want a double bed). Breakfast is not always included in this price, but you are usually expected to have it and often are charged for it regardless. In smaller rural hotels, you may be expected to have your evening meal at the hotel, too.

Hotels Hotels are officially classified from one-star up to four-star/deluxe. France is not dominated by big hotel chains; examples in the upper price bracket include **Frantel, Holiday Inn, Novotel,** and **Sofitel.** The **Ibis** and **Climat de France** chains are more moderately priced. Chain hotels, as a rule, lack atmosphere, with the following exceptions: **Logis de France** has small, inexpensive hotels that can be relied on for minimum standards of comfort, character, and regional cuisine. Look out for the distinctive yellow and green signs. The Logis de France paperback guide is widely available in bookshops (cost: around 45 francs) or from Logis de France, 25 rue Jean-Mermoz, 75008 Paris. **France-Accueil** is another friendly low-cost chain (free booklet from France-Accueil, 85 rue Dessous-des-Berges, 75013 Paris). You can stay in style at any of the 150 members of the prestigious **Relais et Châteaux** chain of converted châteaus and manor-houses. Each hotel is distinctively furnished, provides top cuisine, and often stands in spacious grounds. A booklet listing members is available in bookshops or from Relais et Châteaux (10 pl. de la Concorde, 75008 Paris).

Self-catering Best bets are the **Gîtes Ruraux,** which offer a family or group the possibility of a low-cost, self-catering vacation in a furnished cottage, chalet, or apartment in the country; rentals are by the week or month. For details contact either the **Fédération Nationale des Gîtes Ruraux** (34 rue Godot de Mauroy, 75009 Paris), naming which region interests you, or the **French Government Tourist Office** in London (178 Piccadilly, W1V OAL, tel. 01/491–7622), which runs a special reservation service.

Bed and Breakfast B&Bs, known in France as *Chambres d'Hôte,* are becoming increasingly popular, especially in rural areas. Check local tourist offices for details.

Youth Hostels Given that cheap hotel accommodations in France are so easy to find, there is scarcely any economic reason for staying in a youth hostel, especially since standards in France don't come up to those in neighboring countries. If you enjoy a hostel ambience, however, you may care to note the address of the French headquarters (**Fédération Unie des Auberges de Jeunesse,** 6 rue Mesnil, 75016 Paris).

Villas   The French Government Tourist Offices in New York and London publish extensive lists of agencies specializing in villa rentals. You can also write to **Rent-a-Villa Ltd.** (3 W. 51st St., New York, NY 10019) or, in France, **Interhome** (88 blvd. Latour-Maubourg, 75007 Paris).

Camping   French campsites have a high reputation for organization and amenities, but tend to be jam packed in July and August. More and more campsites now welcome advance reservations; if you're traveling in summer, it makes good sense to book ahead. A guide to the country's campsites is published by the **Fédération Française de Camping et de Caravaning** (78 rue de Rivoli, 75004 Paris).

Ratings   Highly recommended hotels are indicated by a star ★.

Category	Cost*: Major City	Cost*: Other Areas
Very Expensive	over 1,000 francs	over 750 francs
Expensive	500–1,000 francs	350–750 francs
Moderate	250–500 francs	200–350 francs
Inexpensive	under 250 francs	under 200 francs

All prices are for a standard double room for two, including the tax (18.6%) and service charge.

Credit Cards

The following credit card abbreviations are used: AE, American Express; DC, Diners Club; MC, MasterCard; and V, Visa.

2 Portraits of France

France at a Glance:
A Chronology

c 3500 BC	Megalithic stone complexes erected at Carnac, Brittany
c 1500 BC	Lascaux cave paintings executed (Dordogne, southwest France)
c 600 BC	Greek colonists found Marseille
after 500 BC	Celts appear in France
58–51 BC	Julius Caesar conquers Gaul; writes up the war in *De Bello Gallico*
52 BC	Lutetia, later to become Paris, is built by the Gallo-Romans
46 BC	Roman amphitheater built at Arles
14 BC	The Pont du Gard, the aqueduct at Nîmes, is erected
AD 212	Roman citizenship conferred on all free inhabitants of Gaul
406	Invasion by the Vandals (Germanic tribes)
451	Attila invades, and is defeated at Châlons

The Merovingian Dynasty

486–511	Clovis, king of the Franks (481–511), defeats the Roman governor of Gaul and founds the Merovingian Dynasty. Great monasteries, such as those at Tours, Limoges, and Chartres, become centers of culture
497	Franks converted to Christianity
567	The Frankish kingdom is divided into three parts—the eastern countries (Austrasia), later to become Belgium and Germany; the western countries (Neustria), later to become France; and Burgundy
732	Arab expansion checked at the Battle of Poitiers

The Carolingian Dynasty

768–778	Charlemagne (768–814) becomes king of the Franks (768); conquers northern Italy (774); and is defeated by the Moors at Roncesvalles in Spain, after which he consolidates the Pyrenees border (778)
c 782	Carolingian renaissance in art, architecture, and education
800	The pope crowns Charlemagne Holy Roman Emperor in Rome. Charlemagne expands the kingdom of France far beyond its present borders, and establishes a center for learning at his capital, Aix-la-Chapelle (Aachen, in present-day Germany)
814–987	Death of Charlemagne. The Carolingian line continues until 987 through a dozen or so monarchs, with a batch called Charles (the Bald, the Fat, the Simple) and a sprinkling of Louis. Under the Treaty of Verdun (843), the empire is divided in two—the eastern half becoming Germany, the western half, France

The Capetian Dynasty

987	Hugh Capet (987–996) is elected king of France and establishes the principle of hereditary rule for his descendants. Settled

conditions and the increased power of the Church see the flowering of the Romanesque style of architecture in the cathedrals of Autun and Angoulême

1066 Norman conquest of England by William the Conqueror (1066–87)

1067 Work begins on the Bayeaux Tapestry, the Romanesque work of art celebrating the Norman Conquest

c 1100 First universities in Europe include Paris. Development of European vernacular verse: *Chanson de Roland*

1140 The Gothic style of architecture first appears at St-Denis and later becomes fully developed at the cathedrals of Chartres, Reims, Amiens, and Notre-Dame in Paris

c 1150 Struggle between the Anglo-Norman kings (Angein Empire) and the French; when Eleanor of Aquitaine switches husbands (from Louis VII of France to Henry II of England), her extensive lands pass to English rule

1154 Chartres Cathedral is begun; Gothic architecture spreads through western Europe

1204 Fourth Crusade: Franks conquer Byzantium and found the Latin Empire

1257 The Sorbonne university is founded in Paris

1270 Louis IX (1226–70), the only French king to achieve sainthood, dies in Tunis on the seventh and last Crusade

1302–07 Philippe IV (1285–1314), the Fair, calls together the first States-General, predecessor to the French Parliament. He disbands the Knights Templars to gain their wealth (1307)

1309 Papacy escapes from a corrupt and disorderly Rome to Avignon in southern France, where it stays for nearly 70 years

---

The Valois Dynasty

1337–1453 Hundred Years' War between France and England: episodic fighting for control of those areas of France gained by the English crown following the marriage of Eleanor of Aquitaine and Henry II

1348–1350 The Black Death rages in France

1428–31 Joan of Arc (1412–1431), the Maid of Orleans, sparks the revival of French fortunes in the Hundred Years' War, but is captured by the English, and burned at the stake at Rouen

1434 Johannes Gutenberg invents the printing press in Strasbourg, Alsace

1453 France finally defeats England, terminating the Hundred Years' War and the English claim to the French throne

1475 Burgundy at the height of its power under Charles the Bold

1494 Italian wars: beginning of Franco-Habsburg struggle for hegemony in Europe

1515–47 Reign of François I, who imports Italian artists, including Leonardo da Vinci (1452–1519), and brings the Renaissance to France. The palace of Fontainebleau is begun (1528)

1558 France captures Calais, England's last territory on French soil

1562–98 Wars of Religion (Catholics versus Protestants/Huguenots) within France

The Bourbon Dynasty

1589 The first Bourbon king, Henri IV (1589–1610) is a Huguenot who converts to Catholicism and achieves peace in France. He signs the Edict of Nantes, giving limited freedom of worship to Protestants. The development of Renaissance Paris gets under way

c 1610 Scientific revolution in Europe begins, marked by the discoveries of mathematician and philosopher René Descartes (1596–1650)

1643–1715 Reign of Louis XIV, the Sun King, an absolute monarch who builds the Baroque power base of Versailles and presents Europe with a glorious view of France. With his first minister, Colbert, Louis makes France, by force of arms, the most powerful nation-state in Europe. He persecutes the Huguenots, who emigrate in great numbers, nearly ruining the French economy

1660 Classical period of French culture: writers Molière (1622–73), Jean Baptiste Racine (1639–99), Pierre Corneille (1606–84), and painter Nicolas Poussin (1594–1665)

c 1715 Rococo art and decoration develop in Parisian boudoirs and salons, typified by the painter Jean Antoine Watteau (1684–1721) and, later, François Boucher (1703–70) and Jean Honoré Fragonard (1732–1806)

1700 onward Writer and pedagogue Voltaire (1694–1778) is a central figure in the French Enlightenment, along with Jean Jacques Rousseau (1712–78) and Denis Diderot (1713–84), who, in 1751, compiles the first modern encyclopedia. The ideals of the Enlightenment—for reason and scientific method and against social and political injustices—pave the way for the French Revolution. In the arts, painter Jacques Louis David (1748–1825) reinforces revolutionary creeds in his severe neo-Classical works

1756–63 The Seven Years' War loses France most of her overseas possessions, and sees England become a world power

1776 The French assist in the American War of Independence. Ideals of liberty cross the Atlantic with the returning troops to reinforce new social concepts

The French Revolution

1789–1804 The Bastille is stormed on July 14, 1789. Following upon early Republican ideals comes the Terror and the administration of the Directoire under Robespierre. There are widespread political executions—Louis XVI and his queen, Marie Antoinette, are guillotined in 1793. Reaction sets in, and the instigators of the Terror are themselves executed (1794). Napoleon Bonaparte enters the scene as the champion of the Directory (1795–99) and is installed as First Consul during the Consulate (1799–1804)

The First Empire

1804 Napoleon crowns himself Emperor of France at Notre-Dame in the presence of the pope

1805–12 Napoleon conquers most of Europe. The Napoleonic Age is marked by a neo-Classical style in the arts, called Empire, as well as by the rise of Romanticism—characterized by such writers as Chateaubriand (1768–1848) and Stendhal (1783–1842), and the painters Eugène Delacroix (1798–1863) and Théodore Géricault (1791–1824)—which is to dominate the arts of the 19th century

1812–14 Winter cold and Russian determination defeat Napoleon outside Moscow. The emperor abdicates and is transported to Elba (1814)

Restoration of the Bourbons

1814–15 Louis XVIII, brother of the executed Louis XVI, regains the throne after the Congress of Vienna is held to settle peace terms

1815 The Hundred Days: Napoleon returns from Elba and musters an army on his march to the capital, but lacks national support. He is defeated at Waterloo (June 18) and exiled to the island of St. Helena in the South Atlantic

1821 Napoleon dies in exile

1830 Bourbon king Charles X, locked into a pre-revolutionary state of mind, abdicates. A brief upheaval (Three Glorious Days) brings Louis Philippe, the Citizen King, to the throne

1840 Napoleon's remains are brought back to Paris

1846–48 Severe industrial and farming depression helps lead to Louis Philippe's abdication (1848)

Second Republic and Second Empire

1848–52 Louis Napoleon (nephew and step-grandson of Napoleon I) is elected president of the short-lived Second Republic. He makes a successful attempt to assume supreme power and is declared Emperor of France, taking the title Napoleon III

c 1850 The ensuing period is characterized in the arts by the emergence of realist painters—Jean François Millet (1814–75), Honoré Daumier (1808–79), Gustave Courbet (1819–77)—and late Romantic writers—Victor Hugo (1802–85), Honoré de Balzac (1799–1850) and Charles Pierre Baudelaire (1821–87)

1853 Baron Haussmann (1809–91) re-creates the center of Paris, with great boulevards connecting important squares, or *places*

1863 Napoleon III inaugurates the Salon des Refusés in response to critical opinion. It includes work by Edouard Manet (1832–83), Claude Monet (1840–1926), and Paul Cézanne (1839–1906) and is commonly regarded as the birthplace of Impressionism and of modern art in general

The Third Republic

1870–71 The Franco-Prussian War sees Paris besieged, and Paris falls to the Germans. Napoleon III takes refuge in England. The Commune is established, an attempt by the extreme left to seize power. France loses Alsace and Lorraine to Prussia before the peace treaty is signed

1871–1940 Before World War I, France expands her industries and builds up a vast colonial empire in North Africa and Southeast Asia.

Sculptor Auguste Rodin (1840–1917), musicians Maurice Ravel (1875–1937) and Claude Debussy (1862–1918), and writers, such as Stéphane Mallarmé (1842–98) and Paul Verlaine (1844–96), set the stage for Modernism

1874 Emergence of the Impressionist school of painting: Monet, Pierre Auguste Renoir (1841–1919), and Edgar Degas (1834–1917)

1889 The Eiffel Tower is built for the Paris World Exhibition. Centennial of the French Revolution

1894–1906 Franco-Russian alliance (1894). Dreyfus affair: the spy trial and its antisemitic backlash shocks France

1898 Pierre and Marie Curie (1859–1906, 1867–1934) observe radioactivity and isolate radium

1904 The Entente Cordiale: England and France become firm allies

1907 Exhibition of Cubist painting in Paris

1914–18 During World War I, France fights with the Allies, opposing Germany, Austria, Hungary, and Turkey. Germany invades France; most of the big battles (Ypres, Verdun, Somme, Marne) are fought in trenches in northern France. French casualties exceed five million. With the Treaty of Versailles (1919), France regains Alsace and Lorraine and attempts to exact financial and economic reparations from Germany

1918–39 Between wars, Paris attracts artists and writers, including Americans—Ernest Hemingway (1899–1961) and Gertrude Stein (1874–1946). France nourishes major artistic movements: Constructivism, Dadaism, Surrealism, and Existentialism

1923 France occupies the Ruhr, a major industrial area in Germany's Rhine valley

1939–45 At the beginning of World War II France fights with the Allies until invaded and defeated by Germany in 1940. The French government, under Marshal Pétain (1856–1951), moves to Vichy and cooperates with the Nazis. French overseas colonies split between allegiance to the legal government of Vichy and declaration for the Free French Resistance, led (from London) by General Charles de Gaulle (1890–1970)

1944 D-Day, June 6: The Allies land on the beaches of Normandy and successfully invade France. Additional Allied forces land in Provence. Paris is liberated in August 1944, and France declares full allegiance to the Allies

1944–46 A provisional government takes power under General de Gaulle; American aid assists the French recovery

The Fourth Republic

1946 France adopts a new constitution; French women gain the right to vote

1946–54 In the Indochinese War, France is unable to regain control of her colonies in Southeast Asia. The 1954 Geneva Agreement establishes two governments in Vietnam: one in the north, under the Communist leader Ho Chi Minh, and one in the south, under the emperor Bao Dai. U.S. involvement eventually leads to French withdrawal

1954–58 The Algerian Revolution achieves Algeria's independence from France. Thereafter, other French African colonies gain independence

1957 Treaty of Rome establishes the European Economic Community (now known as the European Community—EC), with France a founding member

The Fifth Republic

1958–68 De Gaulle is the first president under a new constitution; he resigns in 1968 after widespread disturbances begun by student riots in Paris

1976 The first supersonic transatlantic passenger service begins with Anglo-French Concorde

1981 François Mitterrand is elected the first Socialist president of France since World War II

1988 Mitterrand is elected for a third term

1989 Bicentennial celebration of the French Revolution

The Art of French Cooking

by Anne Willan

Anne Willan is president and founder of the Ecole de Cuisine La Varenne in Paris. Her food column in the Washington Post is widely syndicated and her books include French Regional Cooking and La Varenne's Cooking Course.

Born British, naturalized American, I am an unabashed chauvinist about French food. To wander through a French open market, the vegetables overflowing from their crates, the fruits cascading in casual heaps on the counter, is a sensual pleasure. To linger outside a bakery in the early morning, watching the fresh breads and croissants being lined up in regimental rows, must awaken the most fickle appetite. Just to read the menu posted outside a modest café alerts the imagination to pleasures to come.

Best of all, the French are happy to share their enthusiasm for good food with others. There are more good restaurants and eating places in France than in any other European country; the streets are lined with delicatessens, butchers, cheese shops, bakeries, and pastry shops selling food. And I have yet to find a Frenchman, cantankerous though he may be, who does not warm to anyone who shows an interest in his national passion for wines and fine cuisine.

Fine cuisine does not necessarily mean fancy cuisine. Masters though French chefs are of the soufflé and the butter sauce, the salmon in aspic, and the strawberry *feuilleté*, such delicacies are reserved for celebration. Everyday fare is much more likely to be roast chicken, steak and *frites*, omelette, or pork chop. Bread, eaten without butter, is mandatory at main meals, while the bottle of mineral water is almost as common as wine.

Where the French do score is in the variety and quality of their ingredients. Part of the credit must go to climate and geography—just look at the length of the French coastline and the part seafood plays in the cooking of Normandy, Brittany, and Provence. Count the number of rivers with fertile valleys for cattle and crops. Olives and fruits flourish in the Mediterranean sun, while from southwest of Paris running up north to the Belgian border is one of the great breadbaskets of Europe.

No one but the French identifies three basic styles of cuisine—classical, nouvelle, and regional—not to mention offshoots like diet cooking *(cuisine minceur)* and women's cooking *(cuisine de femme)*. No other European nation pays so much attention to menus and recipes.

Most sophisticated are the sauces and soufflés, the *mousselines* and *macédoines* of classical cuisine. Starting in the 17th century, successive generations of chefs have lovingly documented their dishes, developing an intellectual discipline from what is an essentially practical art. As a style, classical cuisine is now outmoded, but its techniques form the basis of rigorous professional training in French cooking. In some measure, all other styles of cooking are based on its principles.

Nouvelle cuisine, for instance, is directly descended from the classics. Launched with great fanfare about 20 years ago, it takes a fresh, lighter approach, with simpler sauces and a colorful, almost oriental view of presentation. First-course salads, often with hot additions of shellfish, chicken liver, or bacon, have become routine. For a while, cooks experimented with way-out combinations like vanilla with lobster and chicken with raspberries, but now new-style cooking has settled down, establishing its own classics. Typical are *magrets de canard* (boned duck breast) sautéed like steak and served with a brown sauce of wine or green peppercorns; *pot au feu* made of fish rather than the usual beef; and quiches made with vegetables like spinach and zucchini.

Nouvelle cuisine has swept French restaurants, with somewhat mixed results. When scouting out a place to dine, be wary of flowery adjectives like "fresh-culled" and avoid willfully odd combinations, such as scallops with mango and saffron. The shorter the menu, the more likely the dishes are to be fresh.

Cooks have recently made a refreshing return toward the third, grass-roots style of French cooking, that of the countryside. Indeed, many cooks never left it, for classical and nouvelle cuisines are almost exclusively the concern of professionals and are dominated by men. However, regional dishes are cooked by everyone—chefs, housewives, grandma, and the café on the corner. Here women come into their own, for the best country cooking has an earthy warmth that the French prize as typical of *cuisine de femme*.

The city of Lyon exemplifies the best of regional cuisine. Restaurants are often run by women known as *mères* (mothers) and feature local specialties like poached eggs in *meurette* (red wine sauce), *quenelles* (fish dumplings) in crayfish sauce, sausage with pistachios, and chocolate *gâteau* (cake). The Lyonnais hotly dispute Paris's title of gastronomic capital of France, pointing to the cluster of restaurants surrounding their city that have received the prestigious Michelin stars for excellence. What is more, some of the world's finest wines are produced only 90 miles north, in Burgundy. Certainly, the Lyonnais cooking style is different from Paris, less elitist and more robust.

Lyon may represent the best of French regional cooking, but there's plenty to look for elsewhere. Compare the sole of Normandy, cooked with mussels in cream sauce, with the sea bass of Provence, flamed with dried fennel or baked with tomatoes and thyme. Contrast the butter cakes of Brittany with the yeast breads of Alsace, the braised en-

dive of Picardy with the gratin of cardoons (a type of artichoke) found in the south.

Authentic regional specialties are based on local products.
They have a character that may depend on climate (cream
cakes survive in Normandy but not in Provence) or geography (each mountain area has its own dried sausages and
hams). History brought spice bread to Dijon, legacy of the
days when the dukes of Burgundy controlled Flanders and
the spice trade. Ethnic heritage explains ravioli around
Nice on the Italian border, waffles in the north near Belgium, and dumplings close to Germany. Modern ethnic
influences show up in cities, with many an Arab pastry shop
started by Algerian immigrants and many a restaurant run
by Vietnamese.

Fundamental to French existence is the baker, the
boulanger. From medieval times, legislation has
governed the weight and content of loaves of bread,
with stringent penalties for such crimes as adulteration
with sand or sawdust. Today the government pegs the price
of white bread, and you'll find the famous long loaves a bargain compared with the price of brioche; croissants; or
loaves of wholewheat *(pain complet)*, rye *(pain de seigle)* or
bran *(pain de son)*. White bread can be bought as thin *flûtes*
to slice for soup; as *baguettes;* or as the common, thicker
loaves known simply as *pains*.

Since French bread stays fresh only a few hours, it is baked
in the morning for midday and baked again in the afternoon.
A baker's day starts at 4 AM to give the dough time to rise.
Sadly, there is a lack of recruits, so more and more French
bread is being industrially produced without the right nutty
flavor and chew to the crisp crust. The clue to bread baked on
the spot is the heady smell of fermenting yeast, so sniff out a
neighborhood bakery before you buy.

If bread is the staff of French life, pastry is the sugar icing.
The window of a city pastry shop (in the country, bakery and
pastry shop are often combined) is a wonderland of éclairs and
meringues, madeleines, petits fours, tartlets and puff pastry,
spun sugar, and caramel. You'll find pies laden with seasonal
fruits, pound cakes, nut cakes, and chocolate cakes, plus the
chef's specialty, for he is certain to have one. Survey them
with a sharp eye; they should be small (good ingredients are
expensive) and impeccably alike in color and size (the sign of
an expert craftsman). Last, the window should not be overflowing; because of the high cost, the temptation to cram the
shelves with leftovers from the day before is strong.

The *charcuterie* is almost as French an institution as the
bakery. *Chair cuite* means cooked meat, and a charcuterie
is a kind of delicatessen, specializing in pâtés, terrines,
ham, sausages, and all kinds of cooked and raw pork. A
charcuterie also sells long-lasting salads like cucumber,
tomato, or grated carrot vinaigrette and root celery

(celeriac) *remoulade* (with mustard mayonnaise). Cooked "dishes of the day" may include *coq au vin, choucroute alsacienne* (sauerkraut with smoked pork hock), and a variety of sausages, *cassoulet* (a rich stew of goose, sausage, and beans), or stuffed cabbage. Often you'll also find condiments like pickles, plus a modest selection of wines, cheeses, and desserts, such as rice pudding or baked apple. Only bread is needed to complete the meal, and you're set for the world's best picnic!

French cheese deserves, and gets, close attention. Sometimes whole shops are devoted to this branch of gastronomy. Take a whiff of the pungent odor, brace yourself, and plunge into a complex display of goat, sheep, and cow's milk cheeses, of fresh and aged cheeses, low-fat and high-fat, soft, hard, and blue cheeses.

Choosing a cheese is as delicate a matter as deciding on the right wine. In a good cheese shop you will be welcome to sample any of the cut cheeses, and assistants will help with advice. One cardinal rule is to look for *fromage fermier* (farmer's cheese), a rough equivalent of château-bottled wine. If the label says *lait cru* (raw milk)—even better; only when milk is unpasteurized does the flavor of some cheeses, Camembert, for example, develop properly. Try to keep a cheese cool without refrigeration, and eat it as soon as you can. The delicate soft cheeses like Brie can become overripe in a matter of hours, one reason why it is rare to find a wide-ranging selection of cheese in a restaurant.

All kinds of other specialty stores exist, often for local products. In Dijon, for instance, you'll find shops selling mustards in ornamental pots; in Gascony (near Bordeaux), it's foie gras and canned *confit* (preserved duck or goose). The Provençal hill town of Apt goes in for preserves, and Montélimar, close to the almond orchards of the sheltered Rhône valley, makes nougat.

The most famous concentration of food shops in the world must be clustered around the place de la Madeleine in Paris. On one corner stands Fauchon, dean of luxury food emporiums. Fauchon sells everything from wild mushrooms to handmade candies and the most exotic game pâtés, all wrapped in those gift packages at which the French excel. Just across the square stands Hédiard, specializing in spices, rare fruits, and preserves. Next door is La Maison de la Truffe and Caviar Kaspia, while for cheese, it's a step around the corner to La Ferme Saint-Hubert.

The Madeleine crossroads may be unique, but with a bit of persistence, a more modest version can be found in most French towns in the weekly market, often held in a picturesque open hall that may be centuries old. Markets start early, typically around 8 AM, and often disband at noon. In Paris, street markets continue to thrive in almost every quarter, and although the main wholesale market of Les

Halles has moved to the suburbs, the area around the rue Coquillière is still worth exploring for its maze of truffle vendors, game purveyors, and professional kitchen-equipment outlets.

A market is not just somewhere to absorb local color. You'll see what fish is available and what produce is at its best. Often you'll find little old ladies offering rabbits and herbs, honey, and spice bread baked at home. You'll come across local cheeses and, with luck, find a few specialties like the *pissaladière* onion tart of Provence or the candied chestnuts of Privas, near Lyon.

French markets are still dominated by the season—there is little or no sign of frozen produce and meats. The first baby lamb heralds Christmas, little chickens arrive around Easter, together with kid and asparagus. Autumn excitement comes with wild game—venison, pheasant, and wild boar. Even cheeses look and taste different with the time of year, depending on whether the animals have been fed in or outdoors.

The French light breakfast can come as no surprise; its unbeatable wakeup combination of croissant, brioche, or crusty roll with coffee has swept much of the world. Tourists may be offered a glass of orange juice as well. Traditionally, the coffee comes as *café au lait*, milky and steaming in a wide two-handled bowl for dipping the bread.

If you're an early riser, there's a long wait until lunch, for snacks are not a French habit. The structure of a meal, its timing, and its content are taken seriously. The "grazing" phenomenon of minimeals snatched here and there throughout the day is almost unheard of, and snacks are regarded as spoiling the appetite, not to mention being nutritionally unsound.

However, at noon, you'll be rewarded by what, for most Frenchmen, remains the main meal of the day. In much of the country, everything stops for two hours; children return from school, and museums and businesses lock their doors. The pattern is much the same in large provincial cities. Restaurants, bistros, and cafés are crammed with diners, most of whom eat at least two and often three or more courses.

Lunch keeps French adults going until evening, but you may want to follow the example of schoolchildren, who are allowed a treat on the way home. Often it is *pain au chocolat*, a stick of chocolate stuffed in a length of French bread or baked inside croissant dough. By 8 PM, you'll be ready for dinner and for one of the greatest pleasures France has to offer.

The choice of restaurants in France is a feast in itself. At least once during your trip you may want to indulge in an outstanding occasion. But restaurants are just the beginning. You can also eat out in cafés, bistros, brasseries, fast-food outlets (they, too, have reached France), or *auberges* which range from staid country inns to sybaritic hideaways with helicopter pads and cooking to match.

Simplest is the café (where the expresso machine is king), offering drinks and snacks like *croque monsieur* (toasted ham and cheese sandwich), *oeuf au plat* (baked eggs), *le hot dog*, and foot-long sandwiches of French bread. Larger-city cafés serve hot meals, such dishes as onion soup and braised beef with vegetables, consumed on marble-topped tables to a background of cheerful banter. Like English pubs, cafés are a way of life, a focal point for gossip and dominoes in practically every village.

The name *bistro*, once interchangeable with café, has recently taken a fashionable turn. In cities, instead of sawdust on the floor and a zinc-topped counter, you may find a bistro is designer-decorated, serving new-style cuisine to a trendy, chattering crowd. If you're lucky the food will be as witty and colorful as the clientele. Such spots can be great fun to visit, but watch out for the prices.

With few exceptions, brasseries remain unchanged—great bustling places with white-aproned waiters and hearty, masculine food. Go to them for oysters on the half-shell and fine seafood, for garlic snails, *boudin* (black pudding), sauerkraut, and vast ice-cream desserts. Originally, a brasserie brewed beer, and, since many brewers came from Alsace on the borders of Germany, the cooking reflects their origins.

Training is an important factor in maintaining the standards of French cooking. Professional chefs begin their three-year apprenticeship at age 16, starting in baking, pastry, or cuisine and later branching into specialties like aspic work and sugar sculpture. To be a *chocolatier* is a career in itself. Much more than a manual trade, cooking in France aspires to an art, and its exponents achieve celebrity status. In the 1800s, it was Carême (remembered to this day for the ubiquitous caramel); in the 1900s, it was Escoffier; and today, it is Paul Bocuse and his nouvelle cuisine cohorts. Each decade has its stars, their rise and fall a constant source of eager speculation in the press and at the table.

The importance placed on food in France is echoed by the number of gastronomic societies, from the *Chevaliers du Tastevin* to the *Chaîne des Rôtisseurs* and the *Confrérie des Cordons Bleus*, to mention only three. The French believe that good eating, at whatever level, is an art that merits considerable time and attention. The French have done the hard work, and, as a traveler, you can reap the benefits.

A Survey of French Architecture

by Simon Hewitt

As a student of art history at Oxford, Simon Hewitt wrote a thesis on French Gothic architecture. A wine enthusiast, he has traveled extensively through France's vineyards and contributed articles to several wine trade publications. He has lived in Paris since 1984.

Despite the ravages of wars throughout the centuries, France still is a rich showcase of architecture, with excellent examples from nearly every historical and regional style. Ornate theaters, soaring cathedrals, imposing castles, and graceful châteaus serve as a reminder of French architectural achievements through the ages.

Each region has its own characteristics. The dark red brick of the north stands in contrast to the pink brick of Toulouse; compare the white, chalky stone of the Cognac and Champagne regions with the pink sandstone of the Vosges. Roofs vary as well, from the steep slopes of Alpine chalets to the flat, red-tiled roofs of the Midi and the colorful tile patterns of Burgundy.

Medieval black-and-white timber-framed houses survive in towns north of the Loire, such as Troyes, Dinan, Rennes, and the Petite France sector of Strasbourg. Castles perch grandly on cliffs throughout the southwest, while hilltop villages survey the vineyards and olive groves of Provence in the southeast. Grim gateways repel strangers in the Charente region; flower-strewn balconies welcome them to Alsace. Flemish campaniles, or belltowers, and Spanish gables flourish in the north, while the Germans, armed with their heavy Gothico-Renaissance style, did their best to turn Strasbourg into a western Berlin between 1870 and 1914.

Although the cave paintings at Lascaux in the Dordogne and the free-standing *menhir* rocks of Brittany prove that Frenchmen (or their ancestors, at any rate) have created and constructed since prehistoric times, the first great builders here were the Romans. Their efforts—mostly in ruins—are found throughout France, especially in the south. The amphitheaters of Nîmes and Arles, the theater of Orange, and the Pont du Gard aqueduct in southern France are masterpieces equal to anything Italy has to offer. Towns such as Autun, Saintes, and Reims boast proud Roman arches, and even the sprawling cities of Lyon and Paris house Roman remains.

With occasional exceptions, such as the 5th-century chapel at La Pépiole, near Toulon, the next era to leave its architectural mark was the Carolingian, named after the Emperor Charlemagne, who reigned at the start of the 9th century. Surviving examples include the Basse-Oeuvre at Beauvais and the octagonal abbey church of Ottmarsheim in Alsace.

The massive and stocky Romanesque style that succeeded Carolingian, differed in various ways—with its stone (as opposed to wooden) ceilings or vaults, its introduction of windows high up the walls, and its preference for stone sculpture over superficial ornament like mosaic and painting. Many 10th- and 11th-century Romanesque buildings survive in Burgundy, Alsace, the Auvergne, and western France: The city of Poitiers is particularly rich in Romanesque architecture; notably the intricately carved west front of the church of Notre-Dame-la-Grande.

The airier Gothic style of the great French cathedrals built between the 12th and 16th centuries represented a fundamental departure from Romanesque. The most obvious visual change was that pointed arches replaced round ones. Just as important, though, was a new vaulting structure based on intersecting ribbed vaults, which sprang across the roof from column to column (to the columns both directly and diagonally opposite). Outward thrust was borne by flying buttresses, slender arches linking the outer walls to free-standing columns, often topped by spiky pinnacles. Where Romanesque architecture had thick, blocky walls with little room for window space, Gothic architecture, technically much more sophisticated, replaced stone with stained glass.

Most medieval churches were built in the form of a cross, with two arms, or transepts, that intersect at the crossing (often topped by a tower in Romanesque churches). The nave, divided into bays (the spaces between each column) and flanked on either side by side aisles, formed the main body of the church, with the east end, known as the chancel, containing the choir and altar. Many Gothic churches also have a number of small chapels behind the high altar, forming an outline known as the chevet, or apse.

Romanesque and Gothic churches are divided into three or four distinct vertical sections, like strata. Forestlike rows of pillars, topped by carved capitals, spring from the ground either to a gallery or triforium (an arcade of small columns and arches, originally of stone, later filled with glass), then a clerestory (row of windows) above.

The Romanesque facade was intended as an ornate screen and was sometimes fronted by a large porch (or narthex). The tympanum, a large sculpted panel above the central doorway (usually representing Christ in Judgment or Glory), was retained in the Gothic facade, which also featured huge portals, a circular rose window, a statue gallery, and lofty towers. Other towers, over the crossing or alongside the transepts, gradually lost favor: The stone bulls on top of the many-towered cathedral of Laon mourn a dying breed.

Pointed arches and ribbed vaults were first used in the Gothic style during the 1130s at Sens and at St-Denis—home of Abbot Suger, the leading political figure of his day. Within a decade, local bishops had followed Suger's lead, and huge Gothic cathedrals were under way at Noyon, Senlis, and Laon. As France expanded during the early

Middle Ages from its Parisian epicenter, Gothic went with it. But the Gothic style did not displace Romanesque overnight. Many Romanesque churches survive as crypts beneath later buildings (as at Dijon Cathedral, for example); similarly, Romanesque naves were conserved at Mont-St-Michel, Vézelay, and Le Mans despite the addition of new Gothic chancels, while at Strasbourg Cathedral, the reverse is true and a Romanesque chancel survives.

As Gothic evolved, less and less stone was used, and churches came to assume a delicate, almost skeletal framework. Paris's Sainte Chapelle is the most famous example, though, as a stained-glass showcase, its scale doesn't match that of Metz Cathedral.

Height was another Gothic quest. Roofs soared higher and higher—until that at Beauvais Cathedral came crashing down in 1284. Notre-Dame of Paris is 106 feet high, but later cathedrals are even loftier: Chartres is 114 feet; Bourges, 120 feet; Reims, 124 feet; Amiens, 137 feet; and Beauvais an ill-fated 153 feet (it was never completed, so Amiens reigns as the country's largest cathedral).

The circular rose window was one feature that lasted throughout the Middle Ages, evolving from 13th-century geometric splendor at St-Denis and Notre-Dame in Paris, to a petal-like fluidity during the first half of the 16th century.

The Chambiges family, last in a long line of great Gothic master-masons and glaziers, played a major role in the development of the Flamboyant style. When the Bishop of Beauvais was planning a grandiose transept for his cathedral he sent for Martin Chambiges, tempting him away from Sens and keeping him jealously at Beauvais for 30 years. Some see in the flamelike Flamboyant style the last neurotic shrieks of Gothic decadence. But while its decorative profusion sometimes smacks of sculptural self-indulgence (St-Pierre in Caen is a good example), there are several admirable Flamboyant churches, notably St-Séverin in Paris, and St-Nicolas de Port near Nancy.

In the 16th century, Gothic architecture was subject to the influx of Renaissance ideas, given official encouragement when François I (1515–47) invited the Italian painters and architects Il Rosso, Primaticcio, and Leonardo da Vinci to his court. Renaissance architecture was marked by a return to Classical Roman styles and existed side by side with Gothic throughout the 16th century; in a number of Paris churches you will see Classical columns and ornament superimposed on Gothic structure (St-Etienne-du-Mont, St-Gervais, and St-Eustache are the best examples). While Gothic was first and foremost an ecclesiastical style, many of the chief creations of Renaissance architecture had a civil setting: the châteaus of noblemen, princes, and kings. In the Loire Valley, for instance, fortified medieval castles like Chinon gradually yielded to ideals of comfort and luxury (Cheverny, for example). Along the way, Renaissance proportion and daintiness was mingled with medieval massiveness as at the châteaus of Azay-le-Rideau and Amboise. One of the loveliest showcases of Renaissance architecture is the place des Vosges in Paris, a square whose huge, steep-sloping roofs are a recurring trait of French buildings of the 16th and 17th centuries.

To contrast Renaissance style with Baroque, its successor, compare the pink-brick arcades of the place des Vosges (1612) with the solemn and dignified stone of the place Vendôme, built in 1685 a couple of miles across town. A similar difference can be observed between the intimate château of Fontainebleau (mid-16th century) and the immense palace of Versailles (late 17th century).

Baroque imbued the Classical style with drama and a sense of movement: Take a look at Mansart's dome surging above Paris's Hôtel des Invalides, or the powerful rhythms of Charles Perrault's Louvre facade. Yet only in northern France, under the temporary influence of Spanish occupiers, did Latin exuberance find an outlet, typified in the soaring curves and curls on the colossal belfry of St-Amand-les-Eaux near Lille. The overblown fantasies to which Baroque lent itself in Italy, Spain, southern Germany, and Austria—wild curves, broken outlines, and sculptural overkill—were held firmly in check by the French love of discipline. Whole towns survive to remind us: The rigid planning and identical houses of Richelieu, south of Chinon, are restrained and austere.

The 18th century saw several major provincial building programs in neo-Classical style—a more literal, toned-down interpretation of antique precedent. The state rooms of Strasbourg's Château des Rohan, the charming place Stanislas in Nancy, and the Grand Théâtre and place de la Bourse in Bordeaux are top examples. A number of the more affluent châteaus in the Bordeaux vineyards also date from this time.

Baroque, however, continued to dominate church building until the early 19th century (witness the cathedrals of Nancy and Arras). Many clerics commissioned architects to dress up Gothic buildings in Classical apparel, sticking pilasters on columns or transforming pointed arches into rounded ones. Louis XIV set the tone by remodeling the choir of Notre-Dame in Paris in 1708, but Autun Cathedral —revamped throughout—is the most extreme example of this kind of architectural rethink. Stained-glass windows were even ripped out—an act of stylistic vandalism surpassed only during the French Revolution when thousands of churches were wrecked in the name of the Age of Reason.

Napoleon ushered in the 19th century with the Arc de Triomphe, which remained unfinished for 20 years—

typifying the hesitations of a century bereft of original ideas. Iron made its appearance—most obviously at the Eiffel Tower, most frequently accompanied by glass in train stations and covered markets.

The 19th century bequeathed us Paris as we know it, with Baron Haussmann carving boulevards through the city. Luckily, Haussman's seven-story buildings have proved sufficiently large and imposing to withstand the rapacious onslaughts of modern developers, and central Paris has remained unchanged for a hundred years. But it's not surprising that the showpiece of Haussmann's Paris, the Opéra, is a pompous jumble of styles.

Things perked up at the start of the 20th century. While such Paris landmarks as the Grand and Petit Palais (hastily constructed for the World Exhibition of 1900) and opulent town halls throughout the country were faithful to conservative taste, Emile Gallé and Hector Guimard led an artistic revolution known as Art Nouveau, with sinuous, nature-based forms. The Paris Métro, ornamented by iron railings and canopies, is the most familiar example. A reaction occurred in the straighter lines of art deco, which first turned up at the Théâtre des Champs-Elysées in 1913. At the same time, the French developed a taste for reinforced concrete that they have never lost. It's most imaginative exponent was Swiss-born Le Corbusier, an architectural Picasso whose best work (like the chapel at Ronchamp in eastern France) obeys few established rules.

In the first half of the 20th century, much energy was spent repairing the damage of two world wars: Many towns, particularly in the north, are now lackluster copies of their former selves. The greatest efforts were lavished on restoring cathedrals and other landmarks, a pursuit instigated a century before by Eugène Viollet-le-Duc, without whom any number of cathedrals and churches might have crumbled away.

The most visited postwar building in France is Paris's Futuristic Pompidou Center. Its pipes and workings are on the outside, ensuring that the interior is uncluttered to a fault (the fault being that the exterior is going rusty). In terms of size and mass appeal, the equivalents of cathedrals today may well be sports stadiums; here France again sets the lead, with Paris's Parc des Princes a model for the Olympic arenas of Montreal and Seoul.

Paris's latterday skyscrapers have—with the exception of the Tour Montparnasse—been banished to the city outskirts, notably to La Défense. There, finished only in 1989, the giant glass and concrete arch known as La Tête Défense has cemented a vista that stretches along the avenue de la Grande Armée, past the Arc de Triomphe, down the Champs-Elysées, across the place de la Concorde, and over the Tuileries to the gleaming glass pyramid of the Louvre.

An Introduction to French Wine

by Simon Hewitt

Although France marginally trails Italy as the largest wine-producing country in the world, the reputation of French wines is second to none. That's partly because of luck—the exceptional variety of France's soils and climate—and partly because of 2,000 years of know-how. No one understands better than the French which grapes produce the best wines, and where.

The credentials of individual French wines have been internationally established since at least the 18th century. Back in 1787, Thomas Jefferson went down to Bordeaux and splurged on bottles of 1784 Château d'Yquem and Château Margaux, for prices that were, he reported, "indeed dear." Jefferson knew his wines: In 1855, both d'Yquem and Margaux were officially classified among Bordeaux's top five. In 1986, Jefferson's unopened bottle of d'Yquem rated $56,000 at auction. The Margaux—of which Jefferson boasted "there cannot be a better bottle of Bordeaux" (in fact, it was a half-bottle)—was sold for $30,000 in 1987.

With such eminent roots, it is no surprise the United States is the richest export market for French wines, along with Great Britain (which imports the same in terms of overall value, but twice the quantity). France, like Italy, produces about 20% of the world's wine—over double that of Spain and Russia, and four times as much as the United States. Nearly a quarter of a million people in France make and sell wine, and many more produce it for their own consumption.

Bordeaux's reputation dates from the Middle Ages. From 1152 to 1453, along with much of what is now western France, Bordeaux belonged to England. The light red wine then produced was known as *clairet*, origin of our word "claret." Champagne, on the other hand, has only existed as we know it since 1700, when—thanks to the introduction of strong bottles, cork stoppers, and the blending of wines from different vineyards—its sparkle was first captured by a blind monk, Dom Pérignon. The abbey at Hautvillers, where he lived, is a site of pilgrimage for champagne aficionados. So is the monster oak barrel languishing in the Epernay cellars of the Mercier firm: It has a mind-boggling capacity of 200,000 bottles, and 24 thirsty oxen spent three weeks carting it to the Paris Exhibition in 1889.

Such publicity coups have brought champagne fame, fortune—and problems. Like cognac (a brandy produced in a strictly defined area north of Bordeaux), its name is illegally exploited worldwide by would-be imitators. Producers of the real McCoy fight such fraud in international law courts, but it is a hapless struggle. It has proved easier for French authorities to attack fraud in their own backyard. Thomas Jefferson, who cagily noted that his expensive wines were "bought on the spot and therefore genuine," would have enjoyed perusing today's legal texts. Their bureaucratic aridity may be of no succor to the thirsty tourist, but their role is essential in ensuring that the wine in your glass is precisely what the bottle says it is.

Prominently printed on any self-respecting French wine label is the term *Appellation d'Origine Contrôlée* (often abbreviated AC). Such wines have to meet stringent requirements. Yield, production methods, and geographic limits are meticulously controlled, as are the varieties of grape that are permitted (sometimes one, sometimes several—no fewer than 13 types of grape can be used at Châteauneuf-du-Pape), and the requisite degree of alcohol (all wines must respect a minimum, ranging from 8.5% for the sunless, sharp white Gros Plant Nantais up to 13% for sweet whites like Sauternes). AC wines now account for nearly a third of production, a figure that has doubled in 20 years.

The next category, *Vin Délimité de Qualité Supérieure* (VDQS), accounts for about 10% of French wines. It is a sort of second division for wines that, if they prove their mettle and show signs of steady improvement, may be promoted to the AC category. Then come the *Vins de Pays*, regional titles with fewer restrictions, that account for about 15% of production. The simplest classification is *Vin de Table*, a poor relation in terms of price, if not necessarily quality.

Each bottle tells a tale. Usually, the fancier it is, the more it has to hide. Beware of garish labels. Also, note where the wine was bottled: If it was not bottled on the spot *(mise en bouteille à la propriété/au domaine/au château)* or at least by a local merchant (often the case with Burgundies), it should be treated with suspicion.

Napoleon, incidentally, was partial to unblended Burgundy and, in a fit of alcoholic lucidity, once revealed the secret of his military genius: "No wine—no soldiers!" The English took the rival view of battle before wine: General Palmer celebrated victory over Napoleon at Waterloo by galloping down to Margaux and founding Château Palmer.

The vineyards of Margaux are possibly the ugliest in France, lost amid the flat, dusty plains of Médoc. Bordeaux is better represented at historic St-Emilion, with its cascading cobbled streets, or at Sauternes, where noble rot (a tiny mushroom that sucks water from the grapes, leaving them sweeter) steals up the riverbanks with autumn mists vanish in the summer skies. From the chilly hills of Champagne in the north, to the sun-pelted slopes of the southern Midi, vines cover France. Steep-banked terraces tower above the River Rhône. The vineyards of Alsace sway and ripple into the foothills of the Vosges. Chalky cliffs, cellars, and caves line the softly lit Loire Valley.

Names of wines can be as charming as the scenery. The Loire Valley yields Vin de Pays du Jardin de la France— Country Wine from the Garden of France. Entre-Deux-Mers quaintly translates as Between Two Seas (actually the rivers Garonne and Dordogne). It's difficult to resist flowery Fleurie, lovable St-Amour, sober Bouzy, or—if you overindulge—an early Graves.

Over a hundred different types of grapes exist in France. Some sound delicious. Try wrapping your tongue around Mourvèdre, Bourboulenc, Gewürtztraminer, or Sciacarello. Visualize a bunch of Barbarossa ("red beard"), Folle Blanche ("crazy white"), or Fer ("iron"). Some names are confusing: The Auxerrois grape is used at Cahors, not near Auxerre; the Beaunois is used near Auxerre, not near Beaune; the St-Emilion is used for making cognac, not St-Emilion; while the Melon de Bourgogne has nothing to do with melons or Burgundy (it's a white grape grown near the Atlantic coast).

As you travel, look at the vines: Are they young and slender or old, thick, and gnarled? The older the vine, the fewer grapes and wine it yields, but the better the quality. Not that you'll come across many vines over a hundred years old. The phylloxera bug gnawed its way through them all in the 1870s; the vineyards of France had to be replanted using bug-resistant American grafts.

You can buy local wines from a *co-opérative* (which handles wines from a number of local vine growers) or an individual producer. Co-opératives account for about 45% of the total production, but rarely offer wines of top quality. If you stop at a producer's, though (as you are bidden by many an enticing sign), you can hope to find a warmer welcome, and wines with more character. It is customary to buy at least three bottles, but if you don't like the wine, don't buy it.

Although the big champagne houses in Reims and Epernay organize slick, informative visits, the leading Bordeaux châteaus don't—partly because the Bordelais are notoriously reserved, mainly because they have no need to seduce passers-by (bulk orders account for 99% of their sales). One shudders to think what Thomas Jefferson would have made of the gum-chewing, radio-blaring welcome at Château Lascombes, just a stone's throw from his beloved Château Margaux. You can obtain parsimonious gulps of second-string clarets at the Maison du Vin on the cours du XXX Juillet in central Bordeaux, but, unfortunately, there is nothing to match the Marché aux Vins in the Burgundian town of Beaune, where a string of fine Burgundies can be sampled for a modest sum.

Different occasions warrant different wines. If you're buying wine for a picnic, go for something simple, like a rosé or

Wine Regions

St-Malo
St-Brieuc
Caen
Seine
Paris
Vannes
Rennes
Chartres
Le Mans
Orléans
Angers
Nantes
Blois
POUILLY
Loire Tours
SANCERRE
VAL DE LOIRE
QUINCY
Bourges
HAUT-POITOU
REUILLY
Nevers
Niort
Poitiers
La Rochelle
Montluçon
AUVERGNE
Angoulême
Limoges
Clermont-Ferrand
Bay of Biscay
COGNAC
Périgueux
BORDEAUX
Brive-la-Gaillarde
Aurillac
Bordeaux
Garonne
BERGERAC
Dordogne
CAHORS
Langon
DURAS
Cahors
Rodez
MARMANDAIS
BUZET
GAILLAC
Bayonne
TURSAN
Montauban
Millau
Albi
BEARN
ARMAGNAC
FRONTONNAIS
Pau
Toulouse
LANGUEDOC
IROULEGUY
JURANÇON
MADIRAN
Tarbes
Carcassonne
Narbonne
ROUSSILLON
S P A I N
ANDORRA
Perpignan
N

Reims
CHAMPAGNE
Châlons-sur-Marne
Metz
Nancy
Troyes
Strasbourg
ALSACE
Auxerre
CHABLIS
Mulhouse
Belfort
Dijon
Beaune
Besançon
BOURGOGNE
(Burgundy)
JURA
Mâcon
Saône
Bourg-en-Bresse
SAVOIE
BEAUJOLAIS
Lyon Rhône
Chambéry
Le Puy
Grenoble
Rhône
**CÔTES
DU
RHÔNE**
DIE
Montélimar
VENTOUX
LUBERON
PIERREVERT
BELLET
Nîmes
Avignon
Monte Carlo
Montpellier
Nice
Aix-en-Provence
Cannes
PROVENCE
ane
Marseille
Toulon

WEST
GERMANY

SWITZERLAND

CORSICA
Bastia
Calvi
Corte
Ajaccio

ITALY

0   50 mi

0   75 km

Mediterranean Sea

CORSICA

fruity red (Beaujolais or Gamay de Touraine). Full-bodied reds from the hottest regions of France are likely to knock you out if you drink them at lunchtime. Beware of restaurant wine lists designed to beef up the price of your meal, and always go for the house wine rather than a vague description such as "Bordeaux" or "Côtes du Rhône"; if there's no year or precise origin, you can't expect quality. If wine is made locally, try it; you may not come across it elsewhere, and regional cuisine is invariably tailored to regional wines.

A wide selection of local wines can be compared at any of the special fairs that proliferate in wine regions during the summer. The year's biggest celebration, however, is the appearance of Beaujolais Nouveau on the third Thursday of November. In recent years, as cafés and restaurants from Paris to New York rush the new wine from barrel to counter amid unpalatable fuss and brouhaha, the occasion has acquired a cheap if good-natured gimmickiness that obscures the fact that Beaujolais has been drunk young in the cafés of nearby Lyon since the days of, well, Thomas Jefferson, for example. The Trois Glorieuses, three days of Burgundian jollity centering on a wine auction at the Hospices de Beaune, is also held in November. Wine villages pay tribute to their patron saint on January 22, St-Vincent's Day, and another momentous feast is held at the end of the grape harvest. The harvests, or *vendanges*, begin in September and can last into December. In Sauternes, the grapes have to rot before being picked, and at Château Yquem, up to seven successive manual harvests may be required, with each grape inspected individually and picked only after achieving the right degree of maturity (by which time it looks a foul, shriveled mess).

Other wines to look out for include two from the Jura region of eastern France. *Vin Jaune*, also made from grapes picked late, is kept in oak barrels for six years or more, while yeasts form on the surface; the result is a wine (with a unique, nutty flavor sometimes likened to sherry) that can last for over a hundred years. The grapes that produce the strong, amber-colored *Vin de Paille* are left for two months on straw mats while the juice is drawn out and the sugar concentration intensifies.

Champagne offers tiny quantities of wine without a fizz. Still reds and whites made near Reims are known as Côteaux Champenois while, far to the south, there is even a still pink, Rosé des Riceys: rare, delicious, and expensive. Neither the truly black wine of Cahors or the sweet white Jurançon of the Pyrénées are easy to find, unlike the sand wines *(Vins de Sable)* of Provence, made from vines that creep right down to the beach. There are even vines in and around Paris, at Suresnes and Montmartre, where the harvest is celebrated behind the church of Sacré Coeur on the first weekend of October; unfortunately, the resultant wine is undrinkable!

Don't be a prisoner of fashion. Marketing men have convinced the British that Muscadet is *the* dry white, while Americans jostle for Pouilly-Fumé and Sancerre—fine wines, certainly, but in overhyped demand and, therefore, of poor value. Try instead to ferret out unfamiliar, peasanty wines, concocted by authentic local characters. If you hunt around, you may meet someone like Marcel. Marcel makes illegal wines out of illegal vines in a lost corner of Burgundy that is off both the beaten track and the straight and narrow.

People say—maps and guidebooks say, anyway—there aren't any vines in Marcel's bit of Burgundy. We ambled over the Canal du Nivernais and scrambled up a hill. The hill became a street and the street, a village square. There was a large sign on the square saying "Local Wine."

It was 12:15. The wine merchant was closed for lunch. Till 3. We sidled hopefully into a bar. "Local wine? Not here. Try Gaston by the church."

Gaston sold it all right, and sloshed some into cracked glass beakers. We stared solemnly at the wine and all the flat-hatted old men playing cards in the corner stared solemnly at us. We shared impressions. Unexpected. Perky but pale. Seemed friendly, but you never knew.

Gaston leaned confidentially forward, stroked his moustache, and asked "Want some more?" Yes. "Try that fellow there who's just gone out." Which fellow? "Marcel," said Gaston, adding helpfully, "The one in the flat hat."

Eventually—many country roads and twisty bends later—we tracked Marcel down. Who were we? We'd come about the wine. What wine? His wine. Marcel looked suspicious. His *excellent* wine. Marcel mellowed and got out the key to his cellar. We clattered down the slimy steps, tastebuds tingling. Marcel grabbed a bottle. The wine's freshness came soaring through the dinge. Its sunniness pierced the murk. Marcel tossed back a glass and belched.

We murmured a few clichés of admiration. Marcel downed another glass, receded into the darkest, dirtiest depths of his cellar and rummaged under a heap of jerricans. Out popped a bottle as black as ink. Marcel squirted some into a glass, dashed it back and said, "Let's finish the bottle!"

Drinking this thick, cloying illegality was like being half-strangled in a velvet curtain. We fought our way free and staggered to the car with a crate. Marcel turned his back on us, brandished his francs triumphantly, and watered his garden in celebration.

3 Paris

Introduction

If there's a problem with a trip to Paris, it is the embarrassment of riches that faces the visitor. A city of vast, noble perspectives and winding, hidden streets, Paris remains a combination of the pompous and the intimate. Whether you've come looking for sheer physical beauty, for cultural and artistic diversions, for world-famous shopping, for history, or simply for local color, you will find it here in abundance.

The city's 20 districts, or *arrondissements*, have their own distinctive character, as do the two banks of the Seine, the river that weaves its way through the city's heart. The tone of the *Rive Droite* (Right Bank) is set by spacious boulevards and formal buildings, while the *Rive Gauche* (Left Bank) is more carefree and bohemian.

The French capital is also, for the tourist, a practical city: It's relatively small as capitals go, and its major sites and museums are within walking distance of one another. The city's principal tourist axis is less than 6 kilometers (4 miles) long, running parallel to the north bank of the Seine from the Arc de Triomphe to the Bastille.

There are several "musts" that any first-time visitor to Paris will be loath to miss: the Eiffel Tower, the Champs-Elysées, the Louvre, and Notre-Dame. It is only fair to say, however, that a visit to Paris will never be quite as simple as a quick look at a few landmarks. Every *quartier* has its own treasures, and travelers should adopt the process of discovery—a very pleasant prospect in this most elegant of French cities.

Essential Information

Arriving and Departing by Plane

Airports and Airlines Paris is served by two international airports: **Charles de Gaulle,** also known as Roissy, 26 kilometers (16 miles) northeast of the downtown area, and **Orly,** 16 kilometers (10 miles) south. Major carriers, among them TWA, Pan Am, and Air France, fly daily from the United States, while Air France and British Airways between them offer hourly service from London. For more information on getting to Paris by air, *see* Getting to France in Essential Information.

Between the Airports and Downtown The easiest way to get into Paris from **Charles de Gaulle** (Roissy) airport is on the **RER-B** line, the suburban express train. A free shuttle bus runs between the two terminal buildings and the train station, taking about 10 minutes. Trains to Paris leave every 15 minutes; the fare is 27 francs, and the journey time is 30 minutes. **Buses** run between Charles de Gaulle and the Air France air terminal at Porte Maillot, a half-mile west of the Arc de Triomphe. The fare is 35 francs, and the journey time is about 40 minutes, though rush-hour traffic often makes this a slow and frustrating trip. **Taxis** are readily available; the fare will be around 150 francs, depending on traffic.

From **Orly** airport, the simplest way to get into Paris is on the **RER-C** line; there's a free shuttle bus from the terminal building to the train station, and trains leave every 15 minutes. The

fare is 22 francs, and the journey time is about 25 minutes.
Buses run between Orly airport and the Air France air terminal at Les Invalides on the Left Bank; the fare is 28 francs, and
the trip can take from 30 minutes to an hour. A 25-minute **taxi**
ride costs about 150 francs.

Arriving and Departing by Car, Train, and Bus

By Car It is no surprise in a country as highly centralized as France
that expressways converge on the capital from every direction:
A1 from the north (England/Belgium); A13 from Normandy/
the northwest; A4 from the east; A10 from Spain/the southwest; and A7 from the Alps/Riviera/Italy. Each connects with
the beltway, the *périphérique*, that encircles Paris. Note that
exits from the beltway into the city are named, not numbered.

By Train Paris has five international train stations: **Gare du Nord** (north-
ern France, northern Europe, and England via Calais or
Boulogne); **Gare St-Lazare** (Normandy and England via
Dieppe); **Gare de l'Est** (Strasbourg, Luxembourg, Basle, and
central Europe); **Gare de Lyon** (Lyon, Marseille, the Riviera,
Geneva, Italy); and **Gare d'Austerlitz** (Loire Valley, southwest
France, Spain). The **Gare Montparnasse** serves only western
France (mainly Nantes and Brittany). For train information
from any station, phone 45–82–50–50.

By Bus Paris has no central bus depot. Long-distance bus journeys
within France are rare compared to train travel. The two leading Paris-based bus companies are **Eurolines Nord** (3 av. de la
Porte de la Villette, 19e, tel. 40–38–93–93) and **L'Autobus** (4
bis rue St-Sauveur, 2e, tel. 42–33–86–72).

Getting Around

Paris is relatively small as capital cities go, and most of its prize
monuments and museums are within easy walking distance of
one another in any given area. To help you find your way
around, we suggest you buy a *Plan de Paris par arrondissement*, a city guide with separate maps of each district,
including the whereabouts of métro stations and an index of
street names.

Maps of the métro/RER network are available free from any
métro station and many hotels. They are also posted on every
platform, as are maps of the bus network. Bus routes are also
marked at bus stops and on buses.

By Métro The métro is by far the quickest and most efficient way of getting around the city and runs from 5:30 AM until 1:15 AM.
Stations are recognizable either by a large yellow "M" within a
circle, or by their distinctive, curly green Art Nouveau railings
and archway bearing the full title (Métropolitain).

With 13 lines criss-crossing Paris and its environs, the métro is
fairly easy to navigate. It is essential to know the name of the last
station on the line you take, however, since this name appears on
all signs. A connection (you can make as many as you like on one
ticket) is called a *correspondance*. At junction stations, illuminated orange signs, bearing the name of the line terminus,
appear over the correct corridors for *correspondance*. Illuminated blue signs, marked *sortie*, indicate the station exit. Some
lines and stations in the less salubrious parts of Paris are a bit

risky at night: in particular Lines 2 and 13. In general, however, the métro is relatively safe throughout.

The métro network connects at several points in Paris with the RER network. RER trains, which race across Paris from suburb to suburb, are a sort of supersonic métro and can be great time savers.

All métro tickets and passes are valid for RER and bus travel within Paris. Second-class métro tickets cost five francs each, though a *carnet* (10 tickets for 30 francs) is a better value.

Access to métro and RER platforms is through an automatic ticket barrier. Slide your ticket in and pick it up as it pops up. Keep your ticket during your journey; you'll need it to leave the RER system.

By Bus Paris buses are green and are marked with the route number and destination in front and major stopping-places along the sides. Most routes operate from 6 AM to 8:30 PM; some continue until midnight. Ten night buses operate hourly (1 to 6 AM) between Châtelet and various nearby suburbs. The brown bus shelters, topped by red-and-yellow circular signs, contain timetables and route maps.

Tickets are not available on buses; they must be bought in advance from métro stations or *tabac* shops. If you have individual yellow tickets (as opposed to weekly or monthly tickets), state your destination and be prepared to punch one or more tickets in the red-and-gray machines on board the bus.

By Taxi Paris taxis may not have the charm of their London counterparts—there is no standard vehicle or color—but they're cheaper. Daytime rates (6:30 AM till 9 PM) are around 2.50 francs per kilometer, and nighttime rates are around 3.75 francs. There is a basic charge of 10 francs for all rides. You are best off asking your hotel or restaurant to call for a taxi; cruising cabs can be hailed but are annoyingly difficult to spot. Note that taxis seldom take more than three people at a time.

By Bicycle You can rent bikes in the Bois de Boulogne (Jardin d'Acclimatation), Bois de Vincennes, some RER stations, and from the Bateaux-Mouches embarkation point by place de l'Alma. Or try Paris-Vélo (2 rue du Fer-à-Moulin, 5e, tel. 43–37–59–22). Rental rates vary from about 80 to 140 francs per day, 130 to 230 francs per weekend, and 380 to 780 francs per week.

Important Addresses and Numbers

Tourist Information There's the main Paris tourist office (127 av. des Champs-Elysées, 75008 Paris, tel. 47–23–61–72; open daily 9 AM–8 PM; closed Christmas Day and New Year's Day) and branches at all mainline train stations, except Gare du Montparnasse and Gare St-Lazare.

Embassies U.S. (2 av. Gabriel, 8e, tel. 42–96–12–02), Canada (35 av. Montaigne, 8e, tel. 47–23–01–01), and U.K. (35 rue du Fbg. St-Honoré, 8e, tel. 42–66–91–42).

Emergencies Police (tel. 17), ambulance (tel. 45–67–50–50), doctor (tel. 43–37–77–77), and dentist (tel. 43–37–51–00).

Hospitals The American Hospital (63 blvd. Victor-Hugo, Neuilly, tel. 47–47–53–00 or 47–45–71–00) has a 24-hour emergency service.

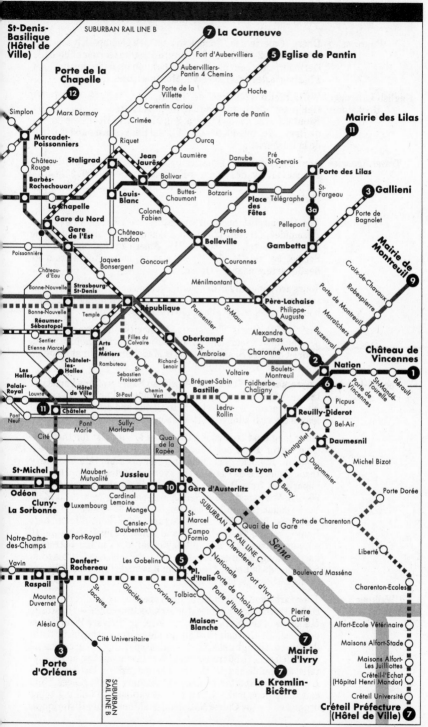

The **Hertford British Hospital** (3 rue Barbes, Levallois-Perret, tel. 47–58–13–12) also offers a 24-hour service.

Pharmacies Dhéry (Galerie des Champs, 84 av. des Champs-Elysées, 8e, tel. 45–62–02–41), open 24 hours; **drugstore** (corner of blvd. St-Germain and rue de Rennes, 6e), open daily until 2 AM; **Pharmacie des Arts** (106 blvd. Montparnasse, 6e).

English-Language Bookstores W.H. Smith (248 rue de Rivoli, 1er, tel. 42–60–37–97), Galignani (224 rue de Rivoli, 1er, tel. 42–60–76–07), **Brentano's** (37 av. de l'Opéra, 2e), **Marshall's Bookshop** (26 rue de Brey, 17e, tel. 40–54–03–05), and **Shakespeare and Co.** (rue de la Bûcherie, 5e).

Travel Agencies **American Express** (11 rue Scribe, 9e, tel. 42–66–09–99) and **Air France** (119 av. des Champs-Elysées, 8e, tel. 42–99–23–64).

Guided Tours

Orientation The two largest bus-tour operators are **Cityrama** (4 pl. des Pyramides, 1er, tel. 42–60–30–14) and **Paris Vision** (214 rue de Rivoli, 1er, tel. 42–60–30–01). **American Express** (11 rue Scribe, 9e, tel. 42–66–09–99) also organizes tours from its headquarters near the Opéra.

Tours are generally in double-decker buses with either a live or tape-recorded commentary (English is available) and last three hours. Expect to pay about 140 francs.

The **RATP** (Paris Transport Authority) has many guide-accompanied excursions in and around Paris. Inquire at its Tourist Service Board (place de la Madeleine, 8e) or at its office (53 quai des Grands-Augustins, 6e).

Special-Interest **Cityrama, Paris Vision,** and **American Express** offer a variety of theme tours ("Historic Paris," "Modern Paris," "Paris-by-Night") lasting from 2½ hours to all day and costing 110 to 270 francs (more if admission to a cabaret show is included).

Hour-long **boat trips** along the Seine are a must for the first-time visitor. Some boats serve lunch and dinner; make reservations in advance. The following services operate regularly throughout the day and in the evening: **Bateaux Mouches** has departures from Pont de l'Alma (Right Bank, 8e, tel. 42–25–96–10); **Vedettes du Pont-Neuf** has departures from Square du Vert Galant (Ile de la Cité, 1er, tel. 46–33–98–38); **Bateaux Parisiens–Tour Eiffel** has departures from Pont d'Iéna (Left Bank, 15e, tel. 47–05–50–00), and **Canauxrama** (tel. 42–39–15–00) organizes half- and full-day canal tours in flat-bottomed barges along picturesque canals in East Paris (departures from 5 bis quai de la Loire, 19e, or from Bassin de l'Arsenal, 12e, opposite 50 blvd. de la Bastille).

Walking Tours There are plenty of guided tours of specific areas of Paris, often concentrating on a historical or architectural topic—"Restored Mansions of the Marais," for instance, or "Private Walled Gardens in St-Germain." The guides are enthusiastic and dedicated, though not always English speaking. Charges range from 30 francs to 50 francs, and tours last about two hours. Details are published in the weekly magazines *Pariscope* and *L'Officiel des Spectacles* under the heading "Conferences." You can sometimes make advance reservations for walking tours organized by the **Caisse Nationale des Monuments Historiques,**

Bureau des Visites/Conférences (Hôtel de Sully, 62 rue St-Antoine, 4e, tel. 48–87–24–14).

Personal Guides International Limousines (182 blvd. Péreire, 17e, tel. 45–74–77–12) has guides with luxury cars or minibuses (taking up to seven passengers) who will take you around Paris and the environs for a minimum of three hours. Reservations are required, and the cost is about 200 francs per hour.

Exploring Paris

Numbers in the margin correspond with points of interest on the Paris map.

Orientation

The best method of getting to know Paris is on foot. With this in mind, we've divided our coverage of Paris into six tours. Use our routes as a base; concentrate on the areas that particularly interest you; and, above all, enjoy to the full the sights, sounds, and smells of this exciting city.

Highlights for First-time Visitors

Arc de Triomphe and Champs-Elysées, Tour 3
Eiffel Tower, Tour 4
The Louvre, Tour 1
Musée de Cluny, Tour 5
Musée d'Orsay, Tour 4
Notre-Dame, Tour 1
Place Vendôme, Tour 3
Beaubourg (Pompidou Center)
Sacré Coeur, Tour 6
Sainte Chapelle, Tour 1

Tour 1: The Historic Heart

Of the two islands in the Seine—the Ile St-Louis and Ile de la Cité—it is the latter that forms the historic heart of Paris. It was here that the earliest inhabitants of Paris, the Gaulish tribe of the Parisii, settled around 250 BC. Whereas the Ile St-Louis is largely residential, the Ile de la Cité remains deeply historic: It is the site of the great, brooding cathedral of Notre-Dame. Few of the island's other medieval buildings have survived, most having fallen victim to Baron Haussmann's ambitious rebuilding of the city in the mid-19th century. Among the rare survivors are the jewel-like Sainte Chapelle, a vision of shimmering stained glass, and the Conciergerie, the grim former city prison.

❶ The tour begins at the western tip of the Ile de la Cité, at the sedate **Square du Vert Galant.** The statue of the *Vert Galant* himself, literally the "vigorous [by which was really meant the amorous] adventurer," shows Henri IV sitting sturdily on his horse. Henri, king of France from 1589 until his assassination in 1610, was something of a dashing figure as well as a canny statesman.

Crossing the Ile de la Cité, just behind the Vert Galant, is the oldest bridge in Paris, confusingly called the **Pont Neuf,** or New

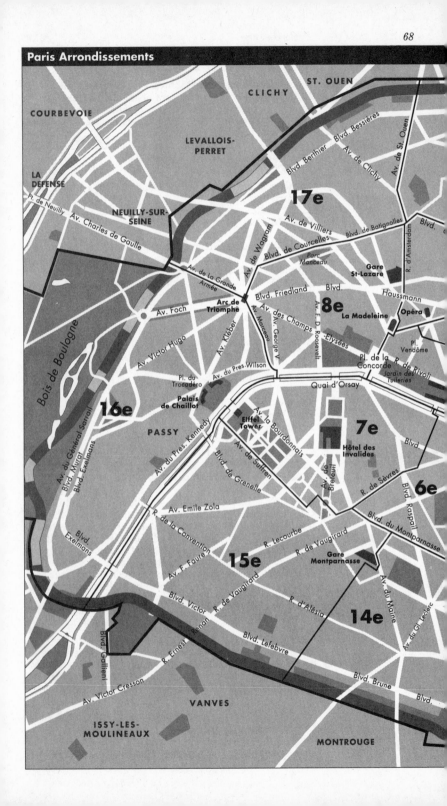

Paris Arrondissements

COURBEVOIE

CLICHY

ST. OUEN

LEVALLOIS-
PERRET

LA
DEFENSE

Pr. de Neuilly

Av. Charles de Gaulle

NEUILLY-SUR-
SEINE

Blvd. Berthier

Blvd. Bessières

Av. de Clichy

Av. de St. Ouen

Blvd.

17e

Av. de Villiers

Av. de Wagram

Blvd. de Courcelles

Blvd. de Batignolles

R. d'Amsterdam

Parc
Monceau

**Gare
St-Lazare**

Av. de La Grande
Armée

Blvd. Friedland

Blvd.

Haussmann

Opéra

**Arc de
Triomphe**

Av. Foch

Av. Kléber

Av. des Champs

8e

La Madeleine

Pl.
Vendôme

Av. F. D. Roosevelt

-Elysées

Av. Victor Hugo

Av. Marceau

Av. George V

Pl. de la
Concorde

R. de Rivoli
Jardin des
Tuileries

Bois de Boulogne

Av. du Pres. Wilson

Pl. du
Trocadéro

**Palais
de Chaillot**

Av. du Général Sarrail

Quai d'Orsay

Av. du Pres. Kennedy

Av. la Bourdonnais

16e

PASSY

**Eiffel
Tower**

Av. de Suffren

7e

Blvd.

Blvd. Murat

Blvd. Exelmans

Blvd. de Grenelle

**Hôtel des
Invalides**

Av. de Breteuil

R. de Sèvres

6e

Av. Emile Zola

R. de la Convention

Blvd.
Exelmans

Av. F. Faure

15e

R. Lecourbe

R. de Vaugirard

Blvd. du Montparnasse

Blvd. Raspail

Blvd. Victor

R. de Vaugirard

R. d'Alésia

**Gare
Montparnasse**

14e

Av. du Maine

Av. du Gl. Leclerc

Blvd. Gallieni

R. Ernest Renan

Blvd. Lefebvre

Blvd. Brune

Blvd.

Av. Victor Cresson

VANVES

**ISSY-LES-
MOULINEAUX**

MONTROUGE

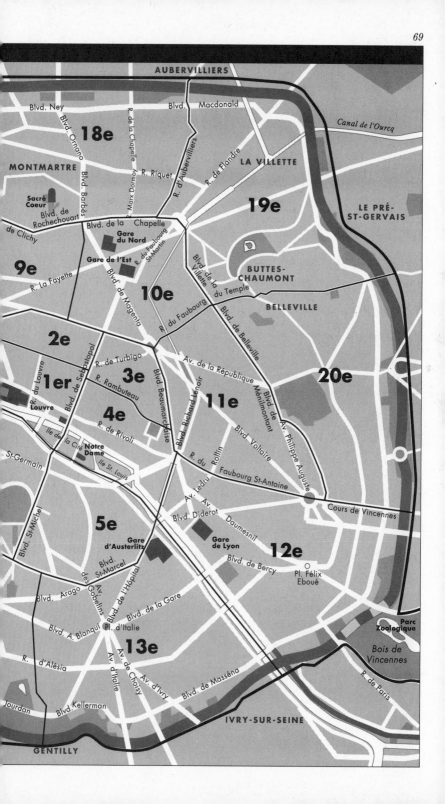

Paris

Bridge. Completed in the early 17th century, it was the first bridge in the city to be built without houses lining either side. Turn left onto it. Once across the river, turn left again and walk down to rue Amiral-de-Coligny, opposite the massive eastern facade of the Louvre. Before heading for the museum, however, stay on the right-hand sidewalk and duck into the church of **St-Germain-l'Auxerrois**. This was the French royal family's Paris church in the days before the Revolution, when the Louvre was a palace rather than a museum. The fluid stonework of the facade reveals the influence of 15th-century Flamboyant Gothic, the final, exuberant fling of the Gothic before the classical take-over of the Renaissance. The unusually wide windows in the nave and the equally unusual double aisles are typical of the style. The triumph of Classicism is evident, however, in the 18th-century fluted columns around the choir, the area surrounding the altar.

The Louvre colonnade across the road screens one of Europe's most dazzling courtyards, the **Cour Carré**, a breathtakingly monumental, harmonious, and superbly rhythmic ensemble. In the crypt below, excavated in 1984, sections of the defensive towers of the original, 13th-century fortress can be seen.

Saunter through the courtyard and pass under the **Pavillon de l'Horloge,** the Clock Tower, and you come face to face with I. M. Pei's **glass pyramid,** surrounded by three smaller pyramids. The pyramid marks the new entrance to the Louvre and houses a large museum shop. It also is the terminal point for the most celebrated city view in Europe, a majestic vista stretching through the Arc du Carrousel, the Tuileries Gardens, across place de la Concorde, up the Champs-Elysées to the towering Arc de Triomphe, and ending at the giant modern arch at La Tête Défense, 2½ miles away. Needless to say, the architectural collision between Classical stone blocks and pseudo-Egyptian glass panels has caused a furor.

Today's **Louvre** is the end product of many generations of work. It began in the mid-13th century, when Philippe Auguste built it as a fortress to protect the city's western flank. The earliest parts of the current building date from the reign of François I at the beginning of the 16th century, while subsequent monarchs—Henri IV (1589–1610), Louis XIII (1610–43), Louis XIV (1643–1715), Napoleon, and Napoleon III—all contributed to its construction. The open section facing the Tuileries Gardens was originally the Palais des Tuileries, the main residence of the royal family in Paris.

Over the centuries, the Louvre has been used as both a royal residence and a home for minor courtiers; at one point, it was taken over by a rabble of artists who set up shop and whose chimneys projected higgledy-piggledy from the otherwise severe lines of the facades. After a stint as headquarters of the French Revolution, the Louvre was finally established, in Napoleon's time, as a museum, though the country's last three monarchs continued to make it their home.

The number-one attraction for most visitors is Leonardo da Vinci's enigmatic *Mona Lisa*, "La Joconde" to the French; be forewarned that you will find it encased in glass and surrounded by mobs of tourists. The collections are divided into seven sections: Oriental antiquities; Egyptian antiquities; Greek and Roman antiquities; sculpture; paintings, prints, and drawings; furniture; and *objets d'art.* Unless you enjoy masochistic 10-hour slogs around museums, don't try to see it all at once. Try, instead, to make repeat visits—the Louvre is free on Sundays. *Palais du Louvre. Admission: 20 frs. adults, 10 frs. for teenagers 13-18, free, children under 13; free Sun. Open daily 9-6, Wed. and Thurs. until 10.*

Running the length of the Louvre's northern side is Napoleon's arcaded rue de Rivoli. Cross it and you're in **place des Pyramides,** face to face with its gilded statue of Joan of Arc on horseback. Walk up rue des Pyramides and take the first left, rue St-Honoré, to the Baroque church of **St-Roch.** The church was completed in the 1730s, the date of the cool, Classical facade. It's worth having a look inside to see the bombastically Baroque altarpiece in the circular Lady Chapel.

Continue up rue St-Honoré to **place André-Malraux,** with its exuberant fountains. The Opéra building is visible down the avenue of the same name, while, on one corner of the square, at the corner of rue Richelieu, is the **Comédie-Française,** the time-honored setting for performances of classical French drama. The building dates from 1790, but the Comédie-Française company was created by Louis XIV in 1680. Those who understand French and who have a taste for the mannered, declamatory style of French acting will appreciate an evening here (*see* The Arts and Nightlife).

To the right of the theater is the unobtrusive entrance to the gardens of the **Palais Royal.** The buildings of this former palace date from the 1630s and are royal only in that the builder, Cardinal Richelieu (1585–1642), magnanimously bequeathed them to Louis XIII. Today, the Palais Royal is home of the French Ministry of Culture and is not open to the public. But don't miss the **gardens,** divided by rows of perfectly trimmed little trees, a surprisingly little-known oasis in the gray heart of the city. There's not much chance that you'll miss the black-and-white striped columns in the courtyard or the revolving silver spheres that slither around in the two fountains at either end, the controversial early-1980s work of architect Daniel Buren. Walk to the end, away from the main palace, and peek into the opulent, Belle-Epoque, glass-lined interior of **La Grand Vefour** (*see* Dining). One of the swankiest restaurants in the city, it's probably the most sumptuously appointed, too.

Around the corner, on rue de Richelieu, stands France's national library, the **Bibliothèque Nationale,** containing over 7 million printed volumes. Visitors can admire Robert de Cotte's 18th-century courtyard and peep into the 19th-century reading room. *58 rue de Richelieu. Open daily noon–6.*

From the library, walk along rue des Petits Champs to the circular **place des Victoires.** It was laid out by Mansart, a leading proponent of French 17th-century Classicism, in 1685, in honor of the military victories of Louis XIV. You'll find some of the city's most upscale fashion shops here and on the surrounding streets.

Head south down rue Croix des Petits Champs. The second street on the left leads to the circular 18th-century **Bourse du Commerce,** or Commercial Exchange. Alongside it is a 100-foot-high fluted column, all that remains of a mansion built here in 1572 for Catherine de Médicis. The column is said to have been used as a platform for stargazing by her astrologer, Ruggieri.

You can easily spot the bulky outline of the church of ⑪ **St-Eustache,** away to the left. It is a huge church, the "cathedral" of Les Halles, built, as it were, as the market people's Right-Bank reply to Notre-Dame. Under construction from 1532 to 1637 and modified over the centuries, the church is a curious architectural hybrid. Its exterior flying buttresses, for example, are solidly Gothic, yet its column orders, rounded arches, and comparatively simple window tracery are unmistakably Classical. Few buildings bear such eloquent witness to stylistic transition.

If Notre Dame and the Louvre represent Church and State, respectively, Les Halles (pronounced "Lay Al") stands for the common man. For centuries, this was Paris's central market. Closed in 1969, it was replaced by a striking shopping mall, the ⑫ **Forum des Halles.** The surrounding streets have since undergone a radical transformation much like the neighboring Marais, and the shops, cafés, restaurants, and chic apartment buildings make it an example of successful urban redevelopment.

Time Out A few blocks south of Les Halles and just north of place du Châtelet is **Le Trappiste,** where 20 different international beers are available on draught, with well over 180 in bottle. Mussels and french fries are the traditional accompaniment, although various other snacks (hot dogs and sandwiches) are also available. There are tables upstairs and on the pavement. *4 rue St-Denis.*

From place du Châtelet cross back over the Seine on the Pontau-Change to the Isle de la Cité. To your right looms the imposing **Palais de Justice,** the Law Courts, built by Baron Haussmann in his characteristically weighty Classical style around 1860. The main buildings of interest on the Ile de la Cité, however, are the medieval parts of the complex, spared by Haussmann in his otherwise wholesale destruction.

The **Conciergerie,** the northernmost part of the complex, was originally part of the royal palace on the island. Most people know it, however, as a prison, the grim place of confinement for Danton, Robespierre, and Marie Antoinette during the French Revolution. Inside (conducted tours only) you'll be shown the guardroom (the Salle des Gens d'Armes), a striking example of Gothic monumentality; the cells, including the one in which Marie Antoinette was held; and the chapel, where objects connected with the ill-fated queen are displayed. *Admission: 24 frs. Open daily 9–6.*

The other perennial crowd puller in the Palais de Justice is the **Sainte Chapelle,** the Holy Chapel, one of the supreme achievements of the Middle Ages: It will most likely be one of the highlights of your trip to Paris. It was built by the genial and pious Louis IX (1226–70) to house what he took to be the Crown of Thorns from Christ's crucifixion and fragments of the True Cross. Architecturally, for all its delicate and ornate exterior decoration, the design of the building is simplicity itself; in essence, no more than a thin, rectangular box, much taller than it is wide. Some clumsy 19th-century work has added a deadening touch, but the glory of the chapel—the stained glass—is spectacularly intact: The walls consist of at least twice as much glass as masonry. Try to attend one of the regular, candle-lit concerts given here. *Admission: 22 frs. adults, 5 frs. children under 17. Open daily 10–6.*

Take rue de Lutèce opposite the Palais de Justice down to place Louis-Lépine and the bustling **Marché aux Fleurs,** the flower market. Around the corner is the most enduring symbol of Paris, the cathedral of **Notre-Dame.** The building was started in 1163, with an army of stonemasons, carpenters, and sculptors working on a site that had previously seen a Roman temple, an early Christian basilica, and a Romanesque church. The chancel and altar were consecrated in 1182, but the magnificent sculptures surrounding the main doors were not put into position until 1240. The north tower was finished 10 years later. Despite various changes in the 17th century, principally the removal of the rose windows, the cathedral remained substantially unaltered until the French Revolution, when much destruction was wrought, mainly to statuary.

Place du Parvis, in front of the cathedral, is the perfect place from which to gaze at the building's famous facade, divided neatly into three levels. The interior of the cathedral, with its vast proportions, soaring nave, and gentle, multicolored light filtering through the stained-glass windows, inspires awe, despite the inevitable throngs of tourists. On the south side of the chancel is the **Treasury,** with a collection of garments, reliquaries, and silver and gold plate. (Admission: 15 frs. Open Mon.–Sat. 10–6, Sun. 2–6). The 387-step climb to the top of the towers is worth the effort for the close-up view of the famous gargoyles and the expansive view over the city. (Entrance via the north tower. Admission: 22 frs. Open daily 10–4:30.)

And if your interest in the cathedral is not yet sated, duck into the **Musée Notre-Dame,** which displays artwork and documents tracing the cathedral's history. *10 rue du Cloître Notre-Dame. Admission: 10 frs. Open Wed. and weekends only, 2:30–6.*

Tour 2: The Marais and Ile St-Louis

The history of the Marais began when Charles V, king of France in the 14th century, moved the French court from the Ile de la Cité. However, it wasn't until Henri IV laid out the place Royale, today the place des Vosges, in the early 17th century, that the Marais became *the* place to live. Following the French Revolution, however, the Marais rapidly became one of the most deprived, dissolute areas in Paris. It was spared the attentions of Baron Haussmann, the man who rebuilt so much of Paris in the mid-19th century, so that, though crumbling, its ancient rose-pink buildings and squares remained intact. Today's Marais once again has staked a convincing claim as the city's most desirable district.

Begin your tour at the **Hôtel de Ville** (City Hall) overlooking the Seine. It was in the square on the Hôtel de Ville's south side that Robespierre, fanatical leader during the period of the French Revolution known as the Reign of Terror, came to suffer the fate of his many victims when a furious mob sent him to the guillotine in 1794. Following the accession of Louis Philippe in 1830, the building became the seat of the French government, a role that came to a sudden end with the uprisings in 1848. In the Commune of 1871, the Hôtel de Ville was burned to the ground. Today's fussy building, based loosely on Renaissance models, went up between 1874 and 1884.

From the Hôtel de Ville, head north across rue de Rivoli and up rue du Temple. On your right, you'll pass one of the city's most popular department stores, the **Bazar de l'Hôtel de Ville,** or BHV as it's commonly known. The first street on your left, rue de la Verrerie, will take you down to the stores, restaurants, and galleries of the rue St-Martin.

16 The Centre National d'Art et de Culture Georges Pompidou, known as the **Beaubourg,** is next. The center hosts an innovative and challenging series of exhibits, in addition to housing the world's largest collection of modern art. Its brash architectural style—it has been likened to a gaudily painted oil refinery—has caused much controversy, however. Many critics think it is beginning to show its age (it only opened in 1977) in a particularly cheap manner: witness the cracked and grimy plastic tubing that encases the exterior elevators, and the peeling skeletal interior supports. Probably the most popular thing to do at the Beaubourg is to ride the escalator up to the roof to see the Parisian skyline unfolding as you are carried through its clear plastic piping. There's a sizable restaurant and café on the roof. Aside from the art collection (from which American painters and sculptors are conspicuously absent), the building houses a movie theater; a language laboratory; an extensive collection of tapes, videos, and slides; an industrial design center; and an acoustics and musical research center. *Plateau Beaubourg. Admission: free. Open Wed.–Mon. noon–10 PM, weekends 10–10, closed Tues. Guided tours: weekdays 3:30, weekends 11.*

Time Out   Don't leave the plateau without stopping for coffee at the **Café Beaubourg** on the corner of rue St-Merri. A staircase takes you up from the first floor to a *passerelle,* or foot bridge, linking the two sides of a mezzanine. The severe high-tech design is lightened by the little glass-top tables, which are gradually being covered with artists' etchings.

Leave plateau Beaubourg by its southwestern corner and head down little rue Ste-Croix de la Bretonnerie to visit the Marais's Jewish quarter, lately rather cloistered as a result of recent bomb attacks. You'll see the more obvious of the area's historical highlights if you take rue Rambuteau, which runs along the north side of the center (to your left as you face the building). The **Quartier de L'Horloge,** the Clock Quarter, opens off the plateau here. An entire city block has been rebuilt, and despite the shops and cafés, it retains a resolutely artificial quality. The mechanical clock around the corner on rue Clairvaux will amuse children, however: St. George defends Time against a dragon, an eagle-beaked bird, or a monstrous crab (symbolizing earth, air, and water, respectively) every hour, on the hour. At noon, 6 PM, and 10 PM, he takes on all three at once.

You are now poised to plunge into the elegant heart of the Marais. The historic homes here are now private residences, but don't be afraid to push through the heavy doors, or *porte-cochères,* to glimpse the discreet courtyards that lurk behind.

From the little market on rue Rambuteau, take the first left, up rue du Temple, to the 17th-century **Hôtel de Montmor**, at no. 79. It was once the scene of an influential literary salon—a part-social, part-literary group—that included the philosopher Descartes (1596–1650) and the playwright Molière (1622–73).

Turn down rue des Haudriettes, continuing until you come to the Hôtel de Soubise, now the **Archives Nationales** (its collections form part of the Musée de l'Histoire de France). The museum's highlights are the papers dating from the revolutionary period, including Marie Antoinette's last letter, the pattern book from which she would select a new dress every morning, and Louis XVI's diary that contains his sadly ignorant entry for July 14, 1789, the day the Bastille was stormed at the start of the French Revolution: *Rien* (nothing), he wrote. You can also visit the apartments of the Prince and Princess de Soubise: Don't miss them if you have any interest in the lifestyles of 18th-century French aristocrats. *60 rue des Francs-Bourgeois. Admission: 12 frs. Open Wed.–Mon. 2–5; closed Tues.*

From the Hôtel de Rohan, built for the Archbishop of Strasbourg in 1705, turn right into rue de la Perle and walk down to the **Musée Bricard de la Serrure,** the Lock Museum. The museum's sumptuous building is perhaps more interesting than the assembled locks and keys within; it was built in 1685 by Bruand, the architect of Les Invalides. But those with a taste for fine craftsmanship will appreciate the intricacy and ingenuity of many of the older locks. One represents an early security system—it would shoot anyone who tried to open it with the wrong key. *Hôtel Bruand, 1 rue de la Perle. Admission: 10 frs. Open Tues.–Sat. 10–noon and 2–5; closed Mon., Aug. and last week of Dec.*

From here, it is but a step to the Hôtel Salé, built between 1656 and 1660, and today the popular **Musée Picasso;** be prepared for long lines. The collection encompasses pictures, sculptures, drawings, prints, ceramics, and other assorted works of art given to the French government after the painter's death in 1973, in lieu of death duties. What's notable about it—other than its being the world's largest collection of works by Picasso—is that these were works that the artist himself owned and especially valued. There are works from every period of his life, as well as paintings by Paul Cézanne, Joan Miró, Pierre Auguste Renoir, Georges Braque, Edgar Degas, Henri Matisse, and others. The palatial surroundings add greatly to the visit. *5 rue de Thorigny. Admission: 21 frs. Open Wed. 9:45 AM–10 PM, Thurs.–Mon. 9:45–5:30; closed Tues.*

Head back down rue de Thorigny, turn left onto rue du Parc Royal, and right onto rue Payenne. This street takes you down to rue des Francs Bourgeois, where the substantial **Hôtel Carnavalet** became the scene, in the late 17th century, of the most brilliant salon in Paris, presided over by Madame de Sévigné. She is best known for the hundreds of letters she wrote to her daughter during her life; they've become one of the most enduring chronicles of French high society in the 17th century. In 1880, the hotel was transformed into the **Musée de l'Histoire de Paris;** its extraordinary exhibits of the Revolution, which have now moved to the neighboring Hôtel Peletier St-Fargeau, include some fascinating macabre models of guillotines. *29 rue* *de Sévigné. Check locally for details of admission charges and hours.*

㉑ Now walk along to **place des Vosges,** a minute or two farther along rue des Francs Bourgeois. Place des Vosges, or place Royale as it was originally known, is the oldest square in Paris: Laid out by Henri IV at the beginning of the 17th century, it is the model for all the later city squares on which most French urban developments are based. The harmonious balance of the square, with its symmetrical town houses of pale pink stone, makes it a pleasant place to spend a hot summer's afternoon. At no. 6 is the **Maison de Victor Hugo,** which commemorates the workaholic French writer.

From place des Vosges, follow rue du Pas de la Mule and turn ㉒ right down rue des Tournelles until you reach **place de la Bastille,** site of the infamous prison. Until 1988, there was little more to see at place de la Bastille than a huge traffic circle and the **Colonne de Juillet,** the July Column. As part of the country-wide celebrations held in July 1989, the bicentennial of the French Revolution, a 3,000-seat **opera house** boasting five moving stages has been put up on the south side of the square. Redevelopment projects have changed what was formerly a humdrum neighborhood into one of the city's most chic and attractive.

The **Bastille** was built by Charles V in the late 14th century and destroyed in 1789 during the French Revolution. The ground plan is marked by paving stones set into the modern square. The Bastille was originally intended not as a prison but as a fortress to guard the eastern entrance to the city. By the reign of Louis XIII (1610–43), however, it was used almost exclusively to house political prisoners, including, in the 18th century, Voltaire and the Marquis de Sade. This obviously political role led the "furious mob" (in all probability no more than a largely unarmed rabble) to break into the prison on July 14, 1789, kill the governor, steal what firearms they could find, and set free the seven remaining prisoners (all of whom were locked up again the next day).

On rue François Miron, just before the Hôtel de Ville, is the ㉓ site of one of the first churches in Paris, **St-Gervais-St-Protais,** named after two Roman soldiers martyred by the Emperor Nero in the 1st century AD. The original church—no trace remains of it now—was built in the 7th century. The present building, a riot of Flamboyant decoration, went up between 1494 and 1598, making it one of the last Gothic constructions in the country. Pause before you go in to look at the facade, put up between 1616 and 1621. While the interior is late Gothic, the exterior is one of the earliest examples of Classical, or Renaissance, style in France.

Don't cross the Seine to Ile St-Louis yet. Take rue de l'Hôtel de Ville to where it meets rue de Figuier. The painstakingly re-㉔ stored **Hôtel de Sens** (1474) on the corner is one of a handful of Parisian homes to have survived since the Middle Ages. With its pointed corner towers, Gothic porch, and richly carved decorative details, it is a strange mixture, half defensive stronghold, half fairytale château. Built at the end of the 15th century for the archbishop of Sens, it was once the home of Henri IV and his queen, Marguerite, philanderers both. While Henri dallied with his mistresses—he is said to have had 56—

at a series of royal palaces, Marguerite entertained her almost equally large number of lovers here. Today, the building houses a fine arts library, the **Bibliothèque Forney** (admission free; open Tues.–Sat. 1:30–8, Sun. 10:30–8:30).

 Cross pont Marie to the residential **Ile St-Louis,** the smaller of the two islands in the heart of Paris, linked to the Ile de la Cité by pont St-Louis. There are no standouts here and no great sights, but for idle strolling, window shopping, or simply sitting on one of the little quays and drinking in the views, the Ile St-Louis exudes a quintessentially Parisian air.

Time Out **Berthillon** has become a byword for delicious ice cream. Cafés all over Ile St-Louis sell its glamorous products, but the place to try them is still the little shop on rue St-Louis en l'Ile. Expect to wait in line. *31 rue St-Louis en l'Ile. Closed Tues.*

Tour 3: From the Arc de Triomphe to the Opéra

This tour takes in grand, opulent Paris; the Paris of imposing vistas; long, arrow-straight streets; and plush hotels and jewelers. It begins at the Arc de Triomphe, standing sturdily at the top of the most famous street in the city, the Champs-Elysées.

Place Charles-de-Gaulle is known by Parisians as **l'Etoile,** the star—a reference to the streets that fan out from it. It is one of Europe's most chaotic traffic circles, and short of a death-defying dash, your only way of getting to the Arc de Triomphe in the middle is to take an underground passage from the Champs-Elysées or avenue de la Grande-Armée.

26 The colossal, 164-foot **Arc de Triomphe** was planned by Napoleon to celebrate his military successes. Unfortunately, the great man's strategic and architectural visions were not entirely on the same plane: When it was required for the triumphal entry of his new empress, Marie Louise, into Paris in 1810, it was still only a few feet high. To save face, he ordered a dummy arch of painted canvas to be put up. (The real thing was finished only in 1836.) Despite recent signs of decay, its elaborate relief sculptures are magnificent. The highlight is the scene by François Rude, illustrated to the right of the arch when viewed from the Champs-Elysées. Called *Departure of the Volunteers in 1792,* it's commonly known as *La Marseillaise* and depicts *Patrie,* or the Motherland, with outspread wings exhorting the volunteers to fight for France.

If you like views, go up to the viewing platform at the top of the monument, from where you can admire the vista down the Champs-Elysées toward place de la Concorde and the distant Louvre. A small museum halfway up the arch is devoted to its history. France's *Unknown Soldier* is buried beneath the archway; the flame is rekindled every evening at 6:30. *Pl. Charles-de-Gaulle. Admission: 25 frs. Open daily 10–6.*

Laid out by landscape gardener Le Nôtre in the 1660s as a garden sweeping away from the Tuileries, the cosmopolitan **Champs-Elysées** occupies a central role in French national celebrations. It witnesses the finish of the Tour de France cycle race on the second-to-last Sunday of July and is the site of vast ceremonies on Bastille Day, July 14 (France's national holiday), and November 11, Armistice Day. Start by walking down from l'Etoile on the left, where 300 yards down, at no. 116-B, is the famous **Lido** nightclub: Foot-stomping melodies in French and English and champagne-soaked, topless razzamatazz pack in the crowds every night. In contrast are the **Prince de Galles** (Prince of Wales) at no. 33 (with the red awning) and the **George V** (with the blue awning), two of the city's top hotels. Farther down on the same side is the neo-Gothic, late 19th-century **American Cathedral of the Holy Trinity.**

At the bottom of the avenue is the place de l'Alma and the Seine. Just across the Alma bridge, on the left, is the entrance to **Les Egouts,** the Paris sewers (admission: 8 frs; open Mon., Wed., and the last Sat. of the month 2–5). If you prefer a less malodorous tour of the city, stay on the Right Bank and head down the sloping side road to the left of the bridge, for the embarkation point of the *Bâteaux Mouches* motorboat tours of the Seine.

Stylish avenue Montaigne leads from the Seine back toward the Champs-Elysées.

Time Out Although power brokers and fashion models make up half the clientele at the **Bar des Théâtres,** its blasé waiters refuse to bat an eyelid. This is a fine place for an aperitif or a swift, more affordable lunch than around the corner at the luxury restaurants on place de l'Alma. *Opposite the Théâtre des Champs-Elysées at 6 av. Montaigne.*

㉗ Two blocks east, along the Champs-Elysées and on the side of avenue Winston-Churchill, sit the **Grand Palais** and the Petit Palais, erected before the Paris World's Fair of 1900. Like the Eiffel Tower, there was never any intention that they would be anything other than temporary additions to the city. Together they recapture the opulence and frivolity of the Belle Epoque. Today, the atmospheric iron-and-glass interior of the Grand Palais plays regular host to major exhibitions. *Av. Winston-Churchill. Admission varies according to exhibition. Usually open 10:30–6:30, often until 10 on Wed.*

㉘ The **Petit Palais** has a beautifully presented permanent collection of lavish 17th-century furniture and French painting, with splendid canvases by Courbet and Bouguereau. Temporary exhibits are often held here, too. The sprawling entrance gallery contains several enormous turn-of-the century paintings on its walls and ceiling. *Av. Winston-Churchill. Admission: 12 frs. adults, 6 frs. children. Open Tues.–Sun. 10–5:30.*

Cross the Champs-Elysées and head down avenue de Marigny to **rue du Faubourg St-Honoré,** a prestigious address in the world of luxury fashion and art galleries. High security surrounds the French president in the **Palais de l'Elysées.** This "palace," where the head of state lives, works, and receives official visitors, was originally constructed as a private mansion in 1718. It has known presidential occupants only since 1873; before then, Madame de Pompadour (Louis XV's influential mistress), Napoleon, Josephine, and Queen Victoria all stayed here. Today, the French government, the *Conseil des Ministres*, meets here each Wednesday. *Not open to the public.*

Just before rue du Faubourg St-Honoré meets rue Royale, head left into rue Boissy d'Anglas. Look for the discreet gateway that leads into the Cité Berryer, an old, courtyard-like passageway lined with restaurants and boutiques. At the far end is rue Royale. This classy street, lined with jewelry stores, **30** links place de la Concorde to the **Eglise de la Madeleine.** With its rows of uncompromising columns, the Madeleine's sturdy neo-Classical edifice looks more like a Greek temple than a Christian church. The only natural indoor light comes from three shallow domes. The inside walls are richly and harmoniously decorated, and gold glints through the murk. The church was designed in 1814 but not consecrated until 1842. The portico's majestic Corinthian colonnade supports a gigantic pediment with a sculptured frieze of the *Last Judgment*. From the top of the steps, stop to admire the view down rue Royale across the Seine.

31 There is a striking contrast between the gloomy locked-in feel of the high-walled rue Royale and the broad, airy **place de la Concorde.** This huge square is best approached from the Champs-Elysées: The flower beds, chestnut trees, and sandy sidewalks of the avenue's lower section are reminders of its original leafy elegance. Place de la Concorde was built in the 1770s, but there was nothing in the way of peace or concord about its early years. From 1793 to 1795, it was the scene of over a thousand deaths by guillotine; victims included Louis XVI, Marie Antoinette, Danton, and Robespierre. The obelisk, a present from the viceroy of Egypt, was erected in 1833. The handsome, symmetrical, 18th-century buildings facing the square include the deluxe **Hôtel Crillon** (far left), though there's nothing so vulgar as a sign to identify it. Facing one side of place de la Concorde are the Tuileries Gardens. Two smallish buildings stand sentinel here. To the left, nearer rue de Rivoli, is the **Jeu de Paume,** now closed but still fondly known to many as the former home of the Impressionists (now in the Musée d'Orsay). The other identical building nearer the Seine is the **32** recently restored **Orangerie,** containing some early 20th-century paintings by Monet and Renoir, among others. *Pl. de la Concorde. Admission: 15 frs. (8 frs. Sun.). Open Wed.–Mon. 9:45–5:15; closed Tues.*

33 As gardens go, the formal and greatly patterned **Jardin des Tuileries** is typically French, a charming place to stroll and survey the surrounding cityscape. Leave the Tuileries by the rue de Rivoli gateway across from rue de Castiglione and the hefty bronze column of place Vendôme.

34 **Place Vendôme** is one of the world's most opulent squares, a perfectly proportioned example of 17th-century urban architecture (by Mansart), now holding numerous upscale jewelers and the **Ritz.** Napoleon had the square's central column made from the melted bronze of 1,200 cannons captured at the battle of Austerlitz in 1805. That's him standing vigilantly at the top.

35 The **Opéra,** begun at the behest of Napoleon III, and completed in 1875 by Charles Garnier, typifies the pompous Second Empire style of architecture. The monumental foyer and staircase are a stage in their own right where, on first nights, celebrities preen and prance. If the lavishly upholstered auditorium (ceiling painted by Marc Chagall in 1964) seems small, it is only because the stage is the largest in the world—over 11,000 square yards. The **Opéra museum,** containing a few paintings and theatrical mementos, is unremarkable. *Admission: 17 frs. Open daily 11–4:30.*

Tour 4: From Orsay to Trocadéro

The Left Bank has two faces: the cozy, ramshackle Latin Quarter (*see* the Left Bank) and the spacious, stately Seventh Arrondissement, covered in this tour. The latest addition to this area is already the most popular: the **Musée d'Orsay,** a stylishly converted train station housing key Impressionist works, as well as important examples of other 19th- and 20th-century schools. The chief artistic attraction here is the collection of Impressionist works, featured on the top floor. Highlights include Monet's *Waterlilies* series and Renoir's *La Moulin de la Galette.* The Post-Impressionists—Paul Cézanne, Vincent Van Gogh, Paul Gauguin, and Henri Toulouse-Lautrec—are all also represented on this floor.

On the first floor, you'll find the work of Edouard Manet and the delicate nuances of Edgar Degas. Pride of place, at least in art-history terms, goes to Manet's *Déjeuner sur l'Herbe,* the painting that scandalized Paris in 1863. Those who prefer modern developments will make for the early 20th-century *Fauves* (meaning wild beasts, the name given them by an outraged critic in 1905)–particularly Henri Matisse, André Derain, and Maurice Vlaminck. Sculpture at the Orsay means, first and foremost, Auguste Rodin. Two further highlights are the faithfully restored Belle Epoque restaurant and the model of the entire Opéra quarter, displayed beneath a glass floor. Prepare for huge crowds: The best times for relatively painless viewing are at lunchtime or on Thursday evening. *1 rue de Bellechasse. Admission: 23 frs., 12 frs. Sun., children under 18 free. Open Tues., Wed., Fri., and Sat., 10:30–6, Thurs. 10:30–9:45, Sun. 9–6.*

Continue along the left bank of the Seine to the 18th-century **Palais Bourbon** (directly across from place de la Concorde), home of the Assemblée Nationale (French Parliament). The colonnaded facade was commissioned by Napoleon. Though it's not open to the public, there is a fine view from the steps across to place de la Concorde and the church of the Madeleine.

Turn down rue de Varenne to the Hôtel Biron, better known as the **Musée Rodin.** The splendid house, with its spacious vestibule and light, airy rooms, retains much of its 18th-century atmosphere and makes a handsome setting for the sculpture of Rodin (1840–1917), including the famous *Thinker* (le Penseur) and *Kiss.* Don't leave without visiting the garden: It is exceptional, both for its rosebushes (over 2,000) and its sculptures. *77 rue de Varenne. Admission: 16 frs., 8 frs. Sun. Open Wed.–Mon. 10–6, 10–5 winter; closed Tues.*

From the Rodin Museum, you can see the **Hôtel des Invalides** along rue de Varenne, founded by Louis XIV in 1674 to house wounded (or "invalid") veterans. Only a handful of old soldiers live there today, but the building houses one of the world's foremost military museums, **Musée de l'Armée,** with a vast collection of arms, armor, uniforms, banners, and military pictures. The **Musée des Plans-Reliefs,** housed on the fifth floor of the right-hand wing, contains a fascinating collection of scale models of French towns made to illustrate the fortifications planned by the 17th-century military engineer, Sébastien de Vauban. The largest and most impressive is Strasbourg, taking up an entire room.

The museums are not the only reason for visiting the Invalides, however. The building itself is an outstanding monumental ensemble in late 17th-century Baroque, designed by Libéral Bruant (1635–97) and Jules Hardouin-Mansart (1646–1708). The main, cobbled courtyard is a fitting scene for the parades and ceremonies still occasionally held here. The most impressive dome in Paris towers over the **Eglise du Dôme** (church of the dome). The Dôme church was designed by Mansart and built between 1677 and 1735. The remains of Napoleon are here, in a series of six coffins, one inside the next, within a bombastic tomb of red porphyry. Among others commemorated in the church are French World War I hero Marshal Foch and fortification-builder Vauban, whose heart was brought to the Invalides at Napoleon's behest. *Hôtel des Invalides. Admission: 23 frs. adults, 11.50 frs. children. Open daily 10–6, 10–4:45 winter. A son-et-lumière (sound and light show) in English is held in the main courtyard on evenings throughout the summer.*

Cross the lawns outside the Dôme church to the place Vauban. A few minutes' walk down the pleasant Champ de Mars will bring you face to face with Paris's best known landmark, the
40 **Eiffel Tower.** Built by Gustave Eiffel for the World Exhibition of 1889, the centennial of the French Revolution, it was still in good shape to celebrate its own 100th birthday. Such was Eiffel's engineering wizardry that even in the strongest winds his tower never sways more than 4½ inches. Today, it is Paris's best-known landmark and exudes a feeling of permanence. As you stand beneath its huge legs, you may have trouble believing that it nearly became 7,000 tons of scrap iron when its concession expired in 1909. Only its potential use as a radio antenna saved the day; it now bristles with a forest of radio and television transmitters. The energetic can stride up the stairs as far as the third deck. If you want to go to the top, 1,000 feet up, you'll have to take the elevator. *Pont d'Iéna. Cost by elevator: 2nd floor, 12 frs.; 3rd floor, 28 frs.; 4th floor, 44 frs. Cost by foot: 7 frs. (2nd and 3rd floors only). Open daily 10 AM–11 PM; mid-Mar.–Aug., Fri. and Sat. 10 AM–midnight.*

Visible just across the Seine from the Eiffel Tower, on the
41 heights of Trocadéro, is the massive, sandy-colored **Palais de Chaillot,** a cultural center built in the '30s. The gardens between the Palais de Chaillot and the Seine contain an aquarium and some dramatic fountains, and the terrace between the two wings of the palace offers a wonderful view of the Eiffel Tower.

The Palais de Chaillot contains four large museums, two in each wing. In the left wing (as you approach from the Seine) are the **Musée de l'Homme,** an anthropological museum, with primitive and prehistoric artifacts from throughout the world (Admission: 16 frs. adults, 8 frs. children. Open Wed.–Mon. 10–5), and the **Musée de la Marine,** a maritime museum with exhibits on French naval history right up to the age of the nuclear submarine (Admission: 18 frs. adults, 9 frs. children. Open Wed.–Mon. 10–6).

The other wing is dominated by the **Musée des Monuments Français,** without question the best introduction to French medieval architecture. Its long first-floor gallery pays tribute to French buildings, mainly of the Romanesque and Gothic periods (roughly AD 1000–1500), in the form of painstaking copies of statues, columns, archways, and frescoes. Substantial sections of a number of French churches and cathedrals are represented here, notably Chartres and Vézelay. Murals and ceiling paintings —copies of works in churches around the country—dominate the other three floors. *Admission: 15 frs., 8 frs. on Sun. Open Wed. –Mon. 9:45–12:30 and 2–5:15.*

The area around the Palais de Chaillot offers a feast for museum
42 lovers. The **Musée Guimet** has three floors of Indo-Chinese and Far Eastern art, including stone Buddhas, Chinese bronzes, ceramics, and painted screens. *6 pl. d'Iéna. Admission: 15 frs., 8 frs. on Sun. Open Wed.–Mon. 9:45–5:10; closed Tues.*

43 Nearby is the **Palais Galliera,** home of the **Musée de la Mode et Costume** (Museum of Fashion and Costume), a late 19th-century town house that hosts revolving exhibits. *10 av. Pierre-Ier-de-Serbie. Admission: 21 frs. Open Tues.–Sun. 10–5:40.*

44 The **Musée de l'Art Moderne de la Ville de Paris** has both temporary exhibits and a permanent collection of modern art. Among the earliest works in the vast galleries are Fauvist paintings by Vlaminck and Derain, followed by Picasso's early experiments in Cubism. Other highlights include works by Robert Delaunay, Georges Braque, and Amedeo Modigliani. There is also a large room devoted to Art Deco furniture and screens; a pleasant, if expensive, museum café; and an excellent bookshop with many books in English. *11 av. du Président-Wilson. Admission: 15 frs., free Sun. for permanent exhibitions only. Open Tues.–Sun. 10–5:40, Wed. 10–8:30.*

Tour 5: The Left Bank

References to the Left Bank have never lost their power to evoke the most piquant images of Paris. Although the bohemian strain the area once nurtured has lost much of its vigor, people who choose to live and work here today are, in effect, turning their backs on the formality and staidness of the Right Bank. As a matter of fact, President Mitterrand himself lives here.

The Left Bank's geographic and cerebral hub is the Latin Quarter, which takes its name from the university tradition of studying and speaking in Latin, a practice that disappeared at the time of the French Revolution. The area is populated mainly by students and academics from the Sorbonne, the headquarters of the University of Paris.

45 **Place St-Michel** is a good starting point for exploring the rich slice of Parisian life that the Left Bank offers. Leave your itineraries at home, and wander along the neighboring streets lined with restaurants, cafés, galleries, old bookshops, and all sorts of clothing stores, from tiny boutiques to haute couture showrooms. If you follow quai des Grands Augustins and then quai de Conti west from St-Michel, you will be in full view of the Ile de la Cité, the Louvre, and the Temple de l'Oratoire (built in 1621 and once one of the most important churches in France) across the Seine.

For an alternative route crowded more with humanity than with traffic, pick up the pedestrian rue St-André des Arts at the southwest corner of place St-Michel. Just before you reach the carrefour de Buci crossroads at the end of the street, turn onto the cour du Commerce St-André. Jean Paul Marat printed his revolutionary newspaper, *L'Ami du Peuple*, at no. 8, and it was here that Dr. Guillotin conceived the idea for a new "humane" method of execution that, apparently to his horror, was used during the French Revolution.

46 Continue to the **carrefour de Buci,** once a notorious Left Bank landmark. By the 18th century, it contained a gallows, an execution stake, and an iron collar for punishing troublemakers. Many Royalists and priests lost their heads here during the bloody course of the French Revolution. Nearby rue de Buci has one of the best markets in Paris. The stands close by 1 PM and are shut on Monday.

Several interesting, smaller streets of some historical significance radiate from the carrefour de Buci. Rue de l'Ancienne-Comédie, which cuts through to the busy place de l'Odéon, is so named because no. 14 was the first home of the now legendary French theater company, the *Comédie-Française*. Across the
47 street sits the oldest café in Paris, the **Procope.** Opened in 1686, it has been a watering hole for many of Paris's literati, including Voltaire, Victor Hugo, and Oscar Wilde. Ben Franklin was a patron, as were the fomenters of the French Revolution—Marat, Danton, Desmoulins, and Robespierre. Napoleon's hat, forgotten here, was encased in a glass dome.

Stretching north toward the Seine is the rue Dauphine, the street that singer Juliet Greco put on the map when she opened the **Tabou jazz club** here in the '50s. The club attracted a group of young intellectuals who were to become known as the Zazous, a St-Germain movement prompting the jazz culture, complete with all-night parties and free love.

The next street that shoots out of the Carrefour (moving coun-
48 ter-clockwise) is rue Mazarine, housing the **Hôtel des Monnaies,** the national mint. Louis XVI transferred the Royal Mint to this imposing mansion in the late 18th century. Although the mint was moved in 1973, weights and measures, and limited-edition coins are still made here. You can see the vast collection of coins, documents, engravings, and paintings at the **Musée Monétaire.** *11 quai Conti. Admission: 10 frs. adults, children free. Open Tues.–Sun. 1–6.*

Next door is the **Institut de France,** one of France's most revered cultural institutions and one of the Left Bank's most impressive waterside sights, with its distinctive dome and commanding position overlooking the quai. It was built as a college in 1661; in the early 19th century, Napoleon stipulated that the Institut de France be transferred here from the Louvre. The **Académie Française,** the oldest of the five academies that comprise the Institut de France, was created by Cardinal Richelieu in 1635. Its first major task was to edit the French dictionary; today, among other functions, it is still charged with safeguarding the purity of the French language. Membership is the highest literary honor in France. Not until 1986 was a woman, author Marguerite Yourcenar, elected to its ranks. *Guided visits are reserved for cultural associations only.*

Just west along the waterfront, on quai Malaquais, stands the
49 **Ecole Nationale des Beaux-Arts,** whose students can usually be seen painting and sketching on the nearby quais and bridges. The school, once the site of a convent, was established in 1816. Allow yourself time to wander into its courtyard and galleries to see the casts and copies of the statues that were once stored

here, or stop in at one of the temporary exhibitions of professors' and students' works. *14 rue Bonaparte. Open daily 1–7.*

Tiny **rue Visconti,** running east–west off rue Bonaparte (across from the entrance to the Beaux-Arts), has a lot of history packed into its short length. In the 16th century, it was known as Paris's "Little Geneva"—named after Europe's foremost Protestant city—because of the Protestant ghetto that formed here. Jean Racine, one of France's greatest playwrights and tragic poets, lived at no. 24 until his death in 1699. Honoré Balzac set up a printing shop at no. 17 in 1826, and the fiery Romantic artist Eugène Delacroix (1798–1863) worked here from 1836 to 1844.

Time Out The terrace at **La Pallette** beckons as you reach the rue de Seine, at the end of rue Visconti. This popular café has long been a favorite haunt of Beaux-Arts students. One of them was allowed to paint an ungainly portrait of the patron, François, which rules over the shaggy gathering of clients with mock authority. *Rue de Seine.*

Farther down the gallery-lined rue de Seine, swing right onto the pretty rue Jacob, where both Wagner and Stendhal once lived. Then turn left onto rue de Fürstemberg, which leads to one of Paris's most delightful and secluded little squares, the place Fürstemberg. Delacroix's studio here has been turned

50 into the charmingly tiny **Musée Eugène Delacroix;** it contains a small collection of sketches and drawings, while the garden at the rear is almost as interesting. *Pl. Fürstemberg. Admission: 10 frs. adults, 5 frs. youths 18–25 and senior citizens over 60, children under 18 free. Open Wed.–Mon. 9:45–12:30 and 2–5:15; closed Tues.*

51 **St-Germain-des-Prés,** Paris's oldest church, began as a shelter for a relic of the True Cross brought back from Spain in 542. Behind it, rue de l'Abbaye runs alongside the former **Abbey Palace,** dating from 990. Interesting interior details include the colorful 19th-century frescoes in the nave by Hippolyte Flandrin, a pupil of the Classical painter Ingres. The church stages superb organ concerts and recitals; programs are displayed outside and in the weekly periodicals *Officiel des Spectacles* and *Pariscope.*

Across the cobbled place St-Germain-des-Prés stands the celebrated **Deux Magots** café, still thriving on its '50s reputation as one of the Left Bank's prime meeting places for the intelligentsia. These days, you're more likely to rub shoulders with tourists than with philosophers, but a sidewalk table still affords a perfect vantage of Left Bank life.

In the years after World War II, Jean-Paul Sartre and Simone de Beauvoir would meet "The Family"—their intellectual clique—two doors down at the **Café de Flore,** on the boulevard St-Germain. Today, the Flore has become more of a gay hangout, but it is a scenic spot that never lacks for action, often in the form of the street entertainers performing in front of the church.

If you now pick up the long rue de Rennes and follow it south, you'll soon arrive in the heart of Montparnasse. The opening of

52 the **Tour Maine-Montparnasse** in 1973 forever changed the face of this former painters' and poets' haunt. The tower, containing offices and a branch of the Galeries Lafayette department store, was part of a vast redevelopment plan that aimed to make the area one of Paris's premier business and shopping districts. As Europe's tallest high rise, it claims to have the fastest elevator in Europe and affords stupendous views of Paris. *Admission: 32 frs. adults, 19 frs. children 5–14, under 5 free. Open daily 9:30 AM–11 PM.*

Up boulevard du Montparnasse and across from the Vavin métro station are two of the better-known gathering places of Montparnasse's bohemian heyday, the **Dôme** and **La Coupole** brasseries. La Coupole opened in 1927 and soon became a home away from home for some of the area's most famous residents, such as Guillaume Apollinaire, Max Jacob, Jean Cocteau, Erik Satie, Igor Stravinsky, and the inevitable Ernest Hemingway.

Head one block north to boulevard du Montparnasse, then turn right for the intersection with boulevard St-Michel, where the verdant avenue de l'Observatoire begins its long sweep up to the Luxembourg gardens. Here you'll find perhaps the most famous bastion of the Left Bank café culture, the **Closerie des Lilas** (*see* Dining). Now a pricy but pretty bar/restaurant, the Closerie remains a staple on all literary tours of Paris, not least because of the commemorative plaques fastened onto the bar, marking the places where renowned writers used to sit. Charles Pierre Baudelaire, Paul Verlaine, Ernest Hemingway, and Guillaume Apollinaire are just a few of the names.

Walk up avenue de l'Observatoire to the **Jardin du Luxembourg** (the Luxembourg Gardens), one of the city's few large parks. Its fountains, ponds, trim hedges, precisely planted rows of trees, and gravel walks are typical of the French fondness for formal gardens. At the far end is the **Palais du Luxembourg** itself, gray and formal, built, like the park, for Marie de Médicis, widow of Henri IV, at the beginning of the 17th century. The palace remained royal property until the French Revolution, when the state took it over and used it as a prison. Danton, the painter Jacques Louis David, and American political philosopher and author Tom Paine (1737–1809) were all detained here. Today, it is the site of the French Senate and is not open to the public.

If you follow rue Vaugirard (the longest street in Paris) one block east to boulevard St-Michel, you will soon be at the place de la Sorbonne, nerve center of the Left Bank's student population. The square is dominated by the **Eglise de la Sorbonne,** whose outstanding exterior features are its 10 Corinthian columns and cupola. Inside is the white marble tomb of Cardinal Richelieu. (The church is open to the public only during exhibitions and cultural events.) The university buildings of La Sorbonne spread out around the church from rue Cujas down to the visitor's entrance on rue des Ecoles.

The **Sorbonne** is the oldest university in Paris—indeed, one of the oldest in Europe—and has for centuries been one of France's principal institutions of higher learning. It is named after Robert de Sorbon, a medieval canon who founded a theological college here in 1253 for 16 students. By the 17th century, the church and university buildings were becoming dilapidated, so Cardinal Richelieu undertook to have them restored; the present-day Sorbonne campus is largely a result of that restoration. For a glimpse of a more recent relic of

Sorbonne history, look for Puvis de Chavannes's painting of the *Sacred Wood* in the main lecture hall, a major meeting point during the tumultuous student upheavals of 1968.

Behind the Sorbonne, bordering its eastern reach, is the rue St-Jacques. The street climbs toward the rue Soufflot, named to honor the man who built the vast, domed **Panthéon,** set atop place du Panthéon. One of Paris's most physically overwhelming sites—it was commissioned by Louis XV as a mark of gratitude for his recovery from a grave illness in 1744—the Panthéon is now a seldom-used church with little of interest except for the crypt, which holds the remains of Voltaire, Emile Zola, and Jean Jacques Rousseau. *Admission to crypt: 22 frs., 18–24s 12 frs., 17 and under 5 frs. Open daily 10–6.*

Up rue St-Jacques and left on the rue des Ecoles is the square Paul Painlevé; behind it lies the entrance to the inimitable **Hôtel et Musée de Cluny.** Built on the site of the city's enormous old Roman baths, the Musée de Cluny is housed in a 15th-century mansion that originally belonged to the monks of Cluny Abbey in Burgundy. But the real reason anyone comes to the Cluny is to see its superb tapestry collection. The most famous series is the graceful *Dame à Licorne* (the *Lady and the Unicorn*), woven in the 15th or 16th century, probably in the southern Netherlands. There is also an exhibition of decorative arts from the Middle Ages; a vaulted chapel; and a deep, cloistered courtyard with mullioned windows, set off by the *Boatmen's Pillar,* Paris's oldest sculpture, at its center. *Admission: 15 frs., 18 frs. Sun. Open Wed.–Mon. 9:45–12:30 and 2–5:15; closed Tues.*

Above boulevard St-Germain, rue St-Jacques reaches toward the Seine, bringing you past the elegant proportions of the church of **St-Séverin,** the parish church of the entire Left Bank during the 11th century. Rebuilt in the 16th century and noted for its width and its Flamboyant Gothic styling, the church dominates a close-knit neighborhood filled with quiet squares and pedestrian streets. Note the splendidly deviant spiraling column in the forest of pillars behind the altar. *Open weekdays 11–5:30, Sat. 11–10.*

Cross to the other side of rue St-Jacques. In square René Viviani, which surrounds the 12th-century church of **St-Julien-le-Pauvre,** stands an acacia that is supposedly the oldest tree in Paris (although it has a rival claim from another acacia at the Jardin des Plantes). This tree-filled square also gives you one of the more spectacular views of Notre-Dame.

Behind the church, to the east, are the tiny, elegant streets of the recently renovated Maubert district, bordered by quai de Montebello and boulevard St-Germain. Rue de Bièvre, once filled with tanneries, is now guarded at both ends to protect President Mitterrand's private residence.

Public meetings and demonstrations have been held in place Maubert ever since the Middle Ages. Nowadays, most gatherings are held inside or in front of the **Palais de la Mutualité** on the corner of the square, also a venue for jazz, pop, and rock concerts. On Tuesday, Thursday, and Saturday, it is transformed into a colorful outdoor food market.

The **Jardin des Plantes,** several blocks southeast, is an enormous swath of greenery containing spacious botanical gardens and a number of natural history museums. It is stocked with plants dating back to the first collections of the 17th century and enhanced ever since by subsequent generations of devoted French botanists. The garden claims to shelter Paris's oldest tree, an *Acacia robinia*, planted in 1636. It also contains a small, old-fashioned zoo, an alpine garden, an aquarium, a maze, and a number of hothouses. *Admission: 16–25 frs. Open Wed.–Mon. 10–5; closed Tues.*

Time Out At the back of the gardens, in place du Puits-de-l'Hermite, you can drink a restorative cup of sweet mint tea in **La Mosquée,** a beautifully kept white mosque, complete with minaret. The Moslem restaurant here serves copious quantities of couscous. The sunken garden and tiled patios are open to the public—the prayer rooms are not—and so are the luxurious *hammams,* or Turkish baths, with massages also available (around 100 francs for both). *Admission: 10 frs. Open Sat.–Thurs., guided tours 9–12 and 2–5.*

Tour 6: Montmartre

On a dramatic rise above the city is **Montmartre,** site of the basilica of Sacré-Coeur—Paris's best-known landmark after the Eiffel Tower—and home to a once-thriving artistic community, now reduced to gangs of third-rate painters clustered in the area's most famous square, the place du Tertre. Despite their presence, and the fact that the fabled nightlife of old Montmartre has fizzled down to some glitzy nightclubs and porn shows, the area still exudes a sense of history.

61 Begin your tour at **place Blanche,** site of the Moulin Rouge. Place Blanche (White Square) takes its name from the clouds of chalky dust churned up by the windmills that once dotted Montmartre (*La Butte,* meaning "mound" or "hillock"). The windmills were set up here not just because the hill was a good place to catch the wind—at over 300 feet, it's the highest point in the city—but because Montmartre was covered with cornfields and quarries right up to the end of the 19th century. Today, only two of the original 20 windmills are intact. The most famous, immortalized by painter Toulouse-Lautrec, is the **Moulin Rouge,** or Red Windmill, built in 1885 and turned into a dance hall in 1900; the place is still trading shamelessly on the notion of Paris as a city of sin (*see* Arts and Nightlife, below).

For a taste of something more authentically French than the Moulin Rouge's computerized light shows, walk up rue Lepic, site of one of the most colorful and tempting **food markets** in Paris (closed Mon.).

Turn left onto rue des Abbesses and walk along to the small **Montmartre cemetery.** It contains the graves of many prominent French men and women including Degas and Adolphe Sax, inventor of the saxophone. The Russian ballet dancer Vaslav Nijinsky is buried here as well.

62 Walk along rue des Abbesses, then turn into rue Tholoze, which leads to the **Moulin de la Galette,** one of the two remaining windmills in Montmartre, now unromantically rebuilt. To reach it you pass **Studio 28:** This seems no more than a scruffy little movie theater, but when opened in 1928 it was the first *art et essai,* or experimental theater, in the world, and has shown

Montmartre

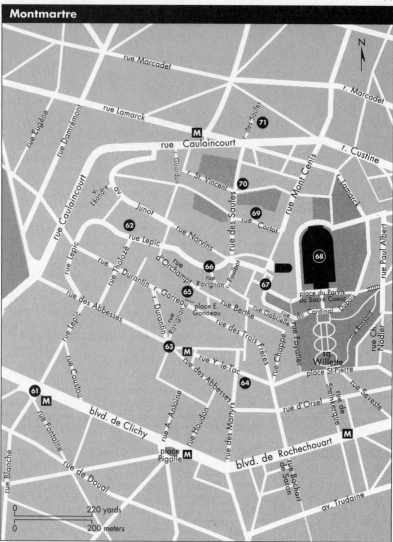

Basilique du Sacré Coeur, **68**

Bateau-Lavoir, **65**

Chapelle de Martyre, **64**

Lapin Agile, **70**

Moulin de la Galette, **62**

Musée de l'Art Juif, **71**

Musée du Vieux Montmartre, **69**

Place des Abbesses, **63**

Place Blanche, **61**

Place Jean-Baptist Clement, **66**

Place du Tertre, **67**

the works of directors like Jean Cocteau, François Truffaut, and Orson Welles before the films' official premieres.

63 Return to rue des Abbesses, turn left and walk to **place des Abbesses.** Though commercial, the little square has the kind of picturesque and slightly countrified architecture that has made Montmartre famous.

There are two competing attractions just off the square. Theater buffs should head down the tiny rue André Antoine. At no. 37, you'll see what was originally the **Théatre Libre,** the Free Theater, which was influential in popularizing the ground-breaking works of naturalist playwrights Henrik Ibsen and August Strindberg. The other attraction is **rue Yvonne-le-Tac,** scene of a vital event in Montmartre's early history and linked to the disputed story of how this quarter got its name. Some say the name Montmartre comes from the Roman temple to Mercury that was once here, called the Mound of Mercury, or *Mons Mercurii.* Others contend that it was an adaptation of *Mons Martyrum,* a name inspired by the burial here of Paris's first bishop, St-Denis. (The popular yet implausible version of his martyrdom is that he was beheaded by the Romans in AD 250 but arose to carry his severed head from rue Yvonne-le-Tac to an area four miles north, now known as St-Denis.) St-Denis is com-
64 memorated by the 19th-century **Chapelle de Martyre** at no. 9. It was in the crypt of the original chapel that the Italian priest Francis Xavier founded the Jesuit order in 1534, a decisive step in the efforts of the Catholic Church to reassert its authority in the face of the Protestant Reformation.

From rue Yvonne-le-Tac, retrace your steps through place des Abbesses. Take rue Ravignon on the right, climbing to the summit via place Emile Goudeau, an enchanting little cobbled
65 square. Your goal is the **Bateau-Lavoir,** or Boat Wash House, at its northern edge. Montmartre poet Max Jacob coined the name for the old building on this site, which burned down in 1970: Not only did it look like a boat, he said, but the warren of artists' studios within were always paint-spattered and in need of a good hosing down. The drab new concrete building also contains art studios, though none so illustrious as those of Cubist painters Picasso and Braque, which were housed here in former years.

66 Continue up the hill to **place Jean-Baptiste Clement.** The Italian painter and sculptor Modigliani (1884–1920) had a studio here at no. 7. Some people have claimed he is the greatest Italian artist of the 20th century, the man who fused the genius of the Italian Renaissance with the modernity of Cézanne and Picasso. Modigliani claimed he would drink himself to death—he eventually did—and chose the wildest part of town in which to do it. Most of the old-time cabarets are gone now, though, and only the Moulin de Paris still reflects a glimmer of the old atmosphere.

Rue Norvins, formerly rue des Moulin, runs behind and parallel to the north end of the square. Turn right, walk past the
67 bars and tourist shops, and you'll reach **place du Tertre.** At most times of the year, you'll have to fight your way through the crowds to the southern end of the square and the breathtaking view over the city. The real drawback here, though, is the swarm of artists clamoring to dash off your portrait. Most are licensed, but there is a fair share of con men. If one produces a

picture of you without having asked first, you're under no obligation to buy it!

La Mère Catherine, the restaurant at the northern end of the square, was a favorite with the Russian cossacks who occupied Paris after Napoleon's 1814 exile to the island of Elba. Little did the cossacks know that when they banged on the tables and shouted "bistro," the Russian word for "quick," they were inventing a new breed of French restaurant. Now fairly touristic, La Mère Catherine is surprisingly good, though prices are high.

Time Out   **Patachou** sounds the one classy note in place du Tertre. It offers exquisite, if expensive, cakes and teas.

It was in place du Tertre that one of the most violent episodes in French history began, which colored French political life for generations. Despite popular images of later 19th-century France—and Paris especially—as a time of freedom and prosperity, the country was desperately divided into two camps for much of this period: a militant underclass, motivated by resentment of what they considered an elitist government, and a reactionary and fearful bourgeoisie and ruling class. In March 1871, the antimonarchist Communards clashed with soldiers of the French government leader Adolph Thiers. The Communards formed the Commune, which ruled Paris for three months. Then, Thiers ordered his troops to take the city, and upwards of 10,000 Communards were executed after the Commune's collapse.

Looming behind the church of St-Pierre on the east side of the **68** square, the **Basilique du Sacré Coeur** was erected by the government in 1873 (after Thiers's death) as a kind of guilt offering for the ruthless killing of the Communards. Even so, the building was, to some extent, a reflection of political divisions within the country, financed by French Catholics, fearful of an anticlerical backlash, and determined to make a grand statement on behalf of the Church. Stylistically, Sacré Coeur borrows elements from Romanesque and Byzantine models, fusing them under its distinctive Oriental dome. The gloomy, cavernous interior is worth visiting for its golden mosaics; climb to the top of the dome for the view over Paris.

More of Montmartre beckons north and west of Sacré Coeur. **69** Take rue du Mont-Cenis down to rue Cortot, site of the **Musée du Vieux Montmartre.** Like the Bateau-Lavoir, the building that is now the museum sheltered an illustrious group of painters, writers, and assorted cabaret artists in its heyday toward the end of the 19th century. Foremost among them were Renoir and Maurice Utrillo, who was the Montmartre painter par excellence. Taking the gray, crumbling streets of Montmartre as his subject matter, Utrillo discovered that he worked much more effectively from cheap postcards than from the streets themselves. Look carefully at the pictures in the museum here and you can see the plaster and sand he mixed with his paints to help convey the decaying buildings of the area. The next best thing about the museum is the view over the tiny vineyard on neighboring rue des Saules. *12 rue Cortot. Admission: 20 frs. Open Tues.–Sat. 2:30–6, Sun. 11–6.*

There's an equally famous Montmartre landmark on the corner **70** of rue St-Vincent, just down the road: the **Lapin Agile,** or the

Nimble Rabbit. It's a bar-cabaret, originally one of the raunchiest haunts in Montmartre. Today, it manages against all odds to preserve at least something of its earlier flavor, unlike the Moulin Rouge.

Behind the Lapin Agile is the **St-Vincent Cemetery** whose entrance is off little rue Lucien Gaulard. It's a tiny graveyard, but serious students of Montmartre might want to visit to see Utrillo's burial place. Continue north on rue des Saules, across busy rue Caulaincourt and you come to the **Musée de l'Art Juif**, the Museum of Jewish Art, containing devotional items, models of synagogues, and works by Camille Pissarro and Marc Chagall. *42 rue des Saules. Admission: 10 frs. adults, 5 frs. students and children. Open Sun.–Thurs. 3–6; closed Fri. and Sat.*

Excursion: Rueil-Malmaison

Rueil-Malmaison is today a faceless, if pleasant, western suburb of Paris, but the memory of star-crossed lovers Napoleon and Josephine still haunts its Malmaison château on avenue Napoléon-Bonaparte. To get there by car, take N13 from Porte Maillot; or, alternatively, catch the RER to La Défense, then switch to the 158A bus, which stops right by the château.

Built in 1622, **La Malmaison** was bought by the future Empress Josephine in 1799 as a love nest for Napoleon and herself (they had married three years earlier). After the childless Josephine was divorced by the heir-hungry emperor in 1809, she retired to La Malmaison and died here on May 29, 1814.

The château has 24 rooms furnished with exquisite tables, chairs, and sofas of the Napoleonic period; of special note are the library, game room, and dining room. The walls are adorned with works by contemporary artists of the day, such as David, Pierre-Paul Prud'hon, and Baron Gérard. Take time to admire the clothes and hats belonging to Napoleon and Joséphine, particularly the display of the empress's gowns. Their carriage can be seen in one of the garden pavilions, and another pavilion contains a unique collection of snuffboxes donated by Prince George of Greece. The gardens themselves are delightful, especially the regimented rows of spring tulips. *Av. du Château. Admission: 21 frs., 11 frs. Sun. Open Wed.–Mon. 10–noon and 1:30–5; closed Tues.*

The **Bois Préau**, which stands close to La Malmaison, is a smaller mansion dating back to the 17th century. It was acquired by Josephine in 1810, after her divorce, but subsequently reconstructed in the 1850s. Today its 10 rooms, complete with furniture and objects from the Empire period, are devoted mainly to souvenirs of Napoleon's exile on the island of St. Helena. *Entrance from av. de l'Impératrice. Admission: 10 frs., 5 frs. Sun. Open Wed.–Mon. 10–noon and 1:30–5; closed Tues.*

For other excursions from Paris, *see* the Ile de France chapter.

Paris for Free

Unfortunately, Paris doesn't offer too many organized sights that can be enjoyed without first digging deep in your pockets. That said, the city is one of the world's most scenic and exciting capitals, and just strolling along, breathing in its rich, romantic atmosphere, is an occupation in which every visitor will want to indulge. A **walk along the Seine** is at the top of the list, whether you're on your first trip or your 51st. One of the rewarding sections is the quayside on the Ile St-Louis, notably the **quai de Bourbon,** at the western end facing Ile de la Citè, from where you'll have some memorable views of Notre-Dame. The streets of **Montmartre** are also rich in Gallic charm, though don't be surprised by the crowds or the many steep streets and flights of steps you'll encounter.

Paris's many parks and gardens can be enjoyed free of charge (the **Tuileries** and the **Jardin du Palais-Royal** are especially delightful), and, of course, the churches of **Sacré-Coeur, La Madeleine,** and **St-Germain-des-Prés** won't break the bank either.

A trip to the city's largest and most attractive cemetery, the 19th-century **Cimetière du Père-Lachaise,** is also a freebie: Cobbled avenues, steep slopes, and lush vegetation contribute to its powerful atmosphere, while inhabitants include Frederic Chopin, Molière, Balzac, and Oscar Wilde, among other luminaries.

On Sunday, the **Louvre**—granddaddy of Paris's many museums—is open free: Expect half of Paris to be in there with you, though!

Except for those galleries with temporary exhibitions, the vast halls of the **Beaubourg** are always open free of charge. Outside, on the plateau Beaubourg, you can be entertained for hours by the fire-eaters, Indian rope tricksters, musicians, mimes, and clowns who gather here during summer months. Similar entertainment can be found on the square in front of St-Germain-des-Prés, on the Left Bank.

And while this isn't strictly speaking free: The price of a cup of coffee will guarantee you a ringside seat in any of Paris's sidewalk cafés, where you can amuse yourself for hours watching the world go by.

What to See and Do with Children

Amusement Parks **Jardin d'Acclimatation.** This charming children's play park in the Bois de Boulogne boasts a miniature train, boat rides, and a zoo. *Admission: 6.80 frs. adults, 3.3 frs. children. Open daily 10–6. Métro: Les Sablons.*

Parc Floral de Paris. The east Paris equivalent of the Jardin d'Acclimatation, the Parc Floral is situated in the Bois de Vincennes, near the château. It features a miniature train, a games area, and miniature golf. *Rte. de la Pyramide, Vincennes. Admission: 4 frs. adults, 2 frs. children under 10. Open daily, summer 9:30–8; winter 9:30–5. Métro: Château de Vincennes.*

Aquariums Fish gazing is a soothing, mesmerizing experience for young and old alike. There are two principal aquariums in Paris: **Aquarium de la Mer et des Eaux** (195 rue St-Jacques, 5e. Admission: 15 frs. adults, 9 frs. children. Open Tues.–Fri. 10–12:30 and 1:15–5:30; weekends 10–5:30. Métro: Luxembourg) and **Aquarium Tropical** (293 av. Daumesnil, 12e. Admission: 20 frs., 10 frs. Sun. Open Wed.–Mon. 9:45–noon and 1:30–5:15. Métro: Porte Dorée).

Boat Trips An hour on the Seine on a *Bateau Mouche* or *Vedette* is a fun way to get to know the capital. The cost is 25–30 francs for adults, 12–15 francs for children under 10. Departures every half-hour from **Square du Vert Galant** (1er. Métro: Pont-Neuf), **Eiffel Tower** (7e. Métro: Bir Hakeim), and **Pont de l'Alma** (8e. Métro: Alma Marceau).

Boating Rowboats can be rented at the **Lac Inférieur** in the Bois de Boulogne and at **Lac des Minimes** and **Lac Daumesnil** in the Bois de Vincennes.

Circus There's no need to know French to enjoy a circus. Tickets range from 40 francs to 120 francs. There are evening and weekend matinee performances. Check for details with **Cirque Pauwels** (Jardin d'Acclimatation, Bois de Boulogne; Métro: Les Sablons) or **Cirque d'Hiver** (110 rue Amelot, 11e, tel. 47–00–12–25; Métro: Chemin Vert).

Museums **Cité des Sciences et de l'Industrie de la Villette.** Children love this extensive and imaginatively laid out museum devoted to industry. *Parc de la Villette. Admission: 30 frs., planetarium 15 frs. extra. Open Thurs. and Fri. 10–6; Tues., Wed. and weekends noon–8. Métro: Porte de la Villette.*

Musée de la Femme et Collection d'Automates. The collection of automata and clockwork dolls bursts into life each afternoon. It's well worth making the short trip to Neuilly, especially since the Jardin d'Acclimatation (*see* above) and Bois de Boulogne are close at hand. *12 rue du Centre, Neuilly. Admission: 9.2 frs. adults, 4.6 frs. children and senior citizens. Guided tours Wed.–Mon. 3 PM. Métro: Pont de Neuilly.*

Musée Grévin. The long-established Boulevard Montmartre museum concentrates on waxwork imitations of the famous, the one in Halles on recapturing the Belle Epoque. *10 blvd. Montmartre, 9e. Admission: 38 frs. adults, 26 frs. children under 14. Métro: rue Montmartre. Forum des Halles, 1 er. Admission: 34 frs. adults, 22 frs. children under 14. Métro: Les Halles. Both open Mon.–Sat. 10:30–7:30, Sun. 1–8.*

Puppet Shows On most Wednesday, Saturday, and Sunday afternoons, **Guignol,** the French equivalent of Punch and Judy, performs at various parks, including Tuileries and the Luxembourg.

Zoos Monkeys, deer, birds, and farm animals star at the **Jardin d'Acclimatation** (*see* above), while the **Ménagerie** in the Jardin des Plantes also boasts elephants, lions, and tigers. *57 rue Cuvier, 5e. Admission: 20 frs. adults, 10 frs. children. Open daily 9–6 (9–5 in winter). Métro: Jussieu.*

Paris's biggest zoo is in the **Bois de Vincennes;** in addition to wild beasts, it includes a museum, films, and exhibitions. *53 av. de St-Maurice, 12e. Admission: 30 frs. adults, 15 frs. children. Open daily 9–6 (9–5 in winter). Métro: Porte Dorée.*

Off the Beaten Track

Buttes-Chaumont. This immensely picturesque park in the downbeat 19th arrondissement of northeast Paris boasts a lake, waterfall, and clifftop folly, or "belvedere." Until town planner Baron Haussmann got his hands on it in the 1860s, the area was a rubbish dump and quarry—hence the steep slopes. *Rue Botzaris. Métro: Buttes-Chaumont.*

Les Catacombes. The Catacombs consist of an extensive underground labyrinth founded by the Romans, who tunneled under much of the Left Bank and into the near suburbs. They were subsequently used to store bones from disused graveyards; then, during World War II, they became the headquarters of the French Resistance. You are well advised to take a flashlight with you. *1 pl. Denfert-Rochereau. Admission: 15 frs., 10 frs. students and seniors. Open Tues.–Fri. 2–4, weekends 9–11 and 2–4. Guided tours on Wed. at 2:45; 20 frs. extra. Métro: Denfert/Rochereau.*

Shopping

Paris lives up to its reputation as one of the world's great shopping capitals. The city boasts great names in haute couture, perfume, and accessories, as well as countless boutiques and department stores. Prices are generally higher than in London or New York, so you may prefer to limit yourself to window shopping.

Shopping Districts A general rule of thumb is that the Left Bank is geared more to small, specialist shops and boutiques, while the Right Bank boasts the high fashion houses, the most ostentatious shops, and the large department stores.

On the Left Bank, **St-Germain-des-Prés** has long been a center for bookshops, ready-to-wear fashion stores, and specialty shops. The nearby **rue de Grenelle** has seen the arrival of chic designers, including Sonia Rykiel and Charles Jourdan. Shoe and fabric shops crowd the **rue des Sts-Pères,** while the rue de **Rennes,** running from St-Germain to Montparnasse, is packed with a variety of clothing stores, many quite inexpensive. The The **Montparnasse Tower** contains several department stores.

On the Right Bank, the modern, three-tiered **Forum des Halles** has recently become a popular shopping spot. The area around the mall contains numerous shops with knick-knacks and clothes. **Place des Victoires** is one of the leading centers of avant-garde Parisian fashion, while the **rue du Faubourg St-Honoré** and the area around the **Champs-Elysées** boast numerous haute couture houses.

The **Opéra** district contains landmark department stores. The **place Vendôme** and the surrounding streets glitter with the city's swankiest jewelry stores.

Shopping Arcades The various shopping arcades scattered around Paris often date back to the 19th century. Many have been splendidly restored, with arching glass roofs, marble flooring, and brass lamps set off to full advantage. Most are conveniently located in the 1st and 2nd arrondisements on the Right Bank.

The **Galerie Vivienne** (4 pl. des Petits Champs, 2e), between the Bourse (Stock Exchange) and Palais Royal, is a delightful place to amble.

Galerie Vero-Dodot (19 rue Jean-Jacques Rousseau, 1er) has painted ceilings and slender copper pillars.

Passage des Panoramas (11 blvd. Montmartre, 2e) is the granddaddy of them all, opened in 1800. You can window-shop here until about 9 PM, when the ornamental gates at either end are closed.

Department Stores Paris has a good selection of department stores, several of which are conveniently grouped on the Right Bank around the Opéra. **Printemps** (64 blvd. Haussmann, 9e) claims to be the "most Parisian department store." Its main rival is **Galeries Lafayette** (40 blvd. Haussmann, 9e), and competition is fierce. Both go out of their way to cater to foreign visitors, and each offers excellent services, including multilingual hostesses, bureaux de change, and sales. For visitors in a hurry, both stores have the added attraction of a series of designer boutiques.

Two other department stores are located on the Right Bank, nearer the Seine. **Samaritaine** (19 rue de la Monnaie, 1er) is the largest department store in Paris, offering a vast range of goods at reasonable prices. As the name implies, the **Bazar de l'Hôtel de Ville** is located across from the Hôtel de Ville (City Hall). Familiarly known as the B.H.V. (pronounced Bay-Ash-Vay), it is great for good-quality household goods.

The Left Bank's sole department store is **Au Bon Marché,** located at the corner of rue de Sèvres and rue du Bac. It's not trendy but has an excellent antiques section.

The budget **Monoprix** and **Prisunic** stores are cheap and cheerful. The largest Prisunic outlets are 109 Champs-Elysées, on the corner of rue La Boétie, 8e; and 56 rue de Caumartin, 9e. Monoprix's handiest outlet for tourists is at 21 av. de l'Opera, 1er.

Markets Every *quartier* in Paris boasts an open-air food market, if only for a few days a week. Sunday mornings, until 1 PM, is usually a good time to go; Monday is the most likely closing day. The local markets usually concentrate on food, but they always have a few brightly colored flower stalls. Some markets have stalls selling antiques, clothing, household goods, and second-hand books. Their lively—sometimes chaotic—atmosphere makes them a sight worth seeing even if you don't want to buy anything.

Many of the better-known markets are located in areas you'd visit for sightseeing. Our favorites are on **rue de Buci,** 6e (open daily); **rue Mouffetard,** 5e; and **rue Lepic** in Montmartre. (The latter two are best on weekends.) The **Marché d'Aligre** (open Sat., Sun., and Mon. mornings) is located beyond the Bastille in the 12th arrondissement. It's not very touristic, but Parisians from all over the city know and love it.

Paris's main **flower market** is located right in the heart of the city on Ile de la Cité, between Notre-Dame and the Palais de Justice. It's open every day except Monday. On Sunday, it becomes a bird market.

The huge **Marché aux Puces** on Paris's northern boundary (Métro: Porte de Clignancourt) is the city's largest flea market. It's not as cheap as days of yore, but it remains a great place to barter, browse, and maybe even buy. The century-old labyrinth of alleyways is packed with antique dealers and junk stalls. *Open Sat., Sun., and Mon.*

Specialty Stores Those wishing to take home china and crockery should head for
Gift Ideas the **rue du Paradis,** 10e; it's lined with china shops selling goods at a wide range of prices. If you need something to put on your dishes, you can procure posh nosh from all over the world at

A la Mère de
Famille, **26**
A La Ville du Puy, **13**
Annick Goutal, **23**
Au Bon Marché, **48**
La Bagagerie, **11**
Bazar de l'Hôtel
de Ville, **41**
Bouchara, **16**
Cacharel, **32**
Carel, **47**
Carré Rive Gauche, **44**
Cartier, **19**
Chanel, **8**
Chaumet, **22**
Chauvet, **37**
Chipie, **40**
Christian Dior, **3**
Christian Lacroix, **4**
Claude Montana, **29**
Daniel Hechter, **38**
Didier Aaron and
Perrin, **5**
Fauchon, **10**
Galeries Lafayette, **18**
Galeries Vero-
Dodot, **34**
Galerie Vivienne, **28**
Givenchy, **1**
Guy Laroche, **2**
Hediard, **9**
Hermès, **7**
Jean Laporte Artisan
Parfumeur, **20**
Karl Lagerfeld, **6**
Kenzo, **31**
Léon, **24**
Lolita Lempika, **42**
Louvre des
Antiquaires, **33**
Maud Frizon, **46**
Le Monde en
Marché, **43**
Monoprix, **25**
Naf Naf, **36**
Passage des
Panoramas, **27**
Pierlot, **35**
Printemps, **14**
Prisunic, **15**
Pucinella, **12**
Samaritaine, **39**
Sephora, **17**
Sonia Rykiel, **45**
TATT, **49**
Van Cleef and
Arpels, **21**
Victoires, **30**

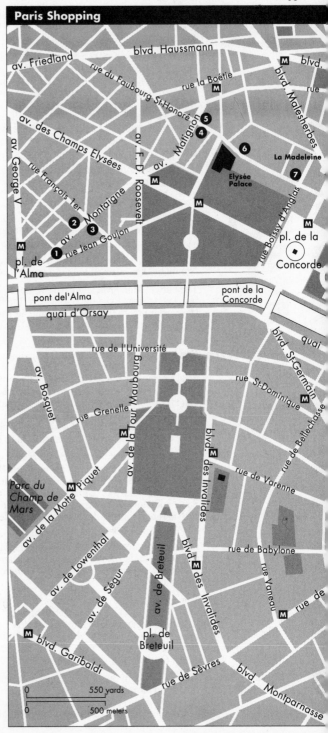

Paris Shopping

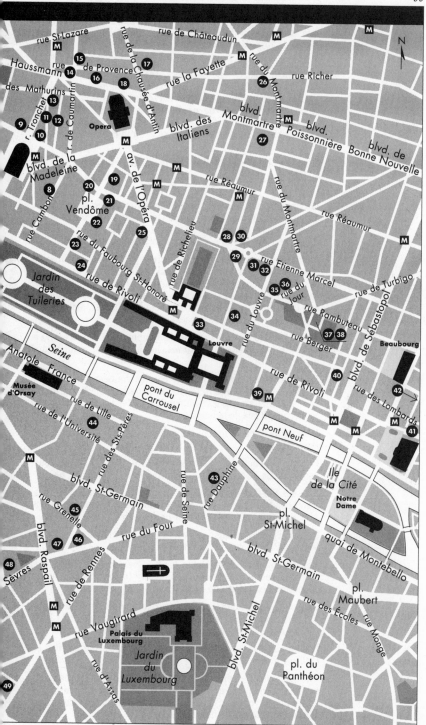

N

rue St-Lazare

rue de Châteaudun

rue Haussmann

rue de Provence

15

14

16

17

18

rue de la Chaussée d'Antin

rue la Fayette

rue du Montmartre

rue Richer

26

des Mathurins

13

r. de Caumartin

blvd. Montmartre

blvd. des Italiens

blvd. Poissonnière

blvd. de Bonne Nouvelle

9

11

12

r. Tronchet

10

Opéra

27

blvd. de la Madeleine

8

rue Cambon

19

20

21

pl. Vendôme

22

av. de l'Opéra

rue Réaumur

rue du Montmartre

rue Réaumur

23

25

rue de Richelieu

28 30

29

31 32

rue Etienne Marcel

rue de Turbigo

24

rue du Faubourg St-Honoré

rue de Rivoli

35 36

rue du Jour

rue Rambuteau

blvd. de Sébastopol

33

34

rue du Louvre

rue Berger

37 38

Beaubourg

Louvre

40

rue de Rivoli

rue des Lombards

42

Jardin des Tuileries

Seine

Anatole France

pont du Carrousel

39

pont Neuf

41

Musée d'Orsay

rue de Lille

rue de l'Université

44

rue des Sts-Pères

rue de Seine

rue Dauphine

43

Ile de la Cité

Notre Dame

blvd. St-Germain

45

rue Grenelle

pl. St-Michel

quai de Montebello

47 46

rue du Four

blvd. St-Germain

48

Sèvres

blvd. Raspail

rue de Rennes

pl. Maubert

rue des Écoles

rue Monge

rue Vaugirard

Palais du Luxembourg

blvd. St-Michel

49

rue d'Assas

Jardin du Luxembourg

pl. du Panthéon

Fauchon and **Hediard,** two upmarket grocers on place de la Madeleine, 8e. (Hard-core sweet-tooths can satisfy cravings at **À la Mere de Famille,** with stores at 1 rue de Provence, 9e, and 35 rue du Fbg. Montmartre, 9e.)

Shoppers looking for fabrics should try **Bouchara** (54 blvd. Haussmann, 9e; 57 rue de Passy, 16e; and 10 av. des Ternes, 17e), the best-known name in Paris for high-quality fabric. Those on a more limited budget may like the wide range of souvenir shops on the **rue de Rivoli,** selling porcelain boxes, imitation Sévres china, busts of Napoleon, and Eiffel Tower memorabilia. **Léon,** at no. 220, has been in business for over a century.

For children, try **Le Monde en Marche** (34 rue Dauphine, 6e), which has a great selection of wooden toys, puppets, and miniatures.

Antiques   **Louvre des Antiquaires** (2 pl. du Palais Royal, 1er) features 250 antique dealers under one roof. On the rue du Faubourg St-Honoré are the internationally known antique dealers—**Didier Aaron and Perrin** and **Alexandre Poniatowski.**

Carré Rive Gauche is a prime hunting ground for antiques on the Left Bank. A number of small dealers are grouped along the narrow, atmospheric streets of rue du Bac, rue de Beaune, rue de Lille, rue de l'Université, rue des Sts-Pères, rue Jacob, and quai Voltaire. These streets also have small, discreet art galleries—with wares at upscale prices.

Accessories   World-famous **Hermès** (24 rue du Faubourg St-Honoré, 8e) is known for exquisite silk scarves, leather goods, jewelry, and haute couture.

Place Vendôme is renowned for having the best and most expensive jewelry stores in town, counting **Van Cleef and Arpels** and **Chaumet** among its occupants. **Cartier** is just around the corner, at 13 rue de la Paix.

Pucinella (10 rue Vignon, 9e) has a delightful selection of old jewelry.

For bags and belts, try **La Bagagerie** (outlets at 41 rue du Four, 6e; 11 rue de Fbg. St-Honore, 8e; and 12 rue Tronchet, 8e).

Rue des Sts-Pères is one place to go in search of shoe shops: **Carel** has been at no. 78 for ages, and **Maud Frizon,** at no. 79, carries numerous styles at well-heeled prices.

Clothing   Chic and pricey young designer creations can be found at **À La Ville du Puy** (36 rue Tronchet, 8e).

Lolita Lempika (corner of rue des Rosiers and rue Paveé, 4e) is one of the newest stars of French ready-to-wear, with a junior collection **Lolita Bis** line located on the opposite corner.

Pierlot (4 rue du Jour, 1er) is a favorite shopping spot for young French career girls, while **Naf Naf** (10 rue du Jour) and **Chipie** (31 rue de la Ferronerie, 1er) offer sporty, trendy clothes.

For the city's cheapest threads, try **TATT,** a Parisian institution (140 rue de Rennes, 6e).

Those looking for something at the other end of the price range might try the **place des Victoires,** where **Victoires** houses the creations of young stylists, and where **Kenzo, Cacharel,** and **Claude Montana** have boutiques.

Sonia Rykiel's small boutique (4 rue de Grenelle, 6e) is highly popular for upscale women's clothes.

Haute couture fiends will head for **rue du Faubourg St-Honoré,** where **Christian Lacroix** and **Karl Lagerfield** keep shop.

Av. Montaigne, near the Champs-Elysées, offers hardy perennials like **Christian Dior** at no. 30, **Guy Laroche** at no. 29, and **Givenchy's** boutique for men at no. 8.

Rue Cambon, in the Opéra district, boasts one of the finest **Chanel** boutiques.

For men, try **Chauvet** (28 pl. Vendôme) or **Daniel Hechter** in Forum des Halles.

Perfume   This tried-and-true Parisian gift is available at **Annick Goutal's** exquisite boutique (24 rue de Castiglione, 1er) or at the chain **Sephora** (outlets at 66 rue Chaussée d'Antin, 9e; 30 av. de l'Italie, 13e; 46 av. Général-Leclerc, 14e; and 15 rue de Passy, 16e). **Jean Laporte Artisan Parfumeur** has two highly original boutiques (5 rue des Capucines, 1er, and 84 bis rue Grenelle, 7e).

Sports and Fitness

Biking   The Bois de Boulogne and the Bois de Vincennes, with their wide leafy avenues, are good places for biking. Bikes can be rented from **Paris Vélo** (4 rue du Fer à Moulin, 5e, tel. 43–37–59–22) for around 80 francs a day or 130 francs a weekend.

Fitness Centers   The best hotel fitness facilities are in the newer properties on the edges of the city center. The Vitatop Club on the top floors of the **Sofitel Paris** (8 rue Louis Armand, 15e, tel. 45–54–79–00) offers a 15-meter pool, sauna, steamroom, and Jacuzzi, plus a stunning view of the Paris skyline. Next door is the **Parc Suzanne Lenglen,** with plenty of room for running, plus indoor and outdoor tennis courts. The **Bristol** (112 rue du Faubourg St-Honoré, 8e, tel. 42–66–91–45) has a large, pool, plus a sauna.

Gyms and aerobic centers have mushroomed in Paris. One of the leading names is **Garden Gym** (65 Champs-Elysées, 8e, tel. 42–25–87–20; 147 bis rue St-Honoré, 1er, near Palais-Royal; and 2 rue Drouot, 9e, near the Opéra).

Jogging   The best inner-city running is in the **Champ-de-Mars,** next to the Eiffel Tower, measuring 1½ miles around the perimeter. Shorter and more crowded routes are found in the **Luxembourg Gardens,** with a one-mile loop just inside the park's fence; in the **Tuileries,** again measuring about one mile; and in the **Parc Monceau,** which has a loop of just under one mile. The **Bois de Boulogne,** on the western edge of Paris, offers miles of trails through woods, around lakes, and across grassy meadows. The equally bucolic **Bois de Vincennes,** on the eastern side of the city, offers a nine-mile circuit or a one-mile loop around the château de Vincennes itself.

Tennis   There are few tennis courts in Paris. Your best bet is to try the public courts in the **Luxembourg Gardens.** There is also a large complex of courts at the "Polygone" sportsground in the **Bois de Vincennes.** It's a 20-minute walk down route de la Pyramide from the château de Vincennes mêtro stop.

The **French Open** is held during the last two weeks in May at the **Roland Garros** stadium on the eastern edge of the Bois de Boulogne (take the métro to Porte d'Auteuil). Center-court tickets are difficult to obtain, especially for the second week; try your hotel or turn up early in the morning (play starts at 11) and buy a general ground ticket.

Dining

Our restaurant recommendations have been compiled under the direction of Jean-Marc Blanchot, editor of UP, a prestigious bilingual magazine distributed in hotels throughout Paris and the Riviera.

Eating out is one of the perennial delights of this most civilized of cities. Some complain that the French capital is overrated gastronomically and that the Parisian restaurateur is resting complacently on his or her laurels. Of course, not every restaurant offers a gastronomic adventure, and bad meals at unconscionable prices are no more unknown in Paris than at home. The important point to remember is that the city's restaurants exist principally to cater to the demanding needs of the Parisians themselves, and any restaurant that fails to meet their high standards is unlikely to stay in business long.

It's dangerous to generalize on such a complex subject, but Paris's most expensive and formal restaurants offer either classical food (characterized by rich sauces) or nouvelle cuisine (characterized by light, fresh produce artfully arranged on your plate); many serve a judicious mixture of the two. In less-expensive places—especially the numerous bistros and brasseries—the food veers more toward classical styles, though it will almost always be less intimidatingly rich than in the temples of classical cuisine. Different regional cuisines are also widely available, most commonly from Normandy.

Almost all restaurants offer two basic types of menu: à la carte and fixed-price (*un menu* to the French). The fixed-price menu will almost always offer the best value, though you will have to eat three or sometimes four courses, and choices will be limited. There's nothing to stop you from choosing only one or two dishes from the à la carte menu, but only the most thick-skinned will want to try this in a top restaurant, especially if it's busy: The wilting look of a Parisian waiter is not something many can happily endure.

Lunch is usually served from noon to 2. You shouldn't have difficulty getting a table in all but the best restaurants if you arrive by 12:30; after 1, however, you may have problems, especially if you want a full three-course meal. Dinner is rarely served before 8, and 9:30 or even 10 is not considered unduly late.

Highly recommended restaurants are indicated by a star ★.

1st Arrondissement
★
Le Grand Véfour. Located under the elegant neo-Classical colonnades at the north end of the gardens of the Palais Royal, Le Grand Véfour has a convincing claim to be regarded as the most sumptuously decorated restaurant in the city. The elegantly incised and painted early 19th-century mirrors reflect the crisp white linen of the tablecloths. Haute cuisine is prepared in the traditional manner; this is not a place for lovers of nouvelle cuisine. Breton lobster with artichokes is a perennial favorite. The fixed-price menu, available only at lunch, offers excellent value. *17 rue de Beaujolais, tel. 42–96–56–27. Reservations essential; book 1 week in advance for Fri. and Sat. dinner. Jacket and tie required. AE, DC, MC, V. Closed Sat. lunch, Sun., and Aug. Very Expensive.*

Le Carré des Feuillants. Anyone with pretensions to be numbered among *le beau monde* will already know that this elegant new restaurant offers one of the city's most talked-about dining experiences. Try for a table in the largest of the three dining rooms; it has a memorable fireplace. The food is predominantly from the southwest of France, one of the richest gastronomic regions of the country. Foie gras, truffles, and young pigeon number among the specialties. The wine list is fabulous. *14 rue de Castiglione, tel. 42-86-82-82. Reservations advised. Dress: casual but elegant. AE, DC, MC, V. Closed Sat. lunch, Sun., and weekends in July and Aug. Expensive.*

★ **Chez Paul.** Lovers of the authentic Parisian bistro—and they don't come much more authentic than this—rejoice at the survival of Chez Paul. It's located on the Ile de la Cité, between the Pont Neuf and the Palais du Justice, on one of the prettiest squares in Paris. Dining on the terrace is an experience to remember. The food is sturdily traditional, with snails, and calf's head in shallot sauce as long-time favorites. *15 pl. Dauphine, tel. 43-54-21-48. Reservations essential. Dress: informal. No credit cards. Closed Mon., Tues., and Aug. Moderate.*

2nd Arrondissement **Drouant.** This elegant restaurant and café is a Paris institution, where France's highest literary prize, the Prix Goncourt, has been awarded since 1914. The glamorous café serves rather traditional bourgeois cuisine, with the accent on seafood. The more sophisticated restaurant offers excellent nouvelle dishes. Try the warm oysters with caviar, the rabbit with spices, or lobster fricassee. *18 rue Gaillon, tel. 42-65-15-16. Reservations advised. Dress: casual but elegant; jacket and tie required in restaurant. AE, DC, MC, V. Closed weekends. Expensive.*

4th Arrondissement **La Colombe.** "The Dove" lives up to its name and is home to 14 white doves. It also offers one of the most charming dining experiences in Paris. The restaurant is set in a beautiful 13th-century house on the Seine, right near Notre-Dame. Try to secure a table on the leafy terrace. The food is predominantly classic, but with nouvelle touches. The good-value fixed-price lunch menu is also available for dinner before 9 PM. *4 rue de la Colombe, tel. 46-33-37-08. Reservations advised. Dress: casual chic. AE, DC, MC, V. Closed Sun. and Mon. lunch. Moderate.*

Coconnas. With its warm Italian decor and early 18th-century paintings of beautiful place des Vosges, the little Coconnas has won plaudits from critics and humble diners alike. Depending on your mood, you can choose either nouvelle dishes or cuisine *à l'ancienne,* solid 19th-century fare with not so much as a hint of nouvelle innovation. Owned and run by the proprietors of the Tour d'Argent (*see* below), the Coconnas has a considerable reputation to live up to. If the overbooking is anything to go by, it obviously does. *2 bis pl. des Vosges, tel. 42-78-58-16. Reservations essential. Dress: informal. AE, DC, MC, V. Closed Mon., Tues., and mid-Dec.–mid-Jan. Moderate.*

★ **Trumilou.** Overlooking the Seine opposite the Ile St-Louis, this very French little bistro is a real find. Despite the harsh lighting, the mood is boisterous and welcoming, with many regulars among the diners. Bright and splashy paintings line the walls. The food is resolutely traditional, with time-honored favorites like *boeuf bourguignon* and sweetbreads. *84 quai de l'Hôtel de Ville, tel. 42-77-63-98. Reservations accepted. Dress: informal. MC, V. Inexpensive.*

Paris Dining

Au Clocher du Village, **1**
L'Assommoir, **11**
Beauvilliers, **12**
Brasserie Lipp, **26**
Le Carré des Feuillants, **6**
Chartier, **9**

Chez Papa, **24**
Chez Paul, **17**
Closerie des Lilas, **28**
Coconnas, **14**
La Colombe, **16**
Le Coupe-Chou, **21**
La Coupole, **29**
De Graziano, **10**
Dôme, **30**

Drouant, **7**
Le Grand Véfour, **8**
Jean-Claude Ferrero, **2**
Joël Robuchon, **3**
Jules Verne, **31**
Lucas-Carton, **5**
Mansouria, **13**

Petit St-Benoit, **25**
La Petite Chaise, **27**
Le Procope, **22**
Saumoneraie, **20**
Taillevent, **4**
Tour d'Argent, **18**
Trumilou, **15**
Vagénende, **23**
Villars Palace, **19**

5th Arrondissement
Tour d'Argent. The Tour d'Argent is the sort of temple to haute cuisine that has serious gourmets quivering in expectation. It offers the complete dining experience, very much in the grand manner. You come not simply for the food—though, after some years of noticeably falling standards, new chef Manuel Martinez has restored this to its previous high peaks—but for the perfect service, the discreetly understated decor, the immense wine list, and the fabled view of Notre-Dame. *15 quai de la Tournelle, tel. 43–54–23–31. Reservations at least 1 week in advance. Jacket and tie required. AE, DC, MC, V. Closed Mon. Very Expensive.*

Le Coupe-Chou. Located in an alley at the foot of the Montagne Ste-Geneviève and the Panthéon, Le Coupe-Chou has uneven floors, bare stone walls, and candlelit alcoves. The mood throughout is great for romantic dining. The food is competent rather than memorable, but it's the magical setting that counts. Have your coffee and *digestif* in the small fire-lit sitting room. *9 rue Lanneau, tel. 46–33–68–69. Reservations advised. Jacket and tie required. MC, V. Closed Sun. Expensive.*

★ **Villars Palace** and **Saumoneraie.** Fish lovers should make for rue Descartes, halfway up the Montagne Ste-Geneviève, to the Villars Palace and the Saumoneraie. They belong to the same owner and, until recently, shared the same entrance. The Villars Palace is the more sophisticated and expensive. Its tasteful modern decor is enhanced by wall mosaics and two aquariums —one fresh water, one sea water—where your dinner swims oblivious of its fate. The Saumoneraie is a more traditional bistro-style haunt, with bare stone walls. Salmon dominates the wide range of fish and seafood dishes. There's also a good-value fixed-price menu. *Villars Palace, 8 rue Descartes, tel. 43–26–39–08. Reservations advised. Dress: casual. AE, DC, MC, V. Expensive. Saumoneraie, 6 rue Descartes, tel. 46–34–08–76. Reservations essential. Dress: informal. MC, V. Moderate.*

6th Arrondissement
★ **Closerie des Lilas.** On the corner of boulevard St-Michel and boulevard du Montparnasse, the Closerie des Lilas has been an essential part of the Left Bank scene since it opened in 1907. Hemingway was here so regularly that a plaque commemorates his favorite spot at the bar. Though the lilacs—*les lilas*—may long since have disappeared from the terrace, the place is just as popular as it was during its salad days in the '30s. Straightforward traditional fare is the staple: Try the oysters. The adjoining brasserie offers much the same food at lower prices. *171 blvd. du Montparnasse, tel. 43–26–70–50. Reservations advised. Dress: informal. AE, DC, MC, V. Expensive.*

Brasserie Lipp. The Brasserie Lipp is perhaps *the* Left Bank restaurant. It's been a favorite haunt of politicians, journalists, and assorted intellectuals for longer than most people can remember. Try for a table on the first floor, but don't be surprised to find yourself relegated to the second-floor dining room. Food, service, and atmosphere are polished. *151 blvd. St-Germain, tel. 45–48–53–91. No phone reservations; expect lines. Dress: informal. AE, DC. Closed first 2 weeks in Aug. Moderate.*

Chez Papa. The refreshing open-plan decor of Chez Papa makes a pleasant change from the bustle and tightly packed tables of most St-Germain restaurants. A shiny black baby-grand piano, surrounded by a host of plants, stands out against the white

walls and high ceiling. There's soft music from 9 every evening.
Cuisine is surprisingly light, considering that the dishes themselves are usually associated with the sturdiest French
traditional food: snails, cassoulet, and pot-au-feu. A good fixed-
price lunch menu makes Chez Papa an ideal lunch spot. *3 rue
St.-Benoît, tel. 42–86–99–63. Reservations advised. Dress: informal. AE, DC, MC, V. Closed Sun. Moderate.*

Vagénende. Dark woods, gleaming mirrors, and super-
professional waiters—perfect in their black jackets and white
aprons—take the Vagénende dangerously close to turn-of-the-
century pastiche. Nonetheless, the superior brasserie food—
seafood and hearty *cuisine bourgeoise*—and the busy atmosphere make this a restaurant to take seriously. The homemade
fois gras and the chocolate-based desserts are outstanding. *142
blvd. St-Germain, tel. 43–26–68–18. Reservations advised.
Dress: informal. AE, MC, V. Moderate.*

★ **Petit St. Benoît.** This is a wonderful place—small, amazingly
inexpensive, always crowded, and with decor that's plain to the
point of barely existing. The food is correspondingly basic, but
quite good for the price. Expect to have to share a table. *4 rue
St-Benoît. No phone reservations. Dress: informal. No credit
cards. Closed weekends. Inexpensive.*

Le Procope. Founded in 1686 by an Italian, Francesco Procopio,
Le Procope is said to be the oldest café in Paris. It was a meeting place for Voltaire in the 18th century and for Balzac and
Victor Hugo in the 19th. In 1987 it was bought by the Blanc
brothers, owners of a number of other popular brasseries.
Though they have given the Procope something of a facelift,
they have promised, practically on pain of death, not to change
the busy and bustling mood or to tamper with the solid *bourgeoise* food. *13 rue de l'Ancienne-Comédie, tel. 43–26–99–20.
Reservations advised. Dress: informal. AE, DC, MC, V. Inexpensive.*

7th Arrondissement **Jules Verne.** Those who think that the food in a restaurant with
a view is bound to take second place to that view should head
tout de suite for the Jules Verne, located, memorably, on the
third floor of the Eiffel Tower. The view, of course, is fantastic,
but the food, too, is superb, featuring inventive combinations of
classic and nouvelle cuisine. Specialties include baked turbot in
vinegar and tarragon, and veal in lemon and vanilla. *Eiffel Tower, tel. 45–55–61–44. Reservations essential; book at least 3
weeks in advance. Jacket and tie required. AE, DC, MC, V.
Expensive.*

La Petite Chaise. What was once a coaching inn, opened in 1680,
has since become one of the most popular restaurants in the
city. While the decor may be on the musty side, the simple,
good-value food, with specialties like seafood pancakes and av-
ocado mousse, is the important factor here. *36 rue de Grenelle,
tel. 42–22–13–35. Reservations advised. Dress: informal. MC,
V. Inexpensive.*

8th Arrondissement
★ **Lucas-Carton.** Many gastronomes maintain that the Lucas-
Carton is absolutely *the* best restaurant in Paris. Are they
right? Who can say? What's beyond doubt, however, is that
Lucas-Carton offers a gastronomic experience equaled in no
more than a handful of restaurants around the world. The decor
is strictly Belle Epoque, all glinting mirrors and crimson seats.
The food, by contrast, is strictly nouvelle, though nouvelle at
its subtle best, which some may find an acquired taste. But

duck with honey and spices or sweetbreads with mixed vegetables prepared by master chef Alain Senderens will probably be a once-in-a-lifetime experience. *9 pl. de la Madeleine, tel. 42-65-22-90. Reservations essential; book at least 3 weeks in advance. Jacket and tie required. MC, V. Closed Sat., Sun., Christmas–New Year's, and Aug. Very Expensive.*

Taillevent. The exquisite mid-19th-century mansion that houses Taillevent provides the perfect, discreet setting for some of the most refined nouvelle food in the city. Specialties like stuffed baby pigeon on a bed of cabbage à la Taillevent provide the sort of gastronomic memory you'll never forget. The wine list boasts over 500 vintages; it's said to be the most extensive in Paris. *15 rue Lamennais, tel. 45-63-39-94. Reservations at least 1 week in advance. Jacket and tie required. MC, V. Closed Sat., Sun., and July 23–Aug. 23. Very Expensive.*

9th Arrondissement **Chartier.** Low prices, simple decor, and classic fare have earned Chartier an enviable reputation as one of the best-value places to eat in Paris. The choice isn't wide, but the food is always hearty and filling. Try the steak tartare if it's on the menu and you're feeling adventurous. *7 rue du Fbg Montmartre, tel. 47-70-86-29. No reservations. Dress: informal. No credit cards. Inexpensive.*

11th Arrondissement **Mansouria.** Despite its off-the-beaten-track location to the west of place de la Bastille, Mansouria is worth the trip if you have any interest in Moroccan food—it's in a class of its own. The decor is fresh and modern, and the service is friendly and relaxed. Try any of the *tagines*, a range of sophisticated spicy Moroccan "stews," and the pigeon "pie" with sugar. *11 rue Faidherbe, tel. 43-71-00-16. Reservations essential. Dress: informal. MC, V. Moderate.*

14th Arrondissement **Dôme.** In the heart of Montparnasse, the Dôme still reigns as one of the city's classic brasseries. Have a drink outside on the terrace before venturing into the ebullient Belle-Epoque interior to enjoy one of the excellent fresh fish platters or the steaming bouillabaise. *108 blvd. du Montparnasse, tel. 43-35-25-81. Reservations essential. Dress: informal. AE, DC, MC, V. Closed Mon. Expensive.*

16th Arrondissement **Joël Robuchon.** Without a doubt, this is one of the very best restaurants in Paris. Joël Robuchon is a chef known for his ★ personalized and exceptionally creative cuisine—*langoustine* (prawn) ravioli with cabbage, potato purée, roasted pig's head, and other dishes are impeccably served in this refined and delightfully decorated restaurant. Reservations must be made months in advance. *32 rue de Longchamp, tel. 47-27-12-27. Jacket and tie required. AE, DC, MC, V. Closed Sat., Sun., and July. Very Expensive.*

Jean-Claude Ferrero. The chic habitués of the upscale 16th arrondissement feel very much at home in this oh-so-classy restaurant. Nouvelle cuisine reigns supreme. Any of the mushroom dishes is excellent; otherwise, try the beef in crusty pastry. The restaurant is located in a stately town house and boasts a charming, plant-filled courtyard. *38 rue Vital, tel. 45-04-42-42. Reservations essential. Jacket and tie required. AE, DC, MC, V. Closed Sat., Sun., May 1–10, 2 weeks in Aug., and Christmas. Expensive.*

★ **Au Clocher du Village.** The simple, country-villagelike interior of the Clocher du Village, with old posters on the walls, wine presses hanging from the ceiling, lace curtains, and a gleaming, brass coffee machine on the bar, provides the perfect complement to simple, well-prepared classic French cuisine. Service is straightforward and friendly. It's a place like this that can make eating out in Paris special. There's nothing very fancy here, yet the whole place exudes that inimitable Gallic culinary flair. *8 bis rue Verderet, tel. 42–88–35–87. Reservations advised. Dress: informal. MC, V. Closed Sat., Sun., and Aug. Moderate.*

18th Arrondissement

Beauvilliers. This is the best luxury restaurant in Montmartre. Chef Michel Deygat has won lavish praise for his nouvelle-inspired dishes; red mullet in green peppers and veal kidneys in a truffle-based sauce are among his specialties. An excellent fixed-price menu (lunch only) keeps prices, which can otherwise be high, within reach. Vast bouquets of fresh flowers add colorful touches to the formality of the three main dining rooms; there's a tiny terrace for summer evenings. *52 rue Lamarck, tel. 42–54–19–50. Reservations essential. Jacket and tie required. MC, V. Closed Sun., Mon. lunch, and first 2 weeks in Sept. Very Expensive.*

Da Graziano. Located right under one of the neighborhood's remaining windmills, Da Graziano offers an exquisite taste of Italy in the heart of Montmartre. Owner Federighi Graziano is as chic as his restaurant—chandeliers, mirrors, and flowers proliferate—and as Tuscan as the cuisine. His fresh pasta is memorable. He also offers a range of French dishes, some named after stars who have dined here. Try the smoked beef *à la* Jean Marais. The inexpensive fixed-price lunch menu makes the climb up the hill well worthwhile. *83 rue Lepic, tel. 46–06–84–77. Reservations essential. Jacket and tie required. MC, V. Closed Feb. Expensive.*

L'Assommoir. L'Assommoir is known not just for its subtle cuisine—there's a superb range of sophisticated fish dishes—but for the personality of owner and chef Philippe Larue, who speaks English to perfection and has a tremendous sense of humor. He has covered the walls of his charming little bistro with samples from his vast collection of paintings. L'Assommoir also has the advantage of being on a peaceful little street away from crowded place du Tertre. *12 rue Girardon, tel. 42–64–55–01. Reservations advised. Dress: elegant casual. MC, V. Closed Sun. evening, Mon., mid-July–mid-Aug., and Christmas. Moderate.*

Lodging

At last count, the Paris Tourist Office's official hotel guide listed 1,090 hotels in 20 inner-city districts, or *arrondissements*, alone. Despite this huge choice, you should always be sure to make reservations well in advance, except, paradoxically, during July and August, when the trade fairs, conventions, and conferences that crowd the city the rest of the year come to a halt.

Our listings have been compiled with the aim of identifying hotels that offer maximum atmosphere, convenience, and comfort. We do not include many chain hotels for the simple reason that those in Paris are little different from those in other major cities. We prefer to list special, one-of-a-kind hotels that will, in themselves, contribute greatly to the charm of your stay. For the most part, hotels on the Right Bank offer greater luxury, or at any rate formality, while those on the Left Bank are smaller and offer more in the way of a certain, old-fashioned Parisian charm.

Other than in the largest and most expensive hotels, almost all Parisian hotels have certain idiosyncrasies. Plumbing can be erratic, though rarely to the point where it becomes a problem. Air-conditioning is the exception rather than the rule. This can cause difficulties chiefly because of noise in summer, when on stuffy, sultry nights you may have no choice but to open the windows. Ask for a room *sur cour*—overlooking the courtyard (almost all hotels have one)—or, even better, if there is one, *sur le jardin*—overlooking the garden.

There is almost always an extra charge for breakfast, anything from about 20 francs per person in the least expensive hotels to 90 francs per person in the most expensive. If you want more than the standard French breakfast of *café au lait* (coffee with milk) and a croissant, the price will almost certainly be increased.

Highly recommended hotels are indicated by a star ★.

1st Arrondissement
★ **Intercontinental-Paris.** An aura of elegant luxury reigns throughout this exquisite late 19th-century hotel, which was designed by the architect of the Paris Opéra, Garnier. Three of its opulent public rooms are official historic monuments. In summer, breakfast on the patio is a delicious experience. Service is impeccable. There are two year-round indoor restaurants —*La Rôtisserie Rivoli* and the *Café Tuileries;* in summer, you can also eat outdoors at the *Terrasse Fleurie. 3 rue de Castiglione, tel. 42–60–37–80. 450 fully equipped rooms and suites, many with Jacuzzis. Facilities: 2 restaurants, bar, patio. AE, DC, MC, V. Very Expensive.*

Normandy. For a combination of Belle-Epoque elegance and an excellent central location near the Palais Royal, the Normandy is hard to beat. Rooms are individually decorated and vary considerably in size. Some of the least expensive ones have shower only. There's a restaurant and a wood-paneled, English-style bar. *7 rue de l'Echelle, tel. 42–60–30–21. 130 rooms, plus 4 large and 4 small suites, most with bath. Facilities: restaurant (closed Sat. and Sun.). AE, DC, MC, V. Expensive.*

2nd Arrondissement
★ **Gaillon-Opéra.** The oak beams, stone walls, and marble tiles of the Gaillon-Opéra single it out as one of the most charming hotels in the Opéra neighborhood. To add to the charm there are plants throughout and a flower-filled patio. There's a small bar but no restaurant. *9 rue Gaillon, tel. 47–42–47–74. 26 rooms and 1 suite, all with bath. Facilities: bar. AE, DC, MC, V. Expensive.*

Montpensier. This handsome 17th-century mansion was transformed into a hotel in 1874. It offers the kind of small hotel charm and character that Paris is known for, as the clientele, many of them regulars, will testify. All the rooms are individually decorated and vary greatly in size. Those on the top floor, for example, are tiny and modern. The location, on an attractive street running parallel to the gardens of the Palais Royal, is ideal. There's no restaurant or bar. *12 rue Richelieu, tel. 42–96–28–50. 37 rooms with bath, 6 without bath. MC, V. Moderate.*

4th Arrondissement ★ **Deux-Iles.** This cleverly converted 17th-century mansion on the residential Ile-St-Louis has long won plaudits for charm and comfort. Flowers and plants are scattered around the stunning hall. The fabric-hung rooms, though small, have exposed beams and are fresh and airy. Ask for a room overlooking the little garden courtyard. There's no restaurant, but drinks are served in the cellar bar until 1 AM. The lounge is dominated by a fine chimneypiece and doubles as a second bar. *59 rue St-Louis-en-Ile, tel. 43–26–13–35. 8 rooms with bath, 9 with shower. Facilities: bar (closed Sun.). No credit cards. Expensive.*

Vieux Marais. As its name implies, this charming, two-star hotel lies in the heart of the Marais. It dates back to the 16th century; today, an elevator takes the strain out of coping with six floors. The rooms and bathrooms are simply decorated in light, refreshing colors and are impeccably clean. Try to get a room overlooking the courtyard. Breakfast is served in a pretty, corn-colored lounge. The staff is exceptionally courteous. *8 rue de Plâtre, tel. 42–78–47–22. 22 rooms with bath, 8 with shower. MC, V. Expensive.*

Place des Vosges. A loyal American clientele swears by the small, historic Place des Vosges, which is located on a charming street just off the exquisite square of the same name. The entrance hall is imposingly grand and is decorated in Louis XIII–style, but some of the rooms are little more than functional. A number of the smaller ones fall into the inexpensive category. There's no restaurant, but there's a welcoming little breakfast room. *12 rue de Birague, tel. 42–72–60–46. 11 rooms with bath, 5 with shower. AE, DC, MC, V. Expensive.*

5th Arrondissement **Elysa.** The Elysa is what the French call a "hôtel de charme." Though the building is not large, most rooms are surprisingly spacious, and all have been renovated; cream-colored furniture is set against pale blue or pink fabrics. There's no restaurant or bar, but you'll find a minibar in every room and a breakfast lounge serving Continental or buffet breakfasts. Moreover, the Elysa is one of the rare hotels in the city with a sauna. *6 rue Gay-Lussac, tel. 43–25–31–74. 25 rooms with bath, 5 with shower. Facilities: sauna. AE, DC, MC, V. Expensive.*

Sorbonne. This pretty, early 18th-century hotel, located right by the Sorbonne, was transformed in 1988 when its handsome stone facade was cleaned. As part of the cleanup, fresh flowers are now put into every room, augmenting their existing simple elegance. There's no restaurant or bar, but the receptionist is English, so you'll have no trouble making dining and entertainment plans. Try for a room overlooking the little garden. *6 rue Victor-Cousin, tel. 43–54–58–08. 10 rooms with bath, 27 with shower. MC, V. Moderate.*

6th Arrondissement ★ **L'Hôtel.** The reputation of the oh-so-chic L'Hôtel shows no sign of waning. This is the place to stay for anyone with aspirations to being numbered among the real sophisticates of Paris. The stunning hall, which is decked out with lavish and cool marbles and features an elegant curved staircase, sets the tone. There are two suites—one, Le Jardin, has a terrace filled with flowers and views of the church of St-Germain-des-Près. Here you can stay in the room where Oscar Wilde died ("I am dying beyond my means") or where music-hall star Mistinguette liked to reside (authentic Art Deco furniture and mirrors crowd the

Bradford, **1**
Crillon, **2**
Deux-Iles, **10**
Elysa, **12**
Gaillon-Opéra, **5**
Grand, **4**
L'Hôtel, **15**
Hôtel d'Angleterre, **16**
Intercontinental-Paris, **3**
Marronniers, **14**
Montpensier, **6**
Normandy, **7**
Pavillon, **18**
Place des Vosges, **9**
Royal, **13**
Sorbonne, **11**
Université, **17**
Vieux Marais, **8**

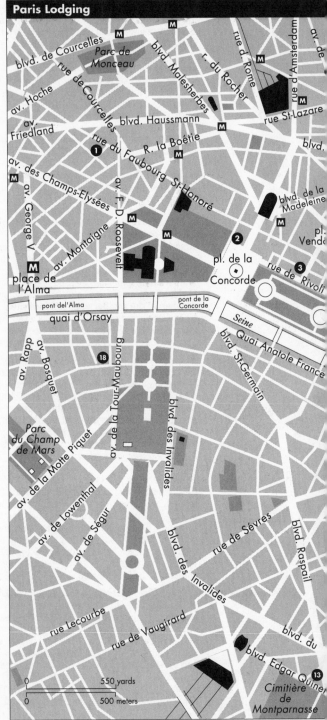

Paris Lodging

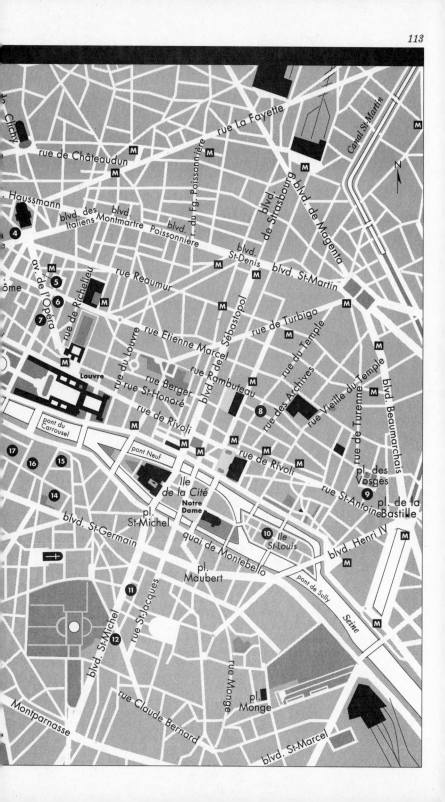

room). Not only is there a restaurant *(Le Belier)*—which is most unusual for a small Left Bank hotel—but it's one of the best in the city, offering delicate nouvelle cuisine. What's more, there's a tree growing up through the ceiling. *Le tout Paris* gathers in the bar—it stays open till 2 AM—especially when the pianist is on duty. *13 rue des Beaux-Arts, tel. 43-25-27-22. 19 rooms and suites, all with bath; 8 rooms with shower. Facilities: restaurant, bar. AE, DC, MC, V. Very Expensive.*

★ **Hôtel d'Angleterre.** Some claim the Hôtel d'Angleterre is the ultimate Left Bank hotel—a little small and shabby, but elegant and perfectly managed. The 18th-century building was originally the British ambassador's residence; later, Hemingway made it his Paris home. Room sizes and rates vary greatly, though all rooms are individually decorated. Some are imposingly formal, others are homey and plain. Ask for one overlooking the courtyard. There's no restaurant, but a small bar has been installed. *44 rue Jacob, tel. 42-60-34-72. 29 rooms with bath. Facilities: bar. AE, DC, MC, V. Expensive.*

★ **Marronniers.** There are few better places in Paris than the Marronniers for great value and atmosphere. Located on appealing rue Jacob, the hotel is reached through a small courtyard. All rooms are light and full of character. Those on the attic floor have sloping ceilings, uneven floors, and terrific views over the church of St-Germain-des-Près. The vaulted cellars have been converted into two atmospheric lounges. There's a bar but no restaurant. *21 rue Jacob, tel. 43-25-30-60. 37 rooms with bath. Facilities: bar. No credit cards. Moderate.*

7th Arrondissement **Université.** This appealingly converted 18th-century town house is located between boulevard St-Germain and the Seine. The rooms have their original fireplaces and are decorated with English and French antiques. Ask for one of the two rooms with a terrace on the sixth floor. Though there's no restaurant, you can rent the vaulted cellar for parties. Drinks and snacks are served all day in the bar or, in good weather, in the courtyard. *22 rue de l'Université, tel. 42-61-09-39. 28 rooms with bath. Facilities: bar. No credit cards. Expensive.*

Pavillon. The entrance to the family-run Pavillon lies behind a garden at the end of an alley off rue St-Dominique, guaranteeing peace and quiet. Although some rooms in this former 19th-century convent are tiny, all have been redecorated and feature Laura Ashley wallpaper and old prints. Breakfast is served in the little courtyard in summer. There's no restaurant or bar, but snacks can be served in your room. *54 rue St-Dominique, tel. 45-51-42-87. 18 rooms, most with shower. MC, V. Moderate.*

8th Arrondissement **Crillon.** There can surely be no more sumptuous a luxury hotel
★ than this regal mansion overlooking place de la Concorde. The Crillon was founded in 1909 by the champagne family Taittinger (who still run it) with the express intention of creating the best hotel in the city. They chose as their setting two adjoining town houses built by order of Louis XV. Renovations in the '80s have added comfort—all rooms are air-conditioned—though not at the expense of the original imposing interior. Mirrors, marbles, tapestries, sculptures, great sprays of flowers, and glistening floors are found in all the public rooms. The expansive bedrooms have judicious mixtures of original and re-

production antiques. The bathrooms are, of course, marble. If you want to enjoy the amazing view over place de la Concorde to the National Assembly, you'll have to reserve one of the palatial suites. Of the three restaurants, the best in *Les Ambassadeurs,* housed in what was originally the Grand Salon and offering the best hotel food in the city. *10 pl. de la Concorde, tel. 42–65–24–24. 189 rooms and suites, all with bath. Facilities: 3 restaurants, bars, private reception rooms. AE, DC, MC, V. Very Expensive.*

Bradford. The Bradford prides itself on providing slightly old-fashioned, well-polished service, in an appealing, fusty atmosphere, the kind that has the many repeat guests coming back year after year. It's no surprise that this is a family-run hotel. An old wooden elevator takes you up from the flower-filled lobby to the rooms. Some are vast, with brass beds and imposing fireplaces. None has a TV; that's not the Bradford style. Drinks are served in the soothing Louis XVI–style lounge on the first floor; there's no restaurant. *10 rue St-Philippe-du-Roule, tel. 43–59–24–20. 49 rooms with bath, 12 with shower. MC, V. Moderate.*

9th Arrondissement **Grand.** The recent restoration of the Grand's honey-colored facade put the final touches on a three-year renovation program that has transformed this 19th-century palace on place de l'Opéra. All rooms have been lavishly redecorated in Art-Nouveau style and are now air-conditioned. The hotel prides itself on its exemplary business facilities, not the least of which are its three restaurants. The *Opéra* is the most formal and imposing, while the *Relais Capucines* offers less intimidatingly grand meals; *Le Patio* serves buffet lunches and breakfast. *2 rue Scribe, tel. 42–68–12–13. 515 rooms and suites with bath. Facilities: 3 restaurants, 2 bars, 13 conference rooms, secretarial services, travel agency, shops, parking. AE, DC, MC, V. Very Expensive.*

14th Arrondissement **Royal.** This small hotel, set in a late 19th-century building on attractive boulevard Raspail, has already won much praise, especially from American guests. The mood throughout is stylish yet simple, with salmon-pink rooms and a wood-paneled, marble-floored lobby filled with plants. You can sit in the small conservatory, where drinks are served; there's no bar or restaurant. *212 blvd. Raspail, tel. 43–20–69–20. 33 rooms and suites with bath, 15 with shower. AE, MC, V. Expensive.*

The Arts and Nightlife

The Arts

The weekly magazines *Pariscope, L'Officiel des Spectacles,* and *7 à Paris,* all published on Wednesday, give detailed entertainment listings. The best place to buy tickets is at the venue itself; otherwise, try your hotel or a travel agency such as **Paris-Vison** (214 rue de Rivoli). Tickets for some events can be bought at the **FNAC** stores (there are special ticket counters in branches at 26 av. de Wagram, near the Arc de Triomphe; and at the Forum des Halles). Half-price tickets for many same-day theater performances are available at the booth next to the Madeleine church.

Theater A number of theaters line the Grands Boulevards between Opéra and République, but there is no Paris equivalent to Broadway or London's West End. Shows are mostly in French. Classical drama is performed at the **Comédie-Française** (Palais-Royal, tel. 40–15–00–15). You can reserve seats in person about two weeks in advance or turn up an hour beforehand and wait in line for returned tickets.

The only place in Paris that you're likely to find English-speaking entertainment is at **Galerie 55,** the English Theater of Paris (55 rue de Seine, 6e, tel. 43–26–63–51). Many of the plays it produces are aimed at audiences of all ages. Seat prices range from 80 francs to 100 francs for adults, 60 francs for children. Call for reservations.

Concerts Until the new Opéra de la Bastille has established itself, the **Salle Pleyel** (252 rue du Fbg. St-Honoré, tel. 45–63–88–73), near the Arc de Triomphe, remains Paris's principal home of classical music. Paris isn't as richly endowed as New York or London when it comes to orchestral music, but the city compensates with a never-ending stream of inexpensive lunchtime and evening concerts in churches. The candlelit concerts held in the **Sainte-Chapelle** are outstanding—make reservations well in advance. Notre-Dame is another church where you can combine sightseeing with good music.

Opera The **Opéra** itself (tel. 47–42–53–71) is a dramatically flamboyant hall, and, with Rudolf Nureyev as artistic director, its ballet choreography has reached new heights. But getting tickets is not always easy. The **Opéra Comique** (the French term for opera with spoken dialogue), close by (5 rue Favart, tel. 42–96–12–20), is more accessible.

The **Théâtre Musical de Paris** (place du Châtelet, tel. 42–21–00–86) offers opera and ballet for a wider audience at more reasonable prices. The **Opéra de la Bastille,** due to open early in 1990, will stage both traditional opera and symphony concerts.

Dance Apart from the traditional ballets sometimes on the bill at the Opéra, the highlights of the Paris dance year are the visits of major foreign troupes, usually to the **Palais des Congrès** at Porte Maillot (tel. 46–40–22–22) or the **Palais des Sports** at the porte de Versailles (tel. 48–28–40–48). The annual **Festival de la Danse** is staged at the **Théâtre des Champs-Elysées** on avenue Montaigne (tel. 47–39–28–26) in October.

Films There are hundreds of movie theaters in the city, and a number of them show English films. Look for the initials "V.O."—they mean original version (not dubbed). Cinema admission runs from 30 to 35 francs. There are reduced rates on Monday; programs change Wednesday. Old and rare films are often screened at the **Pompidou Center** and **Musée de Cinéma** at Trocadéro.

Nightlife

Paris's nightclubs are household names, at least among foreign tourists. Prices can range from 150 francs (simple admission plus one drink) to 500 francs (dinner plus show). For 250–350 francs, you can get a good seat plus half a bottle of champagne.

Cabaret The **Crazy Horse** (12 av. George-V, 8e, tel. 47–23–32–32) is one of the best known for pretty girls and *risqué* dance routines; lots of humor and lots less clothes.

The **Moulin Rouge** (pl. Blanche, 18e, tel. 46–06–00–19) is an old favorite at the foot of Montmartre.

Nearby is the **Folies-Bergère** (32 rue Richer, 9e, tel. 42–46–77–11), not as "in" as it once was, but still renowned for its glitter and its vocal numbers.

The **Lido** (116 bis av. des Champs-Elysées, 8e, tel. 45–63–11–61) stars the famous Bluebell Girls and tries to win you over through sheer exuberance.

Bars and Nightclubs The more upscale Paris nightclubs tend to be both expensive (1,000 francs for a bottle of gin or whisky) and private–in other words, you'll usually need to know someone who's a member to get through the door.

If **L'Apocalypse** (40 rue du Colisée, 8e) is not too full and you look sufficiently slick, you may be allowed in.

Club 79 (79 av. des Champs-Elysées, 8e) is probably the handiest bet for dancing the night away.

For a more leisurely evening in an atmosphere that's part pub, part gentleman's club, try **Harry's Bar** (5 rue Daunou, 2e), a cozy, wood-paneled hangout for Americans, journalists, and sportsmen, which still reeks with memories of Ernest Hemingway, F. Scott Fitzgerald, and Gertrude Stein.

Other places for a fun evening out include:

Caveau des Oubliettes. Traditional folk-singing and ballads are performed in a medieval cellar with Gothic arches and heavy beams. It's very popular with tourists, but still full of energetic charm. *1 rue St-Julien-le-Pauvre, 5e.*

Le Lapin Agile. This is a touristy but picturesque Montmartre setting: hard wooden benches, brandied cherries, and thumping great golden French oldies. *22 rue des Saules, 18e. Admission: 75 frs. Open 9 PM–2 AM.*

La Rôtisserie de l'Abbaye. French, English, and American folksongs are sung to the accompaniment of a guitar in a medieval setting. The action starts around 8 PM; come early or you won't get in. You can dine here, too. *22 rue Jacob, 6e. Closed Sun. Admission: 100–300 frs.*

Jazz Clubs Paris is one of the great jazz cities of the world, with plenty of variety, including some fine, distinctive local coloring. For nightly schedules, consult the specialist magazines *Jazz Hot* or *Jazz Magazine.* Remember that nothing gets going until 10 or 11 PM and that entry prices can vary widely from about 30 francs to over 100 francs.

The Latin Quarter is a good place to track down Paris jazz. The **Caveau de la Huchette** (5 rue de la Huchette, 5e) offers Dixieland in a hectic, smoke-filled atmosphere.

Le Petit Opportun (15 rue des Lavandières-Ste-Opportune, 1er) is a converted Latin Quarter bistro with a cramped, atmospheric basement that sometimes features top-flight American soloists with French rhythm sections. At street level, there is a pleasant bar with recorded music and less expensive drinks.

On the Right Bank is **New Morning** (7 rue des Petites-Ecuries, 10e), a premier venue for visiting American musicians and top French bands.

Discos   **Club Zed** (2 rue des Anglais, 5e) boasts lively dancing and some rock-only evenings.

The long-established **Balajo** (9 rue de Lappe, 11e) is crowded and lots of fun, with plenty of nostalgic '60s sounds some nights.

Les Bains (7 rue du Bourg-l'Abbé, 3e), once a public bathhouse, now specializes in New Wave music and features live music on Wednesday.

4   Ile de France

Introduction

Paris is small as capital cities go, with just under 2 million inhabitants. The Paris region, however, contains about 10 million people—almost one-fifth of France's entire population. That type of statistic conjures up visions of a gray, never-ending suburban sprawl. Nothing could be further from the truth.

The official name for the region sets the tone. "Ile de France" has a poetic ring to it; there is no island here, but the region is figuratively isolated from the rest of France by the three rivers —the Seine, Oise, and Marne—that weave majestic, meandering circles around its limits.

The juxtaposition of the broad, ambling waters of those rivers, along with a quiver of brooks and streams, both defend the area and make it lush. This precious combination has always enticed settlers; an entire country was to spring from the Ile de France fountainhead. Indeed, the kings and clerics who ruled the medieval roost refused to be sequestered in Paris: Castles and palaces went up in the towns of Vincennes, St-Germain-en-Laye, and Provins; abbeys and cathedrals sprang skywards in Chartres, Senlis, and Royaumont.

Ile de France never lost favor with the powerful, partly because its many forests—large chunks of which still stand—harbored sufficient game for even bloated, cossetted monarchs to achieve a regular kill. First Fontainebleau, in humane Renaissance proportions, then Versailles, on a minion-crushing Baroque scale, reflected the royal desire to transform hunting lodges into palatial residences.

The 17th century was a time of prodigious building in the Ile de France—a period that bequeathed a vast array of important sights to admire and explore. The château, gardens, and well-preserved town of Versailles should not be overlooked. But do not neglect Versailles's slightly lesser neighbors; Vaux-le-Vicomte, Dampierre, Rambouillet, and Chantilly would bask in superstar status anywhere else. And, after the crowds of Versailles in midsummer, you will welcome the relative tranquillity of these smaller châteaus.

The architectural impact of the 20th century is discreet in the Ile de France, and you may find it disorienting that so many rural backwaters exist within 30 minutes' drive of the capital. There is no miracle involved with this, however, just some commonsensical forethought: With the Gallic mania for centralized planning, new developments are assigned to restricted areas. Modern architecture students may find food for thought in so-called New Towns like St-Quentin-en-Yvelines (near Versailles), and sociologists won't lack material in the concrete ghettoes of the "red belt" north of Paris (so-called because its working-class population votes heavily communist), but the average visitor can comfortably avoid them.

Essential Information

Important Addresses and Numbers

Tourist Information The regional tourist office for the Ile de France (written enquiries only) is the **Comité Régional de Tourisme d'Ile de France** (101 rue de Vaugirard, 75006 Paris, tel. 42–22–74–43). Local offices are in the following towns: **Barbizon** (41 rue Grande, tel. 60–66–41–87), **Chartres** (7 Cloître Notre-Dame, tel. 16/37–21–54–03), **Fontainebleau** (31 pl. Napoléon-Bonaparte, tel. 64–22–25–68), **Rambouillet** (pl. de la Libération, tel. 34–83–21–21), and **Versailles** (7 rue des Réservoirs, tel. 39–50–36–22).

Travel Agencies **American Express** (11 rue Scribe, Paris, 9e, tel. 42–66–09–99); **Thomas Cook** (32 rue du 4 September, 2e, tel. 42–63–48–48).

Car Rental **Avis** (tel. 45–50–32–31); **Hertz** (tel. 45–51–20–37); **Budget** (tel. 42–29–50–50). All in Paris.

Arriving and Departing

By Plane Visitors to the Ile de France can arrive at either of Paris's two airports: **Charles de Gaulle** (Roissy), 25 kilometers (16 miles) northwest of the city (tel. 48–62–22–80) or **Orly,** 16 kilometers (10 miles) south (tel. 48–84–32–10).

Getting Around

By Car Although a comprehensive rail network ensures that most towns in the Ile de France can make comfortable day excursions from Paris, the only way to criss-cross the region without returning to the capital is by car. There is no shortage of expressways or fast highways, but be prepared for delays close to Paris and during the morning and evening rush hours.

By Train Many of the sights mentioned in our exploring text can be reached by train from Paris. Both regional and mainline (Le Mans-bound) trains leave the **Gare Montparnasse** for Chartres; the former also stop at Versailles, Rambouillet, and Maintenon, Gare Montparnasse is also the terminus for trains to Dreux (Granville line) and for the suburban trains that stop at Beynes, the nearest station to Thoiry.

Some mainline trains from **Gare St-Lazare** stop at Vernon and Mantes-la-Jolie on their way to Rouen and Le Havre. Mantes and Pontoise are termini for the frequent suburban trains from St-Lazare, most of which stop at Conflans-Ste-Honorine. Suburban trains leave St-Lazare for Maisons-Laffitte and Versailles, and the **Gare du Nord** for L'Isle-Adam and Beaumont-sur-Oise. Chantilly is on the main north-bound line from Gare du Nord (Senlis can be reached by bus from Chantilly) and Provins on the Swiss-bound line from **Gare de l'Est.** Fontainebleau—or, rather, neighboring Avon, 1½ miles away (there is a frequent bus service)—is 45 minutes from **Gare de Lyon.**

St-Germain-en-Laye is a terminus of the **RER-A express metro** that tunnels through Paris (main stations at Etoile, Auber, and Les Halles). The handiest of Versailles's three train stations is

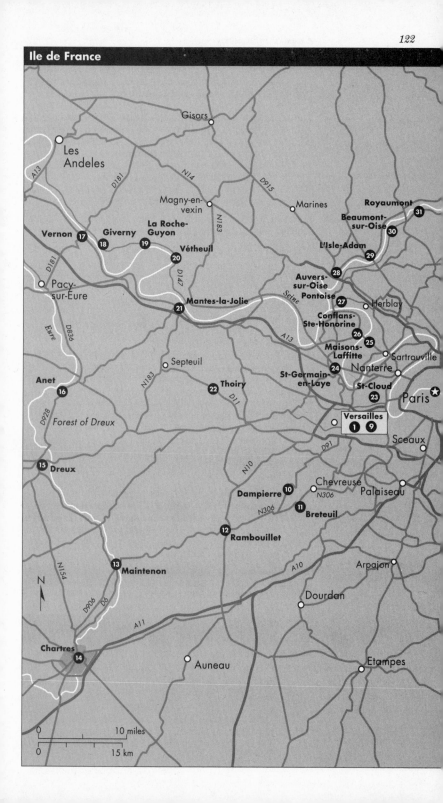

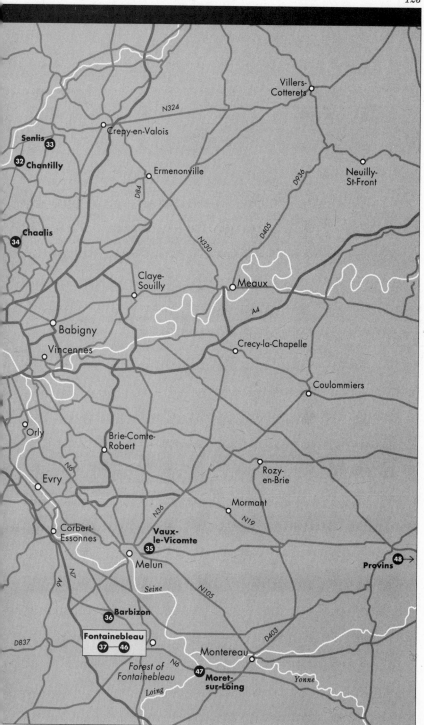

the one reached by the **RER-C** (main stations at Austerlitz, St-Michel, and Invalides).

Guided Tours

Orientation **Paris Vision** (214 rue de Rivoli, 1e, tel. 42–60–30–01) and **Cityrama** (4 pl. des Pyramides, 1e, tel. 42–60–33–54) organize guided visits to a number of sites in the Ile de France region, departing Paris from the place des Pyramides (off rue de Rivoli at the Louvre end of the Tuileries Gardens). Both run half-day trips to Chartres on Tuesday and Saturday afternoons (180 francs), full-day trips to Chartres plus Versailles (290 francs), and half-day trips to Fontainebleau and Barbizon (departures 1:30 Wednesday, Friday, and Sunday; price 195 francs).

Guided excursions to Giverny are organized by **American Express** (11 rue Scribe, 9e, tel. 42–66–09–99) and the **RATP** (Paris Transport Authority): either half-day or full-day when combined with Rouen. The RATP also has guide-accompanied excursions in and around Paris. Inquire at its Tourist Service on the place de la Madeleine (8e, to the right of the church as you face it) or at its office (53 quai des Grands-Augustins, 6e); both are open daily.

Personal Guides For touring in style, get in touch with **International Limousines** (182 blvd. Péreire, 17e, tel. 45–74–77–12). Guides with luxury cars or minibus (taking up to seven passengers) will take you around Paris or the surrounding area for a minimum of three hours for around 200 francs an hour (though call to check details and prices). Advance reservations are obligatory.

Exploring the Ile de France

Numbers in the margin correspond with points of interest on the Ile de France map.

Orientation

Our three tours take you southeast to Fontainebleau, north to Chantilly, and west—the most favored point on the regional touring compass—to Versailles, Chartres, and Giverny. We have occasionally transgressed the administrative limits of Ile de France along the way: Bear in mind that phone numbers in several of the towns—Chartres, Dreux, Giverny, Chantilly, and Senlis—must be prefixed by "16" when you dial from Paris (where applicable, we have included the code). Though they are within striking distance of Paris, the towns of Reims, Laon, Compiègne, and Beauvais are officially part of northern France, and are described in that chapter.

Highlights for First-time Visitors

Chartres Cathedral, Tour 1
Château of Chantilly, Tour 2
Château of Fontainebleau, Tour 3
Claude Monet's house and gardens at Giverny, Tour 1
Château of Vaux-le-Vicomte, Tour 3
Château and gardens of Versailles, Tour 1

Tour 1: West to Versailles, Chartres, Giverny, and Thoiry

No visit to Paris is complete without an excursion to Versailles —easy to get to either by train (*see* Getting Around, above) or car (A13 expressway from Porte d'Auteuil) in about 25 minutes. On this tour, however, Versailles is only the starting point for a trip through the west of the Ile de France, a region of forests, wheat fields, lush valleys, and imposing châteaus.

If, after days of museum lines and crowded métros, you feel a sense of escape as you leave Paris, you won't be the first. Back in the 17th century, Louis XIV, the Sun King, was barely out of his teens when he began to cast his cantankerous royal eye over the Ile de France in search of a new power base. Marshy, inhospitable **Versailles**, 24 kilometers (15 miles) to the west of Paris, was the place of his dreams. Down came its modest royal hunting lodge and up, up, and along went the new château.

Today, the **château** of Versailles seems outrageously big—but it wasn't big enough for the sycophantic army of 20,000 noblemen, servants, and hangers-on who moved in with Louis. A new capital had to be constructed from scratch. Tough-thinking town planners dreamed up vast Baroque mansions and avenues broader than the Champs-Elysées.

It is hardly surprising that Louis XIV's successors soon felt out of sync with their architectural inheritance. Louis XV, who inherited the throne from the Sun King in 1715, transformed the royal apartments into places to live in rather than to pose. The unfortunate Louis XVI—reigning monarch at the time of the French Revolution and subsequent Terror—cowered at the Petit Trianon in the leafy depths of Versailles park, well out of the mighty château's shadow. His queen, Marie Antoinette, lost her head well before her trip to the guillotine in 1793, by pretending to be a peasant shepherdess playing amid the ersatz rusticity of her cute hamlet.

The château was built by French architects Louis Le Vau and François Mansart between 1662 and 1690. Enter through the gilt iron gates from the huge place d'Armes. On the first floor of the château, right in the middle as you approach across the sprawling cobbled forecourt, is Louis XIV's bedchamber. The two wings were occupied by the royal children and princes of the blood, with courtiers making do in the attics.

The highlight for many on the guided tour of the palace is the **Galerie des Glaces** (Hall of Mirrors), fully restored to sparkling glory. It was here, after France's capitulation, that Prince Otto von Bismarck proclaimed the unified German Empire in 1871, and here, too, that the controversial Treaty of Versailles, asserting Germany's responsibility for World War I, was signed in 1919.

The **Grands Apartements** (State Rooms) that flank the Hall of Mirrors retain much of their original Baroque decoration: gilt stucco, painted ceilings, and marble sculpture. Perhaps the most extravagant of these rooms is the **Salon d'Apollon,** the former throne room, dedicated to the sun god Apollo, Louis XIV's mythical hero. Equally interesting are the **Petits Apartements,** where the royal family and friends lived in (relative) intimacy.

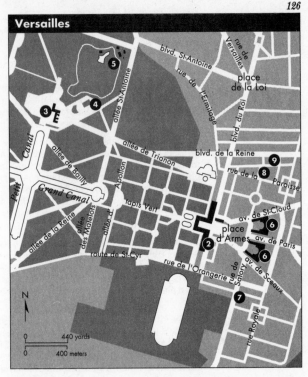

In the north wing of the château can be found the solemn white-and-gold **chapel,** designed by François Mansart and completed in 1710; the miniature **opera house,** the first oval room in France, built by J. A. Gabriel for Louis XV in 1770; and, connecting the two, the 17th-century **Galleries,** with exhibits retracing the château's history. The south wing contains the wide, lengthy **Galerie des Batailles** (Gallery of Battles), lined with gigantic canvases extolling French glory. *Admission: 23 frs. adults, 12 frs. students and senior citizens. Open Tues.– Sun. 10–5; closed Mon.*

After the awesome feast of interior decor, the **park** outside is an ideal place to catch your breath. The gardens were designed by the French landscape architect Le Nôtre, whose work here represents formal French landscaping at its most rigid and sophisticated. The 250-acre grounds include woods, lawns, flower beds, statues, artificial lakes, and fountains galore. They are at their golden-leafed best in the fall, but enticing also in summer —especially on those Sundays when the fountains are in full flow. They become a spectacle of rare grandeur during the **Fêtes de Nuit** floodlighting and firework shows held in July and September. *The grounds are free and open daily. Tel. 39–50– 36–22 for details of the fountains and Fêtes de Nuit.*

If you wander too far into the park woods you can easily get lost. Follow signs to skirt the numerous basins (or ponds) until you reach the **Grand Canal.** Move down the right bank, along gravelly paths beneath high-plinthed statues, until you discover that the canal is in the form of a cross—with two smaller arms known as the **Petit Canal.** At the crossing, bear right toward the Grand Trianon (in all, about a mile from the château).

③ The **Grand Trianon,** built by Mansart in 1687, is a scaled-down, pink-marble pleasure palace now used to entertain visiting heads of state. When there aren't any of them, it's open for visitors to admire its lavish interior and early 19th-century furniture. *Admission: 15 frs. adults, 8 frs. students and seniors; joint ticket for the two Trianons 18 frs. (9 frs. students and senior citizens). Open Tues.–Sun. 10–noon and 2–5; closed Mon.*

④ The **Petit Trianon,** close by, was built by architect Gabriel in the mid-18th century. It is a mansion, not a palace, and modest by Versailles standards—though still sumptuously furnished. It contains mementoes of its most illustrious inhabitant, Marie Antoinette. Look for her initials wrought into the iron railings of the main staircase.

Beyond the Petit Trianon, across the Petit Lac that looks more like a stream as it describes a wriggly semicircle, is the queen's **⑤** so-called hamlet (**Hameau**). With its watermill, genuine lake (Grand Lac), and pigeon loft, this phoney village is outrageously pretty; it was here that Marie Antoinette lived out her romanticized dreams of peasant life. *Admission: 10 frs. adults, 5 frs. students and senior citizens; joint ticket for the two Trianons 18 frs. (9 frs. students and seniors). Open Tues.– Sun. 2–5; closed Mon.*

The town of Versailles is attractive, and its spacious, leafy boulevards make agreeable places to stroll. Facing the château are **⑥** the **royal stables,** buildings of regal dimensions and appearance. Take avenue de Sceaux, to the right, and turn right again along **⑦** rue de Satory, which leads to the **Cathédrale St-Louis,** an austere edifice built between 1743 and 1754 by Mansart's grandson, with notable paintings and an organ loft.

Turn right out of the cathedral, then left down avenue Thiers, which cuts through the town's three major boulevards— avenues de Sceaux, de Paris, and de St-Cloud—to the ancient market square, where rue de la Paroisse heads left to the **⑧** **Eglise Notre-Dame.** This sturdy Baroque monument was built from 1684 to 1686 by Mansart (and is, therefore, older than the cathedral) as parish church for the Sun King's new town. Louis XIV himself laid the foundation stone.

Behind the church, in an imposing 18th-century mansion on **⑨** boulevard de la Reine, is the **Musée Lambinet,** a museum with a wide-ranging collection—a maze of cozy, finely furnished rooms replete with paintings, weapons, fans, and porcelain. *54 blvd. de la Reine. Admission free. Open Tues.–Sun. 2–6; closed Mon.*

The fast N10 heads down from Versailles to another famous château town—Rambouillet (*see below*). But, if you're in no rush, take the attractive D91 south from Versailles through the glades and folds of the Chevreuse Valley to the unspoiled vil- **⑩** lage of **Dampierre,** 18 kilometers (11 miles) away.

The **château** of Dampierre is a handsome, stone-and-brick structure, surrounded by a moat and set 100 yards back from the road behind 18th-century iron railings. Rebuilt in the 1670s by Mansart for the Duc de Luynes, it is still the family seat. Much of the interior has kept its 17th-century decoration—portraits, wood-paneling, furniture, and works of art. But the main staircase, with its trompe-l'oeil murals, and the richly gilded Salle des Fêtes date from the last century. The Salle des Fêtes, on the second floor, contains a huge wall painting by the celebrated artist Jean Auguste Ingres (1780–1867): a mythical evocation of the Age d'Or (Golden Age). The large park was designed by Le Nôtre. *Admission: 32 frs. adults, 24 frs. children and senior citizens. Open Apr.–Oct., daily 2–6:30; closed Nov. –Mar.*

From Dampierre take D58 (signposted to Chevreuse) for 2½ kilometers (1½ miles) before forking off toward N306. A couple of miles farther south (follow signs), close to the village of Choisel, is the steep-roofed château of **Breteuil**. Like the Luynes of Dampierre, the Breteuil family have owned and lived in their château since the early 17th century. And, like the Panouses of Thoiry (*see* below), they have been innovative in their attempts to woo visitors: Life-size wax figures—including the English Queen Victoria's son King Edward VII and one-time guest Marcel Proust, the French novelist (1871–1922)—lurk in many of the rooms.

Interior highlights range from Swedish porcelain to Gobelins tapestries and a richly inlaid Teschen table, encrusted with pearls and precious stones—an 18th-century present to the Breteuils from Austrian Empress Maria Theresa. The basement kitchens contain a gleaming array of copper pots and pewterware, while the vast wooded park boasts picnic areas and playgrounds. *Admission (château): 37 frs. adults, 25 frs. children and seniors. Admission (grounds): 17 frs. adults, 12 frs. children and seniors. Château open daily 2:30–5:30; grounds open daily 11–5:30.*

Get back onto N306 and head southwest to **Rambouillet**, 14 kilometers (9 miles) away. Surrounded by a huge forest, Rambouillet is a haughty town, once favored by kings and dukes. Today, it is home to affluent gentry and, occasionally, President Mitterrand. When the president is not entertaining visiting big-wigs, the château and its grounds are open to all.

Leave your car in the spacious parking lot next to the **Hôtel de Ville** (town hall), an imposing Classical building in red brick, and wander around the corner to the **château**. Most of the buildings you see date from the early 18th century, but the muscular **Tour François I** (Tower of François I), named after the king who breathed his last therein in 1547, once belonged to a 14th-century castle. *Admission: 6 frs. Open Thurs.–Mon. 10–noon and 2–6; closed Tues. and Wed.*

If your appetite for château interiors has already been satisfied, you may forgo Rambouillet's without too guilty a conscience. The château's exterior charms are hidden as you arrive, but if you head to the left of the buildings—and if nature is in bloom—you are in for two pleasant surprises. A splendid lake, with several enticing islands, spreads out for you, beckoning you to explore the extensive grounds beyond. Before you do, however, turn around: There, behind you, across trim flower beds awash with color, is the facade of the château—a sight of unsuspected serenity, asymmetry, and, as more flowers spill from its balconies, cheerful informality.

If time allows, veer left around the lake and carry on until you reach two interesting groups of outbuildings: the **Laiterie de la Reine** (built as a dairy for Marie Antoinette), with its small temple, grotto, and shell-lined **Chaumière des Coquillages** (Shell Pavilion); and the **Bergerie Nationale** (National Sheepfold), site of a more serious agricultural venture; the merino sheep reared here, prized for the quality and yield of their wool, are descendants of beasts experimentally imported from Spain by Louis XVI way back in 1786. *Admission: 9 frs. Laiterie open Jan.–Apr., Thurs.–Mon. 10–noon and 2–6; May–Nov., 10–noon and 2–4; closed Dec. and Tues., Wed. The Bergerie can be visited Sept.–June, Sun. only 2:30–5:30.*

⑬ D906 links Rambouillet to the town of **Maintenon**, 24 kilometers (15 miles) west. The Renaissance **château** of Maintenon once belonged to Louis XIV's mistress, Madame de Maintenon, whose private apartments form the hub of the short interior visit. A round brick tower (14th century) and a 12th-century keep are all that remain of the buildings on the site. The formal gardens ease their way back from the château to the unlikely ivory-covered arches of a ruined aqueduct, one of the Sun King's most outrageous projects. His aim: to provide Versailles (some 50 kilometers/30 miles away) with water from the River Eure. In 1684, 30,000 men were signed up to construct a three-tiered, 3-mile aqueduct as part of the project. Many died of fever in the process, and construction was called off in 1688. *Admission: 22 frs. Open Easter–Oct., Wed.–Sat. 2:30–6, Sun. 10–noon and 2:30–6, closed Tues.; Nov.–Easter, Sat. 2:30–6, Sun. 10–noon and 2:30–6, closed weekdays.*

⑭ The River Eure, accompanied by picturesque D6, snakes southwest from Maintenon to **Chartres**, 19 kilometers (12 miles) away. Try to spot the noble, soaring spires of **Chartres Cathedral** before you reach the town; they are one of the most famous sights in western Europe.

Worship on the site of the cathedral goes back to before the Gallo-Roman period; the crypt contains a well that was the focus of Druid ceremonies. In the late ninth century, Charles II (known as the Bald) presented Chartres with what was believed to be the tunic of the Virgin, a precious relic that attracted hordes of pilgrims. Chartres swiftly became a prime destination for the Christian faithful; pilgrims trek here from Paris to this day.

Today's cathedral mainly dates from the 12th and 13th centuries, having been built after the previous 11th-century edifice burned down in 1194. A well-chronicled outburst of religious fervor followed the discovery that the Virgin's relic had miraculously survived unsinged, and reconstruction moved ahead at breaktaking pace: Just 25 years were needed for the cathedral to rise from the rubble.

The lower half of the facade is a survivor of the earlier Romanesque church: This can be seen most clearly in the use of round arches, rather than the pointed Gothic type. The main door (**Portail Royal**) is richly sculpted with scenes from the Life of Christ, and the flanking towers are also Romanesque. The taller of the two spires (380 feet versus 350 feet) dates from the start of the 16th century; its fanciful Flamboyant intricacy contrasts sharply with the stumpy solemnity of its Romanesque counterpart across the way.

The **rose window** above the main portal dates from the 13th century, while the three windows below it contain some of the finest examples of 12th-century stained glass in France.

The interior is somber, and your eyes will need time to get used to the murk. Their reward: the gemlike richness of the stained glass, with the famous deep "Chartres blue" predominating. The oldest window is arguably the most beautiful: **Notre Dame de la Belle Verrière,** in the south choir. *Pl. Notre-Dame.*

Just behind the cathedral stands the **Musée des Beaux-Arts** (Museum of Fine Arts), a handsome 18th-century building that used to be the Bishop's Palace. Its varied collection includes Renaissance enamels; a portrait of the Dutch scholar Erasmus by German painter Hans Holbein; tapestries; armor; and some fine, mainly French paintings dating from the 17th to the 19th century. There is also an entire room devoted to the forceful 20th-century land- and snowscapes of Maurice de Vlaminck, who lived in the region. *29 cloître Notre-Dame. Admission: 6 frs. adults, 3 frs. students and senior citizens. Open Wed.– Mon. 10–11:45 and 2–5:45; closed Tues.*

The **museum gardens** overlook the old streets that tumble down to the River Eure. Take rue Chantault down to the river, cross over and head right along rue de la Tannerie (which, in turn, becomes rue de la Foulerie) as far as rue du Pont St-Hilaire. From here, there is a picturesque view of the roofs of old Chartres nestling beneath the cathedral. Cross over the bridge and head up to the **Eglise St-Pierre,** whose magnificent windows date back to the early 14th century. There is more stained glass (17th century) to admire at the **Eglise St-Aignan** nearby, just off the rue St-Pierre. Wander at will among the steep, narrow surrounding streets, using the spires of the cathedral as your guiding landmark.

⑮ Thirty-two kilometers (20 miles) northwest of Chartres (via N154) is the charming and ancient town of **Dreux**. The downtown area has several old houses and monuments, notably the **Eglise St-Pierre** on place Métézeau, and the **Beffroi** (Belfry) just across the road. St-Pierre, an interesting jumble of styles with good stained glass and a 17th-century organ loft, presents a curious silhouette, with its unfinished Classical towers, cut off in mid-column. The Beffroi, standing at one end of a lively shopping square, is a hefty tower built 1512–31; there is a fine view from the top. *Pl. Métézeau. Admission: 2 frs. Open Wed., Fri.–Mon. 10–11:30 and 2–5; closed Tues. and Thurs.*

Dreux was a prosperous place in the 16th century—it was awarded the title of Royal Borough in 1556—but the early 19th century conferred lasting glory on the town. In 1816, the Orléans family, France's ruling house from 1830 to 1848, began the construction of a chapel-mausoleum on the hill behind the center of town. The circular chapel, known as the **Chapelle Royale de St-Louis,** is built in sugary but not unappealing neo-Gothic: Superficial ornament rather than structure recalls the medieval style. Unfortunately, the sumptuously decorated interior can be visited only with a French-speaking guide, but no linguistic explanations are needed to prompt wonder at either the Sèvres-manufactured "stained glass"—thin layers of glass, coated with painted enamel (an extremely rare, fragile, and vivid technique)—or the funereal statuary. There may be morbid sentimentality about some of the tombs—an imploring hand reaching through a window to a loved one, or an infant wrapped in a cloak of transparent gauze—but their technical skill and compositional drama belie sculpture's reputation as one of the fustier visual arts. *Rue de Billy. Admission: 18 frs. Open daily 9–11:30 and 2–5 (4 in winter).*

D928 runs straight through the **Forest of Dreux** to the tiny village of **Anet**, 16 kilometers (10 miles) to the north. Only picturesque ruins now remain of what was reputedly the finest **château** of the French Renaissance, begun in 1548 for Henri II's mistress Diane de Poitiers. Her bedchamber can be visited in the Left Wing, the finest surviving building with its 17th-century **Escalier d'Honneur** (Grand Staircase) and tapestries in the **Salle des Gardes** (Guard Room), depicting the adventures of the Huntress Diana. The chapel is of note, thanks to its 16th-century dome, one of the earliest in France. *Admission: 18 frs. Open Easter–Oct., Mon., Wed.–Sat. 2–6:30, Sun. 10–11:30 and 2–6:30, closed Tues.; Nov.–Easter., Sat. 2–5, Sun. 10–11:30 and 2–5, closed weekdays.*

From Anet, keep to the road that winds along the River Eure (D836), and follow signs north to Pacy-sur-Eure, 24 kilometers (15 miles) away. Here D181 heads off to the pleasant old town of **Vernon**, 13 kilometers (eight miles) distant. Together with its pleasant riverside location on the Seine, Vernon boasts several medieval timber-frame houses; the best of which has been chosen by local authorities to house the Tourist Office, in rue Carnot. Alongside is the arresting rose-windowed facade of **Notre-Dame** church. The facade, like the high nave, dates from the 15th century, but the rounded Romanesque arches in the choir attest to the building's 12th-century origins. The church is a fine sight when viewed from behind—Impressionist painter Claude Monet painted it several times from across the Seine.

A few minor Monet canvases, along with other late 19th-century paintings, can be admired in the **Musée Poulain** (Town Museum) at the other end of rue Carnot. This rambling old mansion is seldom crowded, and the helpful curators are happy to explain local history to visitors who are intrigued by the town's English-sounding name. *Rue du Pont. Admission: 5 frs. (free Wed.). Open Tues.–Sun. 2–5:30; closed Mon.*

Most people stop off at Vernon simply because of its proximity to the village of **Giverny** across the Seine (turn right along D5 after the bridge). A place of pilgrimage for art lovers, it was here that Claude Monet lived for the second half of his life and died in 1926 at age 86. After decades of neglect, his pretty pink-washed house, with its green shutters, studios, and, above all, the wonderful garden with its famous lily pond, have been lovingly restored.

Monet was brought up in Normandy, in northwestern France, and, like many of the Impressionists, was stimulated by the soft light of the Seine Valley. After several years at Argenteuil, just north of Paris, he moved downriver to Giverny in 1883, along with his two sons, mistress Alice Hoschedé (whom he later married), and her own six children. By 1890, a prospering Monet was able to buy the house outright; three years later, he purchased another plot of land across the road to continue his gardening experiments, diverting the little River Epte to make a pond.

Soon the much-loved and oft-painted waterlilies and Japanese bridges were special features of Monet's garden. They readily conjure up the image of the grizzle-bearded brushman dabbing cheerfully at his virgin canvas—pioneering a breakup of form that was to have a major impact on 20th-century art.

Provided you steer clear of the tourist battalions that tramp through Giverny on weekends and hot summer days, Monet's house—which you enter from the modest country lane that masquerades as Giverny's major thoroughfare—feels refreshingly like a family home after the formal French châteaus. The rooms have been restored to Monet's original designs: the kitchen with its blue tiles, the buttercup-yellow dining room, Monet's bedroom containing his bed and desk. Walls are lined with the Japanese prints Monet avidly collected, as well as with reproductions of his works.

The exuberant **garden** breaks totally with French tradition, with flowers spilling over the paths. You can reach the enchanting **water garden**, with its lilies, bridges, mighty willow, and rhododendrons, via an attractively decorated tunnel. *84 rue Claude-Monet. Admission: 25 frs. (garden only, 15 frs.). Open Apr.–Oct., Tues.–Sun. 10–noon and 2–6 (garden open 10–6); closed Mon. and Nov.–Mar.*

South of Giverny, the French road network has difficulty matching the extravagant bends of the meandering Seine. If you follow the signs to Mantes, you will next encounter the river at the charming village of **La Roche-Guyon**, dominated by chalky cliffs and its Classical **château** (not open to the public).

A few miles farther on, just after the tumbling village of **Vétheuil**, with its **12th-century church**, the road (now D147) again abandons the riverbank until it reaches prettily named **Mantes-la-Jolie**, these days a sullen suburban town but once favored by 19th-century landscape artist Camille Corot. Corot would set up his easel within sight of the town's principal attraction, the 12th-century church of **Notre-Dame.** The small, circular windows that ring the east end are a rare local characteristic; you may have noticed them at the church of nearby Vétheuil.

N183 runs 13 kilometers (8 miles) south of Mantes to Septeuil, where we suggest you head east along D11 (follow signs to Versailles) to **Thoiry**, 9 kilometers (5½ miles) away.

The **château** of Thoiry, just 40 kilometers (25 miles) west of Paris, makes an excellent day outing in its own right, especially if you are traveling with children. Owners Vicomte de la Panouse and his glamorous American wife Annabelle have restored the château and park to former glory, opening both to the public. The result is a splendid combination of history, culture, and adventure. The superbly furnished 16th-century château has archive and gastronomy museums and overlooks a safari park, where you can picnic with the bears and lions.

The château was built in 1564. Its handsome Renaissance facade is set off by gardens landscaped in typically disciplined French fashion by Le Nôtre. The discipline has unexpected justification: The château is positioned to be directly in line with the sun as it rises in the east at the winter solstice (December 21) and as it sets in the west at the summer solstice (June 21). To heighten the effect, the central part of the château appears to be a transparent arch of light, thanks to its huge glass doors and windows.

The viscountess is a keen gardener and enjoys experimenting in the less-formal **Jardin à l'Anglaise** (English Garden), and in her late-flowering **Autumn Garden.** Visitors are allowed to wander at leisure, although few dare stray from the official footpath through the **animal reserve!** Note that those parts of the reserve containing the wilder beasts—deer, zebra, camels, hippos, bears, elephants, and lions—can be visited only by car.

The reserve hit the headlines when the first ever ligrons—a cross between a lion and a tiger—were born here a few years ago. These new-look beasts (bigger than either a lion or a tiger) are now into their second generation and can be seen from the safety of a raised footbridge in the **Tiger Park.** Nearby, as emus and flamingoes stalk in search of tidbits, there is a **children's play area** that features an Enchanted Burrow to wriggle through and huge netted Cobweb to bounce around in.

Highlights of the château's interior include the **Grand Staircase,** with its 18th-century Gobelins tapestries, and the **Green and White Salons,** with their old, painted harpsichord, portraits, and tapestries. There is an authentic, homey, faintly faded charm to these rooms, especially when log fires crackle in their enormous hearths on damp afternoons.

The distinguished history of the Panouse family—a Comte César even fought in the American Revolutionary War—is retraced in the **Archive Museum,** where papal bulls, Napoleonic letters, and Chopin manuscripts (discovered in the attic in 1973) mingle with missives from Thomas Jefferson and Benjamin Franklin.

The château pantries house a **Museum of Gastronomy,** whose tempting display of *pièces montées*—virtuoso banquet showpieces—re-create the designs of ace 19th-century chef Antoine Carême. Early recipe books, engravings, and old copper pots are also displayed. *Admission: château 25 frs.; animal reserve 58 frs. adults, 49 frs. children; gardens 44 frs. adults, 38 frs. children. Joint ticket for château, reserve, and gardens: 80 frs. adults, 71 frs. children. Open weekdays 10–6, weekends 10–6:30.*

Time Out The **self-service restaurant** at Thoiry is housed in the converted 16th-century château stables. You can break here for a snack or an inexpensive set-menu lunch before attacking the ligrons and other wild beasts. *Open same hours as the Safari Park.*

From Thoiry, get onto D11 once again, and follow the signs back to Paris.

Tour 2: North to St-Germain-en-Laye and Chantilly

Although this second Ile de France tour explores the north of the region, we suggest you again leave Paris by the A13 (Rouen-bound) expressway from Porte d'Auteuil. A spectacular curving bridge soon whisks you across the Seine, past the **㉓** chic suburb of **St-Cloud.** To the right are the steep streets of the old town, pierced by a church spire; to the left, the tumbling wooded St-Cloud Park, once the site of the favorite palace of Napoleon's nephew, Napoleon III; it was burned down by invading Prussians in 1870. Only the ground plan of the former buildings and the imposing, tiered waterfall known as the **Grande Cascade** (designed by architect Jules Hardouin-Mansart, François Mansart's grand-nephew, in the 17th century), now remain. The park commands fine views of Paris and, with its grassy expanses and broad, wooded paths, is a delightful place for walks. The château's history and architecture are retraced in the **Musée Historique** (Historical Museum) by the ceremonial gates (Grille d'Honneur) of the main entrance. *Admission free. Grounds open daily 7 AM–9 PM. Museum open Easter–mid-Nov., Wed. and weekends 2–6; mid-Nov.–Easter 2–5; closed Mon., Tues., Thurs., and Fri.*

Just after St-Cloud, A13 veers right through a depressingly long, dirty tiled tunnel, emerging into a corridor of tall evergreens that lasts several miles. Instead of continuing to Versailles, take the N186 exit just beforehand, sign posted to St-Germain-en-Laye, a further 5 kilometers (3 miles) away.

㉔ The elegant town of **St-Germain-en-Laye**, perched on a hill above the Seine and encircled by forest, has lost little of its original cachet, despite the invasion of wealthy Parisians who commute to work on the RER (the regional express train that puts St-Germain just 30 minutes from the capital). Next to the train station, at the heart of St-Germain, is the town's chief attraction; its stone-and-brick **château.**

Most of the defensive-looking château, with its dry moat and intimidating circular towers, dates from the 16th and 17th centuries. Yet a royal palace has existed here since the early 12th century, when Louis VI—known as *Le Gros* (The Fat)—exploited St-Germain's defensive potential in his bid to pacify the Ile de France. A hundred years later, Louis IX (St-Louis) added the elegant **Sainte-Chapelle,** which is the château's oldest remaining section. The figures on the tympanum (the inset triangular area over the main door) are believed to be the first known representations of French royalty, portraying Louis with his mother, Blanche de Castille, and other members of his family.

Charles V (1364–80) built a powerful defensive keep in the mid-14th century, but from the 1540s, François I and his successors transformed St-Germain into a palace of more domestic and less warlike, vocation. Until 1682—when the court moved to Versailles—it remained the country's foremost royal residence outside Paris. Ever since 1867, the château has housed a major **Musée des Antiquités National** (Museum of Ancient History), holding a trove of artifacts, figurines, brooches, and weapons from the Stone Age through to the eighth century. *Admission: 15 frs. (8 frs. on Sun.). Open Wed.–Mon. 9:45–noon and 1:30–5:15; closed Tues.*

Another place to visit in St-Germain is the tranquil **Musée du Prieuré** (Priory Museum), some 600 yards from the château (follow rue au Pain from the church). This museum is devoted to the work of the artist Maurice Denis (1870–1943) and his fellow Nabis—painters opposed to the naturalism of their 19th-century Impressionist contemporaries. Denis found the calm of the former Jesuit priory suited to his spiritual themes, which he expressed in stained glass, ceramics, and mosaics, as well as oils. *2 bis rue Maurice-Denis. Admission: 20 frs. adults, 10 frs.*

children and senior citizens. Open Wed.–Fri. 10–5:30, week-ends 10–6:30; closed Mon. and Tues.

Six and a half kilometers (4 miles) north of St-Germain along the River Seine, via D157, is the town of **Maisons-Laffitte**. The early Baroque **château** of Maisons, constructed by architect François Mansart from 1642 to 1651, is one of the least known châteaus in the Ile de France. This was not always the case: Sun King Louis XIV came to the housewarming party, and Louis XV (1715–74), Louis XVI (Marie Antoinette's husband, 1774–92), the 18th-century writer Voltaire, and Napoleon all stayed here. The interior clearly met their exacting standards, thanks to the well-proportioned entrance vestibule with its rich sculpture; the winding **Escalier d'Honneur**, a majestic staircase adorned with paintings and statues; and the royal apartments, above, with their parquetry floors and elegant wall paneling. *Admission: 22 frs. adults, 12 frs. students and senior citizens. Open Sun. 2:30–6, Mon., Wed.–Sat. 9–noon and 2:30–6, Tues. 2:30–6.*

Cross the bridge that links Maisons-Laffitte to Sartrouville and take the first left along the banks of the Seine. Parts of this river road, particularly at the neighboring town of La Frette, retain surprising pastoral charm, given the proximity of the industrial suburbs. At Herblay, the road leaves the river; head up through the housing development to the main road and turn left for Conflans, a couple of miles away.

The town of **Conflans-Sainte-Honorine,** 32 kilometers (20 miles) northwest of Paris, reflects the importance of waterways to the Ile de France region. Boats and barges arrive from as far afield as the ports of Le Havre and DunKerque, on France's northern coast, and are often moored up to six-abreast along the mile-long quayside, near the *conflans* (confluence, and hence the town's name) of the rivers Seine and Oise. The **Musée de la Batellerie** (Boat Museum), next to an old church high above the river, explains the historic role of the barges and waterways with the help of its collection of pictures and scale models. *Admission: free. Open Easter–Oct., weekdays 9–noon and 1:30–6 (closed Tues. AM), weekends 3–6; Nov.–Easter, weekdays 9–noon (except Tues.) and 1:30–5, weekends 2–5.*

The road that crosses the Seine at Conflans continues 8 kilometers (5 miles) north toward **Pontoise,** a pleasant old town on the banks of the Oise. One of the town's most illustrious past residents was Impressionist painter Camille Pissarro (1830–1903). Pissarro is the hero of a small **museum** in rue du Château, close to the Hôtel de Ville (Town Hall) and 12th-century **Cathedral of St-Maclou** up in the old town. *Admission: free. Open Wed.–Sun. 2–6; closed Mon. and Tues.*

The tranquil Oise Valley, which runs northeast from Pontoise, retains much of the charm that attracted Pissarro and other Impressionists to this area a century ago. Pissarro, Paul Cézanne, and Vincent van Gogh all worked at the town of **Auvers-sur-Oise,** 6½ kilometers (4 miles) from Pontoise along D4. Van Gogh—whose vibrant *Irises* sold for a record $49 million in November 1987—eked out the last few penniless months of his life in Auvers before committing suicide in a nearby field in July 1890. He lived above what was then a café (at 52 rue du Général-de-Gaulle), and is buried, along with his devoted brother Theo, in the cemetery above the church he made famous in one of his most powerful paintings, *The Church at Auvers* (now at the Musée d'Orsay in Paris). Stop in at the Auvers tourist office, which is a mine of information on the activity of Van Gogh and other painters in the area. *Office de Tourisme, rue de la Sansonne, tel. 30–36–10–06. Open daily 10–noon and 2–6.*

② Six and a half kilometers (4 miles) upstream from Auvers, across the bridge at Parmain, is residentially exclusive **L'Isle-Adam,** one of the most picturesque towns in the entire Ile de France. Paris lies just 25 miles south, but it could be 100 miles and as many years away. There is a sandy **beach** along one stretch of the River Oise and an unassuming local museum, the **Musée Louis Senlecq,** in the main street, which often stages painting exhibitions. *46 Grand Rue. Admission free. Open Apr.–Nov., weekends and Mon. 2–5:30; closed Tues.–Sat.*

③ From L'Isle-Adam, take N322/D922 to the small hilltop town of **Beaumont-sur-Oise**—worth a quick peek if only for its attractive old 12th–13th-century **church of St-Laurent,** transformed into a cathedral by 19th-century French writer Émile Zola as the setting for his romantic novel *Le Rêve* (The Dream). From Beaumont, take D922 to Viarmes, then turn left along D909 to **③** the Cistercian Abbey of **Royaumont,** 2½ kilometers (1½ miles) away. The abbey was founded by the only canonized French King, Louis IX, known as St-Louis, in 1228; five of his eleven children are buried here. Only part of the abbey church still stands (the south transept), which can be visited, along with the ivy-clad cloisters, the refectory where St-Louis served the monks, and the vaulted kitchens. The monks' dormitories, chapter-house, and library are now part of an international cultural center, and are rarely open to the public (tel. 30–35–88–90 for details of the concerts held here in summer). *Admission: 14 frs. Open Easter–Oct., Wed.–Mon. 10–noon and 2–5, closed Tues.; Nov.–Easter, Sun. only, 10–noon and 2–5.*

③ Ten kilometers (6 miles) northeast via D909 lies the town of **Chantilly,** with its haughty, spacious, golden-stoned **château,** sitting snugly behind an artificial, carp-stocked lake. Despite appearances, much of the current building is not old but 19th-century Renaissance pastiche, rebuilt in the 1870s. The lavish interior contains the outstanding **Condé Collection** of illuminated medieval manuscripts, tapestries, furniture, and paintings. The most famous room, the **Santuario,** boasts two celebrated works by Italian master Raphael (1483–1520)—the *Three Ages of Woman* and *The Orleans Virgin*—plus an exquisite ensemble of 15th-century miniatures by the most illustrious French painter of his time, Jean Fouquet (1420–81). Farther on, in the Cabinet des Livres, is the **Book of Hours** of the Duc de Berri, one of the finest medieval manuscripts.

Other highlights of this unusual museum are the **Galérie de Psyché,** with 16th-century stained glass and portrait drawings by Flemish artist Jean Clouet II; the **chapel,** with sculptures by Jean Goujon and Jacques Sarrazin; and the extensive **collection of paintings** by 19th-century French artists, headed by Jean Auguste Ingres. *Admission: 30 frs. adults, 7 frs. children; 12 frs. (park only). Open Easter–Oct., Wed.–Mon. 10–6; Nov.–Easter, 10–5; closed Tues.*

Behind the château is a large **park,** based on that familiar combination of formal bombast (neatly planned parterres and a mighty straight-banked canal) and romantic eccentricity (the

Jardin Anglais [English Garden], with its waterfall, or the make-believe village that inspired Marie Antoinette's version at Versailles).

Across the lake from the château is the Chantilly racecourse, inaugurated in 1834 by the prestigious French Jockey Club. In one corner (to the right as you leave the château) are the majestic 18th-century stables (**Grandes Ecuries**), where up to 240 horses and 400 hounds for stag- and boar hunts could be accommodated in straw-lined comfort. Today, the stables host the **Musée du Cheval** (Horse Museum) and a glittering array of carriages. *Admission: 34 frs. adults, 24 frs. children. Open Wed.–Mon. 10:30–5:30, Tues. 10:30–5:30 only.*

Time Out Since the château of Chantilly is a fair walk from the town's main street, it makes sense to have a quick lunch on the spot—at the self-service **Capitainerie restaurant** in the château's medieval basement (adorned with old kitchen utensils). The buffet is available nonstop from 10:30 through 6:30: mostly salads, cheeses, and desserts, complemented by the occasional hot dish. *Closed Tues.*

Ten kilometers (6 miles) east of Chantilly, along the picturesque, gently turning D924, is **Senlis**, whose crooked, mazelike streets are dominated by the svelte soaring spire of the Gothic cathedral of **Notre-Dame.** Down the lane behind the cathedral is the former church of **St-Pierre,** with its Flamboyant facade, while across place Notre-Dame, the large square beside the cathedral, is the **Fondation Cziffra:** the former church of St-Frambourg, converted into an exhibition center by Hungarian-born pianist Gyorgy Cziffra in 1977, with a small adjoining museum devoted to regional architectural finds. *1 pl. St-Frambourg. Admission: 10 frs. adults, 6 frs. students. Open weekends only 3–6.*

Time Out A few minutes away, down the rue du Châtel, is the 13th-century vaulted **Vert Galant** restaurant. It has a pretty garden where you can sit and have a drink or just order an inexpensive snack. *15 pl. Henri IV.*

Just off N330, some 11 kilometers (7 miles) southeast of Senlis, stand the ruins of the 18th-century abbey of **Chaalis,** built on the site of a 13th-century Cistercian abbey. The landscaped park has been restored to its 18th-century appearance, and the château, which dates from the same period, has an eclectic collection of Egyptian antiquities and medieval paintings, together with three rooms devoted to the 18th-century French philosopher and writer Jean Jacques Rousseau, who died at nearby Ermenonville. *Admission: 14 frs. Open Mon., Wed., Sat. 1:30–6, Sun. 10–noon and 1:30–6; closed Tues., Thurs., and Fri.*

To return to Paris, take D84 about 8 kilometers (5 miles) due south, then pick up signs for Paris on the fast A102.

Tour 3: South to Fontainebleau

Fontainebleau, which forms the hub of our final tour, can be reached from Paris (65 kilometers/40 miles away) in as little as half an hour via A6 and N37. But we urge you not to bypass nearby Vaux-le-Vicomte, best reached from Paris (Porte de

Bercy) via N6, leaving this road at Melun and continuing to Vaux, 5 kilometers (3 miles) northeast, along N36 and D215.

㉟ The château of **Vaux-le-Vicomte** was built between 1656 and 1661 for court financier Nicolas Fouquet. The construction process was decadent, even for those days: Entire villages were razed, 18,000 workmen called in, and ace designers Louis Le Vau, Charles Le Brun, and esteemed landscape architect André Le Nôtre hired to prove that Fouquet's sense of aesthetics matched his business acumen. Unfortunately, his house-warming party was too lavish for the likings of star guest Louis XIV. King Louis threw a fit of jealousy, hurled the tactless Fouquet in jail, and promptly began building Versailles to prove just who was boss.

The high-roofed château, partially surrounded by a moat, is set well back from the roadside behind iron railings topped with sculpted heads. A cobbled avenue winds its way up to the entrance. Stone steps lead to the vestibule, which, given the noble scale of the exterior, seems small. There is no grand staircase, either—the stairs are tucked away in the left wing and lead to a set of rooms that could be described almost as pokey.

Painter Charles Le Brun's lush interior decoration partly compensates: His major achievement is the ceiling of the **Chambre du Roi** (Royal Bedchamber), depicting Time Bearing Truth Heavenwards, framed by stucco work by top sculptors François Girardon and Legendre. Along the frieze you can make out small squirrels—known as *fouquets* in local dialect.

But the château's most impressive room is the **Grand Salon** on the ground floor. With its unusual oval form and 16 caryatid pillars symbolizing the months and seasons, it possesses harmony and style despite its unfinished state (the cupola remains depressingly blank).

An astute exhibition, complete with lifesize wax figures, explains the rise and fall of Nicolas Fouquet. The version is, not surprisingly, favorable to the château's founder—accused by Louis XIV and subsequent historians of megalomania and shady financial dealings, but apparently condemned on little evidence by a court anxious to please the jealous, irascible monarch. The exhibition continues in the basement, whose narrow corridors and stone vaults have, in parts, a suitably dungeonlike feel. The **kitchens** are also down here, a more cheerful sight, with their gleaming copperware and old menus.

Although the château interior lacks majesty, there is no mistaking the grandeur of Le Nôtre's **gardens,** which have been carefully restored. Visit the **Musée des Equipages** (Carriage Museum) in the stables and inspect a host of lovingly restored carriages and coaches. *Admission: 40 frs. adults, 32 frs. students. Gardens only: 15 frs. Open daily 10–6. Candlelight visits 8:30–11PM Sat. May–Sept., admission: 50 frs.*

Time Out | To the right of the château entrance is an imposing barn that has been transformed into a self-serve **cafeteria**. Here, beneath the ancient rafters of a stout wood-beam roof, you can enjoy coffee, cheap pitchers of wine, and good steaks. Insist on *bien cuit* if you don't want your meat too bloodily rare.

From Vaux, return to Melun (take the beltway around the north of the town) and head along D132 (which becomes D64) to

36 **Barbizon,** 10 kilometers (6 miles) south. Barbizon stands on the western edge of the 42,000-acre Forest of Fontainebleau and retains the atmosphere of a small village, despite the intrusion of expensive art galleries, tacky souvenir shops, and weekending Parisians.

Barbizon owes its renown to the colony of landscape painters—Camille Corot, Jean François Millet, and Théodore Rousseau, among others—who lived here from the 1830s on. Their innovative commitment to working outdoors paved the way for the Impressionists, as did their willingness to accept nature on its own terms, rather than use it as an idealized base for carefully structured compositions.

After working hours, the Barbizon painters repaired to the **Auberge du Père Ganne.** The inn still stands—it's now a museum—and you can soak up the arty mood here or at the houses of Millet and Rousseau farther along the single main street (Grande-Rue). *Musée Auberge du Père Ganne, 92 Grande-Rue. Admission free. Open Easter–Oct., Wed.–Mon. 10–5:30, closed Tues.; Nov.–Easter, Wed., Fri., and Sun. only, 10–5:30.*

37 Eight kilometers (5 miles) southeast of Barbizon (via the fast N7) lies the town of **Fontainebleau.** Like Chambord in the Loire Valley or Compiègne to the north, Fontainebleau earned royal esteem as a hunting base. Indeed, a hunting lodge once stood on the site of the current château, along with a chapel built in 1169 and consecrated during exile by Thomas à Becket (1118–70), the now canonized archbishop of Canterbury. Today's château was begun under the flamboyant Renaissance prince François I, the French contemporary of England's Henry VIII.

Although Sun King Louis XIV's architectural energies were concentrated on Versailles, he nonetheless commissioned architect François Mansart to design new pavilions at Fontainebleau, and had Le Nôtre replant the gardens. But it was Napoleon who spent lavishly to make a Versailles, as it were, out of Fontainebleau.

38 Walk past the parterres to the left of the Etang des Carpes (Carp Pond) and turn left into an alley that leads to the **Cour Ovale**—a courtyard shaped like a flattened oval with, at the **39** straight end, the domed **Porte du Baptistère,** an imposing gateway designed by court architect Francesco Primaticcio (1504–70). The gateway's name commemorates the fact that the Dauphin—the male heir to the throne, later to become Louis XIII—was baptized under its arch in 1606. Opposite is the **40** **Cour des Offices,** a large, severe square built at the same time as the place des Vosges in Paris (1609).

The hedge-lined alley continues to the Jardin de Diane (Garden of Diana), with its peacocks and statue of the hunting goddess surrounded by mournful hounds. Cross this informal garden **41** and enter the palace's most majestic courtyard, the **Cour du 42** **Cheval-Blanc,** dominated by the famous **horseshoe staircase** built by Jean Androuet du Cerceau in the early 17th century. Climb the steps to the château entrance.

43 In **Napoleon's apartments** on the second floor, you can ogle at a lock of his hair, his Légion d'Honneur medal, his imperial uniform, the hat he wore on his return from Elba in 1815, and the bed in which he used to sleep.

Cour du Cheval-
Blanc, **41**
Cour des Offices, **40**
Cour Ovale, **38**
Galerie de Diane, **45**
Horseshoe
Staircase, **42**
Napoleon's
Apartments, **43**
Porte du
Baptistère, **39**
Salle de Bal, **46**
Throne Room/Queen's
Bedroom, **44**

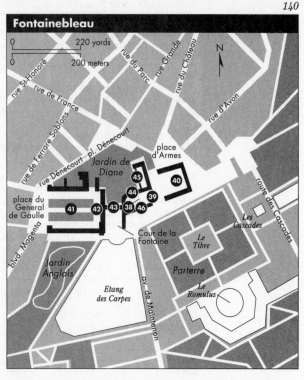

44 There is also a **throne room**—one of Napoleon's foibles, since
the kings themselves were content with the one at Versailles—
and the **Queen's Bedroom,** known as the Room of the Six
45 Maries. The seemingly endless **Galerie de Diane,** built during
the reign of Henri IV (1589–1610), was used as a library. Other
salons boast 17th-century tapestries, marble reliefs by Jacquet
de Grenoble, and paintings and frescoes by the versatile Italian
Francesco Primaticcio (besides being court architect to
François I, he was also a top-rate painter, sculptor, and interi-
or designer).

Jewel of the interior, though, is the ceremonial ballroom—the
46 **Salle de Bal**—nearly 100 feet long, with wood paneling and a
gleaming parquetry floor whose pattern matches that of the
ceiling.

If time permits, complete your visit with a wander around the
leafy **Jardin Anglais** (English Garden) to the right of the Etang
des Carpes. *Admission: 21 frs. adults, 10 frs. children. Open
Wed.–Mon. 9:30–12:30 and 2–5; closed Tues. Gardens open 9–
dusk; admission free.*

Ten kilometers (six miles) southeast of Fontainebleau on N6,
close to the confluence of the rivers Seine and Yonne, is the
47 charming village of **Moret-sur-Loing,** immortalized by Impressionist painter Alfred Sisley, who lived here for 20 years at 19
rue Montmartre (not open to the public), around the corner
from the church of Notre-Dame. Close by, leading off from the
rue du Peintre Sisley, is the thatched **house-museum** of another

illustrious former inhabitant: truculent World War I leader Georges Clemenceau (1841–1929), known as The Tiger. His taste for Oriental art and his friendship with Impressionist Claude Monet, are evoked. *Follow signs to the Grange Batelière. Admission: 17 frs. Open Easter–Nov., daily 2:30–6; closed Dec.–Easter.*

The best view of Moret is from the far banks of the Loing. Cross the narrow bridge (one of the oldest in France and invariably clogged with traffic) to gaze back at the walls, rooftops, and church tower. A good time to visit Moret is on a summer evening when locals stage *son-et-lumière* (sound-and-light) pageants illustrating the village's history.

After crossing the Loing, take N6 for 6½ kilometers (four miles), then turn left along D403 (via Montereau) to the attractive town of **Provins,** another 37 kilometers (23 miles) away. Provins grew up on the hilltop site of a Roman camp before acquiring international renown as a rose-growing center. Under the medieval influence of the counts of Champagne, Provins became an important commercial center, the third most important town in France (after Paris and Rouen) during the Middle Ages. Neither historic hilltop Provins nor the more recent township below are much of an economic dynamo these days, however. Upper Provins sleeps in the past, tucked in behind its defensive walls at the foot of the beefy 12th-century Tour de César, a circular keep on a sturdy mound. Climb to the top for a view of the town. *Admission: 6 frs. Open Mar.–Nov., Mon.–Sat. 9:30–noon and 2–6, Sun. 2–6; Dec.–Feb. until 5.*

Beneath the tower is the 12th-century Gothic church of **St-Quirace,** with its incongruous 17th-century Classical dome. Close by is a pleasant garden, the **Jardin des Brébans.** From here, rue du Palais leads up to place du Châtel, a sloping square with restaurants at the far end. Veer left down rue de Jouy; on the first corner is the 13th-century tithe-barn, or **Grange aux Dîmes,** whose vaulted ground floor contains a collection of stone sculptures. *Admission: 6 frs. Open Easter–Oct., daily 10–noon and 2:30–5; Nov.–Easter until 4:30.*

Rue St-Jean leads to the Porte St-Jean gateway. Here you can survey some of the best-preserved **medieval city walls** in France.

N19 links Provins to Paris, 72 kilometers (45 miles) away.

What to See and Do with Children

Opposite the abbey of Chaalis, 11 kilometers (7 miles) southeast of Senlis, is the **Mer de Sable playground**—a cheerful place for children to play, with its miniature train, giant slide, small zoo, and curious natural "desert" of white sand. *Parc d'Attractions Jean-Richard, Forêt d'Ermenonville, off N330. Admission: 44 frs. Open Apr.–Oct., Tues.–Sat. and weekends 10:30–7, closed Mon. and Fri.; Nov.–Mar., Wed. and weekends only 11–6:30.*

The **Mirapolis Amusement Park** in Cergy, 40 kilometers (25 miles) northwest of Paris, ia a Gallic answer to Disneyland, with all the fun of the fair and a determinedly French flavor. There's no Mickey Mouse or Donald Duck here, though, just characters from French fiction. The hefty entrance fee covers all the rides. *Rte. de Courdimanche, Cergy-Pontoise, RER–A Cergy St-Christophe. Admission: 75 frs. weekdays, 90 frs. weekends. Open Easter–Oct. only.*

The brand-new theme park known as **Park Astérix** takes its cue from a French comic book figure whose adventures are set during the Roman invasion of France 2,000 years ago. Highlights include a mock Romano-Gallic village, a dolphin lake, and a giant roller coaster. *Just off A1 at Plailly, 32 km (20 miles) north of Paris. Admission: 120 frs. adults, 90 frs. children under 12. Open Easter–Oct., Sun.–Fri. 10–6, Sat. 10–10.*

Most children will enjoy a visit to the Animal Reserve and Tiger Park of the **Château de Thoiry** *(see* Tour 1, above).

Off the Beaten Track

Take a short literary pilgrimage down the Seine Valley one Sunday to the little town of **Médan**, where Emile Zola moved in 1877 after the runaway success of his novel *L'Assommoir*. Until recently, his house was used as an orphanage, but it is now open to the public once a week. *26 rue Pasteur. Admission: 15 frs. adults, 10 frs. students and senior citizens. Open Sun. only, 2–5.*

Ecouen, a woody suburb 19 kilometers (12 miles) north of Paris, is known for its château, home of a museum devoted to the Renaissance and particularly strong on 16th- and 17th-century tapestry and furniture from France, Italy, and Holland. *Musée de la Renaissance, Château d'Ecouen. Admission: 15 frs. (8 frs. Sun.). Open Wed.–Mon. 10–12:30 and 2–5:15; closed Tues.*

The Orge Valley southwest of Paris presents an attractive mixture of hills, fields, and forest and two outstanding man-made attractions: an airy 13th-century church in the tiny village of **St-Sulpice de Favières**, and the enticing château of **Le Marais**, with lake, extensive grounds, and a small museum devoted to onetime inhabitant Talleyrand (a romantic but unscrupulous 19th-century diplomat). A car is the only means of access to these two sites, though the RER-C trains from Paris stop at nearby St-Chéron, where taxis can be hired. *Le Marais: open Sun. only in Apr.–Sept., 11–6. Admission: 24 frs.*

Shopping

Most of the Ile de France's working population either commutes to Paris—or plows farmland. There is little in the way of regional specialties, and, with Paris never more than an hour away, serious shopping—particularly for clothes—means heading back to the capital.

Food Items   Versailles is perhaps the region's most commercial town. After visiting the château, you might want to stop in at **Aux Colonnes**, a highly rated *confiserie* with an astounding array of chocolates and candies (14 rue Hoche; closed Mon.). A huge choice of cheeses—including one of France's widest selection of goat cheeses—can be smelt, admired, and eventually purchased from **Eugène Le Gall** (13 rue Ducis; closed Sun. afternoon and Mon.). Stuffed olives, dried fruits, and more exotic spices and teas than you thought existed can be had from **Pamparigouste**

(15 rue des Deux-Portes; closed Sun. afternoon and Mon. morning).

Antiques Anyone in the mood for antique hunting should visit Versailles's passage de la Geôle, site of a good thrice-weekly flea market (10 rue Rameau; open Fri.–Sun. 9–7). Antiques shops in other major towns include **A La Cour Des Adieux** (3 pl. Denecourt, Fontainebleau); **Thenot** (50 av. Foch, Senlis); **Susen Antiquités** (pl. Dauphine, St-Germain-en-Laye); and **Ambiance & Style** (17 rue des Changes, Chartres).

Souvenirs There are notably fine souvenir shops at Vaux-le-Vicomte, Giverny, and Thoiry (where you can sample cookies and jams made by the American viscountess herself).

Gift Items Stained glass being the key to Chartres's fame, enthusiasts may want to visit the **Musée du Vitrail** (17 rue Cloître Notre-Dame), which specializes in the noble art. Pieces range from entire windows to small plaques, and there are books on the subject in English and French.

Sports and Fitness

Bicycling Biking is a fun and healthy way to explore the area; you can rent bicycles from many local train stations, including those of Rambouillet and Fontainebleau. A booklet detailing 16 bike routes in the region can be obtained from the SNCF (tel. 42–61–50–50).

If you like to watch people pedaling more than you enjoy doing it yourself, be in the region on the penultimate Sunday of July, when the **Tour de France** cycle race passes through en route to its Champs-Elysées climax.

Golf Golf is a new, expensive cult sport in France, but there are several clubs open to the general public: **Bougival** (tel. 39–18–43–81), **Chambourcy** (tel. 30–74–45–98), **Fontainebleau** (tel. 64–22–22–95), and **St-Germain-en-Laye** (tel. 34–51–75–90).

Hiking The great forests of Rambouillet, St-Germain, and Fontainebleau are much frequented by walkers; if you'd prefer to go with a group, the local tourist offices (*see* Essential Information) can furnish details of organized hikes.

Horseback Riding Get in touch with one of the following stables (*centre équestre*): 29 rue de l'Arbre Sec, Fontainebleau, tel. 64–22–31–55; rte. Nogent-le-Phaye, Chartres, tel. 37–30–10–10; 23 rue Franklin, St-Germain-en-Laye, tel. 34–51–10–94; or Chemin du Roy, Senlis, tel. 44–53–55–13.

Rock Climbing The region boasts numerous routes, particularly in the Forest of Fontainebleau. For more information, contact the **Club Alpin Français** (Touring Club de France, FSGT, 31 av. C.-Vellefaux, 75010 Paris; tel. 42–01–82–00).

Swimming You'll never be too far away from a public swimming pool. The following are just a few of the options: Stade de la Faisanderie, blvd. Constance, Fontainebleau, tel. 64–22–16–85; Blvd. Courtille, Chartres, tel. 37–28–05–87; 3 rue Léon-Gatin, Versailles, tel. 39–50–65–71.

Dining and Lodging

Dining

With wealthy tourists and weekending Parisians providing the backbone of the region's seasonal clientèle, the smarter restaurants of Ile de France can be just as pricey as their Parisian counterparts. But in smaller towns, and for those prepared to venture only marginally off the beaten tourist track, nourishing, good-value meals are not hard to find. The style of cuisine mirrors that of Paris: There is plenty of variety but few things that can be considered specifically regional. The "local delicacies" cited by earnest textbooks—navarin lamb stew, pâté de Pantin, pig's feet, or vegetable soup—tend to be either banal or obsolete. In season, sumptuous game and asparagus are found in the south of the region; the soft, creamy cheese of Brie hails from Meaux and Coulommiers to the east. More generally, the Ile de France is a prolific producer of vegetables, and at table or the market, you have a right to refuse all but the freshest produce.

Highly recommended restaurants are indicated by a star ★.

Lodging

Remember two things: In summer, hotel rooms are at a premium and reservations are essential; relative lack of choice means that almost all accommodations in the swankier towns—Versailles, Rambouillet, and Fontainebleau—are on the costly side. Take nothing for granted. Picturesque Senlis, for instance, does not have a single hotel in its historic downtown area. Some of the smaller hotels in the region may not accept credit cards, although the Carte Bleue and its international equivalents (MasterCard and Visa) are widely recognized—unlike American Express, often refused in all but the plushest establishments.

Highly recommended hotels are indicated by a star ★.

Barbizon
Dining

Le Relais. Delicious country-French specialties are served here in large portions, and there is a good choice of fixed-price menus. The restaurant is spacious, with a big open fire, and paintings and hunting trophies decorate the walls. The owner is rightly proud of the large terrace where diners can eat in the shade of lime and chestnut trees. *2 av. Charles-de-Gaulle, tel. 60-66-40-28. Reservations essential weekends. Jacket and tie suggested. MC, V. Closed Tues., Wed., Aug. 20–Sept. 5, Dec. 18–Jan. 6. Expensive.*

Lodging
★

Auberge des Alouettes. This delightful family-run 19th-century inn is set in two acres of grounds (which the better rooms overlook). The interior has been redecorated in '30s style, but many rooms still have their original oak beams. The popular restaurant (reservations are essential), with its large open terrace, features light cuisine (no heavy sauces) and barbecued beef in summer. *4 rue Antoine-Barye, 77630, tel. 60-66-41-98. 23 rooms with bath. Jacket and tie required in restaurant. Facilities: tennis. AE, DC, MC, V. Moderate.*

Chantilly **Relais Condé.** What is probably the classiest restaurant in
Dining Chantilly is pleasantly situated opposite the racecourse, in a
★ building that originally served as an Anglican chapel. Reasonably priced menus (105–150 francs) make it a suitable lunch
spot. An extensive wine list and Patrice Lebeau's filling
recipes—*burbet* (freshwater cod) with peppers, veal kidneys in
mustard sauce—warrant a lengthier visit in the evening. *42 av.
du Marechal-Joffre, tel. 16/44–57–05–75. Reservations essential. Jacket and tie required. AE, DC, V. Closed Mon. and
mid-Jan.–mid-Feb. Moderate.*

Les Quatre Saisons. Fresh-air devotees will undoubtedly appreciate this restaurant's flowery terrace, used for dining
alfresco. The set menus are good value, and the mainly Danish-
inspired dishes deliciously light, as befitting Chef Engstrom's
Scandinavian origins. The weekday set menu, at around 100
francs (wine included), is always a good bet. *9 av. Général-
Leclerc, tel. 16/44–57–04–65. Reservations accepted. Dress:
casual. AE, DC, V. Closed Mon. (except holidays) and most of
Feb. Inexpensive/Moderate.*

Lodging **Campanile.** Well run and functional, this modern motel is set in
a quiet, relaxing location just outside Chantilly, on the edge of
the forest. (The forest setting goes far to compensate for the
lack of interior atmosphere.) There's a grillroom for straightforward, if unexciting, meals. *Les Huits Curés, on the N16 to
Creil, tel. 16/44–57–39–24. 47 rooms, some with bath. Facilities: garden, terrace for outdoor dining. V. Moderate.*

Etoile. This small, underwhelming hotel is conveniently placed
on the avenue leading from the train station to the château. It's
cheap and acceptable for a night's stop-over, though your
reception may be somewhat lacking in warmth. *3 av. du
Marechal-Joffre, 60500, tel. 16/44–57–02–55. 10 rooms with
bath. V. Inexpensive.*

Chartres **La Vieille Maison.** Occupying a pretty 14th-century building
Dining just 50 yards from the cathedral, this restaurant is a fine choice
for either lunch or dinner. The decor is intimate, based around
a flower-strewn patio. The menu changes regularly but invariably includes regional specialties—like asparagus or pig's feet
with truffles. The homemade foie gras is superb. Prices,
though justified, can be steep, but the 160- and 220-franc
menus are a good bet. *5 rue au Lait, tel. 16/37–34–10–67. Reservations essential. Jacket and tie required. AE, DC, MC, V.
Closed Mon., Sun. evening, first half Jan., last week July.
Moderate/Expensive.*

Le Buisson Ardent. A wood-beamed, second-floor restaurant,
Le Buisson Ardent offers filling, low-priced menus, imaginative nouvelle food, and a view of Chartres cathedral (it's just
opposite the south portal). Service is gratifyingly attentive.
Try the fruity Gamay de Touraine, an ideal wine for lunchtime.
*10 rue au Lait, tel. 16/37–34–04–66. Reservations accepted.
Dress: casual. AE, DC, V. Closed Sun. evening, Wed. Inexpensive.*

Lodging **Grand Monarque.** The venerable 18th-century Monarque re-
★ cently had a face-lift: 11 rooms were added, and the entrance
hall was completely renovated. Guest rooms have the level of
consistent comfort you expect from a member of two hotel
chains (Best Western and Mapotel); the most atmospheric overlook a small garden or are tucked away in the attic of this
former coaching inn. There's also a classy restaurant, re-

nowned for its nouvelle interpretations of seasonal fare, fowl, and fish. *22 pl. des Epars, 28000, tel. 37–21–00–72. 57 rooms, 52 with bath. Facilities: terrace (used for outdoor dining). AE, DC, MC, V. Moderate/Expensive.*

Dreux
Dining and Lodging

Auberge Normande. This is a modest country hotel, excellently situated on the historic square that links the church to the belfry; ask for a room with a view. A cozy restaurant, belonging to the hotel, is situated a couple of doors farther along the square. *12 pl. Métézeau, 28100, tel. 16/37-50-02-03. 20 rooms, most with shower. DC, MC, V. Closed Christmas–New Year's. Inexpensive.*

Ermenonville
Dining and Lodging
★

Croix d'Or. For lunch or an overnight stop in tiny Ermenonville (just a few miles outside Senlis), why not try the Croix d'Or? Its small rooms and homey restaurant have the welcoming feel of a village inn. *2 rue du Prince-Radziwill, 60950, tel. 16/45-40-00-04. 11 rooms, some with bath or shower. Facilities: garden. MC, V. Restaurant closed Mon. and (winter only) Sun. dinner; hotel closed mid-Dec.–first week Feb. Inexpensive.*

Fontainebleau
Dining
★

Chinois de l'Ile de France. Cheap eating is not the easiest task for Bellifontains (as the town's inhabitants are known), so an address like that of this restaurant needs noting. Chinese cooking is served here, with a fine meat dip the specialty—along with a plethora of set-price menus, each under 100 francs. What the restaurant lacks in style, it makes up for in value: Its prices are modest by Fontainebleau standards (200 francs and up). The Chinois has 25 moderately priced guest rooms, as well. *128 rue de France, tel. 64-22-21-17. Reservations accepted. Dress: casual. AE, DC, MC, V. Inexpensive.*

Le Dauphin. The homey, rustic Dauphin is located near the Hôtel de Ville (Town Hall), just a five-minute walk from the château. Prices are reasonable, and specialties include snails, *confit de canard,* and a variety of homemade desserts. *24 rue Grande, tel. 64-22-27-04. Reservations advised, especially on Sun. Dress: casual. Closed Tues. dinner, Wed., Feb., and Sept. 1–8. Inexpensive.*

Lodging

Hôtel de Londres. The balconies of this tranquil, family-style hotel look out over the château and the Cour des Adieux, where Napoleon bid his troops a fond farewell; the austere 19th-century facade is preserved by government order. Inside, the decor is dominated by Louis XV-style gilt furniture. *1 pl. Général de Gaulle, 77300, tel. 64-22-20-21. 22 rooms, most with bath. Facilities: restaurant, bar, outdoor dining. AE, MC, V. Closed Dec. 20–Jan. 31. Moderate.*

Dining and Lodging
★

Aigle-Noir. This may be Fontainebleau's costliest hotel (rooms from 600 francs up), but you can't go far wrong: Most rooms overlook either the garden or the château and have late 18th- or early 19th-century reproduction furniture to evoke a Napoleonic mood. A thorough modernization program was recently undertaken, affecting the grand hotel restaurant, the **Beauharnais,** as well. The cooking here has the herbal subtlety of nouvelle cuisine, but the portions show none of its traditional parsimony. The menus at 190 and 260 francs are recommended. *27 pl. Napoléon-Bonaparte, 77300, tel. 64-22-32-65. Restaurant reservations required; jacket and tie required. 57 rooms with bath. Facilities: pool, outdoor dining in garden, conference hall. AE, DC, MC, V. Expensive.*

L'Isle-Adam
Dining and Lodging

Le Cabouillet. The riverside Cabouillet aptly reflects the quiet charm of L'Isle-Adam, thanks to its pretty views over the Oise. You can savor these from each of its eight rooms or from the chic restaurant (menus at 160 or 280 francs), where the cooking can be inspired (if it's on the menu, go for the crawfish in Sauternes sauce). *5 quai de l'Oise, 95290, tel. 34–69–00–90. 8 rooms with bath. Restaurant reservations accepted. Dress: casual chic. V. Hotel closed Christmas to early Feb. Restaurant closed Mon. dinner and Tues. Moderate.*

Maintenon
Dining and Lodging
★

Château d'Esclimant. Nineteen kilometers (12 miles) southeast of Maintenon (take D116 to the village of Gallardon, keep an eye out for its magnificent old church and then turn left) is the restored Renaissance Château d'Esclimont. The château is well worth seeking out if you wish to eat (or slumber) like a king (or queen). Set in luxurious grounds, with lawns, a lake, and a huge driveway, this member of the Relais & Châteaux chain is a regular target for smooth-talking and eating Parisian power brokers. The cuisine is sophisticated and varied: Quail, rabbit fricassee, and lobster top the menu. Guest rooms are luxuriously furnished, and there are two private tennis courts and a heated swimming pool. The 16th-century château makes an admirable base for visiting Rambouillet and Chartres (A11 runs close by), both about 24 kilometers (15 miles) away. *St-Symphorien-le-Château, 28700 Auneau, tel. 16/37–31–15–15. 48 rooms with bath. Hotel and dinner reservations recommended. Facilities: restaurant, tennis, pool, fishing. MC, V. Expensive.*

Provins
Dining

Vieux Ramparts. Old wood beams inside and a cheerful, leafy courtyard for outdoor eating in the summer help to create a charming atmosphere at the Vieux Ramparts, housed in an attractive old building in the Ville Haute. The nouvelle menus (125–225 francs) offer good value for the money, and meals are sustaining. *3 rue Couverte, tel. 64–00–02–89. Reservations accepted but not essential. Dress: casual. AE, V. Closed Tues. dinner and late Feb.–first week in Mar. Moderate.*

Rambouillet
Dining

La Poste. You can bank on traditional, unpretentious cooking at this former coaching inn right in the center of town. Until recently, it could only seat 36 diners, but a new room was opened upstairs, doubling the capacity. Service is good, as is the selection of fixed-price menus, weekends included. *101 rue du Général-de-Gaulle, tel. 34–83–03–01. Reservations advised. Jacket and tie required. AE, MC, V. Moderate.*

St-Germain-en-Laye
Dining

La Petite Auberge. The specialty here is farmhouse-style cooking from the Aveyron region of southwest France. Fresh meat is cooked over an open fire throughout the year, and cheerful red wine (Chinon, from the Loire Valley) is drawn straight from the barrel. Game is served in season. *119-bis rue L. Desnoyer, tel. 34–51–03–99. Reservations accepted. Jacket and tie required. V. Closed Tues. dinner, Wed., second half of Mar., and July. Moderate.*

★ **Le Sept Rue des Coches.** The fashionable decor (lacquer and mirrors) and excellent nouvelle cuisine attract an elegant clientele to this restaurant. Insist on the fixed-priced menu unless the marinated salmon or slivers of duck entice you to spend 300 francs à la carte. *7 rue des Coches, tel. 39–73–66–40. Reservations advised. Jacket and tie required. AE, DC, MC, V. Closed Sun. dinner, Mon., and most of Aug. Moderate.*

Lodging
★
La Forestiere. St-Germain is no stopover point for the faint walleted. The town is obsessed with style, and this is its most stylish hotel, a member of the deluxe Relais et Châteaux chain. The forest setting, 18th-century-style furniture, and a fine, if pricey, restaurant, the Cazaudehore (serving fish-based cuisine from southwest France), contribute to a sense of well-being. *1 av. President-Kennedy, 78100, tel. 39–73–36–70. 24 rooms with bath. V. Closed Mon. (except public holidays). Expensive.*

Senlis
Dining
Les Gourmandins. This cozy, two-floored, recently opened restaurant in old Senlis serves some interesting dishes—try the salad with duck and truffles—and offers a fine wine list. The 90-franc fixed-price menu is a bargain for a weekday lunch; dining à la carte can nudge 300 francs. *3 pl. de la Halle, tel. 16/44–60–94–01. Reservations advised. Dress: informal. V. Inexpensive.*

Lodging
Hostellerie Porte-Bellon. This is the closest you'll get to staying a night in the historic center of Senlis. A modest yet efficient hotel, the Porte-Bellon is just a five-minute walk from the cathedral and is close to the bus station. *35 rue Bellon, 60300, tel. 16/44–53–03–05. 20 rooms, most with bath. Facilities: restaurant. V. Closed mid-Dec.–mid-Jan., Fri. (except in summer). Inexpensive.*

Thoiry
Dining and Lodging
Etoile. Handily situated for visitors to Thoiry château and safari park, the Etoile offers a special tourist menu for under 70 francs, as well as a wide choice of à la carte dishes. A garden and a Ping-Pong table add to the hotel's homey appeal. *38 rue de la Porte St-Martin, tel. 34–87–40–21. 12 rooms with bath. AE, DC, MC, V. Closed Mon. and Jan. Inexpensive/Moderate.*

Vernon
Dining and Lodging
★
Château de Brecourt. This 17th-century stone-and-brick château, with its high-pitched roofs and imposing forecourt, is set in extensive grounds 10 kilometers (six miles) south of Vernon along D533 near Douains. Inventive food in the august atmosphere of the tastefully reupholstered dining room makes it a popular spot with visitors to Giverny, just across the Seine from Vernon. And, as similar hotel-cum-châteaus go, guest rooms can represent good value—the smallest start at 350 francs. *Douains, 27120 Pacy-sur-Eure, tel. 16/32–52–40–50. 20 rooms with bath. AE, DC, MC, V. Moderate/Expensive.*

Versailles
Dining
★
Trois Marches. The most famous restaurant in Versailles is also recognized as one of the best in the Ile de France, thanks to its subtle and creative nouvelle cuisine. Even the most sophisticated foodophiles salivate at the thought of Gérard Vié's bisque of lobster, salmon with fennel, or turbot *galette*, impeccably served in a magnificent *hôtel-particulier* (town-house) setting. *3 rue Colbert, tel. 39–50–13–21. Reservations essential. Jacket and tie required. AE, DC, MC, V. Closed Sun. and Mon. Expensive.*

★
Boule d'Or. The Boule d'Or claims to occupy the second-oldest house in Versailles, as well as to be the oldest inn; it was built in 1696. Owner Claude Saillard likes to base his cooking on 17th- and 18th-century recipes, and in the candlelit oak-beamed dining room, you will readily step back in time. The specialty— "The Trilogy" (evenings only)—includes a sole in sauce introduced in 1733, braised beef (1742), and duck fricassee (1654). For the less ambitious, there are simpler lunchtime fixed-price menus. *25 rue Marechal-Foch, tel. 39–50–22–97. Reservations*

essential. *Jacket and tie required. AE, DC, MC, V. Closed Sun. dinner, Mon. Moderate.*

Potager du Roy. There is excellent value in this restaurant run by Philippe Letourneau for Gérard Vié *(see* Trois Marches, above). The cuisine improves constantly, yet prices stay moderate. The bistro and its adjoining terrace get crowded in summer because visitors find the 105- and 150-franc menus hard to resist. *1 rue Marechal-Joffre, tel. 39–50–35–34. Reservations essential. Jacket and tie required. MC, V. Closed Sun., Mon. Moderate.*

Lodging **Trianon Palace.** This deluxe hotel is set in its own huge garden close to the château. A turn-of-the-century creation of imposing size, it has the faded, somewhat fraying charm of an imposing dowager. In a bid to revamp this image, half the guest rooms have been modernized and the furniture replaced. The restaurant has an inventive cuisine, served in fine weather on the huge outdoor terrace. *1 blvd. Reine, 78000, tel. 39–50–34–12. 120 rooms with bath. Facilities: garden, pool. AE, DC, MC, V. Very Expensive.*

Le Versailles. This unpretentious, modern hotel is ideally situated close to the château and warmly recommended if you plan to explore the town on foot (or can't afford the palatial prices of the Trianon, above). Guest rooms have comfort, but no character. No restaurant. *Rue Ste-Anne, 78000, tel. 39–50–64–65. 48 rooms with bath. AE, V. Moderate.*

Home St-Louis. The small, recently modernized Home St-Louis is a good, cheap, quiet bet—close to the cathedral and not too far from the château. There's no restaurant. *28 rue St-Louis, 78000, tel. 39–50–23–55. 27 rooms with bath. V. Inexpensive.*

The Arts and Nightlife

The Arts

With Paris so close, it seems pointless to detail the comparatively minor offerings of the towns of the Ile de France in the domains of theater, music, or cinema *(see* The Arts in chapter 3). There are, however, a number of arts festivals staged in the Ile de France that have earned esteem in their own right. Of these, the largest is the **Festival de l'Ile de France** (mid-May–early July), famed for concerts held at châteaus themselves (for details, tel. 47–23–40–84). There are also music festivals in **Provins** (June), **St-Denis** (mid-May–June, with concerts in the basilica), and at the abbey of **Royaumont** (May–June, tel. 30–35–88–90).

An invaluable list of monthly regional events is the *Tourisme Loisirs* brochure produced by the **Comité Régional du Tourisme Ile-de-France** (137 rue de l'Université, 75007 Paris, tel. 47–53–79–93).

Nightlife

We recommend that anyone interested in painting the town red do so in Paris; there's precious little to choose from in the little towns of the Ile de France. *(See* Nightlife in Chapter 3.)

5 The Loire Valley

Introduction

The Loire is the longest river in France, rising deep in the heart of the southern Massif Central and winding its way north and then west for over 600 miles before reaching the Atlantic at Nantes. Halfway along, just outside the town of Orléans, the river makes a wide, westward bend, gliding languidly through low, rich country known as the Val de Loire—the Loire Valley. In this temperate, "garden" region—a 150-mile stretch linking Orléans with Angers and surrounding valleys—hundreds of châteaus rise from the woods and hollows: For tourists, the words "Loire" and "châteaus" are nearly synonymous.

Until the railroad cut its blackened path through hill and valley, the Loire river provided the area's principal means of transportation. It also acted as an important barrier to invading armies. Cities rose at strategic bridgeheads, and fortresses—the earliest châteaus—appeared on towering hill slopes. As time passed, more palaces grew in the fertile valleys. Under the medieval Plantagenet and Valois kings, the region became the country's power base. And although the nation's capital shifted to Paris around 1600, aristocrats continued to erect luxurious palaces along the Loire until the end of the 18th century. Since that time, many châteaus—too expensive for even the wealthiest to maintain—have fallen to the care of state and local authorities and are now preserved as cultural and historical monuments.

In addition to its abundant châteaus, the Loire Valley offers visitors a host of opportunities for outdoor recreation. Horseback riding, fishing, canoeing, and swimming facilities abound. In the summer, tourists and natives alike flock to concerts, music festivals, fairs, and the celebrated *son-et-lumière* (sound-and-light) extravaganzas held in the grounds of many châteaus. Simply wandering the banks of the placid river and exploring her gentle hills, dotted with woods and fairytale castles bathed in pink and golden light, provides a welcome break for tired city dwellers.

Essential Information

Important Addresses and Numbers

Tourist Information The Loire region has two area tourist offices; both deal with written inquiries only. For Chinon and points east, the regional office is **Comité Régional du Tourisme du Centre-de-Loire** (9 rue St-Pierre-Lentin, 45050 Orléans). For Fontevraud and points west, contact **Comité Régional du Tourisme des Pays-de-Loire** (3 pl. St-Pierre, 44000 Nantes).

The addresses of other tourist offices in major towns mentioned in this chapter are as follows: **Amboise** (quai Général-de-Gaulle, tel. 47–57–09–28), **Angers** (pl. Kennedy, tel. 41–88–69–93), **Blois** (3 av. Jean-Laigret, tel. 54–74–06–49), **Orléans** (blvd. de Verdun, tel. 38–53–05–95), **Saumur** (Pl. de la Bilange, tel. 41–51–03–06), and **Tours** (pl. du Maréchal-Leclerc, tel. 47–05–58–08).

Travel Agencies **American Express** (12 pl. du Martroi, Orléans, tel. 38–53–84–54) and **Wagon-Lits** (9 rue Marceau, Tours, tel. 47–20–40–54).

Car Rental Avis (6 rue Jean Moulin, Blois, tel. 54–74–48–15; 13 rue Sansonnieres, Orléans, tel. 33–62–27–04; and 39 bis blvd. Heurteloup, Tours, tel. 47–05–59–33), **Hertz** (5 rue du Dr.-Desfray, Blois, tel. 54–74–03–03; and 2 rue Fleming, Tours, tel. 47–61–02–54), and **Europcar** (81 rue André-Dessaux, Orléans, tel. 33–73–00–40; and 76 rue Bernard-Pellissy, Tours, tel. 47–64–47–76).

Arriving and Departing

By Plane The closest airports to the Loire Valley are Paris's Charles de Gaulle and Orly.

By Train The Loire region is served by fast, regular trains from Paris and other major cities. Trains run every two hours from Paris's Gare d'Austerlitz to Orléans, Blois, and Tours; from Gare Montparnasse, trains leave for Angers every two hours.

By Car A10 runs from Paris to Orléans—a distance of 130 kilometers (78 miles)—and on to Tours, with exits at Meung, Blois, and Amboise.

Getting Around

By Car Slower but more scenic routes than A10 run from the western Channel ports down through Normandy into the Loire region. You can arrange to rent a car in all the large towns in the region or at train stations in Orléans, Blois, Tours, or Angers.

By Train The Loire region has a good local network. The main line follows the Loire itself, running from Orléans through Blois, Tours, Saumur, and Angers to Nantes.

By Bus Local bus services are extensive and reliable and are a link between train stations and scenic areas off the river. Inquire at tourist offices for information about routes and timetables.

By Bicycle With its gentle hills and lovely vistas, the Loire Valley is ideal for bicycling. For more information, *see* Sports and Fitness.

Guided Tours

Orientation **Accueil de France** in Angers (pl. Président Kennedy) and Blois (pl. du Maréchal-Leclerc) organizes numerous tours of the Loire Valley, including car and bus excursions, and even hot-air balloon and boat trips. The office in Blois also offers equestrian, bike, and horse-drawn carriage tours of the Loire-et-Cher region. **Reservations Loisirs Accueil** in Blois (11 pl. du Château, tel. 54–78–55–50) also arranges guided visits to the region's châteaus, as well as balloon and bicycle trips.

Special-Interest **Cointreau,** that heart-warming liquor, comes from Angers, and the factory welcomes visitors (rue Croix Blanche, 49124 St-Barthelemy d'Anjou, tel. 41–43–25–21). The one-hour tour covers the museum and distillery and includes a tasting. Cost is about 12 francs. A mile downstream from Saumur, on the road to Gennes, the wine-making firms of **Ackerman** (19 rue M-Palustre, 49400 St-Hilaire, tel. 41–50–25–33) and **Veuve Amiot** (21 rue Jean-Ackerman, 49400 St-Hilaire, tel. 41–50–25–24) offer organized tours during which you can watch wine being made by the champagne method. The tours last about an hour.

Anyone interested in mushrooms, a specialty of the region, will be intrigued by an unusual subterranean tour through fossil-filled caverns where edible fungi are grown; it's offered by **La Musée du Champignon** (Mushroom Museum, Flines, rte. de Gennes, tel. 41–50–31–55). Tours are available daily from mid-March through June 10–12 and 2–6; July and August 10–6; and September through mid-November 10–12 and 2–6.

Personal Guides The tourist offices in **Tours** and **Angers** (*see* Tourist Information) arrange city and regional excursions with personal guides. English-speaking guides will conduct visitors around the historic city of **Blois** during a walk that starts from the château at 4; cost is about 30 francs.

Exploring the Loire Valley

Numbers in the margin correspond with points of interest on the Loire Valley map.

Orientation

For touring purposes, we've divided the Loire Valley into two regions: the western Loire, from Angers to Tours, and the eastern Loire, from Amboise to Orléans. If you will be relying on public transportation, it's a good idea to use one of the region's four major cities—Tours, Blois, Angers, or Orléans—as your base or the town of Saumur, about midway between Tours and Angers.

Highlights for First-time Visitors

Amboise, Tour 2
Blois, Tour 2
Chambord, Tour 2
Château d'Useé, Tour 1
Chenonceau, Tour 2
Chinon, Tour 1
Germigny, Tour 2
Saumur, Tour 1
The gardens at Villandry, Tour 1

Tour 1: The Western Loire Valley—Angers to Tours

1 **Angers,** former capital of the Anjou region, lies on the banks of the River Maine, just north of the Loire, about 106 kilometers (66 miles) west of Tours and 210 kilometers (130 miles) from Orléans. In addition to a towering medieval fortress filled with extraordinary tapestries, the town has a fine Gothic cathedral, a choice of art galleries, and a network of pleasant, traffic-free shopping streets. Well served by public transportation, Angers is the starting point for numerous bus, riverboat, hiking, biking, horseback, and ballooning excursions.

The town's principal sights all lie within a compact square formed by the three main boulevards and the River Maine. When you arrive, head for the castle, just off the river between boulevard De Gaulle and quai Ligny. Before you go in, stop at the **Maison du Vin,** the organization representing Anjou's wine producers. It can provide lots of leaflets about wines, sugges-

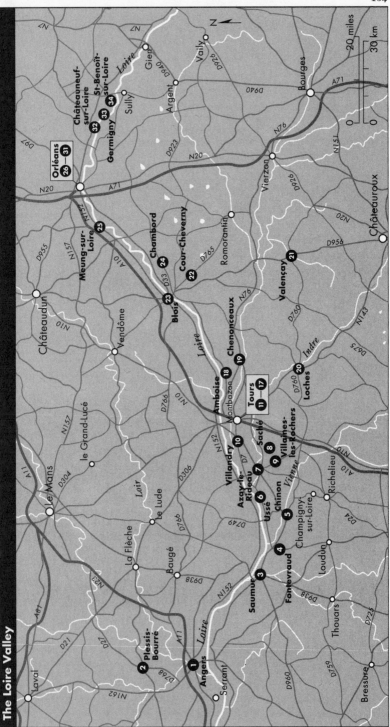

The Loire Valley

154

tions about which vineyards to visit, and even a free sample or two. *5 bis pl. Kennedy.*

The **Château,** a massive shale-and-limestone castle-fortress dating from the 13th century, glowers over the town from behind its turreted moats. The moats are now laid out as gardens, overrun with deer and blooming flowers. As you explore the grounds, note the startling contrast between the thick, defensive walls and the formal garden, with its delicate, white tufa-stone chapel, erected in the 16th century. For a sweeping view of the city and surrounding countryside, climb one of the castle towers.

A new gallery within the castle grounds houses the great **Tapestry of the Apocalypse,** completed in 1390. Measuring 16 feet high and 120 yards long, it shows a series of 70 horrifying and humorous scenes from the Book of Revelations. In one, mountains of fire fall from heaven while boats capsize and men struggle in the water; another shows an intriguing, seven-headed beast. *Pl. Kennedy. Open July and Aug., daily 10–7; Sept.–June, 9:30–noon and 2–5:30. Admission: 22 frs. adults, 12 frs. students and senior citizens, 5 frs. children.*

Just east of the château is the **Cathédrale St-Maurice** (pl. Freppel), a 12th- and 13th-century Gothic cathedral noted for its curious Romanesque facade and original stained-glass windows; you'll need binoculars to appreciate both fully. A few steps north, practically in the cathedral's shadow, lies Angers's large covered food market, **Les Halles** (pl. Mondain; open Tues.–Sun. 9–7). Treat it as a gourmet museum, or stop in for an exotic lunch. A modern shopping mall sits right above it.

Time Out   If you're visiting Les Halles during summer, look out for an impromptu café set up by local fish merchant Jean Foucher. Here you can choose your own sole and have it cooked on the spot, indulge yourself with a platter of *fruits du mer* (shellfish), or enjoy a snack of oysters with a bottle of Anjou wine. Prices are reasonable, the atmosphere quaint and colorful.

Just south of the cathedral, in a house that once sheltered Caesar Borgia and Mary, Queen of Scots, is the **Musée des Beaux-Arts** picture gallery. Among the museum's attractions is an impressive collection of Old Masters from the 17th and 18th century, including paintings by Raphael, Watteau, Fragonard, and Boucher. *10 rue du Musée. Admission: 5 frs. Open Tues.–Sun. 10–noon and 2–6.*

Around the corner, in the refurbished Eglise Toussaint, is the **Musée David d'Angers,** housing a collection of dramatic sculptures by Jean-Pierre David (1788–1859), the city's favorite son. *33 rue Toussaint. Admission: 10 frs. adults, children free. Open Tues.–Sun. 10–noon and 2–6.*

② The château of **Plessis-Bourré** lies 20 kilometers (12 miles) north of Angers by N162 and D768. Built between 1468 and 1473 by Jean Bourré, one of Louis XI's top-ranking civil servants, the château looks like a traditional grim fortress: The bridge across its moat is nearly 50 yards long. Once you step into the central courtyard, however, the gentler mood of the Renaissance takes over.

What makes this place really special is the painted wooden ceiling in the Salle des Gardes (Guard Room). Jean Bourré's hobby was alchemy—an ancient branch of chemistry with more than a touch of the occult—and the ceiling's 24 hexagonal panels are covered with scenes illustrating the craft. Some have overtones of the grotesque dream-world of Renaissance Dutch painter Hieronymus Bosch (1450–1516), while others illustrate folk tales or proverbs. A few must have been painted just for the fun of it: A topless lady steers a land-yacht with wooden wheels (thought to be an allegory of spirit and matter), people urinate ceremoniously (ammonia was extracted from urine), an emaciated wolf takes a bite out of a startled lady (according to folk legend, the wolf's diet was faithful wives, apparently in short supply), and Thurberish dogs gambol in between. You may want to ignore the guide's lecture on furniture and spend your time gazing upward. *Admission: 24 frs. adults, 18 frs. students, 13 frs. children. Open Sept.–Nov. and Apr.–June, Thurs.–Tues. 10–noon and 2–6; Dec.–Mar., Thurs.–Tues. 2–5; closed Wed.*

❸ About 83 kilometers (52 miles) east of Angers by road, and accessible by train, **Saumur** is an excellent base for exploring the western Loire Valley. The town is known for its flourishing mushroom industry, which produces 100,000 tons per year. The same cool tunnels in which the mushrooms grow also provide an ideal storage place for the local *mousseux* (sparkling wines).

You will find an efficient tourist office on place Bilange. Just next door, at the **Maison du Vin de Saumur,** local wine producers show off their products and provide information about visits to local vineyards. *25 rue Beaurepaire. Open summer, Sun., Tues.–Fri. 9–noon and 2–5, closed Mon. and Sat.*

Towering high above town and river is Saumur's elegant, white 14th-century **château.** Though you can reach it by car, it's only a 10-minute walk from the tourist office. The route takes you through the pretty old town and place St-Pierre, with its lively Saturday market.

Time Out When you get to the top of the hill, why not stop off for a picnic on the grass outside the château? If you've forgotten your picnic provisions, there's a café just beside the parking lot.

If the château looks familiar, it's probably because you've seen it in countless reproductions from the famous *Trés Riches Heures* (Book of Hours) painted for the duc de Berri in 1416, now in the Musée Condé at Château de Chantilly (*see* Chapter 4). Inside it's bright and cheerful, with its fairytale gateway and plentiful potted flowers. Two museums, the **Musée des Arts Decoratifs** and the **Musée du Cheval** (Horse Museum), are housed here. The former offers a fine collection of medieval *objets d'art* and 18th- and 19th-century porcelain, while the latter covers the history of the horse, with exhibits ranging from skeletons to saddles. Both are included in the guided tour. Afterwards, climb the **Tour de Guet** (Watch-tower) for an impressive view. *Admission: 18 frs. adults, 10 frs. children and senior citizens. Open July–Sept., daily 9–6:30; Oct. and Apr.–June, daily 9–noon and 2–6; Nov.–Mar., Wed.–Mon. 10–5, closed Tues.*

At **Montreuil-Bellay,** about 17 kilometers (11 miles) south of Saumur on N147, you can visit a 15th-century **château** with majestic towers and pointed roofs. The interior is equally fascinating, offering a fine collection of rich furniture and tapestries, a fully fitted medieval kitchen, and a chapel adorned with frescoes of angelic musicians. For a memorable view, take a stroll in the private gardens; graceful white turrets tower high above the trees and rose bushes, and down below, the little river Thouet winds its lazy way to the Loire. *Pl. des Ormeaux. Admission: 22 frs. Open Apr.–Nov., Wed.–Mon. 10–6; closed Tues.*

Even if the château is closed, be sure to visit the **public gardens** beside the river. Cafés and little restaurants abound.

❹ About 16 kilometers (10 miles) southeast of Saumur is the town of **Fontevraud,** famous for its large, medieval **abbey,** which was of central importance in the histories of both England and France.

Founded in 1099, the abbey offered separate churches and living quarters for nuns, monks, lepers, "repentant" female singers, and the sick. Between 1115 and the French Revolution in 1789, 39 different abbesses—among them a granddaughter of William the Conqueror—directed its operations. The abbey church contains the tombs of Henry II of England; his wife, Eleanor of Aquitaine; and their son, Richard Coeur de Lion— Richard the Lionhearted. Though their bones were scattered during the Revolution, the effigies remain. Napoleon turned the abbey church into a prison, and so it remained until 1963, when historical restoration work—still under way—was begun.

The great 12th-century abbey church is one of the most eclectic architectural structures in France. The medieval section is built of simple stone and topped with a series of domes; the chapter-house, with its collection of 16th-century religious wall paintings (prominent abbesses served as models), is unmistakably Renaissance; and the paving stones bear the salamander emblems of François I. Next to the long refectory, you will find the unusual octagonal kitchen, its tall spire, the **Tour d'Evrault,** serving as one of the abbey's 20 faceted stone chimneys. *Admission: 22 frs. adults, 12 frs. senior citizens, 5 frs. children. Open June–mid-Sept., daily 9–noon and 2–6:30; Sept.–Apr., daily 9:30–12:30 and 2–5.*

❺ **Chinon** lies in the fertile countryside between the Loire and the Vienne rivers, 29 kilometers (18 miles) southeast of Saumur, via Fontevraud. Several trains a day run from Tours, stopping at Azay-le-Rideau on the way. Bicycles can be rented at Chinon station.

The town—birthplace of author François Rabelais (1494–1553) —is dominated by the towering ruins of its medieval **fortress-castle,** perched high above the river Vienne. Though the main tourist office is in the town below, during the summer months a special annex operates from the castle grounds. Both the village and the château stand among steep, cobbled slopes, so wear comfortable walking shoes.

The vast fortress dates from the time of Henry II of England, who died here in 1189 and was buried at Fontevraud. Two centuries later, the castle witnessed an important historical moment: Joan of Arc's recognition of the disguised dauphin, later Charles VII. In the early 17th century, the castle was partially dismantled by its then-owner, Cardinal Richelieu (1585–

1642), who used many of its stones to build a new palace about 24 kilometers (15 miles) away. (That palace no longer exists.)

At Chinon, all but the royal chambers—which house a small museum—is open to the elements. For a fine view of the region, climb the **Coudray Tower,** where, in 1302, leading members of the crusading Knights of Templar were imprisoned before being taken to Paris, tried, and burned at the stake. The **Tour de Horloge,** whose bell has been sounding the hours since 1399, houses a small **Joan of Arc museum.** *Admission: 16 frs. Open Feb–mid-Mar., Wed.–Mon. 10–noon and 2–5, closed Tues.; mid-Mar.–Apr., daily 10–noon and 2–6; June–Sept., daily 10–6; Oct., Wed.–Mon. 10–noon and 2–5, closed Tues.; closed Nov.–Feb.*

Follow the signposted steps down into the old town, or drive your car to the River Vienne pathway. **Place de l'Hôtel**—the main square—is the best place to begin exploring. Stop by the tourist office and pick up a town plan to help you explore the town's fine medieval streets and alleys. While you are there, visit **Le Musée du Vin** (Wine Museum) in the vaulted cellars. This is a fascinating exhibit, full of information on vine growing and wine- and barrel-making. An English commentary is available, and the admission charge entitles you to a sample of the local product. *Admission: 15 frs. Open May–Oct., Fri.–Wed. 10–noon and 2–5; closed Thurs.*

6 About 10 kilometers (6 miles) northeast of Chinon, nestled between the Forest of Chinon and the Loire, is the archetypal fairytale château of Ussé, with its astonishing array of delicate towers and turrets. Tourist literature describes it as the original Sleeping Beauty castle—the inspiration for Charles Perrault's beloved 17th-century story. Though parts of the castle date from the 1400s, most of it was completed two centuries later. It is a flamboyant mix of Gothic and Renaissance styles—stylish and romantic, built for fun, not fighting. Its history supports its playful image: It suffered no bloodbaths—no political conquests or conflicts. And a tablet in the chapel indicates that even the French Revolution passed it by.

After admiring the château's luxurious furnishings and 19th-century French fashion exhibit, climb the spiral stairway to the tower to view the River Indre through the battlements. Here you will also find a waxwork effigy of Sleeping Beauty herself. Before you leave, visit the 16th-century chapel in the garden; its door is decorated with pleasingly sinister skull-and-crossbone carvings. *Admission: 34 frs. Open mid-Mar.–Oct., daily 9–noon and 2–6.*

7 Continuing east about 11 kilometers (7 miles) from Ussé, you soon arrive at **Azay-le-Rideau.** Nestled in a sylvan setting on the banks of the River Indre, this white, 16th-century château was—like Ussé—a Renaissance pleasure-palace rather than a serious fortress.

A financial scandal forced its builder, royal financier Gilles Berthelot, to flee France shortly after its construction in 1520. For centuries, it passed from one private owner to another and was finally bought by the State in 1905. Though the interior offers an interesting blend of furniture and artwork, you may wish to spend most of your time exploring the enchanting private park. During the summer, visitors can enjoy delightful *son-et-lumiere* shows in the castle grounds. *Admission: 22 frs.*

*adults, 12 frs. senior citizens, 5 frs. children. Open Apr.–Sept.,
daily 9:30–noon and 2–6; Oct.–Mar., 9:30–noon and 2–4:45.*

About 6 kilometers (4 miles) east of Azay-le-Rideau is the village of **Saché,** best known for its associations with novelist Honoré de Balzac. Though the town had a real castle during the Middle Ages, the present **château,** built between the 16th and 18th century, is more of a comfortable country house than a fortress. Balzac came here—to the home of his friends, the Marjonnes—during the 1830s, both to write and to escape his creditors. The château houses a substantial **Balzac museum,** with exhibits ranging from photographs to original manuscripts to the coffee pot he used to help keep him going up to 16 hours a day.

Those who have never read Balzac and don't understand spoken French may find little of interest in Saché; those who have, and do, will return to the novels with fresh enthusiasm and understanding. *Admission: 15 frs. Open Feb.–mid-Mar., Thurs.–Tues. 9–noon and 2–5; mid-Mar.–Sept., daily 9–noon and 2–6; Oct.–Nov., Thurs.–Tues. 9–noon and 2–5; closed Dec. and Jan.*

From Saché, it's worth making a brief detour to **Villaines-les-Rochers,** about 6 kilometers (4 miles) southwest, to see the village's interesting **wickerwork cooperative.** Local people have been producing *osier* (or willow) products for centuries. In 1849, when the craft was threatened with extinction, the parish priest persuaded 65 small groups of basketweavers to form France's first agricultural workers' cooperative. Museum exhibits tell the story, and lots of handmade objects—from sofas to cat baskets to babies' rattles—are on sale. *Sociéte Cooperative de Vannerie. Admission: free. Open most of the year, Mon.–Sat. 10–noon and 2–6, Sun. 10–noon and 2–7.*

After leaving Villaines-les-Rochers, head for **Villandry,** following D57 back through Azay-le-Rideau. The **Château de Villandry** stands on the south side of the Loire, about 19 kilometers (12 miles) southwest of Tours. Its extravagant, terraced gardens are well worth a visit.

Both the gardens and the château date from the 16th century, but, over the years, both fell into disrepair. In 1906, Spanish doctor Joachim Carvalla and his wife, American heiress Ann Coleman, bought the property and began a long process of restoration. The gardens were replanted according to a rigorous, geometrical design, with zigzagging hedges enclosing flower beds, vegetable plots, and gravel walks. The result is an aristocratic 16th-century *jardin à la française.* Below an avenue of 1,500 precisely pruned lime trees lies an ornamental lake, filled with swans: Not a ripple is out of place. The aromatic and medicinal garden, with plots neatly labeled in three languages, is especially appealing.

The château itself has a remarkable gilded ceiling—imported from Toledo, in Spain—and a collection of fine Spanish paintings. However, the garden is unquestionably the main attraction, and since it is usually open during the two-hour French lunch break, you can have it to yourself for a good part of the afternoon. *Admission: château and gardens, 24 frs.; gardens only, 17 frs. Château open mid-Mar.–mid-Nov., daily 9–6; garden is open all year, daily 9–sunset (or 8, whichever is earlier).*

About 20 kilometers (12 miles) east of Villandry lies the city of **Tours,** an ideal center from which to tour the Loire Valley's attractions by public transportation. Trains from Tours run along the river in both directions, and regular bus services radiate from here; in addition, the city is the starting point for a variety of organized bus excursions (many with English-speaking guides). The town has mushroomed into a city of a quarter of a million inhabitants, with an ugly modern sprawl of factories, high-rise blocks, and overhead expressway junctions. Nevertheless, the town center remains pleasant and manageable. Travelers with cars may prefer to base themselves in any of a dozen smaller towns within half an hour's drive of Tours (Montbazon, in particular, 10 kilometers/6 miles south, is recommended for its hotels and restaurants—*see* Dining and Lodging, below), but they should certainly explore the city during their stay.

Start your tour at place du Maréchal Leclerc, usually called the **place de la Gare.** Here, you will find the fine Belle Epoque train station, with its cast-iron curlicues, the bus station, and the tourist office. Many of the most convenient hotels are situated here or just around the corner.

The city plan is fairly simple. Turn left from place du Maréchal Leclerc, down boulevard Heurteloup, to reach place Jean-Jaurès; then turn right into rue Nationale. This street holds many of the city's major shops, and if you continue along it for just over half a mile, you reach the River Loire. Turning right near the river end, you soon reach the cathedral, the château, and the Musée des Beaux-Arts. If you turn left, you come to the place Plumereau, and a quaint pedestrian precinct.

The **Cathédrale St-Gatien,** built between 1239 and 1484, reveals a mixture of architectural styles. The stained glass, in particular, deserves binoculars, and you will want to visit the little children's tomb with its kneeling angels, built in memory of the two children of Charles VIII and Anne of Brittany. *Rue Lavoisier. Closed noon–2.*

What is left of the château is of minor interest, but within it, you will find the **Historial de la Touraine**—a group of more than 150 waxwork models representing historical figures, such as St. Martin and Joan of Arc, whose deeds helped shape this region over 15 centuries. There's also a small aquarium. *Quai d'Orleans. Admission: wax museum, 28 frs. adults, 24 frs. students, 18 frs. children; aquarium, 16 frs. adults, 8 frs. children. Open daily, mid-Sept.–mid-Nov. 9–noon and 2–7; mid-Nov.–mid-Mar. 2–6; mid-Mar.–mid-June 9–noon and 2–7; mid-June–mid-Sept. 9–7.*

Next door, in what was once the archbishop's palace, is the **Musée des Beaux-Arts** (Fine Arts Museum). It houses an eclectic selection of treasures: works by Rubens, Rembrandt, Boucher, Degas, sculptor Alexander Calder—even Fritz the Elephant, stuffed in 1902. *18 pl. François Sieard. Admission: 11 frs. adults, 5.50 frs. students, children and senior citizens free. Open Wed.–Mon. 9–12:45 and 2–6; closed Tues.*

Two small museums stand at the river end of rue Nationale: the **Musée des Vins** (Wine Museum) and the **Musée du Compagnonnage** (Guild Museum). You may wish to see the latter, at least. *Compagnonnage* is a sort of apprenticeship-trade-union

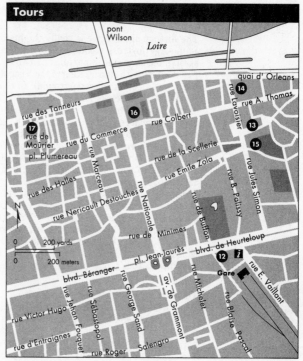

system, and here you see the masterpieces of the candidates for guild membership: virtuoso craftwork, some of it eccentric (an Eiffel Tower made of slate, for instance, or a varnished-noodle château). These stand as evidence of the devotion to craftsmanship that is still an important feature of French life. Both the guild and wine museums are set in and around the cloisters of an old church—a pleasant setting, and you are free to visit them at your own pace. *16 rue Nationale. Admission: 10 frs. adults, 5 frs. students, children free. Open Wed.–Mon. 9–noon and 2–6; closed Tues.*

From rue Nationale, narrow rue du Commerce leads you to the oldest and most attractive part of Tours, the area around **place Plumereau**. It's a great area for strolling, largely traffic free, and full of little squares, open-air cafés, and pricey antiques shops. From place Plumereau, head one block along rue Briconnet, and take the first left into rue des Moûrier. The **Musée Gemmail**, halfway down on the right in the imposing 19th-century Hôtel Raimbault, houses an unusual collection of three-dimensional colored-glass window panels. Depicting patterns, figures, and even portraits, the panels are both beautiful and intriguing, since most of the gemlike fragments of glass come from broken bottles. *7 rue Moûrier. Admission: 12 frs. Open Apr.–mid-Oct., Tues.–Sun. 10–noon and 2:30–6.*

Tour 2: The Eastern Loire Valley— Amboise to Orléans

On the south side of the Loire, about 26 kilometers (16 miles) due east of Tours, is **Amboise**, a picturesque little town with bustling markets, plentiful hotels and restaurants, and a historic **château.**

The history of Amboise is really the history of its château. A Stone-Age fortress stood here, and an early bridge gave the stronghold strategic importance. In AD 503, Clovis, King of the Franks, met with Alaric, King of the Visigoths, on an island (now the site of an excellent campground). In the years that followed, the Normans attacked the fortress repeatedly. The 15th and 16th centuries were Amboise's golden age, and during this time, the château, enlarged and embellished, became a royal palace. Charles VII stayed here, as did the unfortunate Charles VIII, best remembered for banging his head on a low doorway (you will be shown it) and dying as a result. François I, whose long nose appears in so many château paintings, based his court here. In 1560, his son, young François II, settled here with his wife, Mary Stuart (otherwise known as Mary, Queen of Scots), and his mother, Catherine de Médici. The castle was also the setting for the Amboise Conspiracy, an ill-fated Protestant plot organized against François II; visitors are shown where the corpses of 1,200 conspirators dangled from the castle walls. In later years, a decline set in, and demolition occurred both before and after the Revolution. Today, only about a third of the original building remains standing.

The château's interior is partly furnished, though not with the original objects; these vanished when the building was converted to a barracks and then a button factory. The great round tower is reached by a spiral ramp, rather than a staircase; designed for horsemen, it is wide enough to accommodate a small car. You are free to explore the grounds at your own pace, including the little chapel of St-Hubert, with its carvings of the Virgin and Child, Charles VIII, and Anne of Brittany. There are frequent *son-et-lumière* pageants on summer evenings. *Admission: 25 frs. adults, 8 frs. children. Open Sept.–June, daily 9–noon and 2–5; July and Aug., daily 9–6:30.*

Up rue Victor-Hugo, five minutes from the château, is the **Clos Lucé,** a handsome Renaissance manor house. François I lent the house to Leonardo da Vinci, who spent the last four years of his life here, dying in 1519. You can wander from room to room at will. The basement houses an extraordinary exhibition: working models of some of Leonardo's inventions. Though impractical in his own time, perhaps, when technology was limited, they were built recently by engineers from IBM, using the detailed sketches contained in the artist's notebooks. Mechanisms on display include three-speed gearboxes, a military tank, a clockwork car, and even a flying machine. *At the eastern end of rue Victor-Hugo. Admission: 26 frs. adults, 17 frs. children and senior citizens. Open Sept.–June, daily 9–noon and 2–6; July and Aug., daily 9–7.*

Time Out After you've marveled at Leonardo's genius, you can explore the garden and grab a quick bite at the convenient snack bar.

About 10 kilometers (6 miles) south of Amboise lies the village of **Chenonceaux.** (For some reason, the village is spelled Chenonceaux and the château, Chenonceau.) You could happily spend the best part of a day here. From long-ago historical figures, such as Diane de Poitiers, Catherine de Médici, and Mary, Queen of Scots, to a host of modern travel writers, many have called Chenonceau the "most exciting" and the "most romantic" of all Loire châteaus. You are free to wander at your will (there are enough attendants to answer questions). For most of the year, the château is open—unlike many others—all day. Its only drawback is its popularity: If you want to avoid a roomfull of English schoolchildren, take a stroll in the grounds and come back when they stop for lunch.

More pleasure-palace than fortress, Chenonceau was built in 1520 by Thomas Bohier, a wealthy tax collector. When he went bankrupt, it passed to François I. Later, Henri II gave it to his mistress, Diane de Poitiers. After his death, Henri's not-so-understanding widow, Catherine de Médici, expelled Diane to nearby Chaumont and took the château back. It is to Catherine that we owe the lovely gardens and the handsome three-story extension whose arches span the river.

Before you go inside, pick up an English leaflet at the gate. Then walk around to the right of the main building and admire the peaceful, delicate architecture; the formal garden; and the river gliding under the arches. The romantically inclined may want to rent a rowboat and spend an hour drifting. Inside the château are splendid ceilings, colossal fireplaces, and authentic furnishings. Paintings include works by Rubens, Andrea del Sarto, and Correggio. And as you tour the rooms, be sure to pay your respects to former-owner Madame Dupin, whose face is captured in Nattier's charming portrait. Thanks to the great affection Madame Dupin inspired among her proletarian neighbors, the château and its treasures survived the Revolution intact.

A waxwork exhibition (**Musée des Circes**), housed in one of the outbuildings, illustrates four centuries of French history. There are also excellent *son-et-lumière* shows throughout the summer. *Admission: château 30 frs. adults, 20 frs. children; wax museum 5 frs. Open mid-Feb.–mid-Nov., daily 9–5, 6, or 7, depending on the season; mid-Nov.–mid-Feb., daily 9–4:30.*

Time Out   If you feel like spending the day at Chenonceau, refuel in the inexpensive, self-serve restaurant situated in the former stables.

20   About 18 kilometers (11 miles) due south of Chenonceaux lies the town of **Loches**, set on a rocky spur just beside the River Indre. Like Chinon, Loches is a walled citadel dominating a small, medieval village. But although Chinons citadel is a ruined shell, much of Loches's is well preserved and stands as a living part of the town.

As you approach the citadel, the first building you will come across is the church of **St-Ours**: Note its striking roof formed of octagonal pyramids, dating from the 12th century; the doorway sculpted with owls, monkeys, and mythical beasts; and the baptismal font converted from a Roman altar.

The **Logis Royaux**—the château—has a terrace that provides a fine view of the roofs and river below and the towers and swallows' nests above. Inside, keep an eye out for the vicious, two-man crossbow that could pierce an oak door at 200 yards. There are some interesting pictures, too, including a copy of the well-known portrait that shows an extremely disgruntled Charles VII and one of his mistresses, Agnes Sorel, poised as a virtuous Virgin Mary (though semitopless). Her alabaster image decorates her tomb, guarded by angels and lambs. Agnes died in 1450, aged 28, probably the result of poisoning by Charles's son, the future Louis XI. The little chapel was built by Charles VIII for his queen, Anne of Brittany, and is lavishly decorated with sculpted ermine tails, the lady's emblem.

After the tour, amble over to the *donjon*, or tower keep. One 11th-century tower, half-ruined and roofless, is open for individual exploration, though the others require guided supervision. These towers contain dungeons and will delight anyone who revels in prison cells and torture chambers. *Admission: 20 frs. Open Feb.–mid-Mar., Thurs.–Tues. 9–noon and 2–6, mid-Mar.–June, daily 9–noon and 2–6; July and Aug., daily 9–6; Sept. and Oct., Thurs.–Tues. 9–noon and 2–5; closed Nov.–Jan.*

㉑ The town of **Valençay,** with its pleasant château, lies just over 40 kilometers (25 miles) southeast of Chenonceaux and 48 kilometers (30 miles) east of Loches. Though it is some distance south of the Loire, it is well worth a visit.

A palace, rather than a castle, Valençay was started in the 16th century, though most of the surviving structure was added later. Talleyrand (1754–1838), the opportunistic statesman and diplomat, who managed to survive whatever the regime, left his mark here. A young but not very pious bishop under Louis XVI, Talleyrand played a leading role in the Revolution and was foreign minister under Napoleon. After Napoleon's fall he helped reshape Europe at the Congress of Vienna, supporting the return of the Bourbon monarchy. While serving as Napoleon's foreign minister, he was instructed to buy a suitable palace to impress visiting royalty and ambassadors: The result was Valençay. In these grandiose and seductive surroundings, he wove his political spells and enjoyed himself for a quarter of a century. The many rooms open to the public have luscious furnishings and decorations.

The grounds at Valençay include a formal French garden with statues, peacocks, and precisely cut hedges; a park where kangaroos and llamas roam; and the **Musée de l'Automobiles Anciennes,** exhibiting more than 80 polished cars and motorcycles dating from 1898. *Admission: 25 frs. adults, 20 frs. senior citizens, 15 frs. children. Open mid.-Mar.–mid-Nov., daily 9–noon and 2–dusk or 8; mid-Nov.–mid-Mar., weekends and national holidays 9–noon and 1:30–4:30; château closed Nov.–Mar.*

㉒ On your journey north, stop off for an afternoon at the village of **Cour-Cheverny,** just over 20 kilometers (12 miles) outside Blois. The main attraction is the classical **château of Cheverny,** finished in 1634. Its interior, with its painted and gilded rooms, splendid furniture, and rich tapestries depicting the labors of Hercules, is one of the grandest in the Loire region. Patriotic visitors will spot a bronze of George Washington in the gallery, alongside a document bearing his signature. Together, Louis XVI and Washington founded the Society of the Cincinnati, reserved for officers who fought in the War of Independence. Three of the present owner's ancestors were members of the group.

One of the chief delights of Cheverny is that you can wander freely at your own pace. Unfortunately, the gardens are off-limits, as is the Orangery, where the *Mona Lisa* and other masterpieces were hidden during World War II. But you are free to contemplate the antlers of 2,000 stags in a nearby Trophy Room. Hunting, called "venery" in the leaflets, continues vigorously here, red coats, bugles, and all. In the kennels next door, dozens of hounds lounge about waiting for meals. Feeding times—*la soupe aux chiens*—are posted on a noticeboard, and visitors are welcome to watch the dogs eat their dinner. *Admission: 22 frs. adults, 13 frs. children and senior citizens. Open mid-June–mid-Sept., daily 9–6:30; mid-Sept.–mid-June, daily 9:30–noon and 2:30–5.*

㉓ As you leave Cheverny, follow D765 north to **Blois,** a quaint yet convenient touring center off A10, about midway between Tours and Orléans. Perched on a steep hillside overlooking the Loire, its white facades, red-brick chimneys, and blue-slate roofs create a cheerful, tricolor effect. The city is also quite accessible, posing few traffic problems and offering direct train links to Paris and all the major towns along the Loire.

The **château** at Blois is among the valley's finest. Your ticket entitles you to a guided tour—in English when there are enough visitors who can't understand French—but you are more than welcome to wander around without a guide if you visit between mid-March and August. Before you enter the building, stand in the courtyard and admire four centuries of architecture. On one side stands the 13th-century hall and tower, the latter offering a stunning view of town and countryside. The Renaissance begins to flower in the Louis XII wing (built between 1498 and 1503), through which you enter, and comes to full bloom in the François I wing (1515–24). The masterpiece here is the openwork spiral staircase, painstakingly restored. The fourth side is the Classical Gaston d'Orléans wing (1635–38).

At the bottom of the staircase, there's a *diaporama,* an audiovisual display tracing the château's history. Upstairs you'll find a series of enormous rooms with tremendous fireplaces, decorated with the gilded porcupine, emblem of Louis XII; the ermine of Anne of Brittany; and, of course, François I's salamander, breathing fire and surrounded by flickering flames. There are intricate ceilings, carved and gilded paneling, and a sad little picture of Mary, Queen of Scots. In the great council room, the duc de Guise was murdered on the orders of Henri III in 1588. Don't miss the **Musée des Beaux-Arts,** the art gallery, in the Louis XII wing. The miscellaneous collection of paintings from the 16th to the 19th centuries is interesting and often amusing. The château also offers a *son-et-lumière* display most summer evenings. *Admission: 21 frs. adults, 11 frs. children and senior citizens. Open Apr.–Aug., daily 9–6; Sept.–Mar., daily 9–noon and 2–5.*

㉔ The château of **Chambord** lies 18 kilometers (11 miles) east of Blois on D33, in the middle of a royal game forest. The largest of the Loire châteaus, Chambord is also one of the valley's two most popular touring destinations (Chenonceau being the other). But although everyone thinks Chenonceau is extravagantly beautiful, reactions are mixed as to the qualities of Chambord. Chambord is the kind of place William Randolph Hearst would have built if he had enough money: It's been described as "megalomaniac," "an enormous film-set extravaganza," and, in its favor, "the most outstanding experience of the Loire Valley."

A few facts set the tone: the facade is 420 feet long, there are 440 rooms and 365 chimneys, and a wall 32 kilometers (20 miles) long encloses the 13,000-acre forest (you can wander in 3,000 of these, the rest being reserved for wild boar and other game creatures). François I started building in 1519, a job that took 12 years and required 1,800 workmen. His original grandiose idea was to divert the Loire to form a moat, but someone (probably his adviser, Leonardo da Vinci) persuaded him to make do with the River Cosson. François used the château only for short stays; yet, when he first arrived, 12,000 horses were required to transport his luggage, servants, and hangers-on! Later kings also used Chambord as an occasional retreat, and Sun King Louis XIV had Molière perform here. In the 18th century, Louis XV gave the château to Maréchal de Saxe as a reward for his victory over the English and Dutch at Fontenoy in 1745. When not besporting himself with wine, women, and song, the marshal stood on the roof overseeing the exercises of his own regiment of 1,000 cavalry.

Now, after long neglect—all the original furnishings vanished during the French Revolution—Chambord belongs to the nation. Vast rooms are open to visitors (you can wander freely), and have been filled with a variety of exhibits—not all concerned with Chambord, but interesting nonetheless. Children will enjoy repeated trips up and down the enormous **double-helix staircase:** It looks like a single staircase, but an entire regiment could march up one spiral while a second came down the other, and they would never meet. Also be sure to visit the roof terrace, whose forest of towers, turrets, cupolas, gables, and chimneys was described by 19th-century novelist Henry James as "more like the spires of a city than the salient points of a single building."

Chambord also offers a short *son-et-lumière* show, in French, English, and German, successively, on many evenings from mid-May to mid-October. *Admission: 22 frs. adults, 5 frs. children. Open July and Aug., daily 9:30–6:30; Sept.–June, daily 9:30–11:45 and 2–4:30, 5:30, or 6:30 depending on season.*

The remainder of this last leg of our Loire Valley tour follows **㉕** the river itself. **Meung-sur-Loire** lies about 30 kilometers (20 miles) northeast, though you may want to backtrack to Blois and continue along the river road from there. The town's most famous citizen was Jehan de Meung, born in 1260, and author of the best-selling *Roman de la Rose*. (Later, Geoffrey Chaucer produced a well-known English translation.)

The **château** at Meung is part 12th-century fortress, part 18th-century residence. From the 12th century to the French Revolution, it served mainly as the official residence of the bishops of Orléans, although in 1429, Lord Salisbury used it as his headquarters during the seige of Orléans. (When he was killed in the fray, Lord Talbot took over, but could not prevent Joan of Arc from capturing the château.) It was sold off after the French Revolution, and when its present owner, M. Tachon, bought it in 1970, it had stood empty and derelict for years. Tachon began a long process of restoring and furnishing it, filling it with a diverse collection of items ranging from 12th-century antiquities to souvenirs from his own life. The weapons room contains crossbows, World War II submachine guns, and military helmets from the Middle Ages to 1945.

The most unusual part of the château is underground, where the owner is in the process of exploring and reopening a network of tunnels, dungeons, and storehouses, with a chapel and torture chamber. *16 pl. Martroi. Admission: 20 frs. adults, 6 frs. children. Open mid-Mar.–mid-Nov., daily 8:30–5; mid-Nov.–mid-Mar., weekends and national holidays only, 9–5.*

Leaving Meung, follow N152 northeast about 18 kilometers (11 miles) to **Orléans,** a thriving commercial city at the geographic and historical center of France. Its strategic position as a natural bridgehead over the Loire has long made it the target of hostile confrontations and invasions. Julius Caesar slaughtered its inhabitants and burned it to the ground. Five centuries later, Atilla and his Huns did much the same. Next came the Normans; then the Valois kings turned it into a secondary capital. The story of the Hundred Years' War, Joan of Arc, and the siege of Orléans is widely known. During the Wars of Religion (1562–98), much of the cathedral was destroyed, and a century ago, ham-fisted town planners razed many of the city's fine old buildings. During World War II, both German and Allied bombs helped finish the job. Nevertheless, there is much of interest left, and, in recent years, dedicated and sensitive planners have done much to bring the city back to life.

The tourist office is on boulevard de Verdun, just in front of the train station. From here, rue de la République takes you 400 yards south to the main square—the **place du Martroi,** with its statue of Joan of Arc. A block farther south, turn left for the cathedral, down rue Jeanne d'Arc, or continue south down **rue Royale;** the latter is lined with excellent shops of all descriptions. Rue Royale brings you to the quai du Chatelet and the banks of the Loire. Make a left turn here to arrive at the **Nouvelle Halle,** the covered market, with its tempting food displays. (Drivers would do best to park at the Campo Santo, by the cathedral, where there's a large underground parking lot.)

Cathédrale Ste-Croix is a riot of pinnacles and gargoyles, both Gothic and pseudo-Gothic, the whole embellished with 18th-century wedding-cake towers. Novelist Marcel Proust (1871–1922) called it France's ugliest church, but most people find it impressive. Inside you'll see vast quantities of stained glass and 18th-century woodcarving, plus the modern **Chapel of Joan of Arc,** with plaques in memory of the British and American war dead. *Rue Jeanne d' Arc. Open daily 8:30–noon and 2–7.*

The modern **Musée des Beaux-Arts** (the art gallery) is just across the street from the cathedral. Take the elevator to the top and work your way down, viewing works by artists such as Tintoretto, Velásquez, Watteau, Boucher, Rodin, and Gauguin. *1 rue Ferdinand Rabier. Admission: 10 frs. adults, 5 frs. students and senior citizens. Open Wed.–Mon. 10–noon and 2–6; closed Tues.*

Retrace your steps along the rue Jeanne d'Arc and turn left into place Abbé Desnoyers for a visit to Orléans's **Musée Historique.** This Renaissance town house contains both "fine" and "popular" works of art connected with the town's history

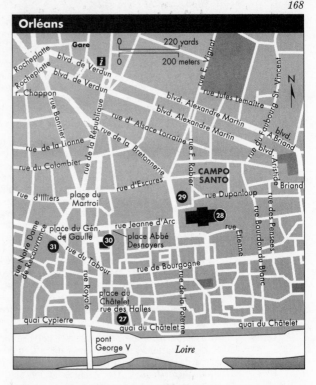

and a remarkable collection of pagan bronzes of animals and dancers. These last were hidden from missionaries in the 4th century and discovered in a sand pit near St-Benoît only in 1861. *Hôtel Cabu, pl. Abbé Desnoyers. Admission: 7 frs. adults, 3.50 frs. students. Open Apr.–Sept., Wed.–Mon. 10–noon and 2–6; Oct.–Mar., 10–noon and 2–5; closed Tues.*

③1 Another block west on rue Jeanne d'Arc, in place du Général de Gaulle, is **La Maison de Jeanne d'Arc.** Seventeen-year-old Joan stayed on the site during the 10-day siege of Orléans in 1429, in a house that underwent many changes before it was bombed flat in 1940. This reconstruction contains exhibits about her life, costumes of her time, and models of siege engines. *Pl. du Général de Gaulle. Admission: 7 frs. adults, 3.50 frs. students. Open May–Oct., Tues.–Sun. 10–noon and 2–6; Nov.–Apr., Tues.–Sun. 2–6; closed Mon.*

③2 About 25 kilometers (15 miles) east of Orléans, the leafy village of **Châteauneuf-sur-Loire** is a convenient base from which to explore the towns and countryside of the eastern Loire.

Though the **château** was destroyed in the French Revolution, its outbuildings and garden survive. Beyond them stretches a delightful public park, laid out *à l'anglaise*—in a "natural" way —with giant tulip trees, magnolias, weeping willows, and rhododendrons, especially beautiful in late May and early June. Little streams snake their way across the parkland, passing benches, shady copses, and scenic picnic spots on their way to the Loire.

You may also want to visit the **Musée de la Marine,** whose exhibits chronicle the history of navigation on the Loire. Paintings, photographs, documents, and model boats illustrate the boatman's life. *In the basement of the Mairie (town hall). Admission: 7.50 frs. adults, 4 frs. students. Open July and Aug., Wed.–Mon. 10–noon and 2–5:30, closed Tues.; June and Sept., Mon. and Wed.–Fri. 2–5:30, closed Tues.; Apr.–May, weekends only, 10–noon and 2–5:30. Other months by appointment.*

33 On the north bank of the Loire, just 5 kilometers (3 miles) southeast of Châteauneuf, is the little village of **Germigny.** Around AD 800, Theodulf, an abbot of St-Benoît, built a tiny **church** here, which is often cited as the oldest in France. A square Byzantine arrangement of rounded arches on square pillars, with indirect lighting filtering from smaller arches above the central square, it was carefully restored to its original condition during the last century. Though Theodulf himself brought most of the original mosaics from Italy, only one— covered in plaster and discovered in 1848—survives. Made of 130,000 cubes of colored glass, it shows the Ark of the Covenant transported by angels with golden halos. The Latin inscription asks us not to forget Theodulf in our prayers. *Open daily 9–noon and 2–5.*

34 The little town of **St-Benoît-sur-Loire** lies about 10 kilometers (6 miles) southeast of Chateâuneuf and 5½ kilometers (3½ miles) from Germigny. Its highlight is the ancient **Abbey of St-Benoît,** often hailed as the greatest Romanesque church in France; village signposts refer to it as *la Basilique.*

St-Benoît, or St. Benedict, was the founder of the Benedictine monastic order. In AD 650, a group of monks chose this safe and fertile spot for their new monastery, returning to Monte Cassino, Italy, to retrieve the bones of St. Benedict with which to bless the site. Despite protests from priests at the church at Monte Cassino, some of the relics remain here, in the 11th-century abbey church bearing his name. Following the Hundred Years' War of the 14th and 15th centuries, the monastery fell into a decline, and the Wars of Religion (1562–98) wrought further damage. During the French Revolution, the monks dispersed and the buildings were destroyed, all except for the abbey church itself, which became the parish church. Monastic life here began anew in 1944, when the monks rebuilt their monastery and regained the abbey church for their own use. The pillars of the tower porch are noted for their intricately carved capitals, and the choir floor is an amazing patchwork of many-colored marble.

Gregorian chants can be heard daily, at mass or vespers, and Sunday services attract worshippers and music lovers from all around. Visitors are welcome to explore the church crypt. *Mass and vespers Sun. 11 and 6:15 PM, Mon.–Sat. noon and 6:15 PM. Guided English-language tours of the monastic buildings can be arranged; inquire at the monastery shop.*

What to See and Do with Children

Older children should enjoy visiting a handful of châteaus— especially **Chambord** (Tour 2), with its extravagant staircase and wild parkland, and the eerie tunnels and dungeons at **Meung** (Tour 2). Make-it-yourself cardboard models of the famous palaces—available in most giftshops—are also popular and help enrich children's visits.

For a fun family outing, try the **Parc Zoologique,** a privately run zoo in a garden setting surrounded by golden limestone quarries. The deer, emu, monkeys—even the vultures—all look happy and well cared for; the hefty admission charge goes to safeguard endangered species. *Rte. de Cholet, 49700 Doué-la-Fontaine, about 16 km/10 mi west of Saumur, tel. 41–59–18–58. Admission: 35 frs. Open May–Sept., daily 9–7; Oct.–Apr., daily 10–12:30 and 2–6.*

Parc Floral de la Source, about 8 kilometers (5 miles) south of Orléans, offers mighty trees, a minizoo, swings, acres of flowers and flowering plants, and a little train that comes in handy when your feet give out. *Parc Floral, 45100 Orléans-la-Source, tel. 38–63–33–17. Admission: 14 frs. (7 frs. winter). Open May –Oct., daily 9–6; Nov.–Apr., daily 2–5.*

Off the Beaten Track

The 16th-century château of **Gué-Péan** is hidden in wooded grounds near the village of Monthou-sur-Cher, about 10 kilometers (6 miles) from Montrichard. It's neither museum nor showcase, but the ancestral home of the Marquis de Keguelin, whose family still lives here. Inside you'll find a miscellany of furniture, paintings, and interesting *objets.* To offset the cost of maintaining the château, the Marquis also runs an excellent bed-and-breakfast service; dinner, if wanted, is often taken in his charming company. *Monthou-sur-Cher, 41400 Montrichard, tel. 54–71–43–01. Open mid-Mar.–Sept., daily 9–5; Oct.–mid-Mar., daily 9–noon and 2–5.*

Thirty-two kilometers (20 miles) northwest of Blois via D957 is the charming town of **Vendôme.** It's not on most tourists' itineraries, but its picturesque appeal amply merits the detour. Vendôme's château is in ruins, but the **gardens** surrounding it offer knockout views of the town center. From place du Château, head up to admire the Flamboyant Gothic abbey church of **La Trinité,** with its unusual 12th-century clock tower and fine stained glass. Take time to stroll through the narrow streets of this enchanting little town.

The fortress-castle of **Châteaudun** lies 45 kilometers (28 miles) northeast of Vendôme via fast N10. Its austere facade is decidedly grim, but the internal courtyard is overlooked by buildings of a more welcoming aspect, thanks to 16th-century restoration work. The interior contains period furniture and tapestries, but the highlight is the **Sainte-Chapelle,** with its collection of 15th-century statues. *Admission: 14 frs. Open Easter–Sept., daily 8–11:45 and 2–6; Oct.–Easter, Sun. 10–11:45 and 2–6.*

The sumptuous moated **Château de Serrant** is only 16 kilometers (10 miles) southwest of Angers, near St-Georges-sur-Loire. Begun in 1546, and gaining additions during the 17th and 18th centuries, it contains lush interiors, paneled and hung with tapestries. The library, holding over 10,000 volumes, is magnificent. Like the château de Gué-Péan, the château is a private residence. *Admission: 22 frs. Open Easter –Oct., Wed.–Mon. 9–11:30 and 2–6; closed Tues.*

Champigny-sur-Veude is just 13 kilometers (8 miles) south of Chinon along D749, but visitors to its **Sainte-Chapelle** (holy chapel) are few. What many miss is some of the best Renaissance stained-glass in the world. The chapel was originally part of a château built between 1508 and 1543 but razed a century later by order of jealous neighbor Cardinal Richelieu. Its 16th-century windows relate scenes from the Passion, Crucifixion, and life of 13th-century French King St-Louis; note the vividness and harmony of the colors, especially the purplish blues. *Admission: 24 frs. Open Apr.–Sept., daily 9–noon and 2–6.*

Five miles farther down D749 is the town of **Richelieu,** founded by Cardinal Richelieu in 1631, along with a huge château intended to be one of the most lavish in Christendom. All that's left of the latter are a few buildings and some parklands, though the town remains a rare example of rigid, symmetrical, and unspoiled Classical town planning, well worth seeing: Its bombastic scale and state of preservation are unique. The severe, straight streets have not changed for 350 years, give or take the occasional traffic sign.

Shopping

Wine The region's extra-special produce is Loire wine. It's not a practical buy for tourists—except for instant consumption—but if wine-tasting tours of vineyards inspire you, enterprising winemakers will arrange shipment to the United States; think in terms of hundreds rather than dozens. Try the **Maison du Vin** in Angers (pl. Président-Kennedy, next to the tourist office), and **Maison des Vins de Touraine** in Tours (4 bis blvd. Heurteloup).

Gift Ideas Loire food specialties include barley sugar *(sucre d'orge)* and prunes stuffed with marzipan *(pruneux fourrés);* both are widely available at food shops throughout the valley. A sweet-toothed specialty of the Orléans district is *cotignac*—an orangey-red molded jelly made from quinces. It, too, can be bought from most local patisseries and is produced almost exclusively by **Gilbert Jumeau** (1 rue Voisinas, St-Ay), 8 kilometers (5 miles) west of Orléans. For fine chocolates, try the **Chocolaterie Royale** in Orléans (53 rue Royale).

Antiques All major towns have high-quality antiques for sale. There are numerous antiques shops in **rue de la Scellerie** in Tours, and you can also pick up some fine pieces at **Au Vieux Tours** (91 rue Colbert). In Saumur, try **Galerie Beaurepaire** (7 rue Beaurepaire); in Fontevraud, **Christian Saulnier** (4 av. Rochechouart). Angers has an interesting **flea market** on Saturdays (pl. Imbach).

Arts and Crafts Gien, on the north bank of the Loire a few miles past Sully and St-Benoît, is a major earthenware center; the factory, **Faïenceries de Gien** (8 pl. Victoire, tel. 38–67–00–05), can be contacted for private visits. In addition to its wines, **La Maison de Touraine** in Tours (4 bis blvd. Heurteloup; closed Sun. and Mon. mornings) offers a wide selection of local products and crafts, including ceramics. For fine wickerwork, visit the shop at the **Société Coopérative de Vannerie** in Villaines-les-Rochers, near Saché.

Sports and Fitness

Bicycling The Loire region is excellent country for biking—not too hilly, not too flat. Bikes can be rented at most train stations, and at dozens of other outlets (try **Au Col de Cygne,** 46 bis rue du Dr-

Fournier, Tours; and **Leprovost,** 13 rue Carnot, Azay-le-Rideau). Loisirs Accueil offices in Blois and Orleans offer organized trips; these often include luggage transportation and camp or youth hostel accommodations. Ask at the nearest tourist office or contact **Loisirs Accueil** (3 rue de la Bretonnerie, Orléans, tel. 38–62–04–88; or 11 pl. du Château, Blois, tel. 54–78–55–50).

Hiking Scenic footpaths abound. Long-distance walking paths *(sentiers de grande randonnée)* pass through the Loire Valley and are marked on Michelin maps with broken lines and route numbers. Tourist offices will supply sketch-maps of interesting paths in their area.

Fishing and Shooting The **Loisirs Accueil** office in Orleans (*see* above) organizes week-long and weekend fishing and shooting outings in the Forest of Orléans. Some include accommodations in two-star hotels.

Horseback Riding The region offers abundant facilities and activities, including pony-trekking trips and week-long equestrian tours. Try **La Poitevinere,** just north of Saumur on N147, tel. 41–52–55–08. You can also rent a horse at **Chambord,** from the former stables of the marshal of Saxe, and ride in the vast National Park surrounding the château (tel. 54–20–31–01).

Water sports Good facilities for canoeing, sailing, fishing, and windsurfing can be found at the **Centre Nautique du Lac de Maine** (tel. 41–73–05–03) in Angers and the **Lac de Loire** (tel. 54–78–82–05) near Blois. The Loire itself has swift and dangerous currents, so swim only at "official" beaches (signposted *plages)*, which are safe and supervised. Package canoeing and kayaking trips can be arranged through local Loisirs Accueil offices (*see* above).

Dining and Lodging

Dining

The Loire region, known as the "garden of France," produces a cornucopia of farm-fresh products, from beef, poultry, game, and fish to butter, cream, wine, fruit, and vegetables. It sends its early crops to the best Parisian tables, yet keeps more than enough for local use. And although Loire wines can't rival the best from Bordeaux and Burgundy, they can be extremely good. Wine makers in Vouvray, Saumur, Chinon, and a variety of other towns produce Anjou and Touraine vintages—mostly white, though some good reds are available in the Chinon-Bourgueil district.

Highly recommended restaurants are indicated by a star ★.

Lodging

Even before the age of the train, the Loire Valley drew visitors from far and wide, anxious to see the great châteaus and sample the sweetness of rural life. Hundreds of hotels of all kinds have sprung up to accommodate today's travelers. At the higher end of the price scale is the **Relais et Châteaux** group; some of their best hotels are converted châteaux. **Chateaux-Hotels Independents** are usually somewhat less expensive, supervised by their live-in owners. Though some are less efficient than ordinary hotels, they offer much individuality and charm. Two smaller groups, the **Château-Accueil** and **La Castellerie,** offer pleasant accommodations for a limited number of guests. Illustrated lists of these groups are available from French Government Tourist Offices abroad, as well as in France. At the lower end of the price scale are the **Logis de France** hotels. These small, traditional hotels are located in towns and villages throughout the region and usually offer terrific value for the money. The Logis de France handbook is available free from French Tourist Offices abroad and for about 30 frs. in French bookshops.

The Loire Valley is one of the country's most popular vacation destinations, so always make reservations well in advance.

Highly recommended hotels are indicated by a star ★.

Amboise
Dining

Manoir St-Thomas. Located between the château and the Clos Lucé, this restaurant occupies a fine Renaissance building with an adjacent garden. Chef François Le Coz serves elegantly traditional food. Try his stewed eels *(matelots d'anguilles)* or his stuffed guinea-fowl breast *(suprême de pintade farci)*. The list of Touraine wines is enticing. *Pl. Richelieu, tel. 47–57–22–52. Reservations advised. Jacket and tie required. AE, DC, MC, V. Closed Mon, first 2 weeks Nov., and mid-Jan.–mid-Feb. Expensive.*

Lodging

Choiseul. Amboise's top hotel also offers a superb restaurant. Choiseul sits on the banks of the Loire, just below the château. Though the guest rooms have recently been modernized, they retain an old and distinctive charm. *36 quai Charles Guinot,37400, tel. 47–30–45–45. 23 rooms with bath. Facilities: restaurant, garden, pool. MC, V. Closed Jan.–mid-Mar. Expensive.*

Château de Pray. This real Louis XII château, with all the lordliness of a bygone era, is situated just outside Amboise on the south bank of the Loire, surrounded by a 25-acre park and a lovely garden. Inside, you'll appreciate the cozy, hunting-lodge ambience. Sixteen elegantly appointed guest rooms are equipped with carved wooden furniture and modern conveniences. The restaurant is only adequate, but diners can enjoy a roaring fire and fine views of the Loire. *On D751, 37400, tel. 47–57–23–67. 16 rooms, 14 with bath. Facilities: restaurant, garden. AE, DC, MC, V. Closed Jan.–mid-Feb. Moderate/ Expensive.*

Angers
Dining
★

Toussaint. Chef Michel Bignon dishes up nouvelle versions of traditional local dishes, plus fine wines, and tasty desserts in a cozy, 400-year-old dining room. Loire river fish with *beurre blanc* is a particular specialty. *7 pl. Kennedy, tel. 41–87–46– 20. Reservations essential. Jacket required. AE, DC, MC, V. Closed Sun., Mon., July 24–Aug. 24, Dec.–New Year's. Moderate.*

Taverne Kanter. This chain restaurant, located at Les Halles covered market, provides simple food and swift service. It's a convenient refueling spot, and the firm's own beer is available on tap. Try the steak and french fries, or the sauerkraut with sausages and ham. *Les Halles, tel. 41–87–93–30. Reservations not required. Dress: casual. V. Inexpensive.*

Lodging

Anjou. In business since 1850, Anjou has recently been redecorated in a vaguely 18th-century style. Each room is individually styled, though all are spacious and feature double-glazed windows. The restaurant, Salamandre, is an affordable place to sample local fare (try the duck with turnips), and has a fine wine list. *1 blvd. Foch, 49000, tel. 41-88-24-82. 51 rooms with bath. Facilities: restaurant. AE, DC, MC, V. Moderate.*

Concorde. You won't find individuality in this standardized chain hotel, but, then again, no problems either. The sound-proof rooms are bright and modern, furnished with a copious amount of white formica. There's a spacious lobby and a good brasserie restaurant. *18 blvd. Foch, 49000, tel. 41-87-37-20. 72 rooms with bath. Facilities: restaurant. AE, DC, MC, V. Moderate/Expensive.*

Azay-le-Rideau
Dining and Lodging

Grand Monarque. Just yards from the château, this mildly eccentric, popular hotel draws hundreds of visitors. It has been in the same family for generations, playing host to celebrities, royals, and tourists alike. Guest rooms are tastefully, individually decorated. The restaurant serves good, traditional food, and the selection of Loire wines is extensive. *Pl. de la République, 37190, tel. 47-45-40-08. 30 rooms, 28 with bath. AE, MC, V. Facilities: restaurant. Restaurant closed mid-Nov.-mid-Mar. Moderate.*

Blois
Dining

La Péniche. This innovative restaurant floats on a Loire barge, where charming chef Germain Bosque serves up beautifully presented fresh seafood specialties. *Promenade du Mail, tel. 57-74-37-23. Reservations advised. Dress: casual. AE, DC, MC, V. Moderate/Expensive.*

★ **La Bocca d'Or.** Original dishes (succulent pigeons, *chaud-froid* of oysters and asparagus) are the order of the day in this stylish, vaulted 14th-century cellar restaurant, presided over by chef Patrice Galland and his genial American wife, Francine. La Bocca d'Or is a small place with a growing reputation, so it's best to reserve a table. *15 rue Haute, tel. 54-78-04-74. Dress: casual. AE, MC, V. Closed Sun., Mon. lunch, and Feb.-early Mar. Moderate.*

Lodging

Anne de Bretagne. A storybook-style French pension decked out with flowers, the Anne de Bretagne offers clean, simple rooms featuring bright bedspreads and curtains. It's a quaint and quiet place to spend a night. *Av. Jean-Laigret, 41000, tel. 54-78-05-38. 29 rooms, most with bath. AE, DC, MC, V. Closed mid-Feb.-mid-Mar. Moderate.*

Chambord
Dining

Le Relais. Residents of Bracieux, 8 kilometers (5 miles) from Chambord, rate this as one of the country's best restaurants.
★ From his gleaming kitchens, chef Bernard Robin produces fine nouvelle cuisine, but connoisseurs savor his simpler dishes: local carp, game in season, and salmon with beef marrow. The attentive staff bring delicious tidbits to keep you busy between courses. *1 av. de Chambord, Bracieux, tel. 54-46-41-22. Reservations required. Jacket and tie required. MC, V. Closed Tues. dinner, Wed., and late Dec.-Feb. Expensive.*

Lodging

St-Michel. Guests enjoy simple and comfortable living in this revamped country house at the edge of the woods across from Chambord château. A few rooms boast spectacular views, and there's a pleasant café-terrace for contemplative drinks. *103 pl. St-Michel, 41250 Bracieux, tel. 54-20-31-31. 39 rooms, 31 with bath. Facilities: tennis, terrace. MC, V. Closed mid-Nov.-Dec. 20. Inexpensive-Moderate.*

Chaumont-sur-Loire
Dining
★

Pont d'Ouchet. This wonderfully inexpensive restaurant-hotel in Onzain is run by a hard-working professional couple, the Cochets. According to Louisette Cochet, her husband Antonin's *moules marinieres* (mussels) are the best in France; take her advice on what to order. In addition to the terrific food, the inn boasts 10 comfortable rooms. *50 Grand Rue, 41150 Onzain, tel. 54–20–70–33. 10 rooms, some with bath. MC, V. Closed Nov.–Feb.; restaurant closed Sun. dinner and Mon. Inexpensive.*

Lodging
★

Domaine des Hauts de Loire. Three kilometers (2 miles) from Onzain, just over the bridge from Chaumont, this exquisite hotel occupies an 18th-century-manor house set amid 180 acres of parkland. The turreted, vine-covered inn boasts high standards: Guest rooms are individually decorated in warm colors and feature antiques and heavy wooden furniture. Service is relaxed and not in the least pretentious. The restaurant is first class. *Rte. d'Herbault, 41150 Onzain, tel. 54–20–72–57. 24 rooms with bath. AE, DC, MC, V. Closed Dec.–Jan. Very Expensive.*

Chenonceaux
Dining and Lodging

Bon Laboureur. In 1882, it won Henry James's praise as a simple, rustic inn. Since then, the Bon Laboureur has come up in the world: It's elegantly modern, with a few old oak beams surviving, and a nice garden where you can eat in summer. The food—especially the fresh fish and the hotel's own garden vegetables—is commendable. *6 rue du Dr. Bretonneau, 37150, tel. 47–23–90–02. 26 rooms with bath. Facilities: restaurant, garden. AE, DC, MC, V. Closed Dec.–mid-Mar. Moderate.*

Chinon
Dining
★

Au Plaisir Gourmand. Gourmets from all around come here to celebrate, and lucky tourists will get a table only if they make reservations (the dining room in this charming old house only seats 30). Chef Jean-Claude Rigollet makes inventive use of fresh, local produce. For a real treat, try the Vienne river trout. Au Plaisir Gourmand gives top quality without frills and features exceptional local wines. *2 rue Parmentier, tel. 47–93–20–48. Reservations essential. Jacket and tie required. MC, V. Closed Sun. dinner, Mon., and last 3 weeks in Feb. Moderate/ Expensive.*

Jeanne de France. Local families and swarms of young people patronize this lively little pizzeria in the town's main square. But it's a far cry from an American pizza joint: Here you can also buy jugfuls of local wine, steaks, and french fries. *12 pl. Général de Gaulle, tel. 47–93–20–12. Reservations not required. Dress: casual. Closed Wed., Jan. Inexpensive.*

Lodging

Château de Marcay. Sophisticated luxury characterizes this 15th-century château, 6 kilometers (4 miles) south of Chinon by D49 and D116. Part of the Relais et Châteaux group, it's run with smooth efficiency. Some rooms are palatial (and cost well over 1,000 francs per night), but an annex contains smaller rooms that go for about half the price. In the original building, much care has been taken to blend modern conveniences with the old beamed and gabled structure. *Marcay, 37500 Chinon, tel. 47–93–03–47. 34 rooms with bath. Facilities: gardens, pool, tennis, restaurant. AE, MC, V. Closed mid-Jan.–mid-Mar. Expensive–Very Expensive.*

Dining and Lodging

Hostellerie Gargantua. In the 15th century, the building housing the Gargantua was a bailiff's palace. Today, this small, quiet hotel offers an array of rooms in various sizes and styles.

Simple good taste prevails throughout. The restaurant, with its charming old dining room and outside tables for summer dining, serves delicious local specialties. *73 rue Haute-St-Maurice, tel. 47–93–04–71. 13 rooms, most with bath. AE, DC, V. Closed mid-Nov.–mid-Mar. Moderate.*

Meung-sur-Loire
Dining and Lodging
★

Auberge St-Jacques. Located on Meung's busy main road, this inn is just a five-minute walk from the château and river. Its restaurant is one of the glories of France, a family-run affair where excellent fresh food is served without fuss at deliciously low prices. Even the cheapest menus are delightful, and the pike soufflé attracts gourmets from all around. The 12 guest rooms are clean and simple. *60 rue Général-de-Gaulle, tel. 38–44–30–39. Reservations advised. Dress: casual. AE, MC, V. Restaurant closed Mon.; hotel and restaurant closed last 2 weeks in Jan. Inexpensive.*

Montbazon
Dining and Lodging
★

Château d'Artigny. One of the most famous of the Relais et Château group inn lies just outside town on D17. Built by the Coty perfume tycoon in 1912 as a vast pseudo-Louis XV house, it is now a suavely run palace-hotel. Ironically, the ambience recalls a perfume ad: Gilt, marble, and plush abound, creating a perfect backdrop for the frequent celebrity guests. The nouvelle restaurant is excellent, and you can jog away the calories in the 60-acre park. *Rte. d'Azay-le-Rideau, 37250 Montbazon, tel. 47–26–24–24. 46 rooms with bath. Facilities: pool, tennis, restaurant, gardens. MC, V. Closed Dec.–early Jan. Expensive.*

★ **Domaine de la Tortinière.** Although this charming little 19th-century château is more intimate and less expensive than the Château d'Artigny, it's hardly a country cousin. The Domaine's brand of elegance is simpler and subtler, but it still has everything you could want in a country hotel. Rooms in the main building exude a quiet, rustic luxury; those in the modern annex are less desirable. The hotel restaurant compares favorably with that of the Artigny. *37250 Montbazon, tel. 47–26–00–19. 14 rooms with bath. Facilities: restaurant, pool, tennis, park. MC, V. Closed mid-Nov.–mid-Mar. Expensive.*

★ **Moulin Fleuri.** Located in a converted watermill 5 kilometers (3 miles) from town, this is really a restaurant with rooms. The Indre sweeps by the garden, and if you've brought a rod, you can fish without a license; if you catch something edible, chef Alain Chaplin may cook it for you. The delightful restaurant offers a tasty inexpensive menu, but it's wiser to budget for "moderate," since you may weaken to such specialties as roast pigeon with acacia honey. Guest rooms are simple but bright. *5 km (3 mi) from town by N10, D287, and D87, 37250 Montbazon, tel. 47–26–01–12. 12 rooms, 8 with bath. AE, MC, V. Restaurant closed Mon.; hotel closed last 2 weeks in Oct. and 3 weeks in Feb. Moderate.*

Orléans
Dining
★

La Crémaillère. Situated in a little street near the Maison de Jeanne d'Arc, Orléans's top restaurant is possibly the best in the valley for seafood of all kinds. Chef Paul Huyart gets the pick of the daily catch from Brittany, from lobster to red mullet, "wild" salmon to turbot. Dishes like *langoustines* (crayfish) in filo pastry with sweet-sour sauce reveal Huyart's ability to innovate. *34 rue Notre-Dame-de-Recouvrance, tel. 38–53–49–17. Reservations recommended. Jacket and tie required. AE, DC, MC, V. Closed Sun. dinner, Mon., and Aug. Expensive.*

L'Assiette. This is a brisk but comfortable place, right on place du Martroi (the main square). Choose your main course (simple grilled meats, mostly), and while it's cooking, help yourself to a wide variety of *hors d'oeuvres* and table wine from the barrel. You're entitled to as much of both as you want—and desserts are "free," too: The price of your meal depends on the main dish. *Pl. du Martroi, tel. 39–53–46–69. Reservations recommended. Dress: casual. AE, DC, MC, V. Inexpensive.*

Saché **Auberge du XIIe Siècle.** You get the best of two eras at this
Dining charming establishment: innovative modern cuisine, plus a genuine 16th-century setting. Situated right on the main square, the Auberge serves a variety of interesting dishes. Try the turbot fillets with oysters and winkles in a vermouth sauce, accompanied by fine Loire wines. In summer, you can dine alfresco. *Saché, 37190 Azay-le-Rideau, tel. 47–26–86–58. Reservations advised. Jacket required. AE, DC, V. Closed Tues. and Feb. Moderate.*

Saumur **La Prieuré.** In a Renaissance manor 8 kilometers (5 miles) out-
Lodging side Saumur on D751, Le Prieuré offers elegant and gracious accommodations. The original structure dates from medieval times. Large guest rooms feature tasteful period decor; the nicest are in the main building, though the garden chalets are luxurious inside. Large windows overlook the Loire, while crystal and silver clink discreetly in the spacious dining room. The restaurant's chef, Jean-Noël Lumineau, prepares delicious nouvelle cuisine, blending imagination with fresh local ingredients. *Chênehutte-les-Tuffeaux, 49350 Gennes, tel. 41–67–90–14. 33 rooms with bath. Facilities: restaurant, garden, tennis, pool. MC, V. Closed early Jan.–early Mar. Expensive.*

Tours **Jean Bardet.** This restaurant is the brainchild and namesake of
Dining Jean Bardet, one of France's top 20 chefs. Try the eight-course
★ *menu degustation*, or from the *carte*, oysters poached in muscadet on a purée of watercress. Or why not a simple grilled lobster, some fine cheese, and a hot baked apple filled with cinnamon ice cream? Bardet was awarded a prize for the best wine list in France in 1988. The inn also has 15 luxurious guest rooms. *57 rue Groison, tel. 47–41–41–11. Reservations essential. Jacket and tie required. AE, DC, MC, V. Expensive.*
Les Tuffeaux. Though it has recently changed hands, this restaurant retains its place as one of Tours's best. Chef Gildas Marsollier has been winning customers with his delicious fennel-perfumed salmon and remarkable desserts. Gentle lighting and a warm, understated decor provide a soothing background. *19 rue Lavoisier, tel. 47–47–19–89. Reservations advised. Jacket required. Closed Sun., Mon. lunch, and part of Jan. Moderate.*

Lodging **Univers.** Once a fine old coaching inn, the Univers, just off place de la Gare, has since been discreetly modernized. J. D. Rockefeller, William Randolph Hearst, Boris Karloff, Sugar Ray Robinson, and the Duke of Windsor have all stayed here; ask to see their entries in the hotel's "golden book." Despite its solemn appearance, the moderately priced restaurant, La Touraine, offers some fine, light dishes. *5 blvd. Heurteloup, 37000, tel. 47–05–37–12. 91 rooms with bath. Facilities: restaurant. Restaurant closed Sat. Expensive–Moderate.*

Valançay *Dining*	**Chêne Vert.** If you want a reliable restaurant serving good, simple meals at rock-bottom prices, look no further. The Green Oak is a basic little tavern offering hearty regional specialties. The four-course meal will fill you up, and in fine weather, you can eat outside. *Rue Nationale, tel. 54–00–06–54. Reservations not required. Dress: casual. Closed Sun. dinner, Sat. (except from July–mid-Sept.), and 3 weeks in June. Inexpensive.*

Lodging
★

Hôtel d'Espagne. A recent addition to the Relais et Châteaux group, this intimate hotel retains the feel of an elegant provincial home. The Fourre family has run it for generations. A former coaching inn, it is built around a landscaped courtyard. Guest rooms are individually decorated, and many feature balconies. *9 rue du Château, 36600, tel. 54–00–00–02. 16 rooms with bath. Facilities: restaurant, garden, pool, tennis. AE, MC, V. Closed Jan.–Feb., Sun. and Mon. in winter. Expensive.*

Villandry
Dining and Lodging

Cheval Rouge. This is a fine old-fashioned hotel whose restaurant is popular with the locals. It boasts an excellent Loire wine list and surprisingly good food, considering its touristy location right next to the château. Good bets are the terrine of foie gras, the calf sweetbreads, and the wood-fired grills. The 20 guest rooms are tidy, and all have bath or shower. *Villandry, 37510 Joué-les-Tours, tel. 47–50–02–07. Reservations advised. Dress: casual. MC, V. Closed Mon. out of season, and Nov.–mid-Mar. Moderate.*

The Arts and Nightlife

Son-et-Lumière

The Loire Valley's favorite form of cultural entertainment is *son-et-lumière* (sound-and-light shows), a dramatic spectacle that takes place after dark on summer evenings on the grounds of major châteaus. Programs sometimes take the form of historical pageants, with huge casts of people in period costume and caparisoned horses, the whole floodlit and backed by music and commentary, often (as at **Amboise**) in English. They may also take the form of spectacular lighting and sound shows, with spoken commentary and dialogue but no visible figures, as at **Chenonceau.** The most magnificent *son-et-lumière* occurs at **Le Lude,** on the River Loir (not the Loire), 48 kilometers (29 miles) northeast of Saumur and 50 kilometers (30 miles) northwest of Tours. Here, more than 100 performers present a pageant chronicling the history of the château and region from the Hundred Years' War on. The spectacle is enhanced by fountains and fireworks.

Open-Air Festivals

For four weeks beginning in mid-June, the **Festival d'Anjou** enlivens the area around Anjou with music, theater, and dance. In July, the château grounds at **Loches** are the setting for a series of open-air concerts. And in the medieval **Grange du Meslay** near Tours, top-class international musicians gather in late June and July for the **Fêtes Musicales de Touraine.**

Nightclubs

Though clubs and discos are not one of the Loire Valley's strong points, the larger cities offer several: In Tours, try **Bourbon's Club** (292 av. de Grammont) and **Pyms** (170 av. de Grammont); in Angers, **Le Boléro** (38 rue S-Laud) and **Le Vénéré** (15 rue de la Roë). If you are visiting Chambord, drive about 8 kilometers (5 miles) north to **Le Carioca,** at Monliveault.

6 Normandy

Introduction

Normandy (or Normandie, as the French spell it), the coastal region lying northwest of Paris, probably has more associations for English-speaking visitors than does any other part of France. William the Conqueror, Joan of Arc, the Bayeux Tapestry, and the D-Day landing beaches have become household names in English, just as they have in French.

Normandy is one of the country's finest gastronomic regions, producing excellent cheeses like Camembert, and Calvados, an apple brandy. The area has become popular with British vacationers not only because it's right across the Channel but because of its charming countryside, from the wild granite cliffs in the west to the long sandy beaches along the Channel coast, from the wooded valleys of the south to the lush green meadows and apple orchards in the center.

Historic buildings—castles, churches, and monuments—crown the Norman countryside as reminders of its rich and eventful past. Following the 1066 invasion of England by the Norman duke, William (the Conqueror), Normandy switched between English and French dominion for several centuries. In Rouen in 1431, Joan of Arc was burned at the stake, marking a turning point in the Hundred Years' War, the last major medieval conflict between the French and the English. The most celebrated building in Normandy is the 8th-century abbey of Mont-St-Michel, erected on a 264-foot mound of granite cut off from the mainland at high tide; it's an architectural marvel and the most visited site in provincial France.

Normandy features 375 miles of coastline bordering the English Channel, four major ports—Le Havre, Rouen, Dieppe, and Cherbourg—and coastal towns with seafaring pasts, such as Honfleur, with its picturesque old harbor, and former fishing villages like Fécamp. Sandwiched between are the beaches of fashionable resorts like Deauville, Cabourg, and Etretat, where visitors can be found reclining in deck chairs, gin and tonic in hand.

Essential Information

Important Addresses and Numbers

Tourist Information Each of Normandy's five *départements* has its own central tourist office: **Alençon** (Orne, 88 rue St-Blaise, tel. 33–28–88–71), **Caen** (Calvados, pl. du Canada, tel. 31–86–53–30), **Evreux** (Eure, 1 pl. de-Gaulle, tel. 32–24–04–43), **Rouen** (Iseine-Maritime, 2 bis rue du Petit-Salut, tel. 35–88–61–32), and **St-Lô** (Manche, Maison du Département, on the road to Lisieux, tel. 33–05–98–70).

Tourist offices of other major towns covered in this chapter are as follows: **Bayeux** (1 rue des Cuisiniers, tel. 31–92–16–26), **Dieppe** (1 blvd. du Général-de-Gaulle, tel. 35–84–11–77), **Fécamp** (front de Mer, tel. 35–29–16–34), **Le Havre** (1 pl. de l'Hôtel-de-Ville, tel. 35–21–22–88), and **Honfleur** (33 cours des Fossés, tel. 31–89–23–30).

Travel Agencies **American Express** (1–3 pl. Jacques-Lelieur, Rouen, tel. 35–98–19–80; 57 Quai George V, Le Havre, tel. 35–42–59–11) and

Havas (25 Grande Rue, Alençon, tel. 33–26–19–34; 54 rue St-Martin, Bayeux, tel. 31–92–14–46; 80 rue St-Jean, Caen, tel. 31–86–04–01; 14 blvd. Nationale, Dieppe, tel. 35–84–28–16).

Car Rental **Avis** (44 pl. de la Gare, Caen, tel. 31–87–73–80; 24 rue Malouet, Rouen, tel. 35–72–77–50), **Europcar** (25 cours de la République, Le Havre, tel. 35–25–21–95), and **Hertz** (8–12 blvd. Gambetta, Dieppe, tel. 35–84–87–87).

Arriving and Departing

By Plane Paris's Charles de Gaulle (Roissy) and Orly airports will be American visitors' closest link with the region. From the United Kingdom, there are regular flights to Caen and Deauville (from London) and to Cherbourg (from Southampton and the Channel Islands).

By Boat Car ferries connect several Normandy ports with England and Ireland. There are crossings to Dieppe from Newhaven, to Le Havre from Portsmouth and Rosslare, and to Cherbourg from Portsmouth, Weymouth, and Rosslare.

By Car The A13 expressway from Paris spears its way to Rouen in 1½ hours and to Caen in 2¼ hours. A13/N13 takes you to Cherbourg via Bayeux in another two hours.

By Train From Paris's St-Lazare station, express trains stop at Rouen and Dieppe, Le Havre, or Fécamp and at Caen and Cherbourg via Evreux and Lisieux. For Mont-St-Michel, take the express from Paris's Montparnasse station to Rennes and switch to a local train.

Getting Around

By Plane Normandy's domestic airports are at Rouen, Le Havre, and Evreux.

By Car A13/N13 travels from Rouen to Cherebourg via Bayeux in two hours. Main roads also branch off from A13 to Le Havre (A15) and Dieppe (N27). To get to Mont-St-Michel, take A11 to Rennes, then N175 north

Guided Tours

Bus and Car Excursions **Viking Voyages** (16 rue Général-Giraud, 14000 Caen, tel. 31–85–52–02) specializes in two-day packages by car, with overnight stays in private châteaus. Itineraries include "Normandy: From Rouen to Cherbourg"; "William the Conqueror's Route"; "Discovering the Manche," which includes a trip to Mont-St-Michel; a "D-Day Beaches" tour; and "From Lisieux to Suisse Normande." An all-inclusive tour, with car and English-speaking driver, is 1,795 francs. The **French Association of Travel Agents** offers a two-day tour of Mont-St-Michel and St-Malo, which includes a visit to Honfleur, the resorts of Deauville and Cabourg, the D-Day beaches, and Caen. The excursion, offered from April to October, costs 1,730 francs; contact **Clamageran Voyages** (29 rue de Buffon, 76000 Rouen, tel. 35–07–39–07) for details.

Train Excursions Both **Cityrama** (214 rue de Rivoli, 75001 Paris, tel. 42–60–31–25) and **Paris-Vision** (4 pl. des Pyramides, 75001 Paris, tel. 42–60–30–14) organize one-day train excursions to Mont-St-Michel, with a two-day option that takes in the châteaus of the

Loire on the second day. Costing 750 francs, the one-day trips leave Paris at 7:15 AM on Saturday, arriving in Mont-St-Michel in time for lunch (included in the cost). Following a guided tour of the mount and the abbey, you return by train to Paris Montparnasse station.

Special-Interest **Viking Voyages** in Caen *(see* above) organizes bike trips around the region, as well as a "Normandy Antiques" tour by car. A two-day bike tour, without guide, costs 995 francs, while a guided antiques excursion costs 1,795 francs. **Trans Canal** in Caen (22 rue de la Hevre, 14780 Lion-sur-Mer, tel. 31–96–00–55) arranges two-hour cruises on Caen's canal.

Personal Guides A number of cities organize their own tours, including Bayeux, Rouen, and Caen, and Le Havre. For details, contact the individual tourist offices *(see* Tourist Information).

Exploring Normandy

Numbers in the margin correspond with points of interest on the Normandy map.

Orientation

We've divided our Norman coverage into three separate tours. The first tour leads northwest from Paris to Rouen, the capital of Upper Normandy. From here, we meander west to the port town of Le Havre before heading up along the impressive coastline of chalky cliffs and pebble beaches known as the Alabaster Coast.

Lower Normandy covers a much larger area, and we explore its sights in two itineraries. The first starts in the market town of Lisieux before heading north to the coastal resort of Honfleur, then west through the region's swankiest resort towns along the Calvados Coast. From here, we turn inland, to Caen and Bayeux. This area saw some of the fiercest fighting after the D-Day landings, as many monuments and memorials testify. The last stop is at the fabled Mont-St-Michel, which lies at the western edge of Normandy.

Finally, there's a scenic drive along the River Orne south of Caen, through the hilly region called Suisse Normande.

Highlights for First-time Visitors

Abbaye aux Hommes, Tour 2
Bayeux Tapestry, Musée de la Tapisserie, Bayeux, Tour 2
Cathédrale Notre-Dame and Old Town, Rouen, Tour 1
D-Day landing beaches, Tour 2
Deauville/Trouville, Tour 2
Honfleur, Tour 2
Musée des Beaux-Arts, Le Havre, Tour 1
Mont-St-Michel, Tour 2

Tour 1: Upper Normandy

Setting out from Paris, take the A13 expressway and branch off left, just after Bonnières-sur-Seine to **Evreux**, capital of the Eure *département*. From the 5th century on, the town was ravaged and burnt by a succession of armies—first the Vandals, then the Normans, the English, and various French kings. World War II played its part as well. These days, the town has been well restored and is embellished by a number of gardens and overgrown footpaths by the banks of the River Iton.

Evreux's principal historic site is the **Cathédrale Notre-Dame,** in the heart of town just off rue Corbeau. Unfortunately, it was an easy victim for the many fires and raids that took place over the centuries; all that's left of the original 12th-century construction are the nave arcades. The lower parts of the chancel date from 1260, the chapels from the 14th century. Still, it's an outstanding example of Flamboyant Gothic inside and out. Don't miss the choir triforium and transept, the 14th-century stained-glass windows in the apse, or the entrance to the fourth chapel. *Pl. Notre-Dame.*

② From Evreux, get on D316 heading for **Les Andelys,** 36 kilometers (21 miles) away on the north bank of the River Seine. The pretty little town is set against magnificent chalky cliffs in one of the most picturesque loops of the River Seine. Overlooking the town from the clifftops and affording spectacular views in both directions are the remains of the **Château de Gaillard,** a formidable fortress built by English king Richard the Lionhearted in 1196. Despite its solid defenses, the castle fell to the French in 1204; it had suffered considerable damage during the assault, and sections were later torn down at the end of the 16th century; only one of its five main towers remains intact. *Admission: 10 frs. Open Thurs.–Mon. 10–noon and 2–5, Wed. 2–5; closed Tues.*

Rather than take the most direct road from Les Andelys to Rouen (D126/D138), continue along D313 around the Seine for about 14 kilometers (9 miles), crossing it at St-Pierre du **③** Vauvry. You can then either stop at the busy town of **Louviers** on the Eure River to see its old houses and its Notre-Dame church or turn straight onto N15, the main road that passes just north of the town. Eight kilometers (5 miles) from Louviers, you cross the Pont de l'Arche, where the Eure and Seine rivers merge; from here, it's another 18 kilometers (11 miles) to Rouen. On the way, you pass through **Bonsecours,** now a suburb of the town and the site of the Basilique Notre-Dame, built in the early 1840s and one of the finest neo-Gothic churches in France.

④ The city of **Rouen** is a blend of ancient and modern, a large part having been destroyed during World War II. Even before its massive postwar reconstruction, the city had expanded outward during the 20th century with the development of industries spawned by its increasingly busy port, now the fifth largest in France. In its more distant past, Rouen gained celebrity when Joan of Arc was burned at the stake here in 1431.

Rouen is known as the City of a Hundred Spires, and many of its important edifices are churches. Lording it over them all, in **⑤** place du Cathédrale, is the magnificent **Cathédrale Notre-Dame,** one of the masterpieces of French Gothic architecture. If you are familiar with the works of Impressionist Claude Monet, you will immediately recognize the cathedral's immense west facade, rendered in an increasingly misty, yet always beautiful, fashion in his series "Cathédrales de Rouen." The original 12th-century construction was replaced after a terrible fire in

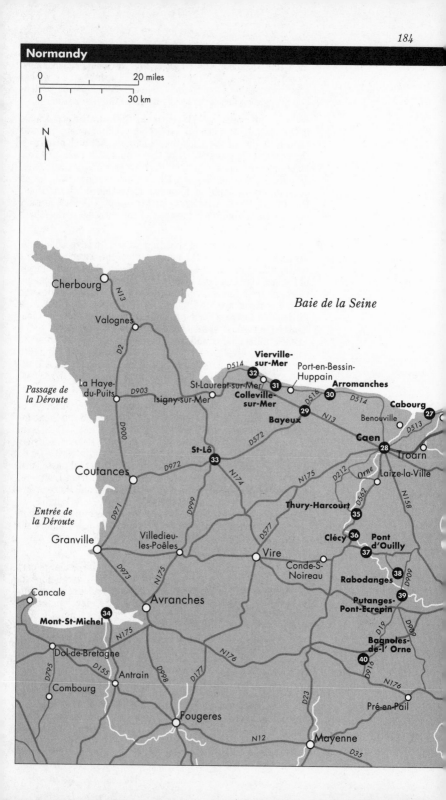

Normandy

0   20 miles

0   30 km

N

Cherbourg

Baie de la Seine

N13

Valognes

D2

Passage de la Déroute

La Haye-du-Puits

D903

Vierville-sur-Mer

D514

32

St-Laurent-sur-Mer

31

Port-en-Bessin-Huppain

Arromanches

30

D516

D514

Cabourg

27

Isigny-sur-Mer

Colleville-sur-Mer

29

N13

Bénouville

D513

Bayeux

D572

Caen

28

Troarn

D900

Coutances

D972

St-Lô

33

N174

D699

N175

D212

Orne

Laize-la-Ville

D562

N158

Entrée de la Déroute

D971

Thury-Harcourt

35

Granville

Villedieu-les-Poêles

D973

N175

D577

Vire

Clécy **36**

Pont d'Ouilly

37

38

D909

Conde-S-Noireau

Rabodanges

39

Cancale

Avranches

Putanges-Pont-Ecrepin

D19

D909

Mont-St-Michel

34

N175

Bagnoles-de-l' Orne

40

D916

N176

Dol-de-Bretagne

D795

D155

Antrain

D998

D177

N176

D19

Combourg

D23

Pré-en-Pail

Fougères

N12

Mayenne

D35

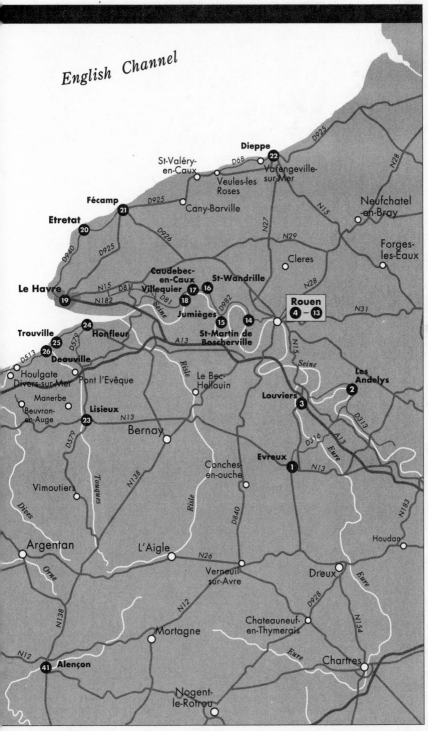

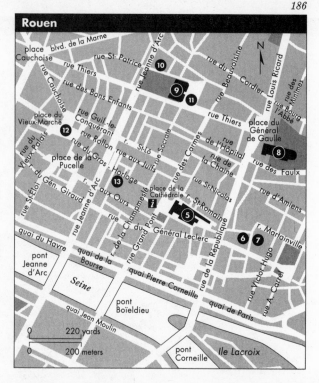

1200; only the left-hand spire, the Tour St-Romain, survived the flames. The imposing 250-foot iron steeple on the right, known as the "Butter Tower," was added in the 15th and 16th centuries and completed in the 17th, when a group of wealthy citizens donated large sums of money—for the privilege of eating butter during Lent.

Interior highlights include the 13th-century choir, with its pointed arcades; vibrant stained glass depicting the crucified Christ (restored after heavy damage during World War II); and massive stone columns topped by some intriguing carved faces. The first flight of the famous Escalier de la Librairie (Booksellers' Staircase) rises up from a tiny balcony just to the left of the transept and is attributed to Guillaume Pontifs, who is also responsible for most of the 15th-century work seen in the cathedral. *Pl. du Cathédrale.*

Leaving the cathedral, head right, and cross rue de la République to place St-Maclou, an attractive square surrounded by picturesque half-timbered houses with steeply pointed roofs. The square's neo-Gothic **Eglise St-Maclou** bears testimony to the wild excesses of Flamboyant architecture; take time to examine the central and left-hand portals under the porchway on the main facade, covered with little bronze lion heads and pagan engravings. Inside, note the 16th-century organ, with its Renaissance woodcarving, and the fine marble columns. *Pl. St-Maclou.*

To the right is the **Aître St-Maclou,** a former ossuary that is one of the last reminders of the plague that devastated Europe dur-

ing the Middle Ages; these days, it holds Rouen's School of Art
and Architecture. The ossuary (a charnel house used for the
bodies of plague victims) is said to have inspired the French
composer Camille Saint-Saëns (1835–1921) when he was working on his *Danse Macabre.* The building's massive double frieze
is especially riveting, carved with some graphic skulls, bones,
and grave diggers' tools. *184–186 rue Martainville.*

Turn right up rue de la République to place du Général-de-
❽ Gaulle, site of the **Eglise St-Ouen,** a fine example of later Gothic
architecture. The stained-glass windows, dating from the 14th
to the 16th century, are the most spectacular features of the
otherwise spare structure. The church's 19th century pipe or-
gans have few equals in France.

Walk west on rue Thiers to get to a cluster of Rouen's fine
❾ museums, the most important of which is the **Musée des Beaux-
Arts** (Fine Arts Museum), on square Vedral. It contains a fine
collection of French paintings from the 17th and 19th centuries,
including works by Claude Monet, Alfred Sisley, and Auguste
Renoir. An entire room is devoted to works by Rouen-born
Théodore Gericault, and some impressive Delacroixs dominate
another. The museum once showcased a superb collection
of Norman ceramics, but these are now housed separately
❿ in the **Musée de la Céramique** (Ceramic Museum), a few steps
down the road. A single ticket will get you into both museums
⓫ and into the **Musée de Ferronerie Le Secq des Tournelles,** right
behind the Musée des Beaux-Arts. This museum claims to possess the world's finest collection of wrought iron, with exhibits
spanning the 3rd century through the 19th. Displays include a
range of items used in daily life, accessories, and professional
instruments used by surgeons, barbers, carpenters, clock-
makers, and gardeners. *Admission: 11 frs. All four museums
are open Thurs.–Mon. 10–noon and 2–6, Wed. 2–6; closed
Tues.*

Continue down rue Thiers, then turn left onto rue Jeanne d'Arc
and head toward place du Vieux-Marché, dominated by the
⓬ thoroughly modern **Eglise Jeanne d'Arc.** Dedicated to the saint,
the church was built on the spot where she was burned to death
in 1431. Not all is spanking new, however; The church is graced
with some remarkable 16th-century glass windows taken from
the former Eglise St-Vincent, destroyed in 1944.

Leading out of place du Vieux-Marché is Rouen's most popular
attraction, the rue du Gros-Horloge. The name of this little
⓭ pedestrian street comes from the **Gros-Horloge** itself, a giant
Renaissance clock house; in 1527, the Rouennais had a splendid
arch built especially for it, and today its golden face looks out
over the street (the ticket to the Musée des Beaux-Arts includes admission to the ornate belfry). Though the ancient
thoroughfare is crammed with boutiques and fast-food joints, a
few old houses, dating from the 16th century, remain. Wander
through the surrounding old town, a warren of tiny streets
lined with over 700 half-timbered houses. Instead of standing
simply as monuments to the past, these cobbled streets have
been successfully transformed into a lively pedestrian shopping precinct, and the old buildings now contain the most
fashionable shops in the city.

The Seine valley between Rouen and Le Havre is full of interesting sights, old and new, dotted amid some lovely scenery.

Within 10 minutes of Rouen, along D982, is the 11th-century
⑭ abbey church of St-George in **St-Martin de Boscherville**. From
here, follow D982 and D65 around the Seine for some 19 kilome-
⑮ ters (12 miles) to **Jumièges** to see the imposing ruins of its once-
mighty Benedictine abbey, the **Abbaye de Jumièges,** founded in
the 7th century and subsequently plundered by Vikings. The
abbey was rebuilt in the 11th century and consecrated in 1067,
but monks lived there until the French Revolution. It was then
auctioned off to a timber merchant, who promptly demolished a
large part of the building to sell the stones. *Admission: 10 frs.*
Open Mon.–Sat. 10–noon and 2–6.

About 16 kilometers (10 miles) farther along the right bank of
⑯ the Seine, in **St. Wandrille,** is another Benedictine abbey. The
Abbaye de St-Wandrille survives as an active monastery to this
day; like Jumièges, it was founded in the 7th century, sacked
(by the Normans), and rebuilt in the 10th century. You can still
hear the monks sing their Gregorian chants at morning Mass if
you're there early in the day (9:25 weekdays and 10 Sunday and
holidays). *Guided tour at 3 and 4 weekdays; cost: 12 frs. adults,*
children free.

From St-Wandrille, it's only a couple of miles to the charming
⑰ little village of **Caudebec-en-Caux**; if the day is sunny, you
should leave the car and walk along the banks of the Seine. The
village's 15th-century Eglise Notre-Dame was described by
French monarch Henri IV (1589–1610) as "the most beautiful
chapel in the kingdom." A huge modern bridge, the Pont de
Brotonne, spans the Seine at Caudebec. Instead of crossing it,
however, drive west around the north bank of the Seine for a
⑱ couple of miles to **Villequier**, a peacefully situated riverside village dominated by its château. Villequier is famous as the place
where 19th-century writer Victor Hugo lost his daughter,
Léopoldine, and her husband, Charles Vacquerie, who
drowned in the Seine's notorious seasonal tidal wave (these
days it is held at bay by a dam). A museum, the **Musée Victor
Hugo,** has been created in the couple's old house; exhibits include the manuscript of Hugo's poem *Contemplations,* a lament
on their deaths. *Rue Ernet-Benet. Admission: 4 frs. Open*
Apr.–Sept., Wed.–Mon. 10–noon and 2–5:30, closed Tues.;
Oct.–Mar., Wed.–Sun. 10–noon and 2–5:30, closed Mon. and
Tues.

Time Out   If the weather's fine when you are in Villequier, stop off for a
light lunch at **Le Grand Sapin.** The food is plain, traditional
fare, but the riverside terrace is delightful. *Rue Louis-Le-*
Gaffric.

⑲ The seaside port of **Le Havre** lies 53 kilometers (33 miles) west
by D81 and N182. A bustling modern town, largely rebuilt after 1945, Le Havre is France's second-largest port (after Marseille). Le Havre was bombarded no less than 146 times during
World War II, and reinforced concrete and bleak open spaces
have not done much for the town's atmosphere. The old seafaring quarter of Ste-Adresse is worth a visit, however. From its
fortress, you have panoramic views of the port and the Seine
estuary.

At the opposite end of the seafront, at the tip of boulevard
François Ier, sits the metal-and-glass **Musée des Beaux-Arts.**

On the ground floor, there's a remarkable collection of Raoul Dufy's work, including oils, watercolors, and sketches. Dufy (1877–1953) was born in Le Havre and devoted a lot of time to his native region: views of Norman beaches and of Le Havre itself. If you can't spend much time in Normandy, go upstairs to have a look at works by one of the forerunners of Impressionism—Eugene Boudin. Boudin's compelling beach scenes and Norman countrysides will give you a taste of what you're missing. *Blvd. Clemenceau. Admission: 14 frs. Open Wed.– Mon. 10–noon and 2–6; closed Tues.*

The first stop on the coast between Le Havre and Dieppe (a stretch known as the Alabaster Coast) is **Etretat**, about 30 kilometers (18 miles) away along D940. The town's white cliffs are almost as famous in France as Dover's are in England. Although the promenade running the length of Etretat's pebble beach has been spoiled by a proliferation of seedy cafés and french-fry stands, the town retains its vivacity and charm. Its landmarks are two arched cliff formations, the **Falaise d'Amont** and the **Falaise d'Aval**, which jut out over the sea on either side of the bay, and a 300-foot needle of rock, the **Aiguille**, which thrusts up from the sea near the Falaise d'Amont. Through the huge archways carved by the sea into the cliffs, you can walk to neighboring beaches at low tide. For a breathtaking view of the whole bay, take the path up to the Falaise d'Aval on the southern side, from where you can hike for miles across the Manneporte hills.

Seventeen kilometers (11 miles) from Etretat along D940 is **Fécamp,** an ancient fishing port that was Normandy's primary place of pilgrimage before Mont-St-Michel stole all the glory. Fécamp no longer has a commercial fishing fleet, but you will still see lots of boats in the private yachting marina. The magnificent **Eglise La Trinité** (just off blvd. de la République) bears witness to the town's religious past. The Benedictine abbey was founded by the duke of Normandy in the 11th century and became the home of the monastic order of the Précieux Sang et de la Trinité (referring to Christ's blood, which supposedly arrived here in the 7th century). Fécamp is also the home of the liqueur Benedictine; the **Musée de la Bénédictine,** seven blocks across town on rue Boufart, was rebuilt in 1892 in a mixture of neo-Gothic and Renaissance styles and remains one of Normandy's most popular attractions. *110 rue Alexandre-le-Grand. Admission: 13 frs. (including a tasting). Open Easter–mid-Nov., daily 9–11:30 and 2–5:30.*

From Fécamp it's about 65 kilometers (40 miles) to Dieppe; take D925 via Cany-Barville to St-Valery-en-Caux and Veules-les-Roses, and then the scenic coast road, D68, the rest of the way. Just before reaching Dieppe, you pass through **Varengeville-sur-Mer.** Look for the tiny church perched on a hill: 20th-century painter Georges Braque—who, with Picasso, is credited with inventing Cubism—is buried in its graveyard.

Dieppe is a charming blend of a fishing and commercial port and a Norman seaside town. The boulevard du Maréchal Foch, a seafront promenade, separates an immense lawn from an unspoiled pebble beach where, in 1942, many Canadian soldiers were killed during the so-called Jubilee raid. Overlooking the Channel, at the western end of the bay, stands the 15th-century **Château de Dieppe,** which dominates the town from its clifftop position. It contains the town museum, well known for its collection of ivories. In the 17th century, Dieppe imported vast quantities of elephant tusks from Africa and Asia, and as many as 350 craftsmen settled here to work the ivory; their efforts can be seen in the form of ship models, nautical accessories, or, upstairs, religious and day-to-day objects. The museum also has a room devoted to sketches by Georges Braque. *Sq. du Canada. Admission: 2 frs. Open mid-Sept.–mid-June, Wed.–Mon. 10–noon and 2–6; closed Tues.*

Tour 2: The Calvados Coast and Mont-St-Michel

㉓ Lisieux is the main market town of the prosperous Pays d'Auge, an agricultural region famous for cheeses named after towns like Camembert, Pont l'Evêque, and Livarot. It is also a land of apple orchards from which the finest Calvados brandy comes. Lisieux emerged relatively unscathed from World War II, though it boasts few historical monuments beyond the **Cathédrale St-Pierre,** built in the 12th and 13th centuries. It is also famous for its patron saint, Ste-Thérèse, who was born and died in the last quarter of the 19th century, having spent the last 10 of her 25 years as a Carmelite nun. Thérèse was canonized in 1925, and in 1954 a basilica—one of the world's largest 20th-century churches—was dedicated to her; to get there from the cathedral, walk down Avenue Victor-Hugo and branch left into Avenue Ste-Thérèse.

㉔ From Lisieux, take D579 north to Pont l'Evêque and stay on that road when it forks right toward **Honfleur,** a distance of 32 kilometers (20 miles). This colorful port on the Seine estuary epitomizes Normandy for many people. It was once an important departure point for maritime expeditions, and the first voyages to Canada in the 15th and 16th centuries embarked from here. Its 17th-century harbor is fronted on one side by two-story stone houses with low, sloping roofs and on the other, by tall, narrow houses, whose wooden facades are topped by slate roofs. The whole town is a museum piece, full of half-timbered houses and cobbled streets.

Honfleur was colonized by French and foreign painters in the 19th century, and the group later known as the Impressionists used to meet in the **St-Siméon Inn,** now a luxurious hotel (*see* Dining and Lodging). Honfleur has also inspired artists of other hues: Charles Baudelaire, the 19th-century poet and champion of Romanticism, wrote his poem *L'Invitation au Voyage* here, while the French composer Erik Satie was born in Honfleur in 1866.

Today, Honfleur is one of the most popular vacation spots in northern France. During the summer, its hotels rarely have vacancies and its cafés and restaurants are always packed. Soak up the seafaring atmosphere by strolling around the old harbor, and pay a visit to the **Eglise Ste-Catherine,** which dominates the harbor's northern corner (rue des Logettes). The wooden church was built by townspeople to show their gratitude for the departure of the English at the end of the Hundred Years' War (1453), when masons and architects were occupied with national reconstruction.

㉕ ㉖ Leave Honfleur by D513 west and follow the coast for 14 kilometers (9 miles) until you arrive at the twin seaside resorts of **Trouville** and **Deauville,** separated only by the estuary of the River Touques. Although Trouville is now considered an overflow town for its more prestigious neighbor, it became one of France's first seaside resorts when Parisians began flocking here in the mid-19th century.

Deauville is a chic watering hole for the French bourgeoisie and would-be fashionable personalities from further afield, who are attracted by its racecourse, its casino, its marina and regattas, its palaces and gardens, and, of course, its sandy beach. The **Promenade des Planches**—the boardwalk extending along the seafront and lined with deck chairs, bars, and striped cabanas —is the place for celebrity spotting. Nevertheless, if you are looking for authenticity rather than glamour, stay in Trouville. It, too, has a casino and boardwalk as well as a bustling fishing port and a native population that makes it a livelier place out of season than Deauville.

Time Out One of the most popular places in Trouville is **Les Vapeurs,** a friendly, animated brasserie with neon-lit '50s decor. It serves good, fresh food at any time, day or night, and both the famous and not-so-famous like to meet here after dark. *160 blvd. Fernand-Moureaux. Closed Tues. dinner and Wed.*

Continue west along D513, which takes you through a number of family seaside resorts, such as Houlgate and nearby Dives-sur-Mer, before reaching the larger and more elegant resort of **㉗** **Cabourg,** just across the River Dives. Cabourg's streets fan out from a central hub near the seafront where the casino and the Grand Hôtel are situated. The early 20th-century novelist Marcel Proust, author of *Remembrance of Things Past,* was a great admirer of the town's pleasant seaside atmosphere, and spent much of his time here. One of his epic's volumes paints a perfect picture of life in the resort, to which the town responded by naming its magnificent seafront promenade after him.

Leave Cabourg by D513, which veers inland and after 24 kilom-**㉘** eters (15 miles) brings you to **Caen,** the capital of Lower Normandy. Caen, with its abbeys and castle, will provide a welcome break from the endless succession of coastal resorts.

William of Normandy ruled from Caen in the 11th century before he conquered England. Nine hundred years later, the two-month Battle of Caen devastated the town in 1944. Much of the city burned in a fire that raged for 11 days, and the downtown area was almost entirely rebuilt after the war.

A good place to begin exploring is at the town's main tourist attraction, the **Abbaye aux Hommes,** a monastery built by William the Conqueror. "The Gentleman's Abbey" was begun in Romanesque style in 1066 and was added to during the 18th century. Note the magnificent facade of the Eglise St-Etienne, whose spareness is enhanced by two 11th-century towers topped by Norman Gothic octagonal spires. Inside, what had been William the Conqueror's tomb was destroyed by 16th-century Huguenots during the Wars of Religion, but the choir still stands; it was the first to be built in Norman Gothic style, and many subsequent choirs were modeled after it. *Pl. Louis-Guillouard. Guided tours of the abbey cost 20 frs. morning, 24 frs. afternoon. Open daily 9–noon and 2–5.*

Head right up Fosses St-Julien to the Esplanade du Château. The ruins of William the Conqueror's **fortress,** built in 1060 and sensitively restored after the war, glower down on all who approach. The castle gardens are a perfect spot for strolling, and the ramparts afford good views of the city. Within the rampart walls lies the **Musée des Beaux-Arts,** a Fine Arts Museum whose impressive collection includes Rembrandts and Titians. Also within the castle are the **Musée de Normandie,** displaying regional arts, and the chapel of St-George. *Entrance by the Porte de Ville. Admission to each: 4 frs. Open Wed.–Mon. 10–1 and 2–5; closed Tues.*

Take rue des Chanoines right to the **Abbaye aux Dames,** the "Ladies Abbey," built by William the Conqueror's wife, Matilda, in 1062. The abbey is now a hospital and not open to visitors, but you can visit its Église de la Trinité. This squat church is a good example of 11th-century Romanesque architecture, though its original spires were replaced by bulky balustrades in the early 18th century. The 11th-century crypt once held Matilda's tomb, which was destroyed during the French Revolution. Note the intricate carvings on columns and arches in the chapel. *Pl. Reine-Mathilde. Admission: 20 frs. afternoons, 24 frs. evenings. Guided tours daily at 2:30 and 4.*

Head back down the rue des Chanoines, and continue on rue Montoir-Poissonnerie. Turning left onto place St-Pierre, you'll come face to face with the Caen Tourist Office. It merits a visit not only for its excellent information resources, but for its splendid site in the **Hôtel d'Escoville,** a 16th-century mansion built by a wealthy town merchant, Nicolas le Valois d'Escoville. The building was badly damaged during the war but has since been restored; the rather austere facade conceals an elaborate inner courtyard, reflecting the Italian influence on early Renaissance Norman architecture.

From Caen, N13 heads 28 kilometers (17 miles) northwest to **Bayeux,** an attractive city steeped in history and the first town to be liberated during the Battle of Normandy. Bayeux's long history stretches back many centuries before World War II, however, and we begin our tour at the **Musée de la Tapisserie,** located in an 18th-century building on rue de Nesmond and showcasing the world's most celebrated piece of needlework, the **Bayeux Tapestry.** The medieval work of art—stitched in 1067—is really a 200-foot-long embroidered scroll, which depicts, in 58 separate scenes, the epic story of William of Normandy's conquest of England in 1066, a watershed in European history. The tapestry's origins remain obscure, though it was probably commissioned from Saxon embroiderers by the count of Kent—also the bishop of Bayeux—to be displayed in his newly built cathedral. Despite its age, the tapestry is in remarkably good condition; the extremely detailed, often homey, scenes provide an unequaled record of the clothes, weapons, ships, and lifestyles of the day. *Centre Culturelle, rue de Nesmond. Admission: 12 frs. (3 frs. for a cassette translation). Open June–Sept., daily 9–7; opening times vary Oct.–May, so check locally.*

Your ticket also gains you entrance to the **Musée Baron Gérard.** Head up rue de Nesmond to rue Larchet, turning left into lovely place des Tribuneaux. The museum contains fine collections of Bayeux porcelain and lace, ceramics from Rouen, and 16th–19th-century paintings. *Pl. des Tribuneaux. Open daily, June –Aug., 9–7; Sept.–mid-Oct. and Mar.–May, 9:30–12:30 and 2 –6:30; mid-Oct.–Mar., 10–12:30 and 2–6.*

Behind the museum, with an entrance on rue de Bienvenu, sits Bayeux's most important historic building, the **Cathédrale Notre-Dame.** Completed in 1077, the cathedral is a fine example of Norman Gothic architecture. A later addition is the portal on the south side of the transept, which depicts the assassination of English Archbishop Thomas Becket in Canterbury Cathedral in 1170, following his opposition to King Henry II's attempts to control the church. Note the whimsical paintings in the nave.

Return to the 20th century by turning left, walking to the place au Blois, and continuing down rue St-Loup. Turn right on boulevard du Général Fabian-Ware, site of the **Musée de la Bataille de Normandie** whose detailed exhibits trace the story of the Battle of Normandy from June 7 to August 22, 1944. The ultramodern museum contains an impressive array of war paraphernalia, including uniforms, weapons, and equipment. *Blvd. Général-Fabian-Ware. Admission: 4 frs. Open, June–Aug., daily 9–7; Sept.–mid-Oct. and Mar.–May, daily 9:30–12:30 and 2–6:30; and mid-Oct.–Mar., daily 10–12:30 and 2–6.*

Operation Overlord, the code name for the Invasion of Normandy, called for five beachheads—named Utah, Omaha, Gold, Juno, and Sword—to be established along the Calvados Coast, to either side of Arromanches. Preparations started in mid-1943, and British shipyards worked furiously through the following winter and spring building two artificial harbors (called Mulberries), boats, and landing equipment. The operation was originally scheduled to take place on June 5, but poor weather caused it to be put back a day.

The British troops that landed on Sword, Juno, and Gold quickly pushed inland and joined with parachute regiments that had been dropped behind the German lines. U.S. forces met with far tougher opposition on Omaha and Utah beaches, however, and it took them six days to secure their positions and meet the other Allied forces. From there, they pushed south and west, cutting off the Cotentin Peninsula on June 10 and taking Cherbourg on June 26. Meanwhile, British forces were encountering fierce resistance at Caen and did not take it until July 9. By then, U.S. forces were turning their attention southward, but it took two weeks of bitter fighting to dislodge the Germans from the area around St-Lô; the town was finally liberated on July 19.

After having boned up on the full story of the Normandy invasion, you'll want to go and see the area where it all took place. There's little point in visiting all five sites, since not much remains to mark the furious fighting waged hereabouts. In the bay of Arromanches, however, some elements of the floating harbor are still visible.

30 Head north from Bayeux along D516 to **Arromanches,** 10 kilometers (six miles) away. Linger here awhile, contemplating those apparently insignificant hunks of concrete protruding from the water, and try to imagine the extraordinary technical feat involved in towing the two floating harbors across the Channel from England. (The other was moored at Omaha Beach but was destroyed on June 19, 1944, by an exceptionally violent storm.) If you're interested in yet more battle documentation, visit the **Musée du Debarquement,** right on the seafront, whose exhibits include models, mock-ups, and photographs depicting the invasion. *Admission: 10 frs. Open mid-June–mid-Sept., daily 9–7; mid-Sept.–mid-June, 9–noon and 2–7.*

From Arromanches, take D514 west.

Time Out About 10 kilometers (6 miles) along, you'll reach Port-en-Bessin-Huppain, a little fishing port that boasts a striking restaurant called **La Marine.** The fish and seafood are fresh, and the upstairs dining room offers terrific views of the port. *Quai Letourneur.*

③ Continue along D514 for another 8 kilometers (5 miles) to **Colleville-sur-Mer,** then turn right to **Omaha Beach,** scene of a bloody battle in which nearly 10,000 American soldiers lost their lives. A little farther along D514, at St-Laurent-sur-Mer, turn right onto D517, which takes you back to the seafront at the site of the **Monument du Débarquement (Monument to the Normandy Landings).** You may want to park the car and stroll around the beaches and the grassy tops of the dunes overlooking them, from where you'll see sad remnants of the war—ruined bunkers, rows of trenches, and the remains of barbed-**③** wire defenses. Continue along ,the beachfront to **Vierville-sur-Mer** which has a monument to the members of the U.S. National Guard who fought in both world wars.

Unless you decide to drive into the Cotentin Peninsula, past Utah Beach and on to Cherbourg, you can conclude your tour of the Calvados Coast either by returning to Bayeux via Isigny-sur-Mer, about 19 kilometers (12 miles) from Vierville, or con-**③** tinuing to **St-Lô,** 29 kilometers (18 miles) from Isigny. Given its sad sobriquet of the "capital of ruins," you won't be surprised that St-Lô played a strategic role in the Battle of Normandy and was almost completely destroyed in July 1944. The town was largely rebuilt after the war, and its only relic of the past is the ruined 13th–17th-century Eglise Notre-Dame.

③ From St-Lô, you are in striking distance of Normandy's most impressive monument, **Mont-St-Michel,** 72 kilometers (45 miles) southwest on the border of Normandy and Brittany.

Take D999, which joins with N175 at Villedieu-les-Poêles, and continue to Avranches; from here, follow the road around the bay to the Abbey of Mont-St-Michel. Before you visit this awe-inspiring monument, be warned that the sea that separates the rock from the mainland is extremely dangerous: It's subject to tidal movements that produce a difference of up to 45 feet between low and high tides, and because of the extremely flat bay bed, the water rushes in at an incredible speed. Also, there are nasty patches of quicksand, so tread with care!

The dramatic silhouette of Mont-St-Michel against the horizon may well be your most lasting image of Normandy. The wonder of the Abbey stems not only from its rocky perch a few hundred yards off the coast (it's cut off from the mainland at high tide), but from its legendary origins in the 8th century and the sheer exploit of its construction, which took over 500 years, from 1017 to 1521. The abbey stands at the top of a 264-foot mound of rock, and the granite used to build it was transported from the Isles of Chausey (just beyond Mont-St-Michel Bay) and Brittany and laboriously hauled up to the site.

Legend has it that the Archangel Michael appeared to Aubert, bishop of Avranches, inspiring him to build an oratory on what was then called Mont Tombe. The original church was completed in 1144, but new buildings were added in the 13th century to accommodate the monks, as well as the hordes of pilgrims who flocked here even during the Hundred Years' War, when the region was in English hands. The Romanesque choir was rebuilt in an ornate Gothic style during the 15th and 16th centuries. The abbey's monastic vocation was undermined during the 17th century, when the monks began to flout the strict rules and discipline of their order, a drift into decadence that culminated in the monks' dispersal, and the abbey's conversion into a prison well before the French Revolution. In 1874, the former abbey was handed over to a governmental agency responsible for the preservation of historical monuments; only within the past 20 years have monks been able to live and work here once more.

A highlight of the abbey is the collection of 13th-century buildings on the north side of the mount. The exterior of the buildings is grimly fortresslike, but inside, they are one of Normandy's best examples of the evolution of Gothic architecture, ranging from the sober Romanesque style of the lower halls to the masterly refinement of the cloisters and the elegance of the refectory.

The climb to the abbey is hard going, but it's worth it. Head first for the Grand Degré, the steep, narrow staircase on the north side. Once past the ramparts, you'll come to the pink-and-gray granite towers of the Châtelet and then to the Salle des Gardes, the central point of the abbey. Guided tours start from the Saut Gautier terrace (named after a prisoner who jumped to his death from it): You must join one of these groups if you want to see the beautifully wrought Escalier de Dentelle (Lace Staircase) inside the church. *Admission: 13 frs. Open mid-May–Sept., daily 9–11:30 and 1:30–6; Oct.–mid-May, Wed.–Mon. 9–11 and 1:30–4, closed Tues.*

The island village, with its steep, narrow streets, is best visited out of season, from September to May. The hordes of souvenir sellers and tourists can be stifling in summer months, but you can always take refuge in the abbey's gardens. The ramparts in general and the North Tower in particular offer dramatic views of the bay.

Tour 3: Suisse Normande

Caen is the best starting place for a trip through Suisse Normande, or Norman Switzerland, a rocky expanse of hills and gullies in the heart of Lower Normandy, containing lots of natural beauty and few man-made wonders. Striking as the scenery is, however, you'll need to exert all your powers of imagination to see much resemblance to the Swiss Alps! Taking D562 south for 45 kilometers (28 miles), you come to **35** **Thury-Harcourt** on the Orne river, the gateway to Suisse Normande. If you're not in a hurry and you enjoy twisting country roads, turn right off D562 at Laize-la-Ville, cross the Orne, and take the more scenic D212, which runs alongside the river and enters Thury-Harcourt from the opposite bank. This little country town is famous for the beautiful gardens of its ruined castle.

36 Continue down D562, following the Orne, to **Clécy**, the area's main tourist center. It's a good base for visiting the sights of

the Orne valley; take the steep roads up to the clifftops overlooking the river, where there are lovely views of the woods on
the other bank.

Time Out You'll find an open-air, riverbank café in Clécy, **La Potinière,**
which is great for drinks or snacks. Pancakes top the bill, either
sweet or with savory fillings like ham and cheese, and there's a
good selection of tarts and homemade ice cream. On Friday
evening, you can enjoy a rowdy musical backdrop of jazz or
rock. *On the river. Closed Oct.–Apr.*

From Clécy, continue for a couple of miles along D562 and then
turn left at Le Fresne onto D1, which winds its way through
㊲ the valley of the Loireau to another riverside resort, **Pont
d'Ouilly,** situated at the point where the River Noireau flows
into the Orne. Heading south along the Orne on D167, veer
right at le Pont-des-Vers onto D43 and head into the most
mountainous part of Suisse Normande to the Roche d'Oëtre;
from here, you'll get the most spectacular views of the craggy
hills that give the region its name.

Continue along D301 for a few miles and then turn left across
the Orne, joining D21 before turning almost immediately right
㊳ along D239 to **Rabodanges.** Turn down any of the side roads
leading to the riverside, where you'll be rewarded with a fine
view of the river gorge (the Gorges de St-Aubert). A little farther upstream is the Rabodanges dam; from here, D121 skirts
the eastern side of the lake. The road crosses the lake by the
㊴ Ste-Croix bridge and brings you to **Putanges-Pont-Ecrépin.**

The river Orne now swings east to Argentan, a peaceful little
town that was badly damaged during the last days of the Battle
of Normandy. Rather than follow the river, however, it's more
rewarding to head south from Putanges, along D909 and then
㊵ D19 to **Bagnoles-de-l'Orne,** the most important spa town in the
region. The town nestles in a beautiful setting overlooking a
lake formed by the River Yée and is surrounded by forests and
parkland that are well worth touring.

㊶ From Bagnoles-de-l'Orne, it's a fairly straight road to **Alençon;**
follow D916 south, then turn left onto N176 to Pré-en-Pail and
take N12 from there. The road runs through the middle of the
Normandie-Maine Nature Park. Alençon lies on the eastern
edge of the park, south of the Forest of Ecouves and west of the
Forest of Perseigne. An attractive town with many historic
buildings, Alençon has been a lace-making center since 1665; by
the end of the century Alençon lace was de rigueur in all fashionable circles. The **Musée des Beaux-Arts et de la Dentelle** (*see*
Shopping) contains a sophisticated collection of lace from Italy,
Flanders, and France, along with paintings from the French
school that span the 17th to the 20th century. *Rue Julien. Admission: 7 frs. Open Tues.–Sun. 10–noon and 2–6.*

Turn right out of the museum and head right again at the corner. Seven blocks down, you'll come to the 14th–15th-century
Eglise Notre-Dame, known for its highly ornate Gothic porch,
erected around 1500. *Rue St-Blaize.*

What to See and Do with Children

The **Parc Zoologique de Clères,** 16 kilometers (10 miles) north of
Rouen, is a wildlife park that's home to over 750 species of

birds, plus a motley assortment of free-roaming antelope, deer, kangaroos, and gibbons. Clères is a tiny village; you can't miss the park. *Admission: 25 frs. adults, 15 frs. children under 15. Open Mar.–May and Sept.–Nov., daily 9–noon and 3:30–sunset; June–Aug., daily 9–sunset.*

A **vintage car museum** is found at Le Bec-Hellouin, southwest of Rouen. Even those who are long past childhood will appreciate the 50 racing and touring automobiles from as early as 1920; the highlights must be the seven Bugattis. *Brionne. Admission: 25 frs. Open 9–noon and 2–7.*

Most Norman resort beaches have supervised play areas where children can happily spend a half-day or so with their peers.

Off the Beaten Track

Connoisseurs of the apple brandy Calvados will be interested in a visit to the **Vallee d'Auge**, on the west side of the Pays d'Auge. This is the heart of Calvados country, between Troarn and Lisieux, through which the River Dives and its tributaries flow. You don't need a fixed itinerary; just follow your nose and look for local farmers offering Calvados for sale. However, there is a pretty, winding route to follow from Manerbe, north of Lisieux, which meanders west along D270, D117, and D85 to Beuvron-en-Auge, where you take D117 again across the River Dives to Troarn. Local Calvados producers will be delighted to let you taste their products, especially if you then buy a few bottles. They use traditional methods to distill the brandy, so you can be sure of finding something superior to the brands available in most shops.

Northwest of Evreux is **Le Bec-Hellouin,** near Brionne. Its famous Abbaye du Bec-Hellouin dates from the 11th century, but the monks were driven out during the French Revolution and the original abbey was demolished during the 19th century. Only the 15th-century St-Nicolas tower, part of the south transept, and the bases of some pillars remain, together with a 13th-century Gothic door and some statues from the 14th and 15th centuries. Next to the abbey is a vintage automobile museum. *(see* What to See and Do with Children). *Abbaye du Bec-Hellouin. Admission: 9 frs. Guided tours only, June–Sept. at 10, 11, 3, 3:45, 4:30, and 5:15; Oct.–May at 11, 3:15, and 4:30.*

Shopping

Lace Handmade lace is a great rarity, and admirers will certainly think it's worth spending some time searching it out. Prices are high, but then, this kind of labor-intensive, high-quality creation never comes cheap. In Alençon, the best places to buy lace are the two museums devoted to it: the **Musée de la Dentelle** (31 rue du Pont-Neuf) and **Musée des Beaux-Arts et de la Dentelle** (pl. Foch). In Bayeux, try the **Centre Normand du Dentelle au Fureau,** on place aux Pommes.

Food Items Normandy is a food-lover's region, and some of the best buying is to be done in food markets and *charcuteries.* Gastronomes will want to drop by **La Ferme Normande** (pl. du Marché, Deauville) for regional delicacies, while those with a weakness for sweets should go straight to **Raten** (115 Grande-Rue, Dieppe).

Spirits It's true that you can buy Benedictine anywhere in the world, but if you've visited the **Musée de la Bénédictine** in Fécamp, the bottle you buy there will have a certain sentimental value (110 rue Alexandre-le-Grand). Calvados is harder to find outside France, and although it's generally available in wine shops around the country, you'll find a wider choice of good-quality Calvados in Normandy itself. If possible, buy Calvados that comes from the Pays d'Auge, the area of Normandy reputed to produce the best (*see* Off the Beaten Track). In Lisieux, the **Distillery du Pere Jules** (rte. des Dives) offers first-rate Calvados.

Antiques Fairs and Markets If you enjoy the hunt as much as the prize, try the following: Caen hosts a bric-a-brac and antiques fair in June, while Cabourg has one in mid-August. Caen also has two morning flea markets: on Sunday in place Courtonne or on Friday in place St-Saveur.

Beaches

Wherever you go on the Normandy coast, you'll look at the chilly waters of the English Channel: Those used to warmer climes may need all their resolve to take the plunge, even on hot, sunny days. The most fashionable Norman resorts lie along the Floral Coast, the eastern end of the Calvados Coast between Deauville/Trouville and Cabourg; it's virtually one long, sandy beach, with the different towns overlapping. The rest of the Calvados Coast is also a succession of seaside resorts, though the beaches that saw the Normandy landings have not been so developed as those farther east. While the resort towns of the western Calvados Coast don't lack for charm, they don't have the character of Honfleur or the unspoiled and rugged beauty of the pebbly Alabaster Coast, stretching from Le Havre to beyond Dieppe. The resorts here are more widely spaced, separated by craggy cliffs, and even in the summer months, beaches are relatively uncrowded. Perched on the clifftops are green fields and woodland where you can amble for hours, breathing the fresh sea air.

Sports and Fitness

Water Sports With its miles of coastline, its rivers, and its lakes, Normandy offers a multitude of water-based activities. Many resorts have yachting marinas, where you can rent sailing dinghies and windsurfers as well as waterski. At the **Deauville Yacht Club** (quai de la Marine, tel. 31-88-38-19), a day in the smallest boat (16 feet) costs just 30 francs, while an 80-foot yacht will set you back only 240 francs. Similar prices are encountered at **Le Club Nautique de Trouville Hennequevelle** (Le Roches Noir, tel. 31-98-52-88). For swimmers, there are 60 outdoor and 20 indoor pools, in addition to the many safe bathing beaches; you can find public swimming pools in Bayeux, Cabourg, Caen, Deauville, Trouville, and Lisieux. The charming resort of Granville, 26 kilometers (16 miles) northwest of Avranches, is a center for aquatic sports; inquire about sailboat jaunts at the **Centre Regional de Nautisme de Granville** (B.P. 124, 50400 Granville, tel. 33-50-18-95). **Lesjesqueux Voile** (3 rue Clement-Desmaisons, 50400 Granville, tel. 33-50-18-97) rents boats and yachts for vacation cruises.

Biking You can rent bicycles from train stations in Bayeux, Caen, Dieppe, and Le Tréport for about 35 francs per day. Or try

Family Home in Bayeux (39 rue du Gal-de-Dais, tel. 31–92–15–22).

Golf The most spectacular golf course in Normandy is at **Le Vaudrueil,** in a park nestling between two branches of the River Eure; the course takes you past the ruins of a number of old castles. Other 18-hole courses are found in Cabourg, Deauville, Etretat, Dieppe, Le Havre, and Rouen; 9 nine-hole courses include Deauville, Houlgate, and Bagnoles-de-l'Orne.

Hiking There are 10 long-distance, signposted itineraries and countless well-indicated footpaths for shorter walks; overnight hostels are found at many points. Contact the **Comité Départemental de la Randonée Pedestre de Seine-Maritime** (B.P. 666, 76008 Rouen).

Horseback Riding Normandy is a leading horseracing and training region, with numerous stud farms, thoroughbred stables, and race courses. The most important race of the year is the Grand Prix at Deauville, on the last Sunday in August. If you prefer riding to watching, contact Upper Normandy's center for equestrian tourism, the **Association Régionale de Tourisme Equestre** in Caen (Chambre d'Agriculture, 4 promenade Mme-de-Sévigné, 14039 Caen, tel. 31–84–47–19).

Rock Climbing There is good rock-climbing country in the Seine Valley and in the region of Suisse Normande; inquire at **C.A.F.** (13 rue Jacques-Durandes, 14000 Caen, tel. 31–93–07–23).

Dining and Lodging

Dining

Normandy is the land of butter, cream cheese, and Calvados, a powerful apple brandy. The Normans are notoriously big eaters: In the old days, on festive occasions, they wouldn't bat an eye at tucking into as many as 24 courses. Between the warm-up and the main course there was a *trou* (hole), often lasting several hours, during which lots of Calvados was downed, giving rise to the expression *le trou normand*.

Many dishes are cooked with rich cream sauces; the description *à la normande* usually means "with a cream sauce." The richness of the milk makes for excellent cheese: *Pont-l'Évêque* (known since the 13th century) is made in the Pays d'Auge with milk that is still warm and creamy, while *Livarot* (also produced for centuries) uses milk that has stood for a while; don't be put off by its strong smell. Then there are the excellent *Pave d'Auge* and the best known of them all, *Camembert*, a relative newcomer, invented by a farmer's wife in the 19th century. Now so popular that it is produced all over France, the best *Camembert* is still made in Normandy (known as *Camembert au lait cru*).

There are many local specialties. Rouen is famous for its *canard à la Rouennaise* (duck in blood sauce); Caen, for its *tripes à la mode de Caen* (tripe); and Mont-St-Michel, for *omelette Mère Poulard*. Then there are *sole dieppoise* (sole poached in a sauce with cream and mussels), excellent chicken from the Vallee d'Auge, and lamb from the salt marshes. Those who like *boudin noir* (blood sausage) have come to the right region, and for seafood lovers, the coast provides oysters, lobster, and shrimp.

Normandy is not a wine-growing area but produces excellent cider. The best comes from the Vallee d'Auge and is 100% apple juice; when poured into the glass, it should fizz a bit but not froth.

Highly recommended restaurants are indicated by a star ★.

Lodging

There are accommodations to suit every taste in Normandy. In the beach resorts, the season is very short, July and August only, but weekends are busy for much of the year; in June and September, accommodations are usually available at short notice.

Highly recommended hotels are indicated by a star ★.

Bagnoles-de-l'Orne
Dining and Lodging
★

Le Manoir de Lys. Elegant guest rooms are decorated with flair at this magnificent Norman manor house, which lords it over a beautifully landscaped park on the edge of a forest. The restaurant has gained a considerable reputation for its cuisine *à la normande. Rte. de Juvigny (a mile from the casino), 61140, tel. 33–37–80–69. 12 rooms with bath. Facilities: tennis, restaurant. AE, V. Closed Jan.–Feb.; restaurant closed Sun. dinner and Tues. Nov.–Mar. Expensive.*

Bois Joli. A less imposing Norman manor house, Bois Joli has been recently renovated, and its cozily stylish guest rooms will make you feel right at home; they're all individually decorated. Peace and quiet reign unchecked here, and the delightful terrace overlooks the hotel's gardens. A piano plays softly in the background while diners tuck into good regional fare in the elegant restaurant. *12 av. Philippe-du-Rozier (opposite the race course), 61140, tel. 33–37–92–77. 20 rooms, 15 with bath. Facilities: restaurant, terrace, garden. AE, DC, MC, V. Closed Jan.–Feb. Moderate.*

Bayeux
Dining and Lodging

Le Lion d'Or. The luxurious Lion d'Or is a handsome '30s creation, conveniently situated in the center of town. Palm trees arch over the garden courtyard, while flowers cascade from balcony window boxes. Rooms are comfortable and well furnished with pretty fabrics. Fine Norman cuisine is served in the chic wood-beamed restaurant, decorated in shades of apricot. Specialties include *andouille chaud Bovary*, no doubt Madame Bovary's own recipe for hot sausages, and fillet of sole in a creamy lobster sauce. *7 rue St-Jean, 14400, tel. 31–92–88–86. 22 rooms with bath. Facilities: restaurant. AE, DC. Moderate.*

Lodging
★

Hôtel d'Argouges. This lovely 18th-century hotel is an oasis of calm in the city center, and many rooms offer views of the well-tended flower garden. The rooms are superb, tastefully furnished in French provincial chic and featuring rustic beamed ceilings. There's no restaurant. *21 rue St-Patrice, 14400, tel. 31–92–88–86. 22 rooms with bath. Facilities: garden. AE, DC, V. Moderate.*

Le Bec-Hellouin
Dining and Lodging
★

Auberge de l'Abbaye. You'll enjoy traditional Norman cooking in this rustic inn, which features beamed ceilings and stone walls hung with ornamental copper pans. Charming Madame Sergent has been in charge for over a quarter of a century; she also has eight delightfully old-fashioned bedrooms but says they are reserved for her diners (though you don't have to stay here to eat at the restaurant). According to one famous TV personality, this restaurant serves the best apple tart in France. *Pl. de l'Eglise, 27800, tel. 32–44–86–02. Reservations advised. Dress: casual. Closed Mon. dinner, Tues. and mid-Jan.–Feb. Moderate.*

Bénouville **Le Manoir d'Hastings.** One of Normandy's most celebrated res-
Dining taurants is situated in a little village 10 kilometers (6 miles)
★ north of Caen. The 17th-century building was originally a Norman priory. In addition to the main dining room, there are 11
private rooms for more intimate (and expensive) occasions.
Aperitifs and coffee are served in the garden. The considerable
reputation of owner-chef Claude Scaviner and his son is based
mainly on their fish and seafood dishes. *18 av. de la Côte-de-
Nacre, tel. 31–44–62–43. Reservations essential. Jacket and
tie required. AE, DC, MC, V. Expensive–Very Expensive.*

Bonsecours **Auberge de la Butte.** Master chef Pierre Herve is renowned for
Dining his subtle way with fish and seafood; his best dishes include
★ poached oysters wrapped in spinach leaves and fricasseed fillet
of sole. The magnificent Norman dining room's half-timbered
walls are adorned with paintings and shining copper pots and
pans, and the ceiling features exposed beams as well. *69 rue de
Paris, tel. 35–80–43–11. Reservations advised. Jacket and tie
required. AE, DC, V. Closed Wed. dinner, Thurs., Sun. dinner, Dec. 22–Jan. 5, and Aug. Expensive.*

Cabourg **Le Grand Hôtel.** This luxurious white stucco hotel is set right
Lodging on the seafront at the heart of town, and many guest rooms
have balconies overlooking the sea. There's a lively piano bar
during the summer season, and the hotel is connected to the casino. Its restaurant, Le Balbec, boasts traditional French
cuisine of a high standard but no great sophistication. *Promenade Marcel-Proust, 14390, tel. 31–91–01–79. 70 rooms with
bath. Facilities: restaurant, bar. AE, DC, V. Restaurant
closed mid-Sept.–June. Very Expensive.*

Caen **La Bourride.** Normandy boasts a number of excellent restau-
Dining rants; La Bourride is one of the best, situated close to the castle
★ down one of Caen's oldest streets. Chef Michel Bruneau's inventive and delicate dishes are inspired mainly by local
produce, but the cooking is essentially modern. The small dining room is typically Norman, with stone walls, beamed
ceilings, and a large fireplace. *15 rue du Vaugueux, tel. 31–93–
50–76. Reservations essential. Jacket and tie required. MC, V.
Closed Sun., Mon., first 3 weeks Jan. and second half Aug. Expensive.*

Dining and Lodging **Château d'Audrieu.** Twenty-four kilometers (15 miles) west of
★ Caen, on the road to Tilly-sur-Seulles, is a property that fulfills
Hollywood's idea of a palatial château. A tree-lined avenue
leads to an imposing, elegant 18th-century facade, which sets
the tone for what lies within. The bedrooms and salons are the
last word in old-world opulence, featuring wall sconces, over-
stuffed chairs, and antiques. The restaurant has an extensive
wine list, and the chef uses produce from the château's own
vegetable garden to create classic French dishes. *14250
Audrieu, tel. 31–80–21–52. 22 rooms with bath. Facilities:
pool, park, restaurant, bar. V. Closed Dec. 20–Jan. 20; restaurant closed Wed., and Thurs. lunch. Very Expensive.*

★ **Le Relais des Gourmets.** One of the best hotels in town also has a
terrific restaurant. The luxurious modern guest rooms are spacious and airy, and an old-world atmosphere reigns in the

public rooms, which are dotted with some charming antiques. The plush restaurant offers a sophisticated level of service and classic local cuisine. The gratinéed lobster with crayfish and turbot with cèpe mushrooms are memorable. Meals are served in the garden during summer months. *13–15 rue de Geôle, 14000, tel. 31–86–06–01. 32 rooms with bath. Facilities: restaurant, garden. AE, DC, MC, V. Restaurant closed Sun. dinner. Expensive.*

Le Dauphin. Despite its downtown location, Le Dauphin offers peace and quiet. The building is a former priory dating from the 12th century, though the guest rooms are briskly modern. Those overlooking the street are soundproofed, while the rooms in back have views of the serene garden courtyard. The service is especially friendly and efficient, both in the hotel and in the excellent, though rather expensive, restaurant, which specializes in traditional Norman cooking. Fish is featured on the menu, though the veal sweetbreads in a mushroom sauce is a good choice as well. *29 rue Gémare, 14000, tel. 31–86–22–26. 21 rooms with bath. Facilities: garden, restaurant. AE, DC, MC, V. Closed mid-July–mid-Aug. and 2 weeks in Feb. Moderate.*

Deauville
Dining and Lodging

Le Royal. This gigantic five-star hotel, overlooking the sea and close to the casino, is stately and more than a trifle self-important. It has a range of guest rooms in various degrees of luxury and two restaurants: Le Royal, a sumptuous dining room in keeping with the establishment's general character, and L'Etrier, more intimate but still very plush, where the emphasis is on *haute cuisine. Blvd. Cornuché, 14800, tel. 31–88–16–41. 310 rooms, 281 with bath. Facilities: pool, sauna, tennis, restaurants. AE, DC, MC, V. Closed mid-Oct.–Easter. Very Expensive.*

Normandy. The Normandy's exterior is a jet-set resort's idea of quaint: Gables and nooks create a sleek rendition of provincial style. Inside, the large guest rooms are rife with antiques and period-style furniture, and many overlook the sea. The restaurant extends into a Norman courtyard surrounded by apple trees. *38 rue Jean-Mermoz, 14800, tel. 31–88–09–21. 348 rooms, 290 with bath. Facilities: restaurant, garden. AE, DC, MC, V. Very Expensive–Expensive.*

Lodging

Le Continental. One of Deauville's oldest buildings is home to this provincial seaside hotel. The owner, Madame Perrot, is brisk and efficient, as is the service. The guest rooms are small and somewhat spartan—but this is Deauville, after all, and for the price you can't do much better. The Continental is handily placed between the port and casino, but it doesn't have a restaurant. *1 rue Désiré-le-Hoc, 14800, tel. 31–88–21–06. 55 rooms, 36 with bath. AE, DC, MC, V. Closed mid-Nov.–mid-Mar. Inexpensive.*

Dieppe
Dining and Lodging

La Présidence. The modern Présidence overlooks the sea and offers airy, well-appointed guest rooms and an "English" bar, Le Verrazane. The delightful restaurant, Le Queiros, is on the fourth floor, where classic, unpretentious, but tasty cooking predominates. *1 blvd. de Verdun, 76200, tel. 35–84–31–31. 88 rooms, 79 with bath. Facilities: restaurant. AE, DC, MC, V. Moderate.*

Duclair

Le Parc. Pierre Le Patezour, one of the region's most acclaimed chefs, has created an excellent restaurant in Duclair, about 20 kilometers (12 miles) west of Rouen, on the road to Caudebec-en-Caux. The dining room features plush, art nouveau decor, and the menu offers classic regional dishes, like *canard à la Rouennaise* (duck in blood sauce). Le Patezour's subtle preparation of fillet of sole is an eye-opener. *721 av. du Président-Coty, tel. 35–37–50–31. Reservations advised. Jacket and tie required. AE, DC, MC, V. Closed Sun. dinner, Mon., and Dec. 20–Jan. 20. Expensive.*

Etretat **Les Roches Blanches.** Expect a warm welcome at this cozily un-
Dining pretentious family-run restaurant near the sea, which has three good-value menus. The house specialty is veal escalope with mushrooms, flambéed in Calvados, and there is a good range of fish and seafood dishes. *Rue Abbé-Cochet, tel. 35–27–07–34. Reservations advised, especially for Sun. lunch. Dress: casual. MC, V. Closed Tues., Wed., and Thurs. (Wed. only July–early Sept.) and Jan. and Oct. Moderate.*

Lodging **Le Donjon.** This charming little château is set in a large park overlooking the resort and offers lovely bay views. The individually furnished guest rooms are huge, comfortable, and quiet. Reliable French cuisine is served with flair in the cozy restaurant. *Chemin de St-Clair, 76790, tel. 35–27–08–23. 7 rooms, 6 with bath. Facilities: pool, restaurant. AE, DC, V. Expensive.*
Dormy House. Thanks to its location halfway up the southern cliff, Dormy House provides dramatic views of the bay. Four buildings, dating from different periods and in a variety of architectural styles, make up the hotel. The large rooms are furnished in oak and sport cheerful floral drapes. Most guests stay on half-board; the restaurant specializes in fish and seafood. *Rte. du Havre, 76790, tel. 35–27–07–88. 32 rooms, 28 with bath. Facilities: restaurant. MC, V. Closed mid-Nov.–Mar. Moderate.*

Fécamp **Auberge de la Rouge.** The quaint Auberge de la Rouge is in a
Dining little hamlet a mile or so south of Fécamp. Its menu features a good mix of classic and modern dishes and includes many local specialties; the lobster is always a good bet. There are eight guest rooms, too. *Commune de St-Léonard, tel. 35–28–07–59. Reservations advised. Dress: casual. AE, V. Closed Sun. dinner and Mon. Moderate.*

★ **L'Escalier.** This delightfully simple little restaurant overlooks the harbor, and serves traditional *cuisine à la Normande.* The several inexpensive fixed-price menus mainly offer fish and seafood. *101 quai Bérigny, tel. 35–28–26–79. Reservations essential in summer. Dress: casual. DC, MC, V. Closed Mon. and 2 weeks in Nov. Inexpensive.*

Honfleur **L'Absinthe.** The Absinthe's 17th-century dining room, with
Dining stone walls and beamed ceilings, is a magnificent setting in which to enjoy chef Antoine Ceffrey's masterly creations, though on sunny days, you'll probably want to eat outside on the terrace. Ceffrey has a delicate way with fish and seafood; try the *burbet*, a freshwater cod, prepared with ginger. *10 quai de la Quarantaine, tel. 31–89–39–00. Reservations advised. Jacket and tie required. AE, DC, MC, V. Closed Mon. dinner and Tues. Sept.–June. Expensive.*

★ **L'Ancrage.** Massive seafood platters top the bill at this delightful old restaurant, which occupies a two-story 17th-century building overlooking the harbor. The cuisine is authentically Norman—simple but good. If you want a change from fish and seafood, try the succulent calf sweetbreads. *12 rue Mont-pensier, tel. 31–89–00–70. Reservations advised, especially in summer. Dress: casual. MC, V. Closed Tues. dinner, Wed., and Jan. Moderate.*

Dining and Lodging **Ferme St-Siméon.** A 19th-century manor house—commonly held to be the birthplace of Impressionism—is set in the park that inspired such 19th-century luminaries as Claude Monet and Alfred Sisley. The guest rooms are individually decorated in a style an ad-man might term "palatial provincial," and a few have Jacuzzis. Pastel colors and floral wallpaper create a gardenlike aura in some rooms, while antiques and period decor are featured in others. The sophisticated restaurant specializes in fish, and in good weather you can eat out on the terrace. Save room for the extensive cheese board. *Rte. Adolphe-Marais, on D513 to Trouville, 14600 Honfleur, tel. 31–89–23–61. 38 rooms with bath. Facilities: tennis, park, restaurant. MC, V. Restaurant closed Wed. lunch Nov.–Mar. Very Expensive.*

★ **Auberge du Vieux Puits.** Twenty kilometers (13 miles) southeast of Honfleur lies a quaint little cottage of a hotel, whose trellised and beamed exterior can't have changed much in the past 300 years. Early admirers included Gustave Flaubert, who gave the hotel a few lines in *Madame Bovary*. The guest rooms make use of heavy wood furniture and pretty curtains and bedspreads to reflect the traditional feel of the architecture. The restaurant offers first-rate cuisine. *6 rue Notre-Dame-du-Pré, 27500 Pont-Audemer, tel. 32–41–01–48. 12 rooms, 6 with bath. V. Closed Dec. 20–Jan. 22. Expensive.*

★ **Le Cheval Blanc.** Occupying a renovated, 15th-century building on the harborfront, this hotel has one of the finest restaurants in town. All the guest rooms have been recently redecorated and offer views of the port. Chef Robert Samson prepares classic yet delicate cuisine that is served with panache in the beautiful Louis XIII–style dining room. Try the seafood and oyster mousse or the sliced turbot in a subtle cider-and-cream sauce. *2 quai des Passagers, 14600, tel. 31–89–13–49. 35 rooms, 14 with bath. Facilities: restaurant. MC, V. Closed last 3 weeks in Jan.; restaurant (tel. 31–89–39–87) closed Mon. and from mid-Nov.–Jan. 31. Moderate.*

Hostellerie Lechat. One of the best-known and -loved establishments in Honfleur stands in a pretty square just behind the harbor in a typical 18th-century Norman building. The spacious guest rooms have been recently renovated in pretty French provincial decor that makes good use of cheerful prints and colors. Foreign guests are given a warm welcome, especially in The American bar. The rustic, beamed restaurant serves top-notch Norman cuisine; lobster features prominently on the menu. *3 pl. Ste-Catherine, 14600, tel. 31–89–23–85. 24 rooms with bath. Facilities: restaurant, bar. AE, DC, MC, V. Restaurant closed Jan., Wed., and Thurs. lunch mid-Sept.–May. Moderate.*

Mont-St-Michel **Mère Poulard.** The hotel of the most celebrated restaurant on
Dining and Lodging the mount consists of adjoining houses whose cozy, second-
★ floor rooms are both comfortable and quiet. The restaurant's reputation derives partly from Mère Poulard's famous omelette (a recipe that originated in the 19th century and requires slow cooking over an open wood fire) and partly from its dramatic location. The young chef successfully combines traditional and nouvelle cuisine, adding his own inventions to the longstanding

house specialties. *50116 Mont-St-Michel, tel. 33–60–14–01. Reservations essential. Jacket and tie preferred. AE, DC, MC, V. Closed Oct.–Mar. Expensive.*

Terrasses Poulard. Monsieur Vannier bought this popular restaurant first, and later acquired its more prestigious sister establishment (above). The hotel is a recent addition, a result of buying up and renovating the neighboring houses to create an ensemble of buildings that exude great charm and character, clustered around a small garden in the middle of the mount. The large restaurant attracts hordes of tourists; If you don't mind being surrounded by fellow Americans, Canadians, and Britons, you'll no doubt enjoy the traditional cuisine. *On the main road opposite the parish church, 50116, tel. 33–60–14–09. 29 rooms with bath. Facilities: library, billiards room, restaurant. AE, DC, MC, V. Moderate.*

Rouen Dining

Bertrand Warin. The most fashionable restaurant in Rouen occupies a 17th-century town house near the old market. Owner-chef Bertrand Warin has created an elegant dining room that contrasts half-timbered walls and Louis XIII chairs with sleek modern furnishings. The tables are widely spaced, and large windows look out onto an illuminated garden. *7–9 rue de la Pie, near the Vieux Marché, tel. 35–89–26–69. Reservations essential. Jacket and tie required. AE, DC, MC, V. Closed Sun. dinner, Mon., Mar., and last 2 weeks in Aug. Expensive.*

★ **La Couronne.** The dining room of this 15th-century Norman building features beamed ceilings, leather-upholstered chairs, wood-paneled walls, and a scattering of sculpture. The traditional Norman cuisine makes few concessions to modernism; specialties include crayfish salad with foie gras and caviar, duck with orange, and turbot in puff pastry. *31 pl. du Vieux Marché, tel. 35–71–40–90. Reservations advised. Jacket and tie required. AE, DC, V. Expensive.*

Gentil. A friendly, bustling bistro, Gentil is located just beside the market and Joan of Arc's memorial church. It has a motherly staff and a huge menu with some worthwhile specialties. This is the place for succulent oysters—there are five or six kinds on the menu—and delicious tripe cooked the local way. There are tables outside in summer. *2 pl. Vieux Marché, tel. 35–71–59–09. Reservations advised. Dress: casual. AE, DC, V. Moderate.*

Dining and Lodging

Pullman Albane. This grandiose modern (1976) hotel, just opposite the train station, has luxurious, comfortable rooms; the best feature '30s-style decor. There's an American bar, and the restaurant, Le Tournebroche, serves classic Norman cooking with creamy and cheesy sauces, as well as plain grilled and spit-roast dishes. *Rue Croix de Fer, 76000, tel. 35–98–06–98. 125 rooms with bath. Facilities: restaurant, bar. AE, DC, MC, V. Expensive.*

Hôtel de Dieppe. Dating from the late 19th century, the Dieppe remains fresh and up-to-date thanks to frequent redecoration. You can take your choice of rooms furnished in breezy modern style or those with antique furniture. The restaurant, Les Quatre Saisons, has a well-earned reputation and offers English-style roasts as well as some traditional French dishes like duck cooked in its blood (which tastes much nicer than it sounds). *Pl. Bernard Tissot, 76000, tel. 35–71–96–00. 42 rooms with bath. Facilities: restaurant, breakfast room. AE, DC, MC, V. Moderate.*

Trouville **Carmen.** This straightforward, unpretentious little hotel is just
Lodging around the corner from the casino. The rooms range from the
plain and inexpensive to the comfortable and moderate. The
restaurant offers good homecooking at value-for-the-money
prices. *24 rue Carnot, tel. 31–88–35–43. 14 rooms, 12 with
bath. Facilities: restaurant. AE, DC, V. Closed Jan., 3rd week
in Apr., and third week in Oct. Restaurant closed Mon. dinner
and Tues. Inexpensive/Moderate.*

The Arts and Nightlife

The Arts

Music Normandy's cultural activities revolve around music, both classical and modern. Many churches host evening concerts, with
organ recitals drawing an especially large number of enthusiasts. Particularly good programs are featured at the church of
St-Ouen in Rouen, **St-Etienne** in Caen, and **St-Pierre** in Lisieux
(get details from the tourist office). Rouen's **St-Maclou** hosts an
annual series of organ recitals in August; even the venerable
abbey of **Mont-St-Michel** gets into the act during July and August. Jazz aficionados will be interested in the **European
Traditional Jazz Festival** held in mid-June at Luneray, 8 kilometers (5 miles) southwest of Dieppe. For those who like spectacle
with their music: the **Théâtre des Arts** in Rouen stages numerous operas (tel. 35–98–50–98).

Festivals A **Joan of Arc Commemoration** takes place in Rouen at the end
of May, featuring a variety of parades, street plays, concerts,
and exhibitions that recall the life—and death—of France's patron saint.

Film One of the biggest cultural events on the Norman calendar is
the **American Film Festival,** held in Deauville during the first
week of September.

Nightlife

The hot spots of Normandy nightlife are, predictably enough,
resorts like Deauville, Trouville, and Cabourg, where discos
and clubs vie for space with casinos.

Casinos There are nearly 30 casinos dotted around the region, five of
which—**Deauville, Forges-les-Eaux, Trouville, Dieppe,** and
Bagnoles-de-l'Orne—rank among France's best, with floor-
shows and cabarets, as well as gaming rooms.

Bars and Try **Le Bar des Jeux** (rue E-Blanc) in Deauville or Dieppe's **Ca-
Nightclubs** **sino** (3 blvd. de Verdun). Night owls will enjoy the smoky
ambience of **Club Melody** in Deauville (13 rue A-Fracasse) and
the jiving crowd at **Le King Créole** (29 blvd. des Belges) in
Rouen.

7 Brittany

Introduction

Thanks to its proximity to Great Britain, its folklore, and its spectacular coastline, Brittany (Bretagne in French) is a favorite destination among English-speaking vacationers. The French love the area, too, but don't worry about hordes of tourists—Brittany's vast beaches aren't easily crowded.

Occupying the bulbous portion of western France that juts far out into the Atlantic, the stubborn, independent-minded Bretons have more in common—both historically and linguistically —with the Celts of Cornwall, Wales, and Ireland than with their French countrymen. Both Brittany and Cornwall claim Merlin, King Arthur, and the Druids as cult figures, while huge Stonehenge-like menhirs and dolmens (prehistoric standing stones) litter the Breton countryside. As in Wales, nationalistic fervor has been channeled into gaining official acceptance for the local language.

Brittany became part of France in 1532, but regional folklore is still very much alive. An annual village *pardon* (a religious festival) will give you a good idea of Breton traditions: Banners and saintly statues are borne in colorful parades, accompanied by hymns, and the whole event is rounded off by food of all sorts. The most famous *pardon* is held on the last Sunday of August at Ste-Anne-la-Palud, near Quimper. The surrounding Finistère (from *Finis Terrae*, or Land's End) département, Brittany's westernmost district, is renowned for the costumes worn on such occasions—notably the lace bonnets, or *coiffes*, which can tower 15 inches above the wearer's head.

Geographically, Brittany is divided in two: maritime Armor ("land of the sea") and hinterland Argoat ("land of the forest"). The north of Brittany tends to be wilder than the south, where the countryside becomes softer as it descends toward Nantes and the Loire. Wherever you go, the coast is close by; the frenzied, cliff-bashing Atlantic surf alternates with sprawling beaches and bustling harbors. Islands, many inhabited and within easy reach of the mainland, are offshore.

Although Brittany's towns took a mighty hammering from the Nazis in 1944, most have been tastefully restored, the large concrete-cluttered naval base at Brest being an exception. Rennes, the only Breton city with more than 200,000 inhabitants, retains its traditional charm, as do the towns of Dinan, Quimper, and Vannes. Many ancient man-made delights are found in the region's villages, often in the form of *calvaries* (ornate burial chapels). Other architectural highlights include castles and cathedrals, the most outstanding examples being those of Fougères and Dol.

Essential Information

Important Addresses and Numbers

Tourist Information The principal regional tourist offices are at **Rennes** (Pont de Nemours, tel. 99–79–01–98), **Brest** (8 av. Georges-Clemenceau, tel. 98–44–24–96), and **Nantes** (pl. du Commerce, tel. 40–35–48–77).

The addresses of other tourist offices in towns mentioned on this tour are as follows: **Carnac** (74 av. des Druides, tel. 97–52–13–52), **Concarneau** (pl. Jean-Jaurès, tel. 98–87–01–44), **Dinan** (6 rue de l'Horloge, tel. 96–39–75–40), **Dinard** (2 blvd Féart, tel. 99–46–94–12), **Dol-de-Bretagne** (3 Grand Rue, tel. 99–48–15–37), **La Baule** (9 pl. de la Victoire, tel. 40–24–34–44), **Morlaix** (pl. des Otages, tel. 98–62–14–94), **Quiberon** (7 rue de Verdun, tel. 97–50–07–84), **Quimper** (3 rue du Roi-Gradlon, tel. 98–95–04–69), **St-Malo** (Esplanade St-Vincent, tel. 99–56–64–48), **Vannes** (1 rue Thiers, tel. 97–47–24–34), and **Vitré** (pl. St-Yves, tel. 99–75–04–46).

Travel Agencies **Thomas Cook** (22 rue du Calvaire, Nantes, tel. 40–48–11–53) and **Wagon Lits** (2 rue Jules-Simon, Rennes, tel. 99–79–45–96).

Car Rental **Avis** (17 av. Clémenceau, La Baule, tel. 40–60–36–28; 3 blvd. des Français-Libres, Brest, tel. 98–43–37–73; 2 blvd. Féart, Dinard, tel. 99–46–94–12; blvd. de Stalingrad, Nantes, tel. 40–74–39–74; and 8 av. de la Gare, Quimper, tel. 98–90–31–34).

Arriving and Departing

By Plane There are domestic airports at Rennes, Brest, Nantes, Morlaix, Dinard, Quimper, and Lorient.

By Car Rennes, the gateway to Brittany, lies 368 kilometers (230 miles) west of Paris. It can be reached in about 4 hours, via Le Mans and the A81/A11 expressways (A11 continues from Le Mans to Nantes).

By Train There are numerous services daily between Paris (Gare Montparnasse) and Rennes (3 ½ hours), four of which stop at Vitre. Nantes is on a direct line from Paris (250 miles in 3½ hours).

Getting Around

By Car Rennes, a strategic base for penetrating Brittany, is linked by good roads to Morlaix and Brest (E50), Quimper (N24/N165), Vannes (N24/N166), Fougéres (N12), and Dinan and St-Malo (N137).

By Train Trains from Paris fork at Rennes on their way to either Brest (via Morlaix) or Quimper (via Vannes). Change at Rennes for Dol and St-Malo; at Dol for Dinan and Dinard (bus link); at Morlaix for Roscoff; at Rosporden, 19 kilometers (12 miles) south of Quimper, for Concarneau; and at Auray for Quiberon. There is regular train service down the west coast from Nantes to La Rochelle and Bordeaux.

Guided Tours

Horizons Européens (France Tourisme, 214 rue de Rivoli, 75001 Paris, tel. 42–60–31–25) organizes seven-day bus tours of Brittany and a 10-day combined tour of Normandy and Brittany; plus a four-day trip to the Celtic Festival in Lorient. Prices are about 650 francs a day all-inclusive. Further details of organized tours of Brittany can be had from the **Maison de la Bretagne** in Paris (Centre Commercial Maine-Montparnasse, 17 rue de l'Arrivée, B.P. 1006, 75737 Paris cedex 15, tel. 45–38–73–15) or the regional tourist offices in Brest (tel. 98–44–24–96) and Quimper (tel. 98–95–04–69).

Exploring Brittany

Numbers in the margin correspond with points of interest on the Brittany map.

Orientation

Our first tour is confined to northeastern Brittany, which stretches from Rennes to the fortified harbor of St-Malo. This region played a frontline role in Brittany's efforts to repel French invaders during the Middle Ages, as can be seen in the massive castles of Vitré, Fougères, and Dinan. Our second tour begins 144 kilometers (90 miles) farther west, at the Channel port of Roscoff, before swinging southeast down the Atlantic coast to the city of Nantes at the mouth of the River Loire. Though Nantes is officially part of the Pays de la Loire, it has historic ties with Brittany, embodied in the imposing Château des Ducs de Bretagne.

Highlights for First-time Visitors

Menhirs and dolmens at Carnac, Tour 2
Ville Close, Concarneau, Tour 2
Dinan (Old Town), Tour 1
Nantes, Tour 2
Rennes, Tour 1
Vitré (Old Town), Tour 1

Tour 1: Northeast Brittany

1 Built high above the Vilaine Valley, **Vitré** (pronounced "V-Tray") is one of the age-old gateways to Brittany: There's still a feel of the Middle Ages about its dark, narrow alleys and tightly packed houses. The town's leading attraction is its formidable **castle,** shaped in an imposing triangle with fat, round towers. An 11th-century creation, it was first rebuilt in the 14th and 15th centuries to protect Brittany against invasion and was to prove one of the province's most successful fortresses; during the Hundred Years' War (1337–1453) the English repeatedly failed to take it, even though they occupied the rest of the town.

Time, not foreigners, came closest to ravaging the castle, which was heavily, though tastefully, restored during the last century. The town hall, however, is an unfortunate 1913 addition to the castle courtyard. You can visit the wing to the left of the entrance, beginning with the Tour St-Laurent and continuing along the walls via Tour de l'Argenterie, with its macabre collection of stuffed frogs and reptiles preserved in glass jars, to Tour de l'Oratoire. *Admission: 6 frs. Open Apr.–June, Wed. –Mon. 10–12 and 2:30–5:30, closed Tues; July–Sept., daily 10 –12 and 1:30–6; Oct.–Mar., Wed.–Fri. 10–12 and 2–5:30, Mon. 2–5:30, closed Tues. and weekends.*

Vitré's castle makes a splendid sight, especially from a vantage point on rue de Fougères across the river valley below. The castle stands at the west end of town, facing the narrow, cobbled streets of the remarkably preserved old town. Rue Poterie, rue d'En-Bas, and rue Beaudrairie, originally the home of tanners (the name comes from *baudoyers*—leather workers), make up a web of medieval streets as picturesque as any in Brittany; take time to stroll through them, soaking up the quaint atmosphere. Fragments of the town's medieval ramparts remain, including the 15th-century **Tour de la Bridolle** on place de la République, five blocks up from the castle. Built in the 15th and 16th centuries, **Notre-Dame** church has a fine, pinnacled south front, and dominates a large square of the same name (you'll have passed it on the left on your way to place de la République).

Thirty-two kilometers (20 miles) due north of Vitré via D178 and D798 is **Fougères**, a traditional cobbling and cider-making center. For many centuries, it was a frontier town, valiantly attempting to guard Brittany against attack. Perhaps one of the reasons for its conspicuous lack of success is the site of the **castle:** Instead of sitting high up on the hill, it spreads out down in the valley, though the sinuous River Nançon does make an admirable moat. The 13-towered castle covers over five acres, making it one of the largest in Europe. Although largely in ruins, it is impressive from both outside and in. The thick walls —up to 20 feet across in places—were intended to resist 15th-century artillery fire, but the castle was to prove vulnerable to surprise attacks and siege. A visit inside the castle walls reveals three lines of fortification, with the cosseted keep at their heart. There are charming views over Fougères from the Tour Mélusine and, in the Tour Raoul, a small shoe museum. The second and third stories of the Tour de Coigny were transformed into a chapel during the 16th century. *East end of town on pl. Raoul II. Admission: 9 frs. Open Apr.–Oct., daily 10–noon and 2–5; closed Nov.–Mar.*

The oldest streets of Fougères are alongside the castle, clustered around the elegant slate spire of **St-Sulpice** (rue de Lusignan), a Flamboyant Gothic church holding several fine altarpieces. A number of medieval houses line rue de la Pinterie, leading directly from the castle up to the undistinguished heart of town.

In the 1790s, Fougères was a center of royalist resistance to the French Revolution. Much of the action in 19th-century novelist Honoré de Balzac's bloodcurdling novel *Les Chouans* takes place hereabouts; the novel's heroine, Marie de Verneuil, had rooms close to the church of **St-Léonard** (follow the river left from the castle), which overlooks the Nançon Valley. Balzac wrote several dramatic scenes in which Marie, a Republican spy, slips down the mazy hillside path below the church to a clandestine rendezvous with the marquess of Montauran, the Royalist leader she had set out to capture but with whom she fell in love. Both path and church, with its ornate facade and 17th-century tower, have changed little; the garden through which the path leads is known today as the **Jardin Public.**

Another man who was inspired by the scenery of Fougères was locally-born Emmanuel de La Villéon (1858–1944), a little-known Impressionist painter. His works are displayed in the **Musée La Villéon,** in one of the oldest surviving houses in hilltop Fougères; to reach it from the Jardin Public, head left past St-Léonard, and cross the square into the adjacent rue Nationale. The over 100 paintings, pastels, watercolors, and drawings suggest serene, underestimated talent. The artist's work ranges from compassionate studies of toiling peasants to pretty landscapes where soft shades of green melt into hazy blue horizons. *51 rue Nationale. Admission: 8 frs. Open*

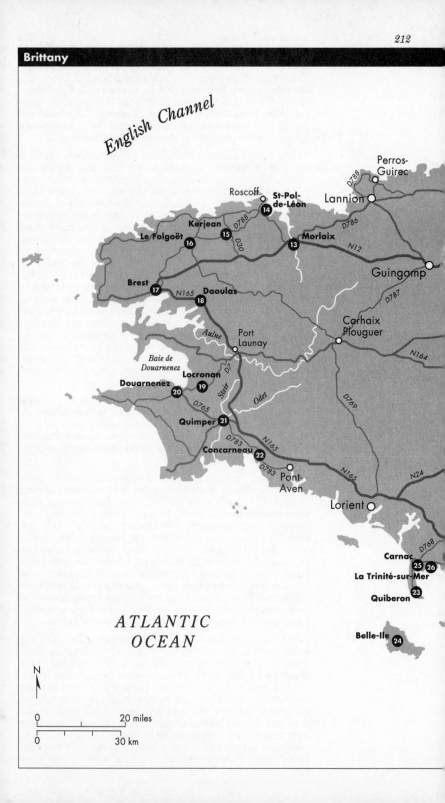

English Channel

Perros-Guirec

Roscoff

St-Pol-de-Léon

Lannion

14

Kerjean

15

Le Folgoët

16

Morlaix

13

Guingamp

Brest

17

N165

Daoulas

18

Aulne

Port Launay

Carhaix Plouguer

N164

Baie de Douarnenez

Locronan

19

Douarnenez

20

D765

Steïr

Odet

D769

Quimper

21

D783

N165

Concarneau

22

D783

Pont-Aven

Lorient

N165

N24

Carnac

25 **26**

La Trinité-sur-Mer

23

Quiberon

ATLANTIC OCEAN

Belle-Ile

24

N

0   20 miles

0   30 km

Golfe de St-Malo

Coutances

Granville

Avranches

D786

St-Brieuc

Cancale
St-Malo 12
Dinard 10 11
Mont-St-Michel

D973

D998

Nançon

Dol-de-Bretagne 8

N176

D266

N137

D795

Dinan 9

La Bourbansais 6
Combourg 7

Fougères 2

N12

D20

Tinténiac

Caradeuc 5
4

Couesnon

D178

D798

Loudéac

N164

St-Meen-le-Grand

Montmuran

N137

N12

Vitré 1

Vilaine

3
Rennes

Pontivy

N24

N168

Josselin

D177

N137

D178

Oust

Elven

Vannes
Auray 27

Rochefort-en-Terre

Chateaubriant

Vilaine

28
Redon

N165

D20

D114

D178

Muzillac

Missillac 29

N171

D51

St-Lyphard

La Baule 30

N165

A11

Loire

St-Nazaire

Nantes
31 38

Golfe du Morbihan

D28

Easter–mid-June, weekends only, 11–12:30 and 2:30–5; mid-June–mid-Sept., daily 10:30–12:30.

❸ Rennes (pronounced "Wren"), lying 48 kilometers (30 miles) southwest, is the traditional capital of Brittany. It has a different flavor from other towns in the region, mainly because of a terrible fire in 1720, which lasted a week and destroyed half the town. The remaining cobbled streets and half-timbered 15th-century houses make an interesting contrast with the Classical feel of Jacques Gabriel's disciplined granite buildings, broad avenues, and spacious squares.

Start at the western end of the old town, bordered by the River Rance. The **Cathédrale St-Pierre,** an early 19th-century building in Classical style, looms above rue de la Monnaie. Stop in to admire its richly decorated interior and outstanding 16th-century Flemish altarpiece. *Pl. St-Pierre. Open Sept.–June, daily 8:30–noon and 2–5; July–Aug., Mon.–Sat. 8:30–noon and 2–5, Sun. 8:30–noon.*

Time Out The swinging youths of Rennes have a nighttime rendezvous at the **Babylone Bar,** next to the cathedral. This isn't a place to linger in, but try it for a tangy, premeal aperitif or cream-and-brandy end-of-evening cocktail. *Rue des Dames.*

The surrounding streets are full of 15th- and 16th-century houses in both medieval and Renaissance styles. Many have been converted for use as shops, boutiques, restaurants, and pancake houses; a lively **street market** is held in and around place des Lices on Saturday morning.

The pedestrian rue Lafayette and rue Nationale lead to the **Palais de Justice** (Law Courts). This palatial building, originally home to the Breton Parliament, was designed in 1618 by Salomon de Brosse, architect of the Luxembourg Palace in Paris, and was the most important building in Rennes to escape the 1720 fire. After admiring its white stone-and-granite facade, venture inside to view the splendid interior. Among its various magnificent halls is the richly carved and painted **Grand' Chambre,** a former parliamentary chamber whose walls are covered with Gobelins tapestries that retrace the history of Brittany. *Pl. du Parlement. Admission: 12 frs. Open Wed.–Mon. 10–noon and 2–6; closed Tues.*

Head down from the Palais de Justice and left across quai Emile-Zola to the **Palais des Musées,** a huge building containing two museums—the **Musée des Beaux-Arts** and **Musée de Bretagne.** The Fine Arts Museum on the second floor houses one of the country's best collections of paintings outside Paris, featuring works by Georges de la Tour, Jean-Baptiste Chardin, Camille Corot, Paul Gauguin, and Maurice Utrillo, to name only a few. The ground-floor Museum of Brittany retraces the region's history, period by period, by way of costumes, models, porcelain, furniture, coins, statues, and shiny push-button visual displays. *20 quai E. Zola. Admission: joint ticket 10 frs. adults, 5 frs. children under 14.*

North of Rennes, the landscape is dotted with hefty castles and enticing châteaus. Twenty-four kilometers (15 miles) away via N137 and D27 is the castle of **Montmuran,** closely associated with Brittany's warrior-hero Bertrand du Guesclin; here, he was knighted in 1354 and married his second wife in 1372. An alley of oak and beech trees leads up to the main 18th-century building, which is surrounded by a moat and flanked by four towers, two built in the 12th century, two in the 14th. You can visit the towers and a small museum devoted to the castle's history. *Admission: 15 frs. Open Easter–Oct., daily 2–7; Nov.–Easter, weekends only, 2–6.*

5 Just 8 kilometers (5 miles) west is **Caradeuc,** a Classical château ambitiously dubbed the "Versailles of Brittany." Visitors can't go inside to check out this claim, unfortunately, but to compensate, explore the surrounding park—Brittany's largest—and admire its statues, flower beds, and leafy alleys. *Admission: 10 frs. Open Apr.–Oct., daily 9–noon and 1:30–8; Nov.–Mar., weekends only, 2–6.*

6 Take D20 to Tinténiac, then N137 north to **La Bourbansais,** a total of 19 kilometers (12 miles) from Caraduec. This castle has remained in the same family since it was founded by local lord Jean de Breil in 1583. It, too, has extensive gardens, containing a small zoo and a pack of hunting hounds. The buildings were enlarged in the 18th century, and the majority of the interior furnishings date from that period. There are fine collections of porcelain and tapestries. *Admission: 32 frs. Castle open Apr.–Oct., daily 2–6; Nov.–Mar., weekends only, 2–6. Park open daily 10–noon and 2–7.*

7 **Combourg,** best known as the boyhood home of Romantic writer Viscount Chateaubriand (1768–1848), is 11 kilometers (7 miles) east along D75 and D794. The thick-walled, four-towered castle dates mainly from the 14th and 15th centuries and contains a roomful of Chateaubriand archives. You can visit the writer's austere bedroom in the Tour du Chat (Cat's Tower). It was here that the adolescent Chateaubriand first gave free rein to his Romantic nature: The tower, he wrote, was haunted by a black cat (the reincarnation of a former Lord of Combourg) who returned on stormy nights as winds battered against the door and owls tapped against the windowpanes with their beaks. The castle's grounds—ponds, woods, and half-tended lawns—are suitably mournful and can seem positively desolate under leaden skies. *Admission: 20 frs., park only 10 frs. Castle open Mar.–Nov., Wed.–Mon. 2–5; closed Tues. Park open Mar.–Nov., Wed.–Mon. 9–noon and 2–5.*

8 Seventeen kilometers (10 miles) north via D795, the ancient town of **Dol-de-Bretagne** looks out from its 60-foot cliffs over Le Marais, a marshy plain stretching across to Mont St-Michel, 21 kilometers (13 miles) northeast. The **Promenade des Douves,** laid out along the northern part of the original ramparts, offers extensive views of Le Marais and Mont Dol, a 200-foot granite mound, three kilometers (two miles) north, legendary scene of combat between St. Michael and the Devil. Unfortunately, the stately trees that line the promenade suffered heavily in the 1987 hurricane, which devastated parts of France and southern Britain.

At the end of the promenade, walk the **Cathédrale St-Samson,** a damp, soaring, fortresslike bulk of granite dating mainly from the 12th to 14th century. This mighty building shows just how influential the bishopric of Dol was in days gone by. The richly sculpted Great Porch, carved wooden choir stalls, and stained glass in the chancel all deserve close scrutiny. *Pl. de la Cathédrale.*

Turn down rue des Ecoles to Dol's picturesque main street, **Grand-Rue des Stuarts,** lined with medieval houses. The oldest, at no. 17, boasts a chunky row of Romanesque arches.

❾ From Dol, take N176 to **Dinan,** 24 kilometers (15 miles) southwest. Dinan has close links with Brittany's 14th-century anti-English warrior-hero Bertrand du Guesclin, whose name is commemorated in countless squares and hostelries across the province. Du Guesclin won a famous victory here in 1359 and promptly married a local girl, Tiphaine Raguenel. When he died in the siege of Auvergne (central France) in 1380, his body was dispatched home to Dinan. Owing to the great man's popularity, however, only his heart completed the journey—his entrails having been confiscated at Le Puy, his flesh in Montferrand, and his bones in Le Mans.

Begin your stroll around the old town at the tourist office, housed in a charming 16th-century building in rue de l'Horloge. For a superb view of the town, climb to the top of the nearby belfry, the **Tour de l'Horloge.** *Admission: 4 frs. Open July–Aug., Mon.–Sat. 10–noon and 2–6.*

Turn left and head half a block along to admire the triangular-gabled wooden houses in **place des Merciers, rue de l'Apport,** and **rue de la Poissonnerie.** With their overhanging balconies and black-and-white half-timbered houses, these cobbled streets are so pretty you may think you've stumbled into a Hollywood movie set. Restore your faith by a visit to the nearby church, the **Basilique St-Sauveur** (turn right out of place des Merciers along rue Haute-Voie, then take the second left into the church square). The church is an entertaining mixture of styles, ranging from the Romanesque south front to the Flamboyant Gothic facade and Renaissance side chapels. Du Guesclin's heart lies in the north transept.

The **Jardin Anglais** (English Garden) is just behind the church; it's not really much of a garden, but its old trees nicely frame the east end of St-Sauveur. More spectacular views are found at the bottom of the garden, which looks down the plummeting Rance Valley to the river 250 feet below.

Leading down to the harbor, rue du Jerzual is a beautifully preserved medieval street, full of boutiques and craft shops, divided halfway down by the town walls and massive Porte du Jerzual gateway.

Time Out Wool yarn by the yard and English cakes and scones by the dozen: That's the unlikely combination you'll find at this strange little American-run outfit, **La Toison d'Or.** Long wooden benches add to the atmosphere, if not the comfort, as you settle down for a cup of coffee and a snack. *Rue du Jerzual.*

Dinan's harbor is somewhat forlorn; although there are sailings in summer up the River Rance to Dinard and St-Malo, abandoned warehouses bear witness to vanished commercial activity. There is, admittedly, an occasional restaurant to brighten the place up, but the irresistible riverbank quaintness deserves greater life.

Stagger back up the hill (it's steep) and turn right, well after the Porte du Jerzual, into rue de l'Ecole. This street leads down to another gateway, the Porte St-Malo, from where the leafy Promenade des Grands Fossés heads left on a tour of the best-preserved section of the town walls. Follow these walls around as far as the **castle**. Here you can visit the two-story Coëtquen Tower and 100-foot 14th-century keep, containing varied displays of medieval effigies and statues, Breton furniture, and local *coiffes* (bonnets). *Porte de Guichet. Admission: 6 frs. Open June–Aug., 9–noon and 2–7, Sept.–Oct. and Mar.– May, 9–noon and 2–6, Nov.–Feb., 2–5; closed Tues.*

Time Out   Just across the Vieux Pont, in what is officially the village of Lanvallay, is **Le Transfert** cocktail bar, whose cool gray decor wouldn't be out of place in some trendy *quartier* of Paris. The cocktails are imaginative and inexpensive, and you can enjoy them in peace and quiet while drinking in the tranquil views over the River Rance and old part of Dinan. *8 bis rue du Four, Lanvallay. Open 6 PM–2 AM.*

🔟 **Dinard**, is a stylish, slightly snobbish vacation resort, 22 kilometers (14 miles) north on D266, or farther away if you follow the picturesque meanderings of the Rance. The town may be fraying on the edges these days, but its picturebook setting on the Rance Estuary opposite St-Malo makes up for any shabbiness. Until the middle of the last century, Dinard was a minor fishing village. It became all the rage, thanks to propaganda from a rich American named Coppinger; avenues were baptized Edward VII and George V as English royalty jumped on the bandwagon. Grand hotels and luxurious villas are still plentiful.

It's not hard to see why uppercrust Edwardians loved the place, with its dramatic cliffs, lush vegetation, bracing coastal walks, and three sandy beaches. To make the most of Dinard's exhilarating setting, head down to the town's southern tip, the **Pointe de la Vicomté,** where cliffs offer panoramic views across the Baie du Prieuré and Rance Estuary. The **Plage du Prieuré**, named after a priory that once stood here, is a sandy beach ringed by yachts, dinghies, and motorboats. The **Clair de Lune Promenade** hugs the seacoast on its way toward the English Channel, passing in front of the small jetty used by boats crossing to St-Malo. Shortly after, the street reaches the **Musée de la Mer** (Marine Museum and Aquarium). Virtually every known species of Breton bird and sea creature is on display here, in two rooms and 24 pools. Another room is devoted to the polar expeditions of explorer Jean Charcot, one of the first men to chart the Antarctic; there are poignant souvenirs of his last voyage, in 1936, from which he never returned. *Claire de Lune Promenade. Admission: 8 frs. Open Pentecost Sun.–Sept., daily 10–noon and 2–6.*

The Clair de Lune Promenade, lined with luxuriant semitropical vegetation, really hits its stride as it rounds the Pointe du Moulinet to the Prieuré Beach. River meets sea in a foaming mass of rock-pounding surf, and caution is needed as you walk along the slippery path. Your reward: the calm and shelter of the **Plage de l'Ecluse,** an inviting sandy beach, bordered by a casino and numerous stylish hotels. The coastal path picks up again on the far side, ringing the Pointe de la Malouine and Pointe des Etêtés before arriving at Dinard's final beach, the **Plage de St-Enogat.**

Little more than a mile from Dinard by water, but 13 kilometers (8 miles) by road, is the ancient walled town of **St-Malo.**

The stone ramparts of this one-time pirate base have stood firm against the Atlantic since the 13th century. The town itself has proved less resistant: A week-long fire in 1944, kindled by retreating Nazis, wiped out nearly all the old buildings. Restoration work was more painstaking than brilliant, but the narrow streets and granite houses of the old town, known as *Intra Muros* ("within the walls") have been satisfactorily recreated, enabling St-Malo to regain its role as a busy fishing port and seaside resort.

North American visitors can pay homage here to Jacques Cartier, who set sail from St-Malo in 1535 to discover the St. Lawrence River and found Quebec. Cartier's tomb is in the church of **St-Vincent** (off Grand-Rue), while his statue looks out over the town ramparts, four blocks away—along with that of swashbuckling corsair Robert Surcouf, hero of many daring 18th-century raids on the British Navy (he's the one pointing an accusing finger over the waves at the enemy). The ramparts themselves date from the 12th century, but were considerably enlarged and modified in the 18th. They extend from the castle in St-Malo's northeast corner and ring the old town, with a total length of over a mile. The views from the ramparts are stupendous, especially at high tide. Five hundred yards offshore is the **Ile du Grand Bé,** a small island housing the somber military tomb of Viscount Chateaubriand, who was born in St-Malo. The islet can be reached by a causeway at low tide, as can the **Fort National,** a massive fortress with a dungeon constructed in 1689 by that military-engineering genius, Sébastien de Vauban. *By the castle. Admission: 8 frs. Open Apr.–Sept., daily 9:30–noon and 2:30–6.*

At the edge of the ramparts, overlooking the Fort National, is **St-Malo Castle,** whose great keep and watchtowers command an impressive view of the harbor and coastline. The castle houses two museums: the **Musée de la Ville,** devoted to local history, and the **Quic-en-Groigne,** a tower where various episodes and celebrities from St-Malo's past are recalled by way of waxwork reconstruction. *Porte St-Vincent. Admission: 5 frs. (Musée de la Ville), 12 frs. (Quic-en-Grogne). Open Apr.–Sept., daily 9:30–noon and 2–6:30; closed Tues. Oct.–Mar.*

⑫ Anyone who enjoys eating oysters should make the 13-kilometer (8-mile) trip east on D355 to **Cancale,** renowned for its oyster beds. You'll find lots of quayside restaurants in which to sample this delicacy. The town's delightful seaside setting is also an attraction.

Tour 2: Brittany's Western Coast

⑬ Our second tour begins at **Morlaix** (pronounced "Morley"), far to the west of St-Malo—144 kilometers (90 miles) by fast N12, considerably longer if you meander along the spectacular coastal road (D786 and D788) via Perros-Guirec and Lannion. Morlaix's town-spanning, 19th-century, two-tiered rail viaduct is an unforgettable sight, 300 yards long and 200 feet high. Though there aren't any major sights in Morlaix, the old town is an attractive mix of half-timbered houses and low-fronted shops that rewards unhurried exploration. The pedestrian Grand' Rue is its commercial heart, lined with quaint 15th-century houses. The **Maison de la Reine Anne,** in adjacent rue du Mur, is a three-story 16th-century building adorned with statuettes of saints.

Just off rue d'Aiguillon, which runs parallel to Grand' Rue, is the town museum, known as the **Musée des Jacobins** because it is housed in the former Jacobin church; an early 15th-century rose window survives at one end as a reminder. The museum's eclectic display ranges from religious statues to archaeological findings and modern paintings. *Pl. des Jacobins. Admission: 10 frs. Open July–Aug., daily 10–noon and 2–6; Apr.–June and Sept.–Oct., Wed.–Mon. 10–noon and 2–6; Nov.–Mar., Wed.–Mon. 10–noon and 2–5.*

⑭ D73 hugs the riverbank north of Morlaix; branch left at Kerdanet and follow signs for **St-Pol-de-Léon**, 10 kilometers (6 miles) farther away. St-Pol is a lively market town dominated by three spires: Two belong to the cathedral, the highest to the Chapelle du Kreisker. The **Ancienne Cathédrale,** built between the 13th and 16th century, is pleasingly proportioned, and its finely carved 16th-century choir stalls are worth a trip inside. Rue du Général-Leclerc, with its large wood-framed houses, links the cathedral to the **Chapelle du Kreisker,** originally used for meetings by the town council. Its magnificent 250-foot 15th-century granite spire, flanked at each corner by tiny spirelets known as *fillettes* ("young girls"), is the prototype for countless Brittany bell towers. From the top there is a rewarding view across the Bay of Morlaix toward the English Channel. *Access to the tower mid-June–mid-Sept., daily 10–noon and 2–5.*

⑮ Just 5 kilometers (3 miles) north of St-Pol along D58 is the burgeoning port of Roscoff. From here, head 24 kilometers (15 miles) southwest toward Brest before turning right onto D30 and making for the nearby 15th-century château of **Kerjean.** With its vast park, ditch, and 40-foot-thick defensive walls, Kerjean at first looks like a fortress until you see the large windows, tall chimney stacks, and high-pitched roofs of its main buildings. The chapel, kitchens, and main apartments, full of regional furniture, may be visited. Temporary exhibitions are held in the stable wing. Notice the old well in the main courtyard. *Admission: 20 frs. Open Sept.–June, Wed.–Mon. 10–noon and 2–7; July–Aug., Wed.–Mon. 10–7.*

⑯ Sixteen kilometers (10 miles) west of Kerjean along D788 is **Le Folgoët** and its splendid **Notre-Dame basilica,** whose sturdy north tower, visible from afar, beckons pilgrims to the *pardon* (religious festival) held here in early September. On this occasion, many pilgrims drink at the Salaün fountain against the wall behind the church; its water comes from a spring beneath the altar, which can be reached through a sculpted porch. Inside the church is a rare, intricately worked, granite roodscreen separating the choir and nave.

⑰ Continue along D788 to the maritime city of **Brest**, 24 kilometers (15 miles) southwest. Brest's enormous, sheltered bay is strategically positioned close to the Atlantic and the English Channel. During World War II, Brest was used by the Germans as a naval base; it was liberated in 1944 by American forces, after a 43-day siege that left the city in ruins. Postwar reconstruction, resulting in long, straight streets of reinforced concrete, has left latterday Brest with the unenviable reputation of being one of France's ugliest cities. Its waterfront, however, is worth visiting for its few old buildings and museums, as well as for dramatic views across the bay toward the Plougastel Peninsula.

Begin your visit at one of the town's oldest monuments, the **Tour Tanguy**. This bulky, round 14th-century tower, once used as a lookout post, is a majestic sight in its own right; the interior contains a museum of local history with scale models of the Brest of yore. *Admission: free. Open Oct.–May, Thurs. and weekends 2–6; June and Sept., daily 2–7; July–Aug., daily 10–noon and 2–7.*

Next to the tower is the River Penfeld and, crossing it, the Pont de Recouvrance, at 95 yards Europe's longest lift-bridge. On the other side, Brest's medieval castle is home to the **Musée de la Marine** (Naval Museum), containing boat models, sculpture, pictures, and naval instruments. A section is devoted to the castle's 700-year history. The dungeons can also be visited. *Admission: 16 frs. adults, 8 frs. children under 12. Open Wed.– Mon. 9:15–noon and 2:20–6; closed Tues.*

A short walk inland leads to the **Musée Municipal** in rue Traverse. French, Flemish, and Italian paintings, spanning the 17th to 20th century, make up the collection. *Rue Emile-Zola. Admission: free. Open Wed.–Sat. and Mon. 10–11:45 and 2– 6:45, Sun. 2–6:45; closed Tues.*

Farther east, overlooking the Moulin Blanc marina, is the brand-new, futuristic **Océanopolis** center. Maritime technology, fauna, and flora are the themes of its exhibits, but the biggest attraction is the aquarium—the largest in Europe. *Admission details and opening times not available as we went to press.*

⓲ Southbound N165, which leaves Brest for Quimper, 104 kilometers (65 miles) away, soon passes through **Daoulas** where you can stop off to admire the *Enclos Paroissial* (literally, "parish enclosure") and the 12th-century Romanesque abbey, with its cloisters and herbal garden. Keep on N165 to Port Launay,
⓳ then branch off southwest along scenic D7 to **Locronan**, a typical old weaving town with a magnificently preserved ensemble of houses, main square, and 15th-century church.

⓴ **Douarnenez**, 10 kilometers (6 miles) west of Locronan via D7, is a quaint old fishing town of quayside paths and narrow streets. Sailing enthusiasts will be interested in the town's biennial classic boat rally in mid-August, when traditionally rigged sailing boats of every description ply the waters of the picturesque Bay of Douarnenez.

㉑ From Douarnenez, take D765 southeast to **Quimper**. This lively commercial town is the ancient capital of the Cornouaille province, founded, it is said, by King Gradlon 1,500 years ago. Quimper (pronounced "Cam-Pair") owes its strange-looking name to its site at the confluence *(kemper* in Breton) of the Odet and Steir rivers. The banks of the Odet make a charming place to stroll. Highlights of the old town include **rue Kéréon**, a lively shopping street, and the stately **Jardin de l'Evêché** (Bishop's Gardens) behind the cathedral in the center of the old town.

The **Cathédrale St-Corentin** is a masterpiece of early Gothic architecture and the second-largest cathedral in Brittany (after that of Dol). Legendary King Gradlon is represented on horseback just below the base of the spires, harmonious mid-19th-century additions to the medieval ensemble. Curiously, the

13th-century choir and 15th-century nave are improperly aligned, probably the result of construction difficulties (or stonemasons' drunkenness). The luminous 15th-century stained glass is particularly striking. *Pl. St-Corentin.*

Two museums flank the cathedral. Works by major masters, such as Rubens, Corot, and Picasso, mingle with pretty landscapes from the local Gauguin-inspired Pont-Aven school in the **Musée des Beaux-Arts** (Fine Arts Museum; *admission 5 frs.; open Wed.–Mon. 9:30–noon and 1–5),* while local furniture, ceramics, and folklore top the bill in the **Musée Départemental** (Regional Museum) in adjacent rue du Roi-Gradlon *(Admission 5 frs.; open mid-Sept.–Apr., Wed.–Sun. 9–noon and 2–5, May–mid-Sept., Wed.–Mon. 9–noon and 2–5).*

Quimper sprang to nationwide attention as an earthenware center in the mid-18th century, when it started producing second-rate imitations of the Rouen ceramics known as *faïence,* featuring blue Oriental motifs. Today's more colorful designs, based on floral arrangements and marine fauna, are still often handpainted. There are guided visits to the main pottery, the **Faïencerie Henriot,** and its museum, situated on the banks of the Odet south of the old town. *Allée de Locmaria. Admission: 12 frs. Open Mon.–Thurs. 9:30–11 and 1:30–4:30; Fri. 9:30–11 and 1:30–3.*

㉒ Pretty **Concarneau,** 21 kilometers (13 miles) from Quimper along D783, stands at the mouth of the Baie de la Forêt, facing south across the Atlantic toward the desolate Islands of Glénan. Concarneau is the third-largest fishing port in France. During its *criée,* an early morning auction held from Monday to Thursday, local fishwives can be heard in full cry as they sell off the recent catch.

The **Ville Close,** the fortified islet in the middle of the harbor, is Concarneau's main attraction. To reach it, you must cross a drawbridge. The islet's narrow streets and huge granite ramparts make for an enjoyable afternoon's roam, though rue Vauban—the main street—contains a lot of tacky souvenir shops; ignore them and concentrate on the fantastic views of the bay. From early medieval times, Concarneau was regarded as impregnable, and the fortifications were further strengthened by the English under John de Montfort during the War of Succession (1341–64). This enabled the English-controlled Concarneau to withstand two sieges by Breton hero Bertrand du Guesclin; the third siege was successful for the plucky du Guesclin, who drove out the English in 1373. Three hundred years later, Sébastien de Vauban remodeled the ramparts and left them as they are today: half a mile long and highly scenic, offering views across the two harbors on either side of the Ville Close. *Admission: 4 frs. Open Easter–Sept., daily 9–7.*

At the end of rue Vauban closest to the drawbridge is the **Musée de la Pêche** (Fishing Museum), occupying an enormous hall in the former arsenal. Here you will encounter historical explanations of fishing techniques from around the world, plus such displays as an antiwhale harpoon gun and a giant Japanese crab. Turtles and fish may be seen in the museum's many aquariums. *Admission: 22 frs. Open Sept.–June, daily 10–12:30 and 2–7; July–Aug., daily 10–8.*

N165 speeds down the coast, past the industrial port of Lorient, as far as Auray. Here, take D768 southwest toward

Carnac at the northern end of the 10-mile long Quiberon Peninsula, dangling off the Brittany coast. The Côte Sauvage (Wild Coast) on the west of the peninsula is a savage mix of crevices, coves, and rocky grottoes lashed by violent seas.

㉓ Quiberon itself is famed for more soothing waters: It is a spa town with fine, relaxing beaches.

Time Out In a country where gourmandism is considered virtually a cultural pursuit, **Henri Le Roux** has taken the art of chocolateering to dizzy heights. Check out his delicious displays—created before your very eyes—at his shop near Quiberon harbor. *18 rue du Port-Maria.*

The cheerful harbor of Port-Maria is the base for boat trips to nearby Belle-Ile, at 11 miles long the largest Brittany island. Because of the cost and inconvenience of reserving car-berths on the ferry, it's best to cross to Belle-Ile as a pedestrian and rent a car—or, better still, a bicycle—on the island.

㉔ Despite being a mere 45-minute boat trip from Quiberon, **Belle-Ile** is much less commercialized, and exhilarating scenery is its main appeal. Near Sauzon, the island's prettiest settlement, is a staggering view across to the Quiberon Peninsula and Gulf of Morbihan from the **Pointe des Poulains,** erstwhile home of the Belle Epoque's femme fatale, actress Sarah Bernhardt. The nearby **Grotte de l'Apothicairerie** is a grotto whose name derives from the local cormorants' nests, said to resemble pharmacy bottles. Farther south, near Port Goulphar, is another dramatic sight—the **Grand Phare** (lighthouse), built in 1835 and rising 275 feet above sea level. Its light is one of the most powerful in Europe, visible from 75 miles across the Atlantic. If the keeper is available, you may be able to climb to the top and admire the view.

㉕ Once back on the mainland, return to **Carnac** at the northern end of Quiberon Bay. Carnac is famed for its beaches and, especially, its **megalithic monuments** dating from the Neolithic/Early Bronze Ages (3500–1800 BC). The whys and wherefores of their construction remain as obscure as those of their English contemporary, Stonehenge, although religious beliefs and astrology were doubtless an influence. The 2,395 menhirs that make up the three *Alignements* (Kermario, Kerlescan, and Ménec) are positioned with astounding astronomical accuracy in semicircles and parallel lines over half a mile long. There are also smaller-scale dolmen ensembles and three tumuli (mounds or barrows), including the 130-yard-long **Tumulus de St-Michel,** topped by a small chapel affording fine views of the rock-strewn countryside. *Guided tours of the tumulus daily Apr.–Sept. Cost: 4 frs.*

㉖ Just east of Carnac lies the yachtsman's paradise of **La Trinité-sur-Mer,** a resort town ringed by sandy beaches and oyster beds, and much favored by wealthy Parisians wanting a vacation home-away-from-home. From La Trinité, head up **㉗** D781 and D28 to Auray, then take N165 east to **Vannes** (pronounced "Van"). Scene of the declaration of unity between France and Brittany in 1532, it's one of the few towns in Brittany to have been spared damage during World War II, so its authentic regional charm remains intact. Be sure to visit the **Cohue** (medieval market hall—now a temporary exhibition center) and the picturesque **place Henri IV** and browse in the small boutiques and antique shops in the surrounding pedestrian streets. The ramparts, Promenade de la Garenne, and medieval washhouses are all set against the backdrop of the much-restored **Cathédrale St-Pierre,** with its 1537 Renaissance chapel, Flamboyant Gothic transept portal, and treasury in the old chapterhouse. *Pl. du Cathédrale. Admission: 3 frs. Treasury open mid-June–mid-Sept., Mon.–Sat. 10–noon and 2–6.*

28 From Vannes, N165 goes to Muzillac, 19 kilometers (12 miles) away, from where D20 veers 43 kilometers (27 miles) east to the little town of **Redon,** built at the junction of the River Vilaine and the Nantes–Brest canal. These days, Redon harbor is used exclusively by pleasure boats, but it was once a busy commercial port. A number of stylish 17th–19th-century mansions, with large windows and wrought-iron balconies, line the adjacent quays. Wood-framed medieval houses can be admired in the main street, Grande Rue, which is dominated by the slender spire and magnificent Romanesque tower of the church of **St-Sauveur,** all that remains of a once-powerful Benedictine abbey.

29 Head due south from Redon, via D114, to **Missillac,** at the edge of the **Grande Brière Regional Park.** This low-lying marshy area, criss-crossed by narrow canals, can be explored either by boat (trips are organized from St-Nazaire) or by car along D51 as you head southwest toward La Baule. Ever since a ducal edict of 1461, La Brière has been the common property of its inhabitants, who live in distinctive and picturesque white thatched cottages. Highlights include the panoramic view from the church tower at **St-Lyphard,** and the curious **Kerbourg dolmen** five kilometers (three miles) south, just off D47.

30 **La Baule,** 18 kilometers (11 miles) from St-Lyphard, is one of the most fashionable resorts in France. Like Le Touquet and Dinard, it is a 19th-century creation, founded in 1879 to make the most of the excellent sandy beaches that extend for six miles around the broad, sheltered bay between Pornichet and Le Pouliguen. A pine forest, planted in 1840, keeps the shifting local sand dunes firmly at bay.

An air of old-fashioned chic still pervades La Baule's palatial hotels, villas, and flowered gardens, but there's nothing old-fashioned about the prices: Hotels and restaurants should be chosen with care. Nightclubbers will be in their element here, while the resort's summer season buzzes with prestigious events like show jumping and classic car contests. The elegant promenade, overlooking the huge beach, is lined with luxury hotels and features a casino.

31 From La Baule head 72 kilometers (45 miles) east, past St-Nazaire and its struggling shipyard, to **Nantes,** a tranquil, prosperous city that seems to pursue its existence without too much concern for what's going on elsewhere in France. Although Nantes is not really part of Brittany—officially it belongs to the Pays de la Loire—the dukes of Brittany were in no doubt that Nantes belonged to their domain, and the castle **32** they built is the city's principal tourist attraction. The **Château des Ducs de Bretagne** is a massive, well-preserved 15th-century fortress with a neatly grassed moat. The duke responsible for building most of it was François II, who led a hedonistic exis-

Cathédrale St-Pierre, **33**
Château des Ducs de Bretagne, **32**
Grand Theater, **36**
Manoir de la Touche, **37**
Musée de Beaux-Arts, **34**
Palais Dobrée, **38**
Passage Pommeraye, **35**

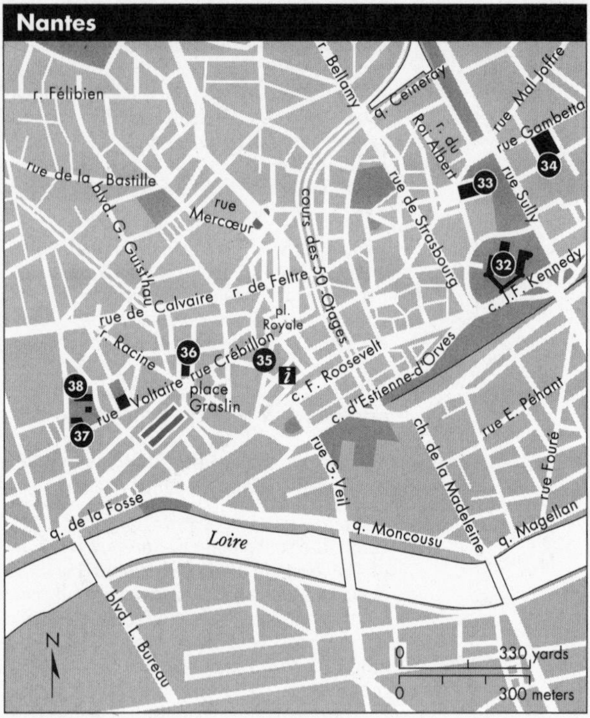

tence here, surrounded by ministers, chamberlains, and an army of servants. Numerous monarchs later stayed in the castle, where, in 1598, Henri IV signed the famous Edict of Nantes advocating religious tolerance.

Within the Harnachement—a separate building inside the castle walls—you'll find the **Musée des Salorges** (Naval Museum), devoted principally to the history of seafaring; a separate section outlines the triangular trade that involved transportation of African blacks to America to be sold as slaves. As you cross the courtyard to the Grand Gouvernement wing, home to the **Musée d'Art Populaire Régional** (Regional Folk Art Museum), look for the old well, where the ducal coat of arms is entwined in some magnificent wrought-iron decoration. The Musée d'Art Populaire features an array of armor, furniture, 19th-century Breton costumes, and reconstituted interiors illustrating the former life in the Vendée region to the south. *Just off rue du Château. Admission: 8 frs., free on weekends. Castle and museums open Sept.–June, Wed.–Mon. 10–noon and 2–6, closed Tues.; July–Aug., daily 10–noon and 2–6.*

33 Opposite the castle is the **Cathédrale St-Pierre,** one of France's latest Gothic cathedrals; building began only in 1434, well after most other medieval cathedrals had been completed. The facade is ponderous and austere, in contrast to the light, wide, elegant interior, whose vaults rise higher (120 feet) than those of Notre-Dame in Paris. In the transept, notice Michel Colombe's early 16th-century tomb of François II and his wife,

Marguerite de Foix, which is one of France's finest examples of funerary sculpture. *Pl. St-Pierre.*

Behind the cathedral, past the 15th-century Porte St-Pierre, is
③④ the **Musée des Beaux-Arts** (Fine Art Museum), with a fine collection of paintings from the Renaissance on, featuring works by Jacopo Tintoretto, Georges de la Tour, Jean-Auguste Ingres, and Gustave Courbet. *10 rue G-Clemenceau. Admission: 8 frs., free on weekends. Open Wed.–Mon. 10–noon and 2–5.*

The cobbled streets around the castle and cathedral make up the town's medieval sector. Across cours des 50 Otages, a broad boulevard, is the 19th-century city. From place Royale stroll and window-shop down busy rue Crébillon. Halfway down on
③⑤ the left is the **Passage Pommeraye,** an elegant shopping gallery erected in 1843. At the far end of rue Crébillon is place Graslin
③⑥ and its 1783 **Grand Theater.**

Time Out   Miniature palm trees, gleaming woodwork, colorful enamel tiles, and painted ceilings have led to **La Cigale** being officially recognized as a *monument historique.* You can savor its Belle Epoque ambience without spending a fortune: The 48- and 100-franc menus are just right for a quick lunch, although the banks of fresh oysters and the well-stacked dessert cart may tempt you to go for a leisurely meal à la carte. *4 pl. Graslin.*

Just along rue Voltaire from place Graslin is the 15th-century
③⑦ **Manoir de la Touche,** once home to the bishops of Nantes. Its
③⑧ medieval silhouette is offset by the mock-Romanesque **Palais Dobrée,** next door, built by arts connoisseur Thomas Dobrée during the last century. Among the treasures within are miniatures, tapestries, medieval manuscripts, and enamels, while one room is devoted to the Revolutionary Wars in Vendée. *Pl. Jean V. Admission: 8 frs., free Sun. Open Wed.–Mon. 10–noon and 2–5; closed Tues.*

What to See and Do with Children

Boat trips make entertaining excursions for old and young alike. Some of the most scenic include the tour of the Golfe du Morbihan (depart from Vannes), sea jaunts from Dinard or St-Malo to the Ile de Cézembre or along the rugged coast to Cap Fréhel, cruises up the River Rance from Dinard to Dinan, and the frequent 10-minute crossings between Dinard and St-Malo. (For information on trips to the numerous islands off the Brittany shore, *see* Off the Beaten Track, below.)

These other attractions are described in the Exploring section:
Château des Ducs de Bretagne, Nantes, Tour 2.
Fougéres Castle, Tour 1.
Grand Phare (Lighthouse), Belle-Ile, Tour 2.
Musée de Bretagne, Rennes, Tour 1.
Musée de la Mer, Dinard, Tour 1.
Musée de la Péche, Concarneau, Tour 2.
Océanopolis, Brest, Tour 2.
Vitré Castle, Tour 1.

Off the Beaten Track

Although our second tour concentrates on Brittany's Atlantic coastline, some travelers may also enjoy visiting the hinter-

land, particularly some of the spectacular castles north of
Vannes. The first of these castles, set in a wooded park 19 kilometers (12 miles) from Vannes via N166, is the **Fortress of
Largoët** near Elven. Its 170-foot 14th-century octagonal keep is
the highest in France; its walls are up to 30 feet thick. Alongside is a faithfully restored 15th-century tower. Henry Tudor
was held prisoner here before his return to England and the
triumphant 1485 military campaign that led to his becoming
Henry VII. *Admission: 10 frs. Open Apr.–Oct., daily 9–6.*

Continue along N166 past Brignac—a round 15th-century tower is all that remains of the fortress that once stood here—to La
Chapelle. The elegant, nearby château of **Le Crêvy** houses a collection of costumes dating from 1730.

Sixteen kilometers (10 miles) northwest along D4 is **Josselin**, a
picturesque medieval town. **Josselin Castle** has two faces. Overlooking the River Oust is a defensive stronghold with three
stout turreted towers linked by austere, near-windowless
walls. The landward facade, however, is a riot of intricate pinnacles, gables, and stone ornament, surrounded by gardens.
You can visit the library, wood-paneled dining room, portrait
gallery, and Grand Salon, with its ornate fireplace (only the
ground floor is open to the public). *Admission: 20 frs. Open
Apr.–May, Wed. and Sun. 2–6; June, daily 2–6; July–Aug.,
daily 10–noon and 2–6; Sept., daily 2–6.*

Another attraction in Josselin is the 500-strong collection of old
dolls displayed in the former castle stables. Many are dressed
in traditional costume; most date back to the 18th century, and
one to the 17th. *Admission: 20 frs. (separate from castle).
Open May–Sept., Tues.–Sun. 10–noon and 2–6; Mar., Apr.,
and Oct.–mid-Nov., Wed. and weekends 10–noon and 2–6.*

The cheerful old town of **Rochefort-en-Terre,** 45 kilometers (28
miles) south of Josselin, boasts a cozy, ivory-clad 14th-century
castle. The interior holds tapestries, armor, chests and old furniture, earthenware statuettes, and paintings by Alfred and
Trafford Klots, American artists who lived here and restored
the castle. *Admission: 12 frs. Open Apr.–May, weekends 10–
12:30 and 2–6:30; June–Sept., daily 10–12:30 and 2–6:30.*

Apart from Belle-Ile, described in our Exploring section, several other islands off the Brittany coast, none more than a few
miles long, can also be visited. Take your pick from these:

Batz, with its tame landscape and sandy beaches. *Frequent
daily crossings from Roscoff. Journey time: 15 minutes.*
Quessant, whose melancholy scenery surrounds an ornitholog-
ical research center for bird enthusiasts. *Crossings daily except Tues. from Brest. Journey time: 90 minutes.*
Molène, where relics of shipwrecks are on display at the old
presbytery. *Crossings daily except Tues. from Brest. Journey
time: 90 minutes.*
Sein, featuring narrow streets and a spectacular setting off the
rugged Pointe de Raz. *Crossings daily except Wed. from
Audierne.*
Glenan Archipelago, a string of eight uninhabited islands and
dozens of rocks and islets. *Frequent crossings in summer from
Concarneau.*
Groix, with its cliffs and sandy beaches. *Daily crossings from
Lorient. Journey time: 45 minutes.*

Houat, highlighted by creeks, dunes, and beaches. *Daily crossings from Quiberon and Vannes. Journey time: 60 minutes.*
Hoedic, a granite outcrop with just 126 inhabitants. *Daily crossings from Quiberon. Journey time: 90 minutes.*

Shopping

Folk Costumes and Textiles
When it comes to distinctive Breton folk costumes, **Quimper** is the best place to look. The streets around the cathedral (notably **rue du Parc**) are full of small shops, several selling the woolen goods (notably thick marine sweaters) in which the region also specializes. Addresses for good textiles in **Rennes** are **Tidreiz** (pl. du Palais) and **Au Roy d'Ys** (29 blvd. de Magenta).

Gift Ideas
The commercial quarter of **Nantes** stretches from place Royale to place Graslin. For antiques, try **Cibot** (7 rue Voltaire). Don't miss chocolate specialist **Georges Gautier** (9 rue de la Fosse), with his *Muscadets Nantais*—grapes dipped in brandy and covered in chocolate. **Quimper** is best known for its *faïence*—hand-painted earthenware—which can be bought at the **Kéraluc Faiencerie** (14 rue de la Troménie on the Bénodet road) or at **HB Henriot** (12 pl. de la Cathédrale). Keep an eye out for such typical Breton products as woven or embroidered cloth, brass and wooden goods, puppets, dolls, and locally designed jewelry.

Markets
Among Brittany's most colorful markets are the ones held at Talensac in **Nantes** and in the streets of old **St-Malo** (Tuesday and Friday only). The most interesting street for arts and crafts is the cobbled, sloping **rue de Jerzual** in **Dinan,** whose medieval houses contain an assortment of wood-carvers, jewelers, leather-workers, glass specialists, and silk painters.

Sports and Fitness

Beaches and Water Sports
From St-Malo to Brest as far as the Côte d'Emeraude, then south to Nantes, the Brittany coast has any number of clean sandy **beaches**—the best are found at Dinard, Perros-Guirec, Trégastel-Plage, Douarnenez, Carnac, and Baule. Resorts offer numerous sports facilities, ranging from **underwater diving** and **spearfishing** to **canoeing** and **sand-sailing** (at St-Pierre Quiberon). To rent **sailboats,** try at St-Malo (tel. 99–40–84–42), Carnac (tel. 97–52–02–41), Douarnenez (**Locamer,** tel. 98–92–38–82), Dinard (**Yacht Club,** tel. 99–46–14–32), or Morlaix (**Loisirs 3000,** tel. 98–88–33–12).

Windsurfing possibilities include Carnac (boards can be rented from **De Petigny** at 90 rte. du Pô, tel. 97–52–02–41), the **Wishbone Club** in Dinard (Pont d'Emeraude), and the **Centre Nautique** in Brest (tel. 98–02–11–93). **Waterskiers** can try Concarneau (tel. 98–97–41–03). Among the region's **swimming pools** are those at Brest, Concarneau, Douarnenez, Morlaix, Quimper, Dinard, and St-Malo.

Horseback Riding
Riding stables include St-Malo (**Société Hippique,** tel. 99–81–20–34), Dinan (tel. 96–27–14–62), Carnac (**Centre Equestre des Menhirs,** tel. 97–55–24–01), and Dinard (**Cercle Equestre de la Cote d'Emeraude,** tel. 99–46–23–57).

Bicycling
Bikes can be rented at the train stations in Brest (tel. 98–44–21–55), Morlaix (tel. 98–88–60–47), and Quimper (tel. 98–80–50–50); in St-Malo, from **Diazo** (tel. 99–40–31–63) or **Rouxel**

(tel. 99–56–14–90); or at Carnac (tel. 97–52–02–33) and Dinard (**Duval Cycles**, 53 rue Gardiner).

Dining and Lodging

Dining

Not surprisingly, Brittany cuisine is dominated by fish and seafood. Shrimp, crayfish, crabs, oysters, and scallops are found throughout the region, but the linchpin of Breton menus is often lobster, prepared in sauce or cream or grilled. Popular meats include ham and lamb, frequently served with kidney beans. Fried eel is a traditional dish in the Nantes district. Brittany is particularly famous for its pancakes, served with both sweet and savory fillings. Washed down with a glass of local cider, they make an ideal basis for a light, inexpensive meal.

Highly recommended restaurants are indicated by a star ★.

Lodging

Brittany's economy is heavily dependent on the tourist industry, and its hotel infrastructure is correspondingly dense. English is more widely spoken here than in many French regions, but since Brittany pulls in visitors from the rest of France and much of northern Europe as well, it is essential to reserve ahead in summer. There are relatively few top-ranking deluxe hotels, however. Dinard, on the English Channel, and La Baule, on the Atlantic, are the two most exclusive resorts.

Highly recommended hotels are indicated by a star ★.

La Baule **L'Espadon.** One of the resort's swankiest restaurants,
Dining L'Espadon has a rooftop location that offers stunning views of land and sea. The decor is starkly elegant, and the cuisine features deft, nouvelle-inspired touches. The grilled sea bass is memorable. *2 av. de la Plage, tel. 40–60–05–63. Reservations advised. Jacket and tie required. AE, DC, V. Closed Sun. dinner, Mon., mid-Nov.–mid-Dec., and 2 weeks in Jan. Moderate/Expensive.*
La Pergola. The inventive finesse of its haute cuisine and the warmth of its welcome have given La Pergola a substantial reputation. The restaurant is conveniently situated in the center of La Baule, next to the casino and a stone's throw from the beach. Meat and fish are prepared with aplomb in a variety of subtle sauces. There is a set menu at 140 francs; allow upward of 200 francs if you eat à la carte. *147 av. des Lilas, tel. 40–24–57–61. Reservations advised. Jacket required. AE, V. Closed Sun. dinner, Mon., and Oct.–Easter. Moderate/Expensive.*

Lodging **Concorde.** This numbers among the least expensive good hotels in pricy La Baule (others charge well over 1,250 francs a night). It's calm, comfortable, recently modernized, and close to the beach (ask for a room with a sea view). There's no restaurant. *1 av. de la Concorde, 44500, tel. 40–60–23–09. 47 rooms with bath. Closed Oct.–Easter. Moderate.*

Belle-Ile **La Forge.** A sure bet for lunch or dinner, La Forge specializes in
Dining traditional cuisine, based on seafood and fish, at affordable prices (menus at 80, 100, or 140 francs). Old wooden beams and remnants of the building's original purpose—a blacksmith—

contribute to the pleasant, rustic atmosphere. *Rte. de Port-Goulphar, Bangor, tel. 91–31–51–76. Reservations essential in summer. Dress: casual. V. Closed Sun. dinner and mid-Nov.–Easter. Inexpensive.*

Cancale
Dining
★

Bricourt. The fishing village of Cancale, 13 kilometers (eight miles) east of St-Malo via D355, is the setting for this popular restaurant. The three intimate dining rooms are furnished in various styles: luxuriant Louis XV (mid-18th century); stylized, Classical-influenced French Empire (circa 1800); and homey, mid-19th century English Victorian. Olivier Roellinger, the highly rated young chef, pays tribute to local seafaring tradition in his subtle preparations of seafood, fish, lamb, or veal with exotic spices. *1 rue Duguesclin, tel. 99–89–64–76. Reservations advised. Jacket required. V. Closed Tues., Wed., and Jan.–Mar. Moderate/Expensive.*

Concarneau
Dining

Le Galion. Flowers, wood beams, silver candlesticks, old stones, and a roaring hearth form a pleasant backdrop to Henri Gaonach's marine *tours de force* at this, one of Concarneau's best fish restaurants. There are menus at 135, 240, and (for famished gourmets) 290 francs. *15 rue St-Guénolé, Ville-Close, tel. 98–97–30–16. DC, V. Closed Sun. evening, Mon. and winter. Moderate/Expensive.*

Lodging

Sables Blancs. A great advantage of this old-fashioned hotel is that all guest rooms feature soul-satisfying views of the sea: The name is derived from the hotel's location near the White Sands *(Sables Blancs)* Beach. The hotel restaurant is adequate, with menus at 59 or 160 francs. *Plage des Sables Blancs, 29110 Concarneau, tel. 98–97–01–39. 48 rooms with bath. Facilities: restaurant. AE, DC, V. Closed Nov.–mid-Mar. Inexpensive/Moderate.*

Dinan
Dining

Relais des Corsaires. The old, hilltop town of Dinan is full of restaurants and pancake houses, but we suggest you wander down to the old port on the banks of the Rance to dine at this spot, quaintly named after the pirates who apparently raided the wharves of Dinan. The 80-franc menu provides an ample four-course meal, with alternative menus at 60 or 125 francs. The à la carte choices, liable to nudge 250 francs, are not as good value. There are two separate, oak-beamed dining rooms; the lush main room with aquarium and attentive, rather unctuous service, communicates by way of a hatch with a smaller room with an impressively long bar, patrolled by Madame Ternisien, the attractive *patronne* who likes to give herself the airs and graces of a *grande dame*. *Le Port, tel. 96–39–79–35. Reservations not required. Dress: casual. AE, DC, V. Inexpensive.*

Dining and Lodging

D'Avagour. This hotel is splendidly situated opposite Dinan Castle's Tour du Connétable and has its own flower garden to boot; most of the cozy guest rooms look out onto either the garden or castle. You can be sure of a warm welcome from the affable owner, Madame Quinton. The hotel attracts numerous foreign guests—American, English, and Italian, in particular. The restaurant, La Poudrière, offers traditional cuisine (shellfish, duck, apple tart) at reasonable prices (56-franc menu at lunchtime, 90- and 150-franc menus in the evening), plus the chance to dine in the garden in warm weather. *1 pl. du Champ-Clos, 22100, tel. 96–39–07–49. 27 rooms with bath. Facilities: restaurant, garden. AE, DC, V. Restaurant closed Sun. during Dec.–Mar. Inexpensive/Moderate.*

Dinard
Dining and Lodging

La Vallée. Prices at this traditional late 19th-century hotel vary from 220 to 350 francs, according to the room. The best have a sea view: The Clair de Lune Promenade and Prieuré Beach are within shouting distance. The hotel itself is decorated in a stockily elegant *fin-de-siècle* style, with an authentic French feel. Expect to pay anything from 100 to 250 francs for your seafood dinner at the hotel restaurant. *6 av. George-V, 35800, tel. 99–46–94–00. 26 rooms with bath. Facilities: restaurant. V. Closed mid-Nov.–mid-Dec., second half of Jan.; restaurant closed Tues. during Oct.–Apr. Moderate.*

Dol-de-Bretagne
Dining and Lodging

Logis de la Bresche Arthur. With its crisp outlines, white walls, and ample glass frontage, the hotel may not be quite as historic as it sounds, but it remains the coziest place in Dol in which to spend a night. Rooms are functional; local character is reserved for the restaurant, where smoked salmon, seafish, and home-prepared foie gras top the menu. *36 blvd. Deminiac, 35120, tel. 99–48–01–44. 24 rooms with bath. Facilities: restaurant. AE, DC, MC, V. Moderate.*

Morlaix
Dining and Lodging
★

Europe. Occupying an old building in the town center, the Europe is easily the best hotel in town, with simple, good-value, modernized guest rooms. Its restaurant (menus at 115 and 210 francs, higher à la carte) provides an exuberant welcome, sumptuous many-mirrored decor, and some exciting recipes featuring lobster, warm oysters, and smoked salmon. *1 rue d'Aiguillon, 29210, tel. 98–62–11–99. 66 rooms with bath. Facilities: restaurant. AE, DC, MC, V. Closed mid-Dec.–mid-Jan. Moderate.*

Nantes
Dining
★

Colvert. This small, modern bistro serves interesting dishes based on seafood or game, according to season. Chef Didier Macoin is an expert at original sauces (lentils and honey to accompany roast pigeon), and the charming waitresses are delighted to explain the intricate differences between the four menus that range from 120 to 250 francs. The 100-franc lunchtime menu, including aperitif, is an excellent value. *14 rue Armand-Brossard, tel. 40–48–20–02. Reservations advised. Dress: casual. V. Closed Sat. lunch, Sun., and Sept. Moderate.*

Mon Rêve. Fine food and a delectable parkland setting are offered at this cozy little restaurant about 8 kilometers (5 miles) east of town. Chef Gérard Ryngel concocts elegantly inventive regional fare (the duck or rabbit in muscadet are good choices), while wife Cecile presides over the dining room with aplomb. *Rte. 751, near Basse-Goulaine, tel. 40–03–55–50. Reservations advised. Dress: casual. AE, DC, MC, V. Closed Sun. dinner, 2 weeks in Feb., and Wed. during Oct.–Mar. Moderate.*

Lodging

Astoria. A conveniently central and unpretentious hotel in a quiet street near both the train station and the castle, the Astorim commands prices (230–280 francs) that are as comfortable as its modern-looking rooms. There's no restaurant. *11 rue Richebourg, 44000, tel. 40–74–39–90. 45 rooms with bath. AE, V. Closed Aug. Moderate.*

Pont-Aven
Dining

La Taupinière. Situated 16 kilometers (10 miles) from Concarneau along D783 on the outskirts of Pont-Aven, this roadside inn has an attractive garden. The food doesn't come cheap (menus start at 220 francs), but, then, chef Guy Guilloux doesn't dabble in mediocrity. Fish, crab, crayfish, and Breton ham (perhaps grilled over the large, open fire) are the bases of his inventions, while his wine cellar is renowned. *Rte. de Concarneau, tel. 98–06–03–12. Reservations essential. Jacket required. AE, DC, V. Closed Mon. dinner, Tues., and mid-Sept.–mid-Oct. Expensive.*

Rennes   **Palais.** The best, though not the most expensive, restaurant in
Dining   Rennes must thank its highly inventive team of young chefs for its considerable reputation. Specialties include roast rabbit and, during winter, fried oysters in crab sauce. The lightish cuisine varies according to season and is offered via two menus (98 and 160 francs). The decor is sharp-edged contemporary, the site conveniently central. *6 pl. du Parlement de Bretagne, tel. 99–79–45–01. Dinner reservations essential. Jacket required. AE, DC, MC, V. Closed Sun. dinner, Mon., and Aug. Moderate.*

★   **Le Grain de Sable.** Situated at the bottom of rue des Dames leading to the cathedral is a thoroughly unusual restaurant. Plants, candelabra, faded photos, and a settee in the middle of the dining room create an ambience that escapes tackiness only by sheer eccentricity (a rocking horse sways in one corner). The cuisine is equally offbeat; expect garlic purée or endive with melted cheese to accompany the grilled meats that dominate the menu. Piped music warbles from opera to Louis Armstrong as the playful waitresses receive noisy reprimands from Hervé in the kitchen. *2 rue des Dames, tel. 99–30–78–18. Reservations advised. Dress: casual. MC, V. Closed Sun., Mon. dinner. Inexpensive.*

Lodging   **Central.** This stately, late 19th-century hotel lives up to its name and sits close to Rennes Cathedral. The individually decorated guest rooms look out over the street or courtyard; ask for one of the latter, as they're quieter. English-speaking guests are frequent. There's no restaurant. *6 rue Lanjuinais, 35000, tel. 99–79–12–36. 43 rooms with bath. V. Moderate.*

Angelina. This little charmer wins on sheer unpretentiousness: friendly welcome, clean rooms, robust breakfasts, and windows double glazed to keep out the noise (it is on Rennes' principal boulevard, within a five-minute walk of the old town). Don't be put off by the fact that the hotel begins on the third floor of an ordinary-looking street block. *1 quai Lamennais, 35100, tel. 99–79–29–66. 25 rooms, some with bath. AE, DC, MC, V. Inexpensive.*

St-Malo   **Café de la Bourse.** Wherever you search for a restaurant in the
Dining   old town of St-Malo, you will feel you are being hemmed into an overcommercialized tourist trap. This restaurant, where prawns and oysters are downed by the shovel, is no exception. However, though its wooden seats and some tacky navigational paraphernalia—ships' wheels and posters of grizzled old sea dogs—are hardly artistic, the large, L-shaped dining room makes amends with genuinely friendly service and a seafood platter for two that includes at least three tanklike crabs, plus an army of cockles, whelks, and periwinkles. *1 rue de Dinan, tel. 99–56–47–17. Reservations accepted. Dress: casual. AE, V. Inexpensive/Moderate.*

Lodging   **La Digue.** Many of the rooms and the breakfast terrace at this hotel face the sea, offering magnificent views over St-Malo's large beach. The largest and most luxurious apartments cost 550 francs a night (the cheapest are under 200 francs). A bar and *salon de thé* (tea room) add to the hotel's attractions. *49 chaussée du Sillon, 35400, tel. 99–56–09–26. 53 rooms, some*

*with bath. Facilities: bar, tea room. AE, V. Closed mid-Nov.–
mid-Mar. Moderate/Expensive.*

Jean-Bart. This clean, quiet hotel next to the ramparts, whose
decor makes liberal use of cool blue, bears the stamp of diligent
renovation: The beds are comfortable, the bathrooms shiny-
modern, but the rooms are a little small. Some rooms boast sea
views. *12 rue de Chartres, 35400, tel. 99–40–33–88. 17 rooms
with bath. MC, V. Closed mid-Nov.–mid-Feb. Moderate.*

Vannes
Dining
Lys. Intricate, light nouvelle cuisine, based on fresh local produce, makes this restaurant a pleasant dinner spot, close to the
agreeable Promenade de la Garenne. The setting, in a late
18th-century Louis XVI style, is at its best by candlelight, with
piano music in the background. *51 rue du Maréchal-Leclerc,
tel. 97–47–29–30. Reservations required. Jacket and tie required. AE, DC, V. Closed Mon., mid-Nov.–mid-Dec., and
Sun. dinner, Oct.–Apr. Moderate.*

Lodging
Image Ste-Anne. This charming hotel is housed in a suitably old,
rustic building in the center of historic Vannes. The warm welcome and comfortable guest rooms make the cost of a night
here (under 250 francs) seem more than acceptable, as a varied
foreign clientele has realized. Mussels, sole in cider, and duck
are featured on the restaurant menu; set menus vary from 65 to
200 francs. *8 pl. de la Libération, 56000, tel. 97–63–27–36. 30
rooms with bath. Facilities: restaurant. MC, V. Restaurant
closed Sun. dinner, Nov.–Mar. Moderate.*

Vitré
Lodging
Chêne Vert. Vitré is badly placed in the hotel stakes, but since
this old town makes such a pleasant overnight stop we feel
obliged to suggest this hotel, which is conveniently accessible
from the road (D857, which links Rennes and Laval), just opposite the train station and a 10-minute stroll through cobbled
streets from Vitré Castle. This is the epitome of a French provincial hotel: creaky stairs, fraying carpets, oversoft
mattresses, and mildly enthusiastic service—all, including a
copious dinner, for next to nothing. Look carefully, however,
and you will notice some intriguing touches—an enormous
model ship on the second floor, for example, or the zinc-plated
walls that submerge the dining room in art deco/ocean-liner
pastiche. *2 pl. de la Gare, 35500, tel. 99–75–00–58. 22 rooms, a
few with bath. Closed mid-Sept.–mid-Oct.; restaurant closed
Fri. dinner and Sat., Oct.–May. Inexpensive.*

The Arts and Nightlife

The Arts

Pardons—the numerous traditional religious parades-cum-
pilgrimages that invariably showcase age-old local costumes—
are the backbone of Breton culture. There are further manifes-
tations of local folklore, often including dancers and folk
singers, at the various Celtic festivals held in summer, of which
the **Festival de Cornouaille** in Quimper (late July) is the biggest.

Theater
The region's principal theaters are the **Théâtre de la Ville** in
Rennes (pl. de la Mairie, tel. 99–28–55–87), the **Théâtre
Châteaubriand** in St-Malo (6 rue Groult-St-Georges, tel. 99–40–
98–05), and the **Théâtre Graslin** in Nantes (rue Scribe, tel. 40–
69–77–18).

Concerts   Of particular note is the **Festival de la Musique Sacrée** (sacred music) held in St-Malo in August.

Nightlife

Bars and Nightclubs   In Saint-Malo: **Le Faubourg** (7 rue St-Thomas), **La Selle** (24 rue Ste-Barbe), or **La Belle Epoque** (11 rue de Dinan). In Rennes, try **Le Pim's Rennes** (27 pl. du Colombier); in Nantes, the piano bar **Le Tie Break** (1 rue des Petites-Ecuries); and in Brest, **Le Nautilus** (rue de Siam).

Jazz Clubs   Two regional jazz venues are the **Cave du Louisiane** in St-Malo (14 rue des Cordiers), and the **Pub Univers** in Nantes (16 rue J.J. Rousseau).

Discos   **Les Chandelles** in Carnac (av. de l'Atlantique) attracts a cosmopolitan crowd and enjoys a reputation as one of the country's leading discos. You could also try the **Slow Club** in St-Malo (chaussee du Sillon) or the **Black Jack** in Dinard (blvd. Wilson).

Casinos   There are casinos in **Dinard** (tel. 99–46–15–71), **Fréhel** (tel. 96–41–49–05), **Perros-Guirec** (tel. 96–23–20–51), **Quiberon** (tel. 97–50–23–57), and **La Baule** (tel. 40–60–20–23).

For Singles   **Le Batchi** in Rennes (34 rue Vasselot) and **L'Interdit** in Nantes (14 rue Menou) cater to men only.

8 Champagne and the North

Introduction

Too few people visit northern France. The sheeplike French head south each year in search of a suntan. The millions of foreign tourists who flock through the Channel ports of Calais, Boulogne, and Dunkerque make a beeline to Paris. But there is plenty in this vast region to see and do, and two themes are common: monuments and memories.

The area was in the frontline of battle during the world wars and suffered heavily. The city of Reims was shelled incessantly during World War I, and such names as the Somme and Vimy Ridge evoke the bloody, deadlocked battles that raged from 1914 to 1918. Cemeteries and war memorials may not be the most cheerful items on a tourist's itinerary, but those we mention have a melancholy, thought-provoking beauty.

The Channel coast—mile upon mile of sandy, empty beaches—is featured in our first tour. It is unfortunate that Calais and Dunkerque, the first ports of call for many visitors to France, are among the country's ugliest towns. The old sectors of neighboring Boulogne are far more appealing while, farther down the coast, there is a startling clash between the narrow streets of the ancient, rickety, walled town of Montreuil and the posh avenues of Le Touquet, a fashionable 19th-century resort.

The north of France is an industrial region, but ignore talk of slag heaps and pollution-spouting smokestacks; heavy industry is highly centralized. This is a green and pleasant land where wooded, restful landscapes predominate. To the east, the plains give way to hills. The grapes of Champagne flourish on the steep slopes of the Marne Valley and on the so-called Mountain of Reims. There are no mountains, of course, even though the mighty mound of Laon is known as the Crowned Mountain because of the bristling silhouette of its many-towered cathedral.

Reims is the only city in Champagne, and one of France's richest tourist venues. The kings of France were crowned in its cathedral until 1825, and every age since the Roman has left an architectural mark. The small nearby towns of Ay and Epernay play an equally important role in the thriving champagne business, which has conferred wealth and, all too often, an arrogant reserve on the region's inhabitants. The down-to-earth folk of the north provide a warmer welcome.

Essential Information

Important Addresses and Numbers

Tourist Information The principal regional tourist offices are in **Lille** (pl. Rihour, tel. 20–30–81–00), **Reims** (rue Guillaume de Machault, tel. 26–47–25–69), and **Amiens** (20 pl. Notre-Dame, tel. 22–91–16–16).

The addresses of other tourist offices in towns mentioned on this tour are as follows: **Abbeville** (26 pl. de la Libération, tel. 22–24–27–92), **Arras** (pl. du Maréchal-Foch, tel. 21–51–26–95), **Boulogne** (Pont Marguet, tel. 21–31–68–38), **Calais** (12 blvd. Clemenceau, tel. 21–96–62–40), **Compiègne** (pl. del'Hôtel-de-

Ville, tel. 44–40–01–00), **Laon** (pl. du Parvis, tel. 23–20–28–
62), **Montreuil-sur-Mer** (pl. Darnétal, tel. 21–06–04–27), **Le
Touquet** (Palais de l'Europe, pl. de l'Hermitage, tel. 21–05–21–
65), **Noyon** (pl. de l'Hôtel-de-Ville, tel. 44–44–21–88),
Pierrefonds (pl. de l'Hôtel-de-Ville, tel. 44–42–81–44), and **St-
Omer** (pl. du Pain-Levé, tel. 21–98–70–00).

Travel Agencies   **Wagons Lits/Thomas Cook,** 1 rue Paul Bert (pl. de l'Hôtel-de-
Ville, Calais, tel. 21–34–79–25; and 74 bis rue Nationale, Lille,
tel. 20–57–72–45).

Car Rental   **Avis** (Hoverport, Boulogne, tel. 21–83–53–71; 36 pl. d'Armes,
Calais, tel. 21–34–66–50; 14 blvd. du Maréchal-Joffre, Reims,
tel. 26–47–40–08), **Europcar** (5 rue du Molinel, Lille, tel. 20–
78–18–18), and **Hertz** (5 blvd. d'Alsace, Amiens, tel. 22–91–
26–24).

Arriving and Departing

By Plane   American visitors should count on arriving at Paris's Charles
de Gaulle or Orly airports; there are direct flights from London's Heathrow to Lille and from Gatwick to Beauvais.

By Car   The A1 expressway from Paris passes close to Compiègne (N32
heads off to Noyon) and Arras before reaching Lille, where
there are expressways to Brussels (E42) and Ghent (E3).

By Train   Trains whistle from Paris to Lille (256 kilometers/160 miles) in
just two hours, stopping at Arras and sometimes continuing to
Brussels. The Paris–Calais train chugs unhurriedly around the
coast, taking nearly three hours to cover 300 kilometers (190
miles) and stopping at Amiens, Abbeville, Etaples (bus link to
Le Touquet four miles away), Montreuil-sur-Mer, and Boulogne. There is frequent daily service from Paris to Compiègne
and Noyon. The train from the Gare du Nord to Laon takes two
leisurely hours to cover 140 kilometers (90 miles). Regular
trains cover the 175 kilometers (110 miles) from Paris (Gare de
l'Est) to Reims in 1½ hours, continuing to Luxembourg.

Getting Around

By Plane   Domestic airports are found at Amiens, Le Touquet, Calais,
Douai, Cambria, Laon, and Reims.

By Car   A26 heads inland from Calais and St-Omer to Arras (where it
intersects with A1), Laon, and Reims, which is directly linked
to Paris by A4. N1 follows the railroad around the coast from
Belgium and Dunkerque through Calais, Boulogne, Mon-
treuilser-Mer, Amiens, and Beauvais to Paris.

By Train   The branch line between Lille and Calais stops at St-Omer.
Trains run daily, though slowly, from Laon to Amiens and
Reims. There are also trains to Reims from Laon and from
Dijon.

Guided Tours

Bus Excursions   The **Nord–Pas de Calais** tourist office in Lille (26 pl. Rihour, tel.
20–57–40–04) is a mine of information about companies that of-
fer bus tours of northern France. **Loisirs-Accueil Nord** (15 rue
du Nouveau-Siècle, Lille, tel. 20–57–00–61) offers bus trips to
Boulogne and Flanders. In the Reims area, the **Comité
Régional de Tourisme et des Loisirs Champagne-Ardennes** (5 rue

de Jericho, Chalons-sur-Marne, tel. 26–64–35–92) has numerous bus excursions around the region, including tours within Reims, "nature" trips to the national parks and forest, and history tours to World War I sites. The cost per day is 200 francs.

Special-Interest **Nuances** (26 pl. Rihour, Lille, tel. 20–40–02–57) offers archaeology and gastronomy tours, ranging from one to five days. One excursion focuses exclusively on the products of the region, including chocolate, cheese, foi gras, and medicinal plants. A two-day tour costs 500 francs. **Loisirs-Accueil Nord** (*see* above) specializes in outdoor pursuits and can arrange fishing and walking tours. It also provides beer-tasting tours.

Personal Guides **Renaissance du Vieux Boulogne** (5 rue Guiale, Boulogne-sur-Mer, tel. 21–92–11–52) arranges trips to Boulogne's old town and port for groups up to four; the cost for two hours is 330 francs.

Exploring Champagne and the North

Numbers in the margin correspond with points of interest on the Champagne and the North map.

Orientation

We have divided the vast region covered in this chapter into two tours. The first covers the north of France proper, stretching from Beauvais up to the English Channel, Lille, and the Belgian frontier. The second covers the Champagne area northeast of Paris, with Reims at its heart.

Highlights for First-time Visitors

Cathédrale Notre Dame, Reims, Tour 2
Cathédrale St-Pierre, Beauvais, Tour 1
Hautvillers, Tour 2
Tour of the ramparts around Laon's old town, Tour 2
Wine towns of the Montagne de Reims, Tour 2
The resort town of Le Touquet, Tour 1
World War I battle sites near Arras, Tour 1

Tour 1: The North

❶ The gateway to the north is the cathedral town of **Beauvais,** 72 kilometers (45 miles) north of Paris on N1. Like Reims and Abbeville, Beauvais still bears the painful scars of two world wars. It was savagely bombed in June 1940, and the ramshackle streets of the old town have resurfaced as characterless modern blocks. One survivor is the beautiful old Bishop's Palace, now the **Musée des Beaux-Arts** (Fine Arts Museum). Within its chambered recesses, you'll find a varied collection of art, embracing painting, ceramics, and regional furniture. Highlights include an epic canvas of the French Revolution by underestimated 19th-century master Thomas Couture, complete with preparatory sketches (all tastefully assembled in a large room once used as the district law court) and the charming attic under the sloping roofs, which easily qualifies as one of the

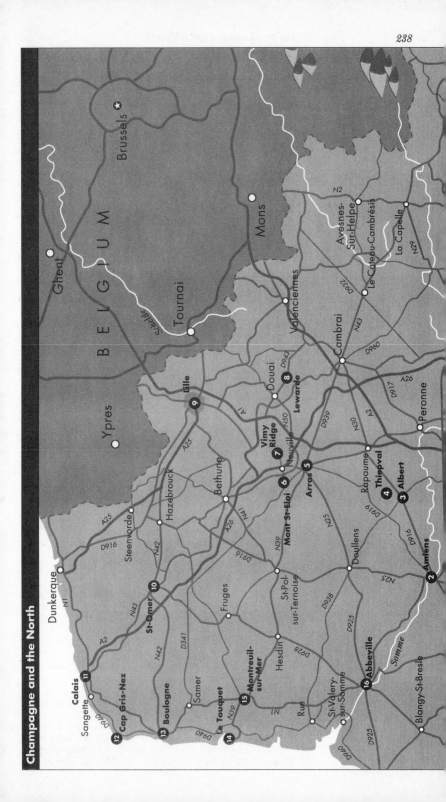

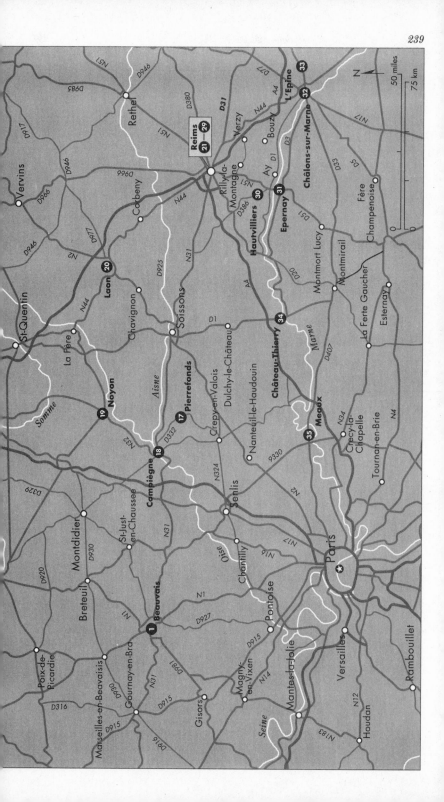

loveliest rooms in all France. *Rue du Musée. Admission: 8 frs.; free Wed. Open Wed.–Mon. 10–noon and 2–6; closed Tues.*

But the town's showpiece is unquestionably the **Cathédrale St-Pierre,** adjacent to the art museum. You may have an attack of vertigo just gazing up at its vaults, which, at 153 feet, are the highest in France. Such daring engineering was not without risk: The choir collapsed in 1284, shortly after completion. The transept, an outstanding example of Flamboyant Gothic styling, was not attempted until the 16th century. It was crowned by an improbable 450-foot spire that promptly came crashing down. With funds rapidly dwindling, the nave was never begun, delivering the final coup de grâce to Beauvais's ambition of becoming the largest church in Christendom. The 10th-century church, known as the **Basse Oeuvre** (closed to the public), juts out impertinently where the nave should have been. *Pl. St-Pierre.*

From 1664 to 1939, Beauvais was one of France's leading tapestry centers; it reached its zenith in the mid-18th century under the direction of renowned artist Jean-Baptiste Oudry. The **Galérie Nationale de la Tapisserie,** a modern museum next to the cathedral, has examples from all periods of the town's tapestry history. *24 rue Henri-Brispot. Admission; 10 frs. Open Mar.–Oct., Tues.–Sun. 9:30–11:30 and 2–6; Nov.–Feb., Tues.–Sun. 9:30–11:30 and 2 to 5.*

② **Amiens,** the capital of Picardy, lies 59 kilometers (37 miles) north of Beauvais via N1. Despite being a catastrophic example of postwar reconstruction, this stolid brick city has a couple of worthwhile attractions. By far the most important is the **Cathédrale Notre-Dame,** the largest church in France. Although it lacks the stained glass of Chartres or the sculpture of Reims, for architectural harmony, engineering proficiency, and sheer size, it has no peer. The soaring, asymmetrical facade boasts a notable Flamboyant Gothic rose window and dominates the nondescript surrounding brick streets. Inside, the overwhelming sensation of space is enhanced by the absence of pews in the nave, a return to medieval tradition. There is no stylistic disunity to mar the perspective: Construction took place between 1220 and 1264, a remarkably short period in cathedral-building terms. One of the highlights of your visit is hidden from the eye, at least until you lift up the choir stalls and admire the humorous, skillful misericord (seat) carvings executed between 1508 and 1518. *Pl. Notre-Dame. Open all day except 10–2.*

Turn left along rue Cormant and take the second right into rue Victor-Hugo. Midway down, you'll discover the **Hôtel de Berny,** an elegant 1634 mansion full of period furniture and devoted to local art and regional history. *36 rue Victor-Hugo. Admission: 10 frs. Open Apr.–Oct., Tues.–Sun. 10–noon and 2–6; Nov.–Mar., Wed. and weekends 2–6.*

Amiens is the major city of the *département* of the Somme, a name forever etched into history as the site of one of the bloodiest battles of World War I. On July 1, 1916, whole regiments of Allied soldiers went "over the top" only to be mowed down by a hail of German machine-gun fire. The major encounters took place northeast of Amiens near **Albert.**

To reach the former Somme battlefields, take D929 from Amiens to Albert, 24 kilometers (15 miles), then D151 north to the

④ British War Memorial at **Thiepval,** 8 kilometers (5 miles) away. This brick memorial, shaped like a triumphal arch, dominates the Ancre Valley and bears the names of the 73,000 British soldiers who were killed nearby. A little over a mile northwest is the **Beaumont-Hamel** memorial park, where trenches, parapets, and barbed wire recall the fighting waged here by Newfoundland regiments in July 1916.

Time Out　The white-painted, vine-covered exterior of **L'Escale,** in the tiny village of Cappy, 16 kilometers (10 miles) southeast of Albert, mark it as a restaurant with a difference. The dining room, decorated with antiques and needlework tablecloths, has the feel of a country cottage, and the menu is illustrated by poems and old photos. The regional dishes (eel, duck, and black pudding) are chosen according to season and accompanied by subtle, refined sauces. *22 Chaussée Léon-Blum.*

⑤ War cemeteries dot the countryside as you head north along D919 to **Arras,** 32 kilometers (20 miles) away. Capital of the historic Artois region between Flanders and Picardy, Arras has grown into something of a sprawling industrial town. Its historic core bears witness to the grandeur of another age, however, when the town enjoyed medieval importance as a trading and clothmaking center.

Grand' Place and **place des Héros,** separated by a short block, are the two main squares, harmonious examples of 17th- and 18th-century Flemish civil architecture. The gabled facades recall those in Belgium and Holland and are a reminder of the unifying influence of the Spanish colonizers of the "Low Lands" during the 17th century. The smaller, arcaded place des Héros is dominated by the richly worked—and much restored—**Hôtel de Ville,** capped by a 240-foot belfry.

Turn left out of the square, then right into rue Paul-Doumer. Walking a block along brings you to the imposing 18th-century premises of a former abbey, now the **Musée des Beaux-Arts.** The Fine Arts Museum houses a rich collection of porcelain and, especially, painting, with several major 19th-century French works. *22 rue Paul-Doumer. Admission: 10 frs. adults, 5 frs. children and senior citizens. Open Wed.–Mon. 10–noon and 2–5:30; closed Tues.*

The 19th-century **Cathédrale St-Vaast,** a short block farther on, is a white-stoned Classical building, every bit as vast as its name (pronounced "va") suggests. It replaced the previous Gothic cathedral destroyed in 1799; though it was half-razed during World War I, restoration was so skillfully done you'd never know.

At first glance you would never guess that Arras was badly mauled during World War I. Not far off, though, are parks and memorials recalling the fierce battles that bled the region to death. Arras is a convenient base for visiting the area's numerous superbly cared-for cemeteries and memorials, which number among the most poignant sights in northern France.

⑥ Eight kilometers (5 miles) northwest of Arras via D341 lies the ruined abbey of **Mont St-Eloi.** Legend has it that this once-vast abbey is connected to Arras by an enormous underground tunnel. Ruined towers are all that remain of the abbey, which was destroyed during the French Revolution. They peer mournfully over the tiny village and surrounding countryside and are visible for miles around. Just 2 miles away, with gentle slopes lined with weeping willows, is the most beautiful and moving of all the French war cemeteries—**La Targette.**

From nearby Neuville-St-Vaast, D55 winds up to the Canadian War Memorial on top of **Vimy Ridge.** Thanks to its woods and lush grass, the Vimy memorial park has become a popular picnicking spot, yet the preserved trenches and savagely undulating terrain are harsh reminders of the combat waged here in 1917. The simple, soaring, white-stone Canadian War Memorial, a cleft rectangular tower adorned with female figures in tearful lament, is highly effective. Its base is inscribed with thousands of names of the fallen.

Head back to Neuville and take D937 right shortly afterward, past the beautiful circular cemetery of the Cabaret Rouge and the village of **Souchez.** Turn left up to **Notre-Dame de Lorette,** a colossal cemetery standing on a windswept hill 500 feet above the plains of Artois. There is a mock-Byzantine church and a huge tower containing a small war museum; from the top of the tower, treat yourself to some superb views of the surrounding countryside.

Get onto southbound A26, branching off at N50 (follow signs for Douai). From Douai, it's just a five-kilometer (three-mile) drive east on D943 to **Lewarde,** whose abandoned coal mine has been skillfully converted into a museum documenting the mining industry. You can admire the beefy mine machinery, stroll around an interesting photographic exhibit, and take a train ride through reconstructed coal galleries. *Admission: 30 frs. adults, 15 frs. children. Open daily 10–4.*

Time Out If you find yourself at the Mining Museum around lunchtime, make for the on-site brasserie, **Le Briquet.** The 95-franc menu is an excellent value: ham from the Ardennes, followed by trout with almonds, guinea fowl (or saddle of lamb), and cheese or dessert. *Closed Jan.–Feb. 8, and Mon. Oct. 10–Christmas.*

Lille, 40 kilometers (24 miles) north, is quickly reached via D943 and the A1 expressway. For a big city supposedly reeling beneath the problems of its main industry, textiles, Lille is a remarkably dynamic, attractive place. The city has had a checkered history, experiencing Flemish, Austrian, and Spanish rule before passing into French hands for good in 1667. Today, it is thoroughly French, apart, perhaps, from its Belgian-like penchant for beer and french fries. Although the downtown area contains several narrow streets full of old buildings, Lille does not boast any outstanding tourist sights. Yet with its choice of shops, restaurants, and museums, it makes an enjoyable overnight rest stop.

Start your tour of the city at the **Hospice Comtesse,** in the northern sector of the old town. Founded by Jeanne de Constantinople, countess of Flanders, as a hospital in 1237, it was rebuilt in the 15th century after a fire destroyed most of the original building. Local artifacts from the 17th and 18th centuries form the backbone of the museum now housed here, but its star attraction is the Salle des Malades (Sick Room), featuring a majestic wooden ceiling. *32 rue de la Monnaie. Admission: 5 frs. adults, children free. Open Wed.–Mon. 10–12:30 and 2–6; closed Tues.*

Follow rue de la Monnaie as it curves right and branch off at rue de la Grand Chaussée. The Grand Place (or, to give it its full name, place du Général-de-Gaulle) is a fitting site for the **Vielle Bourse** (former stock exchange), one of the most charming buildings in central Lille. The quadrangle of elegant, richly worked buildings was erected by Julien Destrée in the 1650s as a commercial exchange to rival those already existing in Belgium and Holland. Just two short blocks down rue de Paris brings you to the sumptuous **Eglise St-Maurice** (on the right), a large, five-aisled church built between the 15th and 19th century.

A block farther along, turn right onto rue du Molinel and continue until you hit the frenzied traffic of boulevard de la Liberté, a vast street that roars through central Lille. Half a block down, on the left, is the **Musée des Beaux-Arts** (Fine Arts Museum), housing a noteworthy collection of Dutch and Flemish painting (Anthony Van Dyck, Peter Paul Rubens, Flemish Primitives, and Dutch landscapists), as well as some works by the Impressionists, a few bombastic 19th-century French painters, and some murkily dramatic Goyas to round it all off. An extensive ceramics section displays some fine examples of Lille faïence, which uses opaque glazing techniques to achieve some remarkable effects. *Pl. de la République. Admission: 5 frs.; free Wed. and Sat. mornings; children free. Open Wed.– Mon. 9:30–12:30 and 2–6; closed Tues.*

Head left out of the art gallery, making for the gigantic **citadel,** which glowers down on the whole of the old town from its perch on the west end of the boulevard. Construction started shortly after that of the Veille Bourse in the mid-17th century; of course that military marvel, Sébastien de Vauban got the commission. Some 60 million bricks were used, and the result is a fortified town in its own right, with monumental towers and walls. These days, the citadel is used as a barracks. *Visits on Sun. during summer months.*

⑩ From Lille, take the A25 expressway toward Steenvorde, then N42 to St-Omer via Hazebrouck. **St-Omer** is a delightful small town, too often neglected by hasty motorists on their way south. It is not the archetypal northern industrial town; with its yellow-brick buildings, it even looks different from its neighbors, and a distinct air of 18th-century prosperity hovers about the place. Stroll through the narrow streets surrounding the Basilique Notre-Dame and, if time allows, visit the **Hôtel Sandelin** on rue Carnot (open Wed.–Sun. 10–noon and 2–5). Now the town museum, the 1777 mansion is furnished with 18th-century furniture and paintings and contains an exceptional collection of porcelain and faïence.

⑪ The port town of **Calais** lies 40 kilometers (25 miles) northeast of St-Omer via N43. Few vestiges remain of the old, once-pretty port that owed its wealth to the lace industry rather than daytrippers (Calais lies just across the English Channel from Dover, 38 kilometers/24 miles away, so it's hardly surprising that nearly eight million visitors flock to it via ferry each year). You won't want to stay here long, but there are a few sights to see before you dash off.

You don't need to be a sculpture fanatic to appreciate Auguste Rodin's bronze **Monument des Bourgeois de Calais,** which lords it over the east end of the Parc St-Pierre next to place Soldat-

Inconnu. The bourgeois in question were townspeople who, in 1347, offered their lives to English king Edward III in a bid to save fellow citizens from merciless reprisals after Calais's abortive attempts to withstand an eight-month siege (Calais was an English possession until 1558 and was the last English toehold in France). Edward's queen, Philippa, intervened on their behalf and the courageous men were spared; Calais, on the other hand, remained in English hands for another 200 years.

Head up traffic-clogged boulevard Jacquard, turning right onto rue Richelieu. Three blocks along, at no. 25, is the **Musée des Beaux-Arts et de la Dentelle** (Fine Arts and Lace Museum, admission: 6 frs.; open Wed.–Mon. 10–noon and 2–5), which contains some fine 19th- and 20th-century pictures, local historical displays, and exhibits documenting the Calais lace industry. Turn left at the next block, making for the much-restored **Eglise Notre-Dame,** where Général de Gaulle was married in 1921. Take time to admire the simple, vertical elegance of the windows and the ornate fan vaulting inside.

D940, running from Calais to Boulogne, winds its picturesque way past vast sandy beaches, Sangette (site of the French terminus for the Channel Tunnel, which, by 1992 should link France and Great Britain), and the cliffs of Cap Gris-Nez and Cap Blanc-Nez. It's worth making the short detour to the **Cap Gris-Nez** for a bracing stroll along the cliff tops beneath the shadow of the lighthouse and ominous outlines of a World War II concrete bunker.

Just before you arrive in **Boulogne** (another stomping ground for cross-Channel visitors), spin off left toward the **Colonne de la Grande Armée.** Work began on this 160-foot marble column in 1804 to commemorate Napoleon's soon-to-be abandoned plans to invade England, but it was finished 30 years later under Louis-Philippe. The 263 steps take you to the top and a wide-reaching panoramic view. If the weather is clear and you're blessed with Napoleonic eyesight, you may be able to make out the distant cliffs of Dover. *Admission free. Open daily 10–noon and 2–5.*

The contrast between the lower and upper sections of Boulogne is startling. The rebuilt concrete streets around the port are gruesome and sinister, but the Ville Haute—the old town on the hill—is a different world, and you can begin to understand why Napoleon chose Boulogne as his base while preparing to cross the channel. The Ville Haute is dominated by the formidable **Notre-Dame** basilica, its distinctive elongated dome visible from far out at sea. Surrounding the basilica are charming cobbled streets and tower-flanked ramparts, dating from the 13th century and offering excellent views. The four main streets of the old town intersect at place Bouillon, where you can see the 18th-century brick town hall, and the Hôtel Desandrouins, where Napoleon spent many long nights pondering how to invade Britain.

Le Touquet, 27 kilometers (17 miles) down the coast from Boulogne via D940, is a total contrast: a superb example of an elegant Victorian seaside resort that sprang out of nowhere in the 19th century, adopting the name Paris-Plage. Mainly because gambling laws were stricter in Victorian England than in France, it soon became clear that Englishmen, not Parisians, were the town's mainstay. A cosmopolitan atmosphere remains, although many Frenchmen, attracted by the airy, elegant avenues and invigorating climate, have moved here for good. To one side lies a fine sandy beach; to the other, an artificial forest planted in the 1850s. A casino, golf course, and racetrack cater to fashionable pleasure.

Time Out   The **Parc de Jeux Aquatiques** has an unpretentious bar and restaurant, as well as numerous watersport facilities; you can shoot the rapids, thunder down a toboggan run, or just relax in the sauna. *Blvd. de la Mer. Admission to waterpark: 50 frs.*

⑮ Despite its seaside-sounding name, **Montreuil-sur-Mer** lies 16 kilometers (10 miles) inland from Le Touquet along N39. This ancient town features majestic walls and ramparts, as well a faded, nostalgic charm to which various authors have succumbed, notably Victor Hugo; an important episode of his epic work *Les Misérables* is situated here.

Whenever citadels and city walls loom on the French horizon, it's a fair bet that Vauban had a hand in their construction. Montreuil is no exception. In about 1690, he supplemented the existing 16th-century towers of the **citadel** with an imposing wall, whose grassy banks and mossy flagstones can be explored at leisure. There are extensive views on all sides. *Admission: 6 frs. Open daily 10–noon and 2–5.*

The old cobbled streets of the town make equally agreeable places to stroll. The **Eglise St-Saulve** (just off rue Carnot; open summer only) boasts some fine paintings and a facade dating, in part, from the 11th century.

⑯ Forty-five kilometers (28 miles) south along N1 is another old town, **Abbeville,** heavily reconstructed after being reduced to rubble in 1940. It makes a fitting epilogue to a tour that began with the huge Gothic cathedrals of Beauvais and Amiens, just 48 kilometers (30 miles) down the Somme. **St-Vulfran's Abbeville,** begun in 1488, was one of the last cathedral-sized churches to be constructed in the Gothic style. Its much-mauled facade, still undergoing renovation, is a riot of Flamboyant Gothic tracery and ornament. It was here that, according to 19th-century art historian John Ruskin, Gothic "laid down and died."

Tour 2: Champagne Country

⑰ One of the first stops for any visitor heading out of the Ile de France to the northeast is **Pierrefonds,** 88 kilometers (55 miles) from Paris and just 14 kilometers (9 miles) southeast of Compiègne. This attractive, lakeside village is dominated by its huge 12th-century **château,** comprehensively restored to imagined former glory by Viollet-le-Duc at the behest of upstart Emperor Napoleon III in the 1860s. What is left is a crenellated fortress with a fairytale silhouette. A visit takes in the chapel, barracks, and the majestic keep holding the lord's bedchamber and reception hall. *Admission: 22 frs. Guided tours only, Apr.–Oct., Wed.–Mon. 9:30–11:15 and 1:30–5:15; Nov.–Mar., until 4.*

⑱ **Compiègne** can be reached from Pierrefonds via D332. A bustling town of some 40,000 people, it stands at the northern limit of the Ile de France forest, on the edge of the misty plains of Picardy: prime hunting country, a sure sign there's a former royal palace in the vicinity. The one here enjoyed its heyday in the mid-19th century under Napoleon III. But the town's history looks both further back—Joan of Arc was held prisoner here —and further forward: The World War I armistice was signed in Compiègne Forest on November 11, 1918.

The 18th-century **palace** was restored by Napoleon I and favored for wild weekends by his nephew Napoleon III, emperor from 1851 to 1870. The entrance ticket includes access to apartments, the Musée du Second Empire, Musée de la Voiture (Car Museum), and the attractive palace park. *Pl. du Palais. Admission: 21 frs. Open Wed.–Mon. 9:30–11:15 and 1:30–4:30; closed Tues.*

One of the central highlights of Compiègne is the late 15th-century town hall, or **Hôtel de Ville,** possessing an exceptional Flamboyant Gothic facade with fine statuary. Make time to visit the **Musée de la Figurine** for its amazing collection of 85,000 lead soldiers depicting military uniforms through the ages. *28 pl. de l'Hôtel de Ville. Admission: 9 frs. Open Apr.–Oct., Tues. –Sun. 9–12 and 2–6; Nov.–Mar. until 5.*

A short distance east of Compiègne, near Rethondes (take N31), is the **Clairière de l'Armistice,** where a railway car was run out on a spur line especially for the signing of the World War I Armistice of 1918, marking the Allied victory. In 1940, the Germans turned the tables on the French, who were made to sign their own surrender to the Nazis—accompanied by Hitler's famous jig for joy. The car you can visit these days is a replica of the original, which was destroyed by the Germans during the war. *Wagon du Maréchal Foch, Forêt de Compiègne. Admission: 5 frs. Open Apr.–Oct., daily 9–noon and 2–6:30; Nov.–Mar. until 5:30.*

⑲ **Noyon,** 26 kilometers (16 miles) northeast of Compiègne on N32, is a frequently overlooked cathedral town that owed its medieval importance to the cult of 7th-century saint Eloi, patron of blacksmiths and a former town bishop. The **Cathédrale St-Eloi** was constructed between 1150 and 1290, and its four-storied nave, intermittent use of rounded as well as pointed arches, and the thin, pointed lancet (as opposed to rose) windows in the austere facade all mark it as one of the earliest attempts at what was to become "The Gothic Cathedral." Note the rounded transepts, another example of pervading Romanesque (and possibly Germanic) influence. Despite the cathedral's size and architectural importance, Noyon itself is virtually unknown, so you can be sure of a peaceful, undisturbed visit.

From Noyon, take N32 and N44 54 kilometers (32 miles) due east to Laon. (Midway along, you'll see signs to St-Quentin, which boasts an excellent hotel/restaurant; *see* Dining and Lodging.)

⑳ **Laon** occupies a splendid hilltop site, and is sometimes referred to as the "crowned mountain"—a reference to the forest of towers sprouting from its ancient cathedral. The site, cathedral, and enchanting old town are worth seeing. Strangely, not many people do; few Parisians, for instance, have ever heard of the place.

In the middle of the old town, just off place Aubry, is **Cathédrale Notre-Dame,** constructed between 1160 and 1235 and a superb example of early Gothic styling. The recently cleaned, light interior gives the impression of order and immense length (120 yards in total). The flat east end, an English-inspired feature, is unusual in France. The upper galleries that extend around the building are typical of early Gothic; what isn't typical is that you can actually visit them (and the towers) with a guide from the tourist office on the cathedral square. The filigree elegance of the five remaining towers is audacious by any standards and rare: Medieval architects preferred to concentrate on soaring interiors, with just two towers at the west end. Even those not usually affected by architecture will appreciate the sense of movement about Laon's majestic west front; compare it with the more placid, two-dimensional feel of Notre-Dame in Paris. Look, too, for the stone bulls protruding from the towers; a tribute to the stalwart 12th-century beasts who carted up blocks of stone from quarries far below.

Time Out   The **café** on place du Parvis is unremarkable in every respect but one: its location, just opposite the cathedral. What better place to drink in one of France's most exciting medieval facades with your morning coffee? *Pl. du Parvis.*

The medieval **ramparts,** virtually undisturbed by passing traffic, provide a ready-made itinerary for a tour of old Laon. Panoramic views, sturdy gateways, and intriguing glimpses of the cathedral lurk around every bend. Another notable survivor from medieval times is the **Chapelle des Templiers,** a small, well-preserved octagonal 12th-century chapel on the grounds of the town museum. *Porte d'Ardon. Admission: 6.50 frs. Open Apr.–Oct., Wed.–Mon. 10–noon and 2–6; Nov.–Mar. until 5.*

Sixteen kilometers (10 miles) south of Laon via N2 lies the **Chemin des Dames,** a hilltop road separating the valleys of the Aisne and the Ailette. The French offensive launched here by Général Nivelle in April 1917 led to futile slaughter, mutiny, and Nivelle's eventual replacement by Marshal Pétain. Leave N2 a couple of miles after Chavignon and follow D18 to **Cerny-en-Laonnois,** where there is a French memorial. Continue to the **Caverne du Dragon,** which was used as an arsenal by the Germans and now is the site of a war museum. Just past Hurtebise, take D985 toward Corbeny; to the right is the **Plateau de Californie,** from whose terrace there is a panoramic view of the scenes of combat. N44 connects Corbeny to Reims, a further 29 kilometers (18 miles) to the south.

㉑ Reims (48 kilometers/30 miles from Laon if you take A26 instead of the meandering route described above) is the capital of the champagne industry. Several major producers are headquartered here, and you won't want to miss the chance to visit the chalky maze of cellars that tunnel under the city center.

Reims is renowned for its cathedral, one of the most famous in France and the age-old setting for the coronations of the French kings (Charles X's was the last, back in 1825). The glory **㉒** of the **Cathédrale Notre-Dame** is its facade: It's so skillfully proportioned you initially have little idea of its monumental size. Above the north (left) door hovers the *Laughing Angel,* a delightful statue whose famous smile is threatening to melt into an acid-rain scowl. Pollution has succeeded war as the ravager

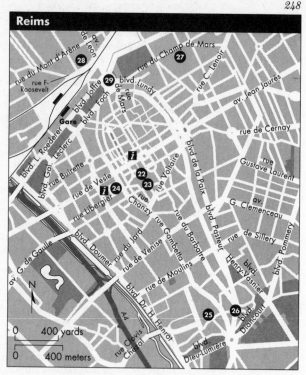

of the building's fabric. Restoration is an ongoing process; take a look in the postcard shops opposite to get an idea of the pounding the cathedral took between 1914 and 1918.

The high, solemn nave is at its best in summer when the plain lower walls are adorned by 16th-century tapestries relating the life of the Virgin. The east-end windows boast stained glass by Marc Chagall. Admire the vista toward the west end, with an interplay of narrow pointed arches of different sizes.

With the exception of the 15th-century towers, most of the original building went up in the 100 years after 1211. A stroll around the outside will reinforce the impression of harmony, discipline, and decorative richness. The east end presents an idyllic sight across well-tended lawns. There are spectacular light shows both inside (40 francs) and outside the cathedral (free) in July and August. *Pl. du Cardinal Luçon.*

23 Next door, the **Palais du Tau** (former archbishop's palace) houses an impressive display of tapestries and coronation robes, as well as several statues "rescued" from the cathedral facade. The second-floor views of Notre-Dame are terrific. *2 pl. du Cardinal-Luçon. Admission: 22 frs. adults, 12 frs. senior citizens, 5 frs. children. Open Tues.–Sun. 2–6.*

Time Out Something out of the ordinary is always happening at the **Café du Palais,** just around the corner from the cathedral: A jazz quartet, a fashion-modeling session, or a screening of a silent movie. There's a piano, a veranda, and a choice of baguette sandwiches with fillings like duck mousse or warm goat cheese. *14 pl. Myron Herrick.*

㉔ Two blocks from the cathedral, on the right, is the **Musée St-Denis,** featuring an outstanding collection of paintings spearheaded by no fewer than 27 Corots and Jacques Louis David's celebrated portrait of Revolutionary leader Jean Paul Marat, who was stabbed to death in his bath by a disillusioned female supporter. *8 rue Chanzy. Admission: 12 frs. Open Wed.–Mon. 10–noon and 2–6.*

㉕ As you leave the museum, turn right and continue along rue Chanzy and rue Gambetta to the 11th-century **Basilique St-Rémi,** honoring the 5th-century saint who gave his name to the city. St-Rémi is nearly as long as the cathedral, and its interior seems to stretch into the endless distance, an impression created by its relative murk and lowness. The airy, four-story Gothic choir contains some fine original 12th-century stained glass.

㉖ Several champagne producers organize visits to their cellars, combining video presentations with guided tours of their cavernous, chalk-hewn underground warehouses. **Taittinger** (9 pl. St-Nicaise; closed weekends Dec.–Feb.) has the most spectacular cellars. Few show much generosity when it comes to pouring samples, though, so we recommend you double back across ㉗ town to **Mumm,** which does. *34 rue du Champ-de-Mars. Open Mar.–Nov., Thurs.–Tues. 9:30–noon and 2–5:30; closed Wed.*

㉘ Head down rue du Champ-de-Mars toward the train station, turn right into avenue de Laon, then left into rue Franklin-Roosevelt. A short way along is the **Salle de Guerre,** where General Eisenhower established Allied headquarters at the end of World War II. It was here, in a well-preserved, map-covered room, that the German surrender was signed in May 1945. *12 rue Franklin-Roosevelt. Admission: 7 frs. adults, 3.50 frs. children. Open Wed.–Mon. 10–noon and 2–6; closed Tues.*

㉙ The **Porte Mars,** an unlikely but impressive Roman arch adorned by faded bas-reliefs depicting Jupiter, Romulus, and Remus, looms up surprisingly just across from the train station.

Your first encounter with the champagne vineyards can be had 10 kilometers (6 miles) south of Reims via N51 on the **Montagne de Reims.** Despite its name, this is no mountain, but a lofty, forest-topped plateau whose slopes are a tangle of vines. D26 winds around the eastern face of the plateau, through wine villages such as Chigny-les-Roses, Rilly-la-Montagne, Mailly-Champagne, and Verzy, each as pretty as its name. Pride of place goes to the unforgettable **Bouzy,** where a fashionable but overpriced still red wine is produced. South of Bouzy, D1 runs along the banks of the River Marne to Ay, once capital of the champagne vineyards; Henry VIII was a keen tippler of its wines.

㉚ To understand why traditional still "wine" became exciting, sparkling "champagne," detour up D386 to nearby **Hautvillers,** a gem of a village and former home of Dom Pérignon (1638–1715), who invented champagne as we know it. This able monk, a cellar master whose blindness enhanced his tastebuds and his sense of smell, is the supposed discoverer of the use of corks for stoppers, the blending of wines from different vineyards, and the systematic (rather than occasional) production of champagne bubbles. Dom Pérignon's simple tomb-slab, in the damp, forlorn village church (all that remains of the former abbey), is a modest memorial to the hero of one of the world's most lucrative drink industries.

㉛ Across the Marne lies **Epernay**, a town that, unlike Reims with its numerous treasures, appears to live for nothing other than champagne. Unfortunately, no relation exists between the fabulous wealth of Epernay's illustrious inhabitants and the drab, dreary appearance of the town as a whole. Most of the champagne houses are spaced out along the long, straight avenue de Champagne and, although their names may provoke sighs of wonder, their functional or overdressy facades are a disappointment.

The attractions are underground, in the cellars. Of the various houses open to the public, **Mercier** offers the best deal; its sculpted, labyrinthine caves contain one of the world's largest wooden barrels (with a capacity of over 200,000 bottles) and can be visited in the speed and comfort of a small train. A generous glass of champagne is your posttrip reward. *75 av. de Champagne. Admission free. Open 10–noon and 2–5.*

Time Out Champagne is not the only Epernay specialty. At **La Chocolaterie,** Monsieur Thibaut performs confectionary miracles before your eyes. If you feel the urge to indulge, take a seat in the adjoining Salon de Thé. *9 rue Gallice. Closed Sun. and Mon.*

Strangely enough, the official administrative center of the champagne industry is not Reims or Epernay but **㉜ Châlons-sur-Marne**. Yet this large town, 35 kilometers (22 miles) east of Epernay along D3, is of principal interest to fans of medieval architecture. The **Cathédrale St-Etienne** is a pure, harmonious 13th-century construction with large nave windows and tidy flying buttresses; the overall effect is marred only by the bulky 17th-century Baroque west front. Of equal merit is the church of **Notre-Dame des Vaux,** with its Romanesque nave and early Gothic choir and vaults.

Another architectural treat lies in wait eight kilometers (five **㉝** miles) east of Châlons along N3 at **L'Epine,** a tiny village dominated by the twin-towered Flamboyant Gothic basilica of **Notre-Dame de l'Epine.** The ornament here, weaving intricate patterns over the facade and spires, seems effortless, while the interior exudes elegance and restraint.

Head back to Epernay and take the north bank of the Marne along D1, which twists its way high above the river valley, providing the most spectacular views of the entire champagne **㉞** vineyard. The vineyard continues almost to **Château-Thierry**, 51 kilometers (32 miles) from Epernay and birthplace of French fable writer La Fontaine. Pay a visit to the ruined castle and old gateway, the Porte St-Pierre, through which Joan of Arc passed in 1429 after delivering the town from the English.

To return from Château-Thierry to Paris, 96 kilometers (60 miles) away, take the direct route along A4. Alternatively, you **㉟** can continue along the banks of the Marne to **Meaux,** site of another venerable medieval cathedral.

What to See and Do with Children

The earnest brick towns and soaring cathedrals that dominate
the landscape can make northern France seem a serious place.
The most obvious source of youthful amusement is found on the
seaside, along the huge, sandy **beaches** that stretch from Calais
to Le Touquet, home to a spectacular watergames center, the
Parc de Jeux Aquatiques. Stop off at **Cap Gris Nez**, as well, for a
walk along the Channel cliffs. The **automated Métro** in Lille fas-
cinates children with its tiny cars and no driver.

The following sights are described fully in the Exploring text.

Mini-train tour of the **Mercier** cellars, Epernay, (Tour 2)
Mining Museum, Lewarde, (Tour 1).
Musée de la Figurine (Toy Soldier Museum), Champiègne,
(Tour 2).

Off the Beaten Track

Midway between the two regions covered in our Exploring section is **Cambrai**, a name the French associate with minty
candies known as *bêtises*. Cambrai would be a typical northern
French industrial town were it not for its white, chalky stone, a
total contrast with the red brick so prevalent elsewhere. Showcasing that stone are age-old town gateways, like the 14th-
century Porte de Paris or the 17th-century Porte Notre-Dame,
and three bell towers—those of St-Géry, the cathedral, and the
former church of St-Martin. Above the sprawling main square
looms the town hall's strange-looking cupola, flanked by an exotic pair of beturbaned attendants who look as if they've just
arrived from India.

Twenty-four kilometers (15 miles) east of Cambrai along N43 is
Le Cateau-Cambrésis. Its most important building is the **Palais
Fénelon**, former home to the archbishops of Cambrai and today
a museum devoted to the artist Henri Matisse (1869–1954),
born in Le Cateau. Along with a number of early oil paintings
and sculptures, there is a superb collection of 50 drawings
selected by Matisse himself, arranged in a carefully lit
room on the second floor. The enthusiastic curator, Dominique
Szymusiak, will show you around (her English is excellent). Reserve a guided tour by calling 27–84–13–15 at least a week
before your visit. *Admission: 12 frs., children under 18 free.
Open Wed.–Sun. 10–noon and 2–5 (6 in winter).*

Shopping

Northern France and shopping are intimately associated in the
minds of many visitors, especially the English. The cross-
channel ferry trip to Calais and Boulogne has become something of an institution, with one rather ignoble aim: to stock up
on as much tax-free wine and beer as is legally and physically
possible. Supermarkets along the coast are admirably large
and well stocked, though you may want to consider local
juniper-based *genièvre* brandy, which is a more original choice.
Boulogne, France's premier fishing port, is famous for its kip-
pers (smoked herring).

Arts and Crafts Calais has been long renowned as a lace-making center. Lace-
shops still abound; try **La Dentellière** (30 blvd. de l'Egalite).

Near Montreuil, the wickerwork tradition prevails at **Régis Quiénot** in Marles-sur-Canche. For individual paintings on silk, visit **C. Decq** at La Calotterie, again near Montreuil. Wooden puppets are a specialty at Amiens, and glazed earthenware is part of St-Omer's historical heritage.

Antiques   Antiques dealers are legion; some of the best buys, though, can be made at the busy auction houses *(commissaires-priseurs)* at Douai, Lille, or Calais.

Champagne   Reims owes its prestige to champagne, and a number of its central shops duly charge sky-high prices. You'll find the best buys at small producers in the villages along the Montagne de Reims between Reims and Epernay (not Bouzy, though).

Sports and Fitness

Beaches and   The northern French coast, from Calais to Le Touquet, is one
Water Sports   long, sandy beach, known as the Côte d'Opale. The **Aqualud** complex on Le Touquet beach (blvd. de la Mer, tel. 21–05–63–59) boasts slides, toboggans, a wave machine, sauna, and solarium.

Apart from ocean swimming (backed up by indoor and outdoor pools throughout the region), you may care to try your hand at speed sailing or handling a sand buggy, those windsurf-boards on wheels that race along the sands at up to 70 mph. Known as *Char à Voile*, the sport can be practiced at Le Touquet, Hardelot, Dunkerque, Bray-Dunes, and Berck-sur-Mer. For details, contact amiable Claude Wantier at the **Drakkars** club in Hardelot, south of Boulogne (tel. 21–91–81–96); the cost is 50–70 francs per hour.

Biking   Bicycles can be rented from many train stations for around 35 francs a day. Get details of special circuits from the **Comité Départemental de Cyclotourisme** (75 rue Louis-Drouart, Les Ageux, 60700 Pont-Ste-Maxence). Mountain biking is also popular in the Noyon area; get in touch with **Patrick Drocourt** (48 rue du Maréchal-Joffre, 60150 Montmacq, tel. 44–76–40–49).

Golf   You'll find courses at Hardelot, Le Touquet (three courses), Wimereux, Lille, and Compiègne.

Horseback Riding   Horseback riding is possible in many places, including Hardelot (tel. 21–83–71–28) and St-Amand-les-Eaux (tel. 27–48–56–62).

Parachuting   Sky-diving thrills can be had at Hardelot (tel. 21–91–81–86).

Dining and Lodging

Dining

The cuisine of northern France is robust and hearty, like that of neighboring Belgium. Beer predominates and is often used as a base for sauces (notably for chicken). French fries and mussels are featured on most menus, and vans selling fries and hot dogs are common sights. Great quantities of fish, notably herring, are eaten along the coast, while inland delicacies include *andouillettes* (chitterling sausages), tripe, and pâté made from duck, partridge, or woodcock. Anyone with a sweet tooth will enjoy the region's ubiquitous macaroons and minty Cambrai *bêtises.* Ham, pigs' feet, gingerbread, and a champagne-based mustard are specialties of the Reims area, as is *ratafia*, a sweet aperitif made from grape juice and brandy. To the north, a glass of *genièvre* (a brandy made from juniper berries and sometimes added to black coffee to make a drink called a *bistoul)* is the typical way to conclude a good meal.

Highly recommended restaurants are indicated by a star ★.

Lodging

Northern France is overladen with old hotels, often rambling and simple, seldom pretentious. Good value is easier to come by than top quality, except in major cities (Amiens, Lille, and Reims) or at Le Touquet, whose Westminster Hotel numbers among the country's best.

Highly recommended hotels are indicated by a star ★.

Amiens **Joséphine.** This unpretentious, good-value restaurant in cen-
Dining tral Amiens is a reliable choice. Solid fare, good wines, and rustic decor (a bit on the stodgy side, like the sauces) pull in many foreign customers, notably the British. *20 rue Sire-Firmin-Leroux, tel. 22–91–47–38. Reservations advised in summer. Dress: casual. AE, V. Closed Sun. dinner, Mon., and 3rd week of Aug. Inexpensive–Moderate.*
Mermoz. Nouvelle and traditional cuisine are skillfully blended by chef Pierre Peroz in a fresh, modern setting close to the train station. There are three menus (100, 115, and 195 francs) and the choice changes according to the season. *7 rue Jean-Mermoz, tel. 22–91–50–63. Reservations advised. Dress: casual. AE, V. Closed Sat. lunch, Sun., and mid-July–mid-Aug. Moderate.*

Lodging **Hôtel de la Paix.** Close to the Picardy Museum, the hotel is housed in a building reconstructed after World War II. Private parking and the view of a nearby church from some of the rooms offset a certain lack of personality, although the breakfast room tries valiantly to suggest an 18th-century Louis XV salon. Foreign visitors are frequent, and English is spoken. *8 rue de la République, 80000, tel. 22–91–39–21. 26 rooms, some with bath. No credit cards. Closed Sun. and mid-Dec.–mid-Jan. Inexpensive.*

Arras **Le Chanzy.** Huge and popular, Le Chanzy offers three set
Dining menus (80, 100, and 150 francs) and as many dining rooms. The restaurant specializes in standard brasserie fare (lunchtime only) and more ambitious gastronomy, based on the roasts in which the chef is expert. There is a vast wine list, and the main room is decked out in a luxuriously flashy '50s-style decor (renovation scheduled). Le Chanzy also has 20 guest rooms. *8 rue Chanzy, tel. 21–71–69–69. Reservations advised. Dress: casual. AE, DC, MC, V. Moderate.*
Maison des Degorres. Two good-value menus (66 and 120 francs), based on traditional French cooking, are offered; there is no selection à la carte. "Classic bourgeois" is the restaurant's preferred description of both its food and its dining room, meaning nondescript but robust. *14 av. Paul-Michonneau, tel. 21–55–36–30. Reservations recommended in summer. Dress: casual. V. Closed Mon. and Oct. Inexpensive.*

Lodging **Univers.** This stylish hotel occupies a converted 18th-century monastery and has a pretty garden and a charming restaurant.

Its central position and views of the courtyard and garden make it a favorite stopover with vacationers heading south. The interior has recently been modernized, but it retains its rustic provincial furniture. *5 pl. de la Croix-Rouge, 62000, tel. 21–71–34–01. 36 rooms, most with bath. Facilities: restaurant, garden. AE, DC, V. Restaurant closed Sun. in Aug. Moderate.*

Boulogne-sur-Mer
Dining
★

Brasserie Liégoise. Good food spiced with delicious nouvelle touches helps this old, established restaurant remain at the forefront of the Boulogne eating scene. The decor is modern,— an eccentric contrast of black and yellow—and so are the prices: 300 francs à la carte and set menus at 150, 200, and 260 francs. Chef Alain Delpierre justifies the expense with delicate sauces and interesting combinations like duck liver with mushrooms. *10 rue Monsigny, tel. 21–31–61–15. Reservations necessary at weekends. Jacket required. AE, DC, MC, V. Closed Wed., and Sun. dinner. Expensive.*

Lodging

Métropole. This small hotel is handy for ferry passengers but, like most of the Ville Basse (lower town), no great architectural shakes. While no exciting views are to be had from this rather faceless '50s building, the guest rooms are adequately furnished and individually decorated. There is no restaurant. *51 rue Thiers, 62200, tel. 21–31–54–30. 22 rooms with bath. Facilities: garden. AE, DC, MC, V. Closed Christmas and New Year's. Moderate.*

Dining and Lodging
★

Cléry. Eight kilometers (5 miles) inland from Boulogne, along N1, is the tiny village of Hesdin-l'Abbé, its 18th-century château now transformed into a stylish hotel. Extensive lawns, lined with tulips, rose beds, and an avenue of trees, create a favorable impression, enhanced by the entrance hall, with its old wooden staircase and wrought-iron banisters. As the vast price range (180–420 francs) indicates, each guest room is different; those in the former stables have been particularly well converted. The restaurant's nouvelle menu features dishes that are pretty rather than substantial, like lobster with pink grapefruit butter. It was here at the château that Napoleon decided to abandon plans to invade England. As you bask in the peace and quiet of the beautiful grounds, you'll understand why: He was better off staying put. *62360 Hesdin-l'Abbé, tel. 21–83–19–83. 18 rooms with bath. Facilities: restaurant, tennis. AE, V. Moderate–Expensive.*

Calais
Dining

Sole Meunière. As its name ("sole fried in butter") suggests, the Sole Meunière is a temple of fish and seafood. Not that anything else could be expected from a restaurant next to Calais harbor! The good-value menus start at 60 francs; the dining room's intimate decor is a medley of soft grays and pinks. *1 blvd. de la Résistance, tel. 21–34–43–01. Reservations advised. Dress: casual. AE, DC, MC, V. Closed Mon. and mid-Dec.–mid-Jan. Inexpensive–Moderate.*

Compiègne
Dining
★

Hostellerie du Royal-Lieu. As befits a once-imperial town, Compiègne boasts a regal restaurant. The luxurious dining room overlooks a terrace and the forest in which Napoleon III used to hunt. The menu (180- and 250-franc set choices are available) is far from dominated by game, however; dishes like snails with dill, turbot with tagliatelli, and pork fillet with tarragon will have you singing the praises of their creator, Monsieur Bonechi. *9 rue de Senlis, tel. 44–20–10–24. Reservations essential. Jacket and tie required. AE, DC, MC, V. Expensive.*

Picotin. Three menus for under 100 francs make the old-fashioned Picotin a good choice for lunch or dinner after you've visited the nearby château. The traditional cuisine (salads, steaks, and chocolate desserts) offers few surprises—or disappointments. *22 pl. de l'Hôtel-de-Ville, tel. 44-40-04-06. Reservations strongly advised. Dress: casual. V. Closed Tues. Inexpensive.*

Laon
Dining

La Petite Auberge. Young chef Marc Zorn dishes up modern, imaginative cuisine at this 18th-century-style restaurant close to the train station in Laon's Ville Basse. The 110-franc menu is a good lunchtime bet. *45 blvd. Pierre-Brossolette, tel. 23-23-02-38. Reservations advised. Dress: casual. AE, DC, V. Moderate.*

Dining and Lodging

Bannière de France. In business since 1685, the old-fashioned, uneven-floored Bannière de France is just five minutes' walk from Laon's picturesque cathedral and the medieval Ville Haute (upper town). The proprietors, Monsieur and Madame Lefèvre, both speak English and offer a warm welcome. Guest rooms are cozy and quaintly decorated, and the restaurant's venerable dining room features sturdy cuisine (trout, guinea fowl) and good-value menus (88, 115, and 190 francs). *11 rue Franklin-Roosevelt, 02000, tel. 23-23-21-44. 18 rooms, a few with bath. Facilities: restaurant. AE, DC, MC, V. Closed Christmas and New Years. Moderate.*

Lille
Dining
★

Devinière. Chef Bernard Devinière has created one of Lille's most fashionable eating places: The welcome is warm, the dining room embellished with cheerful flowers, and the produce fresh and changed according to the season. His nouvelle cuisine receives maximum attention, and the restaurant is frequently packed (with only 30 places, it's one of the city's smallest). *61 blvd. Louis-XIV, tel. 20-52-74-64. Reservations essential. Jacket required. AE, V. Closed Sat. lunch, Sun., and most of Aug. Moderate–Expensive.*

Lodging

Bellevue. This central, elegant hotel has many large, comfortable rooms and the sort of deferential service you can no longer take for granted. It's favored by British travelers and has a leather-lined Bar Anglais to prove it. *5 rue Jean-Roisin, 59800, tel. 20-57-45-64. 80 rooms, most with bath. Facilities: bar. AE, V. Moderate.*

Noyon
Lodging

St-Eloi. Handily situated in a turn-of-the-century building between the station and cathedral, St-Eloi was given a new modern annex in 1978 to help accommodate the flood of northern European visitors. Garden views and reassuring Louis XV–style furnishings are other attributes, as is the fine restaurant, none of whose four menus, starting at 60 francs, will strain your wallet. *81 blvd. Carnot, 60400, tel. 44-44-01-49. 30 rooms, 24 with bath. Facilities: restaurant, garden. MC, V. Closed Christmas; restaurant closed Sun. dinner. Moderate.*

Pierrefonds
Lodging

Etrangers. A small restaurant, serving game in season, and an attractive lakeside terrace make this an ideal halting place beneath the mighty castle of Pierrefonds. The three-story hotel was recently modernized, although it still lacks an elevator; American and Japanese visitors are frequent. *10 rue Beaudon, 60350, tel. 44-42-80-18. 13 rooms, 8 with bath. Facilities: restaurant. MC, V. Closed mid-Jan.–mid-Feb.; restaurant closed Sun. dinner and Mon. from Sept. to mid-Jan. Inexpensive.*

Reims
Dining
★

Boyer–Les Crayères. Gérard Boyer is one of the country's most highly rated chefs. Duck, foie gras in pastry, and truffles figure among his specialties and are complemented by an extensive wine list that pays homage to Reims's champagne heritage. The setting, not far from the Basilique St-Rémi, is magnificent, too: a 19th-century château surounded by an extensive, well-tended park. The decor is opulent, typified by ornate chandeliers, towering ceilings, gilt mirrors, intricate cornices, and glossy paneling. There are 16 luxurious suites as well. *64 blvd. Henry-Vasnier, tel. 26–82–80–80. Reservations essential. Jacket and tie required. AE, DC, MC, V. Closed Mon., Tues. lunch, and Christmas–New Years. Very Expensive.*

Florence. This elegant, well-run restaurant occupies an old, high-ceiling mansion where chef Yves Méjean serves wonderfully light versions of the classical French repertoire. Prices are fair, too, with two menus for under 200 francs. *43 blvd. Foch, tel. 26–47–12–70. Reservations advised. Jacket required. AE, DC, MC, V. Closed part of Feb., most of Aug., and Mon. and Sun. dinner from Nov. to Mar. Moderate.*

★ **Le Vigneron.** This friendly little brasserie in a 17th-century mansion is cozy and cheerful, with two tiny dining rooms that display a jumble of champagne-related paraphernalia—from old advertising posters to venerable barrels and tools of the trade. The food is delightful as well: relatively cheap, distinctly hearty, and prepared with finesse. Try the *andouillettes* (chitterling sausages) and be sure to slather on lots of Reims's delicious mustard made with champagne. *Pl. Paul-Jamot, tel. 26–47–00–71. Reservations strongly advised. Dress: casual. AE, DC, V. Closed Sat. lunch, Sun., Christmas–New Year's, and most of Aug. Inexpensive/Moderate.*

Lodging

Hôtel de la Paix. A modern, eight-story hotel, La Paix boasts admirably equipped, stylish rooms, plus a pretty garden, swimming pool, and a rather incongruous chapel. Its brasserie-style restaurant, Drouet, serves good, though not inexpensive, cuisine (mainly grilled meats and seafood). *9 rue Buirette, 51000, tel. 26–40–04–08. 105 rooms with bath. Facilities: pool, restaurant, chapel. DC, V. Restaurant closed Sun. Moderate.*

Gambetta. The Gambetta experience is not what you'd call out of this world, but, then, the prices are reassuringly down to earth. A location close by Reims's venerable cathedral is the hotel's main claim to fame. Guest rooms are small and somewhat featureless but clean and acceptable for the price. *13 rue Gambetta, 51000, tel. 26–47–41–64. 14 rooms with bath. Facilities: restaurant. V. Restaurant closed Sun. dinner and Mon. lunch. Inexpensive.*

St-Omer
Dining

Le Cygne. Duck *(magret de canard)*, not swan, tops the menu at Le Cygne, in the old sector of St-Omer near the cathedral. There are two menus, one three-course (78 francs), the other four (130 francs). Traditional, regional cooking holds sway. *8 rue Caventou, tel. 21–98–20–52. Reservations accepted. Dress: casual. AE, DC, MC, V. Closed Tues., Sat. lunch, and Dec. 10–31. Moderate.*

Dining and Lodging
★

Moulin de Mombreux. Huge cogs and waterwheels, skillfully integrated into the decor of the open-fire reception area, reflect the 18th-century watermill origins of the Moulin de Mombreux, five kilometers (three miles) west of St-Omer at

Lumbres, close to the A26 expressway. Jean-Marc Gaudry has hoisted these old premises into the top league with his tasteful renovation and even tastier cuisine. Try his warm oysters in champagne, seafood (crayfish and crab), or salmon presented in a beautiful black-and-yellow salmon sauce. There are menus at 175, 275, and 345 francs, though their intricacies could do with an English translation. Silver candlesticks and original wooden beams lend the dining room atmosphere; piped music, plaster-covered walls, and slightly faded flowers take it away again. Six guest rooms occupy the second floor, and there are a further 24 in a new annex across the grounds, where the discreet, if unoriginal, charm of the pastel-shaded rooms is outweighed by the spacious breakfast room, with its large windows and wicker chairs. *62380 Lumbres, tel. 21–39–62–44. 30 rooms with bath. Facilities: restaurant, garden. AE, DC, MC, V. Closed Christmas–New Year's. Expensive.*

St-Quentin
Dining and Lodging
★

Grand. After undergoing head-to-toe restoration the **Grand Hôtel** hopes to underline its status as the best hotel in town. Its restaurant, Le Président, already has a reputation as one of the finest in northern France, with elegant decor and superb nouvelle cuisine. That type of quality doesn't come cheap—290 francs for a truly gastronomic menu—but there is also a menu at 170 francs. *6 rue Dachery, 02100, tel. 23–62–69–77. 26 rooms with bath. DC, V. Closed Aug. 7–22. Restaurant closed Sun. dinner, Mon., first half of Feb., and most of Aug. Expensive.*

Le Touquet
Dining

Flavio. Fish and shellfish star at this elegant restaurant near the casino. Chef Guy Delmotte specializes in lobster and charges 480 francs for his lobster menu—for aficionados only, since the 250- and 350-franc menus will please most. Cut glass, chunky silverware, and original carpets add an appropriate note of chic. *2 av. du Verger, tel. 21–05–10–22. Reservations required except weekday lunch. Jacket and tie required. AE, DC, MC, V. Closed Jan.–Feb., and Wed. during Sept.–June. Very Expensive.*

Dining and Lodging
★

Westminster. The Westminster's mammoth red-brick facade looks as if it were built just a few years ago; in fact, it dates from the 1930s, and like the rest of the hotel has been extensively restored by its new owners, the personable Flament brothers. The hotel offers a modestly priced coffee bar (serving lunch and dinner), a swanky dining room (classic but well-prepared French cuisine), and an "American bar" that serves cocktails for under 50 francs. Try the Westminster Special, a lethal concoction of vodka, blue curaçao, Grand Marnier, and orange juice. The enormous double rooms start at 600 francs—good value—and there is even a bridal suite (1,100 francs) that is the last word in thick-carpeted extravagance. *Av. du Verger, 62520, tel. 21–05–48–48. 115 rooms with bath. Facilities: squash court, indoor pool, Jacuzzi, sauna, solarium, restaurants, bar. AE, DC, MC, V. Very Expensive.*

The Arts and Nightlife

The Arts

Lille is unquestionably the hub of cultural activity in northern France, a lively museum and concert center where exotic happenings can occur at any time—like a recital of traditional music by Tibetan monks, for example. There are various local carnivals, notably the **Dunkerque Carnaval** in February/March, the **Roses Festival** in Arras in May, and the **Kermesse de la Bêtise** festival in Cambrai in early September.

Theater You are unlikely to encounter English-language productions in northern France. Lille's principal theater house is the **Opéra** *(see* below), while the **Théâtre d'Animation Picard** in Amiens (51 rue de Prague, tel. 22–46–29–09) partly overcomes the language barrier with its use of puppets.

Concerts The **Orchestre National de Lille** is a well-respected symphony orchestra (3 pl. Mendès-France, tel. 20–54–67–00).

Opera Lille boasts one of France's few regional opera houses, the **Opéra du Nord** (Pl. du Théâtre, tel. 20–55–48–61).

Nightlife

Bars and Nightclubs We suggest **Chez Marc** (rte. d'Abbeville) or **L'Orange Bleue** (rue du Marché-Lanselles) in Amiens and **Joséphine's Club** (1 pl. des Reignaux) or **Le Majestic** (11 rue des Arts) in Lille.

Cabaret In Amiens, **Le Pétit Paris** combines a cabaret and restaurant (5 blvd. de Beauville), while **Le Boeuf sur le Toit** (rte. d'Abbeville) spices up its act with striptease on Thursday. In Lille, try **Les Dessous de Louise** (pl. Louise-de-Bettignies).

Casinos Gamblers should head for the casinos at **Berck-Plage** (tel. 21–84–09–39), **Boulogne** (tel. 21–83–88–00), **Calais** (tel. 21–96–44–87), **Dunkerque** (tel. 28–59–18–23), and **Le Touquet** (tel. 21–05–16–99).

Discos Good bets include **Penelope** (25 rue de l'Hôpital) in Epernay and **Le Brigith' Bar** (7 blvd. du Général-Leclerc) in Reims.

9 Burgundy

Introduction

For a region whose powerful medieval dukes held sway over large tracts of western Europe and whose glamorous image is closely allied to its expensive wine, Burgundy (Bourgogne in French)—which is just southeast of Paris—can seem a surprisingly rustic backwater, where "life in the fast lane" refers strictly to the Paris-bound A6 expressway.

There's no need to hit the fast lane on either of our two Burgundy tours. The first stretches from Sens in the north to Autun in the south and the River Loire in the west; at the heart of this region is the dark, brooding Morvan Forest. From Sens, we have included a detour to Troyes in the adjacent Champagne region.

In the Middle Ages, Sens, Auxerre, and Troyes came under the sway of the Paris-based Capetian kings, who promptly built mighty Gothic cathedrals in those towns. Burgundy's leading religious monument, however, is the older, Romanesque basilica at Vézelay, once one of Christianity's most important centers of pilgrimage, today a tiny village hidden in the folds of rolling, verdant hills.

Chablis is renowned for its excellent bone-dry white wine, although better values for the money can be had at St-Bris-le-Vineux and Irancy, south of Auxerre. The great wine lands of Burgundy, however, lie farther east and form the backdrop of our second tour. This tour begins at Dijon, the province's only city, which retains something of the opulence it acquired under the rich, powerful dukes of Burgundy who ruled in the late Middle Ages.

Dijon's latterday reputation is essentially gastronomic. Burgundians like to eat well, and outstanding restaurants abound. Game, freshwater trout, ham, goat cheese, *coq au vin*, and mushrooms number among the region's specialties. Local industries at Dijon involve the production of mustard, cassis (blackcurrant liqueur), snails, and—of course—wine.

The famous vineyards south of Dijon—the Côte de Nuits and Côte de Beaune—are among the world's most distinguished and picturesque. Don't expect to unearth many bargains here, but a good place for sampling is the Marché aux Vins in Beaune, a charming old town clustered around the patterned-tile roofs of its medieval Hôtel-Dieu (hospital). Less expensive Burgundies can be found in between Chalon and Mâcon as you head south along the Saône Valley toward the ruined Abbey of Cluny—once a religious center equal in importance to Vézelay.

Essential Information

Important Addresses and Numbers

Tourist Information The principal regional tourist offices are found at **Dijon** (pl. Darcy, close to the cathedral; tel. 80–43–42–12), **Auxerre** (1 quai de la République, tel. 86–52–06–19); and **Mâcon** (1 rue de Lyon, tel. 85–39–43–51).

The addresses of other tourist offices in towns mentioned on this tour are as follows: **Autun** (3 av. Charles-de-Gaulle, tel. 85–

52–20–34), **Avallon** (6 rue Bocquillot, tel. 86–34–14–19), **Beaune** (rue de l'Hôtel-Dieu, tel. 80–22–24–51), **Clamecy** (rue du Grand-Marché, tel. 86–27–02–51), **Cluny** (6 rue Mercière, tel. 85–59–05–34), **Sens** (pl. Jean-Jaurès, tel. 86–65–19–49), **Troyes** (16 blvd. Carnot, tel. 25–73–00–36), and **Vézelay** (rue St-Pierre, tel. 86–33–23–69).

Travel Agencies   **Air France** (pl. Darcy, Dijon; tel. 80–30–66–28), **Thomas Cook** (entre Dauphine, rue Bossuet, Dijon; tel. 80–30–20–20), and **Wagons Lits** (8 av. du Maréchal-Foch, Dijon; tel. 80–45–26–26).

Car Rental   **Avis** (5 av. Foch, Dijon; tel. 80–43–60–76), **Hertz** (18 bis av. Foch, Dijon; tel. 80–43–55–22), and **Europcar** (47 rue Guillaume Tell, Dijon; tel. 80–43–28–44).

Arriving and Departing

By Plane   Dijon has Burgundy's only commercial passenger airport (tel. 80–67–67–67), which operates domestic flights between Paris and Lyon.

By Car   The A6 expressway heads southeast from Paris through Burgundy, passing Auxerre, Avallon, Beaune, and Mâcon.

By Train   The TGV has put Dijon, 290 kilometers (180 miles) away, at just 1½ hours from Paris. There are frequent trains; some continue down to Lyon, though the fastest Paris–Lyon trains do not stop at Dijon or go anywhere near it. There is also a cross-country service linking Dijon to Reims (320 kilometers/200 miles in 3½ hours). Sens is on a mainline route from Paris.

Getting Around

By Train   Train travel is unrewarding, especially since the infrequent cross-country trains chug along at the speed of a legendary Burgundian snail. You'll have to change trains at La Roche-Migenne for Avallon, Auxerre, Clamecy, and Autun, and at Dijon for Beaune.

By Car   Burgundy is best visited by car because its meandering country roads invite leisurely exploration. A38 provides a quick link between Dijon and A6, while A31 heads down from Dijon to Beaune (45 kilometers/27 miles).

Guided Tours

For further information on tours in Burgundy, write to the regional tourist office, **Comité Régional du Tourisme** (4 rue Nicolas-Berthot, 21000 Dijon).

Orientation   **Central Taxi-Radio** of Dijon (tel. 80–41–41–12) offers day-long tours of the city and surrounding area for around 1,000 francs; a minimum of four people is required. Day-long and minibus excursions (with pickups at main train stations) are run by **Sociéte Services 2000** (Ampilly-le-Sec, 21400 Châtillon-sur-Seine, tel. 80–91–36–26).

Special-Interest   Gastronomic weekends, including wine tastings, are organized by **Bourgogne Tour** (11 rue de la Liberté, 21000 Dijon, tel. 80–30–60–40).

Aerial   You can fly over the vineyards between Dijon and Beaune (30 minutes for 150 francs, 120 francs for children under 10) with the **Aéroclub de la Côte d'Or** (tel. 80–35–61–09). In summer months, the **Sociéte Bombard** (Château de Laborde, Meursanges, 21200 Beaune, tel. 80–26–63–30) offers hot-air balloon rides over the surrounding countryside; cost: 600 francs for an hour-long flight, including champagne.

Exploring Burgundy

Numbers in the margin correspond with points of interest on the Burgundy map.

Orientation

Our first tour covers northern Burgundy, stretching from Sens in the north to Autun in the south and the River Loire in the west, with a rewarding detour to the interesting town of Troyes. Our second tour of Burgundy's wine country begins at Dijon before heading south to Mâcon through some of the world's most distinguished and picturesque vineyards.

Highlights for First-time Visitors

Beaune (and a wine-tasting session at the Marché aux Vins), Tour 2

Cathédrale St-Etienne, Sens, Tour 1

Fontenay Abbey, Tour 1

A meal at L'Espérance, Vézelay, Tour 2

Musée d'Art Moderne (Modern Art Museum), Troyes, Tour 1

Palais des Ducs (Ducal Palace), Dijon, Tour 2

Ruins of Cluny Abbey, Tour 2

Troyes, Tour 2

Vézelay (village and basilica), Tour 1

Tour 1: Northern and Western Burgundy

① It makes sense for **Sens** to be your first stop on the way down to Burgundy, since it lies just 112 kilometers (70 miles) from Paris on N6, a fast road that hugs the pretty Yonne Valley south of Fontainebleau.

Sens was for centuries the ecclesiastical center of France and is still dominated by the **Cathédrale St-Etienne,** begun around 1140. You can see the cathedral's 240-foot south tower from far off; the main Paris–Auxerre road forges straight past it. The pompous 19th-century buildings that line this road can give a false impression to visitors in a hurry: The streets leading off it near the cathedral (notably rue Abelard and rue Jean-Cousin) are full of half-timbered medieval houses, and within their midst sits the 13th-century church of **St-Pierre-le-Rond** with its unusual wooden roof and 16th-century stained glass.

The cathedral's sturdy facade used to have two towers; one was destroyed in the 19th century, the other was topped in 1532 by an elegant, though somewhat incongruous, Renaissance campanile, and contains two monster bells. The statue gallery, starring former archbishops of Sens, is a 19th-century addition, but the statue of St. Stephen, between the twin doors of

Burgundy

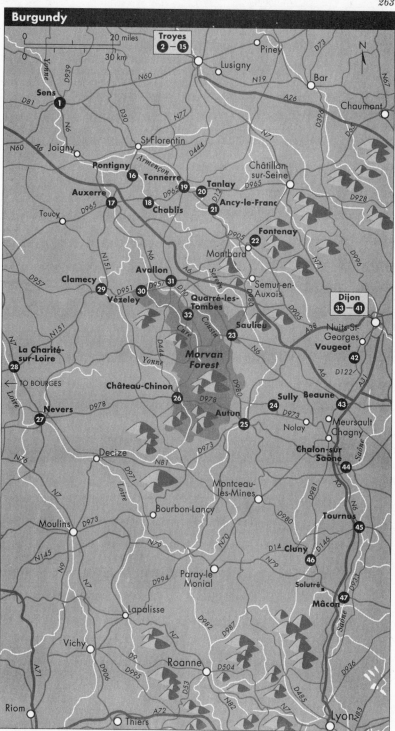

0 — 20 miles
0 — 30 km

Troyes 2 — 15

Piney

Lusigny

Bar

Chaumont

Sens 1

Joigny

St-Florentin

Pontigny 16 **Tonnerre**

Tanlay

Châtillon-sur-Seine

Auxerre 17

18 **Chablis** 19 20

21 **Ancy-le-Franc**

Toucy

Fontenay 22

Montbard

Avallon

Clamecy 29 30 31

Vézelay

Quarré-les-Tombes

Semur-en-Auxois

Dijon 33 — 41

Nuits-St-Georges

32

Saulieu 23

Vougeot 42

La Charité-sur-Loire 28

← TO BOURGES

Morvan Forest

Château-Chinon 26

Sully 24

Beaune

43

Nevers 27

Autun 25

Nolay

Meursault
Chagny

Decize

Chalon-sur-Saône 44

Moulins

Montceau-les-Mines

Tournus 45

Bourbon-Lancy

Cluny 46

Paray-le-Monial

Solutré

Mâcon 47

Lapalisse

Vichy

Roanne

Riom

Thiers

Lyon

the central portal, is thought to date from the late 12th century.

The vast, harmonious interior is justly renowned for its stained-glass windows. The oldest (circa 1200) are in the north choir; those in the south transept were manufactured in 1500 at nearby Troyes and include a much-admired *Tree of Jesse*. The cathedral treasury (access near the sacristy to the south of the choir) is one of the richest in France. It contains a collection of miters, ivories, and gold plate, together with the richly woven gold-and-silver robes of the archbishops of Sens. Robes belonging to Thomas Becket are here as well. Becket fled to Sens from England to escape the wrath of Henry II before returning to his cathedral in Canterbury where, in 1170, he was murdered. Stained-glass windows in the north of the chancel retrace his story. *Pl. de la République.*

The 13th-century **Palais Synodal,** alongside the cathedral, provides a first encounter with Burgundy's multicolored tiled roofs: From its courtyard, there is a fine view of the cathedral's Flamboyant Gothic south transept, constructed by master stonemason Martin Chambiges at the start of the 16th century. (Rose windows were his specialty, as you can admire here.) The Palais Synodal houses a museum with statues, mosaics, and tapestries, but its six grand windows and the vaulted Synodal Hall are outstanding features. *Admission: 12 frs. Open Apr.–Nov. 10–noon and 2–5; closed Wed. Apr.–May and Oct.–Nov.*

② The inhabitants of **Troyes** would be seriously insulted if you mistook them for Burgundians. This old town, 64 kilometers (40 miles) from Sens along N60, is the capital of southern Champagne; as if to prove the point, its historic town center is shaped like a champagne cork. Visitors will be struck by the town's phenomenal number of old buildings, magnificent churches, and fine museums: Few, if any, French town centers contain so much to see and do. A wide choice of restaurants and a web of enchanting pedestrian streets with timber-framed houses add even more to Troyes's appeal.

The center of Troyes is divided in two by quai Dampierre, a broad, busy boulevard. A good place to begin exploring is **place de la Libération,** where quai Dampierre meets the rectangular artificial lake known as the Bassin de la Préfecture. Although Troyes stands on the Seine, it is the capital of the département named after the River Aube, administered from the elegant **③ Préfecture** that gazes across both the lake and place de la Libération from behind its gleaming gilt-iron railings.

But the most charming view from place de la Libération is undoubtedly that of the cathedral, whose 200-foot tower peeps through the trees above the statue and old lamps of the square's **④** central flower garden. The **Cathédrale St-Pierre St-Paul** is just a five-minute walk, in a tumbledown square that, like the narrow surrounding streets, has not changed for centuries.

Perhaps the first thing to strike you about the cathedral will be its resemblance to that of Sens. You'll see this in the incomplete one-towered facade; the small Renaissance campaniles on top of the tower; and the artistry of Martin Chambiges, who worked on Troyes's facade (note the large rose window) around the same time as he did the transept of Sens. Try to see the facade at night, when its floodlit features are thrown into dramatic relief.

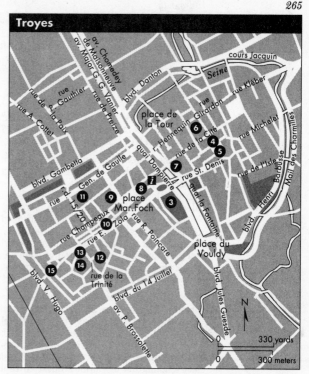

The cathedral's vast five-aisled interior, refreshingly light thanks to large windows and the near-whiteness of the local stone, dates mainly from the 13th century. Like Sens, it has renowned stained glass—fine examples of primitive 13th-century glass in the choir and richly colored 16th-century glass in the nave and facade rose window. Note the arcaded triforium above the pillars of the choir: It was one of the first in France to be glazed rather than filled with stone. *Pl. St-Pierre. Open daily 10–noon and 2–6. Son-et-lumière (sound-and-light) shows are held in the cathedral on Tues., Fri., and Sat. at 10:30 PM, late June–mid-Sept. Admission: 30 frs. adults, 15 frs. children under 16.*

5 To the right of the cathedral is the **Musée d'Art Moderne** (Modern Art Museum), housed in the 16th–17th-century former Bishop's Palace. Its magnificent interior, with huge fireplaces, carved wood-beamed roofs, and Renaissance staircase, plays host to the Levy Collection of modern art, featuring drawings, sculpture, and nearly 400 paintings. The assembly of Fauve works—a short-lived style that succeeded Impressionism at the start of the 20th century—is exceptional, notably the frenzied, hotly colored canvases by Maurice Vlaminck, Georges Braque, and André Derain. *Pl. St-Pierre. Joint ticket covering all town museums: 10 frs. Open Wed.–Mon. 10–5; closed Tues.*

6 On the other side of the cathedral square are the former abbey buildings of the **Musée St-Loup,** containing two museums. The ground-floor display is devoted to natural history, with impressive collections of birds and meteorites; the Musée des Beaux-Arts et Archéologie (Fine Arts and Archaeology Museum) is confusingly spread over two floors. In the former abbey cellars are local archaeological finds, especially gold-mounted 5th-century jewelry and a Gallo-Roman bronze statue of Apollo. There is also a section devoted to medieval statuary and gargoyles. Paintings from the 15th to the 19th century are exhibited on the second floor and include works by Rubens, Anthony Van Dyck, Antoine Watteau, François Boucher, and Jacques-Louis David. *21 rue Chrétien de Troyes. Joint ticket: 10 frs. Open Wed.–Mon. 10–noon and 2–6; closed Tues.*

From the Musée St-Loup, the rue de la Cité, packed with restaurants, leads back to quai Dampierre, passing in front of the **7** superb wrought-iron gates of the 18th-century **Hôtel-Dieu** (hospital), topped with the blue-and-gold *fleurs-de-lys* emblems of the French monarchy. Around the corner is the entrance to the **Pharmacie,** the only part of the Hôtel-Dieu open to visitors. Take time to inspect the former medical laboratory, with its quaint assortment of pewter dishes and jugs, earthenware jars, and painted wooden boxes designed to contain herbs and medicines. *Quai Dampierre. Joint ticket: 10 frs. Open Wed.–Mon. 10–noon and 2–6; closed Tues.*

The cathedral sector north of quai Dampierre seems quiet and drowsy compared to the more upbeat, commercial southern part of Troyes. Cross over from the Hôtel-Dieu and continue **8** down rue Clemenceau to the **Basilique St-Urbain,** built between 1262 and 1286 by Pope Urban IV, who was born in Troyes. St-Urbain is one of the most remarkable churches in France, a perfect culmination of Gothic's quest to replace stone walls by stained glass. Huge windows, containing much of their original glass, ring the church, while the exterior bristles with the thrust-bearing flying buttresses that made this daring structure possible.

Follow rue Urbain-IV down to **place du Maréchal-Foch,** the main square of central Troyes, flanked by cafés, shops, and the **9** delightful early 17th-century facade of the **Hôtel de Ville** (Town Hall). In summer, the square throbs from morning to night as residents and tourists swarm in to drink coffee or eat pancakes in the various cheap restaurants that spill into the rue Champeaux, Troyes's liveliest pedestrian street. Rue **10** Champeaux runs parallel to **St-Jean,** a lengthy church where England's warrior king, Henry V, married Catherine of France in 1420. The church's tall 16th-century choir contrasts with the low earlier nave; the clock tower is an unmistakable landmark of downtown Troyes.

A little farther along rue Champeaux, the **ruelle des Chats** wanders off toward the church of Ste-Madeleine. The *ruelle*, or alley, is the town's narrowest thoroughfare: Its overhanging dwellings practically bump attics. Halfway down is the tastefully restored cour du Mortier d'Or, a tiny medieval courtyard.

Time Out A good place to settle into the medieval ambience of Troyes is the friendly, unpretentious **Bouchon Champenois.** This restaurant serves both light lunches and plentiful evening meals (a four-course menu at 90 francs) in a wood-beamed dining room whose large mirrors reflect the striped timbered patterns of the cour du Mortier d'Or. *Closed Mon.*

⑪ The church of **Ste-Madeleine,** the oldest in Troyes, is best known for its elaborate triple-arched stone rood screen separating the nave and the choir. Only six other such screens still remain in France—most were dismantled during the French Revolution—and this one was carved with panache by Jean Gailde between 1508 and 1517. The church's west tower and main door also date from the early 16th century. *Rue du Général-de-Gaulle.*

Take rue des Quinze-Vingts, which runs parallel to the ruelle des Chats, as far as rue Émile-Zola. Turn right, then second ⑫ left, into rue de la Trinité. The museum known as **Maison de l'Outil** stands at no. 7 in the 16th-century Hôtel de Mauroy. Upstairs is a collection of pictures, models, and tools relevant to such traditional wood-related trades as carpentry, clog making, and barrel making. *7 rue de la Trinité. Joint ticket: 10 frs. Open daily 10–noon and 2–6.*

Close to the Maison de l'Outil, via rue Bordet, is another 16th-⑬ century building: the church of **St-Pantaléon.** A number of fine stone statues, surmounted by canopies, cluster around its pillars. The tall, narrow walls are topped not by stone vaults but by a wooden roof, unusual for such a late church. Just as unexpected are the red-and-white streamers and *Solidarnosc* (Solidarity) banners sometimes found next to the altar: St-Pantaléon is used for services by the Polish community. *Rue de Turenne. Open 10–noon and 2–6 in summer months only; at other times apply to the tourist office.*

The Renaissance Hôtel de Vauluisant, opposite, houses two ⑭ museums. The **Musée Historique** (History Museum) traces the development of Troyes and southern Champagne, with a section devoted to religious art. The **Musée de la Bonneterie** (Textile Museum) outlines the history and manufacturing process of the town's traditional bonnet making industry; some of the bonnets on display are over 200 years old. *Rue de Turenne. Joint ticket: 10 frs. Open daily 10–noon and 2–6.*

Close by, beyond place Jean-Jaurès, is yet another church: that ⑮ of **St-Nicolas.** You may not be tempted by its grimy exterior, but undaunted souls will be rewarded by the chance to scale a wide stone staircase up to an exuberantly decorated chapel and an unexpected view over the nave. Notice the funny little spiral staircase on the left of the nave that appears to vanish into mid-wall.

Leaving Troyes—by far the largest town in this tour—you will soon be plunged back into rural tranquility as you drive southwest along the Auxerre-bound N77. Don't let your sense of ⑯ well-being fog your curiosity, however. **Pontigny,** just 21 kilometers (13 miles) short of Auxerre, can be easily mistaken for another drowsy, dusty village, but its once-proud **abbey** is as large as many cathedrals; in the 12th and 13th centuries, it sheltered three archbishops of Canterbury, including St. Thomas Becket.

The abbey was founded in 1114, but the current church was begun in 1150. The monks belonged to the Cistercian order, which, frowning on the opulence of the rival House of Cluny, fostered buildings of intense sobriety. Small, even-spaced windows render the abbey's silhouette monotonous: The single tower, that of the facade, scrambles almost apologetically to

roof level. The austere, 330-foot interior is divided in two by a
wooden screen. The only ornament is provided by the late-
17th-century wooden choir stalls, carved with garlands and angels.

❼ Auxerre is a small, peaceful town dominated by its **Cathédrale
St-Etienne,** perched on a steep hill overlooking the River
Yonne. The 13th-century choir, the oldest part of the edifice,
contains its original stained glass, dominated by dazzling reds
and blues. Beneath the choir is the frescoed 11th-century Romanesque crypt; alongside is the Treasury, featuring medieval enamels, manuscripts, and miniatures. *Pl. St-Etienne.
Admission to crypt and treasury: 5 frs. each. Open daily 10–
noon and 2–5.*

Fanning out from Auxerre's main square, place des Cordeliers
(just up from the cathedral), are a number of venerable streets
lined by 16th-century houses. Explore these before heading
north toward the town's most interesting church, the former
abbey of **St-Germain,** which stands parallel to the cathedral some 300 yards away. The church's earliest section
above ground is the 11th-century Romanesque bell tower, but
the extensive underground crypt dates back to the 9th century and preserves its original frescoes, some of the oldest in
France. *Pl. St-Germain. Admission: 10 frs. (free Wed.). Guided tours of the crypt, Wed.–Mon. 10–noon and 2–5; closed
Tues.*

❽ Chablis, famous for its white wine, lies just 16 kilometers (10
miles) east of Auxerre along N65 and D965. A pretty village, it
nestles on the banks of the River Serein ("serene") and is protected by the massive, round, turreted towers of the Porte Noël
gateway. Much less welcoming are the inflated prices charged
for local wines by the plentiful village tourist shops! You can
ferret out a better deal at a local producer, and at the same time
scour the surrounding vineyards for dramatic views, as their
towering slopes contrast with the region's characteristic rolling hills.

❾ Continue along D965 from Chablis to the village of **Tonnerre,** 16
kilometers (10 miles) away. The Armançon Valley and 16th-
century houses can be surveyed from the terrace of the church
of St-Pierre, rebuilt, like most of the town, after a devastating
fire in 1556. Tonnerre's chief attraction, the high-roofed **Ancien
Hôpital,** was built in 1293 and has survived the passing
centuries—flames and all—largely intact. The main room, the
Grande Salle, is 250 feet long and retains its oak ceiling; it was
conceived as the hospital ward and later (after 1650) served as
the parish church. The original hospital church leads off from
the Grande Salle; in the adjoining Chapelle du Revestière is a
dramatic 15th-century stone group representing the *Burial of
Christ. Rue du Part. Admission: 10 frs. Open Wed.–Mon. 10–
noon and 2–5; closed Tues.*

Ten kilometers (6 miles) east of Tonnerre lies the château of
❿ Tanlay, built around 1550 and betraying the classical influence
of the Renaissance. The vestibule, framed by wrought-iron
railings, leads to a wood-paneled salon and dining room filled
with period furniture. A graceful staircase leads to the second
floor; notice the frescoed gallery and ornate fireplaces. A small
room in the tower above was used as a secret meeting place by
Huguenot Protestants during the 1562–98 Wars of Religion; its

cupola boasts a fresco of scantily clad 16th-century religious personalities. *Admission: 24 frs. Open Apr.–Nov. 11, Wed.–Mon. 10–noon and 2–5; closed Tues.*

Continue along D965 to Pimelles, then turn right onto D12. Eleven kilometers (seven miles) south is another, slightly earlier château, **Ancy-le-Franc.** The Renaissance styling here has an Italian flavor: The château was built to the designs of Sebastiano Serlio with interior decor by Primaticcio, both of whom worked at the court of French king François I (1515–47). The plain, majestic exterior contrasts with the sumptuous rooms and apartments, many—particularly the magnificent Chambre des Arts—with carved or painted walls and ceilings and their original furniture. Such grandeur won the approval of Sun King Louis XIV, no less, who once stayed in the Salon Bleu. Adjoining the château is a small Musée Automobile featuring vintage cars. *Admission: 24 frs. Open Apr.–Nov. 11, daily 10–noon and 2–5.*

Twenty-nine kilometers (18 miles) southeast along D905 (take D32 at Marmagne, just past Montbard) is the Cistercian abbey of **Fontenay,** founded by St-Bernard in 1118. The same Cistercian criteria applied to Fontenay as to Pontigny: no-frills architecture and an isolated site. By the end of the 12th century, the church and other buildings comprising the monastery were finished. The abbey's community grew to some 300 monks and prospered until the 16th century, when religious wars and administrative mayhem hastened its decline. The abbey was dissolved during the French Revolution and used as a paper factory until 1906. Fortunately the historic buildings emerged unscathed from their industrial use, and, with the help of original plans, Fontenay has since been restored to its former glory.

The abbey is surrounded by extensive gardens dotted with the fountains that gave it its name. The church and cloister are the most important buildings to survive. The church's solemn interior is lit by windows in the facade and a double row of three narrow windows, representing the Trinity, in the choir. A staircase in the south transept leads to the wood-roofed dormitory (spare a thought for the bleary-eyed monks who were frequently obliged to stagger down for services in the dead of night). The chapter house, flanked by a majestic arcade, and the scriptorium, where monks worked on their manuscripts, lead off from the adjoining cloisters. *Admission: 30 frs. Guided visits daily 10–11:30 and 2–4.*

Head back to Montbard and take D980 south to **Saulieu,** 48 kilometers (30 miles) away. The reputation of Saulieu belies its size: It is renowned for good food (Rabelais, that roly-poly 16th-century man of letters, extolled its Gargantuan hospitality) and Christmas trees (a million are packed off from the area each year). The basilica of **St-Andoche** is almost as old as that of Vézelay, though less imposing and much restored. The adjoining **town museum** contains a room devoted to François Pompon, an animal-bronze sculptor whose smooth, stylized creations seem contemporary but pre-date World War II. *Rue Sallier. Admission: 5 frs. Open Wed.–Mon., 10–noon and 2–5; closed Tues.*

On your way south through the brooding Morvan Forest toward Autun, detour to the Renaissance château of **Sully.** Take N6 to Arnay-le-Duc, then D36, turning right for Sully after the village of Vellerot. The turreted château stands in a stately park and is surrounded by a moat, while a monumental staircase leads to the north front and a broad terrace. Marshal MacMahon, president of France from 1873 to 1879, was born here in 1808. *Admission: 5 frs. Visits to the grounds only, Apr.–Nov., daily, 10–noon and 2–5.*

② **Autun**—an important town since Roman times, as you can detect at the well-preserved archways, Porte St-André and Porte d'Arroux, and at the Théâtre Romain, once the largest arena in Gaul. Julius Caesar even referred to Autun as the "sister and rival of Rome itself." Another famous warrior, Napoleon, studied here in 1779 at the military academy (now the Lycée Bonaparte).

D326 links Sully to D973 and, nine kilometers (six miles) later,

Autun's principal monument, however, is its **cathedral,** built from 1120 to 1146 to house the relics of St-Lazarus; the main tower, spire, and upper reaches of the chancel were added in the late 15th century. The influx of medieval pilgrims accounts for the building's size (35 yards wide and nearly 80 yards long). Lazarus's tomb was dismantled in 1766 by canons who were believers in the rationalist credo of the Enlightenment (the period in the 18th century when rational thought took over from superstition). These clergy did their best to transform the Romanesque-Gothic cathedral into a Classical temple at the same time, adding pilasters and classical ornament willy-nilly. Fortunately, some of the best medieval stonework, including the nave capitals and the tympanum above the main door—a *Last Judgment* sculpted by Gislebertus in the 1130s—emerged unscathed. Jean Auguste Ingres's painting depicting the *Martyrdom of St-Symphorien* has been relegated to a dingy chapel in the north aisle of the nave. *Pl. St-Louis.*

Across from the cathedral, the **Musée Rolin** boasts several fine paintings from the Middle Ages and good examples of Burgundian sculpture, including another Gislebertus masterpiece, the *Temptation of Eve,* which originally topped one of the side doors of the cathedral. *Pl. St-Louis. Admission: 7 frs. Open Wed.–Sat., Mon. 10–noon and 2–5, Sun. 10–noon; closed Tues.*

② Our next port of call, **Château-Chinon,** lies 37 kilometers (23 miles) west of Autun along D978. This small town has been in the news during recent years thanks to its former mayor, François Mitterrand, now the French president. One of Mitterrand's legacies is the brash, colorful, and controversial fountain by Niki de St-Phalle, which is in front of the town hall (Mitterrand is responsible, too, for the just-as-controversial glass pyramid standing in the courtyard of Paris's Louvre).

Château-Chinon is capital of the Morvan, and a fine view of the town and forest can be had from the Panorama du Calvaire near square d'Aligre. Costumes and traditions of the Morvan are the subject of the **Musée du Folklore.** *Rue St-Cristophe. Admission: 12 frs. Open Easter–Nov., Wed. and weekends only, 10–noon and 2–5.*

② From Château-Chinon you can either cut north across the Morvan Forest to Clamecy or continue to **Nevers,** 64 kilometers (40 miles) away—Burgundy's western outpost on the banks of the Loire. Nevers is renowned for its ceramics; earthenware has been produced here since the late 16th century, promoted initially by Italian craftsmen. The French Revolution prompted a slowdown in activity, but three traditional manufacturers still remain. An extensive selection of Nevers earthenware, retracing its stylistic development, can be admired at the **Musée Municipal.** *Rue St-Genest. Admission: 2 frs. Open Wed.–Mon. 10–noon and 2–5; closed Tues.*

Part of the medieval walls extend behind the museum, culminating in the intimidating gateway known as the **Porte du Croux** (built 1393), which, thanks to its turrets and huge sloping roof, resembles a small castle. The nearby **Cathédrale St-Cyr-Ste-Juliette,** with its 160-foot square tower, is another sizable building, constructed over several periods of the Middle Ages.

Beyond the cathedral, the **Palais Ducal** has a sumptuous, large-windowed Renaissance facade; unfortunately, its interior is closed to the public. A few hundred yards north, across a park that can be entered from place Carnot, is **St-Gildard's convent,** where Ste-Bernadette of Lourdes (1844–1879) spent the last 13 years of her life. A small museum contains mementoes and outlines her life story (Bernadette claimed to have seen the Virgin several times in 1858 and was canonized in 1933). *Admission: free. Open daily 10–5.*

❷❽ Unlike those of Pontigny and Fontenay, the abbey church of **La Charité-sur-Loire,** 24 kilometers (15 miles) downstream from Nevers, was dependent on Cluny; it was also the country's second-largest church after Cluny when consecrated by Pope Pascal II in 1107. Fire and neglect have taken their toll on the original massive edifice, and these days the church is cut in two, with the single-towered facade separated from the imposing choir and transept by the pretty place Ste-Croix (which occupies the former site of the nave). A fine view of the church exterior can be had from square des Bénédictins, just off the main street (Grande-Rue).

❷❾ From La Charité, head northeast to **Clamecy,** 51 kilometers (32 miles) away. Slow-moving Clamecy is not on many tourist itineraries, but its tumbling alleyways and untouched, ancient houses epitomize *La France Profonde.* Clamecy's multishaped roofs, dominated by the majestic square tower of St-Martin's collegiate church, are best viewed from the banks of the Yonne. The river played a crucial role in Clamecy's development; trees from the nearby Morvan Forest were chopped down and floated in huge convoys to Paris. The history of this curious form of transport *(flottage),* which lasted until 1923, is detailed in the **town museum.** *Rue Bourgeoise. Admission: 4 frs. Open Easter –Oct., 10–noon and 2–5; closed Tues.*

Time Out In homage to the logs that used to be floated downriver from Clamecy to Paris, a log-shaped, sugared-almond candy has long been chewed by Clamecycois, as the local inhabitants are known. You can find your *bûchettes* at the **Avignon** pastry shop (which doubles as a tea room), close to the steps leading up to the church square. *Rue de la Monnaie.*

❸⓿ The picturesque old town of **Vézelay** lies 24 kilometers (15 miles) east of Clamecy along D951. In the 11th and 12th centuries, its celebrated **basilica,** perched at the top of a rocky crag, was one of the focal points of Christendom. Pilgrims poured in to gasp at the relics of St. Mary Magdalene before setting off on the great medieval trek to the shrine of St. James at Santiago de Compostela in northwest Spain.

But decadence lurked. By the mid-13th century, the authenticity of St. Mary's relics was in doubt; others had been discovered in Provence. The decline continued until the French Revolution in the late 18th century, when the basilica and adjoining monastery buildings were sold by the state. Only the basilica escaped demolition and was itself falling into ruin when ace restorer Viollet-le-Duc rode to the rescue in 1840 (he also restored the cathedrals of Laon and Amiens and Paris's Notre-Dame).

Today, the basilica at Vézelay has recaptured its one-time glory and is considered France's most prestigious Romanesque showcase. Nowhere is this more evident than in the nave, whose carved column capitals are imaginatively designed and superbly executed, representing miniature medieval men in all manner of situations—working in the fields, wielding battle swords, or undergoing the tortures of hell.

The basilica exterior is best seen from the leafy terrace to the right of the facade. Opposite is a vast, verdant panorama encompassing lush valleys and rolling hills. In the forefront is the Flamboyant Gothic spire of St-Père-sous-Vézelay, a tiny village a couple miles away, with an excellent restaurant (*see* Dining).

31 Another 13 kilometers (8 miles) east via D957 lies **Avallon,** spectacularly situated on a promontory jutting over the Cousin Valley. The town's old streets and ramparts are pleasant places to stroll, before or after viewing the work of medieval stone carvers whose imaginations ran riot on the portals of the venerable church of St-Lazarus.

The A6 expressway passes close to Avallon and can whisk you north to Paris or south to Dijon and the famous Burgundy vineyards that are part of our second tour. If you have time, however, we suggest you make an excursion from Avallon to the northern part of the **Morvan Regional Park,** whose photogenic lakes, hills, and forest may be viewed around every twisty corner. **32** Take D10 to **Quarré-les-Tombes,** so called because of the empty prehistoric stone tombs discovered locally and eerily arrayed in a ring around the church. The **Rocher de la Pérouse,** 8 kilometers (5 miles) south of Quarré-les-Tombes, is a mighty outcrop worth scrambling up for a view of the Morvan and the Cure Valley.

Tour 2: Wine Country

33 **Dijon,** linked to Paris 314 kilometers (195 miles) away by expressway (A6/A38) and TGV train, is the age-old capital of Burgundy. Throughout the Middle Ages, Burgundy was a duchy that led a separate existence from the rest of France, culminating in the rule of the four "Grand Dukes of the West" between 1364 and 1477. A number of monuments date from this period, such as the Palais des Ducs (Ducal Palace), now largely converted into an art museum.

Dijon's fame and fortune outlasted its dukes, and the city continued to flourish under French rule from the 17th century on. It has remained the major city of Burgundy—the only one, in fact, with over 100,000 inhabitants. Its site, on the major European north-south trade route and within striking distance of

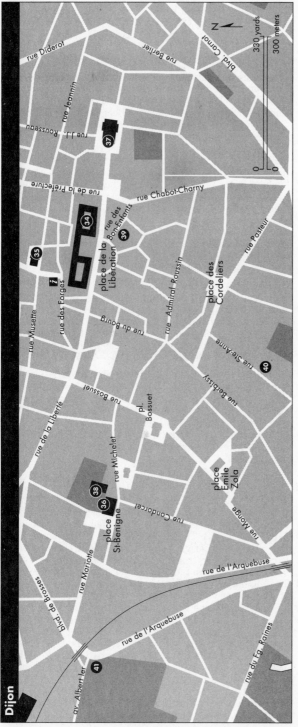

Dijon

Cathédrale
Ste-Bénigne, **36**
Musée
Archéologique, **38**
Musée d'Art Sacré, **40**

Musée d'Histoire
Naturelle et Jardin
Botanique, **41**
Musée Magnin, **39**
Notre-Dame, **35**
Palais des Ducs, **34**
St-Michel, **37**

the Swiss and German borders, has helped maintain its economic importance. So have its numerous gastronomic specialties: snails, mustard, and cassis (a blackcurrant liqueur often mixed with white wine—preferably Burgundy Aligoté—to make Kir, one of France's most popular aperitifs).

㉞ The **Palais des Ducs** is Dijon's leading testimony to bygone splendor. These days, it's home to one of France's major arts museums, the **Musée des Beaux-Arts,** where tombs of two of the aforementioned dukes—Philip the Bold and John the Fearless—spearhead a rich collection of medieval objects and Renaissance furniture. Among the paintings are works by Italian Old Masters, and French 19th-century artists, such as Theodore Géricault and Gustave Courbet, and their Impressionist successors, notably Édouard Manet and Claude Monet. The **ducal kitchens** (circa 1435) with their six huge fireplaces, and the 14th-century chapter house catch the eye, as does the 15th-century **Salle des Gardes** (Guard Room), with its richly carved and colored tombs and late 14th-century altarpieces. The elegant, Classical exterior of the former palace can best be admired from place de la Libération and cour d'Honneur. *Pl. de la Libération. Admission: 15 frs. (free Sun.), ticket valid for all town museums. Open 10–6; closed Tues.*

Further links with Dijon's medieval past are found west of the town center, just off the avenue Albert Ier beyond the train station. Keep an eye out for the exuberant 15th-century gateway to the Chartreuse de Champmol—all that remains of a former charterhouse—and the adjoining **Puits de Moïse,** the so-called Well of Moses, with six large, compellingly realistic medieval statues on a hexagonal base (1395–1405).

㉟ Among the city's outstanding old churches is **Notre-Dame** (rue de la Préfécture), with its elegant towers, delicate nave stonework, 13th-century stained glass, and soaring chancel.
㊱ **Cathédrale Ste-Bénigne** (off rue Mariotte) is comparatively austere; its chief glory is the 10th-century crypt—a forest of
㊲ pillars surmounted by a rotunda. The church of **St-Michel** (rue Rameau) takes us forward 600 years with its chunky Renaissance facade.

Dijon is rich in museums, which can all be visited on a single
㊳ 15-franc ticket. The **Musée Archéologique** (Archaeological Museum), housed in the former abbey buildings of Ste-Bénigne, traces the history of the region through archaeological discoveries (5 rue du Docteru-Maret. Open Wed.–Mon. 9–noon and
㊴ 2–6; closed Tues.). The **Musée Magnin** is a 17th-century mansion showcasing original furniture and furnishings and a variety of paintings from the 16th to the 19th century (4 rue des Bons-Enfants. Open Sun.–Fri. 9–noon and 2–6; closed Sat.).
㊵ The **Musée d'Art Sacré,** devoted to religious art, has a collection of sculpture and altarpieces in the appropriate setting of a former church (17 rue Ste-Anne. Open Sun.–Fri. 9–noon and
㊶ 2–6; closed Sat.). The **Musée d'Histoire Naturelle et Jardin Botanique** encompasses a natural history museum and impressive botanical gardens, with a wide variety of trees and tropical flowers (1 av. Albert Ier. Museum open Wed.–Mon. 2–5; closed Tues.).

Time Out Place Darcy has more to recommend it than the Dijon tourist office in one corner. Gastronomically speaking, this square caters to all tastes and budgets. In addition to the famed **Billoux**

restaurant, a mecca for serious gourmets (*see* Dining and Lodging), you can choose from the bustling **Concorde** brasserie, the quiet bar of the **Hôtel de la Cloche,** the underground **Caveau de la Porte Guillaume** wine and snack bar, or—for those with a sweet tooth—the **Pâtisserie Darcy.**

A31 connects Dijon to Beaune, 40 kilometers (25 miles) south, but you may prefer a leisurely route through the vineyards to racing down the expressway. Chug along D122, past Gevrey-Chambertin, Chambolle-Musigny, and Morey-St-Denis, to **42** **Vougeot.** The **Château du Clos de Vougeot** was constructed by Cistercian monks in the 12th century and completed during the Renaissance; it's famous as the seat of Burgundy's elite company of wine lovers, the *Confrérie des Chevaliers du Tastevin*, who gather here in November at the start of an annual three-day festival, *Les Trois Glorieuses.* You can admire the château's cellars, where ceremonies are held, and ogle the huge grape presses. *Admission: 10 frs. Guided visits daily 10–noon and 2–4:30; closed Christmas–New Year's.*

Wine has been made in nearby **Nuits-St-Georges** since Roman times; its "dry, tonic, and generous qualities" were recommended to Louis XIV for medicinal use. It is appropriate, then, that some of the region's finest vineyards should be owned by the **Hospices de Beaune,** founded in 1443 as a hospital, which carried on its medical activities until 1971, its nurses still sporting their strange medieval uniform. A visit to the Hospices is **43** one of the highlights of a stay in **Beaune.** The hospital's medical history is retraced in a museum whose wide-ranging collections feature some of the weird and wonderful instruments used by doctors back in the 15th century. You can also see Roger Van der Weyden's medieval Flemish masterpiece, *The Last Judgment,* plus a collection of tapestries (though a better series from the late 15th century, relating the life of the Virgin, can be admired in Beaune's main church, the 12th-century **Collégiale Notre-Dame,** just off avenue de la République). Each year, as part of the Trois Glorieuses, an auction of its wines is held at the Hospices on the third Sunday of November, attended by international connoisseurs and dealers. *Rue Deslandes. Museum admission: 13 frs. Open daily 10–noon and 2–5.*

Despite the hordes of tourists, Beaune remains one of the most charming and attractive French provincial towns. There are few more delightful experiences than a visit to one of the town's many wine-tasting cellars, where some of the most famous wines in France can be sampled for next to nothing. Perhaps the most atmospheric place to try the wine is in the candle-lit cellars of the **Marché aux Vins** (rue Nicolas Rolin), where you can taste as much as you please for around 40 francs.

Time Out A good place to find refreshment in the center of Beaune—and drink something other than wine—is the **Bouché** tea room opposite the old belfry. Pastries and homemade ice cream are specialties. *Pl. Monge.*

From Beaune, another scenic route cuts through the vineyards on the way south to Chalon-sur-Saône. Take D973 from Beaune, which soon passes through Pommard, Volnay, and Meursault before continuing to Auxey-Duresses, La Rochepot, and Nolay. From Nolay, N6 scissors through another vineyard, Chassagne-Montrachet, on its way to Chagny. D981 runs south to Rully, past the Mercurey vineyard and the start of the Côte Chalonnaise, which links the vineyards of Burgundy and Beaujolais to Germolles and Givry, where you take D69 to Chalon.

44 **Chalon-sur-Saône** has its medieval heart near the **Eglise St-Vincent**—a former cathedral displaying a jumble of styles—close to the banks of the River Saône. Chalon is the birthplace of Nicéphore Niepce (1765–1833), whose early experiments, developed further by Jacques Daguerre, qualify him as the father of photography. The **Musée Nicéphore Niepce,** a fine museum occupying an 18th-century house overlooking the Saône, retraces the early history of photography and motion pictures with the help of some pioneering equipment. It also includes a selection of contemporary photographic work and a lunar camera used during the U.S. Apollo program. But the star of the museum must be the primitive camera used to take the first photographs in 1816. *Hôtel des Messageries, quai Gambetta. Admission: 5 frs. Open 10–noon and 2–5; closed Tues.*

45 N6 continues down the Saône Valley to **Tournus**, 24 kilometers (15 miles) away, a town that retains much of the charm of the Middle Ages and Renaissance. One of Burgundy's most spectacular and best-preserved Romanesque buildings is the **abbey of St-Philibert.** Despite its massiveness—the nave is supported by unadorned cylindrical pillars over four feet thick—it is spacious and light. No effort was made to decorate or embellish the interior, whose sole hint of frivolity is the alternating red and white stones in the nave arches. The crypt and former abbey buildings, including the cloister and magnificent 12th-century refectory, can also be visited.

Head west from Tournus along picturesque D14 to the fortified hilltop town of Brancion, with its old castle and soaring keep. **46** Shortly after, turn left along D146 to **Cluny,** another 19 kilometers (12 miles) away. The **Abbey of Cluny,** founded in the 10th century, was the biggest church in Europe until Michelangelo built St. Peter's in Rome in the 16th century. Cluny's medieval abbots were as powerful as popes. In 1098, Pope Urban II (himself a Cluniac) assured the head of his old abbey that Cluny was the "light of the world." That assertion, of dubious religious validity, has not stood the test of time, and today, Cluny stands in ruins—a sobering reminder of the temporal limits of human grandeur.

The ruins nonetheless suggest the size and glory of Cluny Abbey at its zenith. Only the Clocher de l'Eau-Bénite (a majestic bell tower) and the right arms of the two transepts, climbing 100 feet above ground, remain. The 13th-century *farinier* (flour mill), with its fine chestnut roof and collection of statues, can also be seen. The gardens contain an ancient lime tree, several hundred years old, named Abélard after the controversial philosopher who sought shelter at the abbey in 1142. No one is sure the tree is quite that old, though! *Admission: 15 frs. (10 frs. Nov.–Easter). Guided visits Easter–Oct., daily 9–noon and 2–5; late morning/early afternoon only the rest of the year.*

Mâcon is a mere 25 kilometers (16 miles) along N79 southeast of Cluny. Stop just outside the town to admire the giant rocky outcrop of **Solutré** on your right, towering above the vineyard of Pouilly-Fuissé, renowned for its white wine. Excavations around the Rock of Solutré have revealed the presence of prehistoric man—and prehistoric horse. So many horses, in fact, that one school of thought asserts that the poor beasts were driven over the top of the cliff to crash to a horrific death below.

47 **Mâcon** is a bustling town, best known for its wine fair in May and for its pesky stone bridge across the Saône, whose low arches are a headache for the pilots of large river barges. The two octagonal towers of the ruined cathedral of St-Vincent loom over the wide quays along the river. The Romantic poet Alphonse de Lamartine (1790–1869) was born in Mâcon.

What to See and Do with Children

Burgundy is a quiet, mainly rural region that lends itself to peaceful pursuits—walks and picnics in the **Morvan Forest** (maybe along the shores of one of its small lakes) or more energetic hikes up the imposing **Rock of Solutré** (Tour 2).

In Troyes (Tour 1), youngsters may be curious to see the yard-wide, overhanging **ruelle des Chats** (alleyway) in the heart of a town whose medieval atmosphere has few peers.

Medieval architecture may be viewed in a new light by a visit to the spectacular **son-et-lumière** (sound-and-light) show at Troyes Cathedral on a summer evening, if the 10:30 starting time isn't too late.

The beautifully restored **abbey of Fontenay** (Tour 1) brings history alive by showing how and where monks lived as well as worshipped.

Musée Nicéphore Niepce, in Chalons-sur-Sâone (Tour 2) will interest children of all ages with its collection of antique camera equipment.

Off the Beaten Track

Burgundy is a convenient launching place for a trip to **Bourges,** just 51 kilometers (32 miles) from La Charité-sur-Loire along N151. The towers of its 13th-century cathedral can be seen on the horizon as you draw near, though, ironically, **Cathédrale St-Etienne** is less easy to spot once you've arrived in the town itself; its asymmetrical facade is hidden away down a narrow street and impossible to photograph. The central portal is a masterpiece of medieval sculpture: cherubim, angels, saints, and prophets cluster in the archway above the tympanum, which contains an elaborate representation of the *Last Judgment.*

The interior is unlike that of any other Gothic cathedral. The forest of tall, slender pillars rising from floor to vaults is remarkable enough, but the unique feature is the height of the side aisles flanking the nave: 65 feet, high enough to allow windows to be pierced above the level of the second side aisle. The cathedral contains some exquisite stained glass, some dating back to its construction. *Off rue du Guichet.*

The center of Bourges, downhill from the cathedral, has been restored to medieval glory. Rue Mirebeau and rue Coursalon, pedestrian-only streets full of timber-framed houses, are charming places to browse and shop. At one end of rue Coursalon, over rue Moyenne—Bourges's busy but less-distinguished main street—is the **Palais Jacques-Coeur,** one of the most sumptuous Gothic dwellings in France. Interior highlights are the vaulted chapel, wooden ceilings covered with original paintings, and the dining room with its wall tapestries and massive fireplace. *Rue Jacques-Coeur. Admission: 10 frs. Open Apr.–Oct., Wed.–Mon. 9–11 and 2–5, Nov.–Mar. 10–11 and 2–4; closed Tues.*

Shopping

Antiques
: The auction houses at Semur-en-Auxois and Dijon are good places to prospect for antiques and works of art; the streets of Tournus are riddled with antique shops.

Clothes
: If there is a place to go on a shopping spree, it's Troyes. Numerous clothing manufacturers are established just outside the town, with the result that clothes prices in stores can be up to 50% cheaper than elsewhere in France. Rue des Bas-Trévois, rue Bégand (leather goods also), and rue Cartalon are good places to look; the best buys on jeans can be had at the **Jeans Outlet Store** (rue du Fbg Croncels).

Food Items
: Shopping is not one of life's major activities in sleepy Burgundy, where eating and drinking are most important. Mustard, snails, and all manner of candies (including chocolate snails—*Escargots de Bourgogne)* may be found without difficulty, especially in the commercial heart of Dijon, with its numerous pedestrian streets. You can get the famous Burgundy wine at a good price if you buy it from an individual producer. Local blackcurrant liqueur (cassis) can be found easily enough anywhere in France for much the same price.

Sports and Fitness

Hiking and Bicycling
: Popular, simple sports in Burgundy start with walking and cycling. Keen hikers should ask for information on paths and circuits from the **Comité Départmental de la Randonnée Pédestre** (B.P.1601, 21000 Dijon cedex, tel. 80–73–81–81). Cycle tours are organized by **La Peurtantaine** (Accueil Morvan Environment, Ecole du Bourg, 71550 Anost, tel. 85–82–77–74). Most tourist offices will be able to give details about recommended routes and where to rent bikes (train stations are a good bet).

Horseback Riding
: Among the numerous establishments that provide lessons or from which you can rent horses are **Locacheval** (Turcey, 21540 Sombernon, tel. 80–33–21–13), **Les Grilles** (89710 St-Fargeau, tel. 86–74–12–11), and the **Ferme du Cheval Roi** (Montceau & Echarnant, 21360 Bligny-sur-Ouche, tel. 80–20–23–81). Horses can be taken out for about 60 francs an hour.

Dining and Lodging

Dining

The Burgundians are hearty eaters; whatever the class of restaurant, you are unlikely to go hungry. Dijon ranks with Lyon as one of the unofficial gastronomic capitals of France. Wealthy Parisian gourmets think nothing of the three-hour drive needed to sample the cuisine of Dijon's Jean-Pierre Billoux or that of Marc Meneau at Vézelay. Game, freshwater trout, ham, goat cheese, *coq au vin*, snails, mustard, and mushrooms number among the region's specialties. Meat is often served in rich, wine-based sauces. There is wine of all types and prices; whites range from cheapish Aligoté to classy Chablis and legendary Meursault and reds, from unpretentious Mâcon to indescribable Gevrey-Chambertin and Romanée-Conti.

Highly recommended restaurants are indicated by a ★.

Lodging

For all its manifold charms, Burgundy is seldom deluged by tourists, and finding accommodations is not the headache it can be on the Riviera or in the Loire Valley. But there are few towns with so many hotels that you can be sure to find something, so always make advance reservations, especially in the "wine country" (from Dijon to Beaune). If you intend to visit Beaune for the Trois Glorieuses wine festival in November, make your hotel reservation several months in advance. Note that nearly all country hotels have restaurants, and you are usually expected to eat in them.

Highly recommended hotels are indicated by a star ★.

Arnay-le-Duc
Dining and Lodging

Chez Camille. Small, quiet, and friendly are words to sum up this hotel on N6 between Saulieu and Beaune. The original 16th-century house has been tastefully renovated and features period furniture and original wooden beams in many rooms. The light, airy restaurant has a glass roof. Traditional Burgundian fare—duck and boar are specialties—figures high on the menu, and there is a thoughtful choice of regional wines. *1 pl. Edouard-Herriot, 21230, tel. 80–90–01–38. 11 rooms with bath. AE, DC, MC, V. Closed Jan. Moderate.*

Autun
Dining

Chalet Bleu. Recently opened in the center of Autun, this restaurant serves solid traditional French cuisine. The setting, complemented by spruce white furniture, is fresh and green and resembles a converted conservatory. Foie gras and beef with shallots are trustworthy choices. *3 rue Jeannin, tel. 85–36–27–30. Reservations advised. Dress: casual. AE, DC, MC, V. Closed Mon. dinner and Tues. Inexpensive.*

Lodging

St-Louis. This comfortable hotel dates from the 17th century; legend has it that Napoleon once slept here. Guest rooms are cozily decorated with a slightly faded charm. The hotel boasts a pleasant patio-garden and its own restaurant. *6 rue Arbalète, 71400, tel. 85–52–21–03. 51 rooms, some with bath. Facilities: restaurant, garden. AE, DC, MC, V. Closed Dec. 20–Feb 2. Inexpensive.*

Auxerre
Dining

Jardin Gourmand. As its name implies, this restaurant features a pretty garden where you can eat *en terrasse* during summer months; the interior, dominated by light-colored oak, is equally congenial. The cuisine is innovative—try the ravioli and foie gras or the duck with blackcurrants—and the service is discreet. *56 blvd. Vauban, tel. 86–51–53–52. Reservations advised. Dress: casual smart. AE, DC, V. Closed part of Feb. and first 3 weeks of Nov.; Sun. dinner Nov.–Mar., and Mon. Moderate.*

Lodging

Le Maxime. This slightly old-fashioned, family-run hotel on the banks of the Yonne is a good bet for anyone who likes the personal touch. The guest rooms are pleasantly decorated, and many offer fine river views. The restaurant is quaintly rustic, with exposed beams and the inevitable row of gleaming copper pots and pans. *2–5 quai Marine, 89000, tel. 86–52–14–19. 25 rooms with bath. Facilities: restaurant, garden. AE, DC, MC, V. Restaurant closed Sat. and part of Feb. Moderate.*

Le Normandie. The picturesque, vine-covered Normandie occupies a grand-looking building conveniently set in the center of Auxerre, a short walk from the cathedral. The guest rooms are unpretentious but of good value and are spanking clean. You can relax in the charming garden, but there is no restaurant on the premises. *41 blvd. Vauban, 89000, tel. 86–52–57–80. 48 rooms with bath. Facilities: garden, garage. AE, DC, MC, V. Inexpensive.*

Avallon
Dining

Morvan. Solid, filling dishes are offered at this folksy eatery just outside town; fish terrine, rabbit, and chocolate cake number among the menu's best. There is an adjoining rock garden. *7 rte. de Paris, tel. 86–34–18–20. Reservations accepted. Dress: casual. DC, V. Closed Sun. evening, Mon., Jan., and second half of Nov. Moderate.*

Dining and Lodging
★

Moulin des Ruats. Part of the prestigious Relais et châteaux group, the Moulin des Ruats is housed in an old flour mill just southwest of Avallon along D427. The guest rooms are decorated with a pretty country-French decor, and many have balconies. Most overlook the River Cousin (in the summer you can eat on the riverbank). Dishes served up in the wood-paneled restaurant are honest and copious: Try the *coq au vin* cooked in local Burgundy wine. *Vallée du Cousin, 89200, tel. 86–34–07–14. 20 rooms, most with bath. Facilities: restaurant, garden. AE, DC, MC, V. Closed Nov.–Feb. Inexpensive.*

Les Capucins. This intimate hotel offers a wide choice of rooms (prices range from 160–320 francs), but is better known for its restaurant, which features four set menus (90–250 francs) dominated by regional cooking. The 180-franc menu is a good value; the duck, trout in flaky pastry, and desserts are excellent. *6 av. Paul-Doumer, 89200, tel. 86–34–06–52. 8 rooms with bath. V. Restaurant closed Wed., Tues. dinner out of season (Nov.–Mar.). Hotel closed third week in Oct. and Christmas–late Jan. Inexpensive/Moderate.*

Beaune
Dining

Auberge St-Vincent. Perhaps the best thing about this restaurant is its admirable setting opposite the Hospices de Beaune. Not surprisingly, it pulls in plenty of tourists, and, consequently, the cuisine and ambience can seem bland. Service, though, is attentive, and the wine list is appropriately lengthy. Prices are reasonable, with kidneys and marinated mullet among the top attractions. *Pl. Fleury, tel. 80–22–42–34. Reservations advised. Casual dress. AE, DC, MC, V. Closed Dec. and Sun. dinner in winter. Inexpensive/Moderate.*

L'Ecusson. Don't be put off by its unprepossessing exterior. This is a comfortable, friendly, thick-carpeted restaurant whose four variously priced menus offer outstanding value. For around 160 francs, for instance, you can dine on rabbit terrine with tarragon followed by leg of duck in oxtail sauce, cheese, and dessert. *2 rue du Lieutenant-Dupuis, tel. 80–22–83–08. Reservations advised. Casual dress. AE, DC, V. Closed Wed. and mid-Feb.–mid-Mar. Inexpensive/Moderate.*

Lodging

La Poste. The front rooms of this traditional French provincial hotel look out over the ramparts and the rear ones over nearby vineyards; not a bad combination! The service is charming; the hotel tastefully renovated; and the long, narrow restaurant, with its gleaming silverware, smacks of tradition. The setting partly compensates for the uninventive cuisine, as does the fabulous wine list. *1 blvd. Clemenceau, 21200, tel. 80–22–08–11. 21 rooms with bath. Facilities: restaurant, terrace. AE, DC, MC, V. Closed Winter. Expensive.*

Central. A well-run establishment with several enlarged and modernized rooms, the Central lives up to its name: It's just around the corner from the Hôtel-Dieu in downtown Beaune. The stone-walled restaurant is cozy—some might say cramped —and the cuisine is reliable. The service is efficient, if a little hurried. The evening meal is obligatory in season (July and August). *2 rue Victor-Millot, 21200, tel. 80–24–77–24. 22 rooms, most with bath. Facilities: restaurant. V, MC. Closed mid-Nov.–Apr. Restaurant closed Wed. except July and Aug. Inexpensive/Moderate.*

Chagny
Dining and Lodging
★

Château de Bellecroix. Located in Chagny, a little town on N6 16 kilometers (10 miles) south of Beaune, the Bellecroix is just what you expect a château to be. It bristles with turrets, is draped in creepers, and is set in its own park. Some of the buildings date from 1199, and the huge dining room, with its majestic fireplace, conjures up the atmosphere of medieval feasts. Salmon with fennel and chocolate cake number among the latterday specialties. Four of the bedrooms are round, set in the towers, and are reached by a picturesque spiral staircase. *71150 Chagny, tel. 85–87–13–86. 15 rooms, some with bath. Facilities: restaurant, park. AE, DC, V. Closed Wed. and Dec. 20–Jan. Moderate.*

Chalon-sur-Saône
Dining and Lodging

St-Georges. Situated close to the train station, a few hundred yards from the town center, the friendly, white-walled St-Georges hotel has been tastefully modernized and possesses many spacious rooms. Its cozy restaurant is known locally for its efficient service and menus of outstanding value. You can't go wrong with the duck in white pepper, foie gras with truffles, or roast pigeon. *32 av. Jean-Jaurès, 71100, tel. 85–48–27–05. 48 rooms, most with bath. AE, DC, MC, V. Moderate.*

Clamecy
Dining and Lodging

Boule d'Or. This down-to-earth country hotel (not particularly comfortable but oh-so-cheap) boasts a delightful setting by the River Yonne. Ask for a room facing the river—there are lovely views of Old Clamecy. The restaurant is housed in a former medieval chapel, which, together with absurdly cheap menus, more than compensates for some apathetic service. *Pl. Bethléem, 58500, tel. 86–27–11–55. 12 rooms, most with bath. Closed Nov.–Mar. Inexpensive.*

Cluny
Dining and Lodging
★

Bourgogne. There's no better place to get into Cluny's medieval mood than the Bourgogne. What remains of the famous abbey is just next door, and the old-fashioned hotel building, which dates from 1817, stands where other parts of the abbey used to be. There is a small garden and a splendid restaurant with sober pink decor and refined cuisine: foie gras, snails, and the more exotic fish with ginger. The evening meal is compulsory in July and August. *Pl. de l'Abbaye, 71250, tel. 85–59–00–58. 14 rooms with bath. AE, DC, V. Closed mid-Nov.–mid-Mar. Restaurant closed for lunch Tues. and Wed., except during July and Aug. Moderate.*

Moderne. Guest rooms at this friendly, unpretentious little hotel are clean and airy, but the Moderne is better known for its peaceful, traditional, waterside restaurant, serving nouvelle cuisine as well as rich Burgundian dishes (fish, saddle of lamb, fillet of beef). You must take dinner at the hotel if you reserve a room between June and October. *Pont-de-l'Etang, 71250, tel. 85–59–05–65. 15 rooms, most with bath. AE, DC, V. Restaurant closed mid-Nov.–mid-Feb. Inexpensive/Moderate.*

Dijon
Dining
★

Jean-Pierre Billoux. Chef Jean-Pierre Billoux has created a restaurant that is arguably the best of many in this most gastronomic of French cities. The stone-vaulted restaurant is magnificently situated in a spacious, restored town house, complete with garden, bar, and chintz-curtained dining room. Service is refined and charming. Specialties include frogs' legs steamed and served with watercress pancakes and guinea fowl with foie gras. *14 pl. Darcy, tel. 80–30–11–00. Reservations essential. Jacket and tie required. AE, DC, MC, V. Closed Sun. dinner, Mon., and mid-Feb.–mid-Mar. Very Expensive.*

Thibert. Like Jean-Pierre Billoux, chef Jean-Paul Thibert has no need to give his restaurant a fancy name. The severely art deco setting is less appealing than that of Billoux, but the cuisine is nearly as refined and imaginative. The menu changes regularly. Cabbage stuffed with snails and prawns with peas and truffles figure among the *tours de force;* sorbets encased in black-and-white mixed chocolate will tempt you to indulge in dessert. Thibert also represents remarkable value for money —for the moment at least. *10 pl. Wilson, tel. 80–67–74–64. Reservations essential. Jacket and tie required. AE, MC, V. Closed Sun., Mon. lunch, and two weeks in both Jan. and Aug. Expensive.*

Pré aux Clercs & Trois Faisans. Situated on the pretty, semicircular square opposite the ducal palace, this venerable eating institution has recently been salvaged after years of indifference. The all-too-classic cuisine (sometimes heavy and dull) is offset by an extensive wine cellar, deferential service, and wood-beamed, stone-walled setting. According to local legend, it was here that Canon Kir invented his famous aperitif (Kir), made with cassis (blackcurrant liqueur) and white (Burgundy Aligoté) wine. *13 pl. de la Libération, tel. 80–67–11–33. Reservations essential. Jacket and tie required. AE, DC, MC, V. Closed Sun. dinner, Tues. Moderate.*

★ **Toison d'Or.** A collection of superbly restored 16th-century buildings belonging to the Burgundian Company of Winetasters forms the backdrop to this fine restaurant, which features a small wine museum in the cellar. Toison d'Or is lavishly furnished and quaint (candlelight *de rigueur* in the evening). The food is straightforward and good value. Try the scallops with ginger-flavored vinaigrette and the nougat and honey dessert. *18 rue Ste-Anne, tel. 80–30–73–52. Reservations not required. Dress: casual. AE, DC, MC, V. Closed Sat. lunch, Sun., part of Feb., most of Aug., and public holidays. Inexpensive.*

Dining and Lodging

Chapeau Rouge. The thick, venerable stone walls of the Chapeau Rouge near Dijon Cathedral encase both a hotel (quiet, well-appointed rooms) and a restaurant, renowned as a haven of classic regional cuisine. New chef Bernard Noël, formerly of the top-ranking Tour d'Argent in Paris, is renowned for his sauces. *22 blvd. de la Marne, 21000, tel. 80–72–31–13. 30 rooms with bath. Facilities: bar, restaurant. AE, DC, MC, V. Reservations necessary for the restaurant. Moderate.*

Ibis-Central. This central, old-established hotel has benefited from joining the Ibis chain: Its sound-proofed, air-conditioned rooms offer a degree of comfort in excess of their price. The adjoining grill room, the Central Grill Rôtisserie, offers a good alternative to the gastronomic sophistication that is difficult to avoid elsewhere in Dijon. *3 pl. Grangier, 21000, tel. 80–30–44–00. 90 rooms, most with bath. AE, DC, MC, V. Restaurant closed Sun. Moderate.*

Sens
Dining and Lodging

Paris & Poste. The newly modernized Paris & Poste is a convenient and pleasant stopping point on the drive down to Burgundy from Paris. The guest rooms are clean, bright, and airy, in line with the hotel's Mapotel connections. The restaurant's helpful service and sumptuous breakfasts confirm the sense of well-being created by the robust evening meal (duck, steak, and snails are high on the various set menus) served in the large, solemn restaurant (its decor is described as "rustic Burgundian"). *97 rue de la République, 89100, tel. 86–65–17–43. 34 rooms with bath. Facilities: restaurant, garden. AE, DC, MC, V. Moderate.*

Croix Blanche. A five-minute walk from the cathedral will bring you to this calm, straightforward hotel. Its two-roomed restaurant (plus veranda) provides three good-value menus, headed by turbot in crayfish sauce, salmon with sorrel, and beef with Roquefort (cheese) sauce. *9 rue Victor-Guichard, 89100, tel. 86–64–00–02. 25 rooms with bath. V. Inexpensive.*

Troyes
Dining

Valentino. Although the restaurant is housed in an old, half-timbered building on a pedestrian street next to the Hôtel de Ville, its flowery interior makes a bold effort to rejoin the 20th century by mimicking art deco chic. Tables are set outside in summer, and oysters are served in winter as a complement to the menu's fish specialties. There is a fine choice of wines to accompany the gastronomic 200- and 300-franc menus. *Cour de la Rencontre, tel. 25–73–14–14. Reservations advised. Jacket and tie required. AE, DC, MC, V. Closed Sun. dinner, Mon., and mid-Aug.–Sept. 10. Expensive.*

Dining and Lodging

Hôtel de France. Some guest rooms here come equipped with fine views of the slender spire of St-Rémy's church; the hotel itself stands on busy quai Dampierre, which bisects the old part of Troyes (easy parking). The rooms are functional and unexciting, but of good value. The hotel restaurant features a bizarre '50s decor that is part jazz club, part cinema, part spaceship; copious five-course meals are served for as little as 125 francs. *18 quai Dampierre, 10000, tel. 25–73–11–95. 60 rooms, 45 with bath. AE, DC, MC, V. Facilities: restaurant. Restaurant closed Sun. dinner Nov.–Apr. Moderate.*

Lodging

Le Marigny. Churches, pancakes, and pizzas dominate the cobbled, half-timbered core of Troyes. Le Marigny sits in their midst, in a quiet street adjacent to the narrow ruelle des Chats. With its tottering gables and uncertain wooden strips, the hotel looks pretty shaky from the outside; creaking floorboards ensure that it's shaky inside, too. The guest rooms are few, small, and faintly run-down. Prices are suitably old-fashioned. There is no restaurant. *3 rue Charbonnet, 10000, tel. 25–73–10–67. 15 rooms, 5 with bath. V. Inexpensive.*

Vézelay
Dining
★

L'Espérance. In the small neighboring village of St-Père-sous-Vézelay, this elegant spot is one of France's premier restaurants. Chef Marc Meneau is renowned for the subtlety and originality of his cuisine and, since he is constantly inventing new combinations, it is difficult to recommend particular dishes; some of his most reputed successes have been with liver of veal, pigeon, and lobster. Madame Meneau is a charming, attentive hostess, and the setting—by a park and stream with Vézelay's hill and basilica in the background—is delightful. L'Espérance also has 17 luxurious guest rooms, and four 1,800-franc suites. *89450 Vézelay, tel. 86–33–20–45. Reservations essential. Jacket and tie required. AE, V. Closed Feb., and Tues. and Wed. lunch. Very Expensive.*

Lodging **Relais du Morvan.** With its delightful setting, Vézelay makes a great place to stay. But it is, after all, a mere village (500 inhabitants) and contains just two hotels. Don't opt for the large, unfriendly, and astronomically expensive Lion d'Or; try instead to reserve a room at the cozy, good-value Relais du Morvan. There is a choice of three very affordable menus in the restaurant. The welcome is cheerful, the rooms functional and unpretentious. *89450 Vézelay, tel. 86–33–25–33. 9 rooms, most with bath. V. Closed mid-Jan.–Feb. Inexpensive.*

The Arts and Nightlife

The Arts

It is perhaps true to say that Burgundy is hotter on folklore than it is on the performing arts. Dijon alone stages a **Festival International de Folklore** (September), a **Bell-Ringing Festival** (mid-August) and an **International Fair of Gastronomy** (November). The Trois Glorieuses in mid-November represent merrymaking for a privileged wine elite.

Cultural activity is best represented by music. The august ruined abbey of Cluny forms the backdrop to the **Grandes Heures de Cluny** in August (tel. 85–59–05–34 for details). Autun Cathedral is the main venue for the **Musique en Morvan** festival in the second half of July, and Nevers the base for **Musique en Nivernais** during September and October. Dijon stages its own **Ete Musical** in June and July. Check local tourist offices for details of the programs.

Nightlife

Nightlife to most Burgundians means staying up late to finish yet another big meal. Since the province's one and only city, Dijon, is one of the most serious eating venues on earth, it is not surprising that nightclubbers can expect a lean time. For a more sedate ambience, try the **New Ambassy** (61 rue de la Liberté) or the **Bahia Brazil** piano bar (39 rue des Godrans). **Le Chic** (107 rue d'Ahuy) and **Le Malibu** (rte. de Troyes) cater to a slightly younger clientele.

10 Lyon and the Alps

Introduction

Even state authorities find it difficult to pin a name on this part of central-eastern France. Their solution, "Lyon-Rhône-Alpes," is hardly poetic, but at least it sums up the major features—the grand city of Lyon, the broad valley of the Rhône, and the towering Alpine mountain range on the frontier with Switzerland and Italy. Although the region is pierced by expressways and high-speed train lines, the pace of life is far from frenzied. Tiny medieval towns sprinkle the landscape, while the only city apart from Lyon is Grenoble, in a majestic setting in the foothills of the Alps.

Lyon is often neglected by drivers pelting down from Paris en route to the Riviera. What they miss is one of the country's most appealing cities, renowned for its historic buildings, quaint *traboule* passageways, and outstanding setting on the banks of the Saône and Rhône rivers. Lyon's also a major gastronomic center, with more good restaurants to the square mile than any other European city outside Paris.

Before reaching Lyon, the Saône flows between the lush hillside of the Beaujolais vineyards and the flat marshland of the Dombes. The Rhône, the great river of southern France, actually trickles to life high up in the Swiss mountains, but it's only at Lyon, where it merges with the Saône, that it truly comes into its own, plummeting due south in search of the Mediterranean. The river's progress south from Lyon is often spectacular, as steep-climbing vineyards conjure up vistas that are more readily associated with the river's Germanic cousin, the Rhine. All along the way, you'll find an abundance of small-town vintners inviting you to sample their wine, without obliging you to buy a crateful. Be warned, though: Rhône wine and the noonday sun make a heady combination.

Roman towns like Vienne and Valence reflect the Rhône's age-old importance as a trading route. To the west lies the Ardèche, a rugged, rustic area where time has stood still; away to the east, the skiing industry has hurtled once-inaccessible Alpine villages into the 20th century.

Essential Information

Important Addresses and Numbers

Tourist Information Contact the **Comité Régional du Tourisme de la Vallée du Rhône** (5 pl. de la Baleine, 69005 Lyon, tel. 78–42–50–04) for information on the Rhône Valley and Lyon, **Maison du Tourisme** (14 rue de la République, B.P. 227, 38019 Grenoble Cedex, tel. 76–54–34–36) for the Isère *départment* and the area around Grenoble, and the **Comité Régional du Tourisme de Savoie–Mont-Blanc** (9 blvd. Wilson, 73100 Aix-les-Bains, tel. 79–88–23–41) for the Alps and the Savoie and Haute-Savoie *départements*.

Local tourist offices in major towns covered in this chapter are **Annecy** (Clos Bonlieu, 1 rue Jean-Jaurès, tel. 50–45–00–33), **Bourgen-Bresse** (6 av. d'Alsace-Lorraine, tel. 74–22–49–40), **Chambéry** (24 blvd. de la Colonne, tel. 79–33–42–47), **Grenoble** (14 rue de la République, tel. 76–54–34–36), **Lyon** (pl. Bellecour, tel. 78–42–25–75, and pl. Carnot, next to the train station, tel. 78–42–22–07), **Montélimar** (allées Champ-de-Mars, tel. 75–01–00–20), **Privas** (av. Chomerac, tel. 75–64–33–35), **Valence** (pl. Leclerc, tel. 75–43–04–88), and **Vienne** (cours Briller, tel. 74–85–12–62).

Travel Agencies **American Express** (6 rue Childebert, Lyon, tel. 78–37–40–69) and **Thomas Cook** (Park Hôtel, 10 pl. Paul Mistral, 38027 Grenoble Cedex, tel. 76–87–15–54, and 48 blvd. Vauban, 26000 Valence, tel. 75–42–02–04).

Car Rental **Avis** (av. du Docteur-Desfrançois, Chambéry, tel. 79–33–58–54, and Airport de Satolas, Lyon, tel. 78–71–95–25) and **Hertz** (8 rue Emile-Gueymard, Grenoble, tel. 76–43–12–92, and 11 rue Pasteur, Valence, tel. 75–44–39–45).

Arriving and Departing

By Plane The international airport at **Satolas**, 26 kilometers (16 miles) from Lyon, is one of France's busiest (for flight information, call 78–71–92–91).

Between the Airport and Downtown Buses leave for the center of Lyon every 20 minutes between 5 AM and 9 PM, and for the train station, every 20 minutes between 6 AM and 11 PM; journey time is 35 minutes, and the fare is 35 francs adults, 17.50 francs children. There's also a bus from Satolas to Grenoble; journey time is just over an hour, and the fare is 100 francs.

By Train The TGV highspeed train to Lyon leaves from Paris's Gare de Lyon station daily and arrives in just two hours.

By Car A6 speeds south to Lyon from Paris (463 kilometers/287 miles away), but be warned that the Tunnel de Fourvière, which cuts through Lyon, is a classic vacationers' hazard, and at peak times you can sit for hours.

Getting Around

By Plane There are domestic airports at Grenoble, Valence, Annecy, Chambéry, and Aix-les-Bains.

By Train Major rail junctions include Grenoble, Annecy, Valence, Vienne, and Montélimar.

By Car Regional roads are fast and well maintained, though smaller mountainous routes can be difficult to navigate in winter, if not impassable.

Guided Tours

Orientation **Lyon Ballade** (8 rue Perrod, 79004 Lyon, tel. 78–27–08–42) offers three-hour minibus tours of the city, with a commentary by tape cassette. Buses leave from place Bellecour, in front of the tourist office, daily at 9:30 and 3; call to reserve your seat. The **French Travel Agents' Association** offers a "Weekend Contract in Lyon," including a tour of the old city, cooking demonstrations, and hotel accommodations. The cost per person in a single room is 2,575 francs; per person in a double room, 2,275 francs. Contact **Sorotour Voyages** (18 rue de Sèze, 69006 Lyon, tel. 78–52–85–38) for reservations.

Special-Interest The Rhône Valley and the Alps offer a variety of special-interest tours, the most relaxing by boat or barge along the region's waterways. **Navig'Inter** (3 rue de l'Arbre, Sec, 69001 Lyon, tel. 78–27–78–02) offers daily boat trips on the Saône, leaving from the quai des Célestins at 2. If you'd like to survey Lyon and Beaujolais from a plane, contact the **Aero-Club du Rhône et du Sud-Est** (Aeroport de Lyon-Bron, 69500 Bron, tel. 78–26–83–97).

Walking Tours The **Office du Tourism** in Lyon (pl. Bellecour, tel. 78–42–25–75) offers guided walks of the city's sights; take your choice of a taped commentary or an English-speaking guide.

Exploring Lyon and the Alps

Numbers in the margin correspond with points of interest on the Lyon and the Alps map.

Orientation

Our exploring tours use Lyon as a base and concentrate on three points of the compass: north toward Burgundy, south down the Rhône Valley, and east into the Alps. The highlights of the relatively inaccessible Auvergne region, to the west, are presented in Off the Beaten Track.

Our first tour concentrates on Lyon itself before heading north into the hilly Beaujolais vineyards, then crossing the Saône to the marshy Dombes area between Bourg-en-Bresse and Lyon. Our second tour heads south from Lyon toward the venerable Rhône towns of Vienne, Valence, and Montélimar and includes an excursion into the dramatic country of the Ardèche, to the west of the river. Last, we move east from Lyon to Grenoble and the Alps, taking in Europe's highest cable car (at Chamonix), Europe's highest mountain (Mont Blanc), and Europe's highest road pass (Col de l'Iseran).

Highlights for First-time Visitors

Cable car ascent from Chamonix, Tour 3
Route de l'Iseran, Tour 3
Grenoble, Tour 3
"Trabouling" in Lyon, Tour 1
Medieval village of Pérouges, Tour 1
Route Panoramique from Tournon, Tour 2
Vienne, Tour 2

Tour 1: Lyon, Beaujolais, and La Dombes

❶ **Lyon** and Marseille both like to claim they are France's "second city." In terms of size and commercial importance, Marseille probably grabs that title. But when it comes to tourist appeal, Lyon's a clear winner.

Lyon's development owes much to the city's exceptional site: halfway between Paris and the Mediterranean and within striking distance of Switzerland, Italy, and the Alps. The site is physically impressive, with steep cliffs dominating the River Saône, which flows parallel to the Rhône before the two converge south of the city center.

Because Lyon has never really had to endure hard times, a mood of untroubled complacency, rather than big-city bustle, prevails. The Lyonnais bask in the knowledge that their city has been important for over 2,000 years, ever since the Romans made it the capital of the occupied province of Gaul, shortly after founding the city in 43 BC. Even the name sounds appropriately proud—until you learn that it derives from the Roman Lugdunum, or "Hill of the Crow."

② Few, if any, crows, rooks, or ravens are found these days on **place Bellecour,** where we begin our tour. This imposing tree-shaded square, midway between the Saône and the Rhône, is one of the largest in France, lent architectural distinction by the symmetrical Classical facades erected along its narrower sides in 1800. The large bronze statue of Louis XIV on horseback is the work of local sculptor Jean Lemot, installed in 1828 to replace the Sun King's original equine statue, which failed to survive the French Revolution.

The city's main tourist office is located in an isolated pavilion in the southeast corner; stop in for a city map and information leaflets. Then cross the square and head 500 yards north along lively rue du Président-Herriot before turning left into rue Grenette. Take the Pont du Maréchal-Juin over the Saône to the old town at the foot of Fourvière Hill, crowned by the imposing silhouette of **Notre-Dame** basilica.

On the right bank of the Saône lies **Vieux Lyon** (Old Lyon), an atmospheric warren of streets and alleys. Turn right after the
③ bridge, then take the first left down a little alley to **place de la Baleine,** a small square lined with 17th-century houses.

Time Out	At one corner of place de la Baleine is a cozy lunch spot, **Aux Trois Maries.** The curious name comes from the carved stone niche on the wall of no. 7, holding statuettes of the Virgin Mary, Mary of Bethany, and Mary Magdalene. *1 rue des Trois-Maries.*

At the far end of place de la Baleine lies **rue St-Jean,** one of the many streets that weave their way around the banks of the Saône. Many of the area's elegant houses were built for the town's most illustrious denizens—bankers and silk merchants—during the French Renaissance under the 16th-century king François I. Originally, they had four stories; the upper floors were added in the last century. Look for the intricate old iron signs hanging over the shop doorways, many of which gave the streets their names.

A peculiarity of the streets of old Lyon are the *traboules,* quaint little passageways that cut under the houses from one street to another. Don't hesitate to venture in; they aren't private. There's a fine example at 24 rue St-Jean, just off place de Baleine (to the left), which leads through to rue du Boeuf via an airy, restored courtyard.

Rue St-Jean was old Lyon's major thoroughfare. Stop in the elegant courtyard of no. 27 on your way north from place de la Baleine to place du Change, where money changers would op-
④ erate during Lyon's medieval trade fairs. The **Loge du Change** church, on one side of the square, was built by Germain Soufflot (best known as architect of the Panthéon in Paris) in 1747.

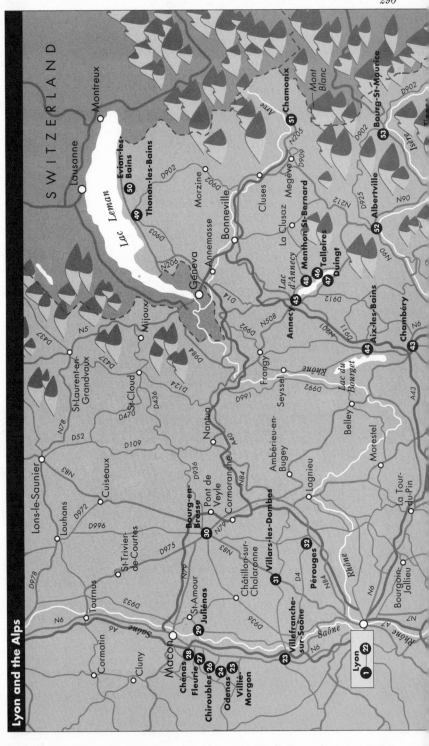

Lyon and the Alps

SWITZERLAND

Montreux

Lausanne

Lac Leman

Evian-les-Bains **50**

Thonon-les-Bains **49**

Morzine

Geneva

Annemasse

Bonneville

Cluses

Megève

La Clusaz

Chamonix **51**

Mont Blanc

Bourg-St-Maurice **53**

Albertville **52**

Menthon-St-Bernard **46**

Talloires **48**

Duingt **47**

Annecy **45**

Lac d'Annecy

Aix-les-Bains **44**

Chambéry **43**

Lac du Bourget

Belley

Morestel

La Tour-du-Pin

St-Laurent-en-Grandvaux

St-Cloud

Mijoux

Frangy

Seyssel

Nantua

Ambérieu-en-Bugey

Lagnieu

Bourgoin-Jallieu

Lons-le-Saunier

Cuiseaux

Louhans

Pont de Veyle

Cormoranche

Bourg-en-Bresse **30**

Châtillon-sur-Chalaronne

Villars-les-Dombes **32**

Pérouges **31**

Rhône

St-Trivier-de-Courtes

Villefranche-sur-Saône **23**

Lyon **1 – 22**

Tournus

St-Amour

Juliénas **29**

Chénas **28**

Fleurie **27**

Chiroubles **26**

Odenas **24**

Villié-Morgon **25**

Mâcon

Cluny

Cormatin

Saône

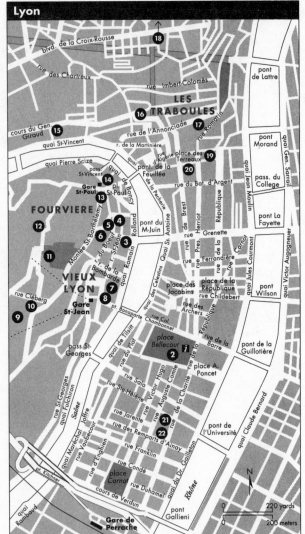

Take rue Soufflot to one side of the church and turn left into rue de Gadagne, where the largest Renaissance ensemble in Lyon is located: the Hôtel de Gadagne, built between the 14th and the 16th century and now home to the **Musée Historique de Lyon.** The first floor of this history museum contains medieval sculpture from long-gone local churches and abbeys, while other floors showcase local furniture, pottery, paintings, engravings, and antique playing cards. On the second floor is the **Musée de la Marionnette** (Puppet Museum), which traces the history of marionnettes from Guignol and Madelon (Lyon's local equivalent of Punch and Judy, created by Laurent Mourguet in 1795) through to contemporary hand and string puppets from across the globe. *10 rue de Gadagne. Admission to both museums free. Open Wed.–Mon. 10:45–6; closed Tues.*

Continue through tiny place du Petit-Collège to rue du Boeuf.

Time Out   The **Cour des Loges** is actually four Renaissance mansions transformed into a luxury hotel. Stop in for a snack at the informal **tapas bar,** and admire the original stone spiral staircase, gigantic roof beams, and ancient sculpted faces that decorate the walls. *6 rue du Boeuf.*

6 One of old Lyon's finest mansions lies farther down rue du Boeuf, at no. 16: the 17th-century **Maison du Crible,** now a high-class restaurant (Tour Rose, *see* Dining and Lodging, below). Venture into its courtyard to glimpse the Tour Rose itself—an elegant, pink-washed tower—and the charming terraced garden. Closeby, at the corner of place Neuve St-Jean, is one of the most famous hanging signs in old Lyon, the work of Giambologna (1529–1608), a renowned French sculptor who honed his skills in Renaissance Italy; the sign portrays the bull for which rue de Boeuf is named. Head down place Neuve and turn right into rue St-Jean. A hundred yards on, turn right into

7 rue de la Bombarde, which leads to the peaceful **Jardin Archéologique** (Archaeological Gardens), with its excavated remains of the four churches that succeeded one another on the spot.

8 Alongside is one church that has withstood the onslaught of time: the **Primatiale St-Jean,** Lyon's somewhat disappointing cathedral. You won't find any soaring roof or lofty spires here. Instead, a stumpy facade is stuck almost bashfully onto the nave, while the interior mishmash has its moments—the 13th-century stained-glass windows in the choir or the variety of window tracery and vaulting in the side chapels—but lacks drama and a sense of harmony. The cathedral dates from the 12th century, and the chancel is Romanesque, but construction continued over three centuries and most of the building is Gothic (note the high pointed windows). Pope John XXII was consecrated here in 1316, and Henri IV married Marie de Médicis here in 1600. The 14th-century astronomical clock, in the north transept, chimes a hymn to St.-Jean (St. John) on the hour from noon to 3 PM as a screeching rooster and other automatons enact the Annunciation.

To the right of the cathedral facade stands the venerable 12th-century **Manécanterie** (choir school); upstairs you'll find a small Treasury museum housing medieval Limoges enamels, fine ivories, and embroidered robes. *70 rue St-Jean. Admission free. Open weekdays 7:30–noon and 2–7:30; weekends 2–5.*

9 To the left of the cathedral as you leave is the **Gare St-Jean;** to continue our tour, take the *ficelle* (funicular railway) that leaves from here on its way to the top of Fourvière Hill. At the top, head along the Montée de Fourvière to the Roman ruins **(Théâtres Romains)** nearby. There are two semicircular theaters here: the **Grand Théâtre,** the oldest Roman theater in France, built in 15 BC to seat 10,000 spectators, and the smaller **Odéon,** with its geometric-patterned tiled flooring. The best time to appreciate the theaters is September, when they are used to stage events during the Lyon International Arts Festival. *Fourvière Hill. Admission free. Open Easter–Oct., weekdays 8–noon and 2–6, Sat. 9–noon and 3–6, Sun. 3–6; Nov.–Easter, weekdays 8–noon and 2–5, Sat. 9–noon and 3–5, Sun. 3–5.*

Since 1933, systematic excavations have unearthed many vestiges of the opulent Roman city of Lugdunum. These remains **⑩** can be viewed in the **Musée de la Civilisation Gallo-Romaine** (Gallo-Roman Museum), which overlooks the theaters. The museum's semisubterranean open-plan design is an unusual showcase for the collection of statues, mosaics, vases, coins, and tombstones. One of the museum's highlights is a large bronze plaque, the **Table Claudienne,** upon which is inscribed part of Emperor Claudius's speech to the Roman Senate in AD 48, conferring senatorial rights on the Roman citizens of Gaul. *Rue Radisson. Admission free. Open Wed.–Sun. 9:30–noon and 2–6; closed Mon. and Tues.*

Head back to the spot where the *ficelle* dropped you off. You won't be able to miss the pompous, late 19th-century basilica of **⑪** **Notre-Dame-de-Fourvière,** which has unfortunately become one of the symbols of Lyon. In terms of its mock-Byzantine architecture and hilltop site, it's a close cousin of Paris's Sacré-Coeur. Both were built for a similar reason: to underline the might of the Roman Catholic Church after the Prussian defeat of France in 1870 had led to the birth of the anticlerical Third Republic. The riot of interior decoration—an overkill of gilt, marble, and colorful mosaics—reveals that the Church had mind-boggling wealth to compensate for its waning political clout. *Fourvière Hill. Open daily 8–noon and 2–6.*

One of the few places in Lyon from where you can't see the Fourvière basilica is the terrace alongside. The plummeting panorama reveals the city laid out on either side of the Saône and Rhône rivers, with the St-Jean cathedral facade in the foreground and the huge glass towers of the reconstructed Part-Dieu business complex glistening behind. For an even more sweeping view—encompassing the surrounding hills—climb the 287 steps of the basilica's **observatory.** *Admission: 6 frs. Open Easter–Oct., daily 10–noon and 2–6; Nov.–Easter, weekends 10–noon and 2–5.*

⑫ Looming beyond the basilica is a skeletal metal tower, **Tour Métallique,** built in 1893 and now used as a television transmitter. Take the stone staircase, **Montée Nicolas-de-Lange,** at the foot of the tower, which leads back down to old Lyon, emerging alongside the St-Paul train station at place St-Paul. Venture **⑬** briefly into rue Juiverie, to the right; the **Hôtel Paterin** at no. 4 is a splendid Renaissance mansion, and the Hôtel Bullioud (no. 8) has a courtyard with an ingenious gallery constructed in 1536 by Philibert Delorme, one of France's earliest and most accomplished exponents of Classical architecture (he worked at the châteaus of Fontainebleau and Chenonceau in the Loire Valley).

⑭ To the left of place St-Paul is the 12th-century church of **St-Paul,** whose octagonal lantern, frieze of animal heads in the chancel, and Flamboyant Gothic chapel are all worth a look. Head around the church, take the St-Vincent footbridge over the Saône, and turn left along quai St-Vincent. Two hundred **⑮** yards along, to the right, is the leafy **Jardin des Chartreux,** a small, leafy park. Cut through the park up to cours du Général-Giraud, then turn right into place Rouville, pausing to admire the splendid view of the river and Fourvière Hill.

⑯ Rue de l'Annonciade leads from place Rouville to the **Jardin des Plantes,** 250 yards away, a haven of peace in this otherwise busy quarter. These luxurious botanical gardens contain remnants of the **Amphithéâtre des Trois Gauls,** a once-huge circular amphitheater built in AD 19. From the gardens, you'll be able to survey the hilly, surrounding **Croix Rousse** district, which once resounded to the clanking of weaving looms that churned out reams of the silk and cloth for which Lyon became famous. By the 19th century, over 30,000 *canuts* (weavers) were working in Lyon; they set up their looms on the upper floors—the brightest—of the tightly packed houses. The houses were so tightly packed, in fact, that the only way to transport the finished fabrics was through the *traboules,* which had the additional advantage of protecting the fabrics from bad weather.

For an impromptu tour of the Croix Rousse, leave the gardens and head along rue Imbert-Colomès as far as no. 20. Here, turn right through the *traboule* that leads to rue des Tables Claudiennes, then veer right across place Chardonnet. Take **(17)** the passage Mermet alongside **St-Polycarpe** church, then turn left into rue Leynaud. A *traboule* at no. 32 leads to montée St-Sébastien. Keep right, cross place Croix-Paquet, and take rue Romarin down to place des Terreaux. Armed with a detailed map, you could spend hours "trabouling" your way across the Croix Rousse, still a hive of activity despite the industrialization of silk and textile production and the ensuing demise of most of the original workshops. Old-time "Jacquard" looms can **(18)** still be seen in action at the **Maison des Canuts;** the weavers—many surprisingly young—are happy to show children how to operate a miniature loom. *12 rue d'Ivry. Admission: 4 frs. Open weekdays 8:30–noon and 2–6:30, Sat. 9–noon and 2–6.*

The north side of the sizable place des Terreaux is lined with **(19)** cafés, from which you can survey the facade of the **Hôtel de Ville** (Town Hall), redesigned by architects Jules Hardouin-Mansart and Robert de Cotte after a serious fire in 1674 (the rest of the building dates back to the early 17th century). In the middle of the square, four majestic horses rear up from a monumental 19th-century fountain by Frédéric Auguste Bartholdi, whose most famous creation is New York's Statue of Liberty. On the south side of the square is the elegant 17th-century front of the former Benedictine abbey, **Palais St-Pierre,** now the city's art museum.

(20) The **Musée des Beaux-Arts** (Fine Arts Museum) showcases the country's largest collection of art after the Louvre. The cloister gardens are studded with various worthy statues, including three works by Rodin: *The Walker, The Shadow,* and *The Bronze Age.* Inside, the wide-ranging collections include enamels, Byzantine ivories, Etruscan statuettes, 4,000-year-old Cypriot ceramics, and a plethora of Egyptian archaeological finds. Amid the usual wealth of Old Master, Impressionist, and modern paintings is a unique collection of works by the tight-knit Lyon School, whose twin characteristics are exquisitely painted flowers and an overbearing mood of religious sentimentality. An entire room is devoted to one of the school's 19th-century luminaries, Louis Janmot, and his mystical cycle *The Poem of the Soul.* Janmot's own tortured soul emerges as you follow his hero's spiritual evolution in a series of immaculately painted visions that seesaw between the heavenly, the hellish, and the downright spooky. *Pl. des Terreaux. Admission free. Open Wed.–Sun. 10:30–6; closed Mon. and Tues.*

From behind the Hôtel de Ville, head south by way of shop-lined rue de la République, which becomes rue de la Charité after place Bellecoeur. Some 300 yards down are two major museums. The **Musée des Arts Décoratifs** (Decorative Arts Museum) occupies an 18th-century mansion, with fine displays of silverware, furniture, *objets d'art*, ceramics, and tapestries. Take time to admire the outstanding array of Italian Renaissance porcelain. *30 rue de la Charité. Admission: 12 frs. (joint ticket). Open Tues.–Sun. 9:30–noon and 2–6.*

㉒ The **Musée Historique des Tissus** (Fabrics Museum) contains a stream of intricate carpets, tapestries, and silks. You'll see Oriental tapestries dating as far back as the 4th century and a fabulous assembly of Turkish and Persian carpets from the 16th to 18th century. European highlights include Italian Renaissance fabrics, Hispano-Moorish cloth from Spain, and 18th-century Lyon silks. A thorough description of the history of cloth down the ages is provided by a "genealogical tree," which covers one wall on the ground floor. *34 rue de la Charité. Admission: 12 frs. (joint ticket). Open Tues.–Sun. 10–noon and 2–5:30.*

Time Out Follow rue de la Charité down to the cours de Vedun, and stop in for an inexpensive lunch at **Brasserie Georges;** it's one of the city's largest and oldest brasseries, still retaining its original mid-19th century painted ceiling. Meals range from hearty veal stew or sauerkraut to more refined fare, dished up at any hour of the day or evening. *30 cours de Vedun.*

㉓ Leaving Lyon, head north along N6 to **Villefranche-sur-Saône,** 25 kilometers (16 miles) away. Villefranche, a lively industrial town, is capital of the Beaujolais wine region, renowned for its Vin Nouveau, the youthful, fruity, red wine eagerly gulped down each year across the globe on the third Thursday of November (date of its official "release").

Not all Beaujolais is so flippant, though. Wine classed as "Beaujolais Villages," with higher alcoholic strength, is produced from a clearly defined region to the northwest of **㉔** Villefranche. Take D43, through part of this region, to **Odenas,** and the start of a narrow strip of land, just 14 miles long, that is home to the nine deluxe Beaujolais wines, known as *crus*, that come close to rivaling the renowned wines of Burgundy produced just to the north. Most villages along the Beaujolais wine road have a *cave* (communal wine cellar) or *co-opérative*, where you can taste and buy the local wine.

Odenas stands in the southernmost and largest vineyard of the Beaujolais *crus:* Brouilly, which produces soft, fruity wine that is best drunk very young. In the middle of the Brouilly vineyard is the imposing Mont Brouilly, a towering hill whose vines produce a tougher, firmer wine, classified as Côte de Brouilly. From Odenas, take D68, via St-Lager, to **㉕** **Villié-Morgon,** in the heart of the Morgon vineyard, whose robust wines age well.

Time Out A short way east of Villié is the 15th-century **Château de Corcelles,** noted for its Renaissance galleries, wrought-iron canopied courtyard well, and the medieval wood-carvings in its chapel. Round off your visit with a trip to the guard room, which has been transformed into a wine-tasting cellar, an atmospheric spot to sample the local wines. *Off D9 from Villié. Open Mon.–Sat. 10–noon and 2:30–6:30.*

D68 threads its way north from Villié-Morgon through the wine villages of **Chiroubles** (rare light wines best drunk young) and **Fleurie** (noted for its elegant flowery bouquet) to **Chénas,** home of two *crus:* the prestigious Moulin à Vent, robust, velvety, and expensive, and Chénas, an underestimated, fruity wine that ages well.

Just two wine villages now remain. **Juliénas** is home to sturdy, deep-colored wines that can be sampled in the atmospheric cellar of the town church, decorated with Bacchanalian scenes (open Wed.–Mon., closed lunchtime). **St-Amour** produces light but firm red wine and a limited quantity of white. A more famous white wine, Pouilly-Fuissé, is produced a few miles north of St-Amour around the village of Fuissé, in the shadow of the Rock of Solutré (*see* the Burgundy chapter).

From St-Amour, take D31/D51 east to Cormoranche, then D933/D28 north through Pont de Veyle to N79, and continue to **Bourg-en-Bresse,** 27 kilometers (17 miles) farther away.

Bourg-en-Bresse is a cheerful town, known for its production of fowl, mainly chicken; they're striking-looking creatures, with plump white bodies and bright blue feet. The town's southeast-lying district, **Brou,** is its most interesting. The church here—**Église de Brou,** a marvel of Flamboyant Gothic—is no longer in religious use but remains open to visitors; it was built between 1506 and 1532 by Margaret of Austria in memory of her husband Philibert le Beau, Duke of Savoy, and their finely sculpted tombs are among the highlights of the richly decorated interior.

Margaret and Philibert can also be seen, kneeling beneath their coats of arms, in the scintillating stained-glass windows in the rounded apse at the east end of the church. More fine glass —and sculpture—can be admired in the side chapels. Don't miss the imaginatively carved oak choir stalls and the exuberant, statue-topped rood-screen separating the choir and the nave.

The church makes a magical setting for *son-et-lumière* (sound-and-light) performances held on Easter and Pentecost Sunday and Monday, and on Thursday, Saturday, and Sunday from early May to the end of September. The nearby **cloisters** house a museum, noted for its paintings: 16th- and 17th-century Flemish and Dutch artists are out in force, alongside 17th- and 18th-century French and Italian masters, 19th-century pictures from the Lyon School, and contemporary works by local artists. There's also an extensive array of richly carved regional furniture, made from local woods (oak, walnut, and cherry). *Blvd. de Brou. Admission to church and museum: 22 frs. Open Apr.–Sept., daily 8:30–noon and 2–6:30; Oct.–Mar., daily 10–noon and 2–4:30.*

La Dombes, the area south of Bourg-en-Bresse, was once covered by an alpine glacier. The glacier gradually eroded the clay soil to create an elaborate grid of lakes and ponds that today attract both anglers and bird-watchers. The **Parc des Oiseaux** at **Villars-les-Dombes,** 29 kilometers (18 miles) south of Bourg-en-Bresse via N83, is one of the finest bird sanctuaries in Europe. Four hundred species of native and exotic birds live and breed here in 56 acres of lakeland. You can visit 435 open-air aviaries, housing every size of species, from waders to birds of prey, and an indoor birdhouse filled with an assortment of vibrantly colored tropical birds. *Admission: 22 frs. adults, 16 frs. students, 10 frs. children. Open Easter–Sept., daily 8:30–7; Oct.–Easter, daily 8:30–dusk.*

Time Out Picnicking isn't allowed in the sanctuary, but stop for a bite to eat in the unpretentious **restaurant-cafeteria.**

N83 continues past the Dombes region's largest lake, the Grand Etang de Birieux, on its way to St-André de Covey, where you should turn left along D4 to **Pérouges,** 21 kilometers (13 miles) away. Pérouges is a wonderfully preserved hilltop village of medieval houses and cobbled streets, surrounded by ramparts. Hand weavers brought it prosperity, but the Industrial Revolution was their downfall; by the end of the 19th century, the population had dwindled from 1,500 to 90, and many old houses were demolished. Fortunately, local conservationists persuaded state authorities to restore and preserve the most interesting houses. Today, a new influx of craftsmen (a potter, bookbinder, cabinetmaker, and weaver) has breathed life back into Pérouges.

Park your car by the main gateway, Porte d'En-Haut, alongside the 15th-century fortress-church. Rue du Prince, the town's main street, leads to the Maison des Princes de Savoie, which has a fine watchtower. Just around the corner is place de la Halle, a pretty square with great charm; in its middle towers a splendid lime tree, planted in 1792. To one side of the square stands the small **town museum,** containing local historical artifacts and a reconstructed weaver's workshop. *Pl. de la Halle. Admission: 15 frs. Open daily 10–noon and 2–6; closed Wed. and Thurs. morning, Oct.–Apr.*

Pérouges is barely 200 yards across, and you should take time to explore its quaint, narrow streets. The rue des Rondes encircles the town; there are fine views over the surrounding countryside from the second gateway, the Porte d'En-Bas (on clear days, you can see all the way to the Alps).

From nearby Meximieux, N84 heads back to Lyon, 32 kilometers (20 miles) away.

Tour 2: The Rhône Valley

Our second tour begins 27 kilometers (17 miles) south of Lyon at **Vienne;** take either N7 (more direct) or the A7 expressway, which meanders along the banks of the Rhône.

Despite being a major road and train junction, Vienne retains a lot of historic charm. It was one of the most important towns of Roman Gaul and a religious and cultural center under its count-archbishops in the Middle Ages. The tourist office stands at the river end of cours Brillier in the leafy shadow of the **Jardin Public** (Public Gardens). Begin your tour here, turning right along quai Jean-Jaurès, beside the Rhône, to the nearby church of **St-Pierre.** Note the rectangular 12th-century Romanesque bell tower with its arcaded tiers. The lower parts of the church walls date from the 6th century.

Head down the left-hand side of the church and turn left again into rue Boson, which leads to the cathedral of **St-Maurice.** Although the religious wars deprived this cathedral of many statues, much of the original decoration is intact; the arches of the portals on the 15th-century facade are richly carved with Old Testament scenes. The cathedral was built between the 12th and 16th century, with later interior additions, such as the splendid 18th-century mausoleum to the right of the altar, which contains the tombs of two of Vienne's archbishops. The entrance to the vaulted passage that once led to the cloisters, but now opens onto place St-Paul, is adorned with a frieze of the zodiac.

Place St-Paul and rue Clémentine bring you to place du Palais and the remains of the **Temple d'Auguste et de Livie** (Temple of Augutus and Livia), thought to date back, in part, to the earliest Roman settlements in Vienne (first century BC). The slender Corinthian columns that ring the temple were filled in with a wall during the 11th century, when the temple was used as a church; today, however, the temple has been restored to its original appearance.

Take rue Brenier to rue Chantelouve, site of a **Roman gateway** decorated with delicate friezes (the last vestige of the city's sizable Roman baths); then continue to rue de la Charité and the **Théâtre Romain.** This was one of the largest Roman theaters in Gaul (143 yards in diameter) and is only slightly smaller than Rome's famed Theater of Marcellus. Vienne's theater was buried under tons of rubble until 1922, but since then, the 46 rows of seating and parts of the marble flooring and frieze on the original stage have been excavated and renovated. Shows and concerts are staged here on summer evenings. *Admission: 7 frs. Open Apr.–mid-Oct., Wed.–Mon. 9–noon and 2–5:30; mid-Oct.–Mar., Wed.–Sat. 10–noon and 2–5, Sun. 1:30–5:30.*

Take rue de la Charité back down to rue des Orfèveres, lined with Renaissance facades, and continue on to the church of **St-André-le-Bas,** once part of a powerful abbey. Extensive restoration was in progress at press time but, if possible, venture inside to see the finely sculpted 12th-century capitals and the 17th-century wooden statue of St. Andrew. The adjacent cloisters are at their best during the summer music festival held here (and at the cathedral) from June to August.

Take the nearby bridge across the Rhône to inspect the excavated Cité Gallo-Romaine, where the Romans built most of their sumptuous private villas. *Admission: 10 frs. Open Apr.–Sept., daily 9–12:30 and 2:30–9; Oct.–Apr., daily 9–noon and 2–5.*

34 Stay on this bank of the Rhône and take N86 south 32 kilometers (20 miles) to the little town of **Serrières,** a traditional stopping point for Rhône river craft. You can see the valley boatmen's way of life from the exhibits at the **Musée des Mariniers du Rhône** (Boatmen's Museum) in the wooden-roofed Gothic chapel of St-Sornin. *Admission: 10 frs. Open Apr.–Oct., weekends 3–6.*

Nearly 10 kilometers (6 miles) south of Serrières along N82, just beyond Peaugres, is the 200-acre **Haut Vivarais Safari Park.** Some 800 animals (including lions, bears, buffalo, bison, tigers, wolves, and camels) can be encountered here—from the safety of your car, with the windows firmly rolled up. Stroll along the separate pedestrian trail to admire tamer beasts like giraffes and ostriches and check out the snakes, crocodiles, and lizards lounging inside their vivarium. The park also has its own bars, cafeteria, souvenir shops, and playground, making it a great place to spend an afternoon if you're traveling with children. *Admission: 46 frs. adults, 30 frs. children. Open Apr.–Oct., daily 9:30–7; Nov.–Mar., daily 11–5.*

35 N82 shortly reaches **Annonay,** a prosperous town that grew up around the leather industry. It's best known, though, as home to the Montgolfier brothers, Joseph and Etienne, who, in 1783, invented the hot-air balloon (known in French as *une montgolfière*). The first flight took place at Annonay on June 4, 1783; it lasted half an hour, and the balloon soared to 6,500 feet. The brothers' exploit is commemorated by an obelisk on avenue Marc-Seguin, although the actual balloon launch took place from place des Cordeliers (close to the tourist office).

The narrow streets and passageways of central Annonay have a lot of character. Local history and folklore are evoked at the **Musée Vivarais César Filhol,** between the Mairie (Town Hall) and Notre-Dame church. *15 rue Béchetoille. Admission: 7 frs. Open June–Aug., Tues.–Sun. 2–6; Sept.–May, Wed. and weekends 2–6.*

36 D578/D532 head southeast to **Tournon,** 37 kilometers (23 miles) away on the banks of the Rhône at the foot of some impressive granite hills. Tournon's chief attraction is its hefty 15th–16th-century **château.** From the chateau's two terraces, there are sumptuous views of the old town, river, and—towering above the village of Tain-l'Hermitage across the Rhône—the steep-climbing vineyards that produce Hermitage wine, one of the Rhône Valley's most refined (and costly) reds. The château houses a museum of local history, the **Musée Rhodanien,** which features an account of the life of Annonay-born Marc Seguin (1786–1875), the engineer who built the first suspension bridge over the Rhône at Tournon in 1825 (the bridge was demolished in 1965). *Admission: 7 frs. adults, 3 frs. children. Open June–Aug., Wed.–Mon. 10–noon and 2–6; Apr.–May and Sept.–Oct., Wed.–Mon. 2–6; closed Tues.*

From Tournon's main square (place Jean-Jaurès), slightly inland from the château, take the signposted "Route **37** Panoramique" in the direction of **St-Romain-de-Lerps.** There are breathtaking views at every turn along this narrow, twisting, clambering road. At the old village of St-Romain, you are rewarded with an immense panorama that, in fine weather, takes in no fewer than 13 *départements* and extends to Mont-Blanc in the east and the whalelike bulk of arid Mont Ventoux to the south.

D287 winds its way down from St-Romain to St-Péray. Looming 650 feet above the plain is the Montagne de Crussol, a white cliff topped by the 12th-century ruins of Crussol Castle. The **38** largish town of **Valence** lies just a couple of miles away along N532. Valence is capital of the Drôme *département* and is the principal fruit-and-vegetable market for the surrounding region. Steep-curbed alleyways—known as *côtes*—extend from the banks of the Rhône to the heart of the old town around the cathedral of **St. Apollinaire.** Although the cathedral was begun in the 12th century in the Romanesque style, it's not altogether as old as it looks: Parts were rebuilt in the 17th century, and the belfry in the 19th. Alongside the cathedral, in the former 18th-century Bishops' Palace, is the **Musée des Beaux-Arts** (Fine Arts Museum), featuring local sculpture and furniture and a collection of 96 red-chalk drawings by deft landscapist Hubert Robert (1733–1808), a master of the picturesque. *Just off rue Sauniere. Admission: 8 frs. (chldren free). Open daily 2–6; also 9–noon on Wed., Sat., and Sun.*

Turn left out of the museum and cross hectic avenue Gambetta to the Champ-de-Mars, a broad terraced garden overlooking the Rhône, where there are fine views across to Crussol Castle. Just below the Champ-de-Mars is the **Parc Jouvet,** with 14 acres of pool and gardens.

Continue 16 kilometers (10 miles) south from Valence along N86 and turn right into D120 just before La Voulte. This attractive road follows the Eyrieux Valley as far as Les Ollieressur-Eyrieux, where you should turn south along D2, under the shade of horse chestnut trees, toward **Privas,** capital of the spectacular Ardeche *departement,* renowned for its rocky gorges and stalagmite-bearing caves (*see* Off the Beaten Track, below).

Privas was a Protestant stronghold during the 16th-century Wars of Religion. In 1629, it was razed by the army of Louis XIII, after a siege lasting 16 days. The **Pont Louis XIII** over the River Ouveze celebrates the kings' reconciliation with Privas, which rose from the dust to become a peaceful administrative town, best known for the production of that delicious French delicacy, the *marron glace* (candied chestnut).

Privas makes a good base for exploring the Ardeche, and the tourist office just off place Charles-de-Gaulle, in the center of town, will provide details of the region's beauty spots. Our tour, meanwhile, continues to another town of sweet-toothed fame: **Montelimar,** the home of the *nougat,* a white or pink candy that usually contains chopped almonds and cherries.

Montelimar, 35 kilometers (22 miles) southeast of Privas (via D2) on the other side of the Rhone, is named fafter the 12th-century fortress of **Mont-Adhemar. This chateau, enlarged in the 14th century, stands in a park surveying the town and valley.** *Admission: 5 frs adults, 2.50 frs. children. Open Wed. 2–7, Thurs.–Mon. 10–noon and 2–7; closed Tuesday.*

You can buy nougat in virtually every shop in town; it makes for a mighty chew, a good idea if you want to keep the children quiet.

Tour 3: Grenoble and the Alps

Whatever the season, the Alpine mountain range is captivating. In winter, the dramatic, snow-carpeted slopes offer some of the best skiing in the world; in summer, chic spas, shimmering lakes, and breathtaking hilltop trails come into their own. The Savoie and Haute-Savoie *departments* occupy the most imprissive Alpine territory, but our tour begins in the Dauphine, with the area's only city: Grenoble.

Grenoble, 104 kilometers (65 miles) southeast of Lyon via A48, is a large, cosmopolitan city whose skyscrapers and forbidding gray buildings may seem intimidating by homey French standards. Along with the city's nuclear research plant, they bear witness to Grenoble's fierce desire to move with the times.

A cable car starting at quai St-Stéphane-Jay whisks you up to the hilltop and its **Fort de la Bastille** (open Apr.–Oct., 9–midnight, Nov.–Dec. and Feb.–Mar., 10–7:30), offering splendid views of the city and river Isère. Walk down rue Maurice-Gignoux, past gardens, cafés, and stone mansions, to the **Musée Dauphinois,** a lively regional museum in a 17th-century convent, featuring displays of local folk arts and crafts. *30 rue Maurice-Gignoux. Admission: 8 frs. Open Wed.–Mon. 9–noon and 2–6; closed Tues.*

Heading left from the museum, make for the church of **St-Laurent,** which contains an atmospherically murky 6th-century crypt (one of the country's oldest Christian monuments) supported by a row of formidable marble pillars. *Rue St-Laurent. Open June–Sept., Wed.–Mon. 10–noon and 2:30–6:30; Oct.–May, by appointment only; closed Tues.*

Art buffs will want to cross the river and pick up rue Bayard, which runs four blocks down to the **Musée de Peinture et de Sculpture** (Painting and Sculpture Museum). The museum showcases an excellent series of 17th-century French and Spanish paintings, plus one of the most exciting modern collections outside Paris, starring Paul Gauguin, Henri Matisse, Amedeo Modigliani, and Pablo Picasso. *Pl. Verdun. Admission: 8 frs. Open Wed.–Mon. 10–noon and 2–6.*

Time Out Leave place Verdun by rue Blanchard and follow it five blocks to **place Grenette,** a lively, flower-strewn pedestrian mall lined with a plethora of sidewalk cafés. It makes a great place to relax and enjoy a *pastis*—an anise-flavored aperitif—while admiring the city's majestic mountain setting.

Take D512 north from Grenoble through the Chartreuse mountain range. Seventeen kilometers (11 miles) from Grenoble, fork left off D512 and follow the small D57-D as far as you can (only a few miles) before leaving your car and making the 30-minute climb to the top of the 6,000-foot Charmant Som peak.
㊷ Your reward: a stimulating view over the **Grande Chartreuse** monastery, 10 kilometers (6 miles) north. The monastery's 12-acre setting, enclosed by wooded heights and limestone crags, is both austere and serene.

Return to D512 and continue north, forking left 8 kilometers (5 miles) along D520-B, just before **St-Pierre-de-Chartreuse;** the Grande Chartreuse is set well back to the right a mile along this road. The monastery, which was to spawn 24 similar charter-houses throughout Europe, was founded by St-Bruno in 1084 according to the ascetic principles of the Benedictine order. It was burned down and rebuilt several times, then finally stripped of its possessions during the French Revolution, when the monks were expelled. The monks were allowed to return several years later and thereupon concocted the sweet Chartreuse liqueur, which soon became a main source of the monastery's income; today, "Green" and "Yellow" Chartreuse are marketed worldwide, though their ingredients remain a closely guarded secret. You can't visit the monastery itself, but stop in at **La Correrie,** next door, to see exhibits on monastic life. You'll also be able to purchase some of the monks' famous brew. *Admission: 10 frs. adults, 5 frs. children. Open Easter–Oct., daily 9–noon and 2–6.*

Return to St-Pierre-de-Chartreuse and continue north along the windy D512 and D912 roads to the elegant old town of **Chambéry,** 40 kilometers (25 miles) away. Stop first for coffee on the pedestrian **place St-Léger** before heading two blocks to visit the 14th-century **Château des Ducs de Savoie.** The château's Gothic Sainte-Chapelle contains some good stained glass and houses a replica of the notorious Turin Shroud, once thought to have been used to wrap up the crucified Christ (but probably, according to recent scientific analysis, a medieval hoax). *Rue Basse du Château. Admission: 10 frs. Guided tours daily at 2:15, Sept.–June, four times daily, July and Aug.*

N201 propels you 14 kilometers (9 miles) north to the gracious spa town of **Aix-les-Bains,** on the eastern shore of Lac du Bourget. Although swimming in the lake is not advised (it's freezing cold), you can sail, fish, play golf and tennis, or picnic in the 25 acres of parkland that stretches along the lakefront. Visit the ruins of the original Roman baths, under the present **Thermes Nationaux** (Thermal Baths), built in 1934 (guided tours only; Apr.–Oct., Mon.–Sat. at 3 PM; Nov.–Mar., Wed. at 3 PM). The Roman Temple of Diana (2nd–3rd century AD) now houses an **archaeology museum** (entrance via the tourist office on place Mollard).

There are half-hour boat trips from Aix-les-Bains across Lac du Bourget to the **Abbaye de Hautecombe,** where mass is celebrated with Gregorian chant. *Cost: 35 frs. Departures from the Grand Pont, Mar.–June and Sept.–Oct., daily at 2:30; July–Aug. at 9:30, 2, 2:30, 3, 3:30, and 4:30.*

Leaving Aix-les-Bains, follow the striking D911 some 24 kilometers (15 miles) to La Charniaz, then turn left along D912, which snakes 24 kilometers (15 miles) farther north alongside the Montagne du Semnoz to **Annecy.**

Annecy stands on the shores of a crystal-clear mountain lake—the Lac d'Annecy—and is surrounded by rugged snow-tipped peaks. The canals, flower-covered bridges, and cobbled pedestrian streets of old Annecy are at their liveliest on market days, Tuesday and Friday, though the town park and the tree-lined boulevard have tranquil, invigorating appeal any day of the week.

There are views over the lake from the towers of the 12th-century **castle,** set high on a hill above the town. Allow a morning or afternoon to make the 40-kilometer (25-mile) drive around the lake, stopping at the picturesque village of **Talloires** and the medieval châteaus at **Duingt** and **Menthon- St-Bernard** (tours every afternoon in July and Aug.; open Thurs. and weekend afternoons only in May, June, and Sept.).

Take N201 north from Annecy and turn off after 18 kilometers (11 miles) into D14, which follows a winding course along Mont Salève to Annemasse 34 kilometers (21 miles) away. From Annemasse, Geneva is just a few minutes away over the Swiss border, but we follow N206/D903 north to **Thonon-les-Bains,** on the banks of Lake Geneva (Lac Léman in French). Thonon and its neighboring sister-spa, **Evian-les-Bains,** have all the trappings (restful parks and lakefront promenades) of chic spa towns. From Evian, there are daily excursions across Lake Geneva to the Swiss town of Lausanne.

Many of the leading Alpine ski resorts lie south of Thonon. A river road (D902) runs 32 kilometers (20 miles) from Thonon to **Morzine. Avoriaz,** renowned for its annual Fantasy Film Festival in January, is reached from Morzine via D338 or by cable car. D902 continues down to Cluses, where the N205 heads left along the Arve Valley to the largish town of **Chamonix** (about 64 kilometers/40 miles from Morzine), the oldest and biggest French winter-sports resort and site of the first Winter Olympics in 1924. The world's highest cable car soars 12,000 feet from Chamonix up the Aiguille du Midi, from where there are staggering views of Europe's loftiest peak, the 15,700-foot **Mont-Blanc.**

N205/D909 leads back down the valley to **Megève,** another major ski resort. From there N212 spears 32 kilometers (20 miles) south through the Arly Valley to **Albertville,** where preparations for the 1992 Winter Olympics are well under way. Stop off at the suburb of **Conflans,** a well-preserved military town, perched precariously on a rocky crag.

Another spectacular road, D925 (becoming D902), heads 61 kilometers (38 miles) east from Albertville to **Bourg-St-Maurice,** a cheerful base for summer vacations, with winter sports catered to at the nearby complexes of **Les Arcs** or **Tignes** (24 kilometers/15 miles south via D902). Tignes features an extensive network of chair lifts and cable cars, which connect it with small resorts like La Daille, Les Boisses, and Les Brévières, as well as the resort of **Val d'Isère,** a favorite among the rich and famous.

The **Route de l'Iseran** (D902) runs from Val d'Isère to Bonneval-sur-Arc, at 9,084 feet the country's highest mountain pass; it's accessible only between July and late October. Along the Iseran Way, a succession of magnificent views unfurl beneath your eyes.

What to See and Do with Children

Lyon is home to an amusing puppet museum, but if your children would like to see the puppets in action, take them to the **Théâtre du Guignol.** *Nouveau Guignol de Lyon, Palais du Conservatoire, rue Louis-Carrand. Children's shows at 3 PM Wed; general performances at 8:30 PM Tues., Thurs., and Fri., and 3 PM Sun.*

The 300-acre **Parc de la Tête d'Or,** on the banks of the Rhône in the north of Lyon, contains a lake, botanical gardens, and a small zoo, as well as facilities for rowing, miniature golf, pony rides, and go-karting. *Take the métro from Perrache train station to Masséna. Admission: free. Open dawn to dusk.*

The following are described fully in our exploring text:

Chair lift at Chamonix, Tour 3
Haut Vivarais Safari Park, Tour 2
Maison des Canuts, Lyon, Tour 1
Musée de la Marionette (Puppet Museum), Lyon, Tour 1
Parc des Oiseaux, Villars-les-Dombes, Tour 1

Off the Beaten Track

Hauterives, 40 kilometers (25 miles) south of Vienne (D538), would be just another quaint village if it weren't for the **Palais Idéal,** one of the weirdest constructions in western Europe. This make-believe palace, constructed entirely of stones and pebbles, was built single-handed by a local postman, Ferdinand Cheval (1836–1924). Although Cheval was haunted by visions of faraway mosques and temples, the result is pure fantasy. It came to be Cheval's lifework: One of the many wall inscriptions reads "1892–1912: 10,000 days, 93,000 hours, 33 years of toil." *Admission 12 frs. adults, 5 frs. children. Open daily 8–8 (closed dusk in winter).*

For a tour of the Auvergne, start at **Le Puy,** 120 kilometers (75 miles) from Privas via N104 and N102, set on a high plateau broken by giant cores of sheer solidified lava, called *puys.* Le Puy's four cores are crowned with man-made monuments: on the lowest, a statue of St. Joseph and the Infant Jesus; on the highest, the 11th-century chapel of St-Michel; on another, a huge statue of the Virgin. Most spectacular is the Romanesque cathedral, **Notre-Dame-du-Puy,** which balances at the top of the fourth narrow pinnacle, approachable only by a long flight of steps. Built of polychrome lava, the cathedral is reminiscent of an Islamic mosque; interior highlights include the statue of the Black Virgin and the Carolingian *Bible of Théodulfe.*

Some 40 kilometers (25 miles) north via N102 and D906 lies the abbey of **Chaise-Dieu,** famous for its splendid red-and-black frescoes of the *Danse Macabre* (Death dancing with the nobility, bourgeoisie, and peasants). The abbey also features 16th-century Brussels and Arras tapestries and 144 carved oak choir stalls.

West of Chaise-Dieu (about 40 kilometers/25 miles via D588) is the town of **Brioude,** whose **St-Julien** basilica is the largest Romanesque church in the Auvergne. Go inside to see the intricately carved column capitals and medieval wall paintings.

The ancient town of **Clermont-Ferrand,** the threshold of the Puy-de-Dome, Auvergne's volcanic region, lies about 100 kilometers (60 miles) north of Brioude via N102 and N9. If you have time for only one excursion in the Auvergne, make it a drive—or walk—to the top of the nearby **Puy-de-Dome volcano,** from whose lofty heights you can take in an extraordinary panorama; extinct volcanoes roll far into the horizon.

Shopping

Clothing and Gift Ideas
Lyon, France's second largest city, makes for the region's best shopping for chic clothing; try the stores on **rue du Président Edouard-Herriot** and **rue de la République** in the center of town. Lyon has maintained its reputation as the French silks-and-textile capital, and all the big-name French and international designers have shops here; Lyonnais designer **Clementine** (18 rue Emile-Zola) is a good bet for well-cut clothes, or, for trendy outfits for youngsters, try **Etincelle** (27 rue St-Jean) in the old town. If it's antiques you're after, wander down **rue Auguste-**

Comte (from place Bellecour to Perrache); you'll find superb engravings at **Caracella** (12 rue du Boeuf) and authentic Lyonnais puppets on **place du Change,** both in the old town.

Food Items Two excellent Lyon *charcuteries* are **Reynon** (13 rue des Archers) and **Vital Pignol** (17 rue Emile-Zola). For chocolates and *patisserie*, try **Bernachon** (42 cours Franklin-Roosevelt). In the Drôme region, the town of **Montélimar** has more nougat shops than cafés; **Chabert et Guillot** (1 rue André-Ducatez) is one of the best.

Arts and Crafts The tiny Ardèche villages of **Thines** and **Les Yans** are popular crafts centers, with several showrooms set up by the **Compagnons de Gerboul,** an association of craftsmen. The medieval village of **Châteauneuf-de-Mazenc** (Drôme) has a particularly pretty arts and crafts shop with a range of handmade jewelry and trinkets.

Sports and Fitness

Skiing The region's most famous ski venue is **Chamonix** (6,063 feet). Most of the slopes are for experienced skiers, but there are plenty of other things to do here: hiking, visiting the casino, or simply admiring the incredible scenery via cable cars. **Val d'Isère** (6,068 feet) ranks as one of Europe's swankiest resorts, with lots of cross-country runs as well as downhill slopes. Nearby **Tignes** is the highest of the Savoie resorts (6,930 feet), with a range of slopes for both beginners and more daring skiers. Family groups should try **Morzine** (3,280 feet), a popular small resort whose gentle slopes are geared to the inexperienced. Chic, expensive **Megève** (3,650 feet) offers a lively night life by way of casino, nightclubs, and restaurants; it also features a particularly impressive network of *téléfériques* (cable cars) and helicopter services. **Courchevel** (6,068 feet) is renowned for its après-ski, while across the mountain, fashionable **Meribel** (5,428 feet) boasts lots of difficult runs; late spring skiing is possible.

Golf Golf clubs are found at **Aix-les-Bains** (av. du Golf), **Annecy** (85 rue du Val Vert), **Chamonix** (rte. de Tines, Les Praz de Chamonix), **Villars-les-Dombes** (Le Clou).

Horseback Riding This is a wonderful region for exploring on horseback. Try the *centres equestres* (stables) at **Aix-les-Bains** (Hippodrome Marlioz), **Chambéry** (rue Sainte-Rose); **Montélimar** (Ile Montmélian), and **Vienne** (Ecuries du Couzon, La Petite Rente).

Swimming The Alpine lakes are pretty chilly for swimming at any time of year, but you'll find warmer water at the following public swimming pools: **Aix-les-Bains** (pl. Daniel Rops), **Albertville** (av. des Chaussures Alpins), **Annecy** (29 rte. Marquisats), **Chambéry** (Nautiparc, rue Eugène-Ducretet), **Grenoble** (rue Lazère-Carnot), **Lyon** (221 rue Garibaldi), and **Valence** (av. Valensolles).

Dining and Lodging

Dining

Lyon is a renowned capital of good cuisine. Gourmets and gourmands both will enjoy the robust local specialties, like *saveloy* (sausage), and *quenelles* (poached fish dumplings). More refined fare is provided by the surrounding regions. The Dombes, extending northeast from Lyon toward Bresse, is rich in game and fowl; chicken, cooked in any number of ways, usually with cream, is a firm favorite. Thrush, partridge, and hare feature prominently on menus as you head south along the Rhône; the *marrons glacés* of Privas and the nougat of Montélimar cater to the sweet tooth. The rivers and lakes of the Alps teem with pike and trout, while the hills are a riot of wild raspberries and blackcurrants during summer months. *Raclette* is a warming Alpine winter specialty: melted cheese served with salami, ham, and boiled potatoes. Licorice-flavored *pastis*, made from anise, is a popular aperitif. A yellowish whiskey-sized measure arrives in a tall glass, accompanied by a pitcher of water: The liquid turns milky when the water is added. Pernod and Ricard are two of the most popular brands.

Highly recommended restaurants are indicated by a star ★.

Lodging

The area covered in our exploring text is too vast for you to make Lyon a central base. But the region is filled with hotels and country inns; at many, you'll be expected to take your evening meal (especially in summer), but this tends to be more a pleasure than an obligation. The Alpine region has an extensive hotel infrastructure—geared primarily to winter visitors, who are invariably expected to take half- or full board *(demi-pension* or *pension complète)*.

Highly recommended restaurants are indicated by a star ★.

Chamonix
Dining and Lodging

Albert I & Milan. The welcoming chalet-style Albert I & Milan is the best-value quality hotel in Chamonix. Many guest rooms have balconies, and all are furnished with elegant period reproductions. The dining room offers stupendous views of Mont Blanc, while the cuisine scales heights of invention and enthusiasm; try the oysters fried with asparagus. *119 impasse du Montenvers, 74400, tel. 50–53–05–09. 30 rooms with bath. Facilities: restaurant, pool, tennis, sauna, Jacuzzi. AE, DC, MC, V. Closed middle 2 weeks of May and Oct. 23–Dec. 9; restaurant closed Wed. out of season. Moderate–Expensive.*

Bourg-en-Bresse
Dining

L'Auberge Bressane. The beauty of this restaurant's location—the terrace looks out on the elegant Brou church—makes up for the rather chilly welcome you'll receive inside. The rustic dining room is an excellent setting in which to enjoy the academic rigor of Jean Pierre Vullin's cooking. The wine list offers more than 300 vintages. Frogs' legs and succulent Bresse chicken with morel mushroom cream sauce are house specialties. *116 blvd. de Brou, tel. 74–22–22–68. Reservations required. Jacket and tie required. AE, DC, V. Closed Mon. dinner, and Tues., Sept.–mid-Mar. Very Expensive.*

★ **La Petite Auberge.** This cozily informal flower-strewn inn is set in the countryside just on the outskirts of town. Motherly Madame Bertrand is a kindly hostess and even provides games for children on the summer terrace. Inside, you'll appreciate chef Philippe Garnier's subtle way with mullet (he grills it in saffron butter) and Bresse chicken (browned in tangy cider vinegar). *St-Just, Ceyzeriat, tel. 74–22–30–04. Reservations accepted. Dress: casual. V. Closed Mon. dinner and Jan. Moderate–Expensive.*

Jacques Guy. The softly lit pastels of the decor and the neoclassical-style furniture lend this restaurant an appealing ambience. The regional cuisine varies with the seasons; poached Bresse chicken with tarragon or bass with red butter sauce both make fine choices. *19 pl. Bernard, tel. 74–45–29–11. Reservations advised. Dress: casual chic. AE, DC, MC, V. Closed Sun. dinner, Mon. Moderate–Expensive.*

Lodging **Terminus.** The best hotel in town is a converted mansion close to the train station. The guest rooms have been renovated with considerable taste and feature traditional French decor; the best room in the house is the two-room suite. The flower garden makes a fine place to relax and sip *pastis*. You'll be given a hearty meal (*saveloy* and seasonal game birds) in the unpretentious restaurant; in fine weather, you can dine outdoors on the terrace. *19 rue Alphonse-Baudin, 01000 Bourg-en-Bresse, tel. 74–21–01–21. 50 rooms with bath. Facilities: restaurant, garden. AE, DC, MC, V. Moderate.*

Hauterives **Le Relais.** The local tourist wonder, the Palais Idéal, is just a
Dining and Lodging stone's throw from this comfortable, rustic inn. The reasonably sized guest rooms feature an unpretentious country look, with chunky wooden desks and headboards and wicker-seated chairs. The same warm, golden color scheme dominates the cozy restaurant, where you can enjoy specialties like roasted partridge or delicately seasoned frogs' legs. Half-board is mandatory during summer months. *26390 Hauterives, tel. 75–68–81–12. 13 rooms with bath. Facilities: restaurant. AE, DC, V. Closed Sun. dinner, Mon., and Jan.–Feb. Moderate.*

Montélimar **Les Hospitaliers.** This tastefully designed modern hotel is in
Lodging the center of the tiny hilltop town of Poët-Laval, 22 kilometers (14 miles) east of Montélimar along D540. With its stone walls and red tile roof, the hotel blends perfectly into the medieval surroundings; there are sweeping views of the valley and mountains from the terrace. In cold weather, you can escape from the tacky '70s decor of the large guest rooms to warm yourself by the immense stone hearth in the sitting room. Local specialties are served in the airy restaurant; thrush pâté with truffles is always a good bet. *Le Vieux Village, Poët-Laval, 26160 La Bégude de Mazenc, tel. 75–46–22–32. 20 rooms with bath. Facilities: restaurant, pool. AE, DC, MC, V. Closed mid-Nov.–Feb. Expensive.*

★ **Relais de l'Empéreur.** Sure enough, Napoleon spent a night here, on April 24, 1814, after his return from exile on the Mediterranean island of Elba—sufficient reason for the hotel to have carved a niche in the hearts of many visitors. The grandiose Empire decor of the guest rooms does its bit as well. There's a stylish, if costly, restaurant, where the Napoleonic heartstrings are tugged to the breaking point (guinea fowl *à la Joséphine*, "imperial" thrush pâté). *1 pl. Marx-Dormoy,*

26000, tel. 75–01–29–00. 38 rooms with bath. AE, DC, MC, V. Closed mid-Nov.–Christmas. Moderate–Expensive.

Lyon **Paul Bocuse.** One of the country's most celebrated gourmet
Dining temples lies 12 kilometers (7 miles) north of town in Collonges-
★ au-Mont-d'Or. The dining room's grand decor is a fitting backdrop for the culinary expertise of larger-than-life chef Paul
Bocuse. Bocuse is often away on the lecture-tour trail, but his
restaurant continues to please its elegantly dressed diners,
who feast on house specialties like truffle soup and succulent
sea bass. The restaurant's reputation means you'll have to reserve a table long in advance; this won't be an impromptu meal.
*50 quai de la Plage, tel. 78–22–01–40. Reservations essential.
Jacket and tie required. AE, DC, V. Very Expensive.*

Léon de Lyon. A mixture of regional tradition (dumplings, hot
sausages) and eye-opening innovation keep this restaurant at
the forefront of the city's gastronomic scene. The restaurant
occupies two floors in an old house full of alcoves and wood paneling. The blue-aproned waiters blend in with the old-fashioned
decor, and dishes such as fillet of veal with celery or leg of lamb
with fava beans will linger in your memory. *1 rue Pleney, tel.
78–28–11–33. Reservations essential. Jacket and tie required.
MC, V. Closed Sun., Mon. lunch, and Dec. 24–Jan. 6. Expensive.*

★ **Tour Rose.** Romantics look no farther. Le Tour Rose is set in
one of the most distinctive 17th-century residences of old Lyon,
inside a mellow pink tower. The dining room decor is sumptuous and sophisticated, with gleaming cutlery and crisp linen
cloths. Chef Philippe Chavent's nouvelle dishes are served with
style in an intimate, candlelit setting. Chavent is a master of
seafood; try the lightly cooked salmon or the sea urchin bisque.
*16 rue du Boeuf, tel. 78–37–25–90. Reservations required.
Jacket and tie required. AE, DC, V. Closed Sun. and Aug. Expensive.*

★ **Café des Fédérations.** For the past 80 years, this sawdust-
strewn café has reigned as one of the city's friendliest eating
spots; expect to be treated like one of the gang. Jocular René
Fulchiron not only serves up deftly prepared Lyonnaise classics like hearty *boudin blanc* (white-meat sausage), he also
comes out to chat with guests and make sure everyone feels at
home. The decor is a homey mix of red-checked tablecloths,
wood paneling, and old-fashioned bench seating. *8 rue du Ma-
jor-Martin, tel. 78–28–26–00. Reservations advised. Dress:
casual. AE, V. Closed Sat., Sun., and Aug. Moderate.*

Chez Sylvain. The old-fashioned decor of Chez Sylvain is a delightful reminder of its days as a favorite neighborhood
beanery. Little has changed since, and the huge wooden counter, turn-of-the-century wall decorations, and original spiral
staircase are the ideal backdrop for Sylvain's robust Lyonnaise
cuisine; the tripe and *andouillettes* (chitterling sausages) are
especially good. *4 rue Tupin, tel. 78–42–11–98. Reservations
accepted. Dress: casual. V. Closed Sun., Mon., and Aug. Inexpensive.*

Lodging **La Cour des Loges.** A team of young Lyonnais architects and
★ Italian interior designers worked for three years to transform
four Renaissance mansions into the most stylish hotel in Lyon.
Four stories of sand-colored stone, an immense courtyard, spiral stone staircases, and exposed roof beams lend a courtly
ambience, while guest rooms are furnished with the best in
modern design furniture and effects. In the cellar, there's an

exclusive wine club, while an informal little *tapas* bar provides an array of appetizer-sized snacks. *6 rue du Boeuf, 69005, tel. 78–42–75–75. 63 rooms with bath. Facilities: bar, pool, Jacuzzi, sauna, health club, wine cellar, boutiques. AE, DC, MC, V. Very Expensive.*

Grand Hôtel des Beaux-Arts. An explosion of columns, seashells, and swags covers the walls of this downtown hotel, conveniently situated next to place Bellecour and the downtown pedestrian area. The authentic Old European mood is further bolstered by an abundance of old leather armchairs. Guest rooms, while on the small side, retain the opulent Belle Epoque atmosphere of the public areas. There's no restaurant. *74 rue du President Edouard-Herriot, 69002, tel. 78–38–09–50. 79 rooms with bath. AE, DC, V. Expensive.*

★ **Morand.** This quiet and delightfully idiosyncratic hotel is located in a residential area of the city. Flowers abound on the pretty inner courtyard that doubles as a breakfast veranda, and the smiles at reception foster a mood of good cheer and friendliness. Guest rooms are on the small side, but feature lots of homey knickknacks. There's no restaurant. *99 rue de Créqui, 69006, tel. 78–52–29–96. 34 rooms, 27 with bath. AE. Inexpensive.*

Pérouges
Dining and Lodging
★
Ostellerie du Vieux Pérouges. This historic Bresson inn is an extraordinary place, even by French standards. Antiques are scattered throughout, and the venerable rustic tone is heightened by glossy wood floors and tables and gigantic stone hearths. You'll be served your meal on chunky pewter plates, by waitresses decked out in colorful folk costume; the crayfish is particularly good. Reserve a room in the geranium-clad 15th-century manor, rather than in the modern annex; those in the former are more spacious, with marble bathrooms and period furniture. *Pl. des Tilleuls, 01800, tel. 74–61–00–88. 28 rooms with bath. Facilities: restaurant. Restaurant closed Thurs. lunch and Wed., Nov.–Mar. Very Expensive.*

Privas
Dining
Lou Esclos. In the countryside, just 5 kilometers (3 miles) southwest of Privas on D2, is a striking modern restaurant with more windows than walls—all looking out over the wild Ardèche landscape. Monsieur Costechareyre serves succulent French cuisine—including goose and snail *feuilleté* (in a flaky pastry)—at a price that's almost too good to be true. *07000 Alissas, tel. 75–65–12–73. Reservations accepted. Dress: casual. AE, V. Closed last week Dec.–Jan. 10. Inexpensive.*

Serrières
Dining and Lodging
Chez Schaeffer. In a sophisticated setting of white wood trim, Chef Bernard Mathé dishes up inventive variants of traditional French dishes: smoked duck cutlet in lentil stew and curried lamb cutlet with morel mushrooms. Don't skimp on dessert; the choice is somewhat overwhelming, but the pistachio cake with bitter chocolate is a clear winner. There are 12 contemporary guest rooms as well. *RN86, 07340, tel. 75–34–00–07. 12 rooms with bath. Reservations required. Jacket and tie required. AE, DC, V. Closed Jan. and 3rd week in Oct. Moderate/Expensive.*

Tournon
Dining
Jean-Marc Reynaud. Tain l'Hermitage, just across the river from Tournon, is the setting for this fine restaurant, which boasts a magnificent view over the Rhône and a comfortable, atmospheric dining room. Brilliantly prepared traditional cuisine is served in the traditionally styled dining room; house specialties include poached egg with foie gras and pigeon fillet

in a blackcurrant sauce. *82 av. du Président Roosevelt, 26600, tel. 75–07–22–10. Reservations advised. Dress: casual. AE, DC, V. Closed Sun. dinner, Mon., and Jan. Moderate.*

Dining and Lodging **Michel Chabran.** This sophisticated hotel/restaurant is decidedly modern; it's on the east bank of the Rhône at Pont de l'Isère, 10 kilometers (6 miles) south of Tournon via N7. The guest rooms, lounge, and dining rooms feature slick Danish-style furniture, elaborate floral displays, and airy plate-glass windows opening onto the private garden. Chabran's cuisine is equally light and imaginative; try his grilled salmon in creamed butter sauce. *Pont de l'Isère, 26600 Tain l'Hermitage, tel. 75–84–60–09. 12 rooms with bath. Facilities: restaurant. V. Closed Sun. dinner and Mon. in winter. Expensive.*

Valence **Pic.** The Pic family are the undisputed kings among Drôme res-
Dining and Lodging taurateurs, with subtle and original recipes to please the most
★ demanding gourmets; try the truffle or bass with caviar. Comfortable, embroidered armchairs; flowering plants on all the tables; wall-to-wall carpeting; and the smiling service of Madame Pic lend a cozy warmth to the peach-colored dining room. In summer you can eat outside on the terrace. Two elegantly furnished guest rooms and two even more opulent suites are available, but you'll have to reserve long in advance. *285 av. Victor-Hugo, 26000, tel. 75–44–15–32. Reservations essential. Jacket and tie required. AE, DC, V. Closed Sun. dinner, Wed., most of Aug., and 2 weeks in Feb. Very Expensive.*

Vienne **Le Bec Fin.** A weekday menu costing under 100 francs makes
Dining the Bec Fin a good lunch spot, as well as a serious dinner venue. The well-run, unpretentious eatery is just opposite the cathedral; its main dishes—steak and freshwater fish—seldom disappoint and occasionally display a deft touch *(burbot, or cod, cooked with saffron)*. The gray-and-white dining room has an understated elegance. *7 pl. St-Maurice, tel. 74–85–76–72. Reservations accepted. Jacket required. MC, V. Closed Sun. dinner and Mon. Moderate.*

Vonnas **Georges Blanc.** It's worth making the 19-kilometer (12-mile)
Dining and Lodging trip from Bourg-en-Bresse west to Vonnas (via D936, D45, and
★ D96) because Georges Blanc must rank as one of the world's best chefs. The simple 19th-century country inn has been embellished with flowers, rugs, grandfather clocks, and antique country furniture and makes a fine setting in which to appreciate Blanc's constantly updated menu. Try the frogs' legs any way he offers them. The wine list is extensive, the desserts superb. There are also 30 guest rooms, ranging from (relatively) simple to downright luxurious. Make your reservations well in advance. *01540 Vonnas, tel. 74–50–00–10. 30 rooms with bath. Facilities: restaurant, pool, tennis, golf, helipad. AE, DC, MC, V. Closed Jan.–mid-Feb.; restaurant closed Wed. and Thurs. (except for dinner June–mid-Sept.). Very Expensive.*

The Arts and Nightlife

The Arts

Lyon is the region's liveliest arts center; *Lyon-Poche,* a weekly guide published on Wednesdays and sold at any newsstand, will give details of the week's cultural events. In Grenoble, pick up the monthly *Grenoble-Spectacles.*

Festivals   September in Lyon sees the internationally renowned **Festival Berlioz** and the **Biennale de la Danse** (staged in alternate years), as well as the **International Puppet Festival**. October brings the **Festival Bach** (tel. 78–72–75–31) and the Contemporary Arts Festival, **Octobre des Arts** (tel. 78–30–50–66). During the second week of October, Lyon stages a pottery fair, **Foire aux Tuppiniers** (tel. 78–37–00–68), while in November, there's a **Music Festival** in Vieux Lyon (tel. 78–28–53–48).

Jazz enthusiasts will want to catch Grenoble's popular **Cinq Jours de Jazz** (Five Days of Jazz) in February or March, and those with classical tastes are catered to during the **Session Internationale de Grenoble-Isère** in June and July. Vienne's cathedral and church host a **Summer Music Festival** throughout June, July, and August.

Theater   The café-theater, a Lyonnais specialty, fuses art with café society; **Espace Gerson** (1 pl. Gerson, tel. 78–27–96–99) or **Café-Théâtre Accessoire** (26 rue de L'Annonciande, tel. 78–27–84–84). More conventional Lyon theaters include **Théâtre Tête d'Or** (24 rue Dunoir, tel. 78–62–76–73); **Théâtre de Lyon** (7 rue des Aqueducs, tel. 78–36–67–67), and **Théâtre des Ateliers** (5 rue du Petit David, tel. 78–37–46–30). And in Grenoble: **Hexagon** (rue des Ayjinards, in the suburb of Meylan, tel. 76–90–00–45) and **Théâtre Municipale** (2 rue Hector-Berlioz, tel. 76–40–06–94).

Music   Lyon's Société de Musique de Chambre (Chamber Music Society) performs at **Salle Molière** (18 quai Bondy, tel. 78–28–03–11).

Nightlife

Lyon is your best bet for nighttime entertainment, with dozens of discos, piano bars, and nightclubs; for a full list of what's available, pick up a copy of the weekly guide, *Lyon-Poche*.

Discos and   Laser beams and video screens make **L'Actuel** (30 blvd. E-
Nightclubs   Deruelle) a frenetic place to dance the night away in Lyon. **Comoedia** (4 rue C-Dullin) is more low key, with a downstairs disco and an old-fashioned piano bar upstairs. Expect anything from the tango to rock and roll at **Jany's Retro Club** (31 rue du Bât-d'Argent), and a trendy crowd at the **19 Club** (19 pl. St-Paul), with its panther-skin seats. Caribbean and African music are featured at **Club Caraïbes** (5 rue Terme).

Bars and Pubs   Lyon's **Hot Club** (26 rue Lanterne) has been going strong for 40 years in a vaulted stone basement that features live jazz. **Ephenon** (21 pl. G-Rambaud) is a more restrained cocktail bar catering to the city's intellectual set. If you'd like a casual game of darts and a pint of bitter, head to the **Albion Public House** (12 rue Ste-Catherine). The **Bouchons aux Vins** wine bar (62 rue Mercière) has over 30 vintages for you to choose from; for a more romantic evening, make it a champagne toast in the intimate, wood-paneled **Metroclub** (2 rue Stella). Fifties fans should try the **Navire Bar** (3 rue Terme).

11 Alsace-Lorraine

Introduction

Alsace-Lorraine, in the northeast corner of France, is often considered to have a single identity, but each of the two regions has its own traditions and economic, social, and geographic peculiarities.

Alsace is heavily German influenced. Regional dialect is still in extensive use: Conversations between locals are incomprehensible even to most Frenchmen. Town names in Alsace sound and look German, and the main daily paper is published in both French and German. The much-resented German occupation of 1870–1918 was limited to Alsace and just the eastern, German-speaking part of Lorraine.

Lorraine, pierced by the cheerful Moselle Valley, is an industrially depressed area whose richest days are past. Its towns and villages possess neither the self-confidence nor the picturesque appeal of those of Alsace, where the tourist industry booms and the economy thrives on excellent transportation links with neighboring Germany and Switzerland.

Strasbourg is the capital of Alsace and unofficial "capital" of Europe, as it is home to European political institutions and a symbol of Franco-German reconciliation. It is a city of great cultural, historic, and architectural interest. The rest of Alsace is over 100 miles long but seldom more than 30 miles wide, squeezed in between the Vosges Mountains and the River Rhine. Much of Alsace is a flat plain; the prettiest parts are the vineyards that nestle amid the Vosges foothills. The Route du Vin (Wine Road) weaves its way through any number of flower-strewn villages, which feature medieval towers, walls, and houses built in the unmistakable red sandstone of the Vosges. These mountains may not possess the craggy majesty of the Alps, but are peppered with ski resorts and dramatic views of lakes and forests.

Noble storks flutter overhead; their distinctively large nests crown the spires of many church towers. Sauerkraut, foie gras, and, more unexpectedly, tobacco, number among the regional specialties. Although France's major breweries are situated here, Alsace is more famous for its white wine, named not by locality but by the variety of grape. The best are elegant, dry Riesling; fragrant Muscat; fruity Tokay; and spicy Gewurtztraminer.

Grapes are scarcer in Lorraine than the plums that are used to make Mirabelle brandy. At the region's heart is another city of great appeal: Nancy, former capital of the dukes of Lorraine and imbued with medieval and neo-Classic elegance. The double-armed Cross of Lorraine was adopted by General de Gaulle's freedom fighters in World War II, but Lorraine has more potent links with World War I: the Battle of Verdun was the bitterest on the Western Front.

Nowhere in France is farther from the sea, so the climate in Alsace–Lorraine is continental: Winters can be extremely cold and summers mighty hot. The Vosges Mountains, which often act as a cloud buffer, ensure that rain is less ferequent in Alsace than in Lorraine.

Essential Information

Important Addresses and Numbers

Tourist Information The principal regional tourist offices are to be found at **Strasbourg** (behind the cathedral, 9 rue du Dôme, tel. 88–22–01–02) and **Nancy** (14 pl. Stanislas, tel. 83–35–22–41). In **Strasbourg**, there is another tourist office, concerned more with the city than with the region (10 pl. Gutenberg, tel. 88–32–57–07).

The addresses of other tourist offices in towns mentioned in this chapter are as follows: **Colmar** (4 rue Unterlinden, tel. 89–41–02–29), **Guebwiller** (5 pl. St-Léger, tel. 89–76–10–63), **Metz** (pl. d'Armes, tel. 87–75–65–21), **Mulhouse** (9 av. du Maréchal-Foch, tel. 89–45–68–31), **Obernai** (Chapelle du Beffroi, pl. du Marche, tel. 88–95–64–13), **Saverne** (Château des Rohan, tel. 88–91–80–47), **Sélestat** (10 blvd. Leclerc, tel. 88–92–02–66), **Toul** (Parvis de la Cathédrale, tel. 83–64–11–69), and **Verdun** (pl. de la Nation, tel. 29–84–18–85).

Travel Agencies **American Express** (30 pl. Kléber, Strasbourg, tel. 88–32–16–34), **Havas Voyages** (28 rue des Grandes Arcades, Strasbourg, tel. 88–32–99–77), and **Thomas Cook** (2 rue Raymond-Poincaré, Nancy, tel. 83–35–06–97).

Car Rental In **Nancy**: Hertz (pl. Thiers, tel. 83–32–13–14) and Europcar (18 rue de Serre, tel. 83–37–57–24) In **Strasbourg**: Avis (Galerie Marchande, pl. de la Gare, tel. 88–32–30–44).

Arriving and Departing

By Plane Most international flights to Alsace land at Mulhouse-Basle airport on the Franco-Swiss border. There are also airports at Strasbourg, Metz, Nancy, and Mirecourt (Vittel/Epinal).

By Car The A4 expressway heads east from Paris to Strasbourg, via Verdun, Metz, and Saverne. It is met by A26, coming down from the English Channel, at Reims. A31 links Metz to Nancy, continuing south to Burgundy and Lyon.

By Train Mainline trains leave Paris **(Gare de l'Est)** every couple of hours for the four-hour, 504-kilometer (315-mile) journey to Strasbourg. Some stop at Toul and all stop at Nancy, where there are connections for Epinal, Gérardmer, and Vittel. Trains run three times daily from Paris to Verdun and more often to Metz (around three hours in each case). Mainline trains stop at Mulhouse (four to five hours) en route to Basle.

Getting Around

By Car N83, a fast, multilane highway that becomes the A35 expressway in parts, shoots through the Plain of Alsace, providing the quickest link between Strasbourg, Colmar, and Mulhouse.

By Train The local trains, which operate several times each day between Strasbourg and Mulhouse (en route to Dijon and Lyon), stop at Sélestat and Colmar.

Guided Tours

Bus Excursions **Horizons Européens** (France Tourisme, 214 rue de Rivoli, 75001 Paris, tel. 42–60–31–25) organizes an excellent seven-day bus tour of Alsace-Lorraine, taking in Verdun, Nancy, Strasbourg, and Colmar, with an excursion to Germany and the Black Forest, for around 5,000 francs inclusive. It also offers three-day trips to Nancy, Strasbourg, and Colmar for 2,000 francs.

Aerial Tours You can take a 15-minute helicopter tour of Nancy with **Tecnavia** (tel. 83–21–09–75) or a plane ride over Strasbourg from the **Aérodrome du Polygone** (tel. 88–34–00–98).

Orientation Tours **Strasbourg Port Authority** (25 rue de la Nuée-Bleue, tel. 88–32–49–15) organizes 75-minute boat tours along the River Ill, which encircles Old Strasbourg; the commentary, though trite, is at least audible, and the views are superb. The fare is 28 francs for adults, 15 francs for children under 16. Departures (every half-hour from 9:30 summer, less frequently in spring and fall) are from the quay on rue de Rohan, just down from place de Château.

Landlubbers might be interested in the 50-minute tour of the old city of Strasbourg by **minitrain,** which leaves place de Château from April to October, daily every half-hour from 9:30. The fare is 20 francs for adults, 12 francs for children under 12.

Exploring Alsace-Lorraine

Numbers in the margin correspond with points of interest on the Alsace and Lorraine maps.

Orientation

Our tour of Alsace-Lorraine begins in Strasbourg, a city of such historic and cultural importance that it is well worth exploring in detail. From here, our second tour takes you through the rest of Alsace, south through the charming villages along the Route du Vin (Wine Road) to Thann, and north again via a 72-kilometer (45-mile) scenic drive past lakes, valleys, and forests along the Route des Crêtes (Crest Road). The third tour covers the region of Lorraine, with a thorough look at the artistic town of Nancy.

Highlights for First-time Visitors

Cathédrale Notre-Dame, Strasbourg, Tour 1
Château des Rohan, Strasbourg, Tour 1
Haut-Koenigsbourg, Tour 2
Issenheim Altarpiece, Musée d'Unterlinden, Colmar, Tour 2
Mont Ste-Odile, Tour 2
Nancy, Tour 3
Toul, Tour 3

Tour 1: Strasbourg

❶ **Strasbourg** is perhaps the most interesting and attractive French city after Paris—an irresistible mixture of old houses,

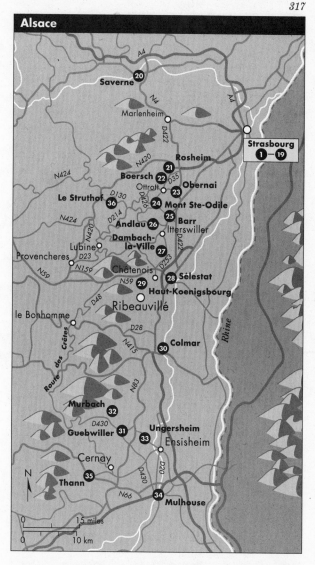

Alsace

waterways, museums, the European Parliament, and, looming above them all, the colossal single spire of the cathedral.

The Romans knew Strasbourg as Argentoratum. After a spell as part of the Holy Roman Empire, the city was united with France in 1681, but retained independence regarding legislation, education, and religion under the honorific title Free Royal City. Since World War II, Strasbourg has become a symbol city, embodying Franco-German reconciliation and the wider idea of a united Europe. It plays host to the European Parliament and Council of Europe and acts as a neutral stomping ground for such controversial political figures as Yasser Arafat, leader of the Palestinian Liberation Organization.

Strasbourg

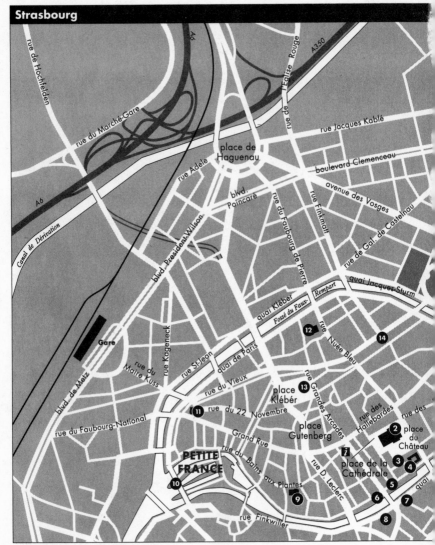

Ancienne Douane, **6**
Cathédrale
Notre-Dame, **2**
Château des Rohan, **4**
Cour du Courbeau, **7**
Musée Alsacien, **8**
Musée Historique, **5**

Musée de l'Oeuvre
Notre-Dame, **3**
Orangerie, **19**
Palais de
l'Université, **17**
Place Broglie, **14**
Place Kléber, **13**

Place de la
République, **15**
Ponts Couverts, **10**
St-Paul, **16**
St-Pierre-le-Jeune, **12**
St-Pierre-le-Vieux, **11**
St-Thomas, **9**

place de
Bordeaux

rue Lauth

blvd. Jacques-Preiss

rue Oberlin

av. de la Paix

rue Schwilgué

rue Ervin

allée de la Robertsau

avenue de l'Europe

18

19

Orangerie

rue Trubner

rue
Schubert

rue de Verdun

rue Schweighauser

15

16

av. de la Forê Noire

av. de la Marseillaise

17

Jardin
Botanique

rue de l'Observatoire

Frères

rue de l'Académie

blvd. de la Victoire

N

des Bateliers

rue de G. Zimmer

rue Blaise Pascal

av. du G. de Gaulle

0   300 yards

0   300 meters

rue Rene Descartes

rue de Londres

At the hub of Strasbourg, on place de la Cathédrale, is the **Cathédrale Notre-Dame,** with its splendid openwork spire. Pink masonry covers the facade. Not content with the outlines of the walls themselves, medieval builders stuck huge, slender, rodlike shafts of stone everywhere: You feel as if you can reach up and snap one off. The spire, finished in 1439, looks absurdly fragile as it tapers skyward like some elongated, 466-foot wedding cake; only the 528-foot spire of Ulm, in West Germany, climbs higher.

The interior presents a stark contrast to the facade. For a start, it is older, virtually finished by 1275. Then, at 105 feet, the nave does not create the same impression of soaring height: Its broad windows emphasize the horizontal rather than the vertical. In the nave, note Hans Hammer's ornately sculpted pulpit (1484–86), with its 50 statuettes, and the richly painted 14th–15th-century organ loft that rises from pillar to ceiling.

Another contrast is apparent within—that between the choir and the nave. The choir is not ablaze with stained glass, but framed by chunky masonry. The original brickwork of the cupola is visible, as if no one had ever gotten around to decorating it. The fact that the choir is raised above the level of the rest of the church heightens the contrast and reinforces an aura of murky mystical sanctity.

The elaborate 16th-century **Chapelle St-Laurent,** to the left of the choir, merits a visit, but most visitors turn to the right to admire the **Angels Column,** an intricate pillar dating from 1230, formed by clustering, tubelike colonnettes harboring three tiers of delicate statues. Nearby, the daring Renaissance machinery of the 16th-century **Astronomical Clock** whirs into action at 12:30 PM daily: Macabre clockwork figures—including a skeletal Father Time and the screeching rooster that reminds the Apostle Peter of his broken promise—enact the story of Christ's Passion. *Admission to clock: 6 frs.*

There is a *son-et-lumière* (sound-and-light) performance in the cathedral every evening from April through the end of September. The text is in French or German, but virtuoso lighting effects pierce any linguistic fog. *Admission: 21 frs. adults, 12 frs. children under 18. Performances at 8:15 and 9:15PM.*

A worthy complement to the cathedral is the **Musée de l'Oeuvre Notre-Dame,** opposite the south front. There is more to this museum than the usual assembly of dilapidated statues rescued from the local cathedral before they fell off. A conscious effort has been made to create a church atmosphere and provide anappropriate setting for the works of art. Part of one room evokes a narrow, low-roofed cloister. A dimly lit, high-walled chamber, reached through a creaky wooden door, is ringed by stone screens with pinnacles and pointed gables. Soon you find yourself in the stonemasons' workshop. A polished wooden staircase leads to a suite of small passages and large rooms, with drawings, stained glass, and gold objects. All the architectural elements of the Renaissance—pediments, spiral pillars, and cornices—can be found on the bulky wardrobes and cupboards produced by local cabinetmakers. There are some fine Old Master paintings as well. *Pl. du Château. Admission: 10 frs. adults, 5 frs. students and children. Open Apr.–Sept., Wed.–Mon. 10–noon and 2–6; Oct.–Mar., Wed.–Sat., Mon. 2–6, Sun. 10–noon; closed Tues.*

4 Alongside the Musée de l'Oeuvre Notre-Dame, between the cathedral and the river, is the **Château des Rohan,** one-time palace of the powerful Rohans, a dynasty of prince-bishops who held both political and spiritual sway over the city and region. The exterior of Robert de Cotte's neo-Classical building (1732–42) is starkly austere. The glamour is inside, in Robert le Lorrain's magnificent ground-floor rooms, led by the great **Salon d'Assemblée** (Assembly Room) and the book- and tapestry-lined **Bibliothèque des Cardinaux** (Cardinals' Library).

The library leads to a series of less august rooms that house the **Musée des Arts Décoratifs** (Decorative Arts Museum) and its elaborate display of ceramics. Works by Hannong, a porcelain manufacturer active in Strasbourg from 1721 to 1782, are comprehensively represented; dinner services by other local kilns reveal the influence of Chinese porcelain in their delicate patterns. Equally interesting are the dishes and terrines in animal form (turkeys and hogs' heads), or table decorations imitating plums and cauliflowers—of doubtful taste but technical *tours de force.* Furniture, tapestries, and silver-gilt complete the collection. *Pl. du Château. Admission: 15 frs. adults, 8 frs. students and children. Open Apr.–Sept., Wed.–Mon. 10–noon and 2–6; Oct.–Mar., Wed.–Sat., Mon. 2–6, Sun. 10–noon; closed Tues.*

About 50 yards north of the cathedral, and running parallel to it, is rue des Hallebardes, Strasbourg's most stylish pedestrian-only shopping street. It leads to **place Gutenberg,** dominated by an elegant three-story building with large windows, constructed 1582–85, now used as the Chamber of Commerce and city tourist office. Johannes Gutenberg (1400–68), after whom the square is named, invented the printing press in Strasbourg in 1434. On one side of his statue, executed in 1840 by sculptor David d'Angers, is a plaque bearing the U.S. Declaration of Independence, in acknowledgment of its influence on French revolutionary soldiers from Alsace.

5 The **Musée Historique** (Local History Museum) stands between place Gutenberg and the river. Wooden floors and beam roofs create a suitably historic atmosphere in which to admire maps, armor, arms, bells, uniforms, printing paraphernalia, cardboard toy soldiers, and two huge relief models of Strasbourg, one made in 1727, the other in 1836. *3 rue de la Grande-Boucherie. Closed for restoration at press time, but due to open in 1990. Open Oct.–Mar., Wed.–Mon. 2–6; Apr.–Sept., Wed.–Mon. 10–noon and 2–6; closed Tues.*

6 The **Ancienne Douane,** opposite, was constructed in 1358 to serve as a customs house. It now houses a brasserie and temporary exhibitions. *Admission: 20 frs. adults, 10 frs. students and children. Open Wed.–Mon. 11–6; closed Tues.*

Time Out Apart from the usual cafés, Alsace is filled with down-to-earth winebars, known as *weinstuben,* serving snacks and local specialties (sauerkraut, sausages, and snails) and wine by the jug. The long, wood-paneled, large-window *weinstub* at the corner of rue du Maroquin and place de la Grande-Boucherie, between the cathedral and the river, makes a cool, seldom-crowded place to pause from museums and monuments.

7 Across the river is the **cour du Courbeau,** a ramshackle 14th-century courtyard whose hostelry once welcomed kings and

8 emperors. Facing the Ancienne Douane is the **Musée Alsacien.** If you want a glimpse of how Alsace families used to live, this is the place to visit. Local interiors—kitchens, bedrooms, and sitting rooms (the latter two often combined)—have been faithfully reconstituted. The diverse activities of blacksmiths, clog makers, saddlers, and makers of artificial flowers are explained with the help of old-time artisans' tools and equipment. *23 quai St-Nicolas. Admission: 10 frs. adults, 5 frs. students and children. Open Oct.–Mar., Wed.–Sat., Mon. 2–6, Sun. 10–noon and 2–6; Apr.–Sept., Wed.–Mon. 10–noon and 2–6; closed Tues.*

Cross the river two bridges farther down to admire the church
9 of **St-Thomas** (quai Finkwiller), particularly the mausoleum of Marshal Maurice of Saxony (1696–1750), a key figure in the 1740–48 War of Austrian Succession. Follow the banks of the River Ill toward the picturesque quarter of **La Petite France,** lined with richly carved, half-timbered Renaissance houses and cobbled streets. The Ill, which branches into sev-
10 eral canals, is spanned by the **Ponts Couverts,** three connected 14th-century covered bridges, each with its tall, stern, stone tower.

11 Quai Turckheim leads to the church of **St-Pierre-le-Vieux,** whose choir is decorated with scenes from the Passion (circa 1500) by local painter Henri Lutzelmann. Follow the quay
12 around to **St-Pierre-le-Jeune,** consecrated in 1320, to admire its painted rood screen, immense choir, and 14th-century frescoes.

Alsace provided the French Revolution with 64 generals and marshals. One of the most famous was Jean-Baptiste Kléber (1753–1800), assassinated in Cairo after being left in charge of Egypt by Napoleon in 1799. Kléber's statue lords it over
13 Strasbourg's busiest square, **place Kléber,** situated up rue des Grandes-Arcades from St-Pierre-le-Jeune.

Time Out Rue des Orfèvres, one of the lively pedestrian streets leading off from rue des Hallebardes, is connected to the noisy, commercial rue des Grandes-Arcades by a cobbled, leafy square— the **place du Marché-Neuf**—seldom discovered by visitors. This peaceful oasis is a fine place to stop for a drink, and its two open-air cafés are open till late at night.

---

14 Rue de l'Outre heads down to another large square, **place Broglie,** home of the city hall, the 18th-century Municipal Theater, and the Banque de France—the last built on the site of the house where the *Marseillaise* (composed by Rouget de Lisle, and originally entitled *Battlesong of the Rhine Army)* was sung for the first time in 1792.

15 The spacious layout and ponderous architecture of **place de la République** have nothing in common, bar the local red sandstone, with the old town across the river. A different hand was at work here, that of occupying Germans, who erected the former Ministry (1902); the Academy of Music (1882–92), ex-Regional Parliament; and the Palais du Rhin (1883–88), destined to be the German imperial palace.

Much of northern Strasbourg bears the German stamp. Head right out of place de la République, past the neo-Gothic church

⑯ ⑰ of **St-Paul,** to the pseudo-Renaissance **Palais de l'Université**—constructed between 1875 and 1885 (though Strasbourg University itself dates from 1621). Heavy, turn-of-the-century houses line allée de la Robertsau, a tree-lined boulevard that would not look out of place in Berlin; follow it six blocks to reach **⑱** the modern **Palais de l'Europe,** designed by Paris architect Henri Bernard in 1977. The Palais houses the European Court of Human Rights and the Council of Europe, founded in 1949 and independent of the European Community (founded in 1957), whose 12 members are joined here by representatives from the traditionally nonaligned countries—Austria, Norway, Sweden, and Switzerland—plus Cyprus, Iceland, Liechtenstein, Malta, and Turkey. The European flag that flutters in front of the Palais—a circle of 12 gold stars on a blue background—was created for the Council of Europe in 1955 and adopted by the European Community in 1986. *Av. de l'Europe. Visits weekdays at 9, 10, 3, 4 and 5.*

Just across the street from the Palais de l'Europe, the **⑲ Orangerie** is a delightful park laden with flowers and punctuated by imperious copper beeches. It contains a lake and, close by, a small reserve of rare birds, including flamingoes and noisy local storks.

Tour 2: Alsace

Leaving **Strasbourg,** take the fast A4 40 kilometers (24 miles) **⑳** northwest to **Saverne,** gateway to the northern Vosges. Its 18th-century **Château des Rohan,** built in red sandstone, is renowned for its majestic north facade, lined by fluted pilasters and a Corinthian colonnade. The right wing houses an interesting museum devoted to archaeology, religious statuary, and local history. *Admission: 8 frs. Open mid-June–mid-Sept., Mon., Wed.–Sat. 2:30–5:30, Sun. 10–noon and 2:30–5:30; closed Tues.*

Head south from Saverne along N4 to **Marlenheim** and the start of the great Alsace **Route du Vin** (Wine Road), which forms the backbone of this tour. Regular signs marked *Route du Vin* will help you keep your bearings on the way due south to Thann, some 60 miles as the crow flies but considerably more on the twisty Wine Road. Nearly all the villages along the route are beautifully maintained, with red geraniums flowing from balconies and carefully preserved old wells.

D422 connects Marlenheim to Wangen, Westhoffen, and **㉑ Rosheim,** the last, a pleasant village with medieval ramparts, gateways, and a sturdy Romanesque church with an octagonal tower. The two-story stone **Heidehuss** is reputedly the oldest construction in Alsace (circa 1170).

㉒ Boersch, 3 kilometers (2 miles) from Rosheim on D35, conserves three medieval gateways and the 16th-century Hôtel de Ville (Town Hall). Just south of Boersch lies the **Château de la Léonardsau,** surrounded by formal and botanical gardens adorned with fountains, statues, and a wide variety of trees. Since 1985, the château has hosted the **Musée du Cheval et de l'Attelage** (Horse and Harness Museum), complete with magnificent 18th- and 19th-century carriages, a blacksmith, and a collection of swords and other arms from the Royal Works at nearby Klingenthal. *Admission: 10 frs. Open Easter–Oct.,*

Tues.–Sun. 2–6, closed Mon.; Nov.–Easter, weekends 2–6, closed weekdays.

㉓ Obernai, one of Alsace's most attractive towns, can be reached from Boersch via D322 (about 6 kilometers/4 miles). At its heart is the medieval place du Marché, dominated by the stout, square 13th-century **Kappellturm Beffroi** (Belfry), topped by a pointed steeple flanked at each corner by frilly openwork turrets added in 1597. The nearby **Puits à Six-Seaux,** constructed in the 1570s, is an elaborate Renaissance well whose name recalls the six buckets suspended from its metal chains. Just behind the belfry is Obernai's **Hôtel de Ville,** rebuilt in 1848 but incorporating much of the original Renaissance building, notably its richly carved balcony.

North of the town hall, the twin spires of the parish church of **St-Pierre-et-St-Paul** compete with the belfry for skyline preeminence. They date, like the rest of the church, from the 1860s, although the 1504 Holy Sepulcher altarpiece in the north transept is a survivor from the previous church, along with some 15th-century stained glass.

D426 from Obernai heads back west to cross the Route du Vin at Ottrott, renowned for its red wine. From Ottrott, D109 **㉔** winds its way 6 kilometers (4 miles) up to the **Mont Ste-Odile,** a 2,500-foot mound that has been an important religious and military site for 3,000 years. An eerie 6-mile long pagan wall, up to 12 feet high and, in parts, several feet thick, rings the summit; its mysterious origins and purpose still baffle archaeologists. The Romans established a settlement here, and at the start of the 8th century, Odile, daughter of Duke Etichon of Obernai, founded a monastery on the same spot after recovering her sight while being baptized (she had been born blind). Odile— venerated as the patron saint of Alsace—died here in AD 720; her sarcophagus rests in the chapel.

The **monastery** still remains, rescued by the bishop of Strasbourg in 1853, after repeated plunder, military vandalism, and the expulsion of its monks in the French Revolution. The bishop's restoration has left us with the current, tidy ensemble of buildings that helps the Mont Ste-Odile rank today alongside Haut-Koenigsbourg (*see* below) as the highspot of the Alsace tourist industry. One of its principal attractions is the splendid view from the clifftop terrace, over the Plain of Alsace toward Strasbourg and the Black Forest over the German border.

㉕ D854 tumbles down the hillside to **Barr,** another 6 kilometers (4 miles) on, a thriving little town surrounded by vines, with some charming narrow streets (notably rue des Cigognes, rue Neuve, and the tiny rue de l'Essieu) and the cheerful Hôtel de Ville. Most buildings in Barr date from after a catastrophic fire of 1678; the only medieval survivor is the Romanesque tower of the Protestant church, St-Martin.

The **Musée de la Folie Marco,** up rue du Dr.-Sultzer from the town hall, is housed in a steep-tiled mansion built by local magistrate Félix Marco in 1763. Despite its name, this is no architectural folly, though jealous villagers may have considered its three large reception rooms to embody a certain crazy extravagance. You can admire lots of original furniture here, plus local porcelain, earthenware, and pewter. One section of the museum explains the traditional process of *schlittage:*

Sleds, bearing bundles of freshly sawn tree trunks, used to be slid down forest slopes along a "corduroy road" made of logs. *Rue du Dr.-Sultzer. Admission: 5 frs. Open July–Sept., Wed.–Mon. 10–noon and 2–6; June and Oct., weekends 10–noon and 2–6.*

Time Out If you're feeling hungry, stop at the **weinstub** on the central square, adjacent to the flower-strewn town hall. You can enjoy an outdoor meal on the veranda, with hefty salads (radish, carrots, egg, and celery) a more-than-adequate substitute for the usual *choucroûte* (sauerkraut) or *charcuterie. Pl. de l'Hôtel de Ville.*

㉖ A small road leads from Barr through the vineyards and the tiny village of Mittelbergheim to **Andlau,** 3 kilometers (2 miles) away. The abbey church of **St-Pierre St-Paul** was built in the mid-12th century after fire had destroyed most of the 11th-century building constructed by Pope Leo IX's niece, Mathilda. The spire above the octagonal bell tower was finished only in 1737, but the abbey's chief glories date back to the 11th century: The west front boasts the richest ensemble of Romanesque sculpture in Alsace. Sculpted vines wind their way around the doorway as a reminder of the time-honored importance of wine to the local economy.

The 15th-century abbey choir stalls are adorned with the coats of arms of the princess abbesses. A statue of a female bear, the mascot of the abbey—bears used to roam local forests and were bred at the abbey until the 16th century—can be seen in the north transept. Legend has it that Queen Richarde founded the abbey in 887 after being enjoined by an angel to construct a church on the spot where a female bear would appear to her.

㉗ Take D253 from Andlau, past the parish church, to the junction with D35. From here, you can enjoy a mouth-watering view down the valley toward Andlau. A mile later, bear left through the over-cute village of Itterswiller (its many restaurants are outrageously expensive) before setting off right toward **Dambach-la-Ville,** a fortified medieval town protected by ramparts and three powerful 13th-century gateways. Dambach is particularly rich in half-timbered, high-roofed houses from the 17th and 18th centuries, mainly clustered around place du Marché and its 16th-century Hôtel de Ville.

㉘ D35 continues to Châtenois, from where it's just a 3-kilometer (2-mile) detour along N59 to **Sélestat,** a busy town with two impressive churches. **St-Foy** dates from between 1155 and 1190; its Romanesque facade remains largely intact (the spires were added in the 19th century), as does the 140-foot octagonal tower over the crossing. Sadly, the interior was mangled during the centuries, chiefly by the Jesuits; their most inspired legacy is the Baroque pulpit of 1733 illustrating the life of the founder of their movement, St. Francis Xavier. Note the Romanesque bas-relief next to the baptistery, originally the lid of a sarcophagus. *Just off rue du Marché Vert.*

Take rue de Babil one block south to the later, Gothic church of **St-Georges.** It, too, has a fine tower, built in 1490 and some 200 feet tall. There is medieval stained glass in the rose window above the south door and in the windows of the choir, telling the tales of Stes. Catherine, Helen, and Agnes.

Head left down rue du Sel to the **Bibliothèque Humaniste**, a major library founded in 1452 and installed in the former Halle aux Blés. Among the precious manuscripts on display are a 7th-century lectionary and a 12th-century Book of Miracles. Altarpieces, jewelry, sculpture, and earthenware are also exhibited. *1 rue de la Bibliothèque. Admission: 6 frs. Open weekdays 9–noon and 2–5, Sat. 9–noon.*

㉙ D159 now makes the steep, twisting climb to **Haut-Koenigsbourg.** This romantic, crag-top castle looks just as a kaiser thought it should: German emperor Wilhelm II was presented with the 13th-century ruins by the town of Sélestat in 1901 and restored them with some diligence and no little imagination—squaring the main tower's original circle, for instance. Today Haut-Koenigsbourg is besieged by tourists and should be avoided on sunny summer days. At other times, the site, panorama, drawbridge, and amply furnished imperial chambers merit a visit. *Admission: 30 frs. Open Apr.–Oct., daily 10–noon and 2–6; Nov.–Dec., Feb.–Mar., daily 10–noon and 2–5; closed Jan.*

㉚ Fast N415 now swoops southeast toward the proud merchant city of **Colmar,** 14 kilometers (9 miles) away. The heart of Colmar remains intact: A web of pedestrian streets fans out from the beefy-towered church of **St-Martin.** To the east lies Grand'Rue, with its 15th-century **Ancienne Douane** (Customs House) and twin-turreted **Maison aux Arcades** (1609). To the south is the pretty, water-crossed district known as **Petite Venise.**

Alongside St-Martin's, on rue Mercière (no. 11), is the **Maison Pfister** (1537), which, with its decorative frescoes and medallions, counts as one of the most impressive dwellings in town. On the other side of rue des Marchands is the **Musée Bartholdi,** former home of Frédéric Auguste Bartholdi, the local sculptor who designed the Statue of Liberty. *30 rue des Marchands. Admission: 7 frs. Open Apr.–Oct., daily 10–noon and 2–6; Nov.–Mar., weekends 10–noon and 2–5; closed weekdays.*

In the nearby **Dominican Church** (pl. des Dominicains) can be seen the Flemish-influenced *Madonna of the Rosebush* (1473) by Martin Schongauer (1445–91), a talented engraver as well as a painter. This work, which hung in St-Martin until it was stolen in 1972, has almost certainly been reduced in size from its original state: A smaller but similar composition (probably a 16th-century copy), now in Boston, shows the Virgin surrounded by a larger, airier garden and surmounted not just by two crown-bearing angels but by God in Heaven. Lifelike birds, buds, thorns, and flowers add life to the gold-background solemnity.

Take rue des Têtes past the Maison des Têtes (1608)—so-called because of the carved heads proliferating on its facade—to the **Musée d'Unterlinden,** France's best-attended provincial museum. The star attraction of this former medieval convent is the **Issenheim Altarpiece** (1512–16) by Martin Grünewald, majestically displayed in the convent's Gothic chapel. The altarpiece was originally painted for the Antoine convent at Issenheim, 32 kilometers (20 miles) south of Colmar, and was believed to have miraculous healing powers over ergot, a widespread disease in the Middle Ages caused by poisonous fungus found in moldy grain. The altarpiece's emotional drama moves away from the stilted restraint of earlier paintings toward the humanistic realism of the Renaissance: The blanched despair of the Virgin, clutched by a weeping St. John, is balanced, on the other side of the cross, by the grave expression of John the Baptist. The blood of the crucified Christ gushes forth, while his face is racked with pain. A dark, simple background heightens the composition's stark grandeur.

The altarpiece was closed and folded according to the religious calendar and contains several other scenes apart from the *Crucifixion:* The *Incarnation* features angelic musicians playing celestial melodies as a white-bearded God, the Father, patrols the heavens; to the left, an incredulous Mary receives the Angel Gabriel; to the right, Christ rises from his tomb amid a bold halo of orange and blue. The third arrangement portrays, to the left, St. Anthony in conversation with St. Paul in a wild overgrown landscape, while to the right, nightmarish beasts, reminiscent of Hieronymous Bosch, compose the tortuous *Temptation of St. Anthony.*

Modern art, stone sculpture, and local crafts cluster around the 13th-century cloisters to complete Unterlinden's folksy charm. *Pl. de la Sinn. Admission: 20 frs. adults, 10 frs. students. Open Apr.–Oct., daily 9–noon and 2–6; Nov.–Mar., Wed.–Mon. 9–noon and 2–5; closed Tues.*

Twenty-five kilometers (15 miles) south on N83 is the **Guebwiller** exit. The town's **Eglise St-Leger** (1180–1280) is one of the most harmonious Romanesque churches in Alsace, though its original choir was replaced by the current Gothic one in 1336. The bare, solemn interior is of less interest than the three-towered exterior. The towers of the facade match—almost: The one on the left has small turrets at the base of its steeple, whereas the one on the right is ringed by triangular gables. The octagonal tower over the crossing looms above them both, topped by a seldom-visited stork's nest.

The surrounding square, home to a lively weekly market, faces rue de la République, Guebwiller's main street. Head left upon leaving the church: 100 yards down the road is the Renaissance **Hôtel de Ville,** with its small spire and crenelated oriel (or bay) window, built by wealthy draper Marquart Hesser. Continue down the main street before turning left into rue de l'Hôpital. The **Dominican Church** is unmistakable, thanks to the thin, lacy lantern that sticks out of its roof like an effeminate chimney. Its large, early 14th-century nave is adorned with frescoes and contains a fine rood screen.

Rue de la République continues to Guebwiller's third and largest church, **Notre-Dame** (1762–85). The church possesses a Baroque grandeur that would not be out of keeping in a chic district of Paris—a reflection of the wealth of the Benedictine abbey at nearby Murbach, whose worldly friars, fed up with country life, opted for the bright lights of Guebwiller in the mid-18th century. The monks—who needed a noble pedigree of at least four generations to take the cloth—outmaneuvered Church authorities by pretending to take temporary exile in Guebwiller while "modernizing" Murbach Abbey, thus circumnavigating the papal permission normally required before abbeys could move. As a token gesture, the crafty clerics smashed the nave of Murbach Abbey, but failed to replace it and refused to budge from their "temporary" home: Instead, they commissioned Louis Beuque to design a new church in Guebwiller—Notre-Dame.

The church's facade, with its double layer of cornice-bearing columns, is devoid of ornament, but for the statues halfway up. The interior is majestic but not overbearing, thanks to the cheerful pale pink of the stone and the survival of much of the original decoration. The gold-and-marble high altar fits in better, perhaps, than does the trick 3-D–effect stucco *Assumption*, which puffs its way out of a half-open coffin behind the altar before splurging over the walls and balcony and making for the roof, an example of Baroque craftsmanship at its most outlandish. *Rue de la République.*

The **Musée du Florival,** on one side of the church square, is housed in one of the 18th-century canon's houses. It has a fine collection of ceramics designed by Théodore Deck (1823–91), a native of Guebwiller and director of the renowned porcelain factory at Sèvres near Paris. *1 rue du 4 Février. Admission: 8 frs. Open May–Oct., weekends 10–noon and 2–6, Mon., Wed.–Fri. 2–6; closed Tues.; Nov.–Apr., weekends only, 10–noon and 2–5:30.*

㉜ D430 now heads up the valley toward Lautenbach; at Buhl, take the exit to **Murbach.** This road is a dead end, so it's all the more surprising to discover a vast rump of a church towering above the hillside. Only the east end remains of the **Eglise St-Léger,** once part of the most powerful abbey in Alsace. Roofs and towers create a geometric interplay of squares and triangles, lent rhythm and variety by those round-arched windows and arcades so loved by Romanesque architects. Note the tympanum above the door to the south transept: Its elongated lions, seen in profile, resemble stone images found more commonly in the Middle East.

Time Out A few miles from Murbach, a small *route forestière* (forest road) heads from Lautenbach up the 2,800-foot col de Boenlesgrab. At the summit, the **Boenlesgrab Inn** commands splendid views down the valley toward Wasserbourg. In an unpretentious setting of wooden benches and checkered tablecloths you'll find a solid, filling *Menu Marcaire,* featuring pies, potatoes, and game in season.

㉝ Make your way back to Guebwiller and take the Ensisheim road, passing over N83, as far as **Ungersheim,** home of the **Ecomusée de Haute-Alsace.** This "open-air museum," a small village created from scratch in 1980, includes 35 historic peasant houses typical of the region, which have been transferred here lock, stock, and barrel (or more precisely, stable, barn, and pigeon loft) to escape demolition. Storks, another example of the local heritage, are nurtured here in a reserve. *Maisons Paysannes d'Alsace. Admission: 27 frs. adults, 10 frs. students, 8 frs. children under 12. Open June–Aug., daily 10–8; Sept.–Nov., Mar.–May., daily 11–6; Dec.–Feb., daily 11–4.*

㉞ From the old town of Ensisheim, D20 spears south to **Mulhouse,** 16 kilometers (10 miles) away. Mulhouse, a pleasant if unremarkable industrial town, is worth visiting for its museums. Dutch and Flemish masters of the 17th–18th centuries top the bill at the **Musée des Beaux-Arts** (Fine Arts Museum, 14 pl. Guillaume Tell; closed Tues). But it is cars and trains that attract most visitors. Some 500 vintage and modern cars, dating from the steam-powered Jacquot of 1878 and spanning 100 different makes, are featured in the **Musée National de l'Automobile.** The highlights are the two Bugatti Royales. Only a handful of these stately cars were ever made; one was auctioned recently for $8 million. *192 av. de Colmar. Admission: 27 frs. adults, 17 frs. students. Open Wed.–Mon. 10–6.*

A reconstructed Stephenson locomotive of 1846 sets the wheels rolling at the **Musée Français du Chemin de Fer** (National Train Museum), a 10-minute walk west down rue J.-Hofer. Rolling stock is spread over 12 tracks, including a vast array of steam trains and the BB 9004 electric train that held the rail speed record of 207 mph from 1955 to 1981. A section of the museum also houses a display of firemen's equipment. *2 rue de Glenn. Admission: 25 frs. adults, 17 frs. students. Open Apr.–Sept., daily 9–6; Oct.–Mar., daily 10–5.*

West of Mulhouse, 16 kilometers (10 miles) along N66, is **Thann.** A local ditty has it that "Strasbourg's spire is the highest, Freiburg's the biggest, and Thann's the finest." The spire of the church of **St-Thiébaut** in Thann is certainly elegant and delicate but, at 254 feet, little over half the height of Strasbourg Cathedral's. St-Thiébaut's square tower was built in 1350, the octagonal spire in 1516; the colored tiles of the roof date only from the 1890s. The Flamboyant Gothic north door and the portals of the facade, still under restoration after the damage inflicted during World War II, boast over 500 sculpted figures.

The interior is relatively high and narrow, with a choir as long as the nave. The 15th–16th-century oak choir stalls, carved with whimsical figures and topped by decorative pinnacles, are the most important in Alsace. Apart from the small Chapelle de la Vierge (Chapel of the Virgin) in the south aisle (1629–31), take a look at the amusing late 15th-century statue of the Virgin and an infant Jesus who chuckles to himself while clutching a bunch of grapes (the statue was donated by local vintners).

D35 wends its way east through the last of the Alsace vineyards to Cernay and the start of the **Route des Crêtes,** the historic Crest Road sliced along the wooded Vosges hilltops during World War I. The road is known successively as D431, D430, D61, and D148 on its spectacular 45-mile path north, accompanied by plummeting views of lake, valley, and forest, from Cernay to the 3,000-foot pass at col du Bonhomme. From here, take D48, then N59 to Bertrimoutier, then turn right up N159 as far as Provenchères and right again onto D23. Just past Lubine, fork left onto D214, which winds its way up the Vosges for 16 kilometers (10 miles) into the Champ du Feu (the Field of Fire). This name is appropriately hellish, given that our next and final stopping point is the concentration camp built by the Nazis at **Le Struthof,** 8 kilometers (5 miles) west along D130. Its barbed wire and modest huts, spread over several levels, remain intact and appear strangely peaceful; a stark, white marble monument recalls their appalling past and purpose. (Admission: 5 frs. Open daily 10–noon and 2–5). Farther down D130 is the innocuous-looking farmhouse that was used as a gas chamber.

Tour 3: Lorraine

Our tour of Lorraine begins in its northwest corner, 3 kilometers (2 miles) from the Belgian frontier, at **Avioth.** If you're

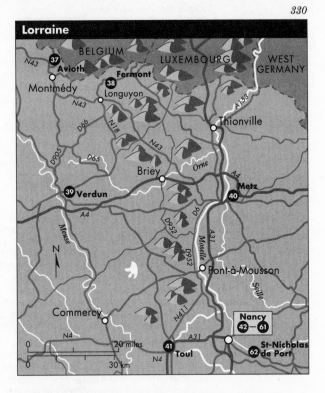

Lorraine

coming from Paris, leave the A4 expressway (which continues to Verdun and Metz; *see* below) at Reims, then take N51 to Charleville-Mézières, 64 kilometers (40 miles) away, completing your trip along A203, N43, and D110 via Sedan.

A sumptuous **basilica** unexpectedly rises above the lowly rooftops of the tiny village of Avioth (population 103). A miraculous statue of the Virgin was discovered here in the 11th century, and the faithful poured in for the next 300 years, which explains the church's surprising richness. Construction of the church lasted from the late 13th century to the early 15th, finishing amid the elaborate stone lace of the Flamboyant Gothic style. The interior contains a 14th-century altar, and recent restoration has revealed medieval frescoes on the choir vaults.

N43 continues east to Longuyon, 34 kilometers (21 miles) from Avioth, from where D17A heads 5 kilometers (3 miles) northeast to the fort of **Fermont,** an imposing memorial to the famous, if ineffective, Maginot Line, built after World War I to defend France's eastern frontier. Although observation posts and concrete bunkers armed with machine guns protrude above ground to stave off would-be aggressors, the main interest of Fermont lies 100 feet under the surface in the galleries once manned by crews 600 strong. Kitchens, dormitories, showers, a soldiers' mess, and sewage and ventilation systems make up a sizable underground town. There is also a museum devoted to the history of the Maginot Line, complete with guns and howitzers. Outside, the ground is still pockmarked with the craters caused by the German shell attack of June 1940. *Admission: 18 frs. adults, 8 frs. children under 14. Open May–Sept., daily 1:30–5; Apr. and Oct., 1:30–4.*

㊴ From Longuyon, head south along N18, D66, D65, and D905 to **Verdun,** 43 kilometers (27 miles) away. A key strategic site along the Meuse Valley, Verdun was besieged by the Prussians in 1792 and 1870, but is famous, above all, for the 18-month battle waged between French and Germans from February 1916 to August 1917, which left over 700,000 dead. Much as the Battle of Stalingrad came to assume symbolic importance during World War II, so Verdun proved to be the turning point of World War I. To this day, the scenes of battle are scarred by undulating terrain and stunted vegetation. Circuits of the major war sites extend on either side of the River Meuse.

Verdun itself, however, is far from the ruined, battered, hastily rebuilt place one might expect. As one of three medieval bishoprics (along with Toul and Metz), it enjoyed much prestige: Verdun's bishops were untitled princes of the Holy Roman Empire. The **Bishop's Palace,** built in the 18th century by Robert de Cotte, is opulent in the extreme, with a vast semicircular Court of Honor to intimidate the unworthy. The adjacent **cathedral,** perched at the highest point of the town, dates from the 1130s, although the Gothic nave was restyled in Classical taste (round, not pointed arches) during the 18th century. The three-sided cloisters that nestle along the south side are mainly Flamboyant Gothic.

Other old buildings in Verdun include the **Hôtel de Ville** (Town Hall; 1623), the **Hôtel de la Princerie** (16th century), Vauban's late 17th-century **citadel,** and two crenelated, neighboring gateways: the **Porte Chaussée** (14th century) and the **Porte Châtel** (13th). A soldier-topped pyramid, above a steep-stepped terrace, provides an imposing war memorial, the **Monument de la Victoire;** a register kept in the crypt contains the names of all who fought at the Battle of Verdun.

㊵ The A4 expressway offers a fast, 72-kilometer (45-mile) link between Verdun and **Metz,** the largest town of northern Lorraine. Despite its industrial background, Metz is officially classed as one of France's greenest cities: Parks, gardens, and leafy squares crop up everywhere. At its heart, towering above the Hôtel de Ville (Town Hall) and the 18th-century place d'Armes, is the **Cathédrale St-Etienne.**

At 137 feet from floor to roof, Metz Cathedral is one of the highest in France. It also is one of the lightest, thanks to nearly 1½ acres of window space. The narrow, 13th–14th-century nave channels the eye toward the dramatically raised 16th-century choir, whose walls have given way to huge sheets of gemlike glass by masters old and modern, including Russian-born artist Marc Chagall (1887–1985). A pair of symmetrical 290-foot towers flank the nave, marking the medieval division between two churches that were merged to form the cathedral. The tower with a fussy 15th-century pinnacle houses **Dame Mutte,** an enormous bell cast in 1605 and tolled on momentous occasions. The Grand Portal beneath the large rose window was reconstructed by the Germans at the turn of the century. The statues of the prophets include, on the right, *Daniel* sycophantically sculpted to resemble Kaiser Wilhelm II (his unmistakable upturned moustachios were shaved off in 1940). *Pl. d'Armes.*

Close by, in a 17th-century former convent, is the **Musée d'Art et d'Histoire** (Art and History Museum); turn left out of the cathedral, and left again up rue Chèvrement. The museum's wide-ranging collections encompass French and German paintings from the 18th century on, military arms and uniforms, and archaeology; local finds evoke the city's Gallo-Roman, Carolingian, and medieval past. Religious works of art are stored in the **Grenier de Chèvrement,** a granary built in 1457, with a many-windowed facade and stone-arcade decoration. *Ancien Couvent des Petits Carmes, rue Chèvrement. Admission: 10 frs., free Wed. Open Wed.–Mon. 10–noon and 2–5; closed Tues.*

Now walk back past the cathedral, continuing on for another two blocks. At one end of the **Esplanade,** an agreeable terraced park overlooking the Moselle, is the 18th-century **Palais de Justice,** noted for the sculpted bas-reliefs in the courtyard (the one on the right portrays the 1783 Peace Treaty between France, England, Holland, and the United States) and its ceremonial staircase with wrought-iron banisters. Farther down the Esplanade is the small, heavily restored church of **St-Pierre-aux-Nonnains** (rue Poncelet). Parts are thought to date from the 4th century, making it the oldest church in France. Neighboring 13th-century **Chapelle des Templiers** (blvd. Poincaré) is also rare: It's the only octagonal church in Lorraine.

41 Leave Metz by D952, which speeds 55 kilometers (33 miles) south along the River Moselle to the charming old town of **Toul,** nestling behind mossy, star-shaped ramparts. The ramshackle streets of central Toul can't have changed much for centuries—not since the embroidered, twin-towered facade, a Flamboyant Gothic masterpiece, was woven onto the **cathedral** in the second half of the 15th century. The cathedral interior, begun in 1204, is long (321 feets), airy (105 feet high), and more restrained than the exuberant facade. The tall, slender windows of the unusually shallow choir sparkle in the morning sunshine.

The cathedral is flanked on one side by 14th-century **cloisters** and, on the other, by a pleasant garden behind the **Hôtel de Ville** (Town Hall), built in 1740 as the Bishop's Palace. Continue down rue de Rigny, turn right onto rue Michâtel, and then take a second right onto rue de Ménin, which winds its way down to the Porte de Metz. Veer left at the gateway, then left again onto rue Gouvion St-Cyr; at no. 25 is the **Musée Municipal** (Town Museum), housed in a former medieval hospital. The museum's well-preserved Salle des Malades (Patients' Ward) dates from the 13th century and displays archaeological finds, ceramics, tapestries, and medieval sculpture. *25 rue Gouvion St-Cyr. Admission: 10 frs. adults, 5 frs. children. Open Wed.–Mon. 10 –noon and 2–6; closed Tues. and mornings in winter.*

Fork right onto rue de la Boucherie, which, over a 300-yard stretch lined with old houses, becomes successively rue du Collège, rue Pont de Vaux, and rue Gengoult. Eventually, rue Sonaire leads off right to the attractive church of **St-Gengoult,** whose choir boasts some of the finest 13th-century stained glass in eastern France. The Flamboyant Gothic cloisters are later than those of the cathedral but equally picturesque. Owing to vandalism, St-Gengoult is open at certain times only. Enquire at the tourist office (next to the cathedral) for details.

42 **Nancy,** 23 kilometers (14 miles) east of Toul via A31, is one of France's richest cities in architectural terms, and the last

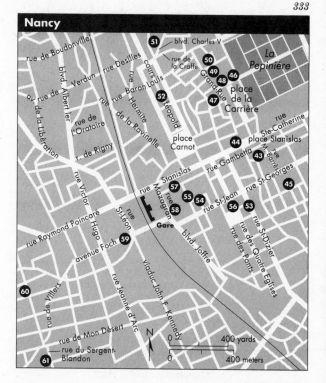

major city we visit on our tour of Lorraine. Medieval ornament, 18th-century grandeur, and Belle Epoque fluidity rub shoulders in a town center that combines commercial bustle with stately elegance.

The symbolic heart of Nancy is **place Stanislas.** The severe, gleaming white Classical facades of this stylish square are lent Rococo jollity by fancifully wrought gilt-iron railings. King Stanislas had a bit of a Rococo history himself. He was offered the throne of Lorraine by his French son-in-law Louis XV, after managing to lose the crown of Poland—twice (once in 1709 and again in 1736).

One side of place Stanislas is occupied by the **Hôtel de Ville** (Town Hall); another houses the **Musée des Beaux-Arts** (Fine Arts Museum). On the ground floor, 19th- and 20th-century pictures by Claude Monet, Edouard Manet, Maurice Utrillo, and the Italian painter Amedeo Modigliani rub shoulders with 150 works in glass and crystal by local Art Nouveau master Antonin Daum. A hefty *Transfiguration* by Rubens adorns the staircase that leads to the second floor and its wealth of Old Masters from the Italian, Dutch, Flemish, and French schools. *Pl. Stanislas. Admission: 12 frs. adults, 8 frs. children; free Wed. for children and students. Open Wed.–Sun. 10:15–12:30 and 1:30–5:45 and Mon. 1:30–5:45; closed Tues.*

Before leaving place Stanislas, take a look down rue Maurice-Barrès (to the left of the Hôtel de Ville) at the twin towers of the **cathedral.** This vast, frigid edifice was built in the 1740s in a chunky Baroque style that has none of the ease and grace of the 18th-century place Stanislas. Its most notable interior feature is a murky 19th-century frescoe in the dome; restoration is promised and sorely needed.

From place Stanislas, the tree-lined place de la Carrière leads
46 down to the colonnaded facade of the **Palais du Gouvernement,** former home to the governors of Lorraine. To the right are some spacious formal gardens known as **La Pépinière;** to the left
47 is the 275-foot spire of **St-Epvre,** a splendid neo-Gothic church rebuilt in the 1860s. Thanks to the efforts of Monsignor Trouillet, an entrepreneurial builder-priest, St-Epvre embodies craftsmanship of a cosmopolitan kind. Most of the 2,800 square yards of stained glass were created by the Geyling workshop in Vienna, Austria; the chandeliers were made in Liège, Belgium; many carvings are the work of Margraff of Munich, Germany; the heaviest of the eight bells was cast in Budapest, Hungary; and the organ, though manufactured by Merklin of Paris, was inaugurated in 1869 by Austrian composer Anton Bruckner.

Opposite St-Epvre is Nancy's principal medieval thoroughfare, Grande-Rue. Note the equestrian statue of Duke Antoine (1512) above the elaborate doorway of the Palais Ducal (Ducal Palace) to the right. The main entrance to the palace, and the Lorraine History Museum which it now houses, is 80 yards farther down the street.

48 The **Musée Historique Lorrain** has a delightfully far-flung assembly of exhibits. Your visit begins in a low terracelike building across the palace lawn, with several showcases of archaeological finds, ranging from Stone-Age implements and ancient pottery to Roman coins and sculpture. Across the courtyard is the poorly indicated entrance to the main building, which welcomes visitors into a long, narrow room lined with medieval statues.

A spiral stone staircase leads up to the palace's most impressive room, the **Galerie des Cerfs;** exhibits here (including pictures, armor, and books) recapture the Renaissance mood of the 16th and 17th centuries—one of elegance and jollity, though not devoid of stern morality, as an elaborate series of huge tapestries, *La Condemnation du Banquet,* exemplify with their allegorical sermon on the evils of drink and gluttony.

The rest of the museum is taken up mainly with paintings, furniture, and an extensive display of porcelain and earthenware. In a series of attic rooms, posters, proclamations, and the inevitable *tricolor* banners retrace local history from Napoleon up to World War I. *64 Grande-Rue. Admission: 15 frs. adults, 10 frs. children. Open mid-June–Sept., Wed.–Mon. 10–noon and 2–6; Oct.–mid-June, Wed.–Mon. 10–noon and 2–5; closed Tues.*

Continue along Grande-Rue to the Couvent des Cordeliers, a
49 former convent that contains the **Musée des Arts et Traditions Populaires.** Its treatment of local preindustrial society is based on reconstituted rural interiors equipped with domestic tools and implements. The dukes of Lorraine are buried in the crypt
50 of the adjoining **Eglise des Cordeliers,** a Flamboyant Gothic church; the intricately sculpted limestone tombs of René II and his wife Philippe de Gueldre are impressive. The octagonal Ducal Chapel was begun in 1607 in Classical style, modeled on the

Chapel of the Medicis in Florence. *Grande-Rue. Admission to chapel: 10 frs. adults, 7 frs. children. Open Easter–Oct., Tues. –Sun. 10–noon and 2–6; Nov.–Easter, Tues.–Sun. 10–noon and 2–5; closed Mon.*

From the medieval to the modern, head down rue de la Craffe to begin an **Art Nouveau tour** of Nancy. Art Nouveau caught fire here at the end of the 19th century, representing a breakaway from decorative stereotype toward an innovative, fluid style of design based on motifs taken from nature.

51 Around the corner from rue de la Craffe, at 1 **boulevard Charles-V**, is a house by Lucien Weisenburger (1904) whose windows, by Jacques Gruber, include one in the form of the **52** double-armed cross of Lorraine. The adjacent **cours Léopold** has another Weissenburger creation (1905) at no. 52, and you'll see more Gruber windows at no. 40.

Continue to the end of cours Léopold, cross place Carnot, turn **53** left onto rue Stanislas, then take a second right onto **rue St-Dizier.** At no. 42 is a bank designed in 1903 by French architects Biet and Vallin; its interior can be inspected during working hours (9–5 weekdays). Make the next left onto rue St-Jean, **54** then a right onto **rue Bénit.** At no. 2 is the first building in Nancy with a metallic structure: not just iron girders, either, but intricately wrought metal pillars, the work of Schertzer to the design of Gutton. There is more stained glass by Gruber, while the exterior decoration tells us the building began life as a seed **55** shop. The next street along, parallel to rue Bénit, is **rue Chanzy;** at no. 9 is another bank, designed by Emile André, with interior furnishings by Majorelle and yet more Gruber windows.

56 Return to rue Stanislas via rue St-Jean and **rue Raugraff.** At **57** no. 86 is a house by Vallin (1906). At no. 40 **rue Henri-Poincaré,** a street running parallel to rue Stanislas, is a commercial building of 1908 by Toussaint and Marchal, with metal structure by Schertzer, glass by Gruber, and wrought iron by Majorelle. The facade is adorned with the Lorraine thistle, while hops— **58** used to make beer—symbolize local breweries. **Rue Mazagran** greets you at the far end of the street with, at no. 5, the Excelsior Brasserie; its rhythmic facade, severe by Art Nouveau standards, is illuminated at night.

59 At the far end of rue Mazagran is **avenue Foch,** a busy boulevard that heads past the train station into a district lined with solid, serious mansions clearly built for Nancy's affluent 19th-century middle class. At no. 41, more ironwork by Majorelle can be admired; yet another architect, Paul Charbonnier, was responsible for the overall design in 1905. At no. 69, the occasional pinnacle suggests Gothic influence on a house built in 1902 by Emile André, who designed the neighboring no. 71 two years later.

60 On the right, past rue de Villers, is **rue Louis-Majorelle.** At no. 1 stands a villa built in 1902 by Paris architect Henri Sauvage for Majorelle himself. Sinuous metal supports seem to sneak up on the unsuspecting balcony like swaying cobras, scrutinizing the spacious windows and reckoning them to be yet further productions of that in-demand glazier Jacques Gruber.

61 End your Art Nouveau survey at the **Musée de l'Ecole de Nancy,** at 36 rue du Sergent-Blandan (head up rue de Villers and cross over rue de Mon-Désert). This airy, turn-of-the-century town house was built by Eugène Corbin, an early patron of the School of Nancy. His personal collection forms the basis of this, the only museum in France devoted to Art Nouveau, and underlines that architecture was not the only vehicle for the expression of Art Nouveau: Lamps, chairs, beds, stained glass, paintings, tables, and silverware are arrayed over two creaky stories. *36 rue Sergent-Blandon. Admission: 12 frs. adults, 6 frs. children. Open Nov.–Mar., Wed.–Mon. 10–noon and 2–6; Apr.–Oct. until 5; closed Tues.*

If you've any appetite left for exploring churches, make the quick trip (20 kilometers, 12 miles) southeast to **St-Nicolas-de-Port,** a small industrial town saved from mediocrity by its colossal **basilica** (1495–1555). Legend has it that a finger of St-Nicholas was brought here during the 11th-century Crusades, and the church was rapidly besieged by pilgrims. Architecture buffs will recognize, in the absence of a triforium (an arcaded story between the nave arches and domed clerestory), the simplified column capitals, and the elaborate rib vaulting, a shining example of Flamboyant Gothic, which here enjoys a final fling before the gathering impetus of the Renaissance movement. But there's no need for specialized knowledge to sense the excitement of the 280-foot onion-domed towers, almost symmetrical but, as was the Gothic wont, not quite. There's excitement inside, too: Daylight floods in through vast windows and cascades around the recently cleaned, honey-colored walls. The slender, free-standing 90-foot pillars in the transept (the "arm" of the church's cruciform shape) are the highest in France.

What to See and Do with Children

Children should be delighted by the newly opened **Nouveau Monde des Schtroumpfs,** a theme park featuring the cuddly blue dwarves known in English as Smurfs. *Chemin des Romaines, Hagondange, just off A31 north of Metz. Admission: 94 frs. adults, 78 frs. children under 12. Open Easter–Oct., weekdays 10–6, Sat. 10–midnight, Sun. 10–8.*

All items listed below are described fully in the Exploring section.
Astronomical Clock, Strasbourg Cathedral, Tour 1
Automobile and Train Museums, Mulhouse, Tour 2
Fort of Fermont, Tour 3
Haut-Koenigsbourg, Tour 2
Horse and Harness Museum, Château de la Léonardsau, near Boersch, Tour 2
Musée Alsacien, Strasbourg, Tour 1
Ungersheim Ecomusée, Tour 2

Off the Beaten Track

Anyone with an interest in glassblowing may be glad to make an excursion to the tiny town of **Passavant-la-Rochère,** 100 kilometers (62 miles) south of Nancy. The **Verrerie de la Rochère** has been in operation since 1475, making it one of the oldest glassworks in France. Next to a roaring furnace, glassblowers respect time-honored techniques and dexterously wield their long metal reeds. A wide selection of glassware is sold in an adjoining 17th-century building with a majestic wooden roof. In a modern gallery, contemporary pictures, sculpture, and tapestries can be admired and purchased. *Admission: free. Open May–Sept., daily 2:30–5:30. No glassblowing Sun. or in Aug.*

Alsace makes a handy base for a day across the Rhine in **West Germany.** Between the elegant spa town of Baden Baden and the historic university center of Freiburg lie the valleys, lakes, and wooded mountains of the Black Forest.

Shopping

Gift Ideas Among the specialties of Alscace that make fine gifts are the handwoven checkered napkins and tablecloths known as **kelches** and the handpainted **earthenware molds** for *Kouglof* bread. These goods can be found throughout this tourist-oriented province, where every pretty village has a souvenir shop of greater or lesser standing. In Obernai, try **Dietrich** (place du Marché) for useful and beautifully crafted household goods.

Glass Glass and crystal are produced by skilled artisans at **Passavant-la-Rochère** (*see* Off the Beaten Track, above) and especially at **Baccarat** (60 kilometers/37 miles east of Nancy on N59), whose town center is dominated by attractive crystal shops.

Shopping Districts The lively city centers of Strasbourg and Colmar are crammed with specialized shops and boutiques. **Rue des Hallebardes** next to the cathedral, adjacent **rue des Grandes Arcades** (with its shopping mall), and **place Kléber** form the commercial heart of Strasbourg; chocolate shops and delicatessens selling local foie gras are delicious places to browse. Nancy has less regional cachet for shoppers, though the streets next to the cathedral are full of life.

Wine In Nancy, at the start of the Grand-Rue and just opposite the Ducal Place, is the Dickensian **La Cave du Roy.** Old wines, champagne, and spirits are arranged in endearing confusion, while mustachioed Monsieur Henné chuckles his way around with Gallic courtesy. His rare red Côtes de Toul is highly recommended.

Sports and Fitness

Bicycling A cyclotourist guide for biking in Lorraine is available from the **Comité Départmental de Cyclotourisme** (33 rue de la République, 54950 Laronxe). Bikes can be rented at many local train stations.

Hiking Hiking in the Vosges Foothills is a rewarding pastime; for a list of signposted trails, contact **Vita** (1 rue Vernet, 75008 Paris).

Horseback Riding There are many possibilities, notably at Kintzheim (tel. 88–82–30–33) and Ensisheim (tel. 89–81–10–10). The **Ferme Equestre Fjord Valoisirs** in Woerth, 35 kilometers (22 miles) north of Strasbourg, organizes excursions on horseback in the Vosges (tel. 88–09–32–20).

Skiing Both downhill and cross-country skiing are possible in winter at Le Bonhomme (altitude 3,300 feet), Gérardmer (3,800 feet), Valley of Munster (up to 4,300 feet), Champ du Feu (3,600 feet), and Le Hohwald (2,800 feet).

Dining and Lodging

Dining

Alsatian cooking is distinctive in its marriage of German and French tastes. It tends to be heavy: *Choucroûte* (sauerkraut), served with ham and sausages, or *Baeckoffe* (a type of potato pie), washed down with a mug of local beer or a pitcher of wine, are a filling means to combat the cold of winter or to fuel up during long walks through the Vosges. But there is some sophistication, too: The local foie gras is admirably accompanied by a glass of Gewurztraminer, preferably late harvested *(vendanges tardives)* for extra sweetness. Riesling, the classic wine of Alsace, is often used to make a sauce that goes so well with trout or chicken. Snails and seasonal game (pheasant, partridge, hare, venison, and boar) are other favorites, as are Munster cheese, salty *Bretzel* loaves, and flaky, brioche-like *Kouglof* bread.

Salmon, pike, eel, and trout can be found in rivers throughout Alsace and Lorraine. Carp fried in breadcrumbs is a specialty of southern Alsace. Lorraine, renowned for its famous quiches, is also known for its dumplings, Madeleine buns, almond candies *(dragées)*, and macaroons. Lorraine shares the Alsatian love of pastry and fruit tarts, often made with mirabelle plums, but resists the German influence manifested in Alsace via *weinstuben* (inns serving wine and snacks or meals, with a passing resemblance to English pubs). Restaurant prices tend to be lower in Lorraine than in Alsace.

Highly recommended restaurants are indicated by a star ★.

Lodging

Hotel accommodations are easier to find in Lorraine than in Alsace, where advance reservations are essential during summer months (especially in Strasbourg and Colmar). Alsace is rich in *gîtes*, or rented country houses, which provide excellent value for families or small groups. Local tourist offices or the regional office in Strasbourg (9 rue du Dôme, tel. 88–22–01–02) can provide full details.

Highly recommended hotels are indicated by a star ★.

Colmar **Schillinger.** Genial Jean Schillinger lords it over one of the
Dining smoothest-run restaurants in Alsace. Impeccable service, velvet upholstery, and gleaming silver cutlery complement an exhaustive wine list and the meticulously prepared fish, or salt-cooked pigeon. Set menus cost 280 or 375 francs, unless you manage a weekday sitting at 190 francs. *16 rue Stanislas, tel. 89–41–43–17. Reservations essential. Jacket and tie required. AE, DC, V. Closed Sun. dinner, Mon. Expensive.*

★ **Buffet de la Gare.** Not all train-station buffets can claim gastronomic fame, but hungry travelers will enjoy this one. With its stained-glass windows, Buffet de la Gare looks more like a church than a station. And the waiters exude pastoral concern, rather than ticket-collecting officiousness: They will happily advise you how best to connect between platters of crayfish or pâte *en croute* (in pastry) and duck in red wine sauce. *Pl. de la*

Gare, tel. 89–41–21–26. *Reservations accepted. Dress: casual. Inexpensive–Moderate.*

Lodging **Hostellerie Le Maréchal.** A maze of corridors connects the
★ three Renaissance town houses that make up this charming hotel near the River Lauch. Some of the rooms are small and are
decorated predominately in light, cheerful colors. Some are en-
dearingly rustic, with exposed beams and curvy walls and
floors, while those in back have good river views. *4–6 pl. des
Six-Montagnes-Noires, 68000, tel. 89–41–60–32. 40 rooms
with bath. Facilities: restaurant, garden. AE, MC, V. Closed
Jan. and Feb. Moderate.*

Colbert. The convenient location is a plus here, halfway between the train station and the ancient town center. Ask for one
of the quieter rooms along rue des Taillandiers. Guest rooms
are well equipped, though the decor is a little loud. *2 rue des
Trois-Epis, 68000, tel. 89–41–31–05. 50 rooms with bath. Facilities: bar. MC, V. Moderate.*

Hirtzbach **Ottié Baur.** Explorers of the Sundgau region, south of Mul-
Dining and Lodging house, are rewarded here with far more *carpe frite* than they
★ can possibly eat. Fried carp, the local specialty, is no delicacy,
but it is unusual, especially when the traditional breadcrumb
batter is replaced by fine semolina. Snails, salmon-trout, and
crayfish salad are other mainstays, and a bottle of Riesling will
wash them all down nicely. Try to reserve a table on the veranda overlooking the garden; the varisectioned dining room has
too much phony dark wood for its own good. Thirteen inexpensive guest rooms are available for overnight stays. *68118
Hirtzbach, 20 km (13 mi) south of Mulhouse on D432, tel. 89–
40–93–22. Reservations recommended. V. Closed Mon. dinner, Tues., Christmas–New Year's, and late June–mid-July.
Moderate.*

Longuyon **Buffet de la Gare.** The train station at Longuyon—an undistin-
Dining and Lodging guished town in the heart of industrial north Lorraine—is an
unexpected focus of attention for marauding gourmets from
neighboring Belgium and Luxembourg. At the station itself, in
the Buffet de la Gare, chubby-cheeked Roland Reinalter,
known locally as "Napo," acts the emperor as far as seasonal
dishes and succulent roasts are concerned. Eight guest rooms
are available for overnight stays. *Pl. de la Gare, 54260, tel. 82–
39–50–85. Reservations recommended. Dress: casual. AE,
DC, MC, V. Closed Fri. dinner, last 2 weeks Sept., and first 2
weeks Mar. Moderate.*

★ **Le Mas.** Opposite Buffet de la Gare is the distinguished, wood-
beamed dining room of Le Mas run by Gérard Tisserant, a former winner of France's coveted Best *Sommelier* (wine waiter)
award. Crayfish in flake pastry, scallops with asparagus, and
lightly peppered Scottish salmon rank among the high spots of
his 260-franc gastronomic menu; simpler pleasures can be had
for just 90 francs during the week. Note that while rooms are
available on either side of the station square, those at Le Mas
are only marginally more expensive and possess greater style.
*Pl. de la Gare, 54260, tel. 82–26–50–07. Reservations essen-
tial. Dress: casual smart. AE, DC, MC, V. Closed Jan.;
restaurant closed Mon. Moderate.*

Metz **La Dinanderie.** Chef Claude Piegiorgi serves clever cuisine—
Dining salmon cooked in mustard and chives or kiwi with lime and ba-
nana sorbet—for modest prices at this intimate restaurant,

just across the River Moselle from Metz Cathedral. *2 rue de Paris, tel. 87–30–14–40. Reservations recommended. Dress: casual. AE, V. Closed Sun., Mon., Christmas–New Year's, mid-Feb., and last 3 weeks Aug. Moderate.*

A La Ville de Lyon. Just behind the cathedral is this new venture in a venerable vaulted setting, well worth checking out for its fabulous wine list (30,000 bottles in stock) and inventive menu. Dishes range from fowl to curried fish, prices from 90 to 250 francs. *7 rue des Piques, tel. 87–36–07–01. Reservations recommended. Dress: casual. AE, DC, MC, V. Closed Sun. dinner, Mon., end of July and most of Aug. Moderate.*

Lodging
★ **Royal Concorde.** The fully modernized Royal Concorde occupies a sumptuous Belle Epoque building not far from the train station and provides a choice of style (old-fashioned luxury versus simpler modernity) and prices (300–500 francs). All rooms are soundproofed. There are two hotel restaurants; a good-value brasserie, Le Caveau, and a higher-class dining room. *23 av. Foch, 57000, tel. 87–66–81–11. 75 rooms with bath. Facilities: 2 restaurants, bar. AE, DC, MC, V. Moderate/Expensive.*

Nancy
Dining
★ **La Capuchin Gourmand.** A sinuous Art Nouveau decor and faultless service set the tone at La Capuchin Gourmand, one of Nancy's finest restaurants. Chef Gérard Veissiére's menu includes such regional specialties as foie gras, game *en casserole*, and an excellent rendition of the classic quiche Lorraine. Local Toul wines make an admirable accompaniment to your meal. *31 rue Gambetta, tel. 83–35–26–98. Reservations essential. Jacket and tie required. AE, V. Closed Sat. dinner, Mon., and first 2 weeks Aug. Expensive.*

Le Gastrolâtre. Admirers of nouvelle cuisine shouldn't pass up a visit to Nancy's most famous purveyor of the art, under the direction of chef Patrick Tanesy. Recommended dishes include salmon—try it any way it's offered—and a delectable fricassee of snails. *39 rue des Maréchaux, tel. 83–35–07–97. Reservations essential. Jacket and tie required. No credit cards. Closed weekends, Christmas–New Year's, and Apr.–mid-May. Moderate–Expensive.*

Manhattan Grill. American '60s charm is promised at Nancy's unlikely sounding Manhattan Grill. In between the earnest posters, mirrors, and hamburgers lurks some competent country French cuisine, and each Thursday there's live music in the cellar. Give this place a try if you're in the mood for a change. It makes quite a contrast with the august medieval buildings along Grand-Rue. *123 Grande-Rue, tel. 83–36–62–71. Reservations accepted. Dress: casual. V. Inexpensive.*

Lodging
★ **Grand Hôtel de la Reine.** This hotel is every bit as swanky as the place Stanislas on which it stands; the magnificent 18th-century building it occupies is officially classified as a historic monument. The guest rooms are decorated in a suitably grand Louis XV style, and the most luxurious look out onto the square. The classic-nouvelle restaurant, Le Stanislas, is costly, although there is a 155-franc menu inclusive of wine. Try the briochelike *kouglof*, a local delicacy made with mirabelle plums. *2 pl. Stanislas, 54000, tel. 83–35–03–01. 52 rooms with bath. Restaurant reservations essential. Jacket and tie required. AE, DC, MC, V. Expensive.*

Central. Next to the train station, and with rooms going for 160 –240 francs a night, the Central makes a less but equally convenient alternative to the Grand Hôtel de la Reine. It is fully modernized, with double glazing to keep out the noise, and has a charming courtyard garden. There's no restaurant. *6 rue Raymond-Poincaré, 54000, tel. 83–32–21–24. 68 rooms with bath. AE, V. Inexpensive.*

Ottrott
Dining
★

L'Ami Fritz. Standing in the hilly village of Ottrott near Obernai, L'Ami Fritz has the stolid heaviness of many an Alsatian *weinstub.* No coincidence, perhaps, since owner Fritz uses this restaurant to showcase his own wine—the famous local Rouge d'Ottrott, a fruity red. Homemade terrine is the highlight of a menu that ranges from steaks and hams to an ice cream crescendo. *Rue du Vignoble, tel. 88–95–80–81. Reservations advised. Dress: casual. AE, DC, MC, V. Closed Wed. and Jan. Inexpensive.*

Strasbourg
Dining

Buerehiesel. The setting can't be bettered—a 17th-century mansion in Strasbourg's leafy Orangerie—but it's the inventive nouvelle cuisine of top French chef Antoine Westermann that really pulls in the customers. His fish cooked in onion and dry Reisling wine is exceptional, as is the poached lobster. Your meal will be pricey, but the fine views over the park come gratis. *4 parc de l'Orangerie, tel. 88–61–62–24. Reservations essential. Jacket and tie required. AE, DC, MC, V. Closed Tues. dinner, Wed., July–early Aug., and Christmas–New Year's. Expensive.*

Crocodile. Chef Emile Jung is celebrated throughout the region for his Alsatian dishes prepared with a delicate nouvelle flair. The restaurant's opulent old-world decor makes a sophisticated backdrop to dishes such as pressed duck and frogs' legs, though if it's on the menu you won't regret choosing the beef Wellington (known to the French as *boeuf en croûte*). *10 rue Outre, tel. 88–32–13–02. Reservations recommended. Jacket and tie required. AE, DC, V. Closed Sun., Mon., first week July–first week Aug., and Christmas–New Year's. Expensive.*

★

Kammerzell. This restaurant glories in its richly carved, wood-framed, 15th-century building—probably the most familiar house in Strasbourg, given its position on the corner of the cathedral square. The shortish menu is served on four stories: Fight your way through the tourist hordes on the terrace and ground floor to one of the atmospheric rooms above, with their gleaming wooden furniture and stained-glass windows. Foie gras and *choucroûte* (sauerkraut) are best bets, while oysters head the seafood that dominates the menu. *16 pl. de la Cathédrale, tel. 88–32–42–14. Reservations recommended. Jacket and tie required. AE, DC, MC, V. Expensive.*

★

Au Gourmet Sans Chiqué. A cheerful welcome can be expected at this intimate, *sans chiqué* (unpretentious) bistro down one of Old Strasbourg's many narrow streets, where herbs and spices are tellingly used by young chef Daniel Klein. The 150-franc menu represents fine value and is complemented by a weekday menu at 90 francs. *15 rue Sainte-Barbe, tel. 88–32–04–07. Reservations advised. Dress: casual. AE, DC, V. Closed Mon., part of Feb., and most of July. Inexpensive–Moderate.*

Lodging

Le Régent Contades. This sleek, modern hotel has only recently opened its doors; it's located just outside the old town in a residential turn-of-the-century district close to the River Ill and its confluence with the narrow River Aar. First-class amenities add to the appeal of the spacious rooms—and prices in excess of 550 francs a night. There's no restaurant. *8 av. de la Liberté, 67000, tel. 88–36–26–26. 20 rooms with bath. Facilities: sauna,* *bar, solarium. AE, DC, V. Closed Christmas–New Year's. Very Expensive.*

★ **Gutenberg.** A 200-year-old mansion is the setting of this charming hotel, just off place Gutenberg and only a few hundred yards from the cathedral. Several rooms, and the reception and breakfast area, have kept their original furniture, underlining a picturesque appeal that once enjoyed the dubious favors of Hitler's Wehrmacht. There's no restaurant. *31 rue des Serruriers, 67000, tel. 88–32–17–15. 50 rooms, most with bath. V. Closed first week Jan. Inexpensive–Moderate.*

Toul
Dining

Le Dauphin. The large, flower-laden dining room was once a G.I. canteen, and the setting (in an industrial sector three miles from the town center) has little of the ambience of historic Toul. Yet Christophe Vohmann entices gourmets with cooking of great finesse—chicken with foie gras or scallops with urchins—for prices that start at 130 francs but soon attain heady heights (300 francs or more) for his most ambitious creations. *Rte. de Villey-St-Etienne, 54200, tel. 83–43–13–46. Reservations advised. Jacket and tie required. V. Closed Sun. dinner and Mon., Jan., and first half of Aug. Expensive.*

Verdun
Dining and Lodging

Coq Hardi. On the banks of the Meuse is this large, steep-roofed hotel furnished in solid regional style. A family-style welcome pervades here and in the large, comfortable restaurant, where lamb and local Ardennes ham figure on the menu (prices start at 150 francs but rise rapidly to 300 francs à la carte). *8 av. de la Victoire, 55100, tel. 29–84–39–41. 40 rooms, most with bath. AE, DC, V. Closed Jan. Restaurant closed Wed. Moderate–Expensive.*

The Arts and Nightlife

The Arts

Many regional towns and villages, especially the wine villages of Alsace, stage festivals in summer. Note the spectacular, pagan-inspired burning of the three pine trees at **Thann** (late June) and the Flower Carnival at **Sélestat** (mid-August). The major regional wine fair is held at **Colmar** (first-half of August); organization is chaotic. There are impressive son-et-lumière performances at the château of **Saverne** and the cathedral of **Strasbourg** (check dates and times locally). The monthly handbook, *Strasbourg Actualités*, is a mine of information on local cultural events.

Theater Leading regional venues are **Strasbourg**—Théâtre National (Salle Hubert Gignoux, av. de la Marseillaise, tel. 88–35–44–52) and Théâtre Municipal (19 pl. Broglie, tel. 88–36–71–12); **Nancy**—Théâtre de la Manufacture (rue du Baron Louis, tel. 83–30–23–32) and Théâtre de Nancy (rue Ste-Catherine, tel. 83–37–65–01); **Metz**—Théâtre Municipal (pl. de la Comédie, tel. 87–75–40–50) and Théâtre Populaire de Lorraine (Ile Saulcy, tel. 87–30–52–78); **Colmar**—Théâtre Municipal (rue Unterlinden, tel. 89–41–29–82); and **Mulhouse** (rue Sinne, tel. 89–45–26–96).

Concerts The annual Festival de Musique is held in **Strasbourg** from June to early July at the modern Palais des Congrès and at the cathedral (tel. 88–32–43–10 for details). There is a rock festival in June, organized by Strasbourg's Centre Culturel (13 pl. André

Maurois), and the city offers summer concerts at the Pavillon Joséphine in the Orangerie. Tuesday evening concerts are held in **Colmar** Collegiate Church in summer. Permanent regional venues and orchestras include Salle Poirel (tel. 83–36–69–93) and Nancy Orchestre Symphonique & Lyrique (pl. Colonel Driant, tel. 83–36–69–93) in **Nancy;** Strasbourg Philharmonic Orchestra (Palais des Congrès, tel. 88–22–15–60) in **Strasbourg;** and Orchestre Philharmine de Lorraine (rue Chambière, tel. 87–32–42–43) in **Metz.**

Opera   Opéra du Rhin (pl. Broglie, tel. 88–36–71–12) in **Strasbourg;** and Opéra de Lorraine (rue Ste-Catherine, tel. 83–37–65–01) in **Nancy.**

Nightlife

Cabaret   In **Nancy:** Cabaret KL (3 rue Gilbert) or Eve (63 rue Jeanne d'Arc). In **Metz:** Le Rio (53 pl. de la Chambre). In **Strasbourg:** L'Aiglon (27 rue Vieux Marché aux Vins).

Bars and   In **Nancy:** Jean Lam (pl. Stanislas), L'Isba (126 rue Jeanne
Nightclubs   d'Arc), or Le Chalet (10 pl. des Vosges). In **Strasbourg:** Charlie's (24 pl. des Halles). In the pretty wine village of **Riquewihr** (14 kilometers/9 miles northwest of Colmar) there is a pleasant piano bar-cum-disco called Le Mequillet (9 av. Méquillet).

Jazz Clubs   In **Nancy:** Rendez-Vous (7 rue St-Dizier) and Les Bacchanales (16 rue de la Primatiale). In **Strasbourg:** Le Funambule (3 rue Klein).

Discos   There is a good choice in **Nancy:** Metro (pl. de la Croix de Bourgogne); New York City (7 rue St-Julien); Club 1900 (19 rue Stanislas); or Tarif de Nuit (3 rue Lafayette). Two of the best bets in **Strasbourg** are the Blue Hawaï (19 rue du Marais-Vert) and Le Chalet (376 rte. de la Wantzeneau). There's a cozy village atmosphere at the Pop Corn disco in **Guebwiller** (169 rue de la République).

12 The Atlantic Coast

Introduction

If there's a formula for enjoying the Atlantic Coast of France and its hinterland, it should include cultural exploration, wine tasting, eating oysters, and relaxing by the sea. Swathes of sandy beaches line the coast: Well-heeled resorts like Biarritz, down by the Spanish border, are thronged with glistening bodies baking in the sun, although those visitors who prefer more solitude won't have any trouble discovering vast, semideserted stretches.

For three centuries of the medieval era, this region was a battlefield in the wars between the French and the English, and the Dordogne and Périgord regions were on the frontline. As a result, castles and châteaus—some ruined, some domesticated —stud the area, with Biron, Hautefort, and Beynac among the best. Robust Romanesque architecture is more characteristic in this area than the airy Gothic style found elsewhere in France: Poitiers showcases the best examples, notably Notre-Dame-la-Grande with its richly worked facade, but Romanesque on the grand scale can also be admired at nearby St-Savin abbey or at the cathedrals of Angoulême and Périgueux. Humble village churches, with distinctive, sturdy towers, perch on verdant hills between Poitiers and Bordeaux, and generations of painters have been inspired by La Rochelle's harbor and imposing fortress-towers.

It's hard not to eat well while visiting the Atlantic Coast. Truffles, walnuts, plums, trout, eel, and myriad succulent species of mushroom jostle for attention on restaurant menus. The goose market in the quaint old town of Sarlat is proof of the local addiction for foie gras. The River Dordogne is home to that rarest of west European fish, sturgeon, whose eggs—better known as caviar—surpass even foie gras as a sought-after delicacy.

The elegant 18th-century city of Bordeaux has tried to diversify its tourist appeal—its May music festival is a major crowd puller—but the city remains synonymous with the wine trade —with the vineyards of Médoc, Sauternes, Graves, Entre-Deux-Mers, and St-Emilion, all within a short drive. Proud châteaus, standing resplendent among the vines, can be visited, although opening hours are irritatingly variable. Wine enthusiasts should note that the *vendages* (grape harvests) usually begin about mid-September in the Bordelais (though you can't visit the wineries at this time). Harvests begin two weeks later in Cognac, the heart of the brandy trade, with its somewhat more dour facades.

In the Gironde *départment* around Bordeaux, forest outnumbers vineyard by four to one; the great Landes pine forest extends all the way from Bordeaux to Spain. Farther north lies the Marais Poitevin, an extraordinary region whose marshy network of rivers and canals is nicknamed Green Venice.

Essential Information

Important Addresses and Numbers

Tourist Information
Suggestions about wine tours and tastings, as well as information on local and regional sights, are available at the **Bordeaux Office de Tourisme**, which also provides a round-the-clock answer service in English (12 cours du XXX Juillet, tel. 56–48–04–61).

The addresses of other tourist offices in towns mentioned on this tour are as follows: **Angoulême** (pl. de la Gare, tel. 45–92–27–57), **Bergerac** (97 rue Neuve d'Argenson, tel. 53–57–03–11), **Biarritz** (1 sq. Ixelles, tel. 59–24–20–24), **Cognac** (16 rue du XIV-Juillet, tel. 45–82–10–71), **Niort** (74 rue d'Alsace-Lorraine, tel. 49–24–76–79), **Poitiers** (350 av. de Nantes, tel. 49–37–83–88), **La Rochelle** (10 rue Fleuriau, tel. 46–41–14–68), **St-Emilion** (pl. des Crénaux, tel. 57–24–72–03), and **Saintes** (Esplanade André-Malraux, tel. 46–74–23–82), and **Sarlat** (pl. de la Liberté, tel. 53–59–27–67).

Travel Agencies
American Express (14 cours de l'Intendance, Bordeaux, tel. 56–81–70–02) and **Thomas Cook** (Gare St-Jean—main train station), Bordeaux, tel. 56–91–58–80).

Car Rental
Avis (59 rue Peyronnet, Bordeaux, tel. 56–92–69–38; 2 blvd. Solferino, Poitiers, tel. 49–58–28–14; and 166 blvd. Joffre, La Rochelle, tel. 46–41–13–55), **Hertz** (pl. de la Gare, Bergerac, tel. 53–57–19–27 and 107 blvd. du Grand Cerf, Poitiers, tel. 49–58–24–24).

Getting Around

By Plane
There are weekly flights from London to Bordeaux and Biarritz and domestic airports at Poitiers, Niort, La Rochelle, Saintes, Angoulême, Dax, and Bergerac.

By Car
As capital of southwest France, Bordeaux boasts superb transport links with Paris, Spain, and even the Mediterranean (A62 expressway via Toulouse). The A10 Paris–Bordeaux expressway passes close to Poitiers, Niort (exit 23 for La Rochelle), and Saintes before continuing toward Spain as A63. Fast N137 connects La Rochelle to Saintes via Rochefort; Angoulême is linked to Bordeaux and Poitiers by the rapid N10; St-Emilion, which can be reached by road only, lies 32 kilometers (20 miles) east of Bordeaux; and D936 runs along the Dordogne Valley to Bergerac.

By Train
The fast and efficient train service between Gare d'Austerlitz and Bordeaux—584 kilometers (365 miles) in 4¼ hours—stops at Poitiers (change for Niort, La Rochelle, and Rochefort) and Angoulême (change for Jarnac, Cognac, and Saintes). Trains run regularly from Bordeaux to Bergerac (80-minute journey) and, just three times daily, to Sarlat (nearly three hours). The main Paris–Northern Spain train line covers the 800 kilometers (500 miles) to Biarritz in 6½ hours.

Guided Tours

Bus Excursions
Horizons Européens (France Tourisme, 214 rue de Rivoli, 75001 Paris, tel. 42–60–31–25) organizes a seven-day bus tour

of Dordogne and Périgord, leaving from Paris and taking in Limoges, castles, wine tastings, and grottoes; cost is about 4,000 francs inclusive. Day trips in a seven-seater minibus are organized Easter through November from Sarlat by **Hep Excursion** (tel. 53–59–05–48); cost is about 140 francs.

Boat Trips The canal-crossed Marais Poitevin area has been described as a rural version of Venice. You can tour the area by boat, starting at the **Benedictine Abbey of Maillezais;** the 45-minute trip has departures between 9 and noon and 2 and 7 from Easter through October, for a cost of 15 francs.

To get a feel for the historic port of **Bordeaux,** the region's largest city, take the 90-minute boat tour that leaves weekdays from the Embarcadères des Quinconces at around 3; cost is about 40 francs.

Special-Interest Tours of the pretty St-Emilion vineyard (including wine tastings) are organized by the **St-Emilion tourist office** (1 pl. Créneaux, tel. 57–24–72–03). Tours last two hours and depart weekdays during summer months from the tourist office at 2 and 4:15; cost is 45 francs.

Walking Tours The tourist office in **Sarlat** (pl. de la Liberté, tel. 53–59–27–67) offers a one-hour walking tour of the town; cost is 10 francs.

Exploring the Atlantic Coast

Numbers in the margin correspond with points of interest on the Atlantic Coast map.

Orientation

We've divided the region into three tours. The first begins in Poitoú-Charentes, a rural area north of Bordeaux, and explores the countryside from St-Savin, to the seacoast town of La Rochelle, and back inland again to Cognac country. Our second tour explores the scenic provinces of Dordogne and Périgord. The vineyards surrounding Bordeaux form the basis of the third tour, which continues south through sand dunes and forested scenery to the coastal resort of Biarritz, near the Spanish border.

Highlights for First-time Visitors

Biarritz, Tour 3
Bordeaux, Tour 3
Marais Poitevin, Tour 1
Poitiers, Tour 1
La Rochelle, Tour 1
La Roque-Gageac, Tour 2
St-Emilion, Tour 2
Sarlat, Tour 2

Tour 1: Poitou-Charentes

The region of Poitou-Charentes occupies the middle band of France's Atlantic coast. Our tour starts just about as far from the sea as regional boundaries will allow: at the tiny village of **St-Savin**, 40 kilometers (25 miles) east of Poitiers.

The large **abbey of St-Savin**, which dates back to the 11th century, is impressive enough from the outside. But it is the interior that beckons, partly for the sculpted ornament—monsters run riot on the column capitals—and mainly for the extensive wall paintings in restrained but skillfully contrasted hues of green and ocher. These frescoes, dating from the building's construction, were painted directly onto the walls, and it's surprising that the thin film of paint has survived the centuries in such fine condition. Swaying folds of cloth and enormous, expressive hands lend life and expression to the numerous figures enacting biblical stories.

Leave St-Savin to the west along N151, making for **Poitiers.** Thanks to its majestic hilltop setting above the River Clain, and its position halfway along the Bordeaux–Paris trade route, Poitiers became an important commercial, religious, and university town in the Middle Ages. Since the 17th century, however, not much has happened in Poitiers, but visitors will find this is no bad thing; stagnation equals preservation, and Poitier's architectural heritage is correspondingly rich.

The church of **Notre-Dame-la-Grande,** in the town center, is one of the most impressive examples of the Romanesque architecture so common in western France. Its 12th-century facade is framed by rounded arches of various sizes and is decorated with a multitude of bas-reliefs and sculptures. The interior is dark. Its painted walls and pillars are not original; such decoration was a frequent ploy of mid-19th century clerics keen to brighten up their otherwise austere churches. *Rue des Cordeliers.*

Just off Grand'Rue, a few hundred yards beyond Notre-Dame-la-Grande, is the cathedral of **St-Pierre,** built during the 13th and 14th centuries. The largest church in Poitiers, it has a distinctive facade featuring two asymmetrical towers, as well as the usual rose window and carved portals. The imposing interior is noted for its 12th-century stained glass, especially the Crucifixion in the chancel, and 13th-century wooden choir stalls, thought to be the oldest in France. *Pl. du Cathédrale.*

Head down Grand'Rue, taking the second left and first right into rue Jean-Jaurès. The town museum, **Musée Ste-Croix,** is a modern building housing archaeological discoveries and European paintings from the 15th to the 19th century, of good, though not outstanding, quality. *Rue St-Simplicien. Admission free. Open Wed.–Mon. 10–11:30 and 2–5:30; closed Tues.*

Next to the museum is the 4th-century **Baptistère St-Jean,** the oldest Christian building in France. Its heavy stone bulk is sunk some 12 feet beneath ground level and consists of a rectangular chamber, used for baptisms, and an eastern end added during the 6th and 7th centuries. The porch, or narthex (restored in the 10th century), is linked to the main building by three archways. Go inside to see the octagonal basin, a larger version of a font for baptism by total immersion, and a collection of sarcophagi and works of sculpture. *Rue Jean-Jaurès. Admission: 8 frs. Open Mar.–Jan., daily 10–12:30 and 2:30–4; Feb., Thurs.–Tues. 10–12:30 and 2:30–4.*

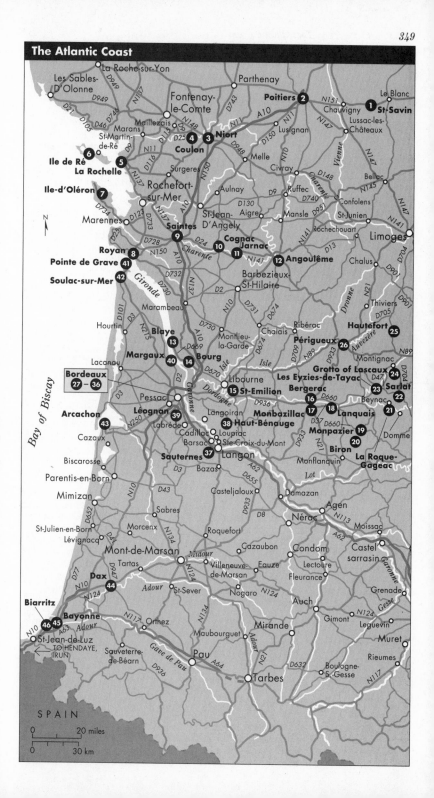

The Atlantic Coast

Make your way back into the town center, pausing to admire the beautifully preserved old houses lining the way, and turn left into rue Carnot. Shortly after this street has become rue de la Tranchée, the oldest of Poitiers's churches, **St-Hilaire-le-Grand,** appears to the right. Parts of St-Hilaire date from the early 11th century. Unfortunately the original church had to be reduced in width in the 12th century when its roof was destroyed by fire; local masons lacked the engineering know-how to cover large expanses with the fireproof stone vaults chosen as a replacement. The semicircular, mosaic-floored choir rises high above the level of the nave. Cupolas, mighty columns, frescoes, and finely carved capitals add to the church's interest. *Rue St-Hilaire.*

3 **Niort,** 72 kilometers (45 miles) down A10, is a complacent, middle-class town best known as the capital of the French insurance business. The massive keep, with its two square towers dominating the River Sèvre, is all that remains of the **castle** built at the end of the 12th century by English kings Henry II and Richard the Lionhearted. Inside there is a museum with an extensive collection of arms and local costumes. *Next to the Vieux-Ponts (Old Bridges). Admission: 10 frs. Open Apr.–Oct., Wed.–Mon 9–noon and 2–6; Nov.–Mar., Wed.–Mon. 9–noon and 2–5; closed Tues.*

Just off the nearby rue Victor-Hugo is the old town hall, a triangular building completed in 1535. It now houses the **Musée du Pilori,** with its collection of local archaeological finds and Renaissance artifacts. The highlight is an ebony chest encrusted with gold and silver. *Just off rue Victor-Hugo. Admission: 10 frs. Open Apr.–Oct., Wed.–Mon. 9–noon and 2–6; Nov.–Mar., Wed.–Mon. 9–noon and 2–5; closed Tues.*

Do an about-face and amble down rue St-Jean, the oldest street in Niort, to the **Musée des Beaux-Arts** (Fine Arts Museum), where tapestries, gold and enamelware, wooden statues and effigies, and 17th–18th century paintings are on display. *Rue St-Jean. Admission: 10 frs. Open Wed.–Thurs. 9–noon and 2–6 (5 in winter).*

West of Niort is the **Marais Poitevin,** an extraordinary region nicknamed "Green Venice" because of its hundreds of canals, lush fields, and rows of hedges. Rent one of the odd-looking local punts (flat, narrow boats maneuvered with a long pole) to

4 get around; you can find them in **Coulon,** a village on the Sèvre Niortaise river 11 kilometers (7 miles) west of Niort along D9. (They cost about 80 francs per hour per boat, maximum six persons.) To explore the region by car or bicycle, a detailed map and sound sense of direction are advisable.

Willows, ash, and alder trees line the rivers and canals; artichokes, onions, melons, and garlic are grown in the fields alongside. There is little but the occasional very pretty village in the way of man-made embellishment, apart from the ruins of the once-mighty **Benedictine Abbaye de Maillezais,** 13 kilometers (8 miles) northwest of Coulon via D9. Maillezais used to be a bishop's seat (transferred to La Rochelle), as well as a powerful monastery. The ruins include the 14th-century cloister and refectory, the 11th-century porch, and the 15th-century transept. There is a fine view from the top of one of the towers. *Admission: 12 frs. Open Nov.–Mar., daily 9–12:30 and 1:30–6; Apr.–Oct., daily 9–8.*

From the abbey, there are 45-minute boat trips through the Marais Poitevin from Easter until the end of October *(see Guided Tours in Essential Information, above).*

Between Maillezais and the Atlantic coast, the Marais Mouillé (wet marsh) gradually dries up and a flat, barren, eerie landscape appears: the Marais Desséché, or dried-out marsh. From Maillezais, head south along D15, then turn right after La Ronde into narrow D262, which hugs the straight banks of the Canal de la Branche as far as Marans, once a thriving seaport but now linked to the sea only by canal. D105 sneaks seaward from Marans. At the first major crossroad, 8 kilometers (5 miles) past Marans, turn left along D9 toward La Rochelle, 16 kilometers (10 miles) away.

⑤ **La Rochelle** is an appealing old town; its ancient streets are centered on its harbor, the remarkably picturesque Vieux Port. Standing sentinel on either side of the harbor are the fortresslike 14th-century towers known as **Tour St-Nicholas** (to the left) and the **Tour de la Chaîne** (to the right). From the top of Tour St-Nicholas, visitors can admire the view over the surrounding bay toward the Ile d'Aix. *Admission: 12 frs.; joint ticket with nearby Tour de la Lanterne, 20 frs. Open Easter–Oct., Wed.–Mon. 10–12:30 and 2:30–6; Nov.–Easter, Wed.–Mon. 2–5; closed Tues.*

Time Out Close to the harbor, in the shadow of the Tour de la Chaîne, **Le Crystal Piano Bar** serves up refreshing sorbets and cocktails against a background of piano music. *54 cours des Dames.*

Take cours des Dames, a spacious avenue lined with sturdy trees and 18th-century houses, back to the Porte de la Grosse Horologe, a massive stone gate marking the entrance to the straight, narrow, bustling streets of the old town. Head down rue du Palais and into rue Gargoulleau. Halfway down on the left is the 18th-century Bishop's Palace, now home to a museum of paintings. Opposite is the **Musée Lafaille**, housed in an elegant mansion and containing extensive collections of rocks, coral, and shellwork. Other items range from a tribal idol from Easter Island in the South Pacific to a giraffe (now stuffed) given as a gift to King Charles X (1824–30). *28 rue Albert-Ier. Admission: 6 frs. Open Apr.–Oct., Tues.–Sun. 10–noon and 2–6; Nov.–Mar., Tues.–Sun. 10–noon and 2–5.*

Farther down rue du Palais (which becomes rue Albert-Ier) is another 18th-century building containing the **Musée du Nouveau-Monde** (New World Museum). Old maps, engravings, watercolors, and even wallpaper evoke the commercial links between La Rochelle and the New World. *10 rue Fleuriau. Admission: 10 frs. Open Wed.–Mon. 10–6; closed Tues.*

⑥ A bridge curves across from La Rochelle to a cheerful island, known as **Ile de Ré**, just 16 miles long and never more than 4 miles wide. Vineyards sweep over the eastern part of the island while oyster beds straddle the shallow waters to the west. The largest village, **St-Martin de Ré** (population 3,000) boasts a lively harbor, and a citadel built by ace military architect Sébastien de Vauban in 1681. Many of its streets also date from the 17th century, and the villagers' low, white houses, often embellished with window boxes full of flowers, are typical of the island as a whole.

The wide, fast N137 speeds down the coast from La Rochelle to Rochefort-sur-Mer, 32 kilometers (20 miles) away. From here, D733 and D123 lead 24 kilometers (15 miles) down the coast to the renowned oyster town of Marennes, at the point where D26 passes over the 2-mile Oléron Viaduct to the **Ile-d'Oléron.** France's second-largest island, after Corsica, it measures 19 miles from end to end, and up to 7 miles across. Sand dunes ring the island to the north and west, while oyster beds line the eastern shores, notably along the route des Huîtres north of the Château d'Oléron, a ruined 17th-century castle. Mainland activity is dominated by the vine; the tangy sweet aperitif, known as *Pineau des Charentes*, is produced by mixing unfermented grape juice with cognac.

Back on the mainland, take D25 around the coast to **Royan,** a commercialized, resort town that was rebuilt—largely in concrete—after being pounded to bits by Nazi shells in 1945. Royan's sheltered bays, sea views, and vast, sandy beaches are its sole remaining attractions, but a brief look should satisfy most visitors.

Head inland along N150 to **Saintes,** a city of stately serenity. Its **cathedral** seems to stagger beneath the weight of its chunky tower, which climbs above the red roofs of the old town. Engineering caution foiled plans for the traditional pointed spire, so the tower was given a shallow dome—incongruous, perhaps, but distinctive. Angels, prophets, and saints decorate the Flamboyant Gothic main door of the cathedral, while the austere 16th-century interior is lined with circular pillars of formidable circumference.

The narrow pedestrian streets clustered around the cathedral contrast with the broad boulevards that slice through the town and over the River Charente, but both are full of life and color. Just across the bridge, to the right, is the impressive Roman **Arc de Germanicus,** built in AD 19. Ahead, reached by rue Arc de la Triomphe, is the sturdy octagonal tower of the **Abbaye aux Dames.** Consecrated in 1047, this abbey church is fronted by an exquisite, arcaded facade, whose portals and capitals, carved with fantastic beasts, deserve more than a quick look. Although the Romanesque choir remains largely in its original form, the rest of the interior is less harmonious, having been periodically restored.

Saintes owes its development to the salt marshes that first attracted the Romans to the area some 2,000 years ago. The Romans left their mark with an arch, which we've already seen, and with an **amphitheater,** now largely grassed over: There are far better preserved examples in France, but few as old. To reach the amphitheater, take the boulevard back across the river and veer left into cours Reverseaux. *Access via rue St-Eutrope.*

Leave Saintes to the east along D24, making for the lichen-covered town of **Cognac,** 27 kilometers (17 miles) away. Compared to Saintes, Cognac seems dull and an unlikely hometown for one of the world's most successful drink trades. You may be disappointed initially by the town's unpretentious appearance, but, like the drink, it tends to grow on you. Cognac owed its early development to the transport of salt and wine along the River Charente. When 16th-century Dutch merchants discovered that the local wine was both tastier and easier to transport if distilled, the town became the heart of the brandy industry and remains so to this day.

The leading monument in Cognac is its former **castle,** now part of the premises of Otard Cognac, a leading distillery. Volatile Renaissance monarch François I was born here in 1494. The castle has changed quite a bit since: The remaining buildings are something of a hodge-podge, though the stocky towers that survey the Charente recall the site's fortified origins. The tour of Otard Cognac combines its own propaganda with historical comment on the drink itself. The slick audiovisuals may seem pretentious, but you will visit some interesting rooms and receive a free taste of the firm's product, which is available for sale at vastly reduced prices. *Admission free. Guided tours daily on the hour 10–noon and 2–5 (not Sun. during Oct.–May).*

Most cognac houses organize visits of their premises and *chais* (warehouses). **Hennessy,** a little farther along the banks of the Charente (note the company's mercenary emblem: an ax-wielding arm, carved in stone), and **Martell** both give polished guided tours, an ideal introduction to the mysteries of cognac. Martell's *chais* are perhaps more picturesque, but the Hennessy tour includes a cheerful jaunt across the Charente in old-fashioned boats. Wherever you decide to go, you will literally soak up the atmosphere of cognac; three percent of the precious cask-bound liquid evaporates every year! This has two consequences: each *chais* smells delicious, and a small, black, funguslike mushroom, which feeds on cognac's alcoholic fumes, forms on walls throughout the town. *Hennessy, rue Richonne, tel. 45-82-52-22. Martell, pl. Martell, tel. 45-82-44-44.*

Rue Saulnier, alongside the Hennessy premises, is the most atmospheric of the somber, sloping, cobbled streets that compose the core of Cognac, dominated by the tower of **St-Léger,** a church with a notably large Flamboyant Gothic rose window. Busy boulevard Denfert-Rochereau twines around the old town, passing in front of the manicured lawns of the town hall and the gravelly drive of the neighboring **Musée du Cognac,** containing good ceramics and Art Nouveau glass, but worth visiting mainly for its section on cognac itself. The history and production of cognac are clearly explained, and one room is devoted to amusing, early advertising posters. *48 blvd. Denfert-Rochereau. Admission free. Open Wed.–Mon. 10–noon and 2:30–5:30; closed Tues.*

⓫ Several cognac firms are found 16 kilometers (10 miles) upriver at the charming village of **Jarnac. Hine** (quai de l'Orangerie, tel. 45-81-11-38) and **Courvoisier** (pl. du Château, tel. 45-35-55-55) organize visits of their riverbank premises, though Hine's cozy buildings in local chalky stone have more appeal than does Courvoisier's bombastic red-brick factory by the bridge. Jarnac is also famous as the birthplace of French President François Mitterrand.

⓬ Twenty-six kilometers (16 miles) east of Jarnac along N141 is **Angoulême,** divided, like many French towns, between an old, picturesque sector perched around a hilltop cathedral and a modern, industrial part sprawling along the valley and railroad below.

Angoulême Cathedral, in place St-Pierre, bears little resemblance to the majority of its French counterparts because of a flattened dome that lends it an Oriental appearance. The cathedral dates from the 12th century, though it was partly destroyed by Calvinists in 1562, then restored in a heavy-handed manner in 1634 and 1866. Its principal attraction is the magnificent Romanesque facade, whose layers of rounded arches boast 70 stone statues and bas-reliefs illustrating the Last Judgment. The interior is austere and massive but of no great interest.

The cathedral dominates the *ville haute* (upper town), known as the "plateau." There are stunning views from the ramparts alongside, and a warren of quaint old streets to explore in the shadow of the Hôtel de Ville (Town Hall), with its colorful garden. Literary enthusiasts may like to note that 19th-century novelist Honoré de Balzac is one of the town's adopted sons; Balzac described Angoulême in his novel *Lost Illusions*.

Tour 2: Dordogne and Périgord

On the first half of this tour, we follow one of the country's longest rivers, the Dordogne, as it meanders inland to Sarlat from its confluence with the River Garonne. The two rivers merge to form the Gironde between Bourg and Blaye, two lesser-known sectors of the Bordeaux vineyard that produce cheerful, light reds and tiny quantities of dry white wine. The small harbor town of **Blaye** (pronounced "Bly"), 48 kilometers (30 miles) north of Bordeaux, is worth a visit, chiefly for its vast riverside **citadel,** over half a mile across, erected by Sébastien de Vauban in the 1680s. From a vantage point at the top of the citadel's Tour de l'Aiguillette, the roving gaze can survey the mighty Gironde estuary and the beginnings of the Atlantic Ocean. Close by are two other towers, all that remain of the medieval Château des Rudel. Ditches and ramparts surround the citadel on the landward side. Beyond, the streets of Blaye soon give way to the Côtes de Blaye vineyard, which extends north to the limits of Cognac country.

D669 runs 14 kilometers (9 miles) along the banks of the Gironde Estuary from Blaye to **Bourg,** with its once-fortified *ville haute* (upper town) perched on top of a chalky cliff and linked by stone stairs to the *ville basse* (lower town), with its harbor on the River Dordogne. There is a fine wooded garden around the **Château de la Citadelle** (former summer residence of the bishops of Bordeaux) and a broad view over the Côtes de Bourg vineyard from its terrace.

Follow D670 southeast of Bourg to **Libourne,** 30 kilometers (19 miles) away and surrounded by some famous vineyards. The tiny vineyards of Fronsac and Canon-Fronsac (producing robust, spicy reds) greet you on your approach from the west. Scattered across the banks of the Dordogne are the vines of Entre-Deux-Mers, which yield crisp, dry, good-value whites. The best is produced beneath the ruins of the Château of Haut-Bénauge near Cadillac (*see* Tour 3, below).

From Libourne, take D244 east to approach the pretty town of St-Emilion across the sun-fired flatness of Pomerol, a land of tiny, twisty lanes and ubiquitous grapevines. The occasional hamlet apologetically interrupts, with scruffy gardens and scraggly dogs. All the wealth is in the earth: Locally produced Château Petrus, made exclusively from Merlot grapes, claims to be the world's most expensive red wine, while the nearby Cheval Blanc vineyard produces one of the two top-ranking St-Emilion wines.

Without any warning, the flatlands break into hills to send you tumbling into **St-Emilion.** This jewel of a town has old buildings of golden stone, ruined town walls, well-kept ramparts offering charming views, and a church hewn into a cliff. Sloping vines invade from all sides, and lots and lots of tourists invade down the middle.

The medieval streets are filled with wine stores and craft shops. Macaroons are a specialty. The local wines offer the twin advantages of reaching maturity earlier than other Bordeaux reds and representing better value for money. Tours of the pretty **St-Emilion vineyard,** including wine tastings, are organized by the *Syndicat d'Initiative* (tourist office) on place des Créneaux, a bulky square with a terrace overlooking the lower part of St-Emilion. A stroll along the 13th-century ramparts helps you appreciate St-Emilion's ancient, unspoiled stone-walled houses, and soon brings you to the Royal Castle, or **Château du Roi,** built by occupying sovereign Henry III of England (1216–72).

Steps lead down from the ramparts to place du Marché, a wooded square where cafés remain open late into the balmy summer night. Lining one side are the east windows of the **Eglise Monolithe,** one of France's largest underground churches, hewn out of the rock face between the 9th and 12th century. *Visits organized by the Syndicat d'Initiative.*

Just south of the town walls is **Château Ausone,** now a winery that is ranked with Cheval Blanc as producing the finest wine of St-Emilion.

As you continue east along D243, you soon find yourself amid the vines of the Côtes de Castillon; the Côtes de Castillon wine is a cheaper and more than palatable alternative to St-Emilion. We are now at the beginning of what English speakers often refer to simply as "The Dordogne," those magical words conjuring up French gastronomy and romantic castles perched above steep valleys.

D936 chugs along the north bank of the river to **Bergerac.** Vines are cultivated here, too, though less expected is the presence of tobacco plantations. Learn about this local industry at the **Musée du Tabac,** a museum housed in the haughty 17th-century Maison Peyrarède near the quayside. The manufacture, uses, and history of tobacco, from its American origins to its spread worldwide, are explained with the help of maps, pictures, documents, and other exhibits, including a collection of pipes and snuff bottles. *Rue de l'Ancien Pont. Admission: 12 frs. Open Tues.–Fri. 10–noon and 2–6, Sat. 10–noon and 2–5, Sun. 2:30 –6:30.*

Head left from the tobacco museum, past place de la Myrpe, to the **Couvent des Récollets,** a former convent. The convent's stone and brick buildings range in date from the 12th to the 17th century and include galleries, a large vaulted cellar, and a cloister, where the Maison du Vin dishes out information on— and samples of—local wines. From the first floor of the convent, treat yourself to a view of the sloping vineyards of Monbazillac across the Dordogne. *Just off pl. de la Myrpe. Ad-*

mission: 12 frs. Visits July–Aug., every hour from 10:30–11:30, and 1:30–5:30; mid-May–June and Sept.–mid-Oct., at 3:30 and 4:30. Closed Mon. and Sun., mid-May–June and Sept.–mid-Oct.

The regional wines of Bergerac range from red and rosé to dry and sweet whites. While you're in town, you might like to purchase a bottle or two of the town's most famous vintage: Monbazillac, a sweet wine, made from overripe grapes, which enjoyed an international reputation long before its Bordeaux rival, Sauternes.

⑰ D13 heads south 8 kilometers (5 miles) from Bergerac to the 16th-century château of **Monbazillac.** Vines grow up to the very doors of this beautifully proportioned, gray stone building, whose squat corner towers pay tribute to the fortress tradition of the Middle Ages but whose large windows and sloping roofs reveal the domesticating influence of the Renaissance. Regional furniture and an ornate, early 17th-century bedchamber enliven the interior. There is—of course—a small wine museum in the cellars. *Admission: 18 frs. Open Apr.–Oct., daily 9:30–noon and 2–6:30; Nov.–Mar., 9:30–noon and 2–5:30.*

⑱ From Monbazillac, head back toward Bergerac and take D37 east along the banks of the Dordogne to the village and turreted château of **Lanquais** (15th–17th century), surrounded by a large garden. The interior is richly furnished throughout and features majestic Italian fireplaces on loan from the Louvre. *Admission: 10 frs. Open Apr.–Oct., Fri.–Wed. 9:30–noon and 2:30–7; closed Thurs.*

⑲ On the opposite side of the Dordogne loom the towers of Baneuil Castle. Keep on the south bank and turn right at Couze along D660, making for the tiny town of **Monpazier,** 27 kilometers (17 miles) away. Monpazier is one of France's best-preserved *bastides* (fortified medieval towns with regimented street plans), built in ocher-colored stone by English king Edward I in 1284 to protect the southern flank of his French possessions. The *bastide* features three stone gateways (of an original six), a large central square, and the church of **St-Dominique,** housing 35 carved wooden choir stalls and a relic of the True Cross. Opposite the church is the finest medieval building in Monpazier, the **Maison du Chapître** (chapter house), once used as a barn for storing grain. Its wood-beam roof is constructed of chestnut to repel web-spinning spiders.

⑳ Five miles south of Monpazier is the hilltop château of **Biron;** its keep, square tower, and chapel date from the Middle Ages, while the Classical buildings were completed in 1730. Highlights of a visit here include monumental staircases, the kitchen with its huge stone slabs, and the tomb of a former owner Pons de Gontaut-Biron (who died in 1524). English Romantic poet Lord Byron (1788–1824) is claimed as a distant descendant of the Gontaut-Biron family that lived here for 14 generations. *Admission: 16 frs. Open Feb.–June and Sept.–Nov., Wed.–Mon. 9–11:30 and 2–6; July–Aug., daily 9–11:30 and 2–6.*

Return to Monpazier and get onto northeast-bound D53, which passes by the château of **Les Milandes,** once owned by the American-born cabaret star of Roaring-Twenties Paris, Josephine Baker (open May–Oct., daily 9:30–11:30 and 2–6). D53 goes by the ruined castle of **Castlenaud** (open May–Nov., daily

10–7). From here, D57 crosses over the Dordogne; turn onto D703, passing the 13th-century castle of **Beynac** (open Apr.– Oct., daily 10–noon and 2:30–7). A short distance upriver, huddled beneath a towering gray cliff, is **La Roque-Gageac,** one of the prettiest and best-restored villages in the Dordogne Valley. Craft shops line its low, narrow streets, which are dominated by the outlines of the 19th-century, mock-medieval Château de Malartrie and the Manoir de Tarde, with its cylindrical turret.

D46 now heads a few miles north to another Dordogne gem, the small town of **Sarlat.** To do justice to its golden-stone splendor, you may want to take advantage of the guided tour offered by the tourist office on place de la Liberté *(see* Guided Tours in Essential Information, above). Rue de la Liberté leads to place du Payrou, occupied on one corner by the pointed-gabled Renaissance house where writer-orator Etienne de la Boétie (1530–63) was born. Diagonally opposite is the entrance to **Sarlat Cathedral.** An elaborate turret-topped tower, begun in the 12th century, is the oldest part of the building and, along with the choir, all that remains of the original Romanesque church. A sloping garden behind the cathedral, the Cour de l'Evêché, affords good views of the choir and contains a strange, conical tower known as the **Lanterne des Morts** (Lantern of the Dead), which was occasionally used as a funeral chapel.

Rue d'Albusse, adjoining the garden, and rue de la Salamandre are narrow, twisty streets that head back to place de la Liberté and the 17th-century town hall. Opposite the town hall is the rickety former church of St-Marie, overlooking place des Oies (where a goose market is occasionally held) and pointing the way to Sarlat's most interesting street, **rue des Consuls.** Among its medieval buildings are the Hôtel Plamon, with broad second-floor windows that resemble those of a Gothic church, and, opposite, the 15th-century Hôtel de Vassal.

Time Out   If you feel like lunch or a snack, make your way to the **Jardin des Consuls,** in the heart of old Sarlat close to the Hôtel Plamon. It's part restaurant, part tea room serving sorbets and pancakes. The stone-walled dining room is pleasant enough, but in sunny weather, cross through it to the idyllic courtyard in back. Soups and *cassoulet* stews head the filling 100-franc menu, best washed down with a young, *Gouleyant* Cahors. *4 rue des Consuls.*

Across the undistinguished rue de la République, which slices Sarlat in two, is the Quartier Ouest, many of whose streets are too narrow to be used by cars. Rue Rousseau saunters past the Chapelle des Récollets and Abbaye St-Claire, to the 16th-century Tour du Bourreau and a remnant of the former town walls.

From Sarlat, D47 twists 21 kilometers (13 miles) west to **Les Eyzies-de-Tayac,** passing the elegant **Château of Puymartin** (open July–Sept., daily 10–noon and 2–6) on the way. Many signs of prehistoric man have been discovered in the vicinity of Les Eyzies; a number of excavated caves and grottoes, some with wall paintings, are open for public viewing. Ask for details of possible visits at the **Musée Nationale de Préhistoire,** where you can also examine many artifacts. The museum's primitive sculpture, furniture, and work tools are presented in an appealing setting: a restored, mainly Renaissance, château. *Admission: 12 frs., 6 frs. Sun., free Wed. Open Apr.–Oct., Wed.–Mon. 9:30–noon and 2–6; Nov.–Mar., Wed.–Mon. 9:30–noon and 2–5; closed Tues.*

㉔ Take D706 up the Vézère Valley to Montignac. Six kilometers (4 miles) away is the famous **Grotto of Lascaux,** whose hundreds of mesmerizing prehistoric wall paintings, thought to be at least 20,000 years old, were discovered by chance in 1940. Unfortunately, the caves have been sealed off to prevent irreparable damage, though portions are reproduced in the Lascaux 2 exhibition center in Montignac. *Admission: 25 frs. Open Tues.–Sun. 10–noon and 2–5.*

㉕ Continue north via D65 and D704 until you reach the château of **Hautefort,** a vast castle surrounded by gardens and presenting a disarmingly arrogant face to the world. The castle's skyline bristles with high roofs, domes, chimneys, and cupolas. The square-lined Renaissance left wing clashes with the muscular, round towers of the right wing, as the only surviving section of the original medieval castle—the gateway and drawbridge—referees in the middle. Most of the buildings date from the 17th century, and contemporary furniture and tapestries adorn the interior. *Admission: 20 frs. Open May–Nov., daily 9–noon and 2–6; Dec.–Apr., Sun. 2–5.*

㉖ **Périgueux,** lying 40 kilometers (25 miles) west via D704/705 (which joins N89), is famous not for a château but for its weird-looking cathedral. The **Cathédrale St-Front** (finished in 1173 but comprehensively restored in the last century) could be on loan from Constantinople, given its shallow, scale-patterned domes and small, elongated, conical cupolas sprouting from the roof like baby minarets. The 200-foot Romanesque tower, one of the finest in southern France, is also topped by a conical dome. You may be struck by similarities with the Byzantine-style Sacré-Coeur in Paris; that's no coincidence—architect Paul Abadie worked on both sites. The interior is cool, vast, and relatively dark. *Pl. de la Clautre.*

Tour 3: Bordeaux to Biarritz

㉗ **Bordeaux,** the capital of southwest France, is renowned world-wide for its wines. Vineyards extend on all sides: Graves and pretty Sauternes to the south; flat, dusty Médoc to the west; and Pomerol and St-Emilion to the east. Stylish châteaus loom above the most famous vines, but much of the wine-making area is unimpressive, with little sign of the extraordinary regional affluence it promotes.

There are signs enough in the city itself, however, where wine shippers have long based their headquarters along the banks of the Garonne. An aura of 18th-century elegance permeates the downtown area, whose fine shops and pedestrian precincts invite leisurely exploration. Take time to head south of the center **㉘** into the **old dockland,** with its narrow, sturdy, low-terraced streets. There is a forbidding feel here and, indeed, Bordeaux as a whole is a less exuberant city than most in France, with an almost British reserve. For a better view of the picturesque **㉙** quayside, stroll across the **Pont de Pierre** bridge spanning the Garonne; built by Napoleon at the start of the 19th century, the bridge makes spectacular viewing itself, thanks to a gracefully curving multitude of arches.

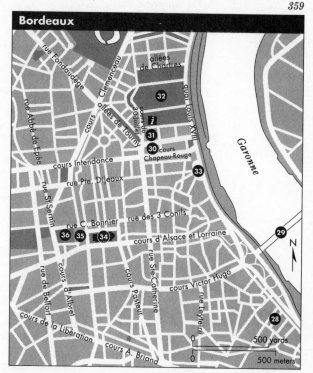

Bordeaux

Two blocks from the riverbank, along cours Chapeau-Rouge, is
the city's leading 18th-century monument: the **Grand Théâtre,**
built between 1773 and 1780 to the plans of architect Victor
Louis. Its elegant exterior is ringed by graceful Corinthian columns and pilasters. The majestic foyer, with its two-winged
staircase and cupola, inspired Charles Garnier's design for the
Paris Opera. The theater-hall itself has a frescoed ceiling and a
shimmering chandelier composed of 14,000 Bohemian crystals;
the acoustics are said to be perfect. *Pl. de la Comédie. Admission: 12 frs. Guided tours mid-July–Sept., Tues.–Fri. at
10:30, 3, and 4:30; Oct.–mid-July, Sat. at 3 and 4.*

The allées de Tourny and cours du 30-Juillet, haughty tree-
lined boulevards, reel off north from the Grand Théâtre. At the
start of the cours du 30-Juillet is the **CIVB,** headquarters of the
Bordeaux wine trade, where information can be had and samples tasted. The **Vinothèque,** opposite, sells Bordeaux by the
bottle to suit every purse. At the far end of the cours is the **Esplanade des Quinconces,** a vast 400-yard-long square overlooking the Garonne.

Turn right from the esplanade and head four blocks along the
quayside. The city's second most important 18th-century landmark after the Grand Théâtre is the three-sided **place de la
Bourse** (1730–55), which looks out over the calm waters of the
Garonne. A provincial reply to Paris's celebrated place Vendôme, the square features airy, large-windowed buildings
designed by the country's most esteemed architect of the era,
Jacques Anges Gabriel.

Time Out Head two blocks down rue F-Philippart to the 18th-century **place du Parlement,** and you'll have no problem finding a promising-looking lunch spot. No fewer than six bistros and restaurants, some with outdoor tables, line the square. Among them are bustling **L'Ombrière** (no. 14); **La Ténarèze** (no. 18), providing rich dishes from Gascony; and expensive **Chez Philippe** (no. 1), one of the city's top fish restaurants. *Most restaurants closed Sun. and Mon.*

34 A maze of narrow streets wend their way from the river to the **Cathédrale St-André,** located in place Pey-Berland. This hefty edifice, 135 yards long, isn't one of France's better Gothic cathedrals, and the outside has a dirty, neglected look to it. The interior, though, rewards your scrutiny as the soaring 14th-century chancel makes an interesting contrast with the earlier, more severe nave. Excellent—albeit grimy—stone carvings adorn the facade (notably that of the Porte Royale, to the right), as well as the 15th-century Pey-Berland Tower that stands nearby.

35 Across the tidy gardens of the luxurious **Hôtel de Ville** (Town Hall) opposite the cathedral, is the busy cours d'Albret and the **36** **Musée des Beaux-Arts.** This fine arts museum has a notable collection of works spanning the 15th–20th centuries, with important paintings by Paulo Veronese *(Apostle's Head)*, Camille Corot *(Bath of Diana)*, and Odilon Redon *(Chariot of Apollo)*, and sculptures by Auguste Rodin. *20 cours d'Albret. Admission: 7 frs. Open Wed.–Mon. 10–noon and 2–6; closed Tues.*

You can find one of the region's most famous châteaus, without even leaving the city. Follow N250 from central Bordeaux (direction Arcachon) for a couple of miles to the district of Pessac, home to the flagship of the Graves vineyard: **Haut-Brion,** producer of the only non-Médoc wine to be ranked a *Premier Cru* (the most elite wine classification). The white, Classical château surveys pebbly soil whose vines yield a celebrated red wine, plus tiny quantities of white. The wines produced at La Mission-Haut Brion, literally across the road, are equally sought after.

Continue from Pessac to the A630 expressway that encircles Bordeaux, then head 32 kilometers (20 miles) south via A62 as far as the Barsac exit. Barsac, a small, innocuous town on the banks of the Garonne, lies 13 kilometers (8 miles) north of the **37** tiny village of **Sauternes.**

Nothing here would tell you that mind-boggling wealth lurks amid the picturesque vine-laden slopes and hollows. Grubby Sauternes has a wine shop where bottles of the celebrated Château d'Yquem gather dust on rickety shelves, next to hand-written pricetags demanding 1,000 francs apiece (about $165 at mid-1989 exchange rates). The bottles do not seem to have been disturbed for years, which, at that price, is hardly surprising.

Making Sauternes is a tricky business. Autumn mists that steal up the valleys promote a form of rot called *pourriture noble,* which sucks moisture out of the grapes, leaving a high proportion of sugar. Not all grapes achieve the required degree of overripeness simultaneously; up to seven successive harvests are undertaken at Château d'Yquem, one mile north of Sauternes village, to assure the optimum selection. This painstaking attention to detail, added to a centuries-old reputation and soil ideally suited to making sweet white wine, enables bottles of d'Yquem to obtain prices more appropriate to liquid gold. If you do splurge on a recent vintage, you may as well lock it away; Château d' Yquem needs to wait a good 10 years before coming into its own and will reward decades of patience.

From Sauternes, take D8 to Langon, cross the Garonne, and head north up the attractive D10, sandwiched between the river and the vineyards of Sainte-Croix-du-Mont, Loupiac, and Cadillac. These villages also produce excellent sweet wines, at a fraction of the cost of prestigious Sauternes.

Meanwhile, 8 kilometers (5 miles) north of Cadillac via D11, a different style of wine is produced beneath the ruins of the 38 Château of **Haut-Bénauge.** The vines here are too far from the Garonne to benefit from the rising early morning damp of the river valley; their grapes prove more suitable for dry white wine—excellent dry white, in fact. Officially, it's the best of the Entre-Deux-Mers region that stretches northeast toward the River Dordogne.

Cross back over the Garonne at Langoiran and head toward Bordeaux (via Labrède and Léognan) through the vineyards of the **Graves** region, so called because of its gravelly soil. The Graves encircles western Bordeaux and is the region's most historic appellation; a lightish red wine known as Clairet (origin of the word "claret," meaning red Bordeaux) was esteemed by English occupiers back in the Middle Ages. White wine—both dry and sweet—is also produced, some of the best at the 39 tiny Domaine de Chevalier in **Léognan.**

A630 skirts Bordeaux, with the N215 exit swiftly announcing the Wine Road, or D2, which slips off north toward Médoc.

Médoc is strange, dusty territory. Even the vines look dusty, 40 and so does the ugly town of **Margaux,** the area's unofficial capital. Yet the soil hereabouts is sown with the seeds of grandeur. The small, arid communes and châteaus of Haut-Médoc feature such venerable names as Margaux, St-Julien, Pauillac, and St-Estèphe. Château Margaux, an elegant, coolly restrained Classical building of 1802, and three wineries at Pauillac—Lafite-Rothschild, Latour, and Mouton-Rothschild—are recognized as producers of *Premiers Crus*, their wines qualifying with Graves's Haut-Brion as Bordeaux's top five reds.

D2 chugs through the less prestigious wine fields of northern, 41 or Bas, Médoc, before merging with N215. **Pointe de Grave,** at the tip of the Médoc peninsula, is the site of an American memorial commemorating the landing of U.S. troops in 1917. From the surrounding sand dunes, there are views over the Gironde Estuary to Royan and back across the Atlantic.

42 Just south of the Pointe de Grave is **Soulac-sur-Mer.** The 12th-century basilica of **Notre-Dame de la Fin-des-Terres** deserves to have an outlandish history, given its name—Our Lady of the Ends of the Earth. It does: By 1800 it had been almost completely embedded in drifting sands and was dug out and restored only 100 years ago.

The entire coast, which stretches down to Spain in a straight line, was once subject to drifting sands. Today, the highest dunes in Europe pile up behind uninterrupted miles of sandy beach. The sands' unpredictable inland advance used to go on at the alarming rate of several yards a year. At the start of the 19th century, efforts were made to stop the sandy invasion by planting a front line of sturdy beach grass with pine trees to the rear. The resulting forest has transformed the hinterland region. The name **Landes,** now synonomous with "enormous pine forest," originally implied a wasteland. This is precisely what the region once was: part sandy desert, part marshy wilderness, whose eccentric inhabitants sported sheepskin jackets and stomped around on stilts. Some still do, mainly for the benefit of the tourists who are attracted to the area by the healthy climate and by the variety of sports activities offered—hiking, fishing, canoeing, sand-skiing, golf, tennis, surfing, sailing, bathing, and water sports of all kinds.

At the start of the century, the coast adopted the name Côte d'Argent, or Silver Coast, in a bid to consolidate its new image. Parallel to this silver coast, a few miles inland, is a chain of lakes connected by streams and canals. The first lake we encounter (take D101 from Soulac) is France's largest: the wild, 12-mile-long **Lac d'Hourtin-Carcans.** The small town of Hourtin, with a marina and 460-yard jetty, stands on its northern shore.

After Hourtin, D3 continues south as the Lake Road to the smaller Lac de Lacanau, which teems with pike, perch, and eel and is linked by the Canal de Lège to the Bassin d'Arcachon, a vast triangular bay named after the town on its southern flank. The bay is renowned both for its rich variety of migratory birds and for its excellent oysters. Many of the oyster beds cluster around the Ile aux Oiseaux, a small island in the middle of the bay.

43 **Arcachon** was "created"—at least as a resort—in the 1850s, when the new railroad connected it with Bordeaux, 64 kilometers (40 miles) away. These days, Arcachon is a lively boating center, with three jetties protruding over its sandy beaches. From boulevard de la Mer, there are good views toward Cap Ferret, across the narrow straits that mark the divide between bay and ocean.

A small lake, 13 kilometers (8 miles) south of Arcachon, the Etang de Cazaux, marks the boundary between the Gironde and Landes *départements*. Oil has been found at Parentis-en-Born, on the eastern shore of the neighboring Etang de Biscarosse. Mimizan, on the southern shore of the Etang d'Aureilhan (the next lake along), was swamped in roving sand during the 18th century; sand still surrounds its ruined Benedictine abbey. Take D652 down to St-Julien-en-Born, then D41 to the charming old village of Lévignacq, with its fortified church and low houses that are typical of the region.

44 D41 joins N10, which branches off toward Dax (as D947) at Castets. **Dax,** known in Roman times as Aquae Tarbellicae, has been famous for 2,000 years on account of its thermal springs. The daughter of Caesar Augustus came here to soothe her aches and pains, the first in a long line of seasonal guests whose numbers have swollen to 50,000 each year, making Dax the country's premier warm-water spa. Steaming water gushes out of the lion-headed Néhé fountain in the center of town. The local mud (containing radioactive algae) is also reputed to have healing qualities.

Dax is an airy town, offering pleasant walks through its parks and gardens and along the banks of the River Adour. Eleventh-century bas-reliefs adorn the east end of the church of St-Paul-les-Dax, while the 17th-century cathedral, built in Classical style, boasts a variety of fine sculpture, some inherited from the previous Gothic building.

45 **Bayonne,** 48 kilometers (30 miles) southwest of Dax via N124 and N10, is the gateway to Basque country, a territory stretching across the Pyrenees to Bilbao in Spain. Bayonne stands at the confluence of the Rivers Adour and Nive; the port of Bayonne extends along the valley to the sea three miles away. You could easily spend an enjoyable few hours here, admiring the town's 13th-century cathedral, cloisters, old houses, and 17th-century ramparts.

46 The celebrated resort of **Biarritz** lies 8 kilometers (5 miles) west of Bayonne on a particularly sheltered part of the Atlantic coast. Biarritz rose to prominence in the 19th century when upstart emperor Napoleon III took to spending his holidays here. You'll soon understand why: The crowded Grande Plage and neighboring Miramar Beach provide fine sand and friendly breakers amid a setting of craggy natural beauty. Biarritz remains a high-brow resort, with no shortage of deluxe hotels or bow-tied gamblers ambling over to the casino. Yet the old down-to-earth charm of the former fishing village remains to counterbalance the uppercrust ambience. The narrow streets around the cozy 16th-century church of St-Martin are delightful to stroll and, together with the harbor of Port des Pêcheurs, offer a tantalizing glimpse of the Biarritz of old.

A 26-kilometer (16-mile) drive along the coast, through the pretty villages of St-Jean-de-Luz and Hendaye, leads to Irun on the Spanish border.

What to See and Do with Children

The Atlantic coast is lined with an almost uninterrupted run of fine, large, sandy **beaches** that are ideal for swimming and sunbathing. Popular resorts are Biarritz, Arcachon, and Royan (Tour 3), though you'll undoubtedly discover less crowded spots for yourself (also *see* Sports and Fitness, below).

Harbor, Musée Lafaille, and **Musée du Nouveau-Monde** (New World Museum), La Rochelle, Tour 1.

Hennessy tour (including boat trip), Cognac, Tour 1.

Boat trip through **the Marais Poitevin** (*see* Guided Tours in Essential Information; also Tour 1, above).

Sarlat Aquarium gives a thorough presentation of the fish that are found in the local rivers: salmon, eels, pike, perch, trout, and even sturgeon, a fish famous for its eggs (caviar) but rarely found outside the waters of the Caspian Sea. *Rue du Commandant-Maratuel. Admission: 15 frs. adults, 9 frs. children. Open mid-June–mid-Sept., daily 10–7; mid-Sept.–mid-June, daily 10–noon and 2:30–6; closed mornings, Nov.–Mar.*

Off the Beaten Track

Limoges is the porcelain collector's mecca, and, at 120 kilometers (75 miles) from Poitiers and 102 kilometers (64 miles) from Angoulême (direct route on N141), it is well worth the detour toward the center of France. In addition to shops filled with

Limoges's delicate porcelain, visit the **St-Etienne Cathedral,** the **Adrien Dubouché Museum** (ceramics), the **Palais Episcopal,** and the **Municipal Museum,** with samples of Limoges china from the 12th century to the present day. Limoges is also the base of David Haviland's **porcelain factory.** This smart American entrepreneur set up shop here in the mid-19th century, and the Haviland hallmark is now synonomous with some of the finest china in Europe. Samples of the group of Limoges porcelain factories and enamel workshops can be seen at the **Limoges-Castel Demonstration Center.** *Av. John-Kennedy, Zone Industrial Magré. Open mid-Apr.–mid-Oct., daily 8:30–6; mid-Oct. –mid-Apr., Mon.–Sat. 8:30–6.*

The historic clifftop village of **Domme** lies across the River Dordogne from La Roque-Gageac. Domme is famous for its *grottes* (caves), where prehistoric bison and rhinoceros bones have been discovered. You can visit the 500-yard-long illuminated galleries, which are lined with stalagmites and stalactites. *Entrance on pl. de la Halle. Admission: 15 frs. Open Apr.–Sept., daily 9–noon and 2–6.*

Shopping

The city of Bordeaux abounds with stylish shops in its commercial heart between the cathedral and Grand Théâtre, where you'll find numerous pleasant pedestrian streets. Other than this section, however, serious shoppers should keep their eyes peeled for likely looking shops in every small town and village.

Food Items The Périgord region owes much of its fame to gastronomic specialties like truffles, *fruits confits* (preserved in brandy), and foie gras (ask for a sealed can, rather than a glass jar, and it will last for months). Similar local goods are found at **Les Maison des Produits Régionaux,** in the Cestras complex on N250 outside Arcachon. For an exceptional selection of cheeses, go to **Jean d'Alos** in Bordeaux (4 rue Montesquieu). If you feel like giving yourself a present that definitely won't last, try some of "the best butter in the world"—available from the **Laiterie Co-Opérative** at Echiré, just north of Niort.

Gift Ideas Regional gifts include embroidery, wooden models, and, more exceptionally, the small green animals made from the stems of the wild angelica found around Poitiers and Niort.

Wine and Spirits An old bottle of Cognac makes a fine souvenir; try **La Cognatheque** in Cognac itself (10 pl. Jean-Monnet). You'll find the same stuff, but infinitely cheaper, at any local producer. A top-ranking Bordeaux is less likely to represent top value, though at the **Vinothèque** in Bordeaux (8 cours du XXX-Juillet) or the **Maison de Tourisme et du Vin,** in Pauillac (north of Bordeaux), you'll have a wide choice.

Sports and Fitness

Beaches and Water Sports The Atlantic coast presents an outstanding, uninterrupted vista of sandy beaches from Rochefort to Royan and from the Pointe de Grave to Biarritz (a stretch known as the **Côte d'Argent:** Silver Coast). Major resorts, offering a welter of sports facilities, are **Royan, Soulac, Carcans, Lacanau,** and **Arcachon.** The **Aquacity** complex (off N250 south of Arcachon, tel. 56–66–39–39), with water slides, wave-machine, and warm-water swimming pool, offers fun for all the family (admission: 65 frs. adults, 50 frs. children under 12).

The lakes that dot the **Landes pine forest** some 30 kilometers (20 miles) from the coast offer various water sports (such as waterskiing or canoeing), as does the stretch of water at **Siorac** between Bergerac and Sarlat.

Bullfighting As you approach the Pyrenees, you step into Basque country, where bullfights are a major sporting occupation. Bullfights are held at **Dax, Mont-de-Marsan,** and **Bayonne;** if you're in the area during the summer months, you can't miss the colorful posters announcing them.

Golf There are courses at **Biarritz** (tel. 59–03–71–80), **Lacanau** (tel. 56–26–35–50), **Bordeaux** (tel. 56–39–10–02), **Arcachon** (tel. 56–54–44–00), and **Cognac** (tel. 45–32–18–17).

Dining and Lodging

Dining

The cuisine of this ocean-facing region centers on fish and seafood. Oysters and mussels are major industries, while carp, eel, sardines, sole, and even sturgeon form the basis of menus in fish restaurants. Heading inland into Périgord, along the Dordogne Valley, you'll find that the cooking becomes richer. Truffles and foie gras lead the way, followed by many types of game, fowl, and mushroom. The versatile wines of Bordeaux make fine accompaniments to most regional dishes, but don't overlook their less prestigious cousins (Bergerac, Monbazillac, Charentes). Cognac is *de rigueur* to finish a meal.

Highly recommended restaurants are indicated by a star ★.

Lodging

In summer, France's western coast provides extreme contrasts of crowds and calm. Vacationers flock to La Rochelle, Royan, Arcachon, Biarritz, and the offshore islands of Ré and Oléron, and for miles around, hotels are booked solid months in advance. Farther inland the situation is easier, but note the dearth of hotel accommodations in Bordeaux. Advance booking is recommended here and in Périgord, whose few towns—Sarlat, Périgueux, and Brantôme—fill up quickly in mid-summer.

Highly recommended hotels are indicated by a star ★.

Angoulême
Dining and Lodging **Hôtel de France.** Set in an old building (part 17th-century), Hôtel de France retains a rustic atmosphere, with lots of wood and stone in evidence. It is extremely well located in the Ville Haute, and there are fine views from the garden. The service is distant, though efficient, and the staff are accustomed to English-speaking visitors. The restaurant serves solid, unpretentious regional cuisine. *1 pl. des Halles, 16000, tel. 45–95–47–95. 47 rooms with bath. Facilities: restaurant, garden. AE, DC, V. Restaurant closed Christmas, New Year, Sun. lunch; and Sat. during Sept.–May. Moderate.*

Bergerac
Dining and Lodging **Bordeaux.** You'll find a curious mixture here: Bordeaux is part typical French provincial hotel, with stocky furniture and ab-

surdly spacious rooms, and part city slicker, with the would-be modern design of the facade and reception area that might have worked a few decades ago but looks strangely unconvincing in a quiet square in a small country town. The recently refitted bathrooms, however, are just fine. The admirable restaurant serves regional dishes with nouvelle inventiveness, though guests are not obliged to eat here. English and American visitors are warmly and frequently welcomed. Rooms facing the garden/courtyard are preferable to those with a view across undistinguished place Gambetta. *38 pl. Gambetta, 24100, tel. 53–57–12–83. 42 rooms with bath. Facilities: pool, restaurant, garden. AE, MC, V. Closed Jan. Restaurant closed Mon. and Sat. during Nov.–Mar. Moderate.*

Biarritz
Dining
★

Café de Paris. This is the most elegant dining room in Biarritz. There is a set menu at 220 francs, but most of chef Pierre Laporte's specialties, including grilled duck liver and *ris de veau* (calf's sweetbread) can be ordered only à la carte, and you will pay up to 500 francs for the privilege. Fish and meats are also available, served with an imaginative nouvelle touch that contrasts with the complacent, fading glory of the Belle Epoque decor. The reasonably priced wine list is strong on Bordeaux. The **Alambic** (tel. 59–24–53–41), at the same address, is a brasserie-type sister restaurant providing a less costly alternative. *5 pl. Bellevue, tel. 59–24–19–53. Closed Sun. dinner, Mon. except during July–Sept., and Jan.–mid-Mar. Reservations essential. Jacket and tie required. AE, DC, V. Expensive–Very Expensive.*

Lodging
★

Palais. This majestic red-brick hotel exudes a stylish, somewhat pompous air. Empress Eugénie, wife of Napoleon III, left her mark here a century ago when she discovered the then-little-known resort of Biarritz. An immense driveway, lawns, and a richly furnished, many-mirrored, semicircular dining room overlooking the sea and superb sandy beach embody a style and luxury that stops just short of decadence. Chef Grégoire creates deft, innovative fare that takes full advantage of subtle herbs and textures. There's also a poolside terrace serving lunch and cocktails. The only drawback is the smallness of some of the rooms. If you can't get in, try the **Miramar** next door (tel. 59–24–85–20): modern, lacking atmosphere, but spacious, and with the same splendid views. *1 av. de l'Impératrice, tel. 59–24–09–40. 117 rooms with bath. Facilities: pool, sauna, solarium, terrace, restaurant, 2 bars. AE, DC, MC, V. Closed mid Oct.–May. Very expensive.*

Windsor. Built in the 1920s, this hotel is handy for the casino and beach and boasts its own restaurant (fish predominates; the cheapest menu is around 100 francs). The guest rooms are modernized and cozy, and some offer sea views. Guests, including many foreigners, tend to come here because they can't afford the Palais or Miramar. *19 blvd. du Général-de-Gaulle, 64200, tel. 59–24–08–52. 37 rooms with bath. Facilities: restaurant. AE, MC, V. Closed mid-Nov.–mid Mar. Moderate–Expensive.*

Bordeaux
Dining
★

Bistrot du Clavel. The recently opened sister restaurant to a center-city establishment of the same name adds a good-value gastronomic note to the undistinguished St-Jean *quartier* near the train station. It is one of the few places in town where you can sample claret by the glass, though any number of fruity young Bordeaux are available by the bottle for under 100 francs. The squeaky-clean modern-rustic decor, varied cuisine (including salmon, pig's feet, and lobster) and true bistro prices—menus at 110 and 130 francs—make this an excellent choice. *44 rue Charles-Domercq, tel. 56–92–91–52. Reservations recommended. Dress: casual. AE, DC, V. Closed Sun., Mon., and second half of July. Inexpensive–Moderate.*

★ **Vieux Bordeaux.** This much-acclaimed nouvelle cuisine haunt lies on the fringe of the old town. Chef Michel Bordage concentrates on fresh produce. His menu is therefore short but of high quality, complemented by three set-price menus at 110, 165, and 210 francs. His fish dishes are particularly good; try the steamed turbot. The wine is good value, the decor modern, and the ambience lively. *27 rue Buhan, tel. 56–52–94–36. Reservations recommended. Dress: casual. AE, V. Closed Sat. lunch, Sun., Aug., and 1 week in Feb. Moderate.*

Ombrière. The friendly Ombrière looks out over one of the finest squares in old Bordeaux; during summer months, you can eat outside. The food is pleasant in an unexciting, brasserie sort of way (steak and fries), but, for central Bordeaux, it is fairly priced, with a set menu at 50 francs. A choice à la carte is unlikely to come to more than 130 francs. *14 pl. du Parlement, tel. 56–44–82–69. Dress: casual. AE, DC, V. Closed Sun., Mon., and Aug. Inexpensive.*

Lodging **Pyrenées.** Located in a turn-of-the-century building close to theater and old town, Pyrenées provides typically earnest provincial comfort (deep, slightly worn armchairs and effusive decor). American and British guests are common. There is no restaurant. *12 rue St-Rémi, 33000, tel. 56–81–66–58. 18 rooms with bath. AE, V. Closed second half Aug. and Christmas–New Year's. Moderate.*

Royal Médoc. This Bordeaux hotel is admirably situated near the majestic Esplanade de Quinconces in the city center, in a building that dates from 1720. English-speaking guests form the backbone of the foreign clientele, attracted by the elegant, neo-Classical architecture and cheerful, efficient service. There is no restaurant. *5 rue de Sèze, 33000, tel. 56–81–72–42. 42 rooms with bath. AE, DC, V. Moderate.*

Cognac
Dining and Lodging
Pigeons Blancs. "White Pigeons," a converted and modernized coaching inn standing in spacious grounds, has been owned by the same family since the 17th century. The welcome is warm, and the hotel is comfortable and intimate. The restaurant is highly rated, offering a choice of three menus of varying sophistication. The most expensive (around 250 francs) will not only titillate your tastebuds but will keep you going for about a week! *110 rue Jules-Brisson, tel. 45–82–16–36. 10 rooms with bath. Facilities: restaurant. Closed Sun. dinner and first half of Jan. Moderate.*

Auberge. The two-story Auberge occupies an old building on a quiet street in the heart of Cognac. The emphasis is on bourgeois comfort; the restaurant, decked out in earnest, mock-18th century (Louis XVI) style, sets the tone. The food has a similarly serious ring to it: copious but unexceptional. *13 rue Plumejeau, 16100, tel. 45–32–08–70. 27 rooms, 20 with bath. Facilities: restaurant. AE, MC, V. Hotel closed Christmas–New Year's, restaurant closed Sat. Inexpensive.*

Coulon
Dining and Lodging
Au Marais. The old village of Coulon is a sound base for exploring the Marais Poitevin, and Au Marais, with its waterside setting and bulky, regional wooden furniture, is its most au-

thentic hotel. The restaurant (150-franc set menu) provides fresh, locally caught eels and snails. English, Belgian, and German guests are frequent. *48 quai Louis-Tardy, 79270, tel. 49-35-90-43. 11 rooms with bath. V. Closed mid-Dec.–mid-Jan.; restaurant closed Sun. dinner and Mon., Sept.–June. Inexpensive–Moderate.*

Les Eyzies
Dining and Lodging
★

Le Centenaire. Although its hotel is stylish, modern, comfortable, and offers numerous amenities, Le Centenaire is known first and foremost as a restaurant. Roland Mazère is rated one of the most accomplished chefs in the whole of Périgord. He adds flair and imagination to the preparation of local specialties: risotto with truffles, foie gras and scampi, and snails with ravioli and gazpacho. The dining room, with its gold-colored stone and wooden beams, retains local character, too, and commands pleasant views across the countryside. *24620 Les Eyzies de Tayac, tel. 53-06-97-18. 23 rooms with bath. Facilities: restaurant, pool, sauna, health club, shopping arcade, garden. Restaurant reservations advised. Jacket required. AE, DC, MC, V. Closed Tues. lunch and Nov.–Mar. Expensive.*

Jarnac
Lodging

Orangerie. If Cognac is filled with tourists or brandy merchants, head up the River Charente to Jarnac and stay at this small, attractive hotel. Several rooms look out across the Charente (far prettier here than in Cognac, anyway), and there is a cheerful garden, although no restaurant. *15 rue Bisquit, 16200, tel. 45-81-13-72. 11 rooms with bath. AE, MC, V. Inexpensive–Moderate.*

Poitiers
Dining

Maxime. This crowd-pleaser lives up to its famous name, thanks to a wide choice of set menus (no fewer than four in the 100–200-franc range), the personal recipes of chef Christian Rougier (foie gras and duck salad, for instance), and a pastel-toned decor featuring interwar frescoes. *4 rue St-Nicolas, tel. 49-41-09-55. Reservations essential. Dress: casual. AE, V. Closed Sat. lunch, Sun., and much of Aug. Moderate.*

Lodging

Europe. An early 19th-century building in the middle of town holds this unpretentious hotel, though some rooms occupy a modern extension. Foreign visitors often stay here, attracted by the traditional decor and competitive prices. There is no restaurant. *39 rue Carnot, 86000, tel. 49-88-12-00. 50 rooms, some with bath. V. Inexpensive.*

La Rochelle
Dining

Pré Vert. Decorated throughout in shades of green, this restaurant is hidden down a discreet pedestrian street close to the harbor. It offers three inexpensive menus (60, 90, and 130 francs) and regional specialties, such as foie gras, eel, and duck. *45 rue St-Nicolas, tel. 46-41-24-43. Reservations advised in summer. Dress: casual. AE, DC, V. Closed Sun., Nov.–Feb. Inexpensive.*

Lodging

Hôtel de Port. The tiny, fully modernized Hôtel du Port, overlooking La Rochelle's picturesque harbor, began life as the home of an 18th-century shipping magnate. It retains both old world charm and inconvenience (no elevator; parking can be difficult). Service is friendly and attentive, and the hotel is popular with Italians. *22 quai Duperré, 17000, tel. 46-41-25-95. 12 rooms with bath. No credit cards. Moderate.*

St-Emilion
Dining

Germaine. Family cooking and regional dishes are featured at this central St-Emilion eatery. The stylish upstairs dining room, candlelit and adorned with flowers, is a pleasant place to enjoy the 90- or 120-franc set menus. Grilled meats and fish are house specialties; for dessert, try the almond macaroons. There's also a terrace for outdoor eating. *Pl. des Crénaux, tel. 57–24–70–88. Reservations advised. DC, V. Closed Sun., Mon., and mid-Dec.–mid-Jan. Moderate.*

Dining and Lodging
★ **Auberge de la Commanderie.** For such a pretty town, St-Emilion is a bit short on accommodations. Luckily, this two-story, 19th-century hotel is admirable in every sense. It is close to the ramparts and has its own garden and views of the vineyards. The rooms are small but clean and individually decorated. The attractive restaurant (90- and 250-franc menus) is much frequented by nonresidents and boasts a good selection of local wines. *Rue des Cordeliers, 33300, tel. 57–24–70–19. 30 rooms, most with bath. Facilities: restaurant, garden. V. Closed mid-Dec.–Jan.; restaurant closed Tues., Sept.–June. Moderate.*

Sarlat
Dining and Lodging
St-Albert. At the edge of the old town, St-Albert provides functional accommodations and a friendly welcome from owner Michel Garrigou. The old-fashioned restaurant, with four menus in the 80–140-franc range, provides some of the best-value meals in small, pretty Sarlat, though the cooking can be on the heavy side. House specialties include duck foie gras with shallots, and *la mique*, a dumpling dish served with pork and vegetables. *10 pl. Pasteur, 24200, tel. 53–59–01–09. 53 rooms with bath. AE, DC, MC, V. Restaurant closed Sun. dinner and Mon., Nov.–mid-Apr. Moderate.*

The Arts and Nightlife

The Arts

The major festival activities in this ocean-bordered region are inspired by the sea. "Fêtes de la Mer"—sometimes including carnival parades—are frequent, with the biggest at **La Rochelle** at Pentecost, **Royan** in late June, and **Arcachon** in mid-August. Drama and music combine to make up the **Festival International de l'Entre-Deux-Mers** (for information call 56–71–51–35).

Theater
The region's principal theaters—inevitably devoted to works in the French language—are at **Poitiers** (1 pl. du Maréchal-Leclerc, tel. 49–88–28–55) and **Bordeaux** (Grand Théâtre, pl. de la Comédie, tel. 56–90–91–60).

Concerts
A wide range of music is available during **Bordeaux's International Musical May**, a leading event in France's cultural calendar. Smaller summer festivals are held at **Saintes** (the **Festival de la Musique Ancienne,** early July) and **Arcachon** (the **International Guitar Festival** in July).

Opera
There are occasional operatic performances at the **Grand Théâtre** in **Bordeaux** *(see* above).

Nightlife

Bars and Nightclubs
Try **L'Aztecal** (61 rue du Pas-St-Georges) or **Les Cricketers** (quai de Paludate) in Bordeaux.

Jazz Clubs
Les Argentiers (7 rue Teulère) is a respected and long-established Bordeaux hangout.

Rock Clubs A late-night venue for raunchy music, complete with videos, is **Le Chat-Bleu** in Bordeaux (28 rue Maurice).

Discos In Bordeaux, try **Sénéchal** (57 bis quai de Paludate); in Arcachon, **Cyclone & Scotch Club** (blvd. de la Plage) or **New Bunny** (4 blvd. Mestrezat); in Niort, **Nouvel Espace** (av. de la Rochelle) or **Club St-Gelais** (43 rue St-Gelais); in Sarlat, **Le Basroc** (av. de la Dordogne); and in Poitiers, **Black House** (195 av. du 8-mai-1945) or the intimate **La Grande Goule** (46 rue du Pigeon-Blanc).

Casinos There are casinos in **Biarritz, Royan, Arcachon,** and on the island of **Oléron.**

13 Toulouse and the Midi-Pyrénées

Introduction

Midi-Pyrénées is France's largest region, stretching 28,500 square miles from the Massif Central in the north to the Spanish border in the south. Mountains, plains, lakes, rivers, verdant hills, and arid limestone plateaus lend the region extreme natural variety. This is the perfect vacation spot for nature lovers and sports enthusiasts; walking, hiking, climbing, horseback-riding, sailing, canoeing, skiing, windsurfing, and rafting are all possible.

The Pyrenees, western Europe's highest mountain range after the Alps, give birth to the Garonne, the great river of Toulouse and Bordeaux. The Garonne is joined by the Aveyron, Lot, and Tarn rivers, which cross the region from east to west, carving out steep gorges and wide green valleys. The Pyrenean foothills are riddled with streams, lakes, and spas established in Roman times. Armagnac brandy has its home among the gently undulating hills of the Gers, while, farther north, hearty red wine has been produced in the rugged country around Cahors for over 2,000 years.

The region has few large towns. Chief among them is Toulouse, an up-beat university center whose energetic nightlife smacks more of Spain (less than two hours' drive away) than the drowsy French provinces. Toulouse, known as the Ville Rose because of its soft pink brick, is an elegant old city. The Canal du Midi, built in the 17th century, meanders through Toulouse and continues east, past the medieval walls of Carcassonne, on its way from the Atlantic to the Mediterranean.

Other highlights range from the picturesque hilltop villages of Cordes and Rocamadour to the fortified medieval bridge at Cahors and the Romanesque basilica perched precariously above the valley at Conques. The religious mecca of Lourdes is here as well, but its football-stadium-like appearance may come as a bit of a disappointment. There are two outstanding art museums, however: the Musée Ingres at Montauban, devoted to one of France's most accomplished pre-Impressionist painters, and the Musée Toulouse-Lautrec at Albi, with its racy testimony to the leading observer of Belle Epoque cabaret. Albi also holds the most impressive monument in the Midi-Pyrénées: the red-brick cathedral of Ste-Cécile, with slits for windows and walls like cliffs.

Essential Information

Important Addresses and Numbers

Tourist Information The regional tourist office for the Midi-Pyrénées (written enquiries only) is the **Comité Régional du Tourisme** (CRT, 12 rue Salambo, 31200 Toulouse, tel. 61–47–11–12). Local tourist offices in other towns covered in this chapter are as follows: **Albi** (pl. Ste-Cécile, tel. 63–54–22–30), **Auch** (1 rue Dessoles, tel. 62–05–22–89), **Cahors** (pl. Aristide-Briand, tel. 65–35–09–56), **Lourdes** (pl. du Champ-Commun, tel. 62–94–15–64), **Montauban** (2 rue du Collège, tel. 63–63–60–60), **Pau** (pl. Royale, tel. 59–27–27–08), **Rodez** (Galerie Foch, tel. 65–68–02–27), and **Toulouse** (Donjon du Capitole, pl. Charles-de-Gaulle, tel. 61–23–32–00).

Travel Agencies **American Express** (Office Catholique De Voyages, 14 chausse du Bourg, Lourdes, tel. 62–94–20–84), **Havas** (73 rue d'Alsace Lorraine, Toulouse, tel. 61–23–16–35), and **Thomas Cook** (Voyages Dépêche, 42 bis rue d'Alsace-Lorraine, Toulouse, 61–23–40–15).

Car Rental **Avis** (pl. de la Gare, Lourdes, tel. 62–34–26–76, Blagnac Airport, Toulouse, tel. 61–30–04–94), **Europcar** (Station Total, av. des Pyrénées, Auch, tel. 62–05–11–43, and 5 av. Chamier, Montauban, tel. 61–63–76–35).

Arriving and Departing

By Plane All international flights arrive at Toulouse's **Blagnac Airport,** a few minutes' drive from the center of town. Regular **Air France** flights link Toulouse to most European capitals, while **Air Inter** runs as many as 30 flights a day during the week between Paris and Toulouse; (for reservations, call 45–39–25–25 in Paris or 61–71–11–10 in Toulouse). **TAT** (Transport Aérien Transregional) offers direct flights from Paris's Orly Airport to Rodez (for reservations, call 46–87–35–53 in Paris or 65–42–20–30 in Rodez).

Between the Buses run regularly (every half hour between 8:15 AM and 8:45
Airport and PM) from the airport to the bus station in Toulouse; single fare is
Downtown 19 francs. Three later buses are available, too at 9:20, 10, and 10:45. From Toulouse bus station to the airport, buses leave at 5:30 AM, 6, 7, 7:30, and then every half hour until 8:30 PM.

By Train There's daily service from Paris–Austerlitz to Toulouse-Matabiau station. Take a **Corail** express, which covers the 446-mile journey in just over six hours; for schedules, call 45–82–50–50 in Paris or 61–62–50–50 in Toulouse. Direct trains from Paris–Austerlitz also serve Auch (over eight hours), Cahors (five to six hours), Carcassonne (seven to eight hours), Montauban (six hours), and Rodez (seven to eight hours).

By Car The fastest route from Paris to Toulouse is via Bordeaux (on A10), then switch to A62; journey time is about nine hours.

Getting Around

By Plane From Toulouse's Blagnac Airport, you can pick up an **Air Inter** flight to one of the two regional airports, at Rodez in the northeast, and Tarbes, near Lourdes (tel. 61–71–11–10 for information).

By Train The French rail network in the southwest provides regular services to all towns.

By Car The A62 expressway slices through the region on its way to the coast at Narbonne. At Toulouse, various highways fan out in all directions: N117 to Pau, N20 to Montauban and Cahors, and N88 to Albi and Rodez.

Guided Tours

The **Comité Régional du Tourisme** *(see* Tourist Information, above) publishes a detailed brochure, *Mille et Une Evasions en Midi-Pyrénées* (1,000 and One Ways to Escape in the Midi-Pyrénées), which provides a host of suggestions for weekends and short organized package vacations throughout the region. The tourist office in **Toulouse** offers a wide range of guided tours in and around the city; guides are knowledgeable and multilingual.

Orientation From July to September, a tour of Toulouse's monuments and historical houses leaves Monday to Saturday from the tourist office at 10 AM; cost is 27 francs. A "Toulouse: Past and Present" bus tour, also leaving from the tourist office, departs at 3 PM and costs 38 francs. A walking tour that takes in the Jacobins church and the private mansions of the St-Rome quarter leaves from the tourist office at 3 PM; cost is 27 francs, plus 5 francs entrance fee to the church's cloister. On Wednesday, a walking tour of the Augustins museum and the rue Croix-Baragnon leaves at 5 PM from the museums's main entrance; cost is 27 francs, plus 5 francs museum admission.

Sightseeing Tours Day-long regional circuits run from May through September, departing from the Toulouse tourist office and costing 110 francs; stops include Rocamadour, Conques, and Cordes, as well as Moissac Abbey, the Ingres museum at Montauban, and the Toulouse-Lautrec museum at Albi.

Exploring Toulouse and the Midi-Pyrénées

Numbers in the margin correspond with points of interest on the Toulouse and the Midi-Pyrénées maps.

Orientation

We have divided this region into four tours. The first takes in southwest France's only city: Toulouse, a lively center emblazened with culture and history. Toulouse can be a base for our three other tours. The most important of these, heading north, caters to many tastes. Nature lovers will savor the rugged Causses plateau and dramatic Tarn and Lot Valleys. Architecture buffs can admire the bravura of Cahors's tower-bridge and Albi's fortress-cathedral. Art enthusiasts will feast on the works of local-born geniuses Jean Auguste Dominique Ingres (in Montauban) and Henri de Toulouse-Lautrec (in Albi). For those with an eye for the picturesque, we'll visit the daringly sited medieval villages of Conques, Cordes, and Rocamadour.

Our third tour moves west from Toulouse into the verdant, once-grand region of Gascony, known more prosaically these days as the Gers *département*, and home of Armagnac brandy. The final tour plunges south to the Pyrenees, taking in snow-capped peaks, mountain passes, thermal spas, and the holy site at Lourdes.

Highlights for First-time Visitors

Cordes, Tour 2
Grande Cascade, Tour 4
Lourdes, Tour 4
Musée Ingres, Montauban, Tour 2
Palais de la Berbie (Toulouse-Lautrec Museum), Albi, Tour 2
Rocamadour, Tour 2
Ste-Cécile, Albi, Tour 2

Ste-Foy, Conques, Tour 2
St-Sernin, Toulouse, Tour 1

Tour 1: Toulouse

1 The ebullient, pink-bricked city of **Toulouse** lies just 60-odd miles from the border with Spain, and its flavor is more Spanish than French. The city's downtown sidewalks and restaurants are thronged way past midnight as foreign tourists mingle with immigrant workers, college students, and technicians from the giant Airbus aviation complex headquartered outside the city.

Place du Capitole, a vast, open square lined with shops and cafés in the city center, is the best spot to get your bearings. One side of the square is occupied by the 18th-century facade of
2 the **Capitole** itself, home of the Hôtel de Ville (Town Hall) and the city's highly regarded opera company. The coats of arms of the Capitouls, the former rulers of Toulouse, can be seen on the balconies in the Capitole's courtyard, and the building's vast reception rooms are open to visitors when not in use for official functions. Halfway up the Grand Escalier (Grand Staircase) hangs a large painting of the *Jeux Floraux*, or Floral Games, organized by the Compagnie du Gai-Savoir—a literary society created in 1324 to promote the local language, Langue d'Oc. The festival continues to this day: Poets give public readings here each May, the best receiving silver- and gold-plated flowers as prizes. The pompous Salle des Illustres, with its late 19th-century paintings, is used for official receptions and uppercrust wedding ceremonies. Weddings are also held in the Salle Gervaise, beneath a series of paintings inspired by the theme of Love at ages 20, 40, and 60; while the men age, the women stay young forever.

Four more giant paintings in the Salle Henri-Martin, named after the artist (1860–1943), show how important the River Garonne has always been to the region. Look out for Jean Jaurès, one of France's greatest socialists (1859–1914), in *Les Rêveurs* (The Dreamers); he's the one wearing a boater and beige-colored coat. *Pl. du Capitole. Admission free. Tel. 61–22–29–22 (ext. 3412) to check opening times. Closed Tues. and weekends.*

Head north from place du Capitole along rue du Taur, lined with tiny shops. Half a block up, the 14th-century church of
3 **Notre-Dame du Taur** was built on the spot where St-Saturnin (or Sernin), the martyred bishop of Toulouse, was dragged to his death in AD 257 by a rampaging bull. The church is famous for its *cloche-mur*, or wall tower; the wall looks more like an extension of the facade than a tower or steeple and has inspired many similar versions throughout the Toulouse region.

4 The basilica of **St-Sernin,** Toulouse's most famous landmark, lies at the far end of rue du Taur. The basilica once belonged to a Benedictine abbey, built in the 11th century to house pilgrims on their way to Santiago de Compostela in Spain. When illuminated at night, St-Sernin's five-tiered octagonal tower glows red against the sky, dominating the city. Not all the tiers are the same: The first three, with their rounded windows, are Romanesque; the upper two, with their pointed Gothic windows, were added around 1300.

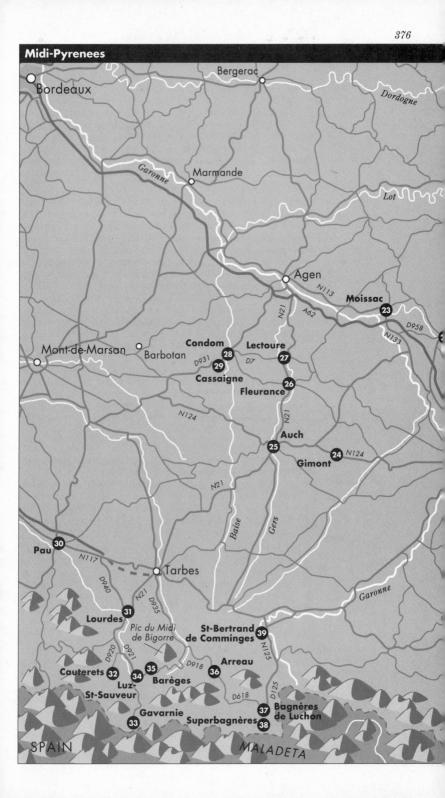

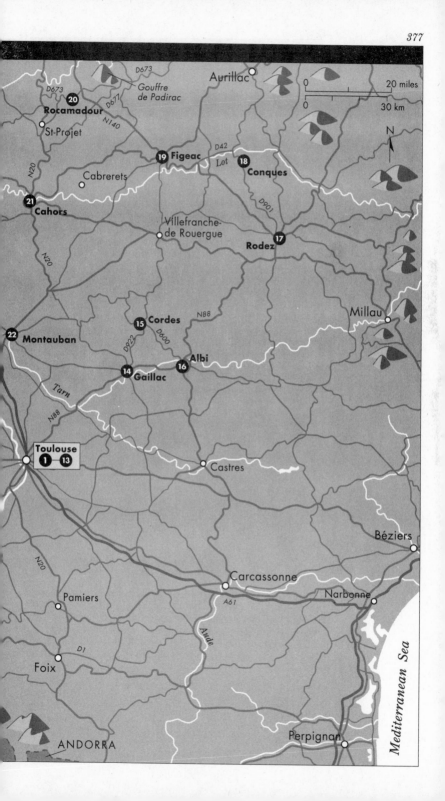

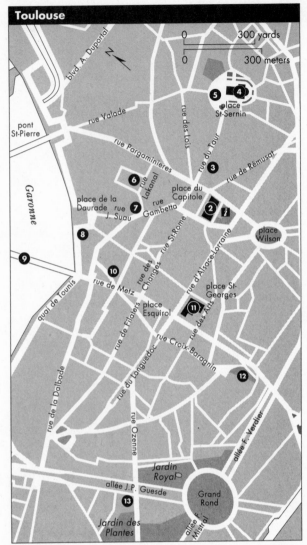

The size of the basilica—particularly the width of the transept, over 68 feet—is striking. It's worth paying the token entry fee to the crypt and ambulatory to admire the tomb of St-Sernin and seven exquisitely preserved marble bas-reliefs of Christ and his apostles, dating from the end of the 11th century. *Rue du Taur. Admission to crypt: 8 frs. Open daily 10–11:30 and 2:30–5:30.*

5 Opposite the basilica is the **Musée St-Raymond,** the city's archaeological museum. The ground floor has an extensive collection of imperial Roman busts, while the second floor is devoted to the applied arts, featuring ancient and medieval coins, lamps, vases, and jewelry. *Pl. St-Sernin. Admission: 15 frs. a-*

dults, children free. Open Wed.–Mon. 8–noon and 2–6; closed Sun. morning and Tues.

❻ Retrace your steps down rue du Taur, turn right at place du Capitole and then left into rue Lakanal to arrive at the **Jacobins church,** built in the 1230s for the Dominicans; the name "Jacobins" was given to the Dominicans in 1217 when they set up their Paris base at the Porte St-Jacques. The church was harmoniously restored in the 1970s, its interior retaining the original orange-ocher tones. The two rows of columns running the length of the nave—to separate the monks from their congregation—is a feature of Dominican churches, though this one is special, since the column standing the farthest from the entrance is said to be the world's finest example of palm-tree vaulting. The original refectory is used for temporary art exhibitions, while the cloisters provide an atmospheric setting for the city's summer music festival.

❼ Around the corner in rue Gambetta stands the **Hôtel de Bernuy,** built during the 16th century when Toulouse was at its most prosperous. Merchant Jean de Bernuy made his fortune exporting pastel, a blue dye made from the leaves of a plant cultivated around Toulouse and Albi and used to color cloth, especially bed linen. Merchant wealth is reflected in the mansion's use of stone, a costly material in this region of brick, and by the octagonal stair tower, the highest in the city. Building such towers was a rarely bestowed privilege, and this one makes its opulent point by rising above the ceiling of the top floor. The Hôtel de Bernuy is now part of a school, but you can wander freely around its courtyard.

❽ Walk down rue Jean-Suau to place de la Daurade and the 18th-century church of **Notre-Dame de la Daurade,** overlooking the River Garonne. The name "Daurade" comes from *doré* (gilt), referring to the golden reflection given off by the mosaics decorating the 5th-century temple to the Virgin that once stood on this site. The flowers presented to the winners of the Floral Games are blessed here.

❾ Take time to saunter along quai de la Daurade, beside the church, and admire the view from **Pont Neuf** across to the left bank. Then head east along rue de Metz. A hundred yards **❿** down, on the left, is the **Hôtel d'Assézat,** built in 1555 by Toulouse's top Renaissance architect, Nicolas Bachelier. The facade is particularly striking: Superimposed classical orders frame alternating arcades and rectangular windows, with ornately carved doorways lurking below. Climb to the top of the tower for splendid views over the city rooftops. *Rue du Metz. Admission free. Open daily 10–noon and 2–6.*

Continue along rue de Metz. The second road on the left (rue des Changes, which becomes rue St-Rome) was once part of the Roman road that sliced through Toulouse from north to south; today, it's a chic pedestrian shopping area. Running parallel is the swinging rue d'Alsace-Lorraine, a center of nightlife, luxury boutiques, and department stores. On the corner of rue d'Alsace-Lorraine and rue de Metz, just beyond busy place **⓫** Esquirol, is the largest museum in Toulouse: the **Musée des Augustins,** housed in a medieval Augustinian convent whose sacristy, chapter house and cloisters provide an attractive set-ting for an outstanding array of Romanesque sculpture and religious paintings by such renowned artists as Spain's

Bartolomé Esteban Murillo (1618–82) and Flemish maestro Pierre-Paul Rubens (1577–1640). *21 rue de Metz. Admission: 6 frs., free Sun. Open Wed.–Mon. 10–noon and 2–6.*

Time Out Around the corner from the Musée des Augustins, on place St-Georges—a delightful little square—is the intimate **Le Père Bacchus,** much frequented by locals. By night it's a popular jazz venue. *20 pl. St-Georges.*

From the Musée des Augustins, cross rue de Metz and head down rue des Arts, then turn left along rue Croix-Baragnin to place St-Etienne, site of both the city's oldest fountain, in marble (16th century), and of the cathedral of **St-Etienne,** erected in stages between the 13th and 17th century. The nave and choir languished unfinished for a lack of funds; they look awkward because they are not properly aligned. A fine collection of 16th- and 17th-century tapestries traces the life of St. Stephen (Etienne, in French).

The broad allée François Verdier leads to the leafy, circular Grand Rond, flanked by the **Jardin Royal** (royal gardens) and **Jardin des Plantes** (botanical gardens)—home of the **Museum d'Histoire Naturelle** (Natural History Museum) and its varied collection of stuffed birds and prehistoric exhibits. *35 allée Jules-Guesde. Gardens open daily dawn to dusk; admission free. Museum open daily 2–6; admission: 6 frs.*

Tour 2: Albi–Rocamadour–Montauban

Leave **Toulouse** by N88 and drive 53 kilometers (33 miles) northeast to **Gaillac,** an old town on the right bank of the Tarn and the center of a long-established vineyard renowned for its versatility. Dry, sweet, and lightly sparkling *(perlant)* white wine are all produced here, as are fruity reds; if you're in the mood to sample some, follow signs to a *dégustation* (tasting session). Some of the earliest winemakers, beginning in the 10th century, were Benedictine monks, whose abbey church stands alongside Pont St-Michel.

From Gaillac, head 24 kilometers (15 miles) north along D922 to the picturebook hilltop village of **Cordes,** built in 1222 by Count Raymond VII of Toulouse. When mists steal up from the Cérou Valley and enshroud the hillside, Cordes appears to hover in mid-air, hence its nickname, Cordes-sur-Ciel (Cordes in the Sky). Cordes is a typical *bastide,* a fortified medieval town built to a strict grid plan. Wander around the ancient streets and admire the restored medieval houses, many peopled by artisans and craftsmen; the best craft shops are found along the main street, **Grande-Rue.** The village's venerable **covered market,** supported by 24 octagonal stone pillars, is also noteworthy, while the nearby well is over 300 feet deep.

Time Out Stop for a drink at one of the cafés on **Terrace de la Bride** and take in the plummeting view over the Cérou Valley. If you want something more substantial, try the delightful terrace of the **Hostellerie du Vieux Cordes;** the *foie gras* is superb. *Rue St-Michel.*

 From Cordes, take pretty D600 to **Albi,** 25 kilometers (16 miles) away. This old town, with its narrow streets and red-brick buildings, has been tastefully preserved. In its heyday, Albi was a major center for Cathars, members of an ascetic religious sect that rejected earthly life as evil and criticized the worldly ways of the Catholic Church. Albi's huge cathedral of **Ste-Cécile**, with its intimidating clifflike walls, resembles a cross between a castle, a power station, and an ocean liner and was meant to symbolize the Catholic Church's return to power after the crusade against the Cathars (or Albigensians, as they came to be known) at the start of the 13th century.

The cathedral's interior is an ornate reply to the massive austerity of the ocher outer walls. Every possible surface has been painted; the leading contributors were a 16th-century team of painters from Bologna, Italy, who splattered the main vault with saints and Old Testament venerati, then lined the bays with religious scenes and brightly colored patterns. The most striking fresco, however, is a 15th-century depiction of the Last Judgment, which extends across the west wall beneath the 18th-century organ loft. Unfortunately, its central section was smashed through in 1693, to make the St-Clair chapel.

Climb the stairway to the right of the altar up to the bell tower. Here, the view takes in the rooftops of the old town and, between the cathedral and the Pont Vieux (Old Bridge) spanning the River Tarn, the **Palais de la Berbie.** Built in 1265 as the Bishops' Palace, it was later transformed first into a fortress, then into a museum honoring Albi's most famous son: Belle Epoque painter Henri de Toulouse-Lautrec (1864–1901).

Toulouse-Lautrec left Albi for Paris in 1882 and soon made his name with racy evocations of the bohemian glamour of the cabarets, music halls, bars, and cafés in and around Montmartre. Despite his aristocratic origins (Lautrec is a town not far from Toulouse), Henri cut a far-from-noble figure. He stood under five feet tall (his growth was stunted by a childhood riding accident) and pursued a decadent life that led to an early grave. The Albi exhibit is the country's largest collection of works by Toulouse-Lautrec. These works are beautifully presented, notably in the lengthy Galérie Ambrie (holding his earliest efforts) and in the rooms leading from the Salon Rose (portraits and lithographs). *Just off pl. Ste-Cécile. Admission: 15 frs. adults, 8 frs. children. Open Easter–Oct., daily 10–noon and 2–6; Nov.–Easter, Wed.–Mon. 10–noon and 2–5; closed Tues.*

Before leaving Albi, stroll around the old town to admire its pedestrian streets and elegant shops. You can also visit Lautrec's birthplace, **Maison Natale de Toulouse-Lautrec** (along boulevard Sibille from the cathedral), to see more of his early works, as well as his personal possessions and memorabilia. *14 rue Henri de Toulouse-Lautrec. Admission: 16 frs. adults, 10 frs. children. Open July–Aug., daily 10–noon and 3–7.*

⑰ Rodez, capital of the Aveyron *département*, sits on a windswept hill 78 kilometers (48 miles) northeast of Albi (via N88), halfway between the arid, limestone Causses plateau and the verdant Ségala hills. On top of the hill in Rodez towers the pink sandstone cathedral of **Notre-Dame,** built over the 13th–15th centuries. Its awesome bulk is lightened by the decorative upper stories, completed in the 17th century, and by the magnificently elaborate 285-foot bell tower. The interior contains ornamental altarpieces, an elaborate 15th-century choir screen, and a 17th-century organ within an intricate wooden casing.

The old but renovated **Cité quarter,** once ruled by medieval bishops, lies behind the cathedral; attractive pedestrian zones have been created around place du Bourg. One of the city's finest medieval mansions can be found on the tiny place de l'Olmet, just off place du Bourg: the 16th-century **House of Armagnac,** with its open courtyard and ornate facade covered in the medallion emblems of the counts of Rodez.

Farther on, at place de la Madeleine, is the 18th-century church of **St-Amans,** featuring finely preserved Romanesque capitals and, inside, some colorful 16th-century tapestries. The extensively modernized **Musée Denys Puech,** an art gallery noted for works by local painters and sculptors, lies just beyond the wide boulevard that encircles the old town. *Pl. Clemenceau. Admission: 15 frs. adults, 10 frs. under-18s. Open Wed.–Sat. and Mon. 10–noon and 3–7; Sun. 3–7; closed Tues.*

18 From Rodez, head 35 kilometers (22 miles) up D901 to **Conques,** whose pretty, ocher-red houses harmonize perfectly with the surrounding rocky gorge. Conques is more than just a picturesque village, however. It holds one of the most outstanding religious monuments in southern France: the Romanesque church of **Ste-Foy.** The church was one of the four principal stopping points on the medieval pilgrimage route that left Le Puy, in central France, for the shrine of St-James at Santiago de Compostela in northwest Spain. Ste-Foy, begun in the early 11th century, enjoyed its heyday in the 12th and 13th centuries. Eventually, though, the flood of pilgrims dried up, taking with it a huge source of revenue for the church's upkeep. In 1561, Ste-Foy was devastated by Protestant hordes at the onset of the Wars of Religion; it then languished in neglect until the 19th century, when the writer and historic-monument enthusiast, Prosper Mérimée, stepped in with plans to salvage it.

Ste-Foy clings to a hill so steep that even driving and walking—let alone building—is a precarious business. Note the intensely dramatic *Last Judgment,* carved over the main portal during the 12th century. The church's interior is high and dignified; the ambulatory around the back was given a lot of wear and tear by medieval pilgrims who were keen on admiring the church's most precious relic: a 10th-century wooden statue of Ste-Foy herself, encrusted with gold and precious stones. Latterday visitors can admire the relic in the Treasury, situated off the recently restored cloisters. Other gold and silver relics testify to the presence of skilled metal workers in Conques from the 9th to the 14th century. The **Musée Docteur Joséph-Fau** (otherwise known as Trésor II), located in an old building opposite the pilgrims' fountain near the church, houses furniture, statues, tapestries and sculpture. *Admission to Trésor and Musée Fau: 17 frs. adults, 14 frs. children. Open Sept.–June, Mon.–Sat. 9–noon and 2–6, Sun. 2–6; July–Aug., Mon.–Sat. 9–noon and 2–7, Sun. 2–7.*

Continue north on D901 for 8 kilometers (5 miles), then turn left onto D42 and wend your way along the beautiful Lot Valley **19** to **Figeac,** 48 kilometers (30 miles) away. Figeac, a charming old town with a lively Saturday morning market, grew up around an abbey in the 9th century, becoming, in turn, a stopping point for pilgrims plodding from Conques to Compostela. Many houses in the older part of town date from the 13th, 14th, and 15th centuries and have been carefully restored. They retain their octagonal chimneys, rounded archways and arcades, and *soleilhos*, open attics used for drying flowers and stocking wood.

The 13th-century **Hôtel de la Monnaie,** a block in from the River Célé, is characteristic of such architecture, an elegant building probably used as a medieval money-changing office; these days, it houses the tourist office and a museum displaying fragments of sculpture and religious relics found in the town. *Pl. Vival. Admission free. Open July–Aug., daily 10–noon and 2:30–6:30; Sept.–June, Mon.–Sat. 3–5.*

Figeac was the birthplace of Jean François Champollion (1790–1832), the first man to decipher Egyptian hieroglyphics. The **Musée Champollion,** in his house near place Champollion (walk right out of place Vival on rue 11-Novembre, take the first left and follow it around as it bends right), contains a casting of the Rosetta Stone, discovered in the Nile Delta; the stone's three inscriptions— two in Egyptian and one in ancient Greek— enabled the mysteries of the pharaonic dialect to be penetrated for the first time. On the ground floor of the museum, a film traces Champollion's life. *4 impasse Champollion. Admission: 15 frs. adults, 8 frs. children. Open May–Sept., Tues.–Sat. 10–noon and 2:30–6:30; and open Christmas and Easter holidays.*

N140 heads 43 kilometers (27 miles) northwest from Figeac, through the Causses de Gramat (an extensive limestone plateau), to **Rocamadour,** a medieval village that seems to defy the laws of gravity as it surges out of a cliff 1,500 feet above the Alzou river gorge.

㉑

Rocamadour first made its name in 1166, when chronicles recorded the miraculous discovery of the body of St-Amadour "quite whole" under a sanctuary. This was a major event: Amadour had died a thousand years earlier and, according to legend, was none other than Zachaeus, the tax collector of Jericho, who had come to live in Gaul as a hermit after Christ had persuaded him to give up his money-grubbing ways. Amadour's body was moved into the church, displayed to pilgrims, and began to work miracles. Its fame soon spread to Portugal, Spain, and Sicily, and pilgrims flocked to the site and climbed the 216-step staircase leading up to the church—on their knees. Making the climb on foot is a sufficient reminder of the medieval penchant for agonizing penance, and today an elevator assists weary souls.

The staircase (and elevator) starts from place de la Carreta; those making their way on foot can pause after the first 141 steps to admire the **Fort,** as the 14th-century Bishops' Palace is invitingly called. The remaining steps lead to tiny place St-Amadour and its seven sanctuaries: the basilica of **St-Sauveur** opposite the staircase; the **St-Amadour crypt** underneath the basilica; the chapel of **Notre-Dame** to the left; the chapels of **John the Baptist, St-Blaise,** and **Ste-Anne** to the right; and the Romanesque chapel of **St-Michel,** built into the overhanging cliff. St-Michel's two 12th-century frescoes—depicting the Annunciation and the Visitation—have survived in superb condition. *Centre d'Acceuil Notre-Dame. English-speaking*

*guide available. Guided tours Mon.–Sat. 9–5; tips at visitors'
discretion.*

The village itself boasts beautifully restored medieval houses.
One of the finest is the 15th-century **Hôtel de Ville** (Town Hall),
near the Porte Salmon, which also houses the tourist office and
a fine collection of tapestries. *Admission free. Open Mon.–Sat.
10–noon and 3–8.*

Time Out Within the ancient stone walls of the **Beau-Site et Notre-Dame**
hotel is an exceptionally cozy restaurant, serving richly flavored regional specialties and other more nouvelle dishes. The
salmon *sashimi* is a good bet, but leave room for some of Madame Menot's homemade desserts. *Rue Roland-le-Preux.*

From Rocamadour, D32/D39/D673 winds 19 kilometers (12
miles) down to St-Projet, there joining the N20 highway to
㉑ Cahors, 26 miles farther on. Cahors, once an opulent Gallo-
Roman town, sits snugly in a loop formed by the River Lot. The
town is perhaps best known for its tannic red wine—often, in
fact, a deep purple, and known to the Romans as "black wine"
—which you can taste at many of the small estates in the surrounding region. The finest sight in Cahors is the **Pont Valentre**
bridge, a spellbinding feat of medieval engineering whose tall,
elegant towers have loomed over the river since 1360.

Rue du Président-Wilson cuts across town from the bridge to
the old quarter of Cahors around the Cathedral of **St-Etienne,**
easily recognized by its cupolas and fortresslike appearance.
The tympanum over the north door was sculpted around 1135
with figures portraying the Ascension and the life of St-
Etienne (St. Stephen). The cloisters, to the right of the choir,
contain a corner pillar embellished with a charmingly sculpted
Annunciation Virgin with long, flowing hair. The cloisters connect with the courtyard of the archdeaconry, awash with
Renaissance decoration and thronged with visitors viewing its
temporary art exhibits.

N20 continues 63 kilometers (39 miles) south from Cahors to
㉒ Montauban, birthplace of the great painter, Jean Auguste
Dominque Ingres (1780–1867). Ingres was the last of the great
French Classicists, who took their cue from Michelangelo, fa-
voring line over color and taking their subject matter almost
exclusively from the antique world. Ingres's personal dislike of
Eugène Delacroix (the earliest and most important French Romantic painter), his sour personality, and (for some) his arid
painting style, with its worship of line and technical draftsman-
ship, led many contemporaries to ridicule his work. These
days, Ingres is undergoing a considerable revival in popularity;
looking at the works in Montauban's Ingres museum, with
their quasiphotographic realism, it's easy to see why.

The **Musée Ingres** is housed in the sturdy brick 17th-century
Bishops' Palace overlooking the River Tarn. Ingres has the second floor to himself; note the contrast between his love of myth
(Ossian's Dream) and his deadpan, uncompromising portrai-
ture *(Madame Gonse),* underscored by a closet eroticism (silky
skinned nudes) that belies the staid reputation of academic art.
The exhibit also includes hundreds of Ingres's drawings, plus
some of his personal possessions—including his beloved violin.

Most of the paintings in the museum are from Ingres's excellent private collection, ranging from his followers (Théodore Chassériau) and precursors (Jacques Louis David) to Old Masters who were active between the 14th and 18th century (displayed on the third floor). *Pl. Bourdelle. Admission: 5 frs. adults, 2.50 frs. students. Open July–Aug., Mon.–Sat. 9:30– noon and 1:30–6, Sun. 1:30–6; Sept.–June, Tues.–Sat. 10– noon and 2–6.*

Take some time to explore the old streets of Montauban, especially the pedestrian zone around the restored place Nationale (home to a lively morning market). Check out the Classical cathedral of **Notre-Dame** on place Roosevelt: Its white stone is an eye-catching contrast to the pink brick of other buildings, while inside lurks a major Ingres painting, the *Vow of Louis XIII*.

㉓ From Montauban, D958/N113 heads west to **Moissac,** 29 kilometers (18 miles) away. Moissac holds one of the region's most remarkable abbey churches, **St-Pierre.** Little is left of the original 7th-century abbey, while religous wars laid waste its 11th-century replacement. Today's abbey, dating mostly from the 15th century, narrowly escaped demolition earlier in this century when the Bordeaux–Sète railroad was rerouted within feet of the cloisters, sparing the precious columns around the arcades, carved in different shades of marble. Each of the 76 capitals has its own unique pattern of animals, geometric motifs, and religious or historical scenes.

The museum, in the corner chapels, houses local religious sculpture and photographs of similar sculpture from throughout the Quercy region. The highlight of the abbey church is the 12th-century south portal, topped with carvings illustrating the Apocalypse. The sides and vaults of the porch are adorned with historical scenes sculpted in intricate detail. *6 bis rue de l'Abbaye. Admission to museum and cloisters: 15 frs. joint ticket. Open daily 9–noon and 2–5 (6 in June and Sept.; 7 in July and Aug.). Museum closed Tues. and Sun. morning.*

Tour 3: Gers

The rural Gers *département*, west of Toulouse, occupies the heart of the former dukedom of Gascony; it's riddled with châteaus—from simple medieval fortresses to ambitious Classical residences—and tiny, isolated villages.

㉔ Take N124 west from Toulouse to **Gimont,** 54 kilometers (34 miles) away. You'll get a good idea of the area's gastronomic riches by browsing in the local shops: Armagnac brandy, *Floc de Gascogne* (an aperitif made with grape juice and Armagnac), goose and duck pâtés, preserves, and foie gras (Aux Ducs de Gascogne is one of France's leading producers of this rich delicacy).

㉕ **Auch,** the capital of Gers, is 24 kilometers (15 miles) west of Gimont via N124. Auch is best known for its Gothic cathedral and quaint alleyways, or *pousterles* (from the French for posterns—*poternes*, the gateways to the medieval fortifications).

The cathedral of **Ste-Marie,** in the center of town, dates from the 15th and 16th centuries. Most of the stained-glass windows in the choir are by Arnaud de Moles, who was working here around 1513, and portray biblical figures and handsome pagan sybils, or prophetesses. The oak choir stalls are especially interesting, carved with over 1,500 figures, both biblical and mythological; the stalls also date from the first half of the 16th century and took 50 years to complete. In June, Auch stages a festival when concerts of classical music are held in the cathedral. *Pl. Salinis. Admission to stalls: 5 frs. Open daily 8–noon and 2–6.*

Cross place Salinis to the terrace overlooking the River Gers. A monumental flight of 232 steps leads down to the riverbank, and there is a statue of D'Artagnan, the musketeer immortalized by Alexandre Dumas, halfway down. Although Dumas set the action of his historical drama *The Three Musketeers* in the 1620s, the true D'Artagnan—Charles de Batz—was born in 1620, probably at Castlemore near Lupiac, and didn't become a musketeer until 1645. Batz adopted the nobler name of D'Artagnan from his mother's family, the Montesquieu, lords of Artagnan and one of the highest-ranking families in Gascony.

On the other side of the cathedral, behind the former Archbishops' Palace (now the Préfecture), is the **Musée des Jacobins,** showcasing one of the country's finest collections of Latin-American art and pre-Colombian pottery, gathered by 19th-century adventurer Guillaume Pujos. The museum also contains Gallo-Roman relics; look for the white marble epitaph dedicated by a grief-stricken mistress to her dog Myia. *Rue Daumesnil. Admission: 5 frs. adults, 2.50 frs. children. Open May–Oct., Tues.–Sun. 10–noon and 2–6; Nov.–Apr., Tues.–Sat. 10–noon and 2–4.*

26 Leave Auch by N21 and follow the Gers Valley 35 kilometers (22 miles) north to Lectoure, via **Fleurance,** a *bastide* town with a regimented street plan. The town's Gothic church of St-Laurent boasts three more stained-glass windows by Arnaud de Moles. Like Auch, **Lectoure** stands on a promontory above

27 the Gers Valley and was once a Roman city and a fortified Gallic town. Archaeologists have a field day combing the area for ancient remains.

Although Lectoure was ravaged in 1473, when Louis XI attacked the fortress and established direct royal rule by killing the last count of Armagnac, there's still plenty to see in its old arched streets: the 13th-century **Fontaine Diane** (fountain) on rue Fontélie for starters. The nearby **Musée Municipal,** installed in the vaulted cellars of the former Episcopal Palace (now the Town Hall), complements the traditional marble tombs, mosaics, and vases with a dramatic collection of 20 pagan altars, discovered in 1640 under the choir of the cathedral. These altars feature Latin inscriptions and heads of the sacrificed bulls (or rams). *Hôtel de Ville. Admission: 20 frs. adults, 5.10 frs. children. Open daily 9–noon and 2–6.*

28 D7 heads west from Lectoure to **Condom,** 21 kilometers (13 miles) away. Condom, the town of seven churches, lies in the heart of Ténarèze, one of the three regions that produce Armagnac (the others: highly rated Bas-Armagnac, around Eauze to the west; and Haut-Armagnac, around Auch). Condom's location on the River Baïse made it an excellent base for exporting the local brandy to Bordeaux or Bayonne on the Atlantic coast.

The musty **Musée de l'Armagnac,** in an 18th-century annex of the former Bishops' Palace in the town center, details the production process from the grape harvest to the barrel. Armagnac is distilled only once (unlike cognac, which is distilled twice); you can inspect the copper stills, or *alambics*, used for distillation. *2 rue Jules-Ferry. Admission: 7 frs. adults, 3.50 frs. children. Open June–Sept., Tues.–Sun. 10–noon and 2–6; Oct.–May, Tues.–Sat. 10–noon and 2–4.*

Time Out The dining room of the **Table des Cordeliers** (a former monastery) is a converted 14th-century chapel, where you can enjoy foie gras, served with fresh pasta, or duck with peaches. *Av. Charles-de-Gaulle.*

㉙ Six kilometers (4 miles) southwest of Condom (take D931/D208) is the château of **Cassaigne,** once the country residence of the bishops of Condom. The vineyards surrounding this 13th-century manor house were originally cultivated for wine, with only the unconsumed leftovers distilled to make brandy (once prescribed by local pharmacists as a disinfectant!). By the 17th century, the English were importing Armagnac in large quantities; ever since, brandy production has been the château's main raison d'être.

Cassaigne has belonged to the same family since 1827. Today, Elvire and Henri Faget organize tours of the château and visits to the 17th-century cellars, where the Armagnac is stored in oak barrels that give it an amber color. There's a small Armagnac museum, and you can taste and buy the brandy in the 16th-century vaulted kitchen. With luck, the slide show on the history of the house and the traditional methods of distillation will be in English as well as French by 1990. *Admission free. Open daily 9–noon and 2–7.*

D142 links Cassaigne to the 12th-century abbey of **Flaran,** just over 4 kilometers (2½ miles) away. In 1971, regional authorities took over the abbey, renovated it, and converted the guests' quarters into a cultural center for temporary exhibits. The abbey was built by Cistercian monks under St-Bernard; the monks' rooms on the second floor, overlooking the cloisters, remain largely unchanged.

The Cistercians preferred to build their abbeys in remote spots, next to a reliable water supply (here, the River Baïse). Have a look at the impressive sacristy, with its ribbed arches, resting on one central column, and at the storeroom, with its exhibit illustrating the medieval routes of pilgrims (two of which crossed the Gers) to Santiago de Compostela. *Valence-sur-Baïse. Admission: 10 frs. adults, 5 frs. children. Open July–Aug., daily 9:30–7; Sept.–June, Wed.–Mon, 9:30–noon and 2–6; closed Tues.*

Tour 4: The Pyrenees

㉚ The elegant town of **Pau,** 160 kilometers (100 miles) southwest of Toulouse, is the historic capital of Béarn, a state annexed to France in 1620. Pau rose to prominence after being "discovered" in 1815 by British officers who were returning from the Peninsular War in Spain and was soon launched as a winter resort. Fifty years later, English-speaking inhabitants made up one-third of Pau's population. They launched the Pont-Long steeplechase, still one of the most challenging in Europe, in

1841; created France's first golf course here, in 1856; and introduced fox hunting to the region.

Paying tribute to Pau's regal past is the **château,** begun in the 14th century by Gaston Phoebus, the flamboyant Count of Béarn. The building was transformed into a Renaissance palace in the 16th century by the beautiful Marguerite d'Angoulême, sister of French king François I. Marguerite's grandson, the future King Henri IV, was born in the château in 1553. Temporary exhibits connected to Henri's life and times are staged regularly here. His cradle—a giant turtle shell—is on show in his bedroom, one of the sumptuous, tapestry-lined royal apartments. Other highlights are the 16th-century kitchens and the imposing dining hall, which could seat up to 100 guests. *Rue du Château. Admission: 21 frs. (10.50 frs. Sun.). Open Apr.-Oct., daily 9:30–11:30 and 2–5:45; Nov.-Mar., daily 9:30–11:30 and 2–4:30.*

On the fourth floor of the château, the **Musée Béarnais** offers an overview of the region, encompassing everything from fauna to furniture to festival costumes. There is a reconstructed Béarn house and displays of such local crafts as cheese- and béret making. *Admission: 6 frs. adults, children free. Open Apr.-Oct., daily 9:30–12:30 and 2:30–6:30; Nov.-Mar., daily 9:30–12:30 and 2:30–5:30.*

③ The quickest and most scenic route from Pau to **Lourdes** (40 kilometers/25 miles southeast) is via N117/D940. Over 3 million pilgrims flock to Lourdes each year, many in quest of a miracle cure for their sickness or handicap. In February 1858, Bernadette Soubirous, a 14-year-old miller's daughter, claimed the Virgin Mary had appeared to her in the **Massabielle grotto** near the Gave de Pau river. The visions were repeated. During the ninth, Bernadette dug at the ground in the grotto, releasing a gush of water from a spot where no spring existed. From then on, pilgrims thronged the Massabielle rock in response to the water's supposed healing powers.

Church authorities reacted skeptically. It took four years of inquiry for the miracle to be authenticated by Rome and a sanctuary erected over the grotto. In 1864, the first organized procession was held. Today, there are six official annual pilgrimages, the most important on August 15. In 1958, Lourdes celebrated the centenary of the apparitions by constructing the world's largest underground church, the basilica of **St-Pie X.** The basilica looks more like a parking lot than a church, but it can accommodate 20,000 people—more than the permanent population of the whole town. Above the basilica stand the neo-Byzantine basilica of **Rosaire** (1889) and the tall, white basilica of **Supérieure** (1871). Both are open throughout the day, but unfortunately, their spiritual function far outweighs their aesthetic appeal.

The area surrounding the churches and grotto (situated between the basilicas and the river) is woefully short on beauty. Out of season, the acres of parking space beneath the basilicas echo like mournful parade grounds to the steps of solitary visitors. Shops are shuttered and restaurants are closed. In season, a milling throng jostles for postcards, tacky souvenirs, and a glimpse of the famous grotto, lurking behind a forest of votive candles struggling to remain aflicker in the Pyrenean breeze.

The Pavillon Notre-Dame, across from the underground basilica, houses the **Musée Bernadette,** with mementoes of her life (she died at a convent in Nevers, Burgundy, in 1879) and illustrated history of the pilgrimages. In the basement is the **Musée d'Art Sacré du Gemmail,** *gemmail* being a modern approach to the stained-glass technique, involving the assembly of broken glass, lit from behind, often by electric light. *72 rue de la Grotte. Admission free. Open July–Nov., daily 9:30–11:45 and 2:30–6:15; Dec.–June, Wed.–Mon. 9:30–11:45 and 2:30–5:45, closed Tues.*

Time Out	Stop in at the **Taverne de Bigorre et Albert;** Chef Claude Moreau prepares a filling stew of cabbage and bacon, or try one of his lighter fish dishes. *21 pl. du Champ-Commun.*

Just across the river are the **Moulin des Boly,** where Bernadette was born on January 7, 1844 (rue Bernadette-Soubrous; open Easter–mid-Oct., daily 9:30–11:45 and 2:30–5:45), and, close to the parish church where she was baptized, the **Cachot,** a shabby little room where Bernadette and her family lived. *15 rue des Petits-Fossés. Admission free. Open Easter–mid-Oct., daily 9:30–11:45 and 2:30–5:30; mid-Oct.–Easter, daily 2:30–5:30.*

Though the story of Bernadette is compelling, Lourdes is lucky to have an authentic historic attraction to complement the commercialized aura of its pilgrim sites. **Lourdes Castle** stands on a hill above the town and can be reached on foot or by escalator. In the 17th and 18th centuries, the castle was used as a prison; now it contains the **Musée Pyrénéen,** one of France's best provincial museums, devoted to popular customs and arts throughout the Pyrenees region, from Bayonne on the Atlantic to Perpignan by the Mediterranean. *Admission: 16.70 frs. adults, 6.30 frs. students, children free. Open Easter–mid-Oct., daily 9–noon and 2–7 (last admission at 6); mid-Oct.–Easter, Wed.–Mon. 9–noon and 2–7.*

㉜ Lourdes is close to several Pyrenean beauty spots. **Cauterets,** 30 kilometers (19 miles) south of Lourdes (via N21/D920), is a spa-resort set deep in the mountains, where you can ski until May. Ever since Roman times, Cauterets's thermal springs have been revered as a miracle cure for female sterility. Virile novelist Victor Hugo (1802–85) womanized here, and Lady Aurore Dudevant—better known as the writer George Sand (1804–76)—discovered the thrill of adultery. Poetic viscount François René Chateaubriand (1768–1848) stayed determinedly chaste, however, pining for his "inaccessible Occitan girl."

Continue south from Cauterets to the **Pont d'Espagne,** where steep-twisting D920 peters out. Continue on foot or by chairlift to the plateau and a view over the bright blue **Lac de Gaube,** fed by the river of the same name.

㉝ Return via Cauterets to Pierrefitte-Nestalas and turn right along D921 and the Gorge de Luz to **Gavarnie,** 30 kilometers (19 miles) away at the foot of the **Cirque de Gavarnie,** one of the world's most remarkable examples of glacial erosion. When the upper snows melt, numerous streams whoosh down from the cliffs to form spectacular waterfalls; the greatest of them—the **Grande Cascade**—drops nearly 1,400 feet. The Cirque presents a daunting challenge to mountaineers; if you've forgotten your climbing boots, a horse or donkey can take you part way into the mountains from the village of Gavarnie.

34 Return along D921 as far as **Luz-St-Sauveur** and turn right along D918. The mountain scenery remains dramatic. The road
35 passes through the lively little spa town of **Barèges** and under the brow of the mighty Pic du Midi de Bigorre, towering nearly 10,000 feet above the Col du Tourmalet pass. Luz-St-Sauveur
36 lies just 18 miles from **Arreau** as the crow flies, and 61 kilometers (38 miles) as the tortuous D918 twists. The finest views—and the sharpest curves—are found toward the Col d'Aspin pass, whose panoramic views of the Pyrenees are unsurpassed.

Another spectacular road, D618, covers the 32 kilometers (20 miles), via the Col de Peyresourde, from Arreau southeast to
37 the largest and most fashionable Pyrenean spa, **Bagnères de Luchon** (better known as just plain Luchon). Thermal waters here cater to the vocal cords: Opera singers, lawyers, and politicians hoarse from electoral promises all pile in. Luchon lies at the head of a lush valley, beneath the ski-resort of
38 **Superbagnères,** reached by a serpentine 12-mile road (D46); on the way up, admire the breathtaking views of the Maladeta mountain range across the border in Spain. The Romans considered Luchon to rank second as a spa only to Naples. A
39 Roman road led directly from Luchon to **St-Bertrand de Comminges** (then a huge town of 60,000), 32 kilometers (20 miles) north on D125/N125. This delightful village, whose inhabitants number just 500 today, is dwarfed beneath the imposing cathedral of **Ste-Marie,** largely 12th-century but extended in the 13th by Bertrand de Got (later Pope Clement V). Old houses, sloping alleyways, and craft shops add to the village's abundant charm.

What to See and Do with Children

At the **Rocher des Aigles** a hundred different species of bird of prey, including condors and vultures as well as eagles, swoop high and low at the command of their expert handlers. *Rte. du Château, tel. 65-33-65-45. Admission: 25 frs. adults, 10 frs. children. Open Apr.–mid-Nov. for demonstrations daily at 11, 3, 4, 5, and 6.*

The following attractions are described in the Exploring and Off the Beaten Track sections:

Boat trip on the Rivière Souterraine, Labouiche, Off the Beaten Track
Gouffre de Padirac, Off the Beaten Track
Grottes de Niaux, near Foix, Off the Beaten Track
Grande Cascade, Tour 4
Musée Béarnais, Pau, Tour 4
Museum d'Histoire Naturelle (Natural History Museum), Toulouse, Tour 1

Off the Beaten Track

At first sight, the **Gouffre de Padirac,** 16 kilometers (10 miles) northeast of Rocamadour via D673/D90, looks like an enormous gaping hole; until the 19th century, locals took the terrifying abyss to be the work of the devil. In 1889, a passage was found leading to underground galleries, and since then, a 14-mile network has been discovered, littered with the bones of mammoths, rhinoceros, and other mammals—some dating back 200,000 years. Elevators take you 200 feet down for an initial encounter with a host of stalagmites, while, farther on, boats cast off on a tour of the subterranean river through a mysterious underworld of chambers and lakes. *Admission: 30 frs. Open Apr.–July and Sept.–mid-Oct., daily 9–noon and 2–6; Aug., daily 7 AM–8 PM.*

Carcassonne, 88 kilometers (55 miles) east of Toulouse along the A61 expressway, boasts Europe's lengthiest medieval town walls. The mighty circle of towers and battlements stands high on a hilltop above the River Aude: a fairytale sight, claimed as the setting for Charles Perrault's story *Puss in Boots.* The earliest sections of wall were built by the Romans in the 5th century, while the Visigoths enlarged the settlement into a true fortress. In the 13th century, French King St-Louis and his son, Philip the Bold, strengthened the fortifications and gave Carcassonne the appearance it has today. The old streets inside the walls are lined with souvenir shops, craft boutiques, and restaurants. The **Château Comtal,** with its **Musée Lapidaire** (stone relics), is worth a visit; the view from the battlements toward the Pyrenees is stunning. *Château Comtal. Admission: 22 frs. adults, 12 frs. senior citizens, 5 frs. children. Open Apr.–Sept., daily 9–6; Oct.–Mar., daily 9:30–noon and 2–5.*

Six kilometers (4 miles) northwest of Foix (via D1) lies the **Rivière Souterraine** (underground river) of Labouiche, whose waters have tunneled through limestone cliffs. The 75-minute boat trip, past fantastically shaped and subtly lit stalactites and stalagmites, culminates in an encounter with a subterranean waterfall. *Admission: 25 frs. Open Easter–July and Sept., daily 9:30–noon and 2–5:30; Aug., daily 9:30–5:30.*

Lying 19 kilometers (12 miles) south of Foix (take D8 from Tarascon-sur-Ariège) are the superb **Grottes de Niaux,** caves containing scores of Magdalenian rock paintings dating back to 20,000 BC. Stylized drawings of horses, deer, and bison line a natural gallery half a mile from the entrance. Now that the famous caves at Lascaux in the Dordogne can be seen only in reproduction, this is the finest assembly of prehistoric art open to the public in France. *Admission: July–Aug., 20 frs. adults, 10 frs. children; Sept.–June, 15 frs. adults, 7.50 frs. children. Open July–Sept., daily 8:30–12:30 and 1:30–5:15; Oct.–June, daily tours at 11, 3, and 4:30.*

Shopping

Gift Ideas Don't leave the Midi-Pyrénées without buying some of the region's renowned foie gras and preserved duck *(confit de canard).* Two manufacturers in particular, **Aux Ducs de Gascogne** (rte. de Mauvezin, Gimont) and **Comtesse de Barry** (rte. Touget, Gimont) offer beautifully packaged tins that make ideal gifts. You'll also find their products in most good grocery stores and general food shops throughout the region.

Spirits Armagnac brandy is distilled throughout the Gers *département.* You'll see signs for *dégustation* (tasting) just about everywhere in the area (you can buy as well as taste), but any good wine and liquor store will have plenty in stock. For a good selection, try **Caves de l'Hôtel de France** (pl. de la Libération) in Auch.

Stores and Boutiques As the area's largest city, Toulouse offers the widest range of shops. The downtown **Centre Commercial St-Georges** (rue du Rempart St-Etienne) is a frenetic, modern shopping mall offering a vast array of clothing, jewelry, books, records—and just about anything else you'd possibly want to buy or admire. For upscale clothes, try the chic shops on **rue St-Rome** and **rue d'Alsace-Lorraine**, home to Toulouse's main department store, **Galeries Lafayette**; like its sister store in Paris, this Galeries Lafayette provides a good range of services for foreign visitors (including overseas shipment), and you can pay with any major credit card.

Sports and Fitness

Canoeing Canoeing is one of the region's most popular sports. Try canoe-kayaking in the rough waters of the Pyrenean torrents or the Tarn and Aveyron gorges or make gentler progress in the peaceful Quercy rivers. The most important bases are at Millau, Rozier-Pyreleau, Najac, Penne, Trébas, Burlats, Albi, St-Juéry, and Laguépie. Contact **Ligue Régionale de Canoë-Kayak** (4 chemin du Château-de-L'Hers, 31000 Toulouse, tel. 61–20–13–96).

Fishing The rivers here teem with trout and salmon. Courses, for beginners and advanced fishermen, are run by **Loisirs Accueil** (Service Pêche, 14 rue Lazéma, 09000 Foix, tel. 61–65–01–15).

Hiking The Midi-Pyrénées offers over 2,000 miles of marked paths for walkers and hikers, all designed to pass natural and historical sights. Local tourist offices have detailed maps, or, for advance information, contact **Comité de Randonnées Midi-Pyrénées** (CORAMIP, 12 rue Salambo, 31200 Toulouse, tel. 61–47–11–12).

Horseback Riding There are more than 120 stables or horseback riding centers in the region; for a full listing, get in touch with **CORAMIP** (*see* Hiking). Two that we recommend are **Poney Club** (Association Vacances, Loisirs Nature, chemin St-Jean, Colomiers, near Toulouse) and the **Centre Equestre et Poney Club** (Degagnac, 46340 Salviac, north of Cahos via D6).

Skiing Skiing—both downhill and cross-country—is often more fun in the Pyrenees than in the Alps; resorts tend to be prettier and certainly are cheaper. There are 26 "stations" along the central part of the range. Contact **Comité Régional Pyrénées Est de sports d'hiver** (1 rue de la Charité, 31000 Toulouse, tel. 61–62–89–25).

Dining and Lodging

Dining

The cuisine in Toulouse and the southwest is rich and strongly seasoned, making generous use of garlic and goose fat. This is the land of foie gras, especially delicious when sautéed with grapes. The most famous regional dish is *cassoulet*, a succulent white bean stew with *confit* (preserved goose), spicy sausage, pork, and sometimes lamb; there are a number of local versions around Toulouse and Carcassonne. Goose and duck dishes are legion: Try a *magret de canard* (a steak of duck breast). Cheaper specialties include *garbure*, mixed vegetables served as a broth or puree; *farci du lauragais*, a kind of pork pancake; and *gigot de sept heures*, a leg of lamb braised with garlic for no fewer than seven hours. Béarn, around Pau, is great eating country, famous for richly marinated stews made with wood pigeon *(civet de palombes)* or wild goat *(civet d'isnard)*. The local *poule au pot* of stuffed chicken poached with vegetables is memorable.

Highly recommended restaurants are indicated by a star ★.

Lodging

Hotels in this vast region range from Mediterranean-style modern to Middle Ages baronial; most are small and cozy, rather than luxurious. Toulouse, the area's only major town, has the usual range of big-city hotels; make reservations well ahead if you plan to visit in spring or fall. As with most of France, many of the hotels we list offer excellent eating opportunities.

Highly recommended hotels are indicated by a star ★.

Albi
Dining

Le Jardin des Quatre Saisons. There are two reasons for this new restaurant's excellent reputation: value for the money and efficient service. Ask the wine waiter to help you choose a bottle from the extensive wine list to accompany one of the chef's fish dishes. House specialties include mussels baked with leeks, or *suprême de sandre* (a type of perch) in wine. Desserts are surprisingly light for this gastronomic region. Try for a table in the garden if the weather's fine. *19 blvd. de Strasbourg, tel. 63–60–77–76. Reservations advised. Jacket and tie required. AE, MC, V. Closed Mon., and Tues. lunch. Inexpensive–Moderate.*

Dining and Lodging

La Réserve. A five-acre park surrounds this delightful hideaway of a hotel, a modern, hacienda-style building with arched windows and terraces extending the length of the facade. All the guest rooms are spacious, but those in the main building have the most charm, with elegant reproduction furniture and lots of pretty knickknacks. The restaurant offers tempting local specialties; the salmon with grapefruit and foie gras lightly fried with apples are good bets. *Rte. de Cordes, 81000 Fonvialane (5 ki/3 mi outside town), tel. 63–60–68–55. 24 rooms with bath. Facilities: restaurant, pool, tennis, park. Restaurant closed Nov.–Mar. AE, DC, MC, V. Expensive.*

Altéa. Ask for a room with a view in this converted 18th-century windmill, opposite the cathedral and overlooking the River Tarn. The ones on the second or fourth floors are best; those on the third and top floors have tiny windows. The hotel's restaurant, Le Moulin (The Windmill), is a stylish place to try regional specialties such as *fritons*, peanut-sized chunks of duck lard in flaky pastry with capers; they're a great deal more appetizing than they sound. Dine on the terrace in summer. *41 bis rue Porta, 81000, tel. 63–47–66–66. 56 rooms with bath. Facilities: restaurant, terrace. AE, DC, MC, V. Moderate.*

Auch
Dining and Lodging
★

France. Be sure to pay a visit to this, the most celebrated restaurant in Gascony. Despite the building's sober facade, the dining room's ambience is as warm and welcoming as at any corner bistro, with a bit of extra plush thrown in for good measure. Renowned chef André Daguin creates traditional Gascon cuisine with a masterly touch; his best dishes include salad with kid's liver and cod in flaky pastry accompanied by a whipped liver sauce. Save room for dessert—chocolates in *Banyuls* (warmed wine). There are 29 guest rooms as well, which wife Jocelyne has decorated with great charm and individuality. *Pl. de la Libération, 32000, tel. 62–05–00–44. Reservations essential. Dress: elegantly casual. Restaurant closed Jan., Sun. dinner, and Mon. AE, DC, MC, V. Expensive.*

Barbotan-les-Thermes
Dining and Lodging

La Bastide Gasconne. One of the country's leading food families —the Guérards—own and run this sumptuously decorated 18th-century manor house, now converted to a fine hotel-restaurant; it's located near an immense lake, close to the spa of Barbotan and 36 kilometers (21 miles) west of Condom. Michel Guérard presides over the magnificent, wood-beamed dining room, and dishes up exceptional nouvelle cuisine; try the fresh foie gras cooked in muslin or ray-wing in a rich mushroom and parsley sauce. Cognac or Armagnac and coffee by the open hearth make a suitably grand finale. Guérard's wife, Christine, is a talented interior decorator, and her elegant taste is shown to advantage in the Gasconne's light, spacious decor. The 36 guest rooms feature a quaint-chic touch, and there are a pool and tennis courts. *Barbaton-les-Thermes, 32150 Cazaubon, tel. 62–69–52–09. Reservations essential. Jacket and tie required. AE. Closed Nov.–Mar. Expensive.*

Cabrerets
Dining and Lodging

La Pescalerie. In a gracious parkland setting on the banks of the Célé (33 kilometers/20 miles northeast of Cahors), La Pescalerie is run with precision by Hélène Combette, a former psychiatrist, while Roger Belcour, a practicing surgeon, acts as maître d'hôtel. Don't panic: The atmosphere is friendly and welcoming and not in the least medicinal. The rustic manor dates from the 16th and 17th centuries, and its shuttered stone facade is cozily inviting. Each guest room features a different decor and its own collection of contemporary paintings, and some of the bathrooms are palatial; antiques are dotted throughout. Rooms on the upper floor are charming, with slanted ceilings and exposed beams. In the restaurant, try the artichoke stew with thin slivers of duck; snails with nuts; and, for dessert, peaches poached in wine. The Cahors wine list is extensive. *A la Fontaine de la Pescalerie, 46330, tel. 65–31–22–55. 10 rooms with bath. Facilities: restaurant, bar, park. AE, DC, MC, V. Closed Nov.–mid-Apr. Expensive.*

Cahors
Dining and Lodging
★

Château de Mercuès. A graceful curving staircase leads up to this majestic stone castle, whose corner towers reach high into the sky. The château, built in the 13th century and former home to the counts of Cahors, lies 8 kilometers (5 miles) outside town on the road to Villeneuve-sur-Lot. There are actually two hotels here: the Mercuès itself, whose guest rooms feature the sort of baronial splendor you'd expect in any self-respecting castle, and the new Cèdres annex, with contemporary furnishings and much less appeal (rooms here cost less, however, and you still get the same fantastic views of the countryside). Chef Pascal Bréant, formerly of Paris's Tour d'Argent, produces food to consistently rave reviews; try his fresh Scottish salmon in butter or potato salad with truffles. And to finish: prunes in Armagnac. *Mercuès, 46090 Cahors, tel. 65–20–00–01. 23 rooms with bath (plus 22 rooms with bath in annex). Facilities: restaurant, terrace, pool, tennis, helipad. AE, DC, MC, V. Closed Nov. and Jan.–Apr. Expensive–Very Expensive.*

Terminus. This small hotel is deep in the heart of truffle country, yet just two minutes' walk from Cahors train station; the restaurant, La Balandre, is the city's best. The decor is mainly Roaring Twenties and the atmosphere is stylishly jazzy, but the windows have turn-of-the-century stained glass. Gilles Marre and his wife, Jacqueline, specialize in truffles but also serve an exceptional fresh cod *brandade* (mousse) and foie gras in flaky pastry. There's a good range of local wines, and the service is sophisticated yet friendly. The 31 guest rooms are cozily traditional in feel. *5 av. Charles de Freycinet-Cahors, 46090, tel. 65–30–01–97. Reservations advised. Dress: elegantly casual. AE, MC, V. Restaurant closed 2 weeks in Feb., 1 week in June, Sun. dinner, Mon., Jan.–Mar., and Sat. lunch, July–Aug. Moderate.*

Carcassonne
Dining

Auberge du Pont-Levis. At the foot of the medieval city gateway, Porte Narbonnaise, the Pont-Levis provides a welcome shelter from the tourist crowds. Chef Henri Pautard serves traditional *cassoulet* stews and foie gras alongside a more inventive terrine marbled with artichokes and leeks, accompanied by a truffle vinaigrette. Otherwise, try the *méli-mélo du pecheur*, a refreshing mix of seafood. In summer, you can eat on the terrace or in the pretty garden. *Porte Narbonnaise, tel. 68–25–55–23. Reservations advised. Jacket required. AE, DC, MC, V. Closed Nov., Feb., Sun. dinner, and Mon. Moderate.*

★ **Le Languedoc.** Candlelit dinners on the Languedoc's terrace are romantic, elegant affairs. Maestro Didier Faugeras offers a range of delicacies, from artichoke hearts and chicken livers in warm vinegar to scallops with cucumbers and chive butter and seasonal game. The same family runs the Montségur, across the street. *32 allée d'Lena, tel. 68–25–22–17. Reservations essential. Jacket and tie required. AE, DC, MC, V. Closed mid-Dec.–mid-Jan., and Mon. and Sun. dinner, Sept.–June. Moderate.*

Lodging
★

Montségur. This pretty little town hotel lies just outside the old city walls. Rooms on the first two floors showcase elaborate Louis XV and XVI period furniture, while those above are more romantic, with gilt-iron bedsteads set under sloping oak beams. *27 allée d'Lena, 11000, tel. 68–25–31–41. 21 rooms with bath. DC, MC, V. Closed mid-Dec.–mid-Jan. Moderate.*

Dining and Lodging

Domaine d'Auriac. Former rugby player Bernard Rigaudis has created a countrified atmosphere in this 19th-century manor house. Room prices vary according to the size and view; larger rooms look out over the magnificent park and vineyards. The dining room is festooned with copper pots and pans and offers traditional Languedoc cuisine. Feast on foie gras poached in Sauterne, anchovies with citronella in salmon *carpaccio*, or local game in season. *Rte. de St-Hilaire, 11009 Auriac, tel. 68–25–72–22. 23 rooms with bath. Facilities: restaurant, pool, garden, tennis, golf. AE, MC, V. Closed last 3 weeks in Jan.; restaurant closed Sun., mid-Oct.–Easter. Expensive.*

Castéra-Verduzan
Dining and Lodging

Ténarèze. The Ténarèze's restaurant, Le Florida, is fast acquiring a reputation nearly as lofty as that of André Daguin's own establishment in Auch. The dining room's setting is unpretentious and completely upstaged by chef Bernard Ramounéda's creative flair. Ramounéda serves his foie gras with grapes, apples, or gooseberries and a glass of Sauterne; offers duck cooked in every possible manner; and presents a sumptuous range of desserts, including ice cream with prunes and Armagnac or peaches with spices. The hotel's 24 inexpensive guest rooms are traditionally decorated, with heavy velvet drapes and lace trim. Castéra-Verduzan is a spa town featuring curative thermal springs. To get there take tree-lined D930 25 kilometers (15 miles) northwest from Auch. *32410 Castéra-Verduzan, tel. 62–68–13–22. Reservations essential. Jacket and tie required. AE, DC, MC, V. Closed Mon., Sun. dinner, and Feb. Expensive.*

Cordes
Dining and Lodging
★

Le Grand Ecuyer. Dramatically set in one of the region's most beautiful villages, Le Grand Ecuyer is a perfectly preserved medieval mansion. The guest rooms contain period furnishings, and a few feature four-poster beds; only the bathrooms are contemporary. Yves Thuriès is one of the southwest's best chefs, and the dining room's elegant decor and ornate silverware provide a stylish background to his inventive recipes. Sample his salmon and sole twist in vanilla puree or the guinea fowl *suprême* in fragrant, flaky pastry. *Rue Voltaire, 81170, tel. 63–56–01–03. 13 rooms with bath. Facilities: restaurant. AE, DC, MC, V. Closed Nov.–Mar.; restaurant closed Mon., Sept.–June. Expensive.*

★ **L'Hostellerie du Vieux Cordes.** This magnificent 13th-century house, belonging to the same family as Le Grand Ecuyer, is set around a charming courtyard, shaded by overhanging trees and dotted with tiny white tables. Inside, the 21 guest rooms are richly decorated, but not nearly as opulent as the vast crimson dining rooms. Bernard Lafuente, Yves Thuriès's brother-in-law, is yet another accomplished chef. For a gastronomic blowout, go for his *Délices de Raymond VII*, a varying multicourse feast. Lighter—and more affordable—specialties include grilled goat cheese in honey, roast salmon with herb vinaigrette and marinated cucumbers, and young pigeon on a bed of red cabbage. *Rue St-Michel, 81170, tel. 63–56–00–12. Reservations advised. Jacket required. AE, DC, MC, V. Closed Mon., Nov.–Easter; hotel closed mid-Jan.–mid-Feb. Moderate.*

Toulouse
Dining

La Belle Epoque. Chef/owner Pierre Roudgé's approach to cooking is novel: Tell him what you don't like and he'll invent your menu on the spot. The ginger-spiced lobster in a flaky pastry is as good as it sounds, while other dishes include cod in leek butter and a light pastry stuffed with asparagus and foie gras. At press time, Roudgé was planning to renovate the 1920s decor, so you'll be able to savor his culinary efforts in a new setting. *3 rue Pargaminières, tel. 61–23–22–12. Reservations advised. Dress: casual. AE, DC, MC, V. Closed Sat. and Mon. lunch, Sun., and July. Moderate.*

Chez Emile. There are two dining rooms at this restaurant, overlooking place St-Georges. The ground floor is modern and elegant, specializing in light, contemporary fish dishes that change daily; if it's on the menu, try the turbot in ginger. Upstairs is a cozy hideaway for those who appreciate a more traditional taste of Toulouse: *cassoulet, magrets de canard* (duck), and other filling fare. *13 pl. St-Georges, tel. 61–21–05–56. Reservations essential. Dress: casual. AE, DC, MC, V. Closed last week in Aug., Sun., and Mon. Moderate.*

★ **Vanel.** French gastronomes have long rated Vanel the top restaurant in Toulouse, and one of the country's finest. Lucien Vanel, now into his sixties and gradually passing control to his talented protégés, is known for his imagination; he's capable of changing the menu completely, overnight. You'll never be disappointed. The decor was more comfortable than exciting, until a recent renovation transformed its Belle Epoque fustiness into modern chic. *22 rue Maurice-Fonvielle, tel. 61–21–51–82. Reservations essential. Jacket and tie required. AE, MC, V. Closed Aug., Sun., and Mon. lunch. Expensive.*

Dining and Lodging **Grand Hôtel de l'Opéra.** This downtown doyen is conveniently
★ located on Toulouse's place du Capitole. The guest rooms are comfortably plush, with calm, soothing colors and modern conveniences; make sure you're not given one of the smaller rooms —they are *very* small. Dominique Toulousy and his wife, Maryse, have made the hotel's Jardins de l'Opéra the most fashionable restaurant in town. Several intimate dining rooms and a covered terrace around a little pond make for undeniable, if slightly overcute, charm. The food is a successful mix of innovation and traditional Gascon fare; try the ravioli stuffed with foie gras and truffles or the *gambas* (jumbo shrimp) baked with artichokes and cheese. For dessert, there's a large selection of homemade patisserie. *1 pl. du Capitole, 31000, tel. 61–21–82–66. 63 rooms with bath. Facilities: restaurant, café, pool, garden. AE, DC, MC, V. Expensive.*

The Arts and Nightlife

The Arts

Toulouse, the region's cultural high spot, is also recognized as one of France's most arty cities. Its classical, lyrical, and chamber music orchestras, dramatic arts center, and ballet are all listed as national companies—no mean feat in this arts-oriented country. So many opera singers have come to sing here at the Théâtre du Capitole or the Halle aux Grains that the city is known as the *capitale du bel canto*. The performing arts season lasts from October until late May, with occasional summer presentations. For information and advance bookings, contact **Théâtre du Capitole** (pl. du Capitole, 31000 Toulouse, tel. 61–23–21–35).

The medieval city of **Carcassonne** has a major arts festival in July, featuring dance, theater, classical music, and jazz; for details, contact the **Théâtre Municipal** (B.P. 236, rue Courtejaire, 11005 Carcassonne Cedex, tel. 68–25–33–13).

Music There are 50 music festivals a year in smaller towns throughout the region; the CRT and larger tourist offices can provide a list of dates and addresses, or contact **Délégation Musicale Régionale** (56 rue du Taur, 31000 Toulouse, tel. 61–23–20–39).

Toulouse is the hometown of Claude Nougaro, one of France's best jazz singers. If you're a blues or boogie buff, take in one of his slick, professional concerts.

Dance Toulouse's **Ballet du Capitole** stages classical ballets, while the **Ballet-Théâtre Joseph Russilo** and **Compagnie Jean-Marc Matos** put on modern dance performances. The **Centre National Chorégraphique de Toulouse** welcomes international companies each year in the St-Cyprien quarter. For a schedule of current programs, get in touch with the city tourist office (*see* Essential Information).

Theater Main theaters in Toulouse are the **Théâtre du Capitole** (pl. du Capitole, tel. 61–23–21–35); **Grenier de Toulouse** (3 rue de la

Digue, tel. 61–42–97–79); **Théâtre du Taur** (69 rue du Taur, tel. 61–21–77–13); **Halles Aux Grains** (pl. Dupuy, tel. 61–22–24–40); and **Théâtre Daniel Sorano** (35 allées Jules Guesde, tel. 61–52–66–87).

Nightlife

Toulouse stays up late. For a complete list of clubs and discos, buy a copy of *Toulouse Pratique*, available at any bookshop or newspaper stand.

Nightclubs L'Art Club (1 rue de l'Echarpe) is a trendy, elegant vaulted brick cellar in the Esquirol quarter; if you like a more intimate setting, try **Le Cendrée** (15 rue des Tourneurs), which has lots of cozy nooks and crannies. **L'Ubu** (16 rue St-Rome) has been the city's top nightspot for 20 years, where the local glitterati and concert and theater stars come to relax. **Victory Clippers Club** (Canal de Brienne, allée de Barcelone) may be a bit daring for some, but liberated couples love it.

Jazz Clubs **Le Café des Allées** (64 allées Charles de Fitte) is a regular hothouse of local musicians. **Café Le Griot** (34 rue des Blanchers) features jazz, blues, and a number of American duos and trios. **La Père Bacchus** (20 pl. St-Georges) is the trendiest spot on the city's trendiest square. At **Le Tilt** (20 rue Denfert-Rochereau) jazz veers to rock and rock becomes jazzy, with an accent on rhythm and blues.

14 The Riviera

Introduction

It's important to begin with a realistic sense of Riviera life so you won't spend your holiday nursing wounded expectations. The Riviera conjures up images of fabulous yachts and villas, movie stars and palaces, and budding Bardots sunning themselves on ribbons of golden sand. The truth is that most beaches, at least east of Cannes, are small and pebbly. In summer, hordes of visitors are stuffed into concrete high rises or roadside campsites—on weekends it can take two hours to drive the last six miles into St-Tropez. Yes, the film stars are here—but in their private villas. When the merely wealthy come, they come off-season, in the spring and fall—the best time for you to visit, too.

That said, we can still recommend the Riviera, even in summer, as long as you're selective about the places you choose to visit. A few miles inland are fortified medieval towns perched on mountaintops, high above the sea. The light that Renoir and Matisse came to capture is as magical here as ever. Fields of roses and lavender still send their heady perfume up to these fortified towns, where craftspeople make and sell their wares, as their predecessors did in the Middle Ages. Some resorts are as exclusive as ever, and no one will argue that French chefs have lost their touch.

It's impossible to get bored along the Riviera. You can try a different beach or restaurant every day. When you've had enough of the sun, you can visit pottery towns like Vallauris, where Picasso worked, and at Grasse, where three-quarters of the world's essences are produced. You can drive along dizzying gorges, one almost as deep as the Grand Canyon. You can disco or gamble the night away in Monte Carlo and shop for the best Paris has to offer, right in Cannes or Nice. Only minutes from the beaches are some of the world's most famous museums of modern art, featuring the works of Fernand Léger, Henri Matisse, Pablo Picasso, Pierre Auguste Renoir, Jean Cocteau —all the artists who were captivated by the light and color of the Côte d'Azur.

Essential Information

Important Addresses and Numbers

Tourist Information The Riviera's regional tourist office is the **Comité Régional du Tourisme de Riviera–Côte d'Azur** (55 Promenade des Anglais, 06000 Nice; written enquiries only). Local tourist offices in major towns covered in this chapter are as follows: **Antibes** (11 pl. Général-de-Gaulle, tel. 93–33–95–64), **Cannes** (Palais des Festivals, 1 La Croisette, tel. 93–39–24–53), **Juan-les-Pins** (5 blvd. Guillaumont, tel. 93–61–04–98), **La Napoule** (rue J-Aulas, tel. 93–49–95–31), **Menton** (Palais de l'Europe, av. Boyer, tel. 93–57–57–00), **Monte Carlo** (2-A blvd. des Moulins, tel. 93–30–87–01), **Nice** (av. Thiers, tel. 93–87–07–07), and **St-Tropez** (quai Jean-Jaurès, tel. 94–97–45–21).

Travel Agencies **American Express** (8 rue des Belges, Cannes, tel. 93–38–15–87; 11 Promenade des Anglais, Nice, tel. 93–87–29–82; and 26 av. du Général-Leclerc, St-Tropez, tel. 94–97–15–27) and **Thomas Cook** (2 av. Monte Carlo, Monte Carlo, tel. 93–25–01–05).

Car Rental Avis (9 av. d'Ostende, Monte Carlo, tel. 93–30–17–53; and 13 blvd. Louis Blanc, St-Tropez, tel. 94–97–03–10), **Europcar** (9 av. Thiers, Menton, tel. 64–39–75–75), and **Hertz** (147 rue d'Antibes, Cannes, tel. 93–48–00–63; and 12 av. du Suede, Nice, tel. 93–87–11–87).

Arriving and Departing

By Plane The area's only international airport is at Nice; for information and reservations, call 93–83–69–11.

By Train Mainline trains from the French capital stop at most of the major resorts; the trip to Nice takes about seven hours.

By Car If you're traveling from Paris by car, you can avoid a lengthy drive by taking the overnight motorail *(train-auto-couchette)* service to Nice, which departs from Paris's Gare de Bercy, five minutes from the Gare de Lyon. Otherwise, leave Paris by A6 (becoming A7 after Lyon), which continues down to Avignon. Here A8 branches off east toward Italy, with convenient exit/ entry points for all major towns (except St-Tropez).

Getting Around

By Train The train is a practical and inexpensive way of getting around the Riviera and stops at dozens of stations.

By Car If you prefer to avoid the slower, albeit spectacularly scenic, coastal roads, opt for the Italy-bound A8.

By Bus Local buses cover a network of routes along the Riviera and stop at many out-of-the-way places that can't be reached by train. Timetables are available from tourist offices, train stations, and the local bus depots *(gare routières)*.

Guided Tours

Bus Tours Two of the largest companies offering 1½-day tours are **Santa Azur** (11 av. Jean-Médicin, 06000 Nice, tel. 93–85–46–81) and **CTM** (Compagnie des Transports Méditerranéens, 5 sq. Mérimée, 06100 Cannes, tel. 93–39–07–68). CTM has a day trip to St-Tropez on Thursday (about 100 francs), as well as a half-day excursion to St-Raphäel and Lac de St-Cassien (about 80 francs); buses leave on Tuesday and Thursday at 8 AM. Santa Azur's one-day tour destinations include Nice (Monday, Wednesday, and Friday; cost 65 francs) and Monaco and the hill town of Eze (Monday, Wednesday, Friday, and Sunday; cost 80 francs).

Boat Tours **Bateaux Gallus 80** (24 quai Lunel, 06000 Nice, tel. 93–55–33–33) offers an enjoyable day-long jaunt to the Iles de Lérins; cost is about 110 francs.

Special-Interest Any tourist office will produce a sheaf of suggestions on gourmandizing, golfing, and walking tours, among others. **Novatours** (14 av. de Madrid, 06400 Cannes, tel. 93–43–45–36) offers tailor-made packages for its clients, though museum tours are a specialty; a three-day/two-night museum tour of Vence and Antibes, including half-board, costs about 2,650 francs.

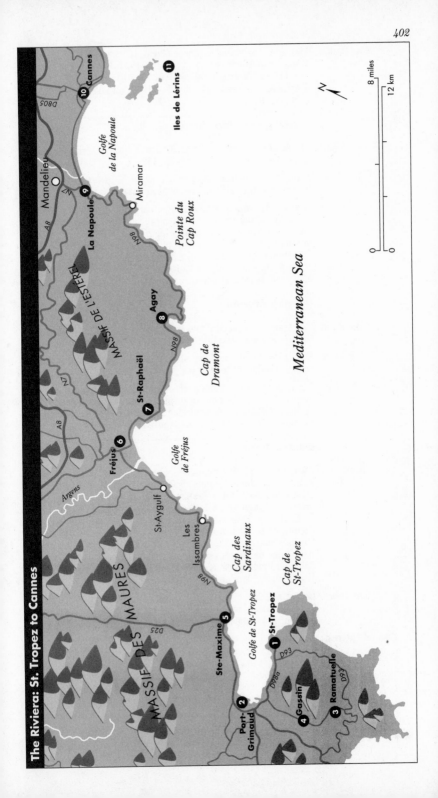

The Riviera: St. Tropez to Cannes

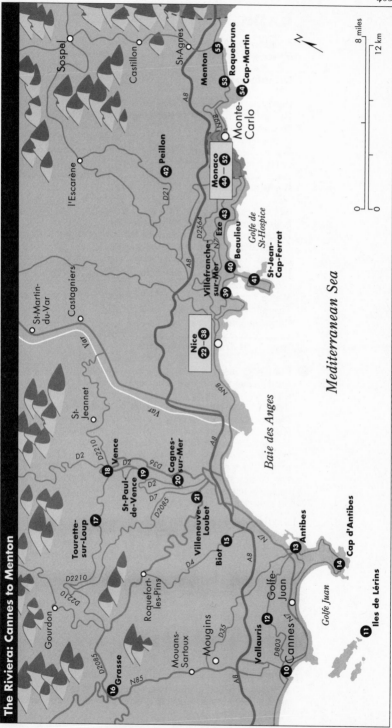

The Riviera: Cannes to Menton

Mediterranean Sea

Exploring the Riviera

Numbers in the margin correspond with points of interest on the Riviera map.

Orientation

Our Riviera text covers the 75 miles between St-Tropez and the Italian border. The first tour concentrates on the Mediterranean coast from St-Tropez to Cannes and Antibes. The second begins with the inland towns of Grasse, Vence, and St-Paul-de-Vence, then rejoins the Mediterranean at Cagnes and continues to Nice and Monaco.

Highlights for First-time Visitors

Sunning on the beach at St-Tropez, Tour 1
A stroll down La Croisette, Cannes, Tour 1
Picasso Museum in the Château Grimaldi, Antibes, Tour 1
A walk along the Cap d'Antibes peninsula, Tour 1
St-Paul-de-Vence, Tour 2
Fondation Maeght, La Gardette, Tour 2
Old Town, Nice, Tour 2
Musée Ephrussi de Rothschild, St-Jean-Cap-Ferrat, Tour 2
The hill village of Peillon, Tour 2
Casino at Monte Carlo, Tour 2

Tour 1. St-Tropez to Antibes

① Old money never came to **St-Tropez,** but Brigitte Bardot did. Bardot came with her director Roger Vadim in 1956 to film *And God Created Woman*, and the resort has never been the same. Actually, the village was "discovered" by the writer Guy de Maupassant (1850–93) and by the French painter Paul Signac (1863–1935), who came in 1892 and brought his friends—Matisse, Pierre Bonnard, and others. What attracted them was the pure, radiant light and the serenity and colors of the landscape. The writer Colette moved into a villa here between the two world wars and contributed to its notoriety. When the cinema people staked their claim in the 1950s, St-Tropez became St-Trop (*trop* in French means "too much").

Anything associated with the past seems either detestable or absurd in St-Tropez, so you may not want to hear the story of how it got its name. In AD 68 a Roman soldier from Pisa named Torpes was beheaded for professing his Christian faith in the presence of the Emperor Nero. The headless body was put in a boat between a dog and a cock and drifted out to sea. The body eventually floated ashore, perfectly preserved, still watched over by the two animals. The buried remains became a place of pilgrimage, which by the 4th century was called St-Tropez. In the late 15th century, under the Genovese, St-Tropez became a small independent republic.

Today Bardot is middle aged, and so is St-Tropez. Most would say Bardot has aged more gracefully.

Whatever celebrities are here are packed away in villas. The people you'll see are mere mortals—many beautiful, many balancing precariously on the far edge of youth, many seriously past their prime. The beaches are filled with every imaginable type of human animal: aggressively cheerful volleyball players searching for meaningful one-night relationships, supergirls with Cartier bracelets, aspiring starlets, middle-aged men with mirrored shades, bare-breasted mothers with children and dogs. The atmosphere is part Benetton, part Tarzan and Jane. In summer, the population swells from 7,000 to 64,000.

Off-season is the time to come, but even in summer you can find reasons to stay. The soft, sandy beaches are the best on the coast. Take an early morning stroll along the harbor or down the narrow medieval streets—the rest of the world will still be comatose from the Night Before—and you'll see just how pretty St-Tropez is, with its tiny squares and its rich, pastel-colored houses bathed in light. There's a weekend's worth of trendy boutiques to explore—to be delighted by or shocked at—and many cute cafés, where you can sit under colored awnings sipping wine and feel very French. Five minutes from town, you're in a green world of vineyards and fields, where you'll see nothing more lascivious than a butterfly fluttering around some chestnut leaves or a grapevine clinging to a farmhouse wall. Above the fertile fields are mountains crowned with medieval villages, where you can come at dusk for wild strawberry tarts and fabulous views. Perhaps it's the soft light, perhaps the rich fields and faded pastels, but nowhere else along the coast will you experience so completely the magic of Provence.

Two cafés on the harbor provide dress-circle seats for admiring the St-Tropez scene: **Le Gorille,** on quai Suffren, and **Sénéquier's,** the café with the big terrace on quai Jean-Juarès, beyond the tourist office. Walk along the harbor, filled with pleasure boats, and along the breakwater (the Môle), and continue to the **Musée de l'Annonciade,** a church converted into a major art museum. The collection of Impressionist paintings is filled with views of St-Tropez by Matisse, Bonnard, Paul Signac, Maurice Vlaminck, and others. *Quai de l'Epi. Admission: 16 frs. adults, 8 frs. children. Open Wed.–Mon. 10–noon and 3–6; closed Tues.*

Rue de la Citadelle leads inland from the tourist office to the **Citadel,** a 16th-century fortress with commanding views from St-Tropez across the bay to Ste-Maxime. In the keep is the **Musée de la Marine,** stocked with marine paintings and ship models, including a Greek galley. *Admission: 12 frs. Open Nov.–Easter, Fri.–Wed. 10–5; Easter–Oct., 10–6; closed Thurs.*

Stroll down Montée Ringrave to **place Carnot,** site of a twice-weekly market (Saturday/Tuesday) and daily games of *boules.* Trendy boutiques are on **rue Sibilli.**

Time Out   Food at the **Café des Arts** may be ordinary, but the café is a popular place to sit and feel part of the in-crowd. *Pl. Carnot. Closed Oct.–Mar.*

Beaches close to town—**Plage des Greniers** and the **Bouillabaisse**—are great for families, but holiday people snub them, preferring a six-mile sandy crescent at **Les Salins** and **Pampellone.** These beaches are about 3 kilometers (2 miles) from town, so it helps to have a car, motorbike, or bicycle.

2 Visitors seem to enjoy a trip through **Port-Grimaud,** a modern architect's idea of a Provençal fishing village-cum-Venice, built out into the gulf for the yachting crowd—each house with its own mooring. Particularly appealing are the harmonious pastel colors, which have weathered nicely, and the graceful bridges over the canals.

3 From St-Tropez, take D93 south 11 kilometers (7 miles) to the old Provençal market town of **Ramatuelle.** The ancient houses are huddled together on the slope of a rocky spur 440 feet above the sea. The central square has a 17th-century church and a huge 300-year-old elm. Surrounding the square are narrow, twisting streets with medieval archways and vaulted passages.

4 From Ramatuelle, follow signs to the old village of **Gassin,** which is less than 3 kilometers (2 miles) away. The ride is lovely, through vineyards and woods, and takes you over the highest point of the peninsula (1,070 feet), where you can stop and enjoy a splendid view. The perched village of Gassin, with its venerable old houses and its 12th-century Romanesque church, has somehow managed to maintain its medieval appearance.

5 D98a runs 6 kilometers (4 miles) west from St-Tropez to join the major coastal highway, the N98, continuing 8 kilometers (5 miles) to **Ste-Maxime**—a family resort with a fine sandy beach.

6 The coastline between Ste-Maxime and Cannes consists of a succession of bays and beaches. Minor resorts have sprung up wherever nature permits—curious mixtures of lush villas, campsites, and fast food stands. **Fréjus,** 19 kilometers (12 miles) farther along N98, was founded by Julius Caesar as Forum Julii in 49 BC, and it is thought that the Roman city grew to 40,000 people—10,000 more than the population today. The Roman remains are unspectacular, if varied, and consist of part of the theater, arena, aqueduct, and city walls.

Fréjus Cathedral dates back to the 10th century, although the richly worked choir stalls are 15th century. The baptistery alongside, square on the outside and octagonal inside, is thought to date from AD 400, making it one of France's oldest buildings. The adjacent cloisters offer an unusual contrast between round and pointed arches.

7 **St-Raphaël,** next door to Fréjus, is another family resort with holiday camps, best known to tourists as the railway stop to St-Tropez. It was here that the Allied forces landed in their offensive against the Germans in August 1944.

The rugged Massif de l'Estérel, between Fréjus and Cannes, is a hiker's joy, made up of volcanic rocks (porphyry) carved by the sea into dreamlike shapes. The harshness of the landscape is softened by patches of lavender, cane apple, and gorse. The deep gorges with sculpted, parasol pines could have inspired Tang- and Sung-Dynasty landscape painters. Drivers can take N7, the mountain route to the north or, as we propose, stay on the N98 coast road past tiny rust-colored beaches and sheer rock faces plunging into the sea.

8 Some 10 kilometers (6 miles) from St-Raphaël is the resort of **Agay,** whose deep bay was once used by traders from ancient Greece. Agay has the best-protected anchorage along the coast. It was here that writer Antoine de Saint Exupéry *(The Little Prince)* was shot down in July 1944 having just flown over his family castle on his last mission. **La Napoule,** 24 kilometers (15 miles) from Agay, forms a unit with the older, inland village of **Mandelieu.** The village explodes with color during the Fête du Mimosa in February and boasts extensive modern sports facilities (swimming, boating, waterskiing, deep-sea diving, fishing, golf, tennis, horseback riding, and parachuting).

Art lovers will want to stop in La Napoule at the **Château de la Napoule Art Foundation** to see the eccentric and eclectic work of the American sculptor Henry Clews. Clews, who saw himself as Don Quixote and his wife as the Virgin of La Mancha, came from a New York banking family. A cynic and sadist, he had, as one critic remarked, a knowledge of anatomy worthy of Michelangelo and the bizarre imagination of Edgar Allan Poe. His work—as tortured as the rocks of the Esterel—shows an infatuation with big bellies and distorted bodies; his nude of a man with a skull between his thighs is not easily forgotten. *Av. Henry-Clews. Admission: 15 frs. Guided visits Mar.–Nov., Wed.–Mon., at 3, 4, and 5.*

Cosmopolitan, sophisticated, smart—these are words that describe the most lively and flourishing city on the Riviera, 6 kilometers (4 miles) farther up the coast. **Cannes** is a resort town—unlike Nice, which is a city—that exists only for the pleasure of its guests. It's a tasteful and expensive breeding ground for yuppies, a sybaritic heaven for those who believe that life is short and that sin has something to do with the absence of a tan.

Picture a long, narrow beach. Stretching along it is a broad, elegant promenade called La Croisette, bordered by palm trees and flowers. At one end of the promenade is the modern Festival Hall, a summer casino, and an old harbor where pleasure boats are moored. At the other end is a winter casino and a modern harbor for some of the most luxurious yachts in the world. All along the promenade are cafés, boutiques, and luxury hotels like the Carlton and the Majestic. Speedboats and waterskiers glide by; little waves lick the beach, lined with prostrate bodies. Behind the promenade lies the town, filled with shops, restaurants, and hotels, and behind the town are the hills with the villas of the very rich.

The first thing to do is stroll along **La Croisette,** stopping at cafés and boutiques along the way. Near the eastern end (turning left as you face the water), before you reach the new port, is the **Parc de la Roserie,** where some 14,000 roses nod their heads. Walking west takes you past the **Palais des Festival** (Festival Hall), where the famous film festival is held each May. Just past the hall is **Place du Général-de-Gaulle,** while on your left is the **old port.** If you continue straight beyond the port on **Allés de la Liberte,** you'll reach a tree-shaded area, where flowers are sold in the morning, *boules* is played in the afternoon, and a flea market is held on Saturday. If instead of continuing straight from the square you turn inland, you'll quickly come to Rue Meynadier. Turn left. This is the old main street, which has many 18th-century houses—now boutiques and specialty food shops, where you can buy exotic foods and ship them.

 You may want to visit the peaceful **Iles de Lérins** (Lerin Islands) to escape the crowds. The ferry takes 15 minutes to **Ste-**

Marguerite, 30 to **St-Honorat** (tel. 93–39–11–82 for information).

Ste-Marguerite, the larger of the two, is an island of wooded hills, with a tiny main street lined with fishermen's houses. Visitors enjoy peaceful walks through a forest of enormous eucalyptus trees and parasol pines. Paths wind through a dense undergrowth of tree heathers, rosemary, and thyme. The main attraction is the dank cell in **Fort Royal,** where the Man in the Iron Mask was imprisoned (1687–98) before going to the Bastille, where he died in 1703. The mask, which he always wore, was in fact made of velvet. Was he the illegitimate brother of Louis XIV or Louis XIII's son-in-law? No one knows.

St-Honorat is wilder but more tranquil than its sister island. It was named for a hermit who came to escape his followers; but when the hermit founded a monastery here in AD 410, his disciples followed and the monastery became one of the most powerful in all Christendom. A pope was among the pilgrims who came to walk barefoot around the island. It's still worth taking this two-hour walk to the **old fortified monastery,** where noble Gothic arcades are arranged around a central courtyard. Next door to the "new" 19th-century monastery (open on request) is a shop where the monks sell handicrafts, lavender scent, and a home-brewed liqueur called Lerina. *Monastère de Lérins. Admission free. Open May–Oct., daily 9:45–4:30; Nov.–Apr. 10:45–3:30. High Mass at the abbey 10:45 Sun.*

From Cannes, take D803 northeast to the pottery-making center of **Vallauris,** 5 kilometers (3 miles) away. Pottery is on sale throughout the village, and several workshops can be visited. Picasso spurred a resurgence of activity when he settled here in 1947 and created some whimsically beautiful ceramics. He also decorated the tunnel-like medieval chapel of the former priory with a fresco entitled *War and Peace. Pl. de la Mairie. Admission: 8 frs. Open Wed.–Mon. 10–noon and 2–6; closed Tues.*

From Vallauris, continue east to **Antibes,** founded as a Greek trading port in the 4th century BC and now a center for fishing and rose growing. Avenue de l'Amiral Grasse runs along the seafront from the harbor to the **market place,** a colorful sight most mornings, and the church of the **Immaculate Conception,** with intricately carved portals (dating from 1710) and a 1515 altarpiece by Nice artist Louis Bréa (c. 1455–1523).

The **Château Grimaldi,** built in the 12th century by the ruling family of Monaco and extensively rebuilt in the 16th century, is reached by nearby steps. Tear yourself away from the sun-baked terrace overlooking the sea to go inside to the Picasso Museum. There are stone Roman remains on show, but the works of Picasso—who occupied the château during his most cheerful and energetic period—hold centerstage; they include an array of paintings, pottery, and lithographs inspired by the sea and Greek mythology. *Pl. du Château. Admission: 15 frs. adults, 8 frs. children and senior citizens. Open Dec.–Oct., Wed.–Mon. 10–noon and 2–6; closed Tues.*

Continue down avenue de l'Amiral Grasse to the St-André Bastion, constructed by Sébastien de Vauban in the late 17th century and home to the **Musée Archéologique.** Here 4,000 years of local history are illustrated by continually expanding displays. *Bastion St-Andre. Admission: 12 frs. adults, 6 frs. children and senior citizens. Open Dec.–Oct., Wed.–Mon. 10–noon and 2–6; closed Tues.*

Antibes officially forms one town (dubbed "Juantibes") with the more recent resort of **Juan-les-Pins** to the south, where beach- and nightlife, patronized mainly by a younger and less affluent crowd than in Cannes, rise to frenetic summer peaks.

⓮ The **Cap d'Antibes** peninsula is rich and residential, with beaches, views, and large villas hidden in luxurious vegetation. Barely two miles long by a mile wide, it offers a perfect day's outing. An ideal walk is along the **Sentier des Douaniers,** the customs officers' path.

From Pointe Bacon, there is a striking view over the Baie des Anges (Bay of Angels) toward Nice; climb up to the nearby Plateau de la Garoupe for a sweeping view inland over the Esterel massif and the Alps. The **Sanctuaire de la Garoupe** (sailors' chapel), has a 14th-century icon, a statue of Our Lady of Safe Homecoming, and numerous frescoes and votive offerings. The lighthouse alongside, which can be visited, has a powerful beam that carries over 40 miles out to sea. *Admission free. Open Nov.–Mar., daily 10:30–12:30 and 2:30–7:30; Apr.–Oct., daily 10:30–12:30 and 2–5.*

Nearby is the **Jardin Thuret,** established by botanist Gustave Thuret (1817–75) in 1856 as France's first garden for subtropical plants and trees. The garden, now run by the Ministry of Agriculture, remains a haven for rare, exotic plants. *Blvd. du Cap. Admission free. Open weekdays 8–12:30 and 2–5:30.*

At the southwest tip of the peninsula, opposite the luxurious Hôtel du Cap d'Antibes (*see* Dining and Lodging, below), is the **Musée Naval & Napoléonien,** a former battery, where you can spend an interesting hour scanning Napoleonic proclamations and viewing scale models of ocean-going ships. *Batterie du Grillon, blvd. du Maréchal-Juin. Admission: 10 frs. adults, 5 frs. children and senior citizens. Open Oct.–Apr., Wed.–Mon. 10–noon and 3–7; Dec.–Mar., Wed.–Mon. 10–noon and 2–5; closed Tues.*

Marineland, Europe's first aquatic zoo, is only a short distance from Antibes. Take N7 north and then head left at La Brague onto D4; Marineland is on the right. Performing dolphins leap into action every afternoon, abetted by a supporting cast of seals, penguins, and sea lions. There is also an amusement park. *Rue Mozart. Admission: 70 frs. adults, 48 frs. children. Open Apr.–Oct. daily 10–9; Nov.–Mar. 11–6; first performance at 2:30.*

Mimosa and roses for the cut-flower market are grown at the ⓯ charming old village of **Biot,** 4 kilometers (2½ miles) up D4. The glassworks at the edge of the village welcomes visitors to observe its glassblowers, but it is wise to call first to check opening times, which vary. *Verrerie de Biot, chemin Combes, tel. 93–65–03–00.*

Artist Fernand Léger (1881–1955) lived in Biot, and hundreds of his paintings, ceramics, and tapestries are on display at the museum here. Léger's stylistic evolution is traced from his early flirtation with Cubism to his ultimate preference for flat expanses of primary color and shades of gray, separated by

thick black lines. *Chemin du Val de Pome. Admission: 15 frs.
adults, 8 frs. senior citizens, children free. Open Apr.–Oct.,
Tues.–Sun. 10–noon and 2–7; Nov.–Mar., 10–noon and 2–6.*

Tour 2: Grasse to Menton

Our tour of the eastern Riviera begins a dozen miles inland at
Grasse. If you are coming from Cannes or Antibes, stop off en
route to admire the dramatic hilltop setting of **Mougins,** a
quaint, fortified town just north of Cannes.

If touring a perfume factory in a tacky modern town is your idea
of pleasure, by all means visit Grasse. If you had visited four
centuries ago, when the town specialized in leather work, you
would have come for gloves. In the 16th century, when scented
gloves became the rage, the town began cultivating flowers and
distilling essences. That was the beginning of the perfume industry. Today, some three-fourths of the world's essences are
made here from wild lavender, jasmine, violets, daffodils, and
other sweet-smelling flowers. Five thousand producers supply
some 20 factories and six cooperatives. If you've ever wondered
why perfume is so expensive, consider that it takes 10,000 flowers to produce 2.2 pounds of jasmine petals and that nearly
one ton of jasmine is needed—nearly 7 million flowers—to
distill 1½ quarts of essence. Sophisticated Paris perfumers
mix Grasse essences into their own secret formulas; perfumes
made and sold in Grasse are considerably less subtle. You
can, of course, buy Parisian perfumes in Grasse—at Parisian
prices.

A new perfume museum, the **Musée International de la Parfum-
erie,** was opened in early 1989, and explains the history and
manufacturing process of perfume. Old machinery, pots, and
flasks can be admired; toiletry, cosmetics, and makeup accessories are on display; and there is a section devoted to perfume's
sophisticated marketing aids, with examples of packaging and
advertising posters. *8 pl. du Cours. Admission: 10 frs. adults,
5 frs. children and senior citizens. Joint ticket for all Grasse
museums: 20 frs. adults, 10 frs. children and senior citizens.
Open Wed.–Mon. 10–6; closed Tues.*

Several perfume houses also welcome visitors for a whiff of
their products and an explanation of how they're made:
Galimard (73 rte. de Cannes, tel. 93–09–20–00); Molinard (60
blvd. Victor-Hugo, tel. 93–36–01–62); and Fragonard (20 blvd.
Fragonard, tel. 93–36–44–65), which is conveniently central
and has its own museum. All perfume houses invite you to purchase their products. *Admission to perfume houses free. Open
daily 9–noon and 2–6.*

The artist Jean-Honoré Fragonard (1732–1806) was born in
Grasse, and many of his pictures, etchings, drawings, and
sketches—plus others by his son Alexandre-Evariste and his
grandson Théophile—are hung in the 17th-century Villa Fragonard, situated close to the perfumerie of the same name. *23
blvd. Fragonard, tel. 93–36–01–61. Admission: 12 frs. adults,
6 frs. children and senior citizens. Joint ticket for all Grasse
museums: 20 frs. adults, 10 frs. children and senior citizens.
Open weekdays 10–noon and 2–5 and the first and last Sun. of
each month.*

The **Musée d'Art et d'Histoire de Provence,** around the corner on
rue Mirabeau, is in an 18th-century mansion with a collection of
Provençal furniture, folk art, tools and implements, and china.
*2 rue Mirabeau. Admission: 12 frs. adults, 6 frs. children
and senior citizens. Joint ticket for all Grasse museums: 20 frs.
adults, 10 frs. children and senior citizens. Open Apr.–Oct.,
Mon.–Sat. 10–noon and 2–6; Dec.–Mar., 10–noon and 2–5.*

From Grasse, strike east along D2085/D2210 toward Vence, 25
kilometers (16 miles) away. About 5 kilometers (3 miles) before you reach Vence is **Tourette-sur-Loup,** whose outer houses
form a rampart on a rocky plateau, 1,300 feet above a valley full
of violets. The town is much less commercialized than many
others in the area; its shops are filled not with postcards and
scented soaps but with the work of dedicated artisans. A rough
stone path takes you on a circular route around the rim of the
town, past the shops of engravers, weavers, potters, and painters. Ask any artisan for a map of the town that locates each of
the shops. Also worth visiting is a single-nave 14th-century
church that has a notable wooden altarpiece.

When you arrive in **Vence,** leave your car on avenue Foch and
climb up to the medieval town (Vielle Ville). The Romans were
the first to settle on the 1,000-foot hill; the **cathedral** (built between the 11th and 18th century), rising above the medieval
ramparts and traffic-free streets, was erected on the site of a
temple to Mars. Of special note are a mosaic by Marc Chagall of
Moses in the bullrushes and the ornate 15th-century wooden
choir stalls.

At the foot of the hill, on the outskirts of Vence, is the **Chapelle
du Rosaire,** a small chapel decorated with beguiling simplicity
and clarity by Matisse between 1947 and 1951. The walls, floor,
and ceiling are gleaming white and pierced by small stained-
glass windows in cool greens and blues. "Despite its imperfec-
tions I think it is my masterpiece . . . the result of a lifetime
devoted to the search for truth," wrote Matisse, who designed
and dedicated the chapel when he was in his eighties and nearly
blind. *Av. Henri-Matisse. Admission free. Open Tues. and
Thur. 10–11:30 and 2:30–5:30.*

A few miles south along D2 is **St-Paul-de-Vence,** a gem of a town
whose medieval atmosphere has been perfectly preserved. Not
even the hordes of tourists—for which the village now exists—
can destroy its ancient charm. You can walk the narrow, cobbled streets in perhaps 15 minutes, but you'll need another
hour to explore the shops—mostly galleries selling second-rate
landscape paintings, but also a few serious studios and
giftshops offering everything from candles to dolls, dresses,
and hand-dipped chocolate strawberries. Your best bet is to
visit in the late afternoon, when the tour buses are gone, and
enjoy a drink among the Klees and Picassos in the Colombe
D'Or (*see* Dining and Lodging, below). Be sure to visit the remarkable 12th-century Gothic church; you'll want to light a
candle to relieve its wonderful gloom. The treasury is rich in
12th–15th-century pieces, including processional crosses, reliquaries, and an enamel Virgin and Child.

At La Gardette, just northwest of the village, is the **Fondation
Maeght,** one of the world's most famous small museums of modern art. Monumental sculptures are scattered around its pine-
tree park, and a courtyard full of Alberto Giacometti's elon-

gated creations separates the two museum buildings. The rooms inside showcase the work of Joan Miró, Georges Braque, Wassily Kandinsky, Bonnard, Matisse and others. Few museums blend form and content so tastefully and imaginatively. There is also a library, cinema, and auditorium. *Admission: 35 frs. adults, 25 frs. children. Open Apr.–Oct., daily 10–12:30 and 3–7; Nov.–Mar., daily 10–12:30 and 2:30–6.*

20 Return to D2 and continue 6 kilometers (4 miles) south to **Cagnes-sur-Mer.** An attractive **château,** once a medieval fortress, is perched high above the modern seaside resort within the walls of Haut-de-Cagnes, the old town. Much of the château's Renaissance decorations—frescoes, plasterwork, and fireplaces—remains intact, and the third floor hosts an art gallery devoted to Mediterranean artists, including Chagall and Raoul Dufy. There's an exciting panorama from the top of the tower. *Pl. du Château. Admission: 5 frs. adults, 3 frs. students. Open Easter–mid-Oct., daily 10–noon and 2:30–7; mid-Nov.–Easter, Wed.–Mon. 10–noon and 2–5; closed Tues.*

The painter Auguste Renoir (1841–1919) spent the last years of his life at Cagnes. His home at Les Collettes has been preserved, and you can see his studio, as well as some of his work. A bronze statue of Venus nestles amid the fruit trees in the colorful garden. *Av. des Collettes. Admission: 5 frs. adults, 3 frs. children. Open Apr.–Oct., daily 2:30–6:30; Nov.–Mar., Wed.–Mon. 2–5.*

21 A mile west of Cagnes is the tiny village of **Villeneuve-Loubet,** worth visiting for its **Fondation Escoffier:** a gourmet shrine that can be fitted in between meals because there's nothing to eat. As kitchen overlord at the London Carlton and the Paris Ritz, Auguste Escoffier (1846–1935) carved out a reputation as Europe's top chef and invented Peach Melba. This museum, in the house where he was born, displays some elaborate pièces montées in sugar and marzipan, and boasts a lip-smacking collection of 15,000 menus. *3 rue Escoffier. Admission: 10 frs. adults, 5 frs. students. Open Dec.–Oct., Tues.–Sun. 2:15–6.*

22 The congested N7 from Cagnes to Nice is enough to put you off the Riviera for life. Tedious concrete constructions assault the eye; the railroad, on one side, and the stony shore, on the other, offer scant respite. Soon, however, you arrive at the Queen of the Riviera—**Nice.**

Nice is less glamorous, less sophisticated, and less expensive than Cannes. It's also older—weathered-old and faded-old—like a wealthy dowager who has seen better days but who still maintains a demeanor of dignity and poise. Nice is a big, sprawling city of 350,000 people—five times as many as Cannes—and has a life and vitality that survive when tourists pack their bags and go home.

Nice is worth a visit, but should you stay here? On the negative side, its beaches are cramped and pebbly. Except for the luxurious Negresco (*see* Dining and Lodging, below), most of its hotels are either rundown or being refurbished for the convention crowd. On the positive side, Nice is likely to have hotel space when all other towns are full and at prices you can afford. It's also a convenient base from which to explore Monte Carlo and the medieval towns in the interior. It does have its share of first-class restaurants and boutiques, and an evening stroll

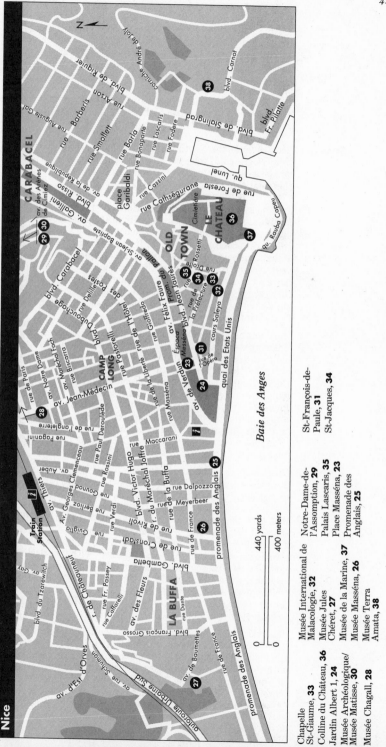

Nice

Baie des Anges

440 yards

400 meters

Chapelle
St-Giaume, **33**
Colline du Château, **36**
Jardin Albert 1, **24**
Musée Archéologique/
Musée Matisse, **30**
Musée Chagall, **28**

Musée International de
Malacologie, **32**
Musée Jules
Chéret, **27**
Musée de la Marine, **37**
Musée Masséna, **26**
Musée Terra
Amata, **38**

Notre-Dame-de-
l'Assomption, **29**
Palais Lascaris, **35**
Place Masséna, **23**
Promenade des
Anglais, **25**

St-François-de-
Paule, **34**
St-Jacques, **34**

through the old town or along the Promenade des Anglais is not easily forgotten.

We suggest you divide your visit of Nice into three minitours, with arcaded **place Masséna,** the city's main square, as a common starting point. First, head west through the fountains and gardens of the **Jardin Albert I** to the **Promenade des Anglais,** built, as the name indicates, by the English community in 1824. Traffic on this multilane highway can be heavy, but once you have crossed to the seafront, there are fine views, across private beaches, of the Baie des Anges.

Time Out Walk as far as the Neptune Plage (beach) and cross over to the **Hôtel Negresco.** If you can't afford to stay here, spend a few dollars on a cup of coffee and think of it as an admission charge to this palatial hotel. *37 Promenade des Anglais.*

Just up rue de Rivoli from the Hôtel Negresco is the **Musée Masséna,** concerned principally with the Napoleonic era and, in particular, the life of local-born general André Masséna (1756–1817), rewarded by Bonaparte for heroic exploits during the Italian campaign with the sonorous sobriquet, *l'Enfant chéri de la victoire* (the Cherished Child of Victory). Sections of the museum evoke the history of Nice and its cherished carnival; there are also some fine Renaissance paintings and objects. *67 rue de France. Admission free. Open Tues.–Sun. 10–noon and 2–5; closed 2 weeks in Nov. or Dec.*

Head left along rue de France, then turn right up avenue des Baumettes to the **Musée Jules Chéret,** Nice's fine arts museum, built in 1878 as a palatial mansion for a Russian princess. The rich collection of paintings includes works by Auguste Renoir, Edgar Degas, Claude Monet, Raoul Dufy, Oriental prints, sculptures by Auguste Rodin, and ceramics by Picasso. Jules Chéret (1836–1932) is best known for his Belle Époque posters; several of his oils, pastels, and tapestries can be admired here. *33 av. des Baumettes. Admission free. Open May–Sept., Tues. –Sun. 10–noon and 3–6; Oct. and Dec.–Apr., Tues.–Sun. 10– noon and 2–5.*

Nice's main shopping street, avenue Jean-Médecin, runs inland from place Masséna; all needs and most tastes are catered to in its big department stores (Nouvelles Galeries, Prisunic, and the split-level Etoile mall). Continue past the train station, then take the first right down to the **Musée Chagall**—built to show off the paintings of Chagall (1887–1985) in natural light. The highlight is the message of the Bible—17 huge canvases covering a period of 13 years, together with 195 prelimary sketches, several sculptures, and nearly 40 gouaches. In summertime, you can buy snacks and drinks in the garden. *Av. du Dr-Ménard. Admission: 15 frs. adults, 8 frs. children and senior citizens; free Wed. Open July–Sept., Wed.–Mon. 10–7; Oct.–July, Wed.–Mon. 10–12:30 and 2–5.30.*

Boulevard de Cimiez heads to the residential quarter of Nice— the hilltop site of **Cimiez,** occupied by the Romans 2,000 years ago. The foundations of the Roman town can be seen, along with vestiges of the arena, less spectacular than those at Arles or Nîmes but still in use (notably for a summer jazz festival). Closeby is the Franciscan monastery of **Notre-Dame-de-l'Assomption,** with some outstanding late-medieval religious pictures; guided tours include the small museum and an audio-visual show on the life and work of the Franciscans. *Admission free. Open weekdays 10–noon and 3–6.*

㉚ A 17th-century Italian villa amid the Roman remains contains two museums: the **Musée Archéologique,** with a plethora of ancient objects, and the **Musée Matisse,** with paintings and bronzes by Matisse (1869–1954), illustrating the different stages of his career. The Matisse Museum is scheduled to reopen in 1990 after a two-year renovation program. *164 av. des Arènes-de-Cimiez, tel. 93–81–59–57 or 93–53–17–70. Admission free. Open May–Sept., 10–noon and 2:30–6:30; Oct.–Apr., 10–noon and 2–5.*

The **old town** of Nice is one of the delights of the Riviera. Cars are forbidden on streets that are narrow enough for their buildings to crowd out the sky. The winding alleyways are lined with faded 17th- and 18th-century buildings, where families sell their wares. Flowers cascade from window boxes on soft pastel-colored walls. You wander down cobbled streets, proceeding with the logic of dreams, or sit in an outdoor café on a Venetian-like square, bathed in a pool of the purest, most transparent light.

㉛ To explore the old town, head south from place Masséna along rue de l'Opéra, and turn left into rue St-François-de-Paule. You'll soon come to the 18th-century church of **St-François-de-Paule,** renowned for its ornate Baroque interior and sculpted decoration.

Time Out Shop for the best crystallized fruits in Nice at **Henri Auer** and have an ice-cream and pastry in his cozy tea room. *7 rue St-François-de-Paule.*

㉜ Rue St-François-de-Paule becomes the pedestrian-only cours Saleya, with its colorful morning market selling seafood, flowers, and orange trees in tubs. Toward the far end of cours Saleya is the **Musée International de Malacologie,** with a collection of seashells from all over the world (some for sale) and a small aquarium of Mediterranean sea life. *3 cours Saleya. Admission free. Open Dec.–Oct., Tues.–Sat. 10:30–1 and 2–6.*

㉝ Next, stroll left up rue la Poissonnerie and pop into the **Chapelle St-Giaume** to admire its gleaming Baroque interior and grand altarpieces. Continue to rue de Jésus; at one end is **㉞** the church of **St-Jacques,** featuring an explosion of painted angels on the ceiling. Walk along rue Droite to the elegant **Palais Lascaris,** built in the mid-17th century and decorated with paintings and tapestries. The palace boasts a particularly grand staircase and a reconstructed 18th-century pharmacy. *15 rue Droite. Admission free. Open Dec.–Oct., Tues.–Sun. 9:30–noon and 2–6.*

㉟ Old Nice is dominated by the **Colline du Château,** a romantic cliff, fortified many centuries before Christ. The ruins of a 6th-century castle can be explored and the views from the surrounding garden admired. A small naval museum, the **Musée de la Marine,** is situated in the 16th-century tower known as the **Tour Bellanda,** with models, instruments, and documents charting the history of the port of Nice. *Rue du Château, tel. 93–80–47–61. Admission free. Open Apr.–Sept., Wed.–Mon.*

10–noon and 2–7; Oct.–Mar., Wed.–Mon. 10–noon and 2–5; closed Tues.

The elevator between Tour Bellanda and the quayside operates daily 9 until 7 in summer and 2 until 7 in winter. The back of castle hill overlooks the harbor. On the other side, along boulevard Carnot, is the **Musée Terra Amata,** containing relics of a local settlement that was active 400,000 years ago. There are recorded commentaries in English and films explaining the lifestyle of prehistoric dwellers. *25 blvd. Carnot, tel. 93–55– 59– 93. Admission free. Open Tues.–Sun. 9–noon and 2–6; closed second half Sept.*

There are three scenic roads at various heights above the coast between Nice and Monte Carlo, a distance of about 19 kilometers (12 miles). All are called "corniches"—literally, a projecting molding along the top of a building or wall. The **Basse** (lower) **Corniche** is the busiest and slowest route because it passes through all the coastal towns. The **Moyenne** (middle) **Corniche** is high enough for views and close enough for details. It passes the perched village of Eze. The **Grande** (upper) **Corniche** winds some 1,300 to 1,600 feet above the sea, offering sweeping views of the coast. The Grande Corniche follows the Via Aurelia, the great Roman military road that brought Roman legions from Italy to Gaul (France). In 1806, Napoleon rebuilt the road and sent Gallic troops into Italy. The best advice is to take the Moyenne Corniche one way and the Grande Corniche the other. The view from the upper route is best in the early morning or evening.

Boulevard Carnot becomes the popular, pretty Basse Corniche (N98), which crawls along the coast from Nice to **Villefranche-sur-Mer,** 4 kilometers (2½ miles) east. The harbor town is a miniature version of old Marseille, with steep narrow streets—one, **rue Obscure,** an actual tunnel—winding down to the sea. The town is a stage set of brightly colored houses—orange buildings with lime-green shutters, yellow buildings with ice-blue shutters—the sort of place where *Fanny* could have been filmed. If you're staying in Nice, include Villefranche on a tour of Cap Ferrat. To see the Cocteau Chapel you'll need to arrive by 4 PM. If you skip the chapel, your best bet is to come at sundown (for dinner, perhaps) and enjoy an hour's walk around the harbor, when the sun turns the soft pastels to gold.

The 17th-century **St-Michael** church has a strikingly realistic Christ, carved of boxwood by an unknown convict. The chapel of St-Pierre-des-Pêcheurs, known as the **Cocteau Chapel,** is a small Romanesque chapel once used for storing fishing nets, which the French writer and painter Jean Cocteau decorated in 1957. Visitors walk through the flames of the Apocalypse (represented by staring eyes on either side of the door) and enter a room filled with frescoes of St. Peter, gypsies, and the women of Villefranche. *Open May–Oct., daily 9–noon and 2–4:30; Nov.–Apr. 9–noon and 2:30–7.*

Beaulieu is just next door to Villefranche, a place for high society at the turn of the century. Stop and walk along the promenade, sometimes called Petite Afrique (Little Africa) because of its magnificent palm trees, to get a flavor of how things used to be.

The one thing to do in Beaulieu is visit the **Villa Kérylos**. In the early part of the century, a rich amateur archaeologist named Theodore Reinach asked an Italian architect to build him an authentic Greek house. The villa, now open to the public, is a faithful reproduction, made from cool Carrara marble, alabaster, and rare fruitwoods. The furniture, made of wood inlaid with ivory, bronze, and leather, is copied from drawings of Greek interiors found on ancient vases and mosaics. *Open July –Aug., daily 3–7; Sept.–June, Tues.–Sun. 2–6.*

41 From Beaulieu, make a detour along D25 around the lush peninsula of **St-Jean-Cap-Ferrat** and visit the 17-acre gardens and richly varied art collection of the **Musée Ephrussi de Rothschild**. The museum reflects the sensibilities of its former owner, Madame Ephrussi de Rothschild, sister of Baron Edouard de Rothschild. An insatiable collector, she lived surrounded by an eclectic but tasteful collection of Impressionist paintings, Louis XIII furniture, rare Sèvres porcelain, and objets d'art from the Far East. *Villa Ile-de-France, tel. 93–01– 33–09. Admission: 25 frs. adults, 15 frs. students, children free. Guided tours only. Open Dec.–Oct., Tues.–Sat. 10–noon and 2–6, Sun. 2–6.*

42 The perched village of **Peillon** is about 10 kilometers (6 miles) inland from Nice. Take D2204, turn right on D21, and turn right again, up the mountain. Of all the perched villages along the Riviera, Peillon is the most spectacular and the least spoiled, a fortified medieval town situated on a craggy mountaintop more than 1,000 feet above the sea. Unchanged since the Middle Ages, the village has only a few narrow streets and many steps and covered alleys. There's really nothing to do here but look—which is why the tour buses stay away. Some 50 families live in Peillon—including professionals from Paris who think it's chic summering in a genuine medieval village and artists who sincerely want to escape the craziness of the world below. Visit the **Chapel of the White Penitents** (key available at the Auberge); spend a half hour exploring the ancient streets, and be on your way back down the mountain to Nice.

Time Out   Stay for lunch or dinner at the charming **Auberge de la Madame**, a short walk from the chapel.

43 Almost every tour from Nice to Monaco includes a visit to the medieval hill town of **Eze**, perched on a rocky spur near the Middle Corniche, some 1,300 feet above the sea. (Don't confuse Eze with the beach town of **Eze-sur-Mer**, which is down by the water.) Be warned that because of its accessibility the town is also crowded and commercial: Eze has its share of serious craftspeople, but most of its vendors make their living selling perfumed soaps and postcards to the package-tour trade.

Enter through a fortified 14th-century gate and wander down narrow, cobbled streets with vaulted passageways and stairs. The church is 18th century, but the small Chapel of the White Penitents dates to 1306 and contains a 13th-century gilded wood Spanish Christ and some notable 16th-century paintings. Tourist and craft shops line the streets leading to the ruins of a castle, which has a scenic belvedere. Some of the most tasteful craft shops are in the hotel/restaurant **Chevre d'Or**.

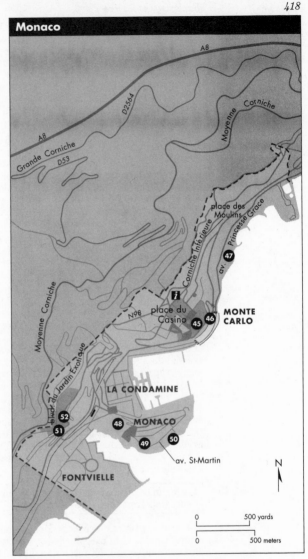

Near the top of the village is a garden with exotic flowers and cacti. It's worth the admission price, but if you've time for only one exotic garden, visit the one in Monte Carlo.

If you're not going to Grasse, the perfume capital of the world (*see* above), consider visiting a branch of a Grasse perfumerie called **La Perfumerie Fragonard,** located in front of the public gardens.

From Eze it's just a short—albeit spectacular—drive up the coast to **Monaco.** The Principality of Monaco covers just 473 acres and would fit comfortably inside New York's Central Park or a family farm in Iowa. Its 5,000 citizens would take up only a small number of seats in the Houston Astrodome. The country is so tiny that residents have to go to another country to play golf.

The present ruler, Rainier III, traces his ancestry back to Otto Canella, who was born in 1070. The Grimaldi dynasty began with Otto's great-great-great-grandson, Francesco Grimaldi, also known as Frank the Rogue. Expelled from Genoa, Frank and his cronies disguised themselves as monks and seized the fortified medieval town known today as the Rock. That was in 1297, almost 700 years ago. Except for a short break under Napoleon, the Grimaldis have been here ever since, which makes them the oldest reigning family in Europe. On the Grimaldi coat of arms are two monks holding swords (look up and you'll see them above the main door as you enter the palace).

Back in the 1850s, a Grimaldi named Charles III made a decision that turned the Rock into a giant blue chip. Needing revenues but not wanting to impose additional taxes on his subjects, he contracted with a company to open a gambling facility. The first spin of the roulette wheel was on December 14, 1856. There was no easy way to reach Monaco then—no carriage roads or railroads—so no one came. Between March 15 and March 20, 1857, one person entered the casino—and won two francs. In 1868, however, the railroad reached Monaco, filled with wheezing Englishmen who came to escape the London fog. The effects were immediate. Profits were so great that Charles eventually abolished all direct taxes.

Almost overnight, a threadbare principality became an elegant watering hole for European society. Dukes and their mistresses and duchesses and their gigolos danced and dined their way through a world of spinning roulette wheels and bubbling champagne—preening themselves for nights at the opera, where artists such as Vaslav Nijinsky, Sarah Bernhardt, and Enrico Caruso came to perform.

Monte Carlo—the modern gambling town with elegant shops, man-made beaches, high-rise hotels, and a few Belle Epoque hotels—is actually only one of four parts of Monaco. The second is the medieval town on the Rock ("Old Monaco"), 200 feet above the sea. It's here that Prince Rainier lives.

The third area is **La Condamine,** the commercial harbor area, with apartments and businesses. The fourth is **Fontveille,** the industrial district on 20 acres of reclaimed land.

Start at the Monte Carlo tourist office just north of the casino gardens (ask for the useful English booklet *Getting Around in The Principality*). The **Casino** is a must-see, even if you don't bet a cent. You may find it fun to count the Jaguars and Rolls-Royces parked outside and breathe on windows of shops selling Saint-Laurent dresses and fabulous jewels. Wandering through a world of gold-leaf splendor are gamblers looking as though they had just stumbled off the bus to Reno or Atlantic City. Beneath the gilt-edged Rococo ceiling, an army of would-be high rollers from Dubuque and Jersey City try their luck at the slot machines.

The main gambling hall, once called the European Room, has been renamed the American Room and fitted with 150 one-armed bandits from Chicago. Adjoining it is the Pink Salon, now a bar where unclad nymphs float about on the ceiling smoking cigarillos. The Salles Privé (private rooms) are for high rollers. The stakes are higher here, so the mood is more sober, and well-wishers are herded farther back from the tables.

On July 17, 1924, black came up 17 times in a row on Table 5. This was the longest run ever. A dollar left on black would have grown to $131,072. On August 7, 1913, the number 36 came up three times in a row. In those days, if a gambler went broke, the casino bought him a ticket home.

The casino opens at 10 AM and continues until the last die is thrown. Ties and jackets are required in the back rooms, which open at 4 PM. Bring your passport.

Place du Casino is the center of Monte Carlo, and it seems in the true spirit of this place that the **Opera House,** with its 18-ton gilt bronze chandelier, is part of the casino complex. The designer, Charles Garnier, also built the Paris Opera.

46 The serious gamblers, some say, play at **Loew's Casino,** nearby. It opens weekdays at 4 PM and on weekends at 1 PM. You may want to try parking here, since parking near the old casino is next to impossible in season.

From place des Moulins there is an escalator down to the Larvotto beach complex, artfully created with imported sand, and the **47 Musée Nationale,** housed in a Garnier villa within a rose garden. This museum has a beguiling collection of 18th- and 19th-century dolls and mechanical automatons, most in working order. *17 av. Princesse Grace, tel. 93-30-91-26. Admission: 22 frs. adults, 12 frs. children. Open 10–12:15 and 2:30–6:30; closed holidays.*

Prince Rainier spends much of the year in his grand Italianate **48 Palace** on the Rock. The changing of the guard takes place here each morning at 11:55, and the State Apartments can be visited in summer. *Admission: 20 frs. adults, 10 frs. children. Joint ticket with Musée Napoléon: 30 frs. adults, 15 frs. children. Open June–Oct., daily 9:30–6:30.*

One wing of the palace, open throughout the year, is taken up by a museum full of Napoleonic souvenirs and documents related to Monaco's history. *Admission: 15 frs. adults, 7 frs. children. Joint ticket with palace apartments: 30 frs. adults, 15 frs. children. Open Tues.–Sun. 9:30–6:30.*

From here, a stroll through the medieval alleyways takes you **49** past the **cathedral,** a neo-Romanesque monstrosity (1875–84), with several important paintings of the Nice school. Continue **50** to one of Monaco's most outstanding showpieces, the **Musée Océanographique**—also an important research institute headed by celebrated underwater explorer and filmmaker Jacques Cousteau. Prince Rainier's great-grandfather Albert I (1848–1922), an accomplished marine biologist, founded the institute, which now boasts two exploration ships, laboratories, and a staff of 60 scientists. Nonscientific visitors may wish to make straight for the well-arranged and generously stocked aquarium in the basement. Other floors are devoted to Prince Albert's collection of seashells and whale skeletons and to Cousteau's diving equipment. *Av. St-Martin, tel. 93-30-15-14. Admission: 45 frs. adults, 23 frs. children. Open daily, July–Aug., 9–9, Sept.–June, 9:30–7.*

Time Out Take the museum's elevator to the roof terrace for a fine view and restorative drink.

A brisk half-hour walk back past the palace brings you to the **Jardin Exotique** (Tropical Gardens), where 600 varieties of cactus and succulents cling to a sheer rock face. The **Museum of Prehistoric Anthropology**, on the grounds, contains bones, tools, and other artifacts. Shapes of the stalactites and stalagmites in the cavernous grotto seem to echo the weird forms of the cacti outside. *Blvd. du Jardin Exotique. Admission: 27.50 frs. adults, 18 frs. senior citizens, 14 frs. children. Open daily 9–7 (dusk in winter).*

Five kilometers (3 miles) northeast of Monaco is the engaging hilltop village of **Roquebrune,** with its steps and narrow streets. The adjacent **Cap-Martin** peninsula is colonized by wealthy villa dwellers. Near the tip, on avenue Winston-Churchill, is the start of a coastal path—promenade Le Corbusier—that leads hardy ramblers to Monte Carlo in 1½ hours.

Next door to Roquebrune is **Menton,** a comparatively quiet all-year resort with the warmest climate on the Riviera. Lemon trees flourish here, as do senior citizens, enticed by a long strand of public and private beaches. Menton likes to call itself the Pearl of the Riviera—beautiful, respectable, and not grossly expensive.

Walk eastward from the casino along promenade du Soleil to the harbor. There is a small 17th-century fort here, where writer, artist, and filmmaker Jean Cocteau (1889–1963) once worked. The fort now houses the **Cocteau Museum** of fantastical paintings, drawings, stage sets and a large mosaic. *Bastion du Port, 111 quai Napoléon III. Admission free. Open Apr.–Oct., Wed–Sun. 10–noon and 2–6; Nov.–Mar., Wed.–Sun. 10–noon and 3–6; closed Mon. and Tues.*

The quaint old town above the jetty has an Italian feel to it. Visit the church of **St-Michel** for its ornate Baroque interior, decorative side chapels, and altarpiece of St-Michael slaying a dragon. Concerts of chamber music are held on the delightful square outside on summer nights.

Higher still is the **Vieux Cimetière** (old cemetery), with a magnificent view of the old town and coast. Here lie Victorian foreigners—Russians, Germans, English—who hoped (in vain, as the dates on the tombstones reveal) that Menton's balmy climate would reverse the ravages of tuberculosis.

Return to the center and the pedestrian rue St-Michel, lined with boutiques and orange trees. In avenue de la République, which runs parallel, is the **Hôtel de Ville** (Town Hall). The room where civil marriage ceremonies are conducted was decorated by Cocteau with theatrically romantic frescoes. A tape in English explains their symbolic meaning. *17 rue de la République. Admission free. Open Mon.–Fri. 8:30–noon and 1:30–5:45.*

Two other places of interest lie at opposite ends of Menton. To the west is the **Palais Carnolès,** an 18th-century villa once used as a summer retreat by the princes of Monaco. The gardens are beautiful, and the collection of European paintings (13th- to 18th-century) is extensive. *3 av. Madone. Admission free. Open Wed.–Sun. 10–noon and 2–6; closed holidays.*

At the other end of Menton, above the Garavan harbor, lie the **Colombières Gardens,** where follies and statues lurk among 15 acres of hedges, yew trees, and Mediterranean flowers.

Chemin de Valleya. Admission: 15 frs. Open Feb.–Sept., daily 9–noon and 3–8 (or sunset if earlier).

The Italian frontier is just a mile away, and the first Italian town, **Ventimiglia** (Vintimille in French), 10 kilometers (6 miles) beyond.

What to See and Do with Children

Zygfolis is a 50-acre amusement park just outside Nice, where children can loop the loop on the roller coaster, whoosh down the water chutes, clop along on the back of a horse, or stuff themselves on the French versions of hot dogs, hamburgers, and Hershey bars. *Colline de Cremat, tel. 93–18–36–36. Admission: 98 frs. (inclusive of all rides and shows). Open July–Aug., daily 10–midnight; Sept.–June, daily 10–8.*

The following attractions are described in our Exploring section:

Automatons at the Musée Nationale, Monte-Carlo, Tour 2
Glassblowers at Biot, Tour 1
Marineland, near Antibes, Tour 1
Musée Océanographique (Museum of Oceanography), Monte Carlo, Tour 2

Off the Beaten Track

Consider a visit to the Italian towns of Ventimiglia and San Remo by train, bus, or car; bring your passport. **Ventimiglia** lies just 10 kilometers (6 miles) over the border and is best known for its colorful Friday flower market, which draws huge crowds (mostly French). If you decide to visit on market day, take the train or bus; there will be no place to park. The elegant town of **San Remo,** just 6 kilometers (4 miles) farther down the coast, still maintains some of the glamour of its late-19th century heyday; compare its casino with that of Monte Carlo. From October to June, you can visit Italy's most important flower market, the Mercato dei Fiori. The old town is an atmospheric warren of alleyways leading up to the piazza Castello, which features a splendid view of the old town.

Costumes, furniture, buildings, and even entire towns often evoke the Stuff of Heroes. Occasionally, so do roads—and one of the most famous roads in France is the **Route Napoléon,** taken by Napoleon Bonaparte in 1815 after his escape from imprisonment on the Mediterranean island of Elba. Napoleon landed at Golfe-Juan, near Cannes, on March 1 and forged northwest to Grasse and through dramatic, hilly countryside to Castellane, Digne, and Sisteron. In Napoleon's day, most of this "road" was little more than a winding dirt track, but now N85 allows drivers to mix history with scenery. Commemorative plaques bearing the imperial eagle stud the route, inspired by Napoleon's remark that "The eagle will fly from steeple to steeple until it reaches the towers of Notre-Dame." That prediction came true. Napoleon covered the 110 miles from the coast to Sisteron in just four days, romped north through Grenoble and Burgundy, and entered Paris in triumph on May 20.

One of the most spectacular roads in France is the **Corniche Sublime** (D71), which runs along the south side of the **Gorges du**

Verdon (Verdon River Gorge), France's answer to the Grand Canyon. To reach the gorge, take the Route Napoléon (N85) from Grasse; turn left after 43 kilometers (27 miles) along D21, which becomes D71 at Comps-sur-Artuby. This is not a road for anyone who is afraid of heights. The narrow lane—just wide enough for two cars to scrape by—snakes its way for 25 miles along the cliffside, 3,000 feet above the tiny River Verdon. At times the river disappears from view beneath the sheer rockface. At the far end of the gorge you arrive at the sparkling blue Lac de Ste-Croix.

Shopping

Clothes Cannes is one of the Riviera's top spots for chic clothing. Some of the most exclusive shops are **Chanel** (5 La Croisette); **Alexandra Scherra** (rond-Point Duboys d'Angers); **Cacharel** (16 rue des Belges); **Révillon** (45 La Croisette); and **St-Laurent** (21 rue d'Antibes). For well-cut menswear, try **Cerruti 1881** (15 rue des Serbes) and **Christian Dior** and **Francesco Smalto** (both at the Hôtel Gray Albion, 38 rue des Serbes).

Food Items Crystallized fruit is a Nice specialty; there's a terrific selection at **Henri Auer** (7 rue St-François-de-Paule). Locals and visitors alike buy olive oil by the gallon from tiny **Alziari**, just down the street at no. 14; the cans sport colorful, old-fashioned labels, and you can also pick up lots of Provençal herbs and spices. For cheese, try **l'Etable** (rue Sade) in Antibes. **Georget** (rue Allard), in St-Tropez, sells delicious handmade chocolates.

Markets St-Tropez's **place des Lices** has a clothing and antique market on Tuesday and Saturday mornings. In addition to plants, Nice's famous flower market at **cours Saleya** also features mounds of fish, shellfish, and a host of other food items; on Monday, there's a flea market at the same spot. In Cannes, a market selling everything from strings of garlic to second-hand gravy boats is held on Saturday on **allées de la Liberté**.

Sports and Fitness

La Napoule is the best place for active sportspeople. As well as facilities for boating, golf, horseback riding, and tennis, there are eight beaches with facilities for waterskiing and jet-skiing (there's a school on the plage du Sweet), and a deep-sea diving club (Club Nautique de L'Esterel) that gives lessons to anyone over age eight.

Biking Bikes can be rented from train stations at **Antibes, Cannes, Juan-les-Pins,** and **Nice.** Two especially scenic trips on fairly level ground are from Nice to the area around Cap d'Antibes and around Cap Ferrat from Cannes. Bikes are ideal at St-Tropez, since the beach is a few miles from town.

Golf There are 18-hole courses at **Cannes, La Napoule, Menton,** and **Monte Carlo** (the last is spectacularly sited on the slopes of Mont Angel).

Horseback Riding Just a couple of miles inland from Mandelieu-La Napoule on N7 is the **Poney Club** (Domaine de Barbossi); children will enjoy the small zoo, as well as the pony rides, while adults can rent horses and, if they like, receive lessons.

Water Sports If you want to get in some sailing while on the Riviera, try **Sportmer** (8 pl. Blanqui) in St-Tropez, and **Yacht Club de**

Cannes (Palm Beach Port) and **Sun Way** (Port de la Napoule) in Cannes. This is a great area for windsurfing; you can rent equipment from **La Club Nautique la Croisettes** (plage Jardin Pierre-Longue, Cannes), **Centre Nautique Municipal** (9 rue Esprit-Violet, Cannes), and **Sillages** (av. Henry-Clews, Mandelieu-La Napoule).

Beaches

If you like your beaches sandy, stick to those between St-Tropez and Antibes; most of the others are pebbly, though Menton and Monaco have imported vast tons of sand to spread around their shores. Private beaches are everywhere. You'll have to pay to use them (usually around 75 francs a day), but you get value for money—a café or restaurant, cabanas and showers, mattresses and umbrellas, and the pleasure of watching the perpetual parade of stylish swimwear and languid egos.

St-Tropez's best beaches are scattered along a three-mile stretch reached by the Routes des Plages; the most fashionable are **Moorea, Tahiti Plage,** and **Club 55.** You'll see lots of topless bathers, and some beaches allow total nudity. If you're traveling with children, try the family beaches at **Ste-Maxime** and **St-Raphaël. La Napoule** has no less than eight beaches, offering facilities for waterskiing, windsurfing, diving, and snorkeling, or you can just swim or stretch out on a lounge chair. One of Cannes's most fashionable beaches belongs to the **Carlton Hotel,** open from March to October, with a glassed-in terrace and heating to offset out-of-season chills. Nice's beaches extend along the Baie des Anges (the Bay of Angels); **Ruhl Place** is one of the most popular, with a good restaurant and facilities for waterskiing, parascending, windsurfing, and children's swimming lessons. Not to be outdone, **Neptune Place** has all that plus a sauna.

Dining and Lodging

Dining

Though prices often scale Parisian heights, the Riviera shares its cuisine with Provence, enjoying the same vegetable and fish dishes prepared with vivid seasonings. The most famous is *bouillabaisse,* a fish stew from around Marseille. Genuine *bouillabaisse* combines *racasse* (scorpion fish), eel, and half a dozen other types of seafood; crab and lobster are optional. Local fish is scarce, however, so dishes like *loup flambé* (sea bass with fennel and anise liqueur), braised tuna, and even fresh sardines are priced accordingly.

With Italy so close, it's no surprise that many menus feature specials like ravioli and potato gnocchi. Try vegetable *soupe au pistou,* an aromatic brew seasoned with basil, garlic, olive oil, and Parmesan cheese; or *pissaladière,* a pastry-based version of pizza, topped with tomato, olives, anchovy, and plenty of onion. Nice claims its own specialties: *pan bagna* (salad in a bun) and *poulpe à la niçoise* (octopus in a tomato sauce). Of the various vegetable dishes, the best is *ratatouille,* a stew of tomatoes, onion, eggplant, and zucchini.

Anise-flavored *pastis* is the Riviera's number one drink.

Highly recommended restaurants are indicated by a star ★.

Lodging

Hotels on the Riviera can push opulence to the sublime—or the ridiculous. Pastel colors, gilt, and plush are the decorators' staple tools in the resort hotels catering to *le beau monde*. The glamour comes hand in hand with hefty price tags, however, and while inexpensive hotels do exist, they're found mainly on the duller outskirts of the big centers and in less fashionable "family" resorts.

Highly recommended hotels are indicated by a star ★.

Antibes
Juan-les-Pins
Dining
★

Bacon. This is the Riviera's top spot for *bouillabaisse* or any other dish that depends on prime fish, simply and perfectly cooked. The Sordello brothers have run Bacon for over 40 years and don't regard a fish as fresh unless it's still twitching—count on eating only the pick of the local catch. Eat outside on the airy terrace overlooking the port. *Blvd. de Bacon, Cap d'Antibes, tel. 93–61–50–02. Reservations essential. Jacket and tie required. AE, DC, MC, V. Closed Sun. dinner, Mon., and mid-Nov.–Jan. Expensive.*

La Bonne Auberge. Chef Jo Rostange and his son Philippe rarely disappoint, with specialties like lobster ravioli, salads of red mullet, and airy soufflés. The dining room is a flower-filled haven of exposed beams, dim lantern-lighting, and rose-colored walls; huge glass windows allow diners a view of the inspired work going on in the kitchen. *Quartier de la Brague, Antibes, tel. 93–33–36–65. Reservations strongly advised. Jacket and tie required. AE, MC, V. Closed Mon. (except for dinner mid-Apr.–Sept.), and mid-Nov.–mid-Dec. Expensive.*

Auberge de l'Esterel. The affable Plumail brothers run the best moderately priced restaurant in Juan-les-Pins, lending a nouvelle twist to local dishes; try the monkfish, and, for dessert, the lemon tart. The secluded garden is a romantic setting for dinner under the stars. There are 15 bedrooms in the small attached hotel. *21 rue des Iles, Juan-les-Pins, tel. 93–61–86–55. Reservations advised. Dress: elegant casual. No credit cards. Closed mid-Nov.–mid-Dec., part of Feb., Sun. dinner, and Mon. Moderate.*

Dining and Lodging

Hôtel du Cap d'Antibes. Crystal chandeliers, gilt mirrors, gleaming antique furniture, and lots of marble make the Cap d'Antibes a glorious testimony to the opulence of another age. Guest rooms are enormous and feature the same impressive decor as the public rooms. The glass-fronted Pavillon Eden Roc is the place for lobster thermidor, washed down with vintage champagne. *Blvd. Kennedy, 06600 Antibes, tel. 93–61–39–01. 130 rooms with bath. Facilities: restaurant, tennis, pool. Closed Nov.–Apr. No credit cards. Very Expensive.*

Juana. This luxuriously renovated '30s hotel sits opposite the casino, just a couple of blocks from the beach. Towering pine trees overhang the grounds and the white marble pool. The restaurant, La Terrasse, is one of the best on the Côte d'Azur; chef Christian Morisset wins praise for his fine seafood creations. Eat outside on the terrace, overlooking the palm trees in the landscaped garden. All the guest rooms are large and individually decorated. *Av. Gallice, 06160 Juan-les-Pins, tel. 93–61–*

08–70. 45 rooms with bath. Facilities: restaurant, bar, pool. No credit cards. Closed late Oct.–mid-Apr. Very Expensive.

Le Mas Djoliba. There are only 14 rooms at this converted Provençal farmhouse, all with a country-house feel. The salon features an airy bamboo-shoot motif, while the guest rooms are painted in a range of pastel shades and feature antique furnishings. Choose between views of the park or the sea. The restaurant is open for dinner only. *29 av. de Provence, 06600 Antibes, tel. 93–34–02–48. 14 rooms with bath. Facilities: restaurant, garden, pool. AE, DC, MC, V. Closed Jan.; restaurant closed Oct.–Mar. Moderate.*

Cannes
Dining

Villa Dionysos. Thanks to chef Claude Verger's culinary talents, an exceptionally accommodating staff, and the dining room's tongue-in-cheek Italianate decor, Villa Dionysos has forged a substantial reputation in the few years since it opened. Dine in the 18th-century Venetian-style dining room or outside on the spectacular terrace. Try the fillet of duck with tarragon sauce or the roast pigeon. *7 rue Marceau, tel. 93–38–79–73. Reservations advised. Dress: casual chic. AE, MC, V. Moderate–Expensive.*

★ **La Mère Besson.** Mix with the locals at this boisterous family eatery that features a range of authentic Provençal fare. Go on Friday for the *aïoli*, a heaped platter of fish, seafood, and boiled vegetables in a thick garlic mayonnaise. Decor borders on the frumpy, but the food is what counts here. *13 rue des Frères-Pradignac, tel. 93–39–59–24. Reservations advised. Dress: casual. AE, MC, V. Closed Sun.; dinner only, July–Aug. Moderate.*

Au Bec Fin. A devoted band of regulars will attest to the quality of this family-run restaurant near the train station. Don't look for a carefully staged decor: It's the spirited local clientele and the homey food that appeal at this cheerful bistro. The fixed-price menus are fantastic value at 69 or 87 francs; try the fish cooked with fennel or the *salade niçoise*. *12 rue du 24-Août, tel. 93–38–35–86. Reservations advised. Dress: casual. AE, DC, MC, V. Closed Sat. dinner, Sun., and Christmas–late Jan. Inexpensive.*

Lodging
★ **Le Fouquets.** If you're looking for a central and comfortable base from which to explore the beach, the shops, the bistros, and the nightclubs, this is the place, located in a quiet, residential area of town. The hotel ambience is welcoming right from the entrance, with its brightly lit archway, plants, and mirrors, to the rooms, decorated in warm shades and decked out with lots of French flounces. All the guest rooms are large and feature covered loggias. There's no restaurant. *2 rond-point Duboys-d'Angiers, 06400, tel. 93–38–75–81. 10 rooms with bath. AE, DC, MC, V. Closed Nov.–Dec. Expensive.*

Mondial. A three-minute walk from the beach takes you to this six-story hotel, a haven for the traveler seeking solid, unpretentious lodging in a town that leans more to tinsel. Many guest rooms offer sea views. There's no restaurant. *77 rue d'Antibes, 06400, tel. 93–68–70–00. No credit cards. Closed Nov. Moderate.*

Roches Fleuries. Escape from the crowds at this pistachio-hued '30s villa, perched on a hillside high above town in the Le Suquet district. Guest rooms are small and unexciting, but the friendly welcome from the English-speaking proprietors and the vine-draped garden are definite pluses. There's no restaurant. *92 rue Georges-Clemenceau, 06400, tel. 93–39–28–78. 24* *rooms, 15 with bath. No credit cards. Closed mid-Nov.–Dec. Inexpensive.*

Dining and Lodging
★

Carlton. Cannes's most elegantly old-fashioned hotel is the gleaming white Carlton, built at the turn of the century right on the seafront. The opulent public rooms feature marble floors, chandeliers, floral bouquets, and glittering mirrors. All the guest rooms are spacious and supremely comfortable, but those in the west wing are best; they're quieter and have terrific views. There are two restaurants: La Côte serves haute cuisine in an imposingly formal atmosphere; the Grill Room is simpler but still impressive. The bar is one of *the* places to mingle with the Riviera's Beautiful People. *58 La Croisette, 06400, tel. 93–68–91–68. 325 rooms with bath. Facilities: restaurants, bar, terrace, private beach. Main restaurant closed Nov.–Christmas. AE, DC, MC, V. Very Expensive.*

Gray d'Albion. This striking contemporary hotel is the last word in state-of-the-art luxury. Its white facade is austere; inside, the atmosphere is ultrasophisticated, with gray and cream walls, and plenty of leather, metal, and mirrors. Guest rooms are fitted out with slick, modern accessories. There's a number of restaurants; the Royal Gray is one of Cannes's most fashionable. *38 rue des Serbes, 06400, tel. 93–68–54–54. 174 rooms with bath. Facilities: 3 restaurants, disco, private beach. AE, DC, MC, V. Restaurant closed Feb., Sun., and Mon. (open Mon. dinner July–Aug.). Very Expensive.*

Martinez. While many of the luxury palace-hotels that cosseted kings and heads of state have receded into history, the Martinez still manages to retain that sybaritic atmosphere of indulgence, despite the fact it wasn't built until the 1920s, a little late for classic status. The Concorde group bought it in 1982 and revamped it in '30s style, while a gentle renovation in 1989 redid 100 bedrooms in cool blue and salmon shades, with wooden furniture and large marble bathrooms. One of the hotel's biggest assets is the Palme d'Or restaurant, whose chef, Christian Willer, draws lavish praise for his choice line of modern cuisine. *73 La Croisette, 06400, tel. 93–94–30–30. 425 rooms with bath. Facilities: restaurants, tennis, pool, beach, bar. Restaurants closed mid-Nov.–Dec., Feb., and Mon. and Tues. lunch. Very Expensive.*

Eze
Dining and Lodging
★

Château de la Chèvre d'Or. Located above Monte Carlo in the medieval hilltop village of Eze, the Chévre d'Or is comprised of a number of ancient houses whose mellow stone walls are set off by terracotta pots brimming with geraniums. The guest rooms, while small, are individually decorated and feature antique furnishings and attractive fabrics and wallpapers; ask for room number 9. The views of Cap Ferrat from the poolside terrace are sensational. The restaurant is dignified, a far cry from some of the Riviera's flashier dining rooms; try the grilled mullet. *Rue du Barry, 06360, tel. 93–41–12–12. 15 rooms with bath. Facilities: restaurant, café, bar, terrace, pool. AE, DC, MC, V. Closed Dec.–Feb. Very Expensive.*

Menton
Dining

Les Arches. Dynamic British expatriate Diana Archer runs this lively bistro on quai Bonaparte; don't be surprised to hear her warbling jazz classics between courses. Diners can choose from a wide variety of Provençal dishes, with a few English favorites tacked on for homesick Britons (try the lemon meringue pie). *31 quai Bonaparte, tel. 95–35–94–64. Reservations advised. Dress: casual. V. Closed Wed., Nov. Inexpensive.*

Dining and Lodging **Auberge de Santons.** Sea views and a peaceful setting on a hill near l'Annonciade Monastery are the lures of this tiny hotel. The spacious white villa was under renovation at press time, but apartments for longer stays should be completed soon. The British owners have studied the art of Oriental cooking, so restaurant specials range from a traditional Chinese banquet to mince pie to Provençal dishes. *Colline de l'Annonciade, 06500, tel. 93–35–94–10. 9 rooms with bath. Facilities: restaurant. AE, MC, V. Moderate.*

Monte Carlo **Port.** Harbor views from the terrace and top-notch Italian food
Dining make the Port a good choice. A large, varied menu includes shrimp, pastas, lasagna, fettucine, fish risotto, and veal with ham and cheese. *Quai Albert 1er, tel. 93–50–77–21. Reservations advised. Dress: casual. AE, DC, MC, V. Closed Mon. and Nov. Moderate.*

★ **Polpetta.** This popular little trattoria is close enough to the Italian border to pass for the real McCoy and is excellent value for money. If it's on the menu, go for the vegetable *soupe au pistou. Rue Paradis, tel. 93–50–67–84. Reservations essential in summer. Dress: casual. V. Closed Thurs.–Sun. and Feb. Inexpensive.*

Lodging **Alexandra.** Shades of the Belle Epoque linger on in this comfortable hotel's spacious lobby and airy guest rooms. Tan and rose colors dominate the newer rooms. If you're willing to do without a private bath, this place sneaks into the Inexpensive category. The friendly proprietress, Madame Larouquie, makes foreign visitors feel right at home. *35 blvd. Princesse-Charlotte, 98000, tel. 93–50–63–13. 55 rooms, 46 with bath. AE, DC, MC, V. Moderate.*

Dining and Lodging **Hôtel de Paris.** Though discreetly modernized, the Hôtel de
★ Paris still exudes the gold-plated splendor of an era in which kings and granddukes stayed here. The restaurant, The Louis XV, stuns you with such royal decor you might not notice the food; but make the effort, since Alain Ducasse is one of Europe's most celebrated chefs. Try his ravioli de foie gras. *Pl. du Casino, 98000, tel. 93–50–80–80. 255 rooms with bath. Restaurant closed Tues., Wed. (except dinner July–Aug.), and Nov.–Dec. Very Expensive.*

Loews. Big, brash, and more than a touch vulgar, Loews has a plush extravagance on a scale Donald Trump would envy. Fountains splash, contemporary rooms are decorated in ice-cream shades, and celebrities mix with sheikhs in the bars, casino, and restaurants. Die-hard football fans can watch the Super Bowl by satellite; those in search of live entertainment should head for the Folie Russe, boasting lines of scantily clad showgirls and mountains of caviar. *12 av. des Spelugues, 98000, tel. 93–50–65–00. 582 rooms with bath. Facilities: restaurants, pool, health spa, casino, Jacuzzi. AE, DC, MC, V. Expensive–Very Expensive.*

Mougins **Moulin de Mougins.** A 16th-century olive mill houses one of the
Dining and Lodging country's top 20 restaurants. Chef Roger Vergé has an ever-
★ changing repertoire, and creates new dishes every season. Some capitalize on traditional regional cuisine, others are innovative concoctions using lobster, caviar, and other ingredients that many crave but few can afford. The intimate beamed dining rooms, with oil paintings, plants, and porcelain tableware, are the perfect setting for world-class fare. Dine outside in summer, under the awnings. There are five elegantly rustic

guest rooms as well. *Notre-Dame-de-Vie, 06250, tel. 93–75–78–24. Reservations required. Jacket and tie required. AE, DC, MC, V. Closed Feb.–Mar., Mon. (except summer), and Thurs. lunch (times are variable). Very Expensive.*

La Napoule
Lodging

Le Domaine d'Olival. There's not the slightest hint of mass production at this charming hotel, whose rooms have been individually designed by the architect-owner. It's small, so make reservations long ahead. All the guest rooms are air-conditioned and have balconies, as well as tiny kitchens. Some suites sleep six, which brings the price per couple down to Moderate. *778 av. de la Mer, 06210, tel. 93–49–31–00. 18 rooms with bath. AE, DC, MC, V. Closed Nov.–mid-Jan. Expensive.*

Dining and Lodging

Loews. Weighing in at just under 200 rooms, this is a pocket edition of the Loews at Monte Carlo, with plenty of marble, plush, and gilt. Guest rooms have sea views and balconies and are decorated in pink and blue, with blond wooden furniture and large bathrooms. Diners at the moderately priced restaurant, Chez Loulou, can gaze out over a flood-lit swimming pool and deliberate between textbook delicacies like caviar, lobster, and vintage champagne; try the grilled fish. *Blvd. Henry-Clews, 06210, tel. 93–49–90–00. 186 rooms with bath. Facilities: pool, casino, restaurants, cabaret, bars, shops, bank, travel agency, tennis. AE, DC, MC, V. Very Expensive.*

Nice
Dining
★

Ane Rouge. The Vidalots run a tight ship. Their tiny restaurant, perched right by the harbor, is always crowded and has been famous for generations as the place to go to for Nice's best fish and seafood. The best bets are the sea bass braised in champagne and the stuffed mussels. *7 quai des Deux-Emmanuel, tel. 93–89–49–63. Reservations advised. Dress: elegant casual. AE, DC, MC, V. Closed Sat., Sun., and mid-July–Sept. Expensive.*

Barale. This is one of Nice's most fashionable restaurants, and eating here is almost like attending a theatrical performance. The tempestuous proprietress and chef, Helen Barale, displays her varied menu on a blackboard hanging in the extraordinary dining room, a warehouse of artifacts and unusual odds and ends. The food blends elements of French cuisine with Italian; try the salade niçoise or the stuffed poached veal. Madame Barale often makes appearances in the dining room and is known to sing to her guests. It sounds a bit hokey, and sometimes half the diners are Japanese, but go in the right mood and you may love it. *39 Beaumont, tel. 93–89–17–94. Reservations essential. Dress: elegant casual. No credit cards. Closed Sun., Mon., and Aug. Moderate.*

★ **La Mérenda.** This noisy bistro lies in the heart of the old town, and its down-to-earth Italo-Provençal food is tremendously good value. The Giustis, who run it, refuse to install a telephone, so go early to be sure of getting a table. House specials include pasta with *pistou* (a garlic-and-basil sauce) and succulent tripe. *4 rue de la Terrasse. Reservations not accepted. Dress: casual. No credit cards. Closed Sat. dinner, Sun., Mon., Feb., and Aug. Inexpensive.*

Lodging

Little Palace. Monsieur and Madame Loridan run the closest thing to a country-house hotel in Nice. The old-fashioned decor, the jumble of bric-a-brac, and the heavy wooden furniture lend an old-world air; some may say it's like stepping onto a film set. *9 av. Baquis, 06000, tel. 93–88–70–49. 36 rooms, 31 with bath. MC, V. Closed Nov. Inexpensive.*

Dining and Lodging

Elysée Palace. This glass-fronted addition to the Nice hotel scene lies close to the seafront; all guest rooms feature views of the Mediterranean. The interior is spacious and ultra-modern, with plenty of marble in evidence. The large restaurant is a sound bet for nouvelle cuisine, enjoyed amid surroundings of contemporary works of art. *59 Promenade des Anglais, 06000, tel. 93–86–06–06. 150 rooms with bath. Facilities: restaurant, pool, sauna, health club, bar, AE, DC, MC, V. Very Expensive.*

★ **Negresco.** Henri Negresco wanted to out-Ritz all the Ritzes when he built this place. There were eight kings at the opening ceremony in 1912, grouped on the 560,000-franc gold Aubusson carpet (the world's largest, naturally) beneath the one-ton crystal chandelier in the great oval salon. No two rooms are the same (except for the bathroom fittings), though all feature antique furniture and individual decor, inspired by various periods from the 16th through the 19th century. New chef Dominique le Stanc forged a name for himself in Monte Carlo and should cement the Chantecler restaurant's reputation as one of France's finest dining rooms. *37 Promenade des Anglais, 06000, tel. 93–88–39–51. 130 rooms with bath. Facilities: 2 restaurants, bar, private beach. Very Expensive.*

★ **Beau Rivage.** Occupying an imposing late-19th-century town house near the cours Saleya, the Beau Rivage is run by the same hotel group (Clef d'Or) as the Elysée Palace (*see* above). While rooms are decorated in a similar modern style, the overall effect is more intimate and personal. Renowned chef Roger Vergé oversees a catering school on the premises; his nouvelle touch can be appreciated in the hotel's fine restaurant. *24 rue St-François-de-Paule, 06000, tel. 93–80–80–70. 110 rooms with bath. Facilities: restaurant, private beach. AE, DC, MC, V. Expensive–Very Expensive.*

St-Paul-de-Vence
Dining and Lodging
★

Colombe d'Or. Anyone who likes the ambience of a country inn will feel right at home here. You'll be paying for your room or meal with cash or credit cards; Picasso, Klee, Dufy, Utrillo—all friends of the former owner—paid with the paintings that now decorate the walls. The restaurant has a very good reputation. The Colombe d'Or is certainly on the tourist trail, but many of the tourists who stay here are rich and famous—if that's any consolation. *06570 St-Paul-de-Vence, tel. 93–32–80–02. 15 rooms with bath. Facilities: restaurant, pool. AE, DC, MC, V. Closed mid-Nov.–late Dec., part of Jan. Expensive.*

St-Tropez
Dining

Bistrot des Lices. You'll find a mix of celebrities and locals at this popular bistro, a hot spot for interesting food, served by a staff as fashionable as the clientele. Bronzed men and glamorous women lounge in the garden or eat inside in the pastel interior. The barman is renowned for his way with a cocktail shaker, high praise in a town where cocktails are a way of life. *3 pl. Carnot, tel. 94–97–29–00. Reservations advised. Dress: elegant casual. DC, V. Closed for lunch July–Aug.; closed Wed. out of season. Moderate.*

Le Girelier. Fish enthusiasts—especially those with a taste for garlic—will enjoy the hearty, heavily spiced dishes at this bustling restaurant, located right on the quai. The fish soup and the giant shrimp are local favorites. *Quai Jean-Jaurès, tel. 94–97–03–87. Reservations not required. Dress: casual. AE, DC, MC, V. Closed mid-Jan.–early Mar. Moderate.*

Lodging **Ermitage.** This is the ideal town hotel, featuring an old-fashioned charm rarely found in modern-day St-Tropez. The guest rooms' white walls are offset by coordinated patterns of strong primary colors on the beds and at the windows. There's no restaurant. *Av. Paul-Signac, 83990, tel. 94–97–52–33. 27 rooms with bath. AE, DC. Moderate.*

Dining and Lodging **Byblos.** The Byblos is the Côte d'Azur's sophisticated answer to Disneyland. Designed with ingenuity, taste, and humor, the complex resembles a Provençal village, with cottagelike suites grouped around courtyards paved with Picasso-inspired tiles and shaded by olive trees and magnolias. Inside, the atmosphere is distinctly New York Casbah, with lots of heavy damask and hammered brass, a leopard-skin bar, and Persian carpets on the dining room ceiling. If you can't afford to stay here, at least go to use the pool (for a steep fee). The restaurant, Le Chabichou, is lucky to have the talented Michel Rochedy as chef; his grilled sardines are memorable. *Av. Paul Signac, 83990, tel. 94–97–00–04. 97 rooms with bath. Facilities: restaurants, pool, nightclub. AE, DC, MC, V. Closed Nov.–Feb.; restaurant closed early Oct.–early May. Very Expensive.*

Le Mas de Chastelas. In an old farmhouse that was once a silkwood farm, guests can enjoy a happy marriage of traditional and modern surroundings. The pink-toned facade, offset by white shutters, is half-hidden behind trees and flowering shrubbery. Inside, white walls, modern furniture, and sculptures by the owner's sister combine to create a cool retreat from the blazing Mediterranean sun. The restaurant is usually filled with a congenial melange of celebrities and well-heeled travelers, the whole show being held together by the friendly personality of the owner, Gérard Racine. *Rte. de Gassin, 83990, tel. 94–56–09–11. 31 rooms with bath. Facilities: restaurant, pool. AE, DC, MC, V. Closed Oct.–Mar. Very Expensive.*

Vence **Château St-Martin.** The secluded, elite St-Martin stands on the
Dining and Lodging site of a crusader castle, surrounded by tall, shady trees and
★ set within spacious grounds. Guest rooms are exquisitely decorated with antiques, needlepoint, and brocade; those in the tower are smaller and less expensive, but feature the same loving attention to detail. There's an excellent restaurant serving Provençal-inspired dishes. *Rte. de Coursegoules, 06140, tel. 93–58–02–02. 25 rooms with bath. Facilities: restaurant, garden, pool, tennis, helicopter landing pad. AE, DC, MC, V. Very Expensive.*

Le Roseraie. While there's no rose garden here, a giant magnolia spreads its venerable branches over the terrace. Chef Maurice Ganier hails from the southwest, as do the ducks that form the basis of his cooking. Polished service and sophisticated menus prove you don't have to be rich to enjoy life in this part of France. There are 12 guest rooms and a swimming pool. *Av. Henri-Giraud, 06140, tel. 93–58–02–20. 12 rooms with bath. Facilities: restaurant, pool. AE, MC, V. Closed Jan.; restaurant closed Tues. and Wed. in low season. Moderate.*

The Arts and Nightlife

The Arts

Festivals
The Riviera's cultural calendar is splashy and star studded, and never more so than during the region's world-famous festivals. The biggest and most celebrated is the **Cannes Film Festival** in May, rivaled by Monte Carlo's arts festival, **Printemps des Arts** (late March through late April). Antibes and Nice both host **jazz festivals** during July, drawing international performers. Menton has a **chamber music festival** in August and a **September music festival** at the Palais d'Europe.

Music and Ballet
Monte Carlo's primary venue for jazz and rock is **Le Chapiteau de Font Vielle** (tel. 93–25–18–68); the **Salle Garnier** (Casino de Monaco, tel. 93–50–76–54) offers both classical music and ballet, as does Nice's **L'Acropolis** (Palais des Arts et de Congrès de Tourisme, Esplanade de Lottre de Tassigny, tel. 93–32–82–82). St-Tropez's major concert hall is the **Salle de la Renaissance** (pl. des Lices, tel. 94–97–48–16). There are frequent jazz and pop concerts at Nice's **Théâtre de Verdure** (Jardins Albert 1er, tel. 93–82–38–68), which relocate to the **Arènes de Cimiez** during summer months.

Opera
The Nice **Opéra** (4 rue St-François-de-Paul, tel. 93–85–67–31) has a season extending from September to June. In Monte Carlo, the **Salle Garnier** (*see* above) hosts operatic performances, most frequently during the spring arts festival.

Theater
A good café-theater in Nice is **Théâtre 12** (12 av. St-Jean-Baptiste, tel. 93–85–40–28). In Monte Carlo, the **Théâtre Princesse Grace** (av. d'Ostende, tel. 93–25–32–27) stages a number of plays during the spring festival; off-season, there's usually a new show each week.

Nightlife

There's no need to go to bed before dawn in any of the Riviera's major resorts, the most fashionable of which are St-Tropez, Cannes, Juan-les-Pins, Nice, and Monte Carlo. Juan-les-Pins draws a young crowd, St-Tropez has gay appeal, while clubs in Cannes, Nice, and Monte Carlo are more expensive and sophisticated. Note that to get into many of the Riviera's nightspots, you'll have to dress the part—or risk being brushed aside by the burly doormen.

Discos and Nightclubs
La Siesta (rte. du Bord de Mer, Antibes) is an enormous setup, with seven dance floors, roulette, bars, and supper places—all dramatically lit by torches; it's open summer season only. The top spot in Cannes is the **Studio-Circus** (blvd. de la République), which admits celebrities, stars, and starlets but not necessarily everyone else. The cabaret shows are legendary, accompanied by lasers and deafening noise. Top-class cabaret is offered at Menton's **Club 06**, at the casino (Promenade de Soleil). In Monte Carlo, head to **Jimmy'z**; it operates from place du Casino from September to June, then moves to premises on avenue Princesse-Grace. The location may be different, but the disco remains expensive and chic, and the clientele is drawn from the elite. The **Navy Club** (plage du Larvotto) is a friendly place whose devotees dance from 11:30 PM to dawn all year (closed Mon.). In the avenue des Spelugues, you'll find **The Living Room**

(at no. 7) and **Tiffany's** (at no. 3); both are popular, crowded, and open year-round. **The Camargue** (6 pl. Charles-Felix, on the cours Saleya) is Nice's trendiest spot, but you'll have to dress sharp to get past the doorman. If you don't make it, try the **Escurial** (29 rue Alphonse-Kerr), a large disco with elaborate lighting effects and the occasional live show. The hottest place in St-Tropez is **Les Caves du Roy** (Byblos Hotel, av. Signac); the decor is stunningly vulgar, but the tres chic clientele don't seem to mind. It's large but always crowded, so look your best if you want to get in.

Casinos There are casinos in **Cannes** (pl. Franklin-Roosevelt), **Nice** (Promenade des Anglais), and **Menton** (Promenade de Soleil), but the Riviera's most famous gambling venue is at **Monte Carlo** (pl. du Casino).

15 Provence

Introduction

As you approach Provence, there is a magical moment when the north is finally left behind: Cypresses and red-tiled roofs appear; you hear the screech of the cicadas and catch the scent of wild thyme and lavender. Even on the modern autoroute, oleanders flower on the central strip against a backdrop of harsh, brightly lit landscapes that inspired the paintings of Paul Cézanne and Vincent Van Gogh.

Provence lies in the south of France, bordered by Italy to the east and the blue waters of the Mediterranean. The Romans called it Provincia—The Province—for it was the first part of Gaul they occupied. Roman remains litter the ground in well-preserved profusion. The theater and triumphal arch at Orange, the amphitheater at Nîmes, the aqueduct at Pont-du-Gard, and the mausoleum at St-Rémy-de-Provence are considered the best of their kind in existence.

Provençal life continues at an old-fashioned pace. Hot afternoons tend to mean siestas, with signs of life discernible only as the shadows under the *platanes* (plane trees) start to lengthen and lethargic locals saunter out to play *boules* (the French version of bocce) and drink long, cooling *pastis*, an anise-based aperitif.

Provence means dazzling light and rugged, rocky countryside, interspersed with vineyards, fields of lavender, and olive groves. Any Provençal market provides a glimpse of the bewildering variety of olives and herbs cultivated, and the local cuisine is pungently spiced with thyme, rosemary, basil, and garlic.

The famous *mistral*—a fierce, cold wind that races through the Rhone Valley—is another feature of Provence. It's claimed that the extensive network of expressways has lessened the mistral's effect, but you may have trouble believing this as the wind whistles around your ears. Thankfully, clear blue skies usually follow in its wake.

The Rhône, the great river of southern France, splits in two at Arles, 15 miles before reaching the Mediterranean: The Petit Rhône crosses the region known as the Camargue on its way to Saintes-Maries-de-la-Mer, while the Grand Rhône heads off to Fos, an industrial port just along the coast from Marseille.

A number of important towns have grown up along the Rhône Valley owing to its historical importance as a communications artery. The biggest is dowdy, bustling Marseille, though Orange, Avignon, Tarascon, and Arles have more picturesque charm. The Camargue, on the other hand, is the realm of birds and beasts; pink flamingoes and wild horses feel more at home among its marshy wastes than people ever could.

North of Marseille lies Aix-en-Provence, whose old-time elegance reflects its former role as regional capital. We have extended Provence's traditional boundaries westward slightly into Languedoc, to include historic Nîmes and the dynamic university town of Montpellier. The Riviera, meanwhile, is part of Provence—but so full of interest that we devote an entire chapter to it.

Essential Information

Important Addresses and Numbers

Tourist Information   Provence's two regional tourist offices accept written enquiries only. **Comité Régional du Tourisme du Languedoc-Roussillon** (20 rue de la République, 34000 Montpellier, tel. 67–92–67–92) will advise on all towns west of the River Rhône, while the remainder of towns covered in this chapter are handled by the **Comité Régional du Tourisme de Provence–Alpes–Côte d'Azur** (Immeuble C.M.C.E., 2 rue Henri-Barbusse, 13241 Marseille, tel. 91–08–62–90).

Local tourist offices for major towns covered in this chapter are as follows: **Aix-en-Provence** (pl. du Général-de-Gaulle, tel. 42–26–02–93), **Arles** (35 pl. de la République, tel. 90–93–49–11), **Avignon** (41 cours Jean-Jaurès, tel. 90–82–65–11), **Marseille** (4 Canebière, tel. 91–54–91–11), **Montpellier** (6 rue Maguelone, tel. 67–58–26–04), **Nîmes** (6 rue Auguste, tel. 66–67–29–11), and **Toulon** (8 av. Colbert, tel. 94–22–08–22).

Travel Agencies   **Thomas Cook** (10 rue Portail Boquier, Avignon, tel. 90–82–20–56; 67 Canabière, Marseille, tel. 91–90–12–46; Midi-Libre Voyages, 20 blvd. de l'Amiral-Courbet, Nîmes, tel. 66–67–45–34) and **Wagons-Lits** (2 pl. Jeanne d'Arc, Aix-en-Provence, tel. 42–27–86–35).

Car Rental   **Avis** (11 cours Gambetta, Aix-en-Provence, tel. 42–21–64–16; 267 blvd. National, Marseille, tel. 91–50–70–11 and 92 blvd. Rabatau, Marseille, tel. 91–80–12–00), **Europcar** (2 bis av. Victor-Hugo, Arles, tel. 90–93–23–24, and 27 av. St-Ruf, Avignon, tel. 90–82–49–85), and **Hertz** (Parking des Gares, rue Jules-Ferry, Montpellier, tel. 67–65–16–45; 39 blvd. Gambetta, Nîmes, tel. 66–76–25–91).

Arriving and Departing

By Plane   The airports at Marseille and Montpellier are served by frequent flights from Paris and London, and there are daily flights from Paris to the smaller airport at Nîmes. Nice (*see* Chapter 14) is only 160 kilometers (100 miles) from Aix-en-Provence, and there are flights direct from the United States. If you are going to rent a car on arrival, the airports of Marseille and Montpellier are equally easy to get away from without driving into either town.

By Car   The A6/A7 expressway (toll road) from Paris is known as the Autoroute du Soleil—the Expressway of the Sun—and takes you straight to Provence, whereupon it divides at Orange.

By Train   Avignon is less than four hours from Paris by high-speed train (TGV); trains depart from Paris's Gare de Lyon station.

Getting Around

By Car   After the A7 divides at Orange, the A9 heads west to Nîmes and Montpellier (765 kilometers/475 miles from Paris), extending into the Pyrenees and across the Spanish border. A7 continues southeast from Orange to Marseille on the coast (1,100 kilometers/680 miles from Paris), while A8 goes to Aix-en-Provence (with a spur to Toulon), and then to the Riviera and Italy.

By Train After the main line divides at Avignon, the westbound link heads to Nîmes, Montpellier (fewer than five hours from Paris by TGV), and points west. The southeast-bound link takes in Marseille (also fewer than five hours from Paris by TGV), Toulon, and the Riviera.

By Bus A moderately good network of bus services links places not served, or badly served, by the railway. If you plan to explore Provence by bus, Avignon is the best base. The town is well served by local buses, and excursion buses and boat trips down the Rhône start from here.

Guided Tours

The regional tourist offices' "52 Week" program pools 52 tours offered by various agencies, allowing visitors to choose from a myriad of tours throughout the year, touching on wine tasting, sailing, hang gliding, golfing, gastronomy, and cultural exploration. Contact **GIE**, Loisirs-Acceuil (Domaine de Vergon, 13370 Mallemort, tel. 90–59–18–05) for details. In addition, local tourist offices can arrange many tours, ranging from one-hour guided walks to excursions taking a week or longer by bus, bicycle, on horseback, or on foot.

Bus Tours The **Comité Départemental du Tourisme** (6 rte. Amarchafes, 13006 Marseille, tel. 91–54–92–66) offers a five-day bus tour called "Decouverte de la Provence," which includes full board in two-star hotels and entry to all places of interest. The tour starts in Marseille, continues to Cassis (from where there is a boat trip in the fjordlike waterways known as *calanques*), and includes a day in the Camargue and visits to Aix-en-Provence, Les Baux, and Arles; the cost is 1,700 francs per person. **Capodano Voyages** (110 blvd. des Dames, 13002 Marseille, tel. 91–91–10–91) offers a "Bouillabaisse Weekend" in Marseille, taking in a trip to the harbor, the Château d'If, and Les Iles de Frioul; the cost is 2,465 francs per person. The **Arles Tourist Office** (35 pl. de la République, tel. 90–93–49–11) employs 15 guide-lecturers to run excursions of the town and region.

Horseback Tours The **Office Municipal de Tourisme** in Marseille features a six-day guided tour on horseback in which you can stay in simple houses or tents. Beginning near Marseille in the hills of the Massif de la Sainte-Beaune, the tour continues through some picturesquely wild countryside, including Cézanne's mountain, La Sainte-Victoire; the cost, including insurance, is 2,560 francs per person. Twenty-seven kilometers (17 miles) from Aix-en-Provence lies **Ranch Lou Maze** (13680 Lancon de Provence, tel. 90–57–74–17), which offers horseback excursions of the Camargue; the cost ranges from 230 to 380 francs a day.

Special-Interest Tours **Capodano Voyages** offers a two-day "Wines of the Sun and Gastronomy" tour that includes Avignon, a trip to the "Wine University" at Suze-la-Rousse, and stops at Orange and Villeneuve-les-Avignon. The price for one person is 1,200 francs, though the price is lower for groups of two or more.

Exploring Provence

Numbers in the margin correspond with points of interest on the Provence map.

Orientation

We have divided Provence into three exploring tours; each follows directly from the other. The marshy Camargue forms the heart of our first tour, which ventures briefly into the Languedoc region to visit the fine old towns of Nîmes and Montpellier before wheeling back across the Camargue to examine the Roman remains at Arles and St-Rémy. The tour finishes at Tarascon on the Rhône. The second tour begins farther up the river valley at Avignon, with its papal palace. This tour falls neatly into the boundaries of the Vaucluse *département*, ranging from Avignon in the south to the Roman towns of Orange and Vaison-la-Romaine to the north; the main natural feature is Mont Ventoux, towering above surrounding plains. The third tour begins in Aix, the historic capital of Provence, then heads south to Marseille and east along the spectacular Mediterranean coast to Toulon.

Highlights for First-time Visitors

Aix-en-Provence, Tour 3
Roman remains at Arles, Tour 1
Palais des Papes (Papal palace), Avignon, (Tour 2)
Roman remains at Nîmes, Tour 1
Pont du Gard, Tour 1
St-Remy-de-Provence, Tour 1
Théâtre Antique, Orange, Tour 2

Tour 1: Nîmes and the Camargue

The first tour starts with a bridge, symbolically linking the 20th century to the Roman grandeur that haunts Provence: the **Pont du Gard,** midway between Avignon and Nîmes off the N86 highway (take D981 at Remoulins; if you arrive by the A9 expressway, take the Remoulins exit).

The Pont du Gard is a huge, three-tiered aqueduct, erected 2,000 years ago as part of a 30-mile canal supplying water to Roman Nîmes. It is astonishingly well preserved. Its setting, spanning a rocky gorge 150 feet above the River Gardon, is nothing less than spectacular. There is no entry fee or guide, and at certain times, you can have it all to yourself: Early morning is best, when the honey-colored stone gleams in the sunlight. The best way to gauge the full majesty of the Pont du Gard is to walk right along the top.

Time Out In the enchanting little medieval town of Uzès, 14 kilometers (9 miles) northwest via D981, the **Alexandry** restaurant is a good choice for an inexpensive bite to eat. *6 blvd. Gambetta.*

Nîmes lies 20 kilometers (13 miles) southwest of the Pont du Gard (via N86) and 24 kilometers (15 miles) south of Uzès (via D979). Few towns have preserved such visible links with their Roman past: Nemausus, as the town was then known, grew to

Provence

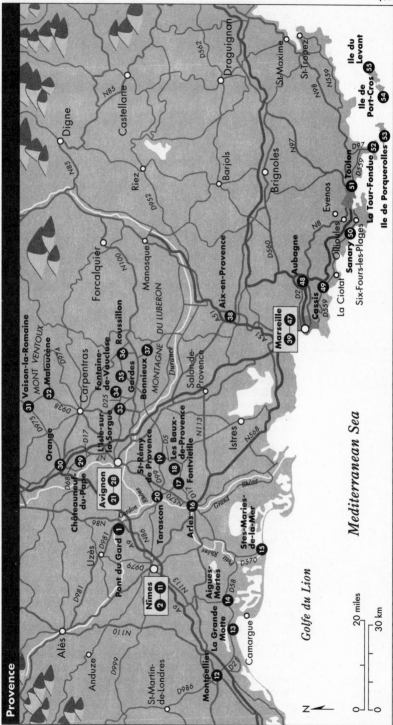

Mediterranean Sea

Golfe du Lion

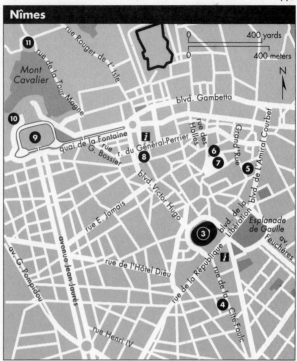

prominence during the reign of Caesar Augustus (27 BC–AD 14)
and still boasts a Roman amphitheater (Arènes), temple (Maison
Carrée), and watchtower (Tour Magne). Luckily, these monuments emerged relatively unscathed from the cataclysmic flash-
flood that devastated Nîmes in 1988, leaving thousands homeless.

③ Start out at place des Arènes, site of the **Arènes,** which is over
140 yards long and 110 yards wide, with a seating capacity of
21,000. Despite its checkered history—it was transformed into
a fortress by the Visigoths and used for housing in medieval
times—the amphitheater has been restored to most of its original splendor. A roof has even been installed to help its latterday
use as a drama and sports stadium (bullfights and tennis tour-
naments are held here). the arena is a smaller version of the
Colosseum in Rome and is considered the world's best-
preserved Roman amphitheater. *Blvd. Victor-Hugo. Admission: 17 frs. adults, 9 frs. children; joint ticket to all monuments and museums: 23 frs. adults, 13 frs. children. Open
mid-June–mid-Sept., daily 8–8; mid-Sept.–Oct. and Apr.–
mid-June, daily 9–noon and 2–6; Nov.–Mar., daily 9–noon
and 2–5.*

④ Take rue de la Cité-Foulc behind the Arènes to the **Musée des
Beaux-Arts** (Fine Arts Museum), where you can admire a vast
Roman mosaic discovered in Nîmes during the last century; the
marriage ceremony depicted in the center of the mosaic pro-
vides intriguing insights into the Roman aristocratic lifestyle.
Old Masters (Nicolas Poussin, Pieter Brueghel, Peter Paul Ru-
bens) and sculpture (Auguste Rodin, and his pupil Emile
Bourdelle) form the mainstay of the collection. *Rue de la Cité*

Foulc. Admission: 15 frs. adults, 8 frs. children, valid for all museums; joint ticket as above. Open daily 9–noon and 1:30–6.

Return to the Arènes and head right, along boulevard de la Libération, which soon becomes boulevard de l'Amiral-Courbet. A hundred and fifty yards down on the left is the **Musée Archéologique et d'Histoire Naturelle,** rich in local archaeological finds, mainly statues, busts, friezes, tools, glass, and pottery. There is an extensive collection of Greek, Roman, and medieval coins. *Blvd. de l'Amiral-Courbet. Admission: 15 frs. adults, 8 frs. children, valid for all museums; joint ticket as above. Open Mon.–Sat. 9–noon and 1:30–6, Sun. 1:30–6.*

Turn right into Grand' Rue behind the museum, then take the second left up toward the **cathedral.** This uninspired 19th-century reconstruction is of less interest than either the surrounding pedestrian streets or the **Musée du Vieux Nîmes** (Museum of Old Nîmes), housed opposite the cathedral in the 17th-century Bishops' Palace. Embroidered garments and woolen shawls fill the rooms in an exotic and vibrant display. Nîmes used to be a cloth-manufacturing center and lent its name to what has become one of the world's most popular fabrics—denim (*de Nîmes*—from Nîmes). Two rooms contain colorful, sometimes grisly, exhibits on the regional sport of bullfighting. *Pl. aux Herbes. Admission: 15 frs. adults, 8 frs. children, valid for all museums; joint ticket as above. Open daily 10–6.*

Head right from the cathedral along rue des Halles, then left down rue du Général-Perrier, to reach the **Maison Carrée.** Despite its name (the "square house"), this is an oblong Roman temple, dating from the 1st century AD. The "temple" has been transformed down the ages into a stable, a private dwelling, a town hall, and a church. Today, the museum contains an imposing statue of Apollo and other antiquities. Take time to admire the exquisite carvings along the cornice and on the Corinthian capitals, which rank as some of the finest in Roman architecture. Thomas Jefferson, an accomplished amateur architect, admired the Maison Carrée's chaste lines of columns so much that he had them copied for the Virginia state capitol at Richmond. *Blvd. Victor-Hugo. Admission: 12 frs. adults, 7 frs. children; joint ticket as above. Open mid-June–mid-Sept., daily 9–7; mid-Sept.–Oct. and Apr.–mid-June, daily 9–noon and 2–6; Nov.–Mar., daily 9–noon and 2–5.*

Rue Molière and rue Boissier lead from the Maison Carrée to the **Jardin de la Fontaine.** This elaborate, formal garden was landscaped on the site of the Roman baths in the 18th century, when the Source de Nemausus, a once-sacred spring, was channeled into pools and a canal. Closeby, you'll see the shattered remnant of a Roman ruin, known as the **Temple of Diana,** while at the far end of the jardin is the **Tour Magne**—a stumpy tower that probably was used as a lookout post, and which, despite losing 30 feet in the course of time, still provides fine views of Nîmes for those energetic enough to trek 140 steps to the top. *Quai de la Fontaine. Admission to Tour Magne: 12 frs. adults, 7 frs. children; joint ticket as above. Open mid-June–mid-Sept., daily 9–7; mid-Sept.–Oct. and Apr.–mid-June, daily 9–noon and 2–6; Nov.–Mar., daily 9–noon and 2–5.*

① Both N113 and the A9 expressway link Nîmes to **Montpellier,** 50 kilometers (30 miles) southwest. Montpellier is a comparatively young town, a mere 1,000 years old; no Romans settled here. Ever since medieval times, Montpellier's reputation has been linked to its university, which was founded in the 14th century. Its medical school, in particular, was so highly esteemed that François Rabelais, one of France's top 16th-century writers, left his native Loire Valley to take his doctorate here. Montpellier remains one of France's premier universities, and a student population of 20,000 peps things up during the school year.

The 17th-century town center has been improved by an imaginative urban planning program, and several streets and squares are now banned to cars. The heart of Montpellier is place de la Comédie, a wide square now freed of traffic jams, much to the benefit of the cafés and terraces laid out before the handsome 19th-century facade of the civic theater.

Boulevard Sarrail leads from the far end of the square, past the leafy Esplanade with its rows of plane trees, to the **Musée Fabre.** The museum's collection of art highlights important works by Gustave Courbet (notably *Bonjour Monsieur Courbet*) and Eugène Delacroix *(Femmes d'Alger)*, as well as paintings by Frédéric Bazille (1841–70)—whose death during the Franco-Prussian War deprived Impressionism of one of its earliest exponents. Older standouts of the museum's varied collection include pictures from the English (Joshua Reynolds), Italian (Raphael), Flemish (David Teniers) and Spanish (Jusepe de Ribera) schools. *Blvd. Sarrail. Admission: 13 frs. (free Wed.). Open Tues.–Sat. 9–12:30 and 1:30–5:30.*

Follow rue Montpelliéret, alongside the museum, into the heart of old Montpellier—a maze of crooked, bustling streets ideal for shopping and strolling. Rue Foch strikes a more disciplined note, slicing straight through to the pride of Montpellier, the **Promenade du Peyrou.** With its wrought-iron railings and majestic flights of steps, this long, broad, tree-shaded terrace has great style. Louis XIV rides triumphant here on his high-plinthed statue, while at the far end an ingenious water tower masquerades behind the carved friezes and Corinthian columns that lend it the appearance of a triumphal arch. Water used to arrive along the **St-Clément aqueduct,** an imposing two-tiered structure 70 feet high and nearly 1,000 yards long. Locals still cluster beneath the aqueduct's arches to drink pastis and play boules.

Just down boulevard Henri IV from the Promenade du Peyrou is France's oldest **botanical garden,** planted by order of Henri IV in 1593. Horticulture buffs will admire the exceptional range of plants, flowers, and trees that grow here, and even nongardeners will appreciate this oasis of peace, where waterlilies float among the lotus flowers. *Admission: free. Gardens open daily 9–noon and 2–5. Greenhouses open weekdays 9–noon and 2–5, Sat. 9–noon.*

The arid, rocky Midi landscape begins to change as you head southeast from Montpellier along D21, past pools and lagoons,
⑬ to **La Grande Motte,** the most lavish of a string of new resorts built along the Languedoc coast. The mosquitoes that once infested this watery area have finally been vanquished, and tourists have taken their place. La Grande Motte was only a

glint in an architect's eye back in the late '60s; since then, its arresting pyramid-shape apartment blocks have influenced several French resorts and host thousands of vacationers each year.

Time Out   Thousands of tons of oysters are cultivated in the nearby Etang (lagoon) de Thau; many end up featured on the menu of the elegant **Alexandre-Amirauté.** You can eat your oysters amid impressive Louis XV surroundings while gazing out over the clear blue waters of the Mediterranean. *Esplanade de la Capitainerie.*

⑭   Thirteen kilometers (8 miles) farther east is **Aigues-Mortes,** an astonishing relic of medieval town planning, created at the behest of Louis IX (St-Louis) in the 13th century. Medieval streets are usually crooked and higgledy-piggledy; at Aigues-Mortes, however, a grid plan was adopted, hemmed in by sturdy walls sprouting towers at regular intervals. Aigues-Mortes was originally a port, and Louis used it as a base for his Crusades to the Holy Land. The sea has long since receded, though, and Aigues-Mortes's size and importance have decreased with it.

Unlike most of the medieval buildings, the **fortifications** remain intact. Walk along the top of the city walls and admire some remarkable views across the town and salt marshes. You can also explore the powerful **Tour de Constance,** originally designed as a fortress-keep, and used in the 18th century as a prison for Protestants who refused to convert to official state Catholicism. One such unfortunate, Marie Durand, languished here for 38 years. Abraham Mazel was luckier. He spent 10 months chiseling a hole in the wall, while his companions sang psalms to distract the jailers. The ruse worked: Mazel and 16 others escaped. *Admission: 22 frs. adults, 12 frs. students and senior citizens, 5 frs. children. Tower and ramparts open Apr.–Oct., daily 9–7; Nov.–Mar. 9:30–noon and 2–5:30.*

Head east on D58 across the haunting, desolate **Camargue:** a marshy wilderness of endless horizons, vast pools, low flat plains, and, overhead, innumerable species of migrating birds. The Camargue is formed by the sprawling Rhône delta and extends over 300 square miles. Much of it is untouched by man; this is a land of black bulls and sturdy, free-roaming gray horses. There are just two towns worthy of the name: Aigues-Mortes and, 32 kilometers (20 miles) southeast via D58/D570, Saintes-Maries-de-la-Mer.

⑮   **Saintes-Maries-de-la-Mer** is a commercialized resort, mainly frequented by British tourists in search of the Camargue's principal sandy beach. Its tiny, dark fortress-church houses caskets containing relics of the "Holy Maries" after whom the town is named. Legend has it that Mary Jacobi (the sister of the Virgin), Mary Magdalene, Mary Salome (mother of the apostles James and John), and their black servant Sarah were washed up here around AD 40 after being abandoned at sea—why, no one knows—by the Jews of Jerusalem. Their adopted town rapidly became a site of pilgrimage, particularly among gypsies. Sarah was adopted as their patron saint, and to this day, gypsies stage colorful pilgrimages to Saintes-Maries in late May and late October, while guitar-strumming pseudogypsies serenade rich-looking tourists throughout the summer.

Take D85-A north from Saintes-Maries through the 30-acre **Parc Ornithologique,** itself part of the vast Réserve Nationale centered on the Etang (lagoon) de Vaccarès. The Parc Ornithologique offers a protected environment to vegetation and wildlife: Birds from northern Europe and Siberia spend the winter here, while pink flamingoes flock in during the summer months. *Admission: 18 frs. Open Mar.–Oct., daily 8–dusk.*

Continue along D85-A until it rejoins D570, then keep north on this road for 25 kilometers (16 miles) until you reach **Arles.** The first inhabitants of Arles were probably the Greeks, who arrived from Marseille in the 6th century BC. The Romans, however, left a stronger mark, constructing the theater and amphitheater (Arènes) that remain Arles's biggest tourist attraction. Arles used to be a thriving port before the Mediterranean receded over what is now the marshy Camargue. It was also the site of the southernmost bridge over the Rhône, and became a commercial crossroads; merchants from as far afield as Arabia, Assyria, and Africa would linger here to do business on their way from Rome to Spain or northern Europe.

Firebrand Dutchman Vincent Van Gogh produced much of his best work—and chopped off his ear—in Arles during a frenzied 15-month spell (1888–90) just before his suicide at 37. Unfortunately, the houses he lived in are no longer standing—they were destroyed during World War II—but one of his most famous subjects remains: the **Pont de Trinquetaille** across the Rhône. Van Gogh's rendering of the bridge, painted in 1888, was auctioned a century later for $20 million.

Local art museums like the **Musée Réattu,** 300 yards from the bridge along quai Marx-Dormoy, can't compete with that type of bidding—which is one reason why no works by Van Gogh are displayed there. Another is that Arles failed to appreciate Van Gogh; he was jeered at and eventually packed off to the nearest lunatic asylum. To add insult to injury: Jacques Réattu, after whom the museum is named, was a local painter of dazzling mediocrity. His works fill three rooms, but of much greater interest is the collection of modern drawings and paintings by Pablo Picasso, Fernand Léger, and Maurice de Vlaminck and the photography section with images by some of the field's leading names. *Rue du Grand-Prieuré. Admission: 13 frs.; joint ticket to all monuments and museums: 33 frs. adults, children free. Open June–Sept., daily 9:30–7; Nov.–Mar., daily 10–12:30 and 2–5; Apr.–May and Oct., daily 9:30–12:30 and 2–6.*

The museum facade, facing the Rhône, dates from the Middle Ages and formed part of a 15th-century priory. Alongside are the ruins of the **Palais Constantin** (same opening times as above), site of Provence's largest Roman baths, the **Thèrmes de la Trouille** (entrance on rue Dominique-Maisto; admission: 12 francs; joint ticket as above).

Most of Arles significant sights and museums are set well away from the Rhône. The most notable is the 26,000-capacity **Arènes,** built in the 1st century AD to showcase circuses and fight-to-the-death gladiator combats. The amphitheater is 150 yards long and as wide as a football field, with each of its two stories composed of 60 arches; the original top tier has long since crumbled, and the three square towers were added in the Middle

Ages. Climb to the upper story for some satisfying views across the town and countryside. Despite its venerable age, the amphitheater still sees a lot of action, mainly Sunday afternoon bullfights. *Rond Point des Arènes. Admission: 10 frs.; joint ticket as above. Open June–Sept., daily 8:30–7; Nov.–Mar., daily 9–noon and 2–4:30; Apr.–May and Oct., daily 9–12:30 and 2–6:30.*

Just 100 yards from the Arènes are the scanty remains of Arles's **Théâtre Antique** (Roman theater); the bits of marble column scattered around the grassy enclosure hint poignantly at the theater's one-time grandeur. The capacity may have shrunk from 7,000 to a few hundred, but the orchestra pit and a few tiers of seats are still used these days for the city's Music and Drama festival each July. *Rue du Cloître, tel. 90–96–93–30 for ticket information. Admission: 10 frs.; joint ticket as above. Open June–Sept., daily 8:30–7; Nov.–Mar., daily 9–noon and 2–4:30; Apr.–May and Oct., daily 9–12:30 and 2–6:30.*

Follow rue de la Calade to place de la République. To the left is the church of **St-Trophime**, dating mainly from the 11th and 12th centuries; subsequent additions have not spoiled its architectural harmony. Take time to admire the accomplished 12th-century sculptures flanking the main portal, featuring the Last Judgment, the apostles, the Nativity, and various saints. Similar sculptured richness embellishes the cloisters (12th and 14th centuries). *Rue de l'Hôtel-de-Ville. Admission to cloisters: 13 frs.; joint ticket as above. Open June–Sept., daily 8:30–7; Nov.–Mar., daily 9–noon and 2–4:30; Apr.–May and Oct., daily 9–12:30 and 2–6:30.*

Opposite St-Trophime is the **Musée d'Art Païen** (Museum of Pagan Art), housed in a former church next to the 17th-century Hôtel de Ville (Town Hall). The "pagan art" displays encompass Roman statues, busts, mosaics, and a white marble sarcophagus. You'll also see a copy of the famous statue the *Venus of Arles;* Sun King Louis XIV waltzed off to the Louvre with the original. *Pl. de la République. Admission: 10 frs.; joint ticket as above. Open June–Sept., daily 8:30–7; Nov.–Mar., daily 9–noon and 2–4:30; Apr.–May and Oct., 9–12:30 and 2–6:30.*

Turn left alongside the Hôtel de Ville into plan de la Cour. A hundred yards down, in a former 17th-century Jesuit chapel, is the **Musée d'Art Chrétien** (Museum of Christian Art). One of the highlights is a magnificent collection of sculpted marble sarcophagi, second only to the Vatican's, that date from the 4th century on. Downstairs, you can explore a vast double gallery built in the 1st century BC as a grain store and see part of the great Roman sewer built two centuries later. *Rue Balze. Admission: 10 frs.; joint ticket as above. Open June–Sept., daily 8:30–7; Nov.–Mar., daily 9–noon and 2–4:30; Apr.–May and Oct., daily 9–12:30 and 2–6:30.*

The **Museon Arlaten,** an old-fashioned folklore museum, is housed next door in a 16th-century mansion. The charming displays include costumes and headdresses, puppets, and waxworks, lovingly assembled by that great 19th-century Provençal poet, Frédéric Mistral. *Rue de la République. Admission: 10 frs.; joint ticket as above. Open June–Sept., daily*

8:30–7; Nov.–Mar., Tues.–Sun. 9–noon and 2–4:30; Apr.– May and Oct., Tues.–Sun. 9–12:30 and 2–6:30.

Head down rue du Président-Wilson opposite the museum to the **boulevard des Luces,** a broad, leafy avenue flanked by trendy shops and sidewalk cafés. Locals favor it for leisurely strolls and aperitifs.

At the eastern end of the boulevard is the **Jardin d'Hiver,** a public garden whose fountains figure in several of Van Gogh's paintings. Cross the gardens to rue Fassin and head left to place de la Croisière and the start of the allée des Sarcophages, which leads to the **Alyscamps,** a Provençal term meaning mythical burial ground. This was a prestigious burial site from Roman times through the Middle Ages. A host of important finds have been excavated here, many of which are exhibited in the town's museums. Empty tombs and sarcophagi line the allée des Sarcophages, creating a powerfully gloomy atmosphere in dull weather.

17 Leave Arles on Avignon-bound N570, and almost immediately turn right along D17 to the striking village of **Fontvieille,** 10 kilometers (6 miles) away and home of the **Moulin de Daudet.** Nineteenth-century author Alphonse Daudet dreamed up his short stories, *Lettres de Mon Moulin,* in this well-preserved, charmingly situated windmill just up D33 on the outskirts of the village. Inside, there's a small museum devoted to Daudet, and you can walk upstairs to see the original grain-grinding system. *Admission: 6 frs. adults, 4 frs. children. Open Apr.– Oct., daily 9–noon and 2–7; Nov.–Dec. and Feb.–Mar., daily 10–noon and 2–5; Jan., Sun. only, 10–noon and 2–5.*

From Fontvieille, take D17 then D78-A to Les Baux-de-Provence 8 kilometers (5 miles) farther on. Half a mile north of Les Baux, off D27, is the **Cathédrale d'Images,** where the majestic setting of the old Baux quarries, with their towering rockfaces and stone pillars, is used as a colossal screen for nature-based film shows (Jacques Cousteau gets frequent billing). *Rte. de Maillane. Admission: 30 frs. adults, 15 frs. children. Open Mar.–Oct., daily 10–7.*

18 **Les Baux-de-Provence** is an amazing place, perched on a mighty spur of rock high above the surrounding countryside of vines, olive trees, and quarries: The mineral bauxite was discovered here in 1821. Half of Les Baux is composed of tiny climbing streets and ancient stone houses inhabited, for the most part, by local craftsmen selling pottery, carvings, and assorted knickknacks. The other half, the Ville Morte (Dead Town), is a mass of medieval ruins, vestiges of Les Baux's glorious past, when the town boasted 6,000 inhabitants and the defensive impregnability of its rocky site far outweighed its isolation and poor access.

Cars must be left in the parking lot at the entrance to the village. Close to the 12th-century church of St-Vincent (where local shepherds continue an age-old tradition by herding their lambs to midnight mass at Christmas) is the 16th-century **Hôtel des Porcelets,** featuring some 18th-century frescoes and a small but choice collection of contemporary art. *Pl. St-Vincent. Admission: 15 frs. (joint ticket with Musée Lapidaire and Ville Morte). Open Easter–Oct., daily 9–noon and 2–6.*

Rue Neuve leads around to the **Ville Morte.** Enter through the 14th-century Tour-de-Brau, which houses the Musée Lapidaire, displaying locally excavated sculptures and ceramics. You can wander at will amid the rocks and ruins of the Dead Town. A 13th-century castle stands at one end of the clifftop, and, at the other, the Tour Paravelle and the Monument Charloun Rieu. From here, you can enjoy a magnificent view of Arles and the Camargue as far as Saintes-Maries-de-la-Mer. *Ville Morte. Admission: 15 frs. (joint ticket with museums). Open daily 9–noon and 2–6.*

Hilly D5 heads 8 kilometers (5 miles) north from Les Baux to the small town of **St-Rémy de Provence,** founded in the 6th century BC and known as Glanum to the Romans. St-Rémy is renowned for its outstanding Roman remains: Temples, baths, forum, and houses have been excavated, while the Mausoleum and Arc Municipal (Triumphal Arch) welcome visitors as they enter the town.

The **Roman Mausoleum** was erected around AD 100 to the memory of Caius and Lucius Caesar, grandsons of the Emperor Augustus; the four bas-reliefs around its base, depicting ancient battle scenes, are stunningly preserved. The Mausoleum is composed of four archways arranged in a square and topped by a circular colonnade. The nearby **Arc Municipal** is a few decades older and has suffered heavily; the upper half has long since crumbled away. You can still make out some of the stone carvings, however; one shows prisoners chained to a tree.

Excavations since 1921 have uncovered about a tenth of the site of the adjacent Roman town. Many of the finds—statues, pottery, and jewelry—can be examined at the town museum, **Le Musée Archéologique,** in the center of St-Rémy. *Hôtel de Sade, rue Parage. Admission: 12 frs. adults, 6 frs. children. Open June–Oct., daily 9–noon and 2–6; Apr.–May and Oct., weekends 10–noon, weekdays 3–6; closed Nov.–Mar.*

Opposite the Hôtel de Sade, in a grand 16th-century mansion, is the **Musée des Alpilles.** It boasts a fine collection of minerals found in the nearby hills (the Alpilles), plus items of regional folklore: costumes, furniture, and figurines. Exhibits also touch on the 16th-century astrologer, Nostradamus, who was born in St-Rémy (his house can be seen on the other side of the church, in rue Hoche, but it's not open to the public). *Pl. Favier. Admission: 12 frs. Open Apr.–Oct., Wed.–Mon. 10–noon and 2–6; Mar. and Nov., weekends 10–noon and 2–4; closed Dec.–Feb.*

Take D99 16 kilometers (10 miles) west from St-Rémy to **Tarascon,** home of the mythical Tarasque, a monster that would emerge from the Rhône to gobble children and cattle. Luckily St. Martha, washed up with the three Maries at Saintes-Maries-de-la-Mer, allegedly tamed the beast with a sprinkle of holy water, after which the inhabitants clobbered it senseless and slashed it to pieces. This dramatic event is celebrated on the last Sunday in June with a colorful parade.

Ever since the 12th century, Tarascon has possessed a formidable **castle** to protect it from any beast or man tempted to emulate the Tarasque's fiendish deeds. The castle's massive stone walls, towering 150 feet above the rocky banks of the Rhône, are among the most daunting in France, and it's not surprising that the castle was used for centuries as a prison.

Since 1926, however, the chapels, vaulted royal apartments, and stone carvings of the interior have been restored to less-intimidating glory. *Admission: 22 frs. adults, 12 frs. senior citizens, 5 frs. children. Open July and Aug., Wed.–Mon. 9–7; Sept.–June guided tours only 9–11 and 2–6 (last tour at 5 in Apr. and May; at 4, Oct.–Mar.); closed Tues.*

It's just 24 kilometers (15 miles) from Tarascon to Avignon and the start of our second tour.

Tour 2: The Vaucluse

A warren of medieval alleys nestling behind a protective ring of chunky towers, **Avignon** is possibly best known for its Pont St-Bénezet, the Avignon bridge that many will remember singing about during their nursery-rhyme days. No one dances across the bridge these days, however; it's amputated in midstream, and has been ever since the 17th century, when a cataclysmic storm washed half of it away. Still, Avignon has lots to offer, starting with the Palais des Papes (Papal Palace), where seven exiled popes camped between 1309 and 1377, after fleeing from the corruption of Rome. Avignon remained papal property until 1791, and elegant mansions and a population of 80,000 bear witness to the town's 18th-century prosperity.

Avignon's main street, rue de la République, leads from the tourist office (41 cours Jean-Jaurès) past shops and cafés to place de l'Horloge and place du Palais, site of the colossal **Palais des Papes.** This "palace" creates a disconcertingly fortress-like impression, underlined by the austerity of its interior decor; most of the furnishings were dispersed during the French Revolution. Some imagination is required to picture it in medieval splendor, awash with color and worldly clerics enjoying what the 14th-century Italian poet Francesco Petrarch called "licentious banquets."

On close inspection, two different styles of building emerge: the severe **Palais Vieux** (Old Palace), built between 1334 and 1342 by Pope Benedict XII, a member of the Cistercian order that frowned on frivolity, and the more decorative **Palais Nouveau** (New Palace), built in the following decade by the arty, lavish-living Pope Clement VI. The Great Court, where visitors arrive, forms a link between the two.

The main rooms of the Vieux Palais are the consistory (council hall), decorated with some excellent 14th-century frescoes by Simone Martini; the Chapelle St-Jean (original frescoes by Matteo Giovanetti); the Grand Tinel, or Salle des Festins, with a majestic vaulted roof and a series of 18th-century Gobelins tapestries; the Chapelle St-Martial (more Matteo frescoes); the Chambre du Cerf, with a richly decorated ceiling, murals featuring a stag hunt, and a delightful view of Avignon; the Chambre de Parement (papal antechamber); and the Chambre à Coucher (papal bedchamber).

The principal attractions of the Palais Nouveau are the Grande Audience, a magnificent two-naved hall on the ground floor, and, upstairs, the Chapelle Clémentine, where the college of cardinals gathered to elect the new pope. *Pl. du Palais des Papes. Admission: 25 frs. adults, 14 frs. students, children free. Guided tours only Mar.–Oct. Open Easter–June, daily 9–*

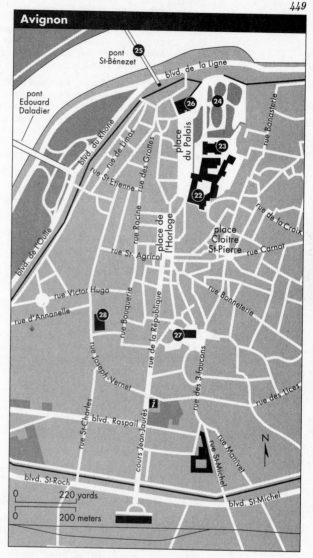

Avignon

12:15 and 2–5:15; July–Sept., daily 9–6; Oct.–Easter, daily 9–11:15 and 2–4:15.

㉓ ㉔ ㉕ The 12th-century **cathedral** alongside contains the Gothic tomb of Pope John XII. Beyond is the **Rocher des Doms,** a large, attractive garden offering fine views of Avignon, the Rhône, and the celebrated **Pont St-Bénezet**—built, according to legend, by a local shepherd named Bénezet in the 12th century. It was the first bridge to span the Rhône at Avignon and was originally 900 yards long. Since the 17th century, only half remains, though it's worth strolling along for the views and a visit to the tiny Chapelle St-Nicolas that juts out over the river.

㉖ The medieval **Petit Palais,** situated between the bridge and the Rocher des Doms garden, was once home to cardinals and archbishops. Nowadays it contains an outstanding collection of Old Masters, led by the Italian schools of Venice, Siena, and Florence (note Sandro Botticelli's *Virgin and Child*). *21 pl. du Palais. Admission: 16 frs. adults, 8 frs. children; free Sun. Open Wed.–Mon. 9:30–noon and 2–6.*

Double back past the Papal Palace and venture into the narrow, winding, shop-lined streets of old Avignon. Halfway down rue
㉗ de la République is the **Musée Lapidaire,** which displays a variety of archaeological finds—including the remains of Avignon's Arc de Triomphe—in a sturdy 17th-century Baroque chapel fronted by an imposing facade. *27 rue de la République. Admission: 7.50 frs. adults, children free. Open daily noon–7.*

Cross rue de la République and turn right into rue Joseph-
㉘ Vernet. A few minutes' walk leads you to the **Musée Calvet,** an elegant 18th-century townhouse featuring an extensive collection of mainly French paintings from the 16th century on; highlights include works by Théodore Géricault, Camille Corot, Edouard Manet, Paul Dufy, Maurice Vlaminck, and the Italian artist Amedeo Modigliani. Greek, Roman, and Etruscan statuettes are also displayed. *65 rue Joseph-Vernet, tel. 90–86–33–84. Closed for renovation at press time; reopening scheduled for mid-1990. Check locally for admission charge and opening times.*

From Avignon, head north to Orange. The most picturesque route, via N7/D17, goes by the hillside village of
㉙ **Châteauneuf-du-Pape,** founded by the popes in the 14th century. The popes knew their wine: The vineyard here is still regarded as the best of the southern Rhône, even though the vines are embedded less in soil than in stones and pebbles. Several producers stage tastings in the village and sell distinctive wine bottles emblazoned with the crossed-key papal crest.

Time Out Inexpensive local wines, filling fare, and a cheerful welcome make **La Mule du Pape** a good choice for lunch. *23 pl. Change. Closed Tues.*

㉚ **Orange,** 10 kilometers (6 miles) north of Châteauneuf via D68, is a small, pleasant town that sinks into total siesta somnolence during hot afternoons but, at other times, buzzes with visitors who are keen on admiring its Roman remains.

The magnificent, semicircular **Théâtre Antique,** in the center of town, is the best-preserved remains of a theatre from the ancient world. It was built just before the birth of Christ, to the same dimensions as that of Arles. Orange's theater, however, has a mighty screen-wall, over 100 yards long and 120 feet high, and steeply climbing terraces carved into the hillside. Seven thousand spectators can crowd in and regularly do for open-air concerts and operatic performances; the acoustics are superb. This is the only Roman theater that still possesses its original Imperial statue, of Caesar Augustus, which stands in the middle of the screen. At nearly 12 feet, it's one of the tallest Roman statues in existence. *Pl. des Frères-Mounet. Admission: 15 frs.; joint ticket with Musée Municipal. Open Apr.–Oct., daily 9–6:30; Nov.–Mar., daily 10–noon and 1:30–5.*

The **Parc de la Colline St-Eutrope,** the banked garden behind the theater, yields a fine view of the theater and of the 6,000-foot Mont Ventoux to the east. Walk up cours A. Briand, turn right at the top, then left immediately after to the venerable **Arc de Triomphe**—composed of a large central arch flanked by two smaller ones, the whole topped by a massive entablature. The 70-foot arch, the third-highest Roman arch still standing, towered over the old Via Agrippa between Arles and Lyon and was probably built around AD 25 in honor of the Gallic Wars. Witness the well-preserved carvings on the north side, recalling the legionaries' battles with the Gauls and Caesar's naval showdown with the ships of Marseille. These days, the arch presides over a busy traffic circle.

③① The D975 heads 27 kilometers (17 miles) northeast from Orange to **Vaison-la-Romaine**. As its name suggests, Vaison was also a Roman town. The remains here are more extensive though less spectacular than those at Orange; they can be explored on either side of the avenue du Général-de-Gaulle. The floors and walls of houses, villas, a basilica, and a theater have been unearthed, and the Roman street plan is partly discernible. Statues and objects are housed in a small museum near the theater. With its lush lawns and colorful flower beds, the entire site suggests a well-tended historical garden. *Admission to remains and museum: 16 frs. adults, 8 frs. students and senior citizens. Open Apr.–Oct., daily 9–7; Nov.–Mar., daily 9–5.*

③② Before leaving Vaison, pause to admire the 2,000-year-old Roman bridge over the River Ouvèze and venture briefly into the medieval town across the river. Then head 10 kilometers (6 miles) south along D938 to **Malaucène**, at the foot of **Mont Ventoux**—a huge mountain that looms incongruously above the surrounding plains. Weather conditions on this sprawling, whalelike bulk—known reverentially as "Le" Ventoux—can vary dramatically. In summer, few places in France experience such scorching heat; in winter, the Ventoux's snow-topped peaks recall the Alps. Its arid heights sometimes provide a grueling setting for the Tour de France cycling race; British bicyclist Tommy Simpson collapsed and died under the Ventoux's pitiless sun in 1967.

③③ D974 winds its way from Malaucène up to the summit, 6,250 feet above sea level. Stay on D974 as it doubles back around the southern slopes of the Ventoux, then follow it southwest from Bédoin toward Carpentras. From here, take D938 south to **L'Isle-sur-la-Sorgue**, 18 kilometers (11 miles) away, where the River Sorgue splits into a number of channels and once turned the waterwheels of the town's silk factories. Silk worms were cultivated locally, one reason for the profusion of mulberry trees in Provence (mulberry leaves being a silkworm's favorite food). Some of the waterwheels are still in place, and you can admire them as you stroll along the banks of the river that encircles the town. The richly decorated 17th-century church is also of interest.

Time Out | A good place for lunch is **Le Pescadou,** an inexpensive restaurant whose shaded terrace overlooks the arms of the Sorgue. There is a wide choice and an excellent-value menu during the week. *Le Partage des Eaux. Closed Mon.*

③④ Tiny D25 leads east from L'Isle-sur-la-Sorgue to **Fontaine-de-Vaucluse**, 8 kilometers (5 miles) away. The "fountain" in question is the site of the River Sorgue's emergence from underground imprisonment: Water shoots up from a cavern as the emerald-green river sprays and cascades at the foot of steep cliffs. This is the picture in springtime or after heavy rains; in the drought of summer, the scene may be less spectacular and infested with tourists.

It's just 6 kilometers (4 miles) from Fontaine-de-Vaucluse to **Gordes** as the crow flies, but drivers have to wind their way south, east, and then north for 16 kilometers (10 miles) on D100-A, D100, D2, and D15 to skirt the impassable hillside. The golden-stoned village of Gordes is perched dramatically on its own hill. At the summit sits a Renaissance **château** with a collection of mind-stretching, geometric-patterned paintings by 20th-century Hungarian-French artist Victor Vasarely. *Admission: 15 frs. adults, children free. Open Wed.–Mon. 10– noon and 2–6; closed Tues.*

In a wild valley some four kilometers (two miles) north of Gordes (via D177) stands the beautiful 12th-century **Abbey of Sénanque.** In 1969, its Cistercian monks moved to the island of St-Honorat (*see* Chapter 14), off the shore of Cannes, and the admirably preserved buildings here are now a cultural center that presents concerts and exhibitions. The dormitory, refectory, church, and chapter house can be visited, along with an odd museum devoted to the Sahara's Tuareg nomads. *Admission: 14 frs. Open July and Aug., Mon.–Sat. 10–7, Sun. 2–7; Sept.–June, Mon.–Sat. 10–noon and 2–5, Sun. 2–5.*

Return to Gordes and strike 10 kilometers (6 miles) east along D2/D102 to another hilltop village, **Roussillon,** whose houses are built with a distinctive orange-and pink-colored stone: This is ocher country, and local quarrying has slashed cliffs into bizarre shapes. **Bonnieux,** 11 kilometers (7 miles) south of Roussillon (D149), is equally picturesque. Climb to the terrace of the old church (not to be confused with the big 19th-century one lower down) for a sweeping view north that takes in Gordes, Roussillon, and the nearby château of Lacoste, now in ruins but once home to that notorious aristocrat, the Marquis de Sade.

Time Out The **Prieuré's** setting—a charming old priory in the pretty hilltop village of Bonnieux—is its main appeal. The simple Provençal dishes are made memorable by the accompanying panoramic views. *Closed Tues. and Thurs. lunch.*

Aix-en-Provence, starting point for our third tour, lies 48 kilometers (29 miles) southeast.

Tour 3: The Marseille Area

Many villages, but few towns, are as well preserved as the traditional capital of Provence: elegant **Aix-en-Provence.** The Romans were drawn here by the presence of thermal springs; the name of Aix originates from *Aquae Sextiae* (the waters of Sextius) in honor of the consul who reputedly founded the town in 122 BC. Twenty years later, a vast army of Germanic barbarians invaded the region but were defeated by General Marius at a neighboring mountain, known ever since as the Montagne Sainte-Victoire. Marius remains a popular local first name to this day.

Aix-en-Provence numbers two of France's most creative geniuses among its sons: Impressionist Paul Cézanne (1839–1906), many of whose paintings feature the nearby countryside, especially Montagne Sainte-Victoire, and novelist Emile Zola (1840–1902), who, in several of his works, described Aix (as "Plassans") and his boyhood friendship with Cézanne.

The celebrated **cours Mirabeau,** flanked by intertwining plane trees, is the town's nerve center, a gracious, lively avenue with the feel of a toned-down, intimate Champs-Elysées. It divides old Aix into two, with narrow medieval streets to the north and sophisticated, haughty 18th-century mansions to the south. Begin your visit at the west end of cours Mirabeau (the tourist office is closeby at 2 place de la Libération). Halfway down is the **Fontaine des Neuf Canons** (Fountain of the Nine Cannons), dating from 1691, then, farther along, the **Fontaine d'Eau Thermale** (Thermal Water), built in 1734.

Any route through the quaint pedestrian streets of the old town, north of cours Mirabeau, is rewarding. Wend your way up to the **Cathédrale St-Sauveur.** Its mishmash of styles lacks harmony, and the interior feels gloomy and dilapidated, but you may want to inspect the remarkable 15th-century triptych by Nicolas Froment, entitled *Tryptique du Buisson Ardent (Burning Bush),* depicting King René (duke of Anjou, Count of Provence, and titular king of Sicily) and Queen Joan kneeling beside the Virgin. Ask the sacristan to spotlight it for you (he'll expect a tip) and to remove the protective shutters from the ornate 16th-century carvings on the cathedral portals. Afterward, wander into the tranquil Romanesque cloisters next door to admire the carved pillars and slender colonnades.

The adjacent Archbishops' Palace is home to the **Musée des Tapisseries** (Tapestry Museum). Its highlight is a magnificent suite of 17 tapestries made in Beauvais that date, like the palace itself, from the 17th and 18th centuries. Nine woven panels illustrate the adventures of the bumbling Don Quixote. *28 pl. des Martyrs de la Résistance. Admission free. Open Wed.– Mon. 9:30–noon and 2–6, Tues. 2–6.*

Return past the cathedral and take rue de la Roque up to the broad, leafy boulevard that encircles Old Aix. Head up avenue Pasteur, opposite, then turn right into avenue Paul-Cézanne, which leads to Cézanne's studio, the **Musée-Atelier de Paul Cézanne.** Cézanne's pioneering work, with its interest in angular forms, paved the way for the Cubist style of the early 20th century. No major pictures are on display here, but his studio remains as he left it at his death in 1906, scattered with the great man's pipe, clothing, and other personal possessions, many of which he painted in his still lifes. *19 av. Paul-Cézanne. Admission: 7 frs. adults, 5 frs. senior citizens and children. Open Wed.–Mon. 10–noon and 2:30–6; closed Tues.*

Time Out   Good addresses for picnic provisions are the **Olivier** *charcuterie* (rue Jacques-de-la-Roque near the cathedral) and the **Brémond** *patisserie* (36 cours Mirabeau, on the corner of rue du Quatre-Septembre).

Make your way back to cours Mirabeau and cross into the southern half of Aix. The streets here are straight and rationally planned, flanked by symmetrical mansions imbued with classical elegance. Rue du Quatre-Septembre, three-quarters of the way down cours Mirabeau, leads to the splendid **Fontaine**

des Quatre Dauphins, where sculpted dolphins play in a fountain erected in 1667. Turn left along rue Cardinale to the **Musée Granet,** named after another of Aix's artistic sons: François Granet (1775–1849), whose works are good examples of the formal, at times sentimental, style of art popular during the first half of the 19th century. Granet's paintings show none of the fervor of Cézanne, who is represented here with several oils and watercolors. An impressive collection of European paintings from the 16th to the 19th century, plus archaeological finds from Egypt, Greece, and the Roman Empire, complete the museum's collections. *13 rue Cardinale. Admission: 12 frs. Open Apr.–Oct., Wed.–Mon. 10–noon and 2–6; Nov.–Mar., Wed.–Mon. 2–6; closed Tues.*

The quickest, most effective route by car between Aix and Marseille is the toll-free A51 expressway, provided you avoid the heavy morning and evening rush-hour traffic.

㊴ Marseille is not crowded with tourist goodies, nor is its reputation as a dirty big city entirely unjustified, but it still has more going for it than many realize: a craggy mountain hinterland that provides a spectacular backdrop, superb coastal views of nearby islands, and the sights and smells of a Mediterranean melting pot where different peoples have mingled for centuries —ever since the Phocaean Greeks invaded around 600 BC. Today North African immigrants add an exotic touch.

Marseille is the Mediterranean's largest port. The sizable, ugly industrial docks virtually rub shoulders with the intimate, picturesque old harbor, the **Vieux Port,** packed with fishing boats **㊵** and pleasure craft: This is the heart of Marseille, with avenue La Canebière leading down to the water's edge.

Pick up your leaflets and town plan at the tourist office (4 La Canebière) and peruse them on a café terrace overlooking the Vieux Port. Until the mid-19th century, this was the center of maritime activity in Marseille. These days, a forest of yacht and fishing-boat masts creates an impression of colorful bustle. Restaurants line the quays, and fishwives spout indecipherable Provençal insults as they serve gleaming fresh sardines each morning. The Marseillais can be an irrascible lot: Louis XIV built the Fort St-Nicolas, at the entry of the Vieux Port, with the guns facing inland to keep the citizens in order.

㊶ Marseille's pompous neo-Byzantine **cathedral** stands around the corner, but it is of considerably less interest than the **㊷ ㊸ Basilique St-Victor** across the water, in the shadow of the **Fort St-Nicolas** (which can't be visited). With its powerful tower and thick-set walls, the basilica resembles a fortress and boasts one of southern France's oldest doorways (circa 1140), a 13th-century nave, and a 14th-century chancel and transept. Downstairs, you'll find the murky 5th-century underground crypt, with its collection of ancient sarcophagi. *Rue Sainte.*

A brisk half-mile walk up boulevard Tellène, followed by a trudge up a steep flight of steps, will bring you to the foot of **㊹ Notre-Dame de la Garde.** This church, a flashy 19th-century cousin of the Sacré Coeur in Paris and Fourvière in Lyon, features a similar hilltop location. The expansive view, clearest in early morning (especially if the mistral is blowing), stretches from the hinterland mountains to the sea via the Cité Radieuse, a controversial '50s housing project by Swiss-born architect Le Corbusier. The church interior is generously endowed with

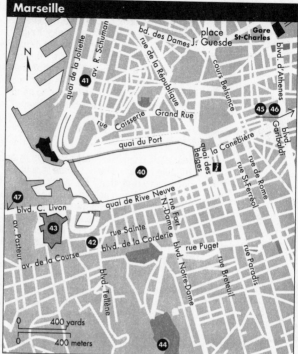

Marseille

bombastic murals, mosaics, and marble, while, at the top of the tower, the great gilded statue of the Virgin stands sentinel over the old port, 500 feet below. *Blvd. A. Aune.*

Return to the Vieux Port and venture along the legendary **La Canebière**—the "Can O' Beer" to prewar sailors—where stately mansions recall faded glory. La Canebière has been on the slide in recent years, but cafés and restaurants continue to provide an upbeat pulse.

Continue past such busy shopping streets as rue Paradis, rue St-Ferréol, and rue de Rome, and turn right into boulevard Garibaldi to reach **cours Julien,** a traffic-free street lined with sidewalk cafés, restaurants, bookshops, and boutiques. The atmosphere is that of a scaled-down St-Germain-des-Prés wafted from Paris to the Mediterranean.

Return to La Canebière and, when you reach the undistinguished church of St-Vincent de Paul, fork left along cours Jeanne-Thierry (which becomes boulevard Longchamp) to the imposing **Palais Longchamp,** built in 1860 by the same architect as Notre-Dame de la Garde, Henri Espérandieu (1829–74). The palais is home to the **Musée des Beaux-Arts** (Fine Arts Museum); its collection of paintings and sculptures includes works by 18th-century Italian artist Giovanni Battista Tiepolo, Rubens, and French caricaturist and painter Honoré Daumier. *Admission: 6 frs. adults, 3 frs. students and senior citizens. Open daily 10–5.*

Marseille is no seaside resort, but a scenic 5-kilometer (3-mile) coast road (Corniche du Président J. F. Kennedy) links the

Vieux-Port to the newly created Prado beaches in the swanky parts of southern Marseille. There are breathtaking views across the sea toward the rocky Frioul Islands, which can be visited by boat. Ninety-minute trips leave the Vieux-Port hourly in summer and frequently in winter to visit the **Château d'If**, a castle in which various political prisoners were held captive down the ages. Alexandre Dumas condemned his fictional hero, the count of Monte Cristo, to be shut up in a cell here, before the wily count made his celebrated escape through a hole in the wall. *Admission included in the boat fare (29 frs.). Open June–Sept., daily 8:30–noon and 1:30–6:30; Oct.–May, daily 8:30–noon and 1:30–4.*

48 Head east from Marseille along D2 to **Aubagne**, 16 kilometers (10 miles) away. The headquarters of the French Foreign Legion is situated along D44A (turn left off D2 just before you reach Aubagne). The legion was created in 1831 and accepts recruits from all nations, no questions asked. The discipline and camaraderie instilled among its motley team of adventurers, criminals, and mercenaries has helped the legion forge a reputation for exceptional valor—a reputation romanticized by songs and films in which sweaty deeds of heroism are performed under the desert sun. The **Musée du Képi Blanc,** named after the legionaries' distinctive white caps, does its best to polish the image by way of medals, uniforms, weapons, and photographs. *Caserne Viénot. Admission: free. Open June–Sept., Tues.–Sun. 9–noon and 2–5; Oct.–May, Wed. and weekends only, 9–noon.*

49 Head south from Aubagne via D559/D1 to the fishing village of **Cassis**, 11 kilometers (7 miles) away. Cafés, restaurants, and seafood shops cluster around its harbor and three beaches, at the foot of Europe's highest cliff, the 1,300-foot Cap Canaille. Boats leave the harbor from quai St-Pierre to visit the neighboring *calanques*—long creeks that weave their way between towering white-stone cliffs. The farthest of the three calanques visited by boat, **En-Vau,** is the most intimidating; you may want to walk back from here along the scenic footpath.

50 From Cassis, a daring clifftop road runs along the top of Cap Canaille to the shipbuilding base of La Ciotat, 13 kilometers (8 miles) away. Stay on D559 for another 19 kilometers (12 miles), through Bandol, to **Sanary,** whose old streets and charming seafront invite discovery. At neighboring Six-Fours-les-Plages, spin right on D616, around the Cap Sicié peninsula, in search of more fine panoramas and a colossal view across the Bay of Toulon.

51 **Toulon** is France's leading Mediterranean naval base. Leave your car in the underground parking lot at place de la Liberté, head along boulevard de Strasbourg, and turn right after the theater into rue Berthelot. This street leads into the pedestrian streets that constitute the heart of old Toulon. Shops and colorful stalls make it an attractive area by day, but avoid it at night.

Time Out Good-value menus and a cozy setting make **La Ferme,** situated on a small square at the harbor end of cours Lafayette, a sensible choice for a filling lunch. *6 pl. Louis-Blanc. Closed Sun. and Aug.*

Avenue de la République, an ugly array of concrete apartment blocks, runs parallel to the waterfront, where yachts and pleasure boats—some available for trips to the Iles d'Hyères *(see below)* or around the bay—add bright splashes of color. At the western edge of the quay is the **Musée Naval,** with large models of old and new ships, figureheads, paintings, and other items related to Toulon's maritime history. *Pl. Monsenergue. Admission: 16 frs. adults, 8 frs. children. Open Wed.–Mon. 9–noon and 2–5; closed Tues.*

Mighty hills surround Toulon. **Mont-Faron,** towering 1,600 feet above sea level, is the highest of all; its steep slopes veer up just outside the town. You can drive to the top, taking the circular route du Faron in either direction, or make the six-minute ascent by cable car from boulevard de l'Amiral Jean-Vence (operates 9:15–noon and 2:15–6, closed Mon., Sept.–May; call 94–92–68–25 to check operating times in winter or bad weather).

㊿ Head east from Toulon along D559 to Hyères-Plage, then turn right along D97 to **La Tour-Fondue** at the tip of the narrow Giens peninsula. Boats leave here frequently (every half hour in July and August) for the nearby island of Porquerolles. *Crossing time 20 min.; round-trip fare 50 frs.*

㊱ At five miles long, **Ile de Porquerolles** is the largest of the Iles d'Hyères, an archipelago spanning some 20 miles. Although the village of Porquerolles has several small hotels and restaurants, the main reason for coming here is simply to escape from the hustle of the modern world. Filmmakers love the island and use it as a handy base for shooting tropical or South Sea Island—type scenery. You can stroll across the island from the harbor to the lighthouse *(le phare)* in about 90 minutes, or head east among luxuriant flowers and thick woods.

㊴ Boats for two of the other islands in the archipelago leave from Hyères-Plages and, farther round the coast, from Port-de-Miramar and Le Lavandou. The smaller of the two, **Ile de Port-Cros,** is classed as a national park and offers delightful, **㊵** well-marked nature trails. The **Ile du Levant** is long and rocky, and much less interesting; the French navy has grabbed part of it, and much of the rest is occupied by the Heliopolis nudist camp.

What to See and Do with Children

The Wild West has invaded Provence at the **O.K. Corral,** a huge amusement park that piles on the thrills by way of roller coasters, ferris wheels, and rootin' tootin' cowboy shows. Roy Rogers might do a double take at the less-than-authentic flavor —more Gallic than "Gunsmoke"—but children love it nonetheless. *11 km (7 mi) west of Aubagne on N8, just beyond Cuges-les-Pins, tel. 42–73–80–05. Admission: 55 frs. adults, 40 frs. children. Open June, daily 10:30–6:30; July–Aug., daily 10:30–7:30; Apr.–May and Sept., weekends 10:30–6:30; Mar. and Oct., Sun. 10:30–6:30.*

The following attractions are covered in the Exploring text:
Boat tour of the calanques by Cassis *(see* Tour 3)
Cathédrale d'Images, near Les Baux-de-Provence *(see* Tour 1)
Moulin de Daudet, Fontvielle *(see* Tour 1)
Museon Arlaten, Arles *(see* Tour 1)

Parc Ornithologique, north of Saintes-Maries-de-la-Mer (*see* Tour 1)

Children might also enjoy the raucous flavor of the Marseille fish market (*see* Tour 3) (also, *see* Shopping).

Off the Beaten Track

Our exploring toure bypasses Six-Fours-les-Plages on its way from the pretty harbor of Sanary to the dramatic Cap Scié peninsula. While Six-Fours is a sprawling town of limited interest, three nearby sites deserve a visit. The first is at Six-Fours itself, or, really, above it. The **Fort of Six-Fours,** at the top of a steep hill that has seemed even more rugged since fire destroyed its pine forest in 1987, can be seen for miles around. Although the fort is a private military base which can't be visited, the views across the Bay of Toulon are stupendous. Nearby is the former parish church of **St-Pierre,** featuring a Romanesque nave and a rich medieval altarpiece by Louis Bréa. Archaeological finds to the right of the entrance have revealed Roman walls built on the site.

Just north of Six-Fours (take D63 and turn left following signs marked *Monument Historique)* is the small stone chapel of **Notre-Dame de Pépiole,** hemmed in by pines and cypresses. While the chapel doesn't seem particularly interesting from a distance, it is, in fact, one of the oldest Christian buildings in France, dating from the 5th century. The simple interior has survived the years in remarkably good shape, although the colorful stained glass that fills the tiny windows is modern—composed mainly of broken bottles! *Chapel open most afternoons.*

Continue 5 kilometers (3 miles) north (via D11) to Ollioules and take N8 (direction Le Beausset) through the spectacular **Gorge d'Ollioules;** the three-mile route twists its scenic way beneath awesome chalky rockfaces. Turn right along D462 to pay a visit to the village of **Evenos,** a patchwork of inhabited, and ruined houses dominated by an abandoned clifftop castle.

Shopping

Gift Ideas *Santons,* colorful painted clay figures traditionally placed around a Christmas crib, make excellent gifts or souvenirs. There are literally hundreds of characters from which to choose, ranging from Mary, Joseph, and the Wise Men to fictional characters and notable personalities, both historic and contemporary. While santons can be found throughout the region (especially at Aubagne), the best places to purchase them are **Paul Fouque** (cours Gambetta, Aix-en-Provence) or **Atelier Ferriol** (2 chemin de Barriol, Arles).

Two specialties of Aix-en-Provence are deliciously fragrant soaps with natural floral scents and *calissons d'Aix,* ingeniously sculpted high-quality marzipan made of almonds and eggs. At **La Provence Gourmande** (66 rue Boulagon) you'll find a vast selection of soaps, as well as herbs, spices, and calissons d'Aix, while **À La Reine Jeanne** (cours Mirabeau) specializes in marzipan. Delicately patterned Provençal print fabrics made by Souleiado are beautiful and can be bought in lengths or already fashioned into dresses, scarves, tea cosies, and other accessories. You can find the prints in better-quality shops throughout the region, though Arles and Aix-en-Provence seem to have cornered most of the market.

Markets **Aix-en-Provence** has several markets that are a delight to explore: the flower market on Tuesday, Thursday, and Saturday mornings at place de l'Hôtel-de-Ville; the fruit and vegetable market every morning at place Richelme; and the fruit, vegetable, and herb market on Tuesday, Thursday, and Saturday mornings at place des Prêcheurs. Visit the antique market on Tuesday, Thursday, and Saturday mornings at place de Verdun. At **Arles,** fruit, vegetables, and household goods are sold on Wednesday and Saturday mornings in the boulevard de Lices, while **Marseille's** famous fish market is held on Monday through Saturday mornings at the Vieux Port. The flower market at **Nîmes** is open Monday mornings at boulevard J.-Jaurès, and you can purchase fruit, herbs, honey, and truffles at **Orange** on Thursday mornings in cours Aristide-Briand. Finally, in **Toulon,** there's a celebrated fish, fruit, and household goods market from Monday to Saturday mornings in rue LaFayette near the harbor.

Sports and Fitness

Biking Bikes can be rented from train stations at Aix-en-Provence, Arles, Avignon, Marseille, Montpellier, Nîmes, and Orange; cost is about 35 francs per day. Contact the **Comité Départemental de Federation Française de Cyclo** (2 rue Lavoisier, Avignon) for a list of the area's more scenic bike paths.

Bullfighting Provence's most popular spectator sport is bullfighting, both Spanish-style or the kinder *course libres*, where the bulls themselves have star billing and are often regarded as local heroes (they always live to fight another day). There are Spanish-style spectacles in the Roman arenas at Rond-Point des Arènes in **Arles** and at place des Arènes in **Nîmes.** *Course libres* are also held at Nîmes, and in nearly all the surrounding little villages throughout the summer.

Golf Golf is still considered a pastime for the rich, and you will find many more golf courses on the Riviera. However, Provence has an excellent course at La Grande Motte (tel. 67–56–05–00) and another near Aix-en-Provence (**Golf International du Château de l'Arc,** Rousset, tel. 42–53–28–38). Eighteen kilometers (11 miles) east of Hyéres is **Golf de Valcrof** (Valcrof, La Londe, tel. 94–66–81–02).

Hiking This has become newly popular in France, and you'll find blazed trails (discreet paint marks on rocks) on the best routes. Contact the **Comité Départemental** (63 av. C-Franck, Avignon) for a detailed list of trails and outfitters.

Horseback Riding Practically every locality in Provence has stables where horses can be rented. **Cheval Nomade** (col du Pointu, Bonnieux, tel. 90–74–40–48) specializes in tours on horseback (also, *see* Guided Tours under Essential Information). In Avignon, **Barthelasse** (Chemin du Mont Blanc, tel. 90–85–83–48) offers lessons for children at **Le Pony Club,** a children's riding school, in addition to renting horses to more experienced equestrians.

Water Sports You can windsurf and sail at La Grande Motte, Les-Saintes-Maries-de-la-Mer, Carry-le Rouet and Martigues (near Marseille), Cassis, Hyéres-Plage, and the island of Porquerolles, where equipment and sailboats can be rented. In Hyéres, the **Wanaco School of Windsurf and Sunboards** (5 Centre de Nautisme, tel. 94–57–77–20) rents sailboats from 300 francs for the day, while a windsurfer costs from 320 francs.

Dining and Lodging

Dining

Provence has more than its share of France's top restaurants. Thank tourism for this: Nature didn't intend Provence to be a gastronomic paradise. There are no deep, damp pastures for cattle and no chill rivers for salmon. In the old days, cooking was based on olive oil, fruit, and vegetables grown in valleys where summer irrigation is possible; salt cod was another staple, while the heady scent and flavor of garlic and wild herbs from stony, sun-baked hills improved the scanty meat dishes. The current gastronomic scene is a far cry from this frugality: Wealthy tourists demand caviar and champagne, and Parisian chefs have obligingly created internationally renowned restaurants to satisfy them. Still, there's a lot to be said for simple Provençal food on a vine-shaded terrace. Have a *pastis*, that pale green, anise-based aperitif, accompanied by black olives, or try the *tapenade*, a delicious paste of capers, anchovies, olives, oil, and lemon juice, best smeared on chunks of garlic-rubbed bread. Follow it up with *crudités* (raw vegetables served with *aïoli*, a garlicky mayonnaise), and a simple dish of grilled lamb or beef, washed down with a bottle of chilled rosé. Locals like to end their meal with a round of goat cheese and fruit.

The Provençal image comes through in a love of color; bell peppers, eggplant, zucchini, saffron, and tomatoes crop up everywhere. Fish is very trendy these days. A trip to the fish market at Marseille will reveal the astronomical price of the fresh local catch; in the Mediterranean there are too few fish chased by too many boats. Steer clear of the multitude of cheap Marseille fish restaurants, though, many with brisk ladies out front who deliver throaty sales pitches; any inexpensive fish menu must use frozen imports. The Marseille specialty of *bouillabaisse* is a case in point: Once a fisherman's cheap stew of spanking-fresh specimens too small or bony to put on sale, it has now become a celebration dish, with heretical additions like lobster. The high-priced versions can be delicious, but avoid the cheaper ones, undoubtedly concocted with canned, frozen, and even powdered ingredients.

Highly recommended restaurants are indicated by a star ★.

Lodging

Accommodations are varied in this much-visited part of France, ranging from luxurious *mas* (converted farmhouses) to modest downtown hotels convenient for sightseeing. Service is often less than prompt, a casualty of the sweltering summer heat. Reservations are essential for much of the year, and many hotels are closed during winter.

Highly recommended hotels are indicated by a star ★.

Aix-en-Provence
Dining
★

Le Clos de la Violette. Aix's best restaurant lies in a residential district north of the old town. You can eat under the chestnut trees or in the charming, airy dining room. Chef Jean-Marc Banzo uses only fresh, local ingredients in his nouvelle and traditional recipes. Try the *saumon vapeur*, an aromatic steamed salmon. The weekday lunch menu is moderately priced and well worth the trek uptown. *10 av. de la Violette, tel. 42–23–30–71. Reservations advised. Jacket required. AE, MC, V. Closed Sun., Mon. lunch, most of Nov., and late Feb.–early Mar. Expensive.*

Brasserie Royale. This noisy, bustling eatery on cours Mirabeau serves up hearty Provençal dishes amid a background din of banging pots, vociferous waiters, and tumultuous cries for more wine. The best place to eat is in the glassed-in patio out front, so you can soak up the Champs-Elysées-style atmosphere of the leafy boulevard while enjoying your meal. *17 cours Mirabeau, tel. 42–26–01–63. Reservations advised. Dress: casual. AE, V. Inexpensive.*

Lodging

Paul Cézanne. Georges Delorme runs this stately town-house hotel, and his taste for antiques and ornate furnishings has made it a civilized and sophisticated place. Each guest room is individually decorated with lots of marble, gilt, and period furniture. There's no restaurant. *40 av. Victor-Hugo, 13100, tel. 42–26–34–73. 42 rooms with bath. AE, MC, V. Expensive.*

★

Nègre-Coste. A cours Mirabeau location makes this hotel both a convenient and an atmospheric choice; it's extremely popular, so make reservations long in advance. The elegant 18th-century town house has been completely modernized, but features a luxurious old-world decor that extends to the guest rooms as well as the public areas. The views from the front rooms are worth the extra bit of noise. There's no restaurant. *33 cours Mirabeau, 13100, tel. 42–27–74–22. 37 rooms with bath. AE, DC, MC, V. Moderate.*

Arles
Dining

Le Vaccarès. In an upstairs restaurant overlooking place du Forum, chef Bernard Dumas serves classical Provençal dishes with a touch of invention and some particularly good fish creations. Try his mussels dressed in herbs and garlic. The dining room decor is as elegant as the cuisine. *Pl. du Forum, tel. 90–96–06–17. Reservations advised. Dress: casual. MC, V. Closed end of Dec.–end of Jan., Sun., and Mon. Moderate.*

Lodging

Arlatan. Follow the signposts from place du Forum to the picturesque street holding this 15th-century house, former home of the counts of Arlatan. Antiques, pretty fabrics, and lots of tapestries and elegant furniture lend it a gracious atmosphere. There's no restaurant, but the attractive garden goes a long way to compensate. *26 rue du Sauvage, 13200, tel. 90–93–56–66. 42 rooms with bath. Facilities: garden. AE, DC, MC, V. Expensive.*

Dining and Lodging
★

Jules César. This elegant hotel was originally a Carmelite convent, and many guest rooms overlook the attractive 17th-century cloisters. Rooms are tastefully decorated with antiques, and the garden is an oasis of tranquility. The restaurant, Lou Marques, is the most fashionable eating place in Arles, thanks to new chef Patrick Fer, who pleases his international clientele with nouvelle cuisine and traditional Provençal dishes. If you've never eaten tripe, try his *pieds et paquets*. *Blvd. des Lices, 13200, tel. 90–93–43–20. 52 rooms with bath. Facilities: restaurant, garden, pool. AE, DC, MC, V. Closed end of Nov.–Dec. 23. Expensive.*

★ **Mas de la Chapelle.** A 16th-century farmhouse surrounded by pretty gardens is the setting of this fine hotel-restaurant, a great spot to stay overnight or to use as a base from which to explore the area. It features an ancient chapel that has been skillfully converted into a cozy restaurant, decorated with Aubusson tapestries and original 18th-century stained glass. The menu varies; the seasonal game dishes are a good bet, or try the *coquilles St.-Jacques*. *Petit Route de Tarascon, 13200, tel. 90–93–23–15. 13 rooms with bath. Facilities: restaurant, riding, tennis, park. MC, V. Moderate.*

Avignon **Hièly-Lucullus.** According to most authorities, this numbers
Dining among the top 50 restaurants in France. The upstairs dining
★ room has a quiet, dignified charm and is run with aplomb by Madame Hiély. Husband Pierre's greater delights include crayfish tails in scrambled eggs hidden inside a puff-pastry case. Save room for the extensive cheese board. *5 rue de la République, tel. 90–86–17–07. Reservations essential. Dress: elegantly casual. AE, V. Closed most of Jan., last 2 weeks in June, Mon. (except July–mid-Aug.) and Tues. Moderate.*

Dining and Lodging **Europe.** This noble 16th-century town house became a hotel in Napoleonic times. In fact, the great man himself was one of the very first customers; since then, everyone from crowned heads of state to Robert and Elizabeth Browning has stayed here. Lovers of gracious living find it an excellent value; the guest rooms are spacious, filled with period furniture, and feature lavishly appointed modern bathrooms. Make reservations well ahead. The restaurant, La Vieille Fontaine, features respectable regional cuisine, and you can eat outside in the stone courtyard. Gourmands will want to try the chicken with wild mushrooms or the duck liver. *12 pl. Crillon, 84000, tel. 90–82–66–92. 46 rooms with bath. Facilities: restaurant. AE, DC, MC, V. Expensive.*

★ **Les Frênes.** The thumbnail-size town of Montfavet, 5 kilometers (3 miles) outside Avignon, is the setting for this luxurious hotel-restaurant. The country house features gardens to ramble in, splashing fountains, and individually decorated guest rooms; style ranges from subtle modern to Art Deco. Whatever the period of decor, each room is distinctive and equipped with every modern convenience. The excellent restaurant specializes in stylish country cuisine; the pigeon with black truffles in a puff-pastry case is always a good bet. *Av. Vertes Rives, 84140 Montfavet, tel. 90–31–17–93. 17 rooms with bath. Facilities: garden, pool, restaurant, tennis, sauna, golf. AE, DC, MC, V. Closed end of Nov.–early Mar. Expensive.*

Les Baux-de- **L'Oustau de Baumanière.** An idyllic setting under chalky-white
Provence cliffs, sumptuous guest rooms, and exquisite food makes this a
Dining and Lodging place of pilgrimage for lovers of the good life. The restaurant,
★ one of the top 20 in France, occupies an old Provençal farmhouse; you'll be served your meal in a cavernous room decked out with ornate furniture and resembling a luxurious crypt.

Try a plump pigeon stuffed with foie gras or some simple local thyme-fed lamb. The guest rooms are fit for a monarch—Queen Elizabeth II has slept here. *13520 Les Baux-de-Provence, tel. 90–54–33–07. 25 rooms with bath. Facilities: restaurant, tennis, pool, riding. Restaurant reservations essential. AE, DC, MC, V. Closed late Jan.–early Mar.; restaurant closed Wed., Thurs. lunch Sept.–June. Very Expensive.*

Gordes
Dining
★

Comptour du Victuailler. You'll find only 10 tables at this tiny restaurant in the village center, which serves elegantly simple meals using only the freshest local ingredients. The fruit sorbets are a revelation. *On the main street, tel. 90–72–01–31. Reservations essential. Dress: casual chic. AE, DC, MC, V. Closed mid-Nov.–mid-Dec., mid-Jan.–mid-Mar., and Tues. and Wed., Sept.–May. Moderate.*

Dining and Lodging
★

Domaine de l'Enclos. Small, private stone cottages make up this charming hotel; they have deceptively simple exteriors, but inside, you'll find them luxurious in a quaint, countrified way. The restaurant serves remarkably good nouvelle dishes; the menu varies with the seasons, but if it's offered, try the excellent aromatic duck. *Rte. de Sénanque, just outside Gordes, tel. 90–72–08–22. 14 rooms with bath. Facilities: restaurant, pool, tennis. AE. Closed Nov.–Easter; restaurant closed Mon. to nonguests. Expensive.*

Ile de Porquerolles
Dining and Lodging
★

Mas du Langoustier. This luxurious hideout lies amid some stunningly lush terrain at the westernmost point of the island, 3 kilometers (2 miles) from the harbor. Anchor your yacht, and Monsieur Richard will pick you up in a handy launch; arrive by ferry, and he'll send a car to meet you. The rooms are delightful, the views superb. Hotel guests must eat their meals here (no hardship), but the restaurant is open to nonresidents, too. Chef Jean-Louis Vosgien uses a delicate nouvelle touch with his seafood dishes; try the fresh sardines in ginger, or the grilled red mullet or lobster. *83400 Ile de Porquerolles, tel. 94–58–30–09. 60 rooms with bath. Facilities: restaurant, tennis, private beach. AE, DC, MC, V. Closed mid-Nov.–mid-June. Expensive.*

Marseille
Dining

Aux Mets de Provence. This restaurant is virtually a local institution. Hiding behind a blank exterior is an austere upstairs dining room whose menu is limited to one basic meal that has been virtually served for 50 years. You start with a spoonful of frozen olive oil to clear your palate, and glasses of the appropriate wine appear with each dish. The three-hour feast includes grilled fish and a seasonal game course, though chicken or duck sometimes make an appearance. You can't smoke, and don't ask for salt and pepper. The food is good, though critics say not quite as good these days. *18 quai Rive-Neuve, tel. 91–33–35–38. Reservations advised. Jacket required. AE, DC. Closed Sun. and Mon. Expensive.*

★

Chez Fonfon. The Marseillais come here for the best *bouillabaisse* in the world, and past diners lured by the top-quality seafood have included John Wayne and Nikita Khrushchev. "Fonfon" is the chef, sometimes known as Alphonse Mounier; he's thinking of retirement but a successor is being trained to his rigorous standards. The restaurant is located on the corniche J. F. Kennedy, which twists its scenic path around the edges of the Mediterranean; the great sea views come gratis. *140 Vallon des Auffes, tel. 91–52–14–38. Reservations strongly* *advised. Jacket and tie required. AE, DC, MC, V. Closed Oct., Christmas–New Year's, Sat. and Sun. Expensive.*

Dining and Lodging ★ **Sofitel.** The Sofitel possesses more appeal than most modern chain hotels, mainly because of the idyllic views across the old fort to the Vieux Port. Rooms with a balcony are more expensive, but the pleasure of an outdoor breakfast in the morning sunshine—possible most of the year—is worth a splurge. The top-floor restaurant, Les Trois Forts, boasts stunning panoramic views and delicious Provençal fare; the red mullet, flavored with pepper, is superb. *36 blvd. Charles-Livon, 13001, tel. 91–52–90–19. 127 rooms with bath. Facilities: pool, restaurant. AE, DC, MC, V. Closed Aug. Expensive.*

Lodging ★ **Pullman Beauvau.** Right on the Vieux Port, a few steps from the end of the Canebière, the Beauvau is the ideal town hotel. The 200-year-old former coaching inn was totally modernized in 1986, and its charming, old-world opulence is enhanced by wood paneling, designer fabrics, fine paintings, genuine antique furniture—and exceptional service. The best rooms look onto the Vieux Port. There's no restaurant, but you can start your day in the cozy breakfast room. *4 rue Beauvau, 13001, tel. 91–54–91–00 (to make reservations toll free from the U.S. call 800/223–9868; in the UK, 01/621–1962). 71 rooms with bath. Facilities: bar, breakfast room. AE, DC, MC, V. Expensive.*

Montpellier **Dining** **Le Chandelier.** The only complaints here concern the prices à la carte; service is impeccable, the trendy pink decor is more than acceptable, and the inventive cuisine is delicious. Try the lobster in lasagne or the pigeon. There's a sound wine list, and the cinnamon-honey ice cream makes a fine end to your meal. *3 rue Leenhart, tel. 67–92–61–62. Reservations advised. Dress: casual. AE, DC, MC, V. Closed part of Feb., first 2 weeks Aug., Sun., and Mon. lunch. Moderate/Expensive.*

★ **Hotel Montpelliérian des Vins du Languedoc.** The local wine producers run this little restaurant, which occupies a stone-vaulted cellar. The food is simple—you can have a plate of mixed *charcuterie* or just bread and cheese—but the choice of wines with which to wash down your meal runs the gamut of Languedoc vintages. *7 rue Jacques-Coeur, tel. 67–60–42–41. No reservations. Dress: casual. No credit cards. Closed Sun., Mon. Inexpensive.*

Nîmes **Dining** ★ **Nicolas.** Locals have long known about this homey place, which is always packed; you'll hear the noise before you open the door. A friendly, frazzled staff serves up delicious *bourride* (a garlicky fish soup) and other local specialties—all at unbelievably low prices. *1 rue Poise, tel. 66–67–50–47. Reservations strongly advised. Dress: casual. MC, V. Closed Mon., first 2 weeks July, and mid-Dec.–first week Jan. Inexpensive.*

Dining and Lodging ★ **Impérator.** This little palace-hotel, just a few minutes' walk from the Jardin de La Fontaine, has been totally modernized in excellent taste. Most guest rooms retain a quaint Provençal feel, and all are cozy but spacious. If this hotel were suddenly whisked to the Riviera, you would expect to pay twice as much for the pleasure of staying here. The fine restaurant, L'Enclos de la Fontaine, is Nîmes's most fashionable eating place, where chef Didier Thibaud provides inventive dishes like iced, dill-perfumed *langoustine* (crayfish) soup, and calves' liver with blackcurrant sauce and Calvados-soaked apples. The moderately priced set menus are bargains, but you can easily order your way into the expensive level. *Quai de la Fontaine, 30000, tel. 66–21–90–30. 59 rooms with bath. Facilities: restaurant. AE, DC, MC, V. Restaurant closed Sat. lunch. Expensive.*

★ **Louvre.** Occupying a 17th-century house on a leafy square near the Roman arena, the Louvre is the best sort of carefully run provincial hotel. The guest rooms are spacious and have high ceilings, and they manage to retain the feel of a private house; ask for one that faces onto the courtyard. The restaurant serves well-prepared traditional cuisine. The most tempting dishes are at the moderate level, though the inexpensive menu is a remarkably good deal. Seafood addicts will enjoy the lobster or the mussels in a flaky pastry crust. *2 sq. de la Couronne, 30000, tel. 66–67–22–75. 33 rooms with bath. Facilities: restaurant. AE, DC, MC, V. Moderate.*

Orange **Le Pigraillet.** One of Orange's best lunch spots is Le Pigraillet
Dining on the Chemin Colline St-Eutrope at the far end of the gardens.
★ You may want to eat in the garden, but most diners seek shelter from the mistral in the glassed-in terrace. The modern cuisine includes crab ravioli, foie gras in port, and duck breast in the muscat wine of nearby Beaumes-de-Venise. *Colline St-Eutrope, tel. 90–34–44–25. Reservations advised. Jacket required. AE, DC. Closed Dec.–Feb., Sun. dinner, and Mon. Moderate/Expensive.*

Le Bec Fin. While hardly elegant, Le Bec Fin is a perfect example of a small-town restaurant, serving local specialties to tourists and locals alike. Try the rabbit with mustard for a real taste of Provençal cooking at its best. *14 rue Segond-Weber, tel. 90–34–14–76. Reservations not required. Dress: casual. No credit cards. Closed Thurs., Fri., and Nov. Inexpensive.*

St-Rémy-de-Provence **Château des Alpilles.** This lavishly appointed 19th-century châ-
Lodging teau lords it over a fine park. In its heyday, it counted statesmen and aristocrats among its guests. The crowd these days is almost as sophisticated, and the guest rooms offer the best in classic luxury. Decorators have gone wild with plush carpeting and wood furniture to enhance the elegant ambience. Many rooms are equipped with kitchenettes. *13210 St-Rémy-de-Provence, tel. 90–92–03–33. 16 rooms with bath. Closed Jan.–mid-Mar. AE, DC, MC, V. Facilities: pool, tennis, gardens. Expensive.*

★ **Château de Roussan.** A manicured 15-acre park makes a lush setting for this 18th-century mansion, a mile outside town on the road to Tarascon. Originally a country retreat for the Roussan family, the château was converted to a hotel just after World War II. Today, it seems so well preserved it's almost spooky. The interior is quiet and gracious and appears virtually unaltered, save for the newly renovated bathrooms. The guest rooms are large and comfortable, and many feature pleasant parkland views. There's no restaurant. *Rte. de Tarascon, 13210 St-Rémy-de-Provence, tel. 90–92–11–63. 12 rooms with bath. Facilities: park. V. Closed late Oct.–late Mar. Moderate/Expensive.*

The Arts and Nightlife

The Arts

Theater and Music   The summer music and drama festivals at Aix-en-Provence, Arles, Avignon, and Orange attract top performers. At Aix, the **International Arts and Music Festival,** with first-class opera, symphonic concerts, and chamber music, flourishes from mid-July to mid-August; its principal venue is the Théâtre de l'Archevêché in the courtyard of the Archbishops' Palace (pl. des Martyrs de la Résistance). At Arles, the **Music and Drama Festival** takes place in July in the Théâtre Antique (rue de la Calade/rue du Cloutre). Avignon's prestigious **International Music and Drama Festival,** held during the last three weeks of July, is centered on the Grand Courtyard of the Palais des Papes (pl. du Palais, tel. 90–86–33–84). The **International Opera Festival** in Orange, during the last two weeks of July, takes place in the best-preserved Roman theater in existence, the Théâtre Antique (pl. des Frerès Mounet).

Opera and concerts are performed throughout the year in Aix-en-Provence's 18th-century Théâtre Municipale (rue de l'Opera, tel. 42–38–07–39), while Montpellier presents similar spectacles at the 19th-century Théâtre des Treize Ventes (pl. de la Comédie, tel. 67–52–77–17).

Nightlife

Provence is a disappointing provincial backwater as far as razzle-dazzle nightlife goes; if you've come to the south of France hoping to paint the place red—keep heading east to the Riviera. Your best bets for clubs and discos are those towns that have a major student population—like Aix-en-Provence, Marseille, and Montpellier—or the seaside resorts of La Grande Motte and Saintes-Maries-de-la-Mer. Most night spots open and close with alarming frequency, but at press time, Marseille's two cabaret-nightclubs were still going strong: **Au Son des Guitares** and **L'Abbaye de la Commanderie** (both on rue Corneille). In Montpellier, we suggest **Le Rimmel** (4 bis rue de Baussairolles); in La Grande Motte, **Capacabana** (Grand Travers, rte. des Plages). Marseille also has a noteworthy jazz club, **Blue Note** (25 rue Fort Notre-Dame), while one of the town's more exciting dance venues is the **Roll's Club** (76 corniche J. F. Kennedy). Finally, for those who thrive on roulette and blackjack, go to **The Casino,** open from 3 PM to 2 AM (pl. Jeanne d'Arc, Aix-en-Provence).

16 Corsica

Introduction

The island of Corsica lies in the heart of the Mediterranean, only 50 miles west of the Italian mainland, and just seven miles north of the island of Sardinia; Menton, on France's border with Italy, lies about 120 miles northeast. Ancient Greeks called Corsica Kallisté, "The Most Beautiful," while less-effusive English invaders nicknamed it the Scented Isle. But it was that most famous Corsican, Napoleon Bonaparte, who paid the island its greatest compliment: "I would recognize Corsica with my eyes closed," he declared, referring to the heady scent of myrtle, honeysuckle, lavender, eucalyptus, cyclamen, and wild mint that carries far out to sea.

Aside from the island's natural perfume, the first thing that strikes visitors, whether they arrive by air or sea, is the dramatic backbone of mountain ranges, which rise abruptly from the coastal shelf to loom high over beaches and bays. The approach by air is superb: Ajaccio, the island's capital, resembles an amphitheater, with the port occupying the stage and the houses perched where the seats would be. The island's sprawling sandy beaches are fringed with palm trees, ancient buildings, and cafés; Genoese watchtowers stud the coast, and houses and boats alike glitter with wild, bright hues of red, green, yellow, and blue.

Corsica seems more Italian than French. Over the centuries, it has served as a meeting point for myriad civilizations and was a hotly contested prize for successive waves of hostile invaders. In 1077, the Pisans wrested control; in the 15th century, Genoa established supremacy. In 1769, Genoa sold her rights in Corsica to France, and the island has been a French *département* ever since.

Corsica's main appeal is its scenery, a wild, rugged landscape covered with jagged, forested mountains. Perched in the foothills and nestled in the valleys are tiny villages that haven't changed since the Middle Ages, give or take the occasional traffic light. Many of the smaller bays are inaccessible other than by boat.

The best way to appreciate the island is to drive along the entire coastal circuit, venturing inland to admire the remote rural regions and picturesque villages, with their stone fortresslike houses topped by heavy slate roofs and pierced by narrow windows; tiny alleys masquerade as village streets, better suited to donkeys and goats than four-wheeled traffic. Though the main roads are full of hairpin curves and daredevil drivers, breathtaking views reward the effort.

Late spring and early fall are favorite times to visit, when the moderate temperature (61°–68°F) is ideal for exploring both inland and coastal areas. Corsica enjoys the longest beach season in France, from early May to November. Many visitors flock here during the celebrated "white spring," from mid-April to mid-June, when the island's ubiquitous white heather is in full bloom. Avoid visiting in July and August, when Corsica is overrun with tourists and there are no hotel vacancies.

Essential Information

Important Addresses and Numbers

Tourist Information The **Agence Régionale du Tourisme et des Loisirs** (ARTL, 22 cours Grandval, Ajaccio, tel. 95–51–15–23) can provide information about all areas of the island. Local tourist offices are as follows: **Ajaccio** (Hôtel de Ville, pl. Foch, tel. 95–21–40–87), **Bastia** (pl. St-Nicholas, tel. 95–31–00–89), **Bonifacio** (rue des Deux Moulins, tel. 95–73–11–88), **Calvi** (Port de Plaisance, tel. 95–65–16–67), and **Sartène** (cours Saranelli, tel. 95–77–05–37).

Travel Agencies **Havas** (1 av. du 1er-Consul, Ajaccio, tel. 95–21–49–66) and **Ollandini** (9 av. Maréchal-Sébastiani, Bastia, tel. 95–31–44–04).

Car Rental **Avis** (quai Comparetti, Bonifacio, tel. 95–73–01–28), **Europcar** (1 rue du Nouveau Port, Bastia, tel. 95–31–59–29) and **Hertz** (8 cours Grandval, Ajaccio, tel. 95–21–70–94, and 2 rue du Maréchal, Calvi, tel. 95–65–06–64).

Arriving and Departing

By Plane Corsica has four major airports, in Ajaccio, Bastia, Calvi, and Figari. **Air France** (tel. 45–35–61–61 Paris; 95–21–00–61 Ajaccio) and **Air Inter** (tel. 45–39–25–29 Paris; 95–21–64–06 Ajaccio) offer daily service between Paris and Ajaccio, Bastia, and Calvi. In addition, **TAT** (Transport Aérian Transrégional, tel. 46–87–35–53 Paris; 95–71–01–20 Figari) flies to Figari from Paris.

Between the Airports and Downtown The airports at Ajaccio and Bastia run regular *navette* bus services to and from town. At Figari, a bus meets all incoming flights and will take passengers as far as Bonifacio and Porto-Vecchio for 35 francs. If you arrive at Calvi, take a taxi into the town center.

By Ferry **SNCM** (Société Nationale Maritime Corse Méditérranée, tel. 42–66–60–19) runs a regular ferry service (twice daily in the low season; more frequently during peak summer months) from Marseille, Nice, and Toulon to Ajaccio, Bastia, Calvi, L'Ile-Rousse, and Propriano; crossings take from five to 10 hours.

Getting Around

By Plane **Air Corse** (tel. 95–20–61–30), **Air Transport Méditérranée** (tel. 95–76–04–99), and **Kyrnair** (tel. 95–20–52–29) offer interisland flights throughout the year.

By Car While driving is undoubtedly the best way to explore the island's scenic stretches, note that winding, mountainous roads and uneven surfaces can as much as double your expected traveling times.

By Train Corsica's simple train network consists of one main route and two branch lines. The main line runs from Ajaccio, in the west, to Corte, in the central valley, then divides at Ponte Leccia. From here, one line continues to L'Ile-Rousse and Calvi in the north and the other to Bastia, in the northeast. Another daily service runs directly between Ajaccio and Bastia, the island's two largest cities. During the summer months, a train-tram service connects Calvi and L'Ile-Rousse, stopping at numerous beaches and resorts (for information, call 95–32–60–06 in Bastia or 95–65–00–61 in Calvi).

By Bus   The local bus network is geared to residents, who use it in the morning and evening to get to and from work; afternoon buses are few and far between.

Guided Tours

Orientation Tours   **Ollandini** (3 pl. de Gaulle, Ajaccio, tel. 95–21–01–86) is one of Corsica's largest bus tour companies, with branches all over the island. Typical half-day bus excursions from Ajaccio visit the prehistoric site at Filitosa, taking in the Col de Bella-velle, Pila-Canale, Taravo Valley, Pietrosella, Isobella, and Porticcio. The most attractive whole-day excursion includes a trek along the breathtaking Scala di Santa Regina, Calacuc-cia, the forest of Valdoniello, and a lunch break at the Col de Vergio.

Boat Tours   Much of Corsica's most spectacular scenery is best viewed from the water. Boats leave regularly from Ajaccio for the Iles Sanguinaires ("Bloody Islands"—named for the red hue of the rocks in the setting sun), which lie just off the tip of the peninsula. The three-hour trip starts twice daily (at 9 and 2), leaving from the Bar du Golfe, below place Foch (for information, call 95–21–06–95). From Bonifaccio, you can visit the Dragon Grottoes and Venus's Bath (boats that make one-hour trips set out every 15 minutes during July and August) and the Lanezzi Islands (boats leave from outside the Hôtel La Caravelle, tel. 95–75–05–43). Whole-day tours leave from Calvi and visit Girolata, Scandola, and the Golfe de Porto. Boats depart at 9 AM, mid-May through September, and return at about 4:30 (contact **Autocare Mariani** in Calvi, tel. 95–65–02–55).

Aerial Tours   **Corse Aero Service** (Figari Airport, tel. 95–23–21–42) offers a series of sightseeing flights that cover the southern half of the island; an hour's flight costs 600 francs. **Bastia Aeroclub** (tel. 95–36–24–85) features tours over the island's central region.

Exploring Corsica

Numbers in the margin correspond with points of interest on the Corsica map.

Orientation

Our tour begins in the bustling port of Bastia, on the northeastern coast, and moves west, creeping inland to the Balagne region before reaching the popular resort town of Calvi. Our second tour actually describes two alternate, but equally dramatic, routes. Both veer inland to start; one branches off to reach Ajaccio by the coastal road and the other snakes down through the center of the island. Our final circuit explores the southern tip before swinging north to Alèria on the eastern coast.

Highlights for First-time Visitors

Ajaccio, Tour 2
The Asco Valley, Tour 2
Hill towns of the Balagne, Tour 1
Bonifacio, Tour 3
Calvi, Tour 1
Menhir statues at Filitosa, Tour 3
Scala di Santa Regina (D84), Tour 2

Tour 1: The Northern Coast

❶ We begin our tour in **Bastia,** whose name derives from *bastaglia,* or fortress. The Genoese built a prodigious one here in the 14th century as a stronghold against pugnacious inland natives and other potential invaders from across the Tuscan Straits. Today, as the island's commercial nerve center and largest town, the city has fallen to a new strain of invaders; a full 50% of Corsica's visitors, as well as over half its maritime traffic, pass through each year. Despite its reputation as the island's industrial center, with sprawling suburbs, modern tower blocks, and laundry-decked tenements, the city retains much of the color and flavor of a bustling Mediterranean port.

Start your tour in the atmospheric **Terra-Vecchia** (Old Town), at place St-Nicholas, bounded on one side by cafés and shops and on the other, by the sea. Head right, along the waterfront, until you reach quai du Premier Bataillon de Choc. Most of the quayside buildings date from the 17th and 18th centuries, but their once-impressive facades are badly in need of restoration. To the right is the **place de l'Hôtel de Ville,** enlivened each morning by a bustling outdoor market where black-swathed grandmothers haggle over the price of fish and fruit.

A few hundred yards up boulevard Général-de-Gaulle, to the right, stands the **Chapelle de l'Immaculate Conception,** occupying a pebble-studded square. Step inside to admire the church's ornate 18th-century interior: The walls are covered with a riot of woodcarvings, gold, and marble, and the ceiling is vibrantly frescoed. A copy of the *Immaculate Conception,* by 17th-century Spanish painter Bartolomé Murillo, adorns the altar, while the sacristy houses numerous relics used by Corsican religious cults between the 15th and 19th century. *Blvd. Général-de-Gaulle.*

Walking left from the Chapelle de l'Immaculate Conception and around the old port brings you to the city's **Terra-Nova** (New Town), dominated by its 16th-century **citadel.** If it's a clear day, climb to the top for a sweeping view of the islands of Capraja, Elba, Pianosa, and Monte-Cristo; in the distance, you'll be able to make out Italy's Tuscan hills.

While you are at place de la Citadelle, stop in at the **Genoese Governors' Palace,** whose vaulted, colonnaded galleries today house the **Musée d'Ethnographie Corse,** with collections detailing Corsican daily life and history. There are also archaeological, botanical, and anthropological exhibits, and a lifelike mock-up of a shepherd's hut. One of the museum's major attractions is an 18th-century rebel flag bearing the elaborate national coat of arms: a Moor's head in profile, bound by a white

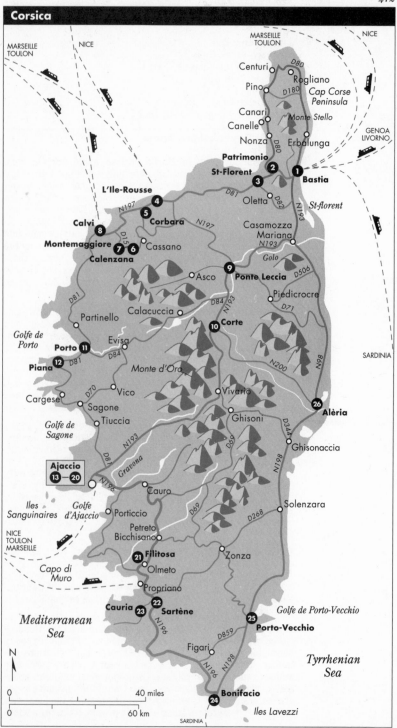

Corsica

MARSEILLE
TOULON

NICE

MARSEILLE
TOULON

NICE

Centuri
Rogliano
D80
Pino
D180
*Cap Corse
Peninsula*
Canari
Monte Stello
Canelle
Nonza
D80
Erbalunga
GENOA
LIVORNO
Patrimonio
St-Florent 2
1 **Bastia**
3
D81
Oletta
D82
St-florent
L'Ile-Rousse 4
N193
N197
5
Corbara
N197
Cassano
Casamozza
Mariana
Calvi 8
N193
Montemaggiore 7 6
Golo
Calenzana
Asco
9 **Ponte Leccia**
D506
Piedicrocre
D84
N193
D71
Calacuccia
Corte
D81
10
Partinello
Evisa
N98
*Golfe de
Porto*
Porto 11
D81
D84
Monte d'Oro
N200
SARDINIA
Piana 12
Vico
D70
Vivario
Cargese
Sagone
26
Tiuccia
Ghisoni
Alèria
*Golfe de
Sagone*
N193
D69
D344
Ghisonaccia
Gravona
N193
Ajaccio
13 — 20
N196
Cauro
D69
N198
Solenzara
*Iles
Sanguinaires*
*Golfe
d'Ajaccio*
Porticcio
D268
NICE
TOULON
MARSEILLE
Petreto
Bicchisano
Filitosa
21
Zonza
*Capo di
Muro*
Olmeto
Propriano
Golfe de Porto-Vecchio
Cauria
22
23 **Sartène**
25
N196
Porto-Vecchio
*Mediterranean
Sea*
D859
Figari
*Tyrrhenian
Sea*
N
N198
N196
0   40 miles
0   60 km
Bonifacio
24
Iles Lavezzi
SARDINIA

band enclosed in a crowned shield, supported by a pair of winged, cloven-hoofed giants. Outside, the palace's courtyard is the setting for local festivities and colorful historical pageants. Behind the ancient defense tower, a tiny flight of steps leads to the governors' private hanging gardens, an intimate green oasis offering a superb view over the old port to the towers of St-Jean-Baptiste. *Pl. du Donjon la Citadelle. Admission: 5 frs. Open Apr.-Oct., Mon.-Sat. 9-noon and 2-6; Nov. -Apr., Mon.-Sat. 9-noon and 2-5.*

Opposite the museum, a network of cobbled alleyways rambles across the citadel to the 15th-century church of **Ste-Marie** (rue Notre-Dame). Inside, textbook baroque abounds in an explosion of gilt decoration. The church's 18th-century silver sculpture depicting the Assumption is paraded through the streets of the Terra-Vecchia each August 15, at the head of a solemn religious procession. Just behind Ste-Marie stands the **Chapelle Sainte-Croix;** with its sumptuous Baroque interior, it looks more theater than church. The chapel owes its name to its major attraction, the "Christ of Miracles," a blackened oak crucifix discovered by fishermen in 1428 and venerated to this day by Bastia's fishing community. *Just off pl. Guasco.*

As you set off west by car along D81, you'll have dramatic views of mountains looming to the north, which form the backbone of the wild **Cap Corse peninsula** *(see* Off the Beaten Track, below). Before turning toward St-Florent, 23 kilometers (14 miles) **②** from Bastia, stop in the little town of **Patrimonio,** lying among acres of vineyards that stretch into the distance, a centuries-old source of some of Corsica's best red, white, and rosé wines. You'll find lots of local producers happy to sell you a bottle or two.

③ The resort town of **St-Florent** nestles in the crook of the Golfe de St-Florent, between the rich Nebbio Valley and the Desert des Agriates, an expanse of barren rocks sloping into the sea. The 13th-century limestone church of **Santa Maria Assunta** stands in isolated splendor among the vines, less than a mile from town. The church is one of only two Pisan cathedrals remaining on the island; though its bell tower crumbled in the 19th century, Santa Maria Assunta ranks as one of the most interesting Romanesque monuments Corsica has to offer. The facade and interior columns feature sculpted capitals depicting human masks, snakes, snail shells, and mystical animals with flowing manes and fierce-looking teeth. In the apse, notice the gilt statue of St-Flor, a martyred Roman soldier; his relics are displayed in a glass case nearby.

D81 snakes about 20 kilometers (12 miles) west from St-Florent **④** to the small resort town of **L'Ile-Rousse.**

Time Out   **Napoléon Bonaparte** is a rambling 18th-century palace-hotel, whose dining room, Le Picine, serves simple, satisfying meals against a backdrop of green foliage and starched white tablecloths. *3 pl. Paoli.*

From L'Ile-Rousse, pick up N197 and drive about 10 kilometers (6 miles) south into the ancient Roman region of **Balagne**. This western *Terre des Seigneurs* (Land of Lords) remained a feudal society right up to the French Revolution, and even today its population remains more insular than other Corsican folk.

Balagne long boasted a higher standard of living than other regions in Corsica, thanks, in part, to the area's rich agricultural resources. Oil, olives, barley, cheese, and grapes made more than a few fortunes for the Balagne gentry; the region is dotted with hill villages whose crumbling mansions hint at the wealth of former denizens.

⑤ D151 boasts a number of postcard-perfect towns. In **Corbara,** the first major village south of L'Ile-Rousse, sinister passageways and shady alleys recall Hollywood images of southern Spain. In the villages of Calenzana, Casano, Montemaggiore, Aregno, and Lumio you'll find myriad churches, many built by wealthy nobles when the island was under Pisan rule (1077–1284). The 11th-century church of **Ste-Restitute,** half a mile **⑥** from **Calenzana** on the road to Montemaggiore, is particularly interesting. The church's white marble, granite-topped 4th-century altar is backed by two 13th-century frescoes depicting Ste-Restitute's life. Legend has it that the saint was martyred here, and when the people of Calenzana began building a church on another site, the stone blocks were moved each night by two huge white bulls, to be discovered here the next morning. Apparently, this happened several times before the Calenzanais finally got the divine message and changed building sites.

⑦ The chapel at **Montemaggiore,** a few miles west, has its own legend. The steps beside it are a monument to Miguel Manara, better known as Don Juan. Born in Seville to Corsican parents in 1627, the womanizing Miguel returned to Corsica at the height of his infamy to seduce his half-sister, Vannina. Vannina's screams of protest awakened the family, and the frustrated rake was forced to flee the village, escaping down these very steps.

⑧ Continue northwest along D151 until you reach **Calvi,** one of Corsica's most sophisticated resort towns and the closest port to mainland France. Like that of Bastia, Calvi's location has long made it a strategic spot for warriors and tourists alike. The Middle Ages saw numerous struggles between local clans, while during the 18th century, Calvi endured assaults from Corsican nationalists, the most prominent being the celebrated patriot Pasquale Paoli.

Today's Calvi sees an annual summertime invasion of French and Italian visitors, drawn by the resort's four miles of white sand beaches flanked with graceful umbrella pines, a perfectly carved bay, and a busy marina.

Calvi's major attraction is the **Genoese citadel,** perched on a rocky promontory at the tip of the bay; the citadel's ramparts are the natural place to begin your tour of the city. As you cross the drawbridge, notice the plaque above; the inscription—*Citivas Calvi semper fidelis* (Calvi always faithful)—reflects the town's unswerving allegiance to Genoa. Calvi remained Genoese for centuries, even after the rest of the island had declared independence.

Next to the citadel is the **Oratoire de la Confrérie St-Antoine,** a 15th-century chapel showcasing Calvi's religious art. The wide collection of sacred objects spans the 16th through 19th century, and many items were discovered in recent excavations. *Admission: 4 frs. Open July–mid-Sept., Mon.–Sat. 10–noon and 3–6.*

Time Out Stop at **Club Tao,** in the former Bishops' Palace at the citadel, to wine, dine, or just listen to the music that fills the ocher-colored 16th-century vaults from 7 PM til 3 AM. *Pl. de la Citadelle.*

Stroll down the elegant quai Landry, lined with attractive bayside cafés and restaurants. Rue Clemenceau and boulevard Wilson, just behind, are major shopping streets. As you explore the narrow, winding streets of the old town, stop at the 13th-century church of **St-Jean-Baptiste** on place d'Armes, which contains an interesting marble baptismal font dating from the Renaissance. Look up at the dome to see the rows of seats screened by grillwork; the chaste women of Calvi's upper classes would sit here saying their prayers, protected from the hot glances of any lusty young peasant who might happen to look up.

Tour 2: Two Scenic Routes to Ajaccio

The route south from Calvi takes in a feast of varied scenery. Head east along N197 about 8 kilometers (5 miles) south of the coast. Follow the road south to the village of **Ponte Leccia,** standing between the spectacular regions of the Gorges de l'Asco and the Castigniccia. The **Asco Valley** runs west to an awe-inspiring barrier of mountains, whose colors vary from a red-mauve to a dark purple-gray, depending on the time of day. As you travel, the maquis-covered valley gives way to deep, granite gorges hung with sweet-smelling juniper. The Asco region's foothills are studded with beehives, and honey and cheese abound in the village shops. This is a land of tradition, where shepherds and goatherds practice the age-old winter ritual of "transhumance," taking their flocks to graze in the pastures of Balagne or on the rocks of Agriates and remaining with them until the summer heat signals them back to the mountains.

We offer two alternative routes from the island's center to Ajaccio. The first, and fastest, option is to follow N193 through Corte to Ajaccio. **Corte,** the biggest inland city in Corsica, has long been associated with the island's struggle for independence against the Genoese. The city's old town proves more austere than picturesque, however, and only hard-core history buffs should plan to linger here for a look at the 15th-century citadel. N193 runs 80 kilometers (50 miles) through the center of the island along the Vecchio Valley and over the Col de Vizzavona. In places, the junglelike chestnut, beech, and pine forests transform the road into little more than a thin green tunnel burrowing through the undergrowth. Along the way, stop for a superb view of the majestic Monte d'Oro, whose purple bulk looms against the skyline. As you enter the Gravona Valley, an unending chain of ridges alters the landscape at every turn.

Time Out Stop off in the village of Vivario, whose relaxed **Café-Restaurant des Amis** is the perfect place for a light lunch or mid-afternoon snack. The menu features local produce. *About 12 kilometers (7 miles) south of Corte.*

For a less efficient but even more dramatic route, pick up D84 just before you reach Corte and head west for the coastal towns of Porto and Piana, about 80 kilometers (50 miles) away. Known as the **Scala di Santa Regina** (Staircase of the Sainted Queen), the road is one of the most spectacular on the island; it's also one of the wildest and most difficult to navigate, particularly in winter. The route follows the twisty path of the River Goli, which has carved its way through layers of red granite, forming dramatic gorges and waterfalls; jagged needles of rock rise threateningly on all sides. Local legend has it that the Santa Regina mountains were the setting for the desperate struggle between St. Martin and the Devil—good versus evil—the theme of many traditional Corsican songs and poems. The road passes through two forests, the Forêt de Valdo-Niello and the Forêt d'Aitone, before descending to the Golfe de Porto. Porto and Piana lie on either side of the deep blue gulf, separated by an enormous red *calanche,* or jagged rock outcropping, that counts as one of the most extraordinary natural sites in France.

⑪ **Porto** is somewhat garish and self-consciously spruced, with an abundance of neon-lit hotels and restaurants; the village of
⑫ **Piana,** about 8 kilometers (5 miles) away, is much more welcoming. In addition to offering a series of breathtaking views of the Golfe de Porto, Piana serves as an excellent base for scenic walks. Visit the old fortress at the top of Capo Rosso to admire the craggy rocks that jut up from the bay.

Leaving Piana, pick up D81 and follow it about 35 kilometers
⑬ (21 miles) south along the coast to **Ajaccio,** which sits snugly on a protected bay surrounded by green mountains and rocky crags. High-rise buildings and overpasses loom as you approach this booming commercial city—Napoleon's birthplace and Corsica's modern capital.

⑭ Begin your tour at **place Maréchal-Foch,** the city's main square
⑮ planted firmly on the waterfront. Stop into the **Hôtel de Ville** (Town Hall), whose Empire-style Grand Salon is hung with portraits of a long line of Bonapartes. Exhibits include a fine bust of Letizia, Napoleon's formidable mother, and a bronze death mask of the emperor himself; the frescoed ceiling portrays Napoleon's meteoric rise to fame. The Salle des Medailles (Medal Room) displays a handsome collection of coins and medals. *Pl. Maréchal-Foch. Admission: 4 frs. Open Apr.–Oct., Mon.–Sat. 9–noon and 2:30–5:30; Nov.–Mar., Mon.–Sat. 9–noon and 2–5.*

⑯ Walk across the square and turn down rue Bonaparte. The **Maison Bonaparte** (the Bonaparte House) is a small, intimate museum in a modest 18th-century row house in rue St-Charles, overlooking place Letizia; Napoleon was born here on August 15, 1769. The museum features original Louis XV and XVI interiors, decorated by Letizia Bonaparte herself. In addition, glass cases display mementoes belonging to Napoleon and his father Carlo; another room contains portraits and cameos of the Bonaparte clan. Other highlights include the two family trees, one spanning nearly 200 years (1769–1959), the other a tiny 19th-century plaque over the chimney, woven out of human hair. *Rue St-Charles. Admission: 10 frs. Open Apr.–Oct., Tues.–Sat. 9–noon and 2–6, Mon. 2–6, Sun. 9–noon; Nov.–Mar., Tues.–Sat. 10–noon and 2–5, Sun. 10–noon, Mon. 2–5.*

Turn left outside the Maison Bonaparte and continue two
⑰ blocks to the 16th-century **cathedral,** where Napoleon was bap-

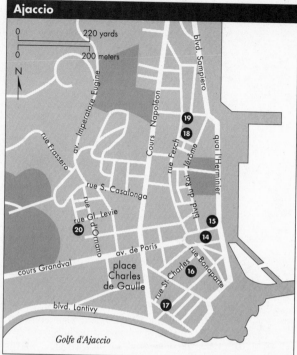

tized. Inside, you'll see Eugène Delacroix's famous painting *Virgin at the Sacre Coeur*, while the marble statue of *Notre-Dame-de-la-Misericorde*, Ajaccio's patron saint, has a place of honor opposite. *Rue Forcioli-Conti.*

Time Out   After visiting the cathedral, make your way down the **Plage St-François** and stop at one of the many cafés, restaurants, or ice cream parlors lining the quayside.

Before leaving Ajaccio, work your way back through the narrow streets to place Maréchal-Foch. Four blocks up rue Fesch is **⑱** the Renaissance-style **Chapelle Impériale,** built in 1857 by Napoleon's nephew, Napoleon III, to accommodate the tombs of the Bonaparte family. (The great man himself isn't buried here, however; his bombastic tomb is housed in Paris's Hôtel des Invalides.) A Coptic crucifix, taken from Egypt during the general's 1798 campaign, hangs over the chapel's main altar. **⑲** Opposite is one of the island's finest museums, the **Musée Fesch,** showcasing a superb collection of early Italian paintings. At press time, the museum was closed for renovation, so check locally for opening times and admission. *Rue Fesch, tel. 95–21–48–17.*

If you're interested in Corsican military history, make a trip to **⑳** **A Bandera,** a tiny museum in rue Général-Levie. To get there from Musée Fesch, walk back down rue Fesch, turn right toward cours Napoleon, then take the first left and first right, finally turning left into rue d'Ornano. The museum has a collection of documents, maps, uniforms, and armaments that illustrates the island's long and important history as a Mediterranean military station. *1 rue Général-Levie. Admission: 15 frs. Open June–Sept., Mon.–Sat. 10–noon and 3–7; Oct.–May, Mon.–Sat. 10–noon and 2–6.*

Tour 3: Ajaccio to Alèria

㉑ Leaving Ajaccio, follow N196 20 kilometers (12 miles) southeast to **Filitosa,** site of Corsica's largest collection of megalithic *menhir* statues. Bizarre, life-size stone figures rise up almost menacingly from the undulating terrain, many with human faces that have been eroded and flattened with time. A small museum on the site houses a variety of fascinating archaeological specimens, including the figure of Scalsa Murta, whose delicately carved spine and rib cage make it difficult to believe the statue dates from some 3,000 years before the birth of Christ. During the peak summer season (June through August), English-speaking guides are on hand to show visitors around. *Filitosa, tel. 95–74–00–91. Admission: 20 frs. Open Easter–mid-Oct., daily 9:30–7:30. Phone for information about winter hours.*

Time Out Stop at the pleasant museum **café** and soak up the prehistoric ambience over a light lunch or snack.

㉒ Following N196 about 16 kilometers (10 miles) southeast from Filitosa, you arrive at the hillside town of **Sartène.** Founded by the Genoese in the 16th century, Sartène has survived Barbary pirates and internal feuding among the town's leading families. Centuries of fighting have left the town with an almost spooky atmosphere; as you draw near, a line of tall, 18th-century granite houses rises in surly greeting.

The most interesting part of town is the **Vieux Sartène** (Old Town), just behind the ancient ruined ramparts. Start at place de la Libération, which is flanked by palms, elms, and intimate cafés. Locals traditionally gather here at night, and, more often than not, you'll find them engaged in heated—and incomprehensible—political discussions. To one side of the square is the Hôtel de Ville (Town Hall) the former Genoese Governors' Palace, whose facade is decorated with an ornate coat of arms. For a taste of the Middle Ages, follow the vaulted passageway through the building to place du Maggiu and the old quarter of **Santa Anna,** an eerie warren of narrow, cobbled streets lined with granite houses. Scarcely 100 yards from the Town Hall, down a steep and winding street, a 12th-century watchtower stands out in stark contrast to the modern apartment blocks behind.

For a look at some prehistoric relics, venture further afield to the **Musée Archéologique Départemental de Prehistoire Corse** (Archaeology Museum), a short distance outside town in Sartène's former prison. Sartène is the center for research on the island's prehistory, and the museum offers a fine collection of artifacts. *Admission: 8 frs. Open mid-June–mid-Sept., Mon.–Sat. 10–noon and 2–6; mid-Sept.–mid-June, Mon.–Sat. 10–noon and 2–4.*

About 10 kilometers (6 miles) southwest of Sartène lies the Cauria Plateau, a region that is rich in megalithic statues and

formations. Follow N196 south along the River Loreto, then
turn off onto tiny D48 to arrive at **Cauria.** Leave your car here
and set off on foot along the maquis-covered paths, where grazing goats share the countryside with spectacular remains. One
of the best preserved ruins is the **Dolmen Fontanaccia funeral
chamber,** discovered in 1840.

Backtracking to N196, continue south toward Bonifacio. As you
pass Roccapino, you'll probably see parked cars lining the cliffs,
their passengers taking in the spectacular **Rocher du Lion**
(Lion Rock), a glowing pink granite formation at the top of a
promontory. About 11 kilometers (7 miles) farther is another
rock formation, perched precariously among the mountains—
Omo di Cagna (The Cagna Man).

About 16 kilometers (10 miles) south of the N196 exit to Figari
looms the ancient fortress-town of **Bonifacio,** the southernmost
town in France. At its feet lies a handsome, fjordlike harbor
carved from the limestone cliffs. The city is just eight miles
from Sardinia, and local speech is heavily influenced by the accent and idiom of the neighboring Italian island. Don't be
surprised if you find the inhabitants difficult to understand—
many Corsicans do.

Established in the 12th century as Genoa's first Corsican
stronghold against the Moors, Bonifacio remained Genoese
through centuries of battles and sieges; these days, the town
contains many reminders of past military conflicts. As you explore the area, think of Homer's *Odyssey;* it was here, in the
bottleneck harbor at Bonifacio, that Ulysses's fleet was supposedly bombarded by the vicious Laestrygonians.

From the port-side village hamlet in the center of town, follow
the broad cobbled ramp up to the fortified **citadel** and the **Vielle
Ville** (Old Town). The citadel, which overlooks the harbor and
the Straits of Bonifacio, has long been the city's main defensive
post, and from 1963 to 1983 served as the main garrison of the
French Foreign Legion. Wander down to the tip of the promontory for a look at the ruins of the Franciscan monastery. As you
walk about, note the circular silos that were used to hoard food
and supplies, testimony to the plight of a city constantly under
siege. *Pl. de la Citadelle. Admission: 5 frs. Open June–mid-
Sept., daily 9–7.*

Finding hotel accommodations in Bonifacio during the peak
season can be difficult, since the sheltered, sandy beaches of
southeastern Corsica draw thousands of summer visitors.
You're more likely to find lodging at the large tourist resort of
Porto-Vecchio, about 27 kilometers (17 miles) north on N198.
Though the town itself is of limited interest, the **Golfe de Porto-
Vecchio** is lined with beautiful beaches and backs onto Corsica's
largest cork-oak forest. The walled old town features a network
of medieval streets, now given over to bistros, boutiques, and
cafés.

Time Out   While in Porto-Vecchio, it's worth making a special detour to
one of the island's most famous hotels, **Grand Hôtel de Cala
Rossa,** at the northernmost tip of the gulf *(see* Dining and
Lodging, below). Even if you can't afford to stay here, stop in
for lunch; the food is light and refined, and you can eat your
meal on a shady terrace among the fragrant pines overlooking

the bay. *8 kilometers (5 miles) outside town; Lecci de Porto-Vecchio.*

Leaving Porto-Vecchio, follow N198 60 kilometers (36 miles) north, skirting the marshy eastern plain, to the Roman city of **Alèria**, whose chief attraction is its rich archaeological heritage. Just outside town, on a pine-tree-studded plateau, is the 16th-century **Fort de Matra.** On the ground floor is the **Musée d'Alèria,** housing a fascinating collection of relics from Classical times, including some well-preserved Etruscan *rhytons,* or drinking cups, discovered in a 5th-century tomb nearby. Detailed exhibits chronicle daily life in Roman Alèria. One rather grisly display is the skeleton of an unfortunate prisoner who died around 50 BC; he was discovered curled in his tomb with his ankles still locked in heavy cuffs and chains. *Fort de Matra. Admission: 7 frs. Open Apr.–Oct., daily 8–noon and 2–7; Nov.–Mar., Mon.–Sat. 8–noon and 2–5.*

What to See and Do with Children

Corsica's **beaches** provide the best island entertainment for children *(see* Beaches, below). Or take them to the **Acqua Cyrné Gliss** water park in Porticcio, just south of Ajaccio, which offers water slides, swimming pools, and plenty of organized aquatic games. *Stragnolo RD 55, 20166 Porticcio. Admission: 63 frs. Open mid-June–mid-Sept., daily 10:30–7.*

Many children are fascinated by the megalithic *menhir* statues at **Filitosa,** Tour 3.

Off the Beaten Track

The rugged **Cap Corse peninsula** points like an accusing finger toward France's south coast, and its wild scenery and atmospheric villages make a rewarding day's exploration. A scenic coastal road (D80) runs right around the peninsula, skirting either side of a mountain range that culminates at the Monte Stello, soaring skyward near the tiny port of **Erbalunga** on the east coast. Erbalunga is one of the cap's prettiest villages, and its tiny houses tumble to the water's edge. Going north, the scenery grows wilder as the maquis covers the slopes. The road cuts across the tip of the peninsula from the fishing port of Macinaggio to its hinterland counterpart, **Rogliano.** A tiny road (D353) on the other side of the peninsula leads down to the picturesque 18th-century port of **Centuri,** an excellent spot for underwater diving.

The only other road that crosses the peninsula (D180) climbs to the Col de Sante Lucie pass and the **Tour de Sénèque,** a tower to which the luckless Sénèque was supposedly exiled after having seduced Roman Emperor Claudius's niece. The west coast of the Cap Corse peninsula offers several pretty villages, notably **Pino, Canari,** and **Cannelle. Nonza** is the largest of the west-coast villages; its location is particularly appealing, overlooking the sea and a stretch of blue-gray beaches on one side and an expanse of terraced vineyards on the other.

Shopping

Arts and Crafts Corsica's rich forests have led to the development of healthy arts and crafts and cottage industries. Many craftsmen are still hidden away on Cap Corse *(see* Off the Beaten Track, above) or inland mountain villages, producing beautifully carved pipes, letter openers, and other decorative objects using the wood of the surrounding chestnut and juniper trees. If the sweet scent of the maquis appeals to you, why not take some home, sewn up in attractive little bags; stop in at any of the tiny shops set back off the Corsican roads advertising "Essences du Maquis." As you wander up to the citadel in Bonifacio, you'll pass lots of small shops selling a wide range of objects, handcarved from sweet-smelling juniper wood—anything from miniature cars to smooth pebble shapes intended to keep moths out of the laundry cupboard; **Pierres de Cade** offers an especially good selection.

The villages of the Balagne region are also good hunting grounds for local crafts. **Casa di l'Artigiani** at Pigna, 8 kilometers (5 miles) from L'Ile-Rousse, offers a wide range of items, from local honey and jams to handknitted sweaters, silk scarves, local pottery, and watercolors. The **Poterie d'Olette** at Nebbio, between St-Florent and Oletta, sells a variety of handsome clay designs; choose from pots, dinner services, or painted lampstands.

Sports and Fitness

Bicycling Rental shops include **Locacycles** (40 blvd. Grazoni, Bastia) and **Avis** (Hôtel Marina Viva, Porticcio).

Hiking While the opportunities for scenic strolls are many and varied, the island's forests are not well maintained, and you may find yourself beating down the undergrowth even on well-marked trails. Leaflets covering walking paths are available from most tourist offices; ask for *Da Paese a Paese* ("From Village to Village") maps and brochures. The **Association "I Muntagnoli Corsi"** (quartier Santa-Maria, 20122 Quenza) offers two- and three-day guided hikes through the mountain and lake areas.

Horseback Riding Corsican equestrian trails are actually former mule paths. There are numerous stables, including **Poney-Club d'Ajaccio** (Centre de Randonnées Equestres, rte. de Sartène, embranchement de Bastia), **La Jument Pie** (rte. de Calvi, 20260 Lumio), and **Société Hippique Urbaine de Bastia La Marana** (Plaine de Montesoro, 20200 Bastia).

Water Sports Corsica is an ideal place for water-sports enthusiasts because it offers 16 "Sub-Aqua" clubs for underwater diving, swimming, and fishing. In Ajaccio, try the **Club des Calanques** (Hôtel des Calanques, rte. des Sanguinaires) or, in Bonifacio, the **Club Atoll** (to contact the manager, M. Ferrari, call 95–73–02–83). If you'd like to get in some sailing, contact the **Tahiti Nautic Club d'Ajaccio** (plage du Ricanto) or, in Bastia, the **Rugby Club Bastiais** (Cala Biancah, 20290 Borgo). Canoeing, kayaking, and rafting are popular pastimes on inland mountain rivers; for details, write the **Association Municipale de Ponte-Leccia** (20218 Ponte Leccia).

Beaches

The island's coastline offers astonishing variety: from the long, white stretches of sand along the eastern plain to the steep, rocky creeks of the rugged west coast; from the wild, undeveloped beaches of Cap Corse to the commercial tourist beaches

near Calvi or Propriano. The most unusual and attractive
beaches back onto the maquis and the forest; when the wind is
offshore, the heady scent of juniper and pine is sensational.
Even in July and August, when the popular beaches of seaside
resorts (Calvi, L'Ile Rousse, St-Florent, Propriano, Porto
Vecchio) are swarming with tourists, you can always find privacy in one of the numerous little creeks on the west coast or
north of Porto-Vecchio on the east coast.

Dining and Lodging

Dining

Corsica isn't known for luxurious restaurants or haute cuisine,
but local food is tasty and the helpings more than lavish. Seafood is abundant and delicious, whether grilled, baked, broiled,
or fried. Oysters, crayfish, and sardines are island staples, and
local fishermen's wives produce a rich *bouillabaisse* called
aziminu.

The island also offers a variety of local cheeses and *charcuterie*.
The best known cheese is *brocciù* (pronounced "brucho"), used
in both sweet and savory dishes; others to look for are the mild
basteliccacis and the *bleu de Corse*. Notable *charcuterie* products include *figatelli* (small, dry pork sausages), salami
sausages, and pork *lonzu* (fillet) or *coppa* (shoulder). Traditional stews of pork, lamb, or blackbird feature prominently on
menus and are often accompanied by a *pebronata* sauce of bell
peppers, garlic, and tomatoes. Other island specialties include
kid drenched in herbs and wild, chestnut-fed boar. Visitors
with sweet tooths will appreciate the local fritters, tarts, and
cookies, with enticing names like *pisticcine*, *canestrone*, *rappi*,
and *pane biscottu*.

Highly recommended restaurants are indicated by a star ★.

Lodging

Corsican hotels are generally clean and modern, though service
may be haphazard. Prices are high—marginally less than the
Côte d'Azur and the Riviera—though few hotels can be classed
as "deluxe." Most close for half the year (October or November
through Easter). During the peak season (July and August),
most insist on half-board or even full-board terms. Many will
provide a convenient packed lunch for guests who venture into
remote areas of the countryside, where restaurants are few; it's
a good idea to take advantage of the service, but check your hotel bill for every item.

Highly recommended hotels are indicated by a star ★.

Ajaccio
Dining

Auberge de Prunelli. Pisciatello, about 11 kilometers (7 miles)
from Ajaccio, is the setting for this authentic Corsican inn on
the banks of the Prunelli river. Hosts Santa and Mathea serve a
range of homey Corsican meals, including *omelette au brocciù*
and delicious roast kid. The atmosphere is cheerful, especially
if the fire's blazing in the hearth. *Pisciatello, tel. 95–20–02–75.
Reservations required. Dress: casual. No credit cards. Closed
Mar. and Oct.–Nov. Moderate.*
Côte d'Azur. Don't be disappointed if there's no space in the
oak-beamed ground-floor dining room; there are two other din-

ing rooms upstairs. The crayfish salad, fish "sausages," and lobster stews all are fine choices. *12 cours Napoléon, tel. 95-21-50-24. Reservations required. Dress: casual. AE, DC, MC, V. Closed Sun. and mid-June–mid-July. Moderate.*

Lodging **Eden Roc.** Ajaccio's best four-star hotel is in the city's most exclusive suburb, 8 kilometers (5 miles) from the center of town. The hotel overlooks the gulf of Ajaccio and the islands at the tip of the peninsula; extraordinary sunsets are guaranteed. Large guest rooms and sumptuous suites abound, all facing south and decorated with chic simplicity. *Rte. des Iles Sanguinaires, 20000, tel. 95-52-01-47. 42 rooms with bath. Facilities: garden, pool, restaurant, piano bar, health spa, sauna, Jacuzzi. AE, DC, MC, V. Expensive–Very Expensive.*

Bastia **Lavozzi.** Diners will enjoy a view over Bastia's old port as they
Dining make their choice of a host of fish and seafood specials. Wall-to-wall carpeting and white, rough-cast plaster walls enhance Lavozzi's charm. The cuisine is traditional Corsican; try the devilfish in mint or sardines in *brocciù* cheese. *8 rue St-Jean, tel. 95-31-05-73. Reservations required. Jacket and tie required. AE, DC, MC, V. Closed Sun. and Feb.–Mar. Expensive.*

★ **Chez Assunta.** Corsican and Mediterranean specialties—lots of seafood salads and grilled fish—are served in this brick-vaulted former chapel, once part of a Genoese private mansion. If it's on the menu, go for the baked rabbit. *4 pl. de la Fontaine Neuve, tel. 95-31-67-06. Reservations required. Dress: casual chic. AE, DC, MC, V. Closed Sun. dinner and Jan.–Feb. Moderate.*

Lodging **L'Alivi.** A striking contemporary hotel, L'Alivi, is less than a mile north of town, in Pietra Nera. The guest rooms are stylishly furnished with plenty of chrome and glass; those nearest the beach feature vast sliding windows and balconies overlooking the sea. On clear days, you can see the Italian islands and Tuscany. There's no restaurant. *Palagaccio, 20200, tel. 95-31-61-85. 35 rooms with bath. V. Closed Christmas–New Year's. Expensive.*

Posta Vecchia. An old building overlooking the port was renovated and transformed into the Posta Vecchia hotel in 1978. The unpretentious guest rooms are decorated with floral wallpapers and print bedspreads, while the wood-beamed ceilings add a rustic touch. Some rooms are small; the best are in the main house, facing the port. There's no restaurant. *Quai des Martyrs, 20200, tel. 95-32-32-38. 49 rooms with bath. AE, DC, MC, V. Moderate.*

Calvi **Ile de Beauté.** One of Calvi's most celebrated restaurants, Ile
Dining de Beauté has been pulling in the crowds since 1929; it's on the
★ quayside, right next to the port. The original wood paneling lends the dining room a classical ambience, while the terrace catches Calvi's festive atmosphere. The menu features a range of fish specials, including lobster fricassee; meat eaters should try the beef *feuilleté* (in a pastry case) stuffed with cepe mushrooms. *Quai Landry, tel. 95-65-00-46. Reservations strongly advised. Jacket and tie required. AE, DC, MC, V. Closed Wed. (except July and Aug.) and Oct.–Apr. Expensive.*

★ **Abri Côtier.** This place is as refreshing by day as it is romantic by night. At lunchtime or on warm summer evenings, you can eat on the covered terrace overlooking the port. When the weather gets cooler, dine indoors in the large dining room, where apricot linen and chunky silver cutlery set the tone. For a light lunch, order the salmon rolls. House specials include fish dishes of all sorts, grilled, baked, or covered in refined sauces. Save room for the homemade desserts. *Quai Landry, 95–65–12–76. Reservations advised. Dress: casual chic. AE, DC, MC, V. Closed Oct.–Apr. Moderate.*

Lodging   **Balanea.** The best feature of the modern Balanea is its port-side setting, from which you can watch the fishing boats chug in and out of the harbor. The stark modern decor lacks character, but the guest rooms are air-conditioned and some are spacious. It's worth the extra cost to have a room with a bay view; try to reserve one of the penthouse rooms. There's no restaurant, but breakfast is served on a balcony overlooking the port. *6 rue Clemenceau, 20260, tel. 95–65–00–45. 40 rooms with bath. Facilities: bar. AE, DC, MC, V. Moderate–Expensive.*

Dining and Lodging
★   **Magnolia.** Massive floral bouquets decorate the cream-colored lobby, and stained-glass windows cast shimmering pools of light onto the central, banistered staircase of this elegant, turn-of-the-century hotel. Outside there's a pleasant garden-patio, shaded by fragrant magnolias and pines. Each guest room has a different monochromatic decorative scheme, though all feature built-in closets and beds framed by niches. There's no restaurant. *Pl. du Marche, 20260, tel. 95–65–19–16. 13 rooms, 10 with bath. Facilities: bar, garden. AE, DC, V. Expensive.*

Le Signoria. This rustic, country inn occupies a park some 5 kilometers (3 miles) outside town. The 17th-century homestead has been fitted out with bedrooms, large bathrooms, and a swimming pool that is directly accessible from the ground-floor rooms. Le Signoria also boasts a fine restaurant, decorated in rosy stucco; specialties include lobster and other seafoods. *Rte. de la Forêt de Bonifato, 20260, tel. 95–65–23–73. 10 rooms with bath. Facilities: restaurant, pool, garden. AE, MC, V. Closed Oct.–Easter. Expensive.*

Centuri
Dining and Lodging
★   **Le Vieux Moulin.** If you're after old-world charm and an authentic Corsican flavor, Le Vieux Moulin is the place to try. The main house was built in 1870 as a private residence; the eight-room annex is more recent, but no less inviting, with bougainvillea cascading from its balconies. The friendly staff will arrange boat rides and fishing trips around the coast of the wildly dramatic Cap Corse peninsula, and there's a tennis court and small golf course nearby. The restaurant specializes in seafood; try the *bouillabaisse. Centuri Port, 20235, tel. 95–35–60–15. 14 rooms with bath. Facilities: restaurant. AE, DC, MC, V. Closed Nov.–Mar. Inexpensive.*

Corte
Dining and Lodging
★   **Auberge de la Restonica.** This Swiss chalet à la Corse lies in the heart of a remote, wooded valley, hemmed in by rocky peaks. The lobby/living room is reminiscent of a hunting lodge, with red-tiled floors, stone walls, and chunky wooden furniture arranged around a massive hearth; the dining-room terrace looks out over a cascading stream. The restaurant offers a good-value set menu, with specials like fresh river trout and herb tart. *Rte. de la Restonica, 20250, tel. 95–46–09–58. 10 rooms with bath. AE, MC, V. Closed Nov.–Feb. Inexpensive–Moderate.*

Piana
Dining and Lodging   **Capo Russo.** The four-star Capo Russo sits high in the hills overlooking the Golfe de Porto, just yards from the famous *calanche* rocky outcropping. The views—whether seen from

your room, the outdoor pool, or the restaurant's terrace—are mind-bogglingly dramatic. Unfortunately, the modern guest rooms are functional, rather than charming. *20115 Piana, tel. 95–27–82–40. 70 rooms with bath. Facilities: restaurant. AE, DC, MC, V. Closed mid-Oct.–Mar. Moderate–Expensive.*

Les Roches Rouges. On the hillside just below the Capo Russo, this rambling old mansion caters to an essentially British clientele. Don't be misled by the crumbling facade: The current owners took over only a few years ago and are still renovating. Most guest rooms are sparse and monastic, but the irrepressible owner, Mady, the eccentric British atmosphere, and the hotel's stunning location, make Les Roches Rouges a definite winner. The vast Imperial-style restaurant is classified as a historical monument; go for the fish soup or the grilled lobster. *20115 Piana, tel. 95–27–81–81. 20 rooms with bath. Facilities: restaurant. AE, DC, MC, V. Closed Nov.–Mar. Moderate.*

Porticcio
Dining and Lodging
★

Le Maquis. The evocatively named Maquis ranks as one of the island's finest *hôtels de charme*. The quaint, ivy-covered building reaches down to its own private beach, and sea-level rooms open directly onto arch-covered patios. West-facing rooms and terraces capture the stunning sunsets over the hills beyond Ajaccio. The candlelit restaurant, L'Arbousier, features hand-hewn beams and white plaster walls, decorated with an ornate gilt mirror; tile floors and wicker chairs add to the rustic elegance. The food is a blend of traditional and nouvelle: fish tartare, scrambled eggs with truffles, *coquilles St-Jacques*, or fresh *tagliatelles* all make fine choices. *20000 Porticcio, tel. 95–25–05–55. 27 rooms with bath. Facilities: restaurant, pool, tennis, private beach. AE, DC, MC, V. Expensive–Very Expensive.*

Sofitel Thalassa. In so superb a setting overlooking the Gulf of Ajaccio, it's a shame that this hotel is such a plain, functional-looking building. If you're looking for straight relaxation and excellent service, however, you'll excuse the hotel's leaden architecture and overplush decor. Candlelit dinners on the terrace of the vast Le Caroubier restaurant—offering French cuisine and Corsican specialties—help compensate as well. *20166 Porticcio, tel. 95–25–00–34. 100 rooms with bath. Facilities: restaurant, pool, tennis, piano bar, disco, solarium, thalassotherapy, water sports. AE, DC, MC, V. Restaurant closed Dec. Expensive–Very Expensive.*

Porto-Vecchio
Dining and Lodging
★

Grand Hôtel de Cala Rossa. This mansion-hotel is one of the island's finest hotels, showcasing modern design at its best. Nothing jars, from the curves of the heavy white walls to the choice of contemporary paintings lining the corridors. Rooms vary greatly in price, but all are luxurious. An early morning breakfast outside under the trees, just yards from the beach, will make you forget your sightseeing plans. Corsican-style nouvelle dishes are featured in the restaurant; you can't go wrong with the roast kid or the fresh-mint omelette. *8 kilometers (5 miles) outside town, 20137 Lecci de Porto-Vecchio, tel. 95–71–61–51. 50 rooms with bath. Facilities: restaurant, terrace, tennis. AE, DC, MC, V. Closed Nov.–Apr. Moderate–Very Expensive.*

Hôtel du Roi Théodore. This modern hotel is run with smooth efficiency. From the covered balconies—each room has its own —views extend over the ocean and sandy beaches. The guest rooms, reception, and bars are decorated in a Moorish-influenced style, with white walls and furnishings and dark wood trim. The restaurant serves Corsican and international specialties. *Rte. de Bastia, 20137, tel. 95–70–14–94. 40 rooms with bath. Facilities: restaurant, pools, tennis, Ping-Pong. AE, DC, MC, V. Closed mid-Oct.–Mar. Moderate/Expensive.*

Santa Giulia
Dining and Lodging

Moby Dick. The Moby Dick's interior designer had an eye for sophisticated simplicity: White stucco walls, white marble lamps, and blue comb-painted doors. The modern hotel is virtually surrounded by water and sandy beaches, and the guest rooms offer views of the sea and mountains. The restaurant serves a good-value buffet lunch and both a "normal" and *gastronomique* (gargantuan) menu at dinner. The crayfish is delicious. *Santa Giulia 20137, Porto Vecchio, tel. 95–70–21–18. 44 rooms with bath. Facilities: restaurant. AE, DC, MC, V. Closed Oct.–Apr. Moderate–Expensive.*

The Arts and Nightlife

The Arts

Music and Festivals

Singing plays an important role in both traditional and daily island life. You'll doubtless come across impromptu café gatherings where the locals are singing their hearts out, giving impressive renderings of a traditional *paghiella* (a three-voice harmony), a *voceru* (funeral chant), or a *chjiama e rispondi* duel (in which two singers rival each other in a lyrical Ping-Pong match, throwing questions and answers in an attempt to outdo each other by the wit, beauty, or rhyme of their invention).

The island has two major **carnivals,** one in Bastia in April and the other in Ajaccio in May, when the towns come alive with song, costumed processions, and outdoor theater. Both towns feature similar festivities throughout the summer, reaching a climax on August 15, when Ajaccio celebrates Napoleon's birthday. Other island festivals include an **Italian Film Festival** in Bastia in February; a **Jazz Festival** in Calvi in June; **pop concerts** in Porto-Vecchio in July and August; a classical **International Music Meeting** in Ajaccio in July; and an **International Music Festival** in Bastia in late August/early September, when the music varies from classical to jazz.

Nightlife

Cabaret

For traditional Corsican cabarets, try **Le Pavillon Bleu** (cours Grandval) and **Le Lido** (plage St-François, blvd. Lantivy) in Ajaccio and in Bastia, **U'Rataghiu** (rue Carnot) and **U'Fanale** (Le Vieux Port).

Piano Bars

In Ajaccio, we recommend **Le Petit Caporal** (9 pl. Foch), **Le Palm Beach** (rte. des Sanguinaires), and **Le Santa Lina** (Espace Santa Lina). In Bastia, try **L'Alba** (22 quai des Martyrs); in Calvi, **Chez Tao** (pl. de la Citadelle).

GO WHERE YOU WANT TO GO, SAY WHAT YOU WANT TO SAY with *Living Language* TRAVELTALK™

- make hotel reservations
- ask directions to the local castle
- order an edible meal
- find the perfect sweater

JUST NEED TO BRUSH UP?

Try **Living Language Plus®**. Refresh and improve your conversational ability with this intermediate-level course. The 90-minute cassette contains 10 lively dialogues in English and the foreign language, so the tape may be used alone or with the 32-page booklet included in the package. Only $9.95 each.

Conversion Tables

Clothing Sizes

Men
Suits To change American suit sizes to French suit sizes, add 10 to the American suit size.
To change French suit sizes to American suit sizes, subtract 10 from the French suit size.

U.S.	36	38	40	42	44	46	48
French	46	48	50	52	54	56	58

Shirts To change American shirt sizes to French shirt sizes, multiply the American shirt size by 2 and add 8.
To change French shirt sizes to American shirt sizes, subtract 8 from the French shirt size and divide by 2.

U.S.	14	14½	15	15½	16	16½	17	17½
French	36	37	38	39	40	41	42	43

Shoes French shoe sizes vary in their relation to American shoe sizes.

U.S.	6½	7	8	9	10	10½	11
French	39	40	41	42	43	44	45

Women
Dresses and Coats To change U.S. dress/coat sizes to French dress/coat sizes, add 28 to the U.S. dress/coat size.
To change French dress/coat sizes to U.S. dress/coat sizes, subtract 28 from the French dress/coat size.

U.S.	4	6	8	10	12	14	16
French	32	34	36	38	40	42	44

Blouses and Sweaters To change U.S. blouse/sweater sizes to French blouse/sweater sizes, add 8 to the U.S. blouse/sweater size.
To change French blouse/sweater sizes to U.S. blouse/sweater sizes, subtract 8 from the French blouse/sweater size.

U.S.	30	32	34	36	38	40	42
French	38	40	42	44	46	48	50

Shoes To change U.S. shoe sizes to French shoe sizes, add 32 to the U.S. shoe size.
To change French shoe sizes to U.S. shoe sizes, subtract 32 from the French shoe size.

U.S.	4	5	6	7	8	9	10
French	36	37	38	39	40	41	42

French Vocabulary

Words and Phrases

	English	French	Pronunciation
Basics	Yes/no	Oui/non	wee/no
	Please	S'il vous plaît	seel voo play
	Thank you	Merci	mare-**see**
	You're welcome	De rien	deh ree-**en**
	Excuse me, sorry	Pardon	pahr-**doan**
	Sorry!	Désolé(e)	day-zoh-**lay**
	Good morning/afternoon	Bonjour	bone-**joor**
	Good evening	Bonsoir	bone-**swar**
	Goodbye	Au revoir	o ruh-**vwar**
	Mr. (Sir)	Monsieur	mih-see-**oor**
	Mrs. (Ma'am)	Madame	meh-**dahm**
	Miss	Mademoiselle	mad-mwa-**zel**
	Pleased to meet you	Enchanté(e)	on-shahn-**tay**
	How are you?	Comment allez-vous?	ko-men-tahl-ay-**voo**
Numbers	one	un	un
	two	deux	dew
	three	trois	twa
	four	quatre	**cat-ruh**
	five	cinq	sank
	six	six	seess
	seven	sept	set
	eight	huit	wheat
	nine	neuf	nuf
	ten	dix	deess
	eleven	onze	owns
	twelve	douze	dues
	thirteen	treize	trays
	fourteen	quatorze	ka-torz
	fifteen	quinze	cans
	sixteen	seize	sez
	seventeen	dix-sept	deess-**set**
	eighteen	dix-huit	deess-**wheat**
	nineteen	dix-neuf	deess-**nuf**
	twenty	vingt	vant
	twenty-one	vingt-et-un	vant-ay-**un**
	thirty	trente	trahnt
	forty	quarante	ka-**rahnt**
	fifty	cinquante	sang-**kahnt**
	sixty	soixante	swa-**sahnt**
	seventy	soixante-dix	swa-sahnt-**deess**
	eighty	quatre-vingts	cat-ruh-**vant**
	ninety	quatre-vingt-dix	cat-ruh-vant-**deess**
	one-hundred	cent	sahnt
	one-thousand	mille	meel
Colors	black	noir	nwar
	blue	bleu	blu
	brown	brun	brun

	green	vert	vair
	orange	orange	o-**ranj**
	red	rouge	rouge
	white	blanc	blahnk
	yellow	jaune	jone

Days of the Week	Sunday	dimanche	dee-**mahnsh**
	Monday	lundi	lewn-**dee**
	Tuesday	mardi	mar-**dee**
	Wednesday	mercredi	mare-kruh-**dee**
	Thursday	jeudi	juh-**dee**
	Friday	vendredi	van-dra-**dee**
	Saturday	samedi	sam-**dee**

Months	January	janvier	jan-**vyay**
	February	février	feh-vree-**ay**
	March	mars	mars
	April	avril	a-**vreel**
	May	mai	my
	June	juin	jwan
	July	juillet	jwee-**ay**
	August	août	oot
	September	septembre	sep-**tahm**-bruh
	October	octobre	oak-**toe**-bruh
	November	novembre	no-**vahm**-bruh
	December	décembre	day-**sahm**-bruh

Useful Phrases	Do you speak English?	Parlez-vous anglais?	par-lay vooz ahng-**glay**
	I don't speak French	Je ne parle pas français	jeh nuh parl pah fraun-**say**
	I don't understand	Je ne comprends pas	jeh nuh kohm-prahn **pah**
	I understand	Je comprends	jeh kohm-**prahn**
	I don't know	Je ne sais pas	jeh nuh say **pah**
	I'm American/British	Je suis américain/anglais	jeh sweez a-may-ree-**can**/ahng-**glay**
	What's your name?	Comment vous appelez-vous?	ko-mahn voo za-pel-ay-**voo**
	My name is . . .	Je m'appelle . . .	jeh muh-**pel** . . .
	What time is it?	Quelle heure est-il?	kel ur et-**il**
	How?	Comment?	ko-**mahn**
	When?	Quand?	kahnd
	Yesterday	Hier	yair
	Today	Aujourd'hui	o-zhoor-**dwee**
	Tomorrow	Demain	deh-**man**
	This morning/afternoon	Ce matin/cet après-midi	seh ma-**tanh**/set ah-pray-mee-**dee**
	Tonight	Ce soir	seh **swar**
	What?	Quoi?	kwah

What is it?	Qu'est-ce que c'est?	kess-kuh-**say**
Why?	Pourquoi?	poor-**kwa**
Who?	Qui?	kee
Where is . . .	Où est . . .	oo ay
the train station?	la gare?	la gar
the subway station?	la station de métro?	la sta-syon deh may-**tro**
the bus stop?	l'arrêt de bus?	la-ray deh **booss**
the terminal (airport)?	l'aérogare?	lay-ro-**gar**
the post office?	la poste?	la post
the bank?	la banque?	la bahnk
the . . . hotel?	l'hôtel . . .?	low-**tel**
the . . . museum?	le musée . . .?	leh mew-**zay**
the hospital?	l'hôpital?	low-pee-**tahl**
the elevator?	l'ascenseur?	la-sahn-**seur**
the telephone?	le téléphone?	leh te-le-**phone**
Where are the restrooms?	Où sont les toilettes?	oo son lay twah-**let**
Here/there	Ici/lá	ee-**see**/la
Left/right	A gauche/à droite	a goash/a drwat
Is it near/far?	C'est près/loin?	say pray/lwan
I'd like . . .	Je voudrais . . .	jeh voo-**dray**
a room	une chambre	ewn **shahm**-bra
the key	la clé	la clay
a newspaper	un journal	un joor-**nahl**
a stamp	un timbre	un **tam**-bruh
I'd like to buy . . .	Je voudrais acheter . . .	jeh voo-**dray** ahsh-**tay**
cigarettes	des cigarettes	day see-ga-**ret**
matches	des allumettes	days a-loŏ-**met**
city plan	un plan de ville	un plahn de la **veel**
road map	une carte routière	ewn cart roo-tee-**air**
magazine	une revue	ewn reh-**view**
envelopes	des enveloppes	dayz ahn-veh-**lope**
writing paper	de papier à lettres	deh-pa-pee-ay a **let**-ruh
airmail writing paper	de papier avion	deh pa-pee-ay a-vee-**own**
postcard	une carte postale	ewn cart post-**al**
How much is it?	C'est combien?	say comb-bee-**en**
It's expensive/cheap	C'est cher/pas cher	say sher/pa sher
A little/a lot	Un peu/beaucoup	un puh/bo-**koo**
More/less	Plus/moins	ploo/mwa
Enough/too (much)	Assez/trop	a-**say**/tro
I am ill/sick	Je suis malade	jeh swee ma-**lahd**

Call a doctor	Appelez un docteur	a-pe-lay un dohk-**tore**
Help!	Au secours!	o say-**koor**
Stop!	Arrêtez!	a-ruh-**tay**

Dining Out

A bottle of . . .	une bouteille de . . .	ewn boo-**tay** deh
A cup of . . .	une tasse de . . .	ewn tass deh
A glass of . . .	un verre de . . .	un vair deh
Ashtray	un cendrier	un sahn-dree-**ay**
Bill/check	l'addition	la-dee-see-**own**
Bread	du pain	due pan
Breakfast	le petit déjeuner	leh pet-**ee** day-zhu-**nay**
Butter	du beurre	due bur
Cocktail/aperitif	un apéritif	un ah-pay-ree-**teef**
Dinner	le dîner	leh dee-**nay**
Fixed-price menu	le menu	leh may-**new**
Fork	une fourchette	ewn four-**shet**
I am on a diet	Je suis au régime	jeh sweez o ray-**jeem**
I am vegetarian	Je suis végétarien(ne)	jeh swee vay-jay-ta-ree-**en**
I cannot eat . . .	Je ne peux pas manger de . . .	jeh nuh puh pah mahn-**jay** deh
I'd like to order	Je voudrais commander	jeh voo-**dray** ko-mahn-**day**
I'd like . . .	Je voudrais . . .	jeh voo-**dray**
I'm hungry/thirsty	J'ai faim/soif	jay fam/swahf
Is service/the tip included?	Est-ce que le service est compris?	ess keh leh sair-veess ay comb-**pree**
It's good/bad	C'est bon/mauvais	say bon/mo-**vay**
It's hot/cold	C'est chaud/froid	say sho/frwah
Knife	un couteau	un koo-**toe**
Lunch	le déjeuner	leh day-juh-**nay**
Menu	la carte	la cart
Napkin	une serviette	ewn sair-vee-**et**
Pepper	du poivre	due **pwah**-vruh
Plate	une assiette	ewn a-see-**et**
Please give me . . .	Donnez-moi . . .	doe-nay-**mwah**
Salt	du sel	dew sell

Spoon	une cuillère	ewn kwee-**air**
Sugar	du sucre	due **sook**-ruh
Wine list	la carte des vins	la cart day **van**

Menu Guide

English	*French*
Set menu	Menu à prix fixe
Dish of the day	Plat du jour
Drink included	Boisson comprise
Local specialties	Spécialités locales
Choice of vegetable accompaniment	Garniture au choix
Made to order	Sur commande
Extra charge	Supplément/En sus
When available	Selon arrivage

Breakfast

Jam	Confiture
Croissants	Croissants
Honey	Miel
Boiled egg	Oeuf à la coque
Bacon and eggs	Oeufs au bacon
Ham and eggs	Oeufs au jambon
Fried eggs	Oeufs au plat
Scrambled eggs	Oeufs brouillés
(Plain) omelet	Omelette (nature)
Rolls	Petits pains

Starters

Anchovies	Anchois
Aromatic sausage	Andouille(tte)
Assorted cold cuts	Assiette anglaise
Assorted pork products	Assiette de charcuterie
Small, highly seasoned sausage	Crépinette
Mixed raw vegetable salad	Crudités
Snails	Escargots
Ham (Bayonne)	Jambon (de Bayonne)
Bologna sausage	Mortadelle
Devilled eggs	Oeufs à la diable
Liver purée blended with other meat	Pâté
Tart with a rich, creamy filling of cheese, vegetables, meat or seafood	Quiche (lorraine)
Cold sausage	Saucisson
Pâté sliced and served from an earthenware pot	Terrine
Cured dried beef	Viande séchée

Salads

Diced vegetable salad	Salade russe
Endive salad	Salade d'endives
Green salad	Salade verte
Mixed salad	Salade panachée
Tuna salad	Salade de thon

Soups

Cold leek and potato cream soup	Vichyssoise
Cream of . . .	Crême de . . .
Cream of . . .	Velouté de . . .
Hearty soup	Soupe
day's soup	*du jour*
French onion soup	*à l'oignon*
Provençal vegetable soup	*au pistou*
Light soup	Potage
mashed red beans	*condé*
shredded vegetables	*julienne*
potato	*parmentier*
Fish and seafood stew	Bouillabaisse
Seafood stew (chowder)	Bisque
Stew of meat and vegetables	Pot-au-feu

Fish and Seafood

Bass	Bar
Carp	Carpe
Clams	Palourdes
Cod	Morue
Creamed salt cod	Brandade de morue
Crab	Crabe
Crayfish	Ecrevisses
Eel	Anguille
Fish stew from Marseilles	Bourride
Fish stew in wine	Matelote
Frog's legs	Cuisses de grenouilles
Herring	Harengs
Lobster	Homard
Mackerel	Maquereau
Mussels	Moules
Octopus	Poulpes
Oysters	Huîtres
Perch	Perche
Pike	Brochet
Dublin bay prawns (scampi)	Langoustines
Red mullet	Rouget
Salmon	Saumon
Scallops in creamy sauce	Coquilles St-Jacques
Sea bream	Daurade
Shrimps	Crevettes
Sole	Sole
Squid	Calmar
Trout	Truite
Tuna	Thon
Whiting	Merlan

Methods of Preparation

Baked	Au four
Fried	Frit
Grilled	Grillé
Marinated	Mariné
Poached	Poché
Sautéed	Sauté

| Smoked | Fumé |
| Steamed | Cuit à la vapeur |

Meat

Beef	Boeuf
Beef stew with vegetables, braised in red Burgundy wine	Boeuf bourguignon
Brains	Cervelle
Chops	Côtelettes
Cutlet	Escalope
Double fillet steak	Chateaubriand
Kabob	Brochette
Kidneys	Rognons
Lamb	Agneau
Leg	Gigot
Liver	Foie
Meatballs	Boulettes de viande
Pig's feet	Pieds de cochon
Pork	Porc
Rib	Côte
Rib or rib-eye steak	Entrecôte
Sausages	Saussices
Sausages and cured pork served with sauerkraut	Choucroute garnie
Steak (always beef)	Steak/steack
Stew	Ragoût
T-bone steak	Côte de boeuf
Tenderloin steak	Médaillon
Tenderloin of T-bone steak	Tournedos
Tongue	Langue
Veal	Veau
Veal sweetbreads	Ris de veau

Methods of Preparation

Very rare	Bleu
Rare	Saignant
Medium	A point
Well-done	Bien cuit

Baked	Au four
Boiled	Bouilli
Braised	Braisé
Fried	Frit
Grilled	Grillé
Roast	Rôti
Sautéed	Sauté
Stewed	A l'étouffée

Game and Poultry

Chicken	Poulet
Chicken breast	Suprême de volaille
Chicken stewed in red wine	Coq au vin
Chicken stewed with vegetables	Poule au pot
Spring chicken	Poussin
Duck/duckling	Canard/caneton
Duck braised with oranges and orange liqueur	Canard à l'orange

Fattened pullet	Poularde
Fowl	Volaille
Guinea fowl/young guinea fowl	Pintade/pintadeau
Goose	Oie
Partridge/young partridge	Perdrix/perdreau
Pheasant	Faisan
Pigeon/squab	Pigeon/pigeonneau
Quail	Caille
Rabbit	Lapin
Turkey/young turkey	Dinde/dindonneau
Venison (red/roe)	Cerf/chevreuil

Vegetables

Artichoke	Artichaut
Asparagus	Asperge
Brussels sprouts	Choux de Bruxelles
Cabbage (red)	Chou (rouge)
Carrots	Carottes
Cauliflower	Chou-fleur
Eggplant	Aubergines
Endive	Endives
Leeks	Poireaux
Lettuce	Laitue
Mushrooms	Champignons
Onions	Oignons
Peas	Petits pois
Peppers	Poivrons
Radishes	Radis
Spinach	Epinards
Tomatoes	Tomates
Watercress	Cresson
Zucchini	Courgette
White kidney/French beans	Haricots blancs/verts
Casserole of stewed eggplant, onions, green peppers, and zucchini	Ratatouille

Spices and Herbs

Bay leaf	Laurier
Chervil	Cerfeuil
Garlic	Ail
Marjoram	Marjolaine
Mustard	Moutarde
Parsley	Persil
Pepper	Poivre
Rosemary	Romarin
Tarragon	Estragon
Mixture of herbs	Fines herbes

Potatoes, Rice, and Noodles

Noodles	Nouilles
Pasta	Pâtes
Potatoes	Pommes (de terre)
matchsticks	*allumettes*
mashed and deep-fried	*dauphine*
mashed with butter and egg yolks	*duchesse*
in their jackets	*en robe des champs*

french fries	*frites*
mashed	*mousseline*
boiled/steamed	*nature/vapeur*
Rice	Riz
boiled in bouillon with onions	*pilaf*

Sauces and Preparations

Brown butter, parsley, lemon juice	Meunière
Curry	Indienne
Egg yolks, butter, vinegar	Hollandaise
Hot pepper	Diable
Mayonnaise flavored with mustard and herbs	Tartare
Mushrooms, red wine, shallots, beef marrow	Bordelaise
Onions, tomatoes, garlic	Provençale
Pepper sauce	Poivrade
Red wine, herbs	Bourguignon
Vinegar, egg yolks, white wine, shallots, tarragon	Béarnaise
Vinegar dressing	Vinaigrette
White sauce	Béchamel
White wine, mussel broth, egg yolks	Marinière
Wine, mushrooms, onions, shallots	Chasseur
With goose or duck liver purée and truffles	Périgueux
With Madeira wine	Madère

Cheeses

Mild:	Beaufort
	Beaumont
	Belle étoile
	Boursin
	Brie
	Cantal
	Comté
	Reblochon
	St-paulin
	Tomme de Savoie
Sharp:	Bleu de Bresse
	Camembert
	Livarot
	Fromage au marc
	Munster
	Pont-l'évêque
	Roquefort
Swiss:	Emmenthal
	Gruyère
	Vacherin
Goat's milk:	St-marcellin
	Valençay
Cheese tart	Tarte au fromage
Small cheese tart	Ramequin
Toasted ham and cheese sandwich	Croque-monsieur

Fruits and Nuts

Almonds	Amandes
Apple	Pomme
Apricot	Abricot
Banana	Banane
Blackberries	Mûres
Blackcurrants	Cassis
Blueberries	Myrtilles
Cherries	Cerises
Chestnuts	Marrons
Coconut	Noix de coco
Dates	Dattes
Dried fruit	Fruits secs
Figs	Figues
Grapefruit	Pamplemousse
Grapes green/blue	Raisin blanc/noir
Hazelnuts	Noisettes
Lemon	Citron
Melon	Melon
Orange	Orange
Peach	Pêche
Peanuts	Cacahouètes
Pear	Poire
Pineapple	Ananas
Plums	Prunes
Prunes	Pruneaux
Raisins	Raisins secs
Raspberries	Framboises
Strawberries	Fraises
Tangerine	Mandarine
Walnuts	Noix
Watermelon	Pastèque

Desserts

Apple pie	Tarte aux pommes
Baked Alaska	Omelette norvégienne
Caramel pudding	Crème caramel
Chocolate cake	Gâteau au chocolat
Chocolate pudding	Mousse au chocolat
Custard	Flan
Ice cream	Glace
Layer cake	Tourte
Pear with vanilla ice cream and chocolate sauce	Poire Belle Hélène
Soufflé made with orange liqueur	Soufflé au Grand-Marnier
Sundae	Coupe (glacée)
Water ice	Sorbet
Whipped cream	Crème Chantilly
Creamy dessert of egg yolks, wine, sugar, and flavoring	Sabayon
Puff pastry filled with whipped cream or custard	Profiterole

Index

Personal Itinerary

Departure *Date*

Time

Transportation

Arrival *Date*   *Time*

Departure *Date*   *Time*

Transportation

Accommodations

Arrival *Date*   *Time*

Departure *Date*   *Time*

Transportation

Accommodations

Arrival *Date*   *Time*

Departure *Date*   *Time*

Transportation

Accommodations

Personal Itinerary

Arrival *Date*   *Time*

Departure *Date*   *Time*

Transportation

Accommodations

Arrival *Date*   *Time*

Departure *Date*   *Time*

Transportation

Accommodations

Arrival *Date*   *Time*

Departure *Date*   *Time*

Transportation

Accommodations

Arrival *Date*   *Time*

Departure *Date*   *Time*

Transportation

Accommodations

Personal Itinerary

Arrival *Date*   *Time*

Departure *Date*   *Time*

Transportation

Accommodations

Arrival *Date*   *Time*

Departure *Date*   *Time*

Transportation

Accommodations

Arrival *Date*   *Time*

Departure *Date*   *Time*

Transportation

Accommodations

Arrival *Date*   *Time*

Departure *Date*   *Time*

Transportation

Accommodations

Personal Itinerary

Arrival *Date*   *Time*

Departure *Date*   *Time*

Transportation

Accommodations

Arrival *Date*   *Time*

Departure *Date*   *Time*

Transportation

Accommodations

Arrival *Date*   *Time*

Departure *Date*   *Time*

Transportation

Accommodations

Arrival *Date*   *Time*

Departure *Date*   *Time*

Transportation

Accommodations

Personal Itinerary

Arrival *Date*   *Time*

Departure *Date*   *Time*

Transportation

Accommodations

Arrival *Date*   *Time*

Departure *Date*   *Time*

Transportation

Accommodations

Arrival *Date*   *Time*

Departure *Date*   *Time*

Transportation

Accommodations

Arrival *Date*   *Time*

Departure *Date*   *Time*

Transportation

Accommodations

Addresses

Name	*Name*
Address	*Address*
Telephone	*Telephone*
Name	*Name*
Address	*Address*
Telephone	*Telephone*
Name	*Name*
Address	*Address*
Telephone	*Telephone*
Name	*Name*
Address	*Address*
Telephone	*Telephone*
Name	*Name*
Address	*Address*
Telephone	*Telephone*
Name	*Name*
Address	*Address*
Telephone	*Telephone*
Name	*Name*
Address	*Address*
Telephone	*Telephone*
Name	*Name*
Address	*Address*
Telephone	*Telephone*

Addresses

Name	*Name*
Address	*Address*
Telephone	*Telephone*
Name	*Name*
Address	*Address*
Telephone	*Telephone*
Name	*Name*
Address	*Address*
Telephone	*Telephone*
Name	*Name*
Address	*Address*
Telephone	*Telephone*
Name	*Name*
Address	*Address*
Telephone	*Telephone*
Name	*Name*
Address	*Address*
Telephone	*Telephone*
Name	*Name*
Address	*Address*
Telephone	*Telephone*
Name	*Name*
Address	*Address*
Telephone	*Telephone*

Notes

Fodor's Travel Guides

U.S. Guides

Alaska
Arizona
Atlantic City & the
  New Jersey Shore
Boston
California
Cape Cod
Carolinas & the
  Georgia Coast
The Chesapeake Region
Chicago
Colorado
Dallas & Fort
  Worth

Disney World & the
  Orlando Area
Florida
Hawaii
Houston &
  Galveston
Las Vegas
Los Angeles, Orange
  County, Palm Springs
Maui
Miami, Fort Lauderdale,
  Palm Beach
Michigan, Wisconsin,
  Minnesota

New England
New Mexico
New Orleans
New Orleans (Pocket
  Guide)
New York City
New York City (Pocket
  Guide)
New York State
Pacific North Coast
Philadelphia
The Rockies
San Diego
San Francisco

San Francisco (Pocket
  Guide)
The South
Texas
USA
Virgin Islands
Virginia
Waikiki
Washington, DC
Williamsburg

Foreign Guides

Acapulco
Amsterdam
Australia, New Zealand,
  The South Pacific
Austria
Bahamas
Bahamas (Pocket
  Guide)
Baja & the Pacific
  Coast Resorts
Barbados
Beijing, Guangzhou &
  Shanghai
Belgium &
  Luxembourg
Bermuda
Brazil
Britain (Great Travel
  Values)
Budget Europe
Canada
Canada (Great Travel
  Values)
Canada's Atlantic
  Provinces
Cancun, Cozumel,
  Yucatan Peninsula

Caribbean
Caribbean (Great
  Travel Values)
Central America
Eastern Europe
Egypt
Europe
Europe's Great
  Cities
Florence & Venice
France
France (Great Travel
  Values)
Germany
Germany (Great Travel
  Values)
Great Britain
Greece
The Himalayan
  Countries
Holland
Hong Kong
Hungary
India, including Nepal
Ireland
Israel
Italy

Italy (Great Travel
  Values)
Jamaica
Japan
Japan (Great Travel
  Values)
Jordan & the
  Holy Land
Kenya, Tanzania,
  the Seychelles
Korea
Lisbon
Loire Valley
London
London (Great
  Travel Values)
London (Pocket Guide)
Madrid & Barcelona
Mexico
Mexico City
Montreal &
  Quebec City
Munich
New Zealand
North Africa
Paris
Paris (Pocket Guide)

People's Republic of
  China
Portugal
Rio de Janeiro
The Riviera (Fun on)
Rome
Saint Martin &
  Sint Maarten
Scandinavia
Scandinavian Cities
Scotland
Singapore
South America
South Pacific
Southeast Asia
Soviet Union
Spain
Spain (Great Travel
  Values)
Sweden
Switzerland
Sydney
Tokyo
Toronto
Turkey
Vienna
Yugoslavia

Special-Interest Guides

Health & Fitness
  Vacations
Royalty Watching

Selected Hotels of
  Europe

Selected Resorts and
  Hotels of the U.S.
Shopping in Europe

Skiing in North America
Sunday in New York

Help us evaluate hotels and restaurants for the next edition of this guide, and we will send you a free issue of Fodor's newsletter, TravelSense.

Title of this guide:

1 Hotel ❑   Restaurant ❑   *(check one)*

Name

Number/Street

City/State/Country

Comments

2 Hotel ❑   Restaurant ❑   *(check one)*

Name

Number/Street

City/State/Country

Comments

3 Hotel ❑   Restaurant ❑   *(check one)*

Name

Number/Street

City/State/Country

Comments

General Comments

Please complete for a free copy of TravelSense

Name

Number/Street

City/State/Zip

Business Reply Mail

First Class   Permit Nº 7775   New York, NY

Postage will be paid by addressee

Fodor's Travel Publications

201 East 50th Street
New York, NY 10022